ABC's of Relationship Selling Through Service

SEVENTH CANADIAN EDITION

CHARLES M. FUTRELL
Texas A & M University

RAJ AGNIHOTRI
Iowa State University

MICHAEL T. KRUSH
Kansas State University

MARK VALVASORI
Mohawk College

NICOLE ROURKE
St. Clair College

Mc Graw Hill

ABC'S OF RELATIONSHIP SELLING THROUGH SERVICE
Seventh Canadian Edition

ISBN-13: 978-1-25-927079-6
ISBN-10: 1-25-927079-3

1 2 3 4 5 6 7 8 9 M 23 22 21 20

Printed and bound in Canada.

Product Director: Rhondda McNabb
Portfolio Manager: Jade Fair
Marketing Manager: Emily Park
Content Developer: Sarah Fulton
Portfolio Associate: Tatiana Sevciuc
Senior Supervising Editor: Jessica Barnoski
Photo/Permissions Editor: Alison Lloyd Baker
Copy Editor: Janice Dyer
Plant Production Coordinator: Heitor Moura
Manufacturing Production Coordinator: Jason Stubner
Cover Design: Lightbox Visual Communications, Inc.
Interior Design: Liz Harasymczuk
Cover Image: © John Fedele/Getty Images
Page Layout: Aptara®, Inc.
Printer: Marquis

About the Authors

Dr. Charles M. Futrell The late Dr. Charles M. Futrell was a professor of marketing in the Mays Business School at Texas A&M University in College Station, Texas. Dr. Futrell held a BBA, MBA, and PhD in marketing. Professor Futrell's books, research, and teaching were based on his extensive work with sales organizations of all types and sizes. He was a former salesperson turned professor. Before beginning his academic career, Professor Futrell worked in sales and marketing capacities for eight years with the Colgate Company, The Upjohn Company, and Ayerst Laboratories. This broad and rich background has resulted in numerous invitations to serve as a speaker, researcher, and consultant to industry.

Dr. Futrell's research in personal selling, sales management, research methodology, and marketing management appeared in numerous national and international journals. An article in the summer 1991 issue of the *Journal of Personal Selling & Sales Management* ranked Charles as one of the top three sales researchers in America. He was also recognized in *Marketing Education,* Summer 1997, as one of the top 100 best researchers in the marketing discipline. Professor Futrell served as the American Marketing Association's chair of the Sales and Sales Management Special Interest Group (SIG) for the 1996–97 academic year. He was the first person elected to this position.

Charles received a number of awards as a testament to his work. In 2005, the AMA Sales and Sales Management Special Interest Group (SIG) presented Charles with its Lifetime Achievement Award for commitment to excellence and service in the area of sales. Charles was the recipient of Sales & Marketing Executives International's (SMEI) Educator of the Year in 2007; and the American Marketing Association's Sales Management Special Interest Group awarded Charles the Lifetime Excellence in Teaching Award in 2012.

Dr. Futrell wrote or co-wrote eight successful books for the college and professional audience. Two of the most popular books were Fundamentals of Selling: Customers for Life through Service, and this book, ABC's of Relationship Selling through Service, now in its thirteenth edition, both published by McGraw-Hill/Irwin. Over 300,000 students worldwide learned from Professor Futrell's books.

Dr. Raj Agnihotri is the dean's fellow in marketing and the director of sales initiative at Ivy College of Business, Iowa State University. Previously, Raj held the first John Merrill Endowed Professorship in Consultative Sales at the University of Texas at Arlington and Robert H. Freeman Professor of Sales Leadership and marketing chair at Ohio University. Before entering academia, Raj held a number of sales and marketing positions with start-up ventures to major global corporations. He currently serves on the advisory boards of several technology startups based in the US and Europe. Raj is also involved in executive education and has given sales seminars to industry professionals from North America, Brazil, Europe, and India. He served on the faculty of Samson Global Leadership Program at Cleveland Clinic from 2014 to 2017 and taught health administrators from across the world.

Raj has published over 35 articles in leading scholarly journals and has presented papers at over 50 national and international conferences. He serves on the editorial review board of *Industrial Marketing Management, Journal of Business Research,* and *Marketing Management Journal*. A recipient of the prestigious 2011 James M. Comer Award for the best contribution to selling and sales management theory, Raj's dissertation on salesperson competitive intelligence won the 2010 Best Dissertation Award from American Marketing Association. Raj has also received the 2017 Citation of Excellence Award from Emerald, the 2012 Bright Idea Award from NJPRO Foundation, the 2012 Stanley Hollander Award from Academy of the 2017 Doctoral Students' Mentor of the Year award from College of Business at UT Arlington, the 2012 Advisor of the Year Award from William Paterson University, the 2010 McGraw-Hill/Steven J. Shaw Award from Society for Marketing Advances, and the 2008 Next Gen Award from AMA Sales SIG and University of Houston.

Raj is a passionate teacher, and he was awarded the 2014 Hormel Excellence in Teaching Award for his innovative teaching practices. He has also received Golden M Teaching Award in marketing at Kent State University. A firm believer in experiential learning, Raj launched Maverick Sales Club at UT-Arlington, Consumer Research Center at Ohio University, Professional Sales Club at William Paterson University of New Jersey, among other initiatives.

Raj lives with his beautiful wife, Manusmriti, and their two lovely daughters, Sia and Aarna, in Ames, Iowa. Raj's family is his biggest source for strength, comfort, and inspiration. Raj remains grateful to his parents for teaching him the importance of hard work and kindness.

Mike Krush (University of Nebraska-Lincoln) serves on the College of Business Administration faculty at Kansas State University and is associated with its National Strategic Selling Institute (NSSI).

Dr. Krush has taught sales and a range of marketing classes at the undergraduate and graduate level at multiple universities including North Dakota State University, St. Cloud State University, and the University of Nebraska-Lincoln.

In terms of sales education, Dr. Krush championed and initiated the Center for Professional Selling Sales Technology at North Dakota State University–the only academic center dedicated to developing the sales skills of college students within the North Dakota University System. The Sales Education Foundation consistently recognized NDSU on its list of top universities for sales education. When serving as its director, Dr. Krush championed the application of the Center for Professional Selling and Sales Technology for full membership within the University Sales Center Alliance, a consortium of sales centers dedicated to advancing the sales profession via teaching, research, and outreach.

Prior to his academic career, Dr. Krush served as a brand manager at the Kimberly-Clark Corporation, one of America's largest publicly held corporations. His responsibilities included areas of strategic marketing for a $600 million brand. In addition, he has conducted marketing and sales operations in the financial services domain, consulted with start-up and existing firms, and written a book on career preparation.

From a research perspective, Dr. Krush was one of three national award winners of the Institute for the Study of Business Market's Doctoral Support Award for his dissertation in business-to-business marketing. Dr. Agnihotri, Dr. Krush, and their colleagues were also recognized by Industrial Marketing Management in 2016 for the Best Article Award.

Dr. Krush's research has been published in a variety of journals, including the *Journal of the Academy of Marketing Science,* the *Journal of Business Research,* the *Journal of Personal Selling and Sales Management,* the *European Journal of Marketing, Industrial Marketing Management, The Journal of Business Ethics,* and the *Journal of Business and Industrial Marketing*. Mike is blessed with an amazing wife, Joan, and two fantastic kids.

Mark Valvasori is a professor in the Business Management program at Mohawk College of Applied Arts and Technology in Hamilton, Ontario. He holds a degree in business administration with a major in marketing from Saint Francis Xavier University in Antigonish, Nova Scotia. Professor Valvasori began his business career with the T. Eaton Company of Canada and spent three years self-employed in franchise development and sales for a national outdoors-adventure game.

Professor Valvasori's academic career spans 30 years as an educator. In addition to being a full-time professor at Mohawk College, he has developed and facilitated many seminars, workshops, and training programs in the areas of marketing, sales, and customer service.

When Professor Valvasori isn't teaching or writing, he is very active in his community. He is an elected trustee on the Hamilton-Wentworth Catholic District School Board and also volunteers with many community-based organizations.

Nicole Rourke is a professor in the Business Administration Marketing program at the Zekelman School of Business and IT at St.Clair College in Windsor, Ontario. She graduated from the University of Windsor with an Honours Bachelor of Commerce degree and while working in the marketing field, completed her Masters of Business Administration degree from Wayne State University in Detroit, Michigan. Professor Rourke worked in brand management and various marketing roles at Hiram Walker and Sons in both the United States and Canada, working on brands such as Kahlúa, Canadian Club, Malibu Coconut Rum, Cutty Sark Scotch, and many others. Her marketing experience allowed her to work closely with the U.S. and global sales divisions, and she continues to use those examples in her teaching at the college.

Professor Rourke has been teaching in the post-secondary field for 14 years and enjoys coaching students in marketing competitions, including the Ontario Colleges Marketing Competition and the Vanier Business Case Competition. Recently, she was honoured to be the recipient of the Award of Excellence at the OCMC in 2019. She has been teaching the Multi-Media Sales Presentations course for 12 years and loves using *ABC's of Relationship Selling through Service* in the classroom. Professor Rourke feels that sales is one of the most rewarding courses to teach to college students, as it provides them with invaluable lessons in business acumen and confidence that are unique to the selling class.

Professor Rourke is thrilled to be a part of the writing team for this seventh edition of *ABC's of Relationship Selling through Service*!

Contents in Brief

Contents

CASE

PART 3

The Relationship Selling Process 161

CHAPTER 6

Prospecting—The Lifeblood of Selling 162

CASES

CHAPTER 7

The Pre-Approach—Planning Your Sales Call and Presentation 194

CASES

CHAPTER 8

The Approach—Begin Your Presentation Strategically 226

CASES

CHAPTER 9

The Presentation—Elements of Effective Persuasion 266

CASES

CHAPTER 10

Objections—Welcome Your Prospect's Concerns 302

CHAPTER 11

Closing—the Beginning of a New Relationship 340

CHAPTER 12

Follow-up—Maintain and Strengthen the Relationship 378

Preface

Welcome to the Seventh Canadian Edition of *ABC's of Relationship Selling through Service!*

With great excitement, we are presenting the Seventh Canadian edition of *ABC's of Relationship Selling through Service*. As selling continues to grow as a profession, the importance of sales education continues to increase in its acceptance and expansion within academia. Increasing sales and profits is up to the sales personnel—the people who represent their employers through interacting with present or prospective customers. Sales professionals today must strive to create a long-term business relationship, which implies that they form close relationships with clients. Prospective customers want to buy from someone who cares about their needs. People do business with the people they trust, and they trust the people they know.

This and previous editions of *ABC's of Relationship Selling through Service* were driven by the advice of sales experts and professional reviewers. The revisions to this text are guided by our conversations with sales students, practitioners, and sales educators. This has resulted in several changes to the book over the last few editions, including changes in objectives as well as many welcome topic additions. Believing, as many do, that ethical behaviour is becoming paramount in modern business practices, the topic of sales ethics appears frequently throughout the text. It has a prominent place in the chapter sequencing, and students are provided with many opportunities to consider their own sales ethics through the many ethical dilemmas presented throughout the text. The new edition also includes an enhanced focus on sales professionalism, improvements in sales technology such as CRM systems, social media tools, and recent trends in sales, including emotional intelligence, artificial intelligence, and predictive analysis.

The structure of this book lends itself to the practical aspects of selling and delivers them in a process-oriented fashion. You will find practical selling tips and many opportunities to reflect on the various issues facing today's salespeople. Student success profiles have been updated to reflect how many graduates end up working in sales and consider a variety of career pathways for sales students. Articles authored by seasoned sales professionals provide words of wisdom from the real world. In addition, you will find an updated and expanded discussion of the technology available to salespeople to help them look after their customers more effectively and efficiently. Also included in this edition is enhanced coverage of the use of social media in the world of professional selling. Most students are familiar with social media such as Instagram, Twitter, Facebook, and LinkedIn, among others; in the text, you will learn how they are used by professional salespeople today.

One of the goals of this Seventh Canadian Edition is to give students the up-to-date information they need to compete in today's fast-paced, competitive, demanding, and increasingly electronic marketplace. *ABC's of Relationship Selling through Service* is written by salespeople turned teachers. The authors have many years of experience applying the concepts discussed in this book. Over the years, they have taught the concepts of selling to many thousands of college students, businesspeople, and industry sales personnel, continually developing and using the strategies, practices, and techniques presented in this textbook. Every day, they spend time interacting with professional salespeople and sharing insights with colleagues and students. This book is the result of these experiences.

The Philosophy behind This Book

The title should help you understand the philosophy of this book. A student of sales should understand the fundamentals—the basics—of personal selling. *All of them*. We do not advocate one way of selling as the best route to success. There are many roads to reaching one's goals!

We *do* believe that a salesperson should have an assortment of selling skills and should be very knowledgeable, even an expert, in the field. Based on the situation, the salesperson determines the appropriate actions to take for a particular prospect or customer. No matter what the situation, however, the basic fundamentals of selling can be applied. It can be said that this is a process-driven sales textbook. Understanding the basic sales process will enable readers to tackle a variety of sales positions.

There is little room any longer for high-pressure, manipulative selling. The salesperson is a problem solver, a helper, a solution provider, a service provider, a relationship builder, and an adviser to the customer. If the customer has no need, the salesperson should accept that and move on to help another person or firm. If the customer has a need, however, the salesperson should and must go for the sale. All successful salespeople we know believe that once they determine the customer is going to buy someone's product–and that their product will satisfy that customer's needs–it is their job to muster all their energy, skill, and know-how to make that sale. That is what it's all about!

It is the authors' hope that after studying this text, the reader will say, "There's a lot more to selling than I ever imagined." It is hoped that this material will help many people to earn a living through selling as a rewarding occupation and career. Finally, the communication skills that will be acquired by reading this text can be used in all aspects of life. Once learned, selling skills will help a person be a better communicator throughout life.

Basic Organization of the Book

We have worked hard to ensure that this edition of *ABC's of Relationship Selling through Service* will provide students with the basic foundation for understanding all of the major components of selling. The chapters are divided into four parts:

- ***Selling as a Profession.*** Emphasizes the history, careers, rewards, and duties of professional salespeople and illustrates the importance of the sales function to the organization's success. It also examines the social, ethical, and legal issues in selling.
- ***Preparation for Relationship Selling.*** Presents the background information salespeople use to develop their sales presentations.
- ***The Relationship Selling Process.*** At the heart of the book, this part covers the entire selling process from prospecting to follow-up. State-of-the-art selling strategies, practices, and techniques are presented in a "how-to" fashion.
- ***Keys to a Successful Selling Career.*** Explores the importance of the proper use and management of time and sales territory, along with an examination of different types of sales jobs.

What's New in This Edition?

The Seventh Canadian Edition of *ABCs of Relationship Selling through Service* emphasizes the importance of ethical behaviour in sales and a sales philosophy of unselfishly treating others as you would like to be treated without expecting reciprocity. In addition, the popular Sales Success Stories–twelve of which are new to this edition–spotlight recent graduates, tracing their career pathways and offering their advice as a feature at the beginning of each chapter.

Other changes to the Seventh Canadian Edition include:

Chapter 1:

- Updated sales salary data
- Streamlined exploration of various careers in selling and a new chart with salaries and years of experience (Exhibit 1.2)
- New survey ***Do You Have What it Takes?***, a personal reflection survey for students
- Added social media platforms as an example of what a sales professional does
- Updated importance of selling for small businesses

Chapter 2:

- Updated ethical, legal, and discretionary examples
- New content explaining moral development (Exhibits 2.3 and 2.4)
- New *Making the Sale* box on **PIPEDA**
- New *Social Media Insights* involving ethical concerns for salespeople using social media
- New *Selling Tip* box looking at **Values and Ethics Code for the Public Sector**
- New *Making the Sale* box examines tied selling by banks in Canada

Chapter 3:

- New content explaining **why people buy a product** (Exhibit 3.3)
- Expanded comparison between consumer and organizational buying contexts (Exhibit 3.4)
- Added content on how salespeople help buyers understand a better situation is available (Exhibit 3.5)
- New *Selling Tips* box on **discovering needs in organizational buying**
- New *Ethical Dilemma* on what would you do in a particular sales situation

Chapter 4:

- New *Selling Tips* box about communicating with **Indigenous People in Canada**
- New content on professional communication (Exhibit 4.9)
- Updated **social media use statistics**
- Updated examples on appropriate length of handshakes
- New *Social Media Insights* box
- Added content on **Snapchat** and **Instagram**

Chapter 5:

- Added content on questions salespeople should ask to better understand their customers (Exhibit 5.1)
- Added content under "Know Your Channels of Distribution" and "Know Your Product's Pricing and Discount Policies"
- New content providing examples of prices and discounts that salespeople discuss (Exhibit 5.3)
- Added content on **CRM technology**
- Added content on **the Cloud**

Chapter 6:

- New content on prospecting guidelines and prospecting using social media
- New content on **how to apply CRM technology to prospecting**
- New *Facing a Sales Challenge* box with an **entrepreneurial approach**
- New content examining prospecting methods that work (Exhibit 6.4)
- New *Selling Tips* box on why qualifying a lead is important
- New *Ethical Dilemma* on the ethics of using confidential information to make a sale
- New terms and content on **social selling** and **social listening**

Chapter 7:

- New content on how to build trust (Exhibit 7.1)
- New *Selling Tip* box discussing what is a solution
- New content on **The Customer Relationship Model** (Exhibit 7.3)
- New content on topics to consider in planning (Exhibit 7.7)
- New *Selling Experiential Exercise*

Chapter 8:

- Added sales presentations methods
- New content on training usage phases over time (Exhibit 8.15)
- New content on *Group Presentations*
- New *Selling Tips* box outlining a checklist for group presentations
- New *Selling Tips* box on negotiation

Chapter 9:

- Added checklist for visuals
- New content on *The Sales Presentation Goal Model* (Exhibit 9.15)
- New *Selling Tips* box on developing trust
- New content on **presentations** (Exhibits 9.10 and 9.11)
- New *Selling Tips* on using videoconferencing technology

Chapter 10:

- New type of objection added (**hidden objections**) (Exhibit 10.6)
- New content on techniques for meeting objections
- New content about what to do after the meeting
- New content on preparing for objections (Exhibit 10.2)
- New content on handing objections (Exhibit 10.3) and examples of objections (Exhibit 10.5)
- Added *Ethical Dilemma* box examining how to deal with a customer setting a condition for a sale
- New content outlining a method to overcome objections (Exhibit 10.9)
- New content describing how to rephrase objections as questions (Exhibit 10.10)

Chapter 11:

- New content on the probability close
- Revised content to include an **entrepreneur** example (Exhibit 11.11)
- Added information on cross-selling

Chapter 12:

- Revised objective for updated content on customer satisfaction, retention, and engagement
- New content on technology and sales service (Exhibit 12.2)
- Added content on **words of sales wisdom and sales proverbs** (Exhibit 12.8)

Chapter 13:

- Expanded content on self-management (Exhibit 13.10)
- New discussion on **emotional intelligence (EI)** and its importance in today's workplace
- Added content on why salespeople need to segment their accounts by size, including the 80/20 principle
- Expanded content on return on time invested
- New trends in sales, including **artificial intelligence** and **predictive analysis**
- New *Ethical Dilemma* box on how to deal with a decline in productivity

Chapter 14:

- Updated retail sales data
- Added content on **crowdfunding** and **crowdsourcing**
- New crowdfunding questions for sales application and further exploring the sales world

This edition of the *ABC's* contains current information from the Canadian Professional Sales Association (CPSA), including its Code of Ethics. This organization is leading the way for Canadian salespeople, offering many benefits and educational opportunities for its members. As well, this edition includes up-to-date descriptions and salary information for different kinds of sales professionals in Canada.

Text and Chapter Pedagogy

Many reality-based features are included in this Seventh Canadian Edition to stimulate learning. One major goal of this book is to offer better ways to convey sales knowledge to the reader. To do this, the text includes numerous special features:

Sales Success Stories. Each chapter opens with a success story of a Canadian college or university graduate who has gone on to succeed in professional selling. This will show readers that there is indeed a light at the end of the tunnel.

Selena Ujj
St. Clair College,
Zekelman School of
Business and IT,
Windsor, Ontario.

Source: Courtesy of Selena Ujj

A Sales Success Story

Selena Ujj graduated from the Business Marketing program at St. Clair College, Zekelman School of Business and IT, in 2018. The program has helped her get to where she is in her career: Security Adviser and Investment Representative for London Life and Quadrus. Even in her early twenties, Selena knew building relationships would be essential to her success.

Selena did not initially consider the financial investment field after graduation, but a recruiter introduced her to it after contacting her on LinkedIn. After hearing about the position and the kind of work she would be doing, Selena was intrigued. She investigated further and spoke to her mother's adviser, a representative of Freedom 55 Financial, a branch of London Life. Her mother's adviser discussed all the pros and cons of the job with Selena. The rest is history, and Selena now works in a field that she loves and that challenges her on a daily basis.

LEARNING OBJECTIVES

Successful salespeople are knowledgeable individuals. Many salespeople are experts in their field. After studying this chapter, you should be able to:

LO1 Explain the importance of knowledge to sales professionals and determine various sources of sales knowledge.

LO2 Discuss the general areas of knowledge needed for increased sales success.

LO3 Understand the importance of features, advantages, and benefits.

LO4 Develop a FAB worksheet.

LO5 Develop and use a unique selling proposition.

LO6 Explain the purpose of planogram software for many types of salespeople.

LO7 Explain the main technologies used by salespeople.

Chapter Topics and Objectives. Each chapter begins with a clear statement of learning objectives and an outline of major chapter topics. These devices provide an overview of what is to come and can also be used by students to see whether they understand and have retained important points.

Sales Challenge/Solution. The text portion of each chapter begins with a real-life challenge that sales professionals face. The challenge pertains to the topic of the chapter and will heighten students' interest in chapter concepts. The challenge is resolved at the end of the chapter, where chapter concepts guiding the salesperson's actions are highlighted.

FACING A SALES CHALLENGE

You are proud of the products you sell and tell everyone they are the top-line of the industry, the best on the market, light years ahead of the competition. Of course you have worked for the company for only two weeks. But the sales training course you took last week clearly convinced you that your products are much better than any others. During one presentation on a new detergent for washing machines, you concentrated on discussing the quality of the product: how well it cleans, its environmental safety, how much users like its pleasant scent. The grocery store buyer said, "I couldn't care less about the quality of your products."

Why did the buyer respond in a negative way? What is the buyer interested in?

(Continued at end of chapter.)

MAKING THE SALE

DO YOU HAVE ANY OF THESE LISTENING HABITS?

No one is perfect. We all have some bad listening habits that we get away with when we talk to our family and friends. In a business context, however, leave these bad habits behind and practise active listening. To gain insight into your listening habits, read through this list of common irritating listening habits and be honest with yourself; notice what you are guilty of and use this awareness to begin eliminating them.

- You do all the talking.
- You interrupt when people talk.
- You never look at the person talking or indicate that you are listening.
- You start to argue before the other person has a chance to finish.
- You constantly feel obligated to digress with a story, since everything that is said reminds you of an experience you've had.
- You finish sentences for people if they pause too long.
- You wait impatiently for people to finish so that you can interject something.
- You work too hard at maintaining eye contact and make people uncomfortable.
- You look as if you are appraising the person talking to you, looking him or her up and down.
- You overdo the feedback you give—too many nods of your head and "uh-huhs."

Making the Sale. These boxed items explore how salespeople, when faced with challenges, use innovative ideas to sell.

Selling Tips. These boxes offer the reader additional selling tips for use in developing their role-plays.

SELLING TIPS

NEGOTIATION

- When you give up something, try to gain something in return. When you give something for nothing, there is a tendency for people to want more. In all fairness to you and your prospect, balance what you give and receive. For example, "I'll lower the price if you pay in full within 30 days," or "I'll give you 10 percent off, but you will be charged for additional services such as training."
- Look for items other than price to negotiate. For example, gain some flexibility by offering better terms, payment plans, return policies, and delivery schedules; lower deposits or cancellation fees; or implementation and training programs. Often these items are provided for less than your company would lose if you lowered the price.
- Do not attack your prospect's demand; look for the motive behind it. Never tell a prospect their demand is ridiculous or unreasonable. Remain calm and ask for the reason behind the desire.
- Do not defend your position; ask for feedback and advice from the prospect. If you meet resistance to an offer, don't be defensive. Say something like, "This is my thinking. What would you do if you were in my position?"

ETHICAL DILEMMA

I APPRECIATE YOUR BUSINESS

People buy from you for many reasons, but primarily because of your excellent products and the service you and your company provide to customers. You follow the Golden Rule: "Do unto others as you would have them do unto you." You feel that customers put the food on your table. They are responsible for the good income you earn. You appreciate that and always try to show your gratitude for their trust and business.

You have occasionally been taking one of your customers, whom you like personally, out to lunch. Recently, this customer's purchases have increased from $50,000 to $650,000 a year. You want to show your appreciation by buying your customer two season tickets for the local Canadian Football League team. The buyer and his spouse are avid football fans. However, if your other clients and co-workers found out, they might view the gift as unprofessional.

What would be the most ethical action to take?

1. Get a season ticket for yourself and for your client. That way, you can always justify it as a "business meeting" if people ask.
2. Buy your client and his spouse the season tickets. You are just trying to show your appreciation for his business.
3. Do not buy the season tickets. It is unprofessional to mix work and social ties. Instead, write your client a nice thank-you letter stating that you appreciate his continued business.

Do you have any other suggestions?

Ethical Dilemma. These challenging exercises provide students an opportunity to experience ethical dilemmas faced in the selling job. Students should review the definition and explanation of ethical behaviour in Chapter 2 before discussing the ethical dilemmas.

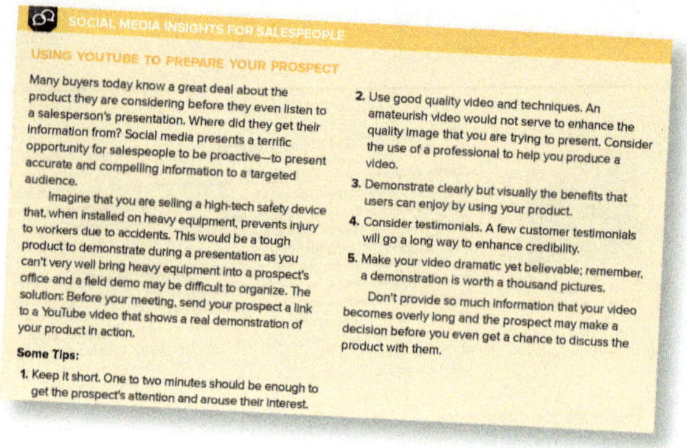

SOCIAL MEDIA INSIGHTS FOR SALESPEOPLE

USING YOUTUBE TO PREPARE YOUR PROSPECT

Many buyers today know a great deal about the product they are considering before they even listen to a salesperson's presentation. Where did they get their information from? Social media presents a terrific opportunity for salespeople to be proactive—to present accurate and compelling information to a targeted audience.

Imagine that you are selling a high-tech safety device that, when installed on heavy equipment, prevents injury to workers due to accidents. This would be a tough product to demonstrate during a presentation as you can't very well bring heavy equipment into a prospect's office and a field demo may be difficult to organize. The solution: Before your meeting, send your prospect a link to a YouTube video that shows a real demonstration of your product in action.

Some Tips:

1. Keep it short. One to two minutes should be enough to get the prospect's attention and arouse their interest.
2. Use good quality video and techniques. An amateurish video would not serve to enhance the quality image that you are trying to present. Consider the use of a professional to help you produce a video.
3. Demonstrate clearly but visually the benefits that users can enjoy by using your product.
4. Consider testimonials. A few customer testimonials will go a long way to enhance credibility.
5. Make your video dramatic yet believable; remember, a demonstration is worth a thousand pictures.

Don't provide so much information that your video becomes overly long and the prospect may make a decision before you even get a chance to discuss the product with them.

Social Media Insights for Salespeople. These boxes explore the potential uses of social media to benefit the salesperson.

Selling Globally. These boxed items take the idea of sales one step further and allow readers to see what happens or should happen when selling outside Canada.

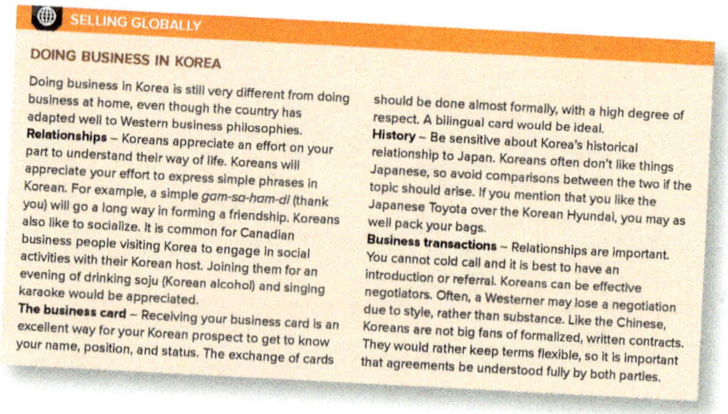

SELLING GLOBALLY

DOING BUSINESS IN KOREA

Doing business in Korea is still very different from doing business at home, even though the country has adapted well to Western business philosophies.
Relationships – Koreans appreciate an effort on your part to understand their way of life. Koreans will appreciate your effort to express simple phrases in Korean. For example, a simple *gam-sa-ham-di* (thank you) will go a long way in forming a friendship. Koreans also like to socialize. It is common for Canadian business people visiting Korea to engage in social activities with their Korean host. Joining them for an evening of drinking soju (Korean alcohol) and singing karaoke would be appreciated.
The business card – Receiving your business card is an excellent way for your Korean prospect to get to know your name, position, and status. The exchange of cards should be done almost formally, with a high degree of respect. A bilingual card would be ideal.
History – Be sensitive about Korea's historical relationship to Japan. Koreans often don't like things Japanese, so avoid comparisons between the two if the topic should arise. If you mention that you like the Japanese Toyota over the Korean Hyundai, you may as well pack your bags.
Business transactions – Relationships are important. You cannot cold call and it is best to have an introduction or referral. Koreans can be effective negotiators. Often, a Westerner may lose a negotiation due to style, rather than substance. Like the Chinese, Koreans are not big fans of formalized, written contracts. They would rather keep terms flexible, so it is important that agreements be understood fully by both parties.

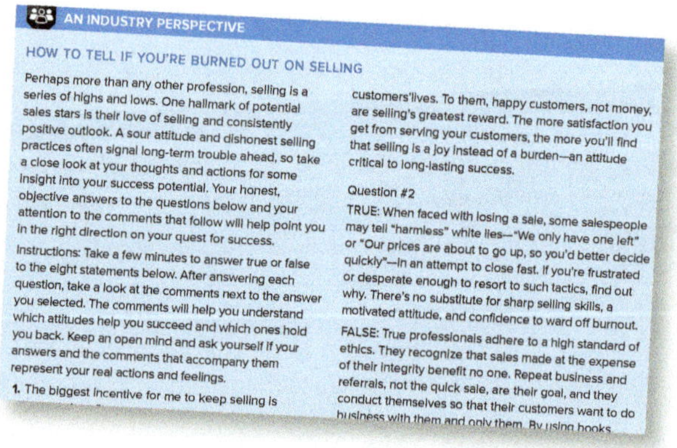

AN INDUSTRY PERSPECTIVE

HOW TO TELL IF YOU'RE BURNED OUT ON SELLING

Perhaps more than any other profession, selling is a series of highs and lows. One hallmark of potential sales stars is their love of selling and consistently positive outlook. A sour attitude and dishonest selling practices often signal long-term trouble ahead, so take a close look at your thoughts and actions for some insight into your success potential. Your honest, objective answers to the questions below and your attention to the comments that follow will help point you in the right direction on your quest for success.

Instructions: Take a few minutes to answer true or false to the eight statements below. After answering each question, take a look at the comments next to the answer you selected. The comments will help you understand which attitudes help you succeed and which ones hold you back. Keep an open mind and ask yourself if your answers and the comments that accompany them represent your real actions and feelings.

1. The biggest incentive for me to keep selling is

customers'lives. To them, happy customers, not money, are selling's greatest reward. The more satisfaction you get from serving your customers, the more you'll find that selling is a joy instead of a burden—an attitude critical to long-lasting success.

Question #2

TRUE: When faced with losing a sale, some salespeople may tell "harmless" white lies—"We only have one left" or "Our prices are about to go up, so you'd better decide quickly"—in an attempt to close fast. If you're frustrated or desperate enough to resort to such tactics, find out why. There's no substitute for sharp selling skills, a motivated attitude, and confidence to ward off burnout.

FALSE: True professionals adhere to a high standard of ethics. They recognize that sales made at the expense of their integrity benefit no one. Repeat business and referrals, not the quick sale, are their goal, and they conduct themselves so that their customers want to do business with them and only them. By using books

Industry Perspectives. Included in every chapter, these are articles written by seasoned, professional sales experts. They offer a real-life perspective and many practical tips for aspiring or professional salespeople.

Key Terms for Selling/Glossary. Learning the selling vocabulary is essential to understanding today's sales world. This is facilitated in three ways. First, key terms are boldfaced and completely defined where they first appear in the text. Second, each key term is listed at the end of each chapter. Third, a glossary summarizing all key terms and definitions appears at the end of the book for handy reference.

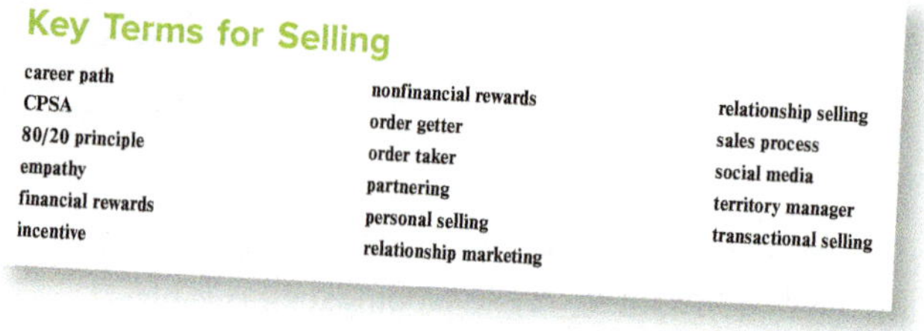

Key Terms for Selling

career path	**nonfinancial rewards**	**relationship selling**
CPSA	**order getter**	**sales process**
80/20 principle	**order taker**	**social media**
empathy	**partnering**	**territory manager**
financial rewards	**personal selling**	**transactional selling**
incentive	**relationship marketing**	

Chapter Summary. Each chapter closes with a summary of key issue designed to help students distinguish between main and supporting ideas.

EXHIBIT 3.6

Match the buyer's needs to the product's benefits and emphasize them in the sales presentation.

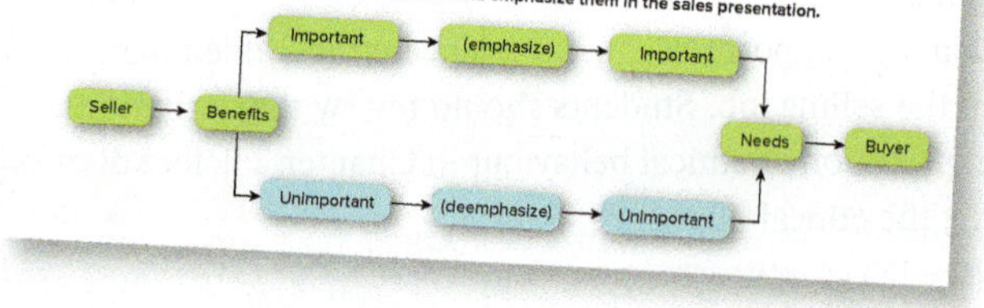

Exhibits. Many aspects of selling tend to be confusing at first. "What should I do?" and "How should I do it?" are two questions frequently asked by students in developing their role-plays. To enhance students' awareness and understanding, many exhibits have been included throughout the book. These exhibits consolidate key points, indicate relationships, and illustrate selling techniques.

Sales Online Exercise. Challenging students to look outside the classroom, the sales online exercises provide access and insight into the most current sales techniques and practices available.

Sales Online Exercise

1. Can You Improve Your Presentation?

The most challenging, rewarding, and enjoyable aspect of the sales job is the sales presentation. An effective presentation completely and clearly explains all aspects of a salesperson's proposition as it relates to a buyer's needs. To learn more about effective presentations, use your favourite search engine to search for sites to improve your presentation skills. Share your tips with the class.

2. Researching Prospects

The more information you have about a potential customer, the better. If your prospect is a large, internationally recognized organization, you can retrieve information from many sources, including the following:

Google: www.google.com

The *Globe and Mail* Report on Business: www.globeandmail.com/business

The Financial Post: www.nationalpost.com/financialpost

Bloomberg Businessweek: www.businessweek.com

LinkedIn: www.linkedin.com

Facebook: www.facebook.com

Twitter: www.twitter.com

Sales Application Learning Exercises (SALES). At the end of appropriate chapters, this multi-part, sequential exercise guides students through the process of preparing an effective sales presentation.

CASE 4–1

SKAGGS MANUFACTURING

John Alvez arrived promptly for his 10:00 a.m. meeting with Martha Gillespie, the buyer for Skaggs Manufacturing. At 10:15, when she hadn't arrived, John asked her secretary if she was out of the office for the morning. The secretary smiled and said, "She'll probably be a few minutes late." John resented this delay and was convinced that Martha had forgotten the appointment.

Finally, at 10:20, Martha entered her office, walked over to John, said hello, and promptly excused herself to talk to the secretary about a tennis game scheduled for that afternoon. Ten minutes later, Martha led John into her office. At the same time, a competing salesperson entered the office for a 10:30 appointment. With the door open, Martha asked John, "What's new today?" As John began to talk, Martha began reading letters on her desk and signing them. Shortly after that, the telephone began to ring, whereupon Martha talked to her husband for 10 minutes.

As she hung up, Martha looked at John and suddenly realized his frustration. She promptly buzzed her secretary and said, "Hold all calls." She got up and shut the door. John again began his presentation when Martha leaned backward in her chair, pulled her golf shoes out of a desk drawer, and began to brush them.

About that time, the secretary entered the office and said, "Martha, your 10:30 appointment is about to leave. What should I tell him?" Martha replied, "Tell him to wait; I need to see him." Then she said, "John, I wish we had more time. Look, I think I have enough of your product to last until your next visit. I'll see you then. Thanks for coming by."

John quickly rose to his feet, did not shake hands, said "OK," and left.

QUESTIONS

1. What nonverbal cues did the salesperson, John Alvez, experience when contacting Martha Gillespie?
2. If you were John Alvez, how would you have handled the situation?

Cases for Analysis. Each chapter ends with brief but substantive cases for student analysis and class discussion. These cases provide an opportunity for students to apply concepts to real events and to sharpen their diagnostic skills for sales problem solving.

Playing the Role. At the end of each chapter, students are presented with a real-life sales problem. They are then asked to assume a particular role and dramatize their solution to the problem.

Sales Application Questions. The sales application questions are a complementary learning tool that enables students to check their understanding of key issues, think beyond basic concepts, and determine areas that require further study.

Further Exploring the Sales World. These projects ask students to go beyond the textbook and classroom to explore what's happening in the real world. Projects can be altered or adapted to the instructor's school location and learning objectives for the class.

Award-Winning Technology

McGraw-Hill Connect

McGraw-Hill Connect® is an award-winning digital teaching and learning solution that empowers students to achieve better outcomes and enables instructors to improve efficiency with course management. Within Connect, students have access to SmartBook®, McGraw-Hill's adaptive learning and reading resource. SmartBook prompts students with questions based on the material they are studying. By assessing individual answers, SmartBook learns what each student knows and identifies which topics they need to practise, giving each student a personalized learning experience and path to success.

Connect's key features also include analytics and reporting, simple assignment management, smart grading, the opportunity to post your own resources, and the Connect Instructor Library, a repository for additional resources to improve student engagement in and out of the classroom.

Instructor Resources for *ABC's of Relationship Selling through Service*, Seventh Canadian Edition:

- Instructor's Manual
- Test Bank
- Microsoft® PowerPoint® Presentations

Application-Based Activities

The Connect Application-Based Activities are highly interactive and automatically graded application- and analysis-based exercises wherein students immerse themselves in a marketing environment, analyze the situation, and apply their knowledge of marketing strategies. Students progress from understanding basic concepts to assessing and solving complex real-world scenarios.

Acknowledgements

I was thrilled to be asked to work on this textbook by Sara Braithwaite. Without her confidence and trust in me, I would not be writing this today, so to Sara—thank you! The professionals at McGraw-Hill Ryerson were a pleasure to work with and I enjoyed meeting many of them throughout this process. I also want to give a huge shout out to Sarah Fulton, who helped guide me through this process and was instrumental in the writing, editing, and completion of this text. We worked really well together and have similar values in what we wanted to include in this new edition, so I am extremely grateful to have her as an editor. I look forward to many more editions with Sarah as my guide.

I want to give a special acknowledgement to my family, especially my husband Bernie, and my children, Maddie and Charlie, who supported my writing endeavours and continue to encourage me daily. Your support is truly appreciated. I also want to thank my parents, Paul and Carole Predhomme, who left us far too soon, but who continue to guide me by having established early-on the importance of ethical and professional behaviours, which is at the forefront of many selling topics in this textbook.

In this edition of *ABC's*, I wanted to include some current events and topics such as Indigenous corporate training and crowdfunding, along with others. Unfortunately, new corporate unethical events continue to arise, some of which were included in this text, which emphasizes the continued importance of ethical behaviour in selling. Students need to understand the impact of their behaviours in the corporate world and strive to achieve a strong moral code in business leadership positions.

We reached out to college-students-turned-sales-professionals from across Canada and had them provide their insights into the real world of professional selling. It is amazing to hear about the sales successes across the country and learn about the diversity of sales stories that relate back to the ABC's textbook. A recurring theme among these professionals was the importance of service in the success of salespeople. To these sales professionals, I say thank you for the inspiration!

A special thank-you must go to the thousands of students I've taught in my 14 years at St. Clair College who always inspire me and keep me learning. Many have encouraged me to write over the past years, so I am thrilled to acknowledge them in this book. I love hearing about their successes and look forward to continuing to keep in touch with them and writing about their successes in sales and marketing in future editions.

I must also thank the many reviewers who took the time to provide input during the development of this textbook. Your comments and suggestions were highly valued and helped in the topic choices we made.

Finally, a special thank you goes out to a few of my colleagues who help me with either contacting past students or listening to me as I evaluated different additions to this text:

Barry Rivard, St.Clair College
Keith Barnwell, Sheridan College
Garry Glatter, St.Clair College
Shannon Cox, Douglas College
Veronica Barris, St.Clair College
Jim Neubauer, Algonquin College
Kevin Hood, University of Waterloo
Terri Champion, Niagara College
Anthony Mancini, St.Clair College
George Dracopoulos, Concordia University
David Moscovitz, Vanier College
Ed McHugh, Nova Scotia Community College

Nicole Rourke
St.Clair College

PART ONE

Selling as a Profession

The first part of *ABC's of Relationship Selling through Service* is written to give readers an overview of the sales profession. Many students, in various business programs, will hesitate if asked whether they want to pursue a career in sales upon graduation. The reasons for this vary greatly, but upon examination it always seems to be that there is a common misconception about the profession itself. This is largely due to the fact that many college students have had limited exposure to the profession other than perhaps part-time sales clerk jobs in retail stores.

Part 1 explores the sales profession itself, identifying the many types of selling careers available as well as the different rewards that a sales career offers. Readers will also learn how and where ethics and ethical behaviour tie in with a sales career.

This part includes:

Source: © Shutterstock/Monkey Business Images

CHAPTER 1

The Life, Times, and Career of the Professional Salesperson

Ryan Eddy
St. Clair College, Zekelman School of Business and IT, Windsor, Ontario.
Source: Courtesy of Ryan Eddy.

A Sales Success Story

Ryan Eddy worked in the automotive industry building seats at an assembly plant for seven years, but soon realized he wanted more of a career than "working on the production line." He decided to head to college and enrolled in the Business Administration Marketing program at St. Clair College, Zekelman School of Business.

Upon graduating in 2012, Ryan accepted a sales position at Provincial Chrysler in Windsor, Ontario, using the sales skills he learned in college as well as his experience from building seats for cars to establish credibility in the automotive industry. After six years in this position, Ryan is the top selling car salesperson at the company and keeps exceeding his personal goals for sales.

As Ryan states, "Success in my sales career has come from being self-driven, self-motivated, and extremely competitive. I am also constantly working at my craft to get better." He compares salespeople to professional athletes. "Just like professional baseball players who practise their swing and defence on a daily basis in order to get better, professional salespeople should practise their craft as well. Learning a new close or a new way to handle an objection will help you become better. And if you are not getting better, you are getting worse."

Ryan also emphasizes that "Sales is a career, not a job. A job is something you have to do to earn money, whereas a career is something you wish to do and you are passionate about. Because sales is a career, you have to think long term with every deal you are involved in. Long-term thinking and a focus on learning have allowed me to have success to this point. My advice to anyone looking to get into a sales position would be to do the same. Find something you like or enjoy doing and it will make it much easier to sell. When you have a passion for your product or service, your customers will sense that and you will reap the benefits."

MAIN TOPICS

What Is Selling?

Why Choose a Sales Career?

Is a Sales Career Right for You?

Success in Selling—What Does It Take?

Relationship Selling

Do You Have What it Takes?

Sales Jobs Are Different

What Does a Professional Salesperson Do?

Relationship Marketing

Building Relationships through the Sales Process

LEARNING OBJECTIVES

This chapter introduces you to the rewarding career of professional selling. After studying this chapter, you should be able to:

LO1 Define and explain the term *selling*.

LO2 Explain why everyone sells, even you.

LO3 Discuss the reasons that people might choose a sales career.

LO4 Identify the many different types of sales jobs and discuss their responsibilities.

LO5 Discuss the rewards inherent in a sales career.

LO6 Define the characteristics that are needed for success in building relationships with customers.

LO7 List and explain the 10 steps in the sales process.

FACING A SALES CHALLENGE

Chin Lee graduated from Conestoga College with a degree in computer technology. After graduation, Chin was hired by a major technology-oriented company in eastern Canada as a computer technician. After three years in this position, he decided that it was time for a change; he requested and was given a transfer to the sales department.

"My first love was computers. I went to school to become an expert in technology but this became a bit boring after a few years. When I moved to sales, I was very frightened at first as I didn't have a lot of practice dealing with people and their problems, but I soon learned that my technical knowledge allowed me to become very proficient at solving customer problems. The more I worked with people, the more I enjoyed it. It was exciting and very rewarding."

Chin never looked back. Before long, he had become one of the leading producers in the sales department. With that came many financial and personal rewards, as well as job offers from some of his client companies. However, Chin felt he had the perfect job and decided to stay put.

(Continued at end of chapter.)

David Ogilvy, one of the fathers of modern advertising, said it best: "We sell or else." His implication was that nothing happens in business until someone sells something and an exchange takes place. The efforts of salespeople have an impact on virtually every field of business. Selling is an honourable, challenging, and rewarding career.

Chapter 1 examines the reasons why people choose sales careers, and provides information about factors critical for success in sales.

LO1 What Is Selling?

personal selling: The personal communication of information to persuade a prospective customer to buy something that satisfies that individual's needs.

Many people consider *selling* and *marketing* synonymous. However, selling is actually only one of many marketing components. In business, **personal selling** refers to the personal communication of information to persuade a prospective customer to buy something—a good, service, idea, or something else—that satisfies the individual's needs on a personal level, or on a business level when an individual is purchasing for a company.

This definition of selling involves one person communicating with an individual or a group to make a sale. The salesperson often works with prospects or customers to examine their needs, provide information, suggest a product to meet their needs, and provide after-sale service to ensure long-term satisfaction.

LO2 Everybody Sells!

If you think about it, everyone is involved with selling. Children develop communication skills early in life to get what they want. When you want something or want someone to do something, you use your natural selling skills. When you attempt to get a date, ask for a pay raise, urge your professor to raise your mark, provide cost-effective solutions to buyers, or deal with customer service representatives in large companies, you are using personal selling skills. Perhaps after completing this

MAKING THE SALE

SOCIAL MEDIA

Brett Legein, a senior sales representative for an electrical supply manufacturer, sells electrical supplies to major accounts across Canada. Brett loves the job as he is a very sociable individual and he gets to meet and interact with a variety of customers on a daily basis.

In recent years Brett has found that his sales have been levelling off and he has been losing ground to some of his competitors. As a relative old-timer, with a vast amount of product knowledge, he was a little perplexed as to why this was happening. At a company party, Brett was speaking with some of his younger colleagues who had often come to him in the past for product advice so he decided to pick their brains about some of the techniques that they were using to grow their own sales accounts.

Eva Spencer, one of the newer and most productive reps in the company, had some good advice for Brett. Her suggestion was that Brett should take the plunge and start using social media to cultivate more sales. He was initially reluctant but agreed to give it a try. Brett first signed up for Twitter and LinkedIn, two giants in the social media realm. Before long, he became proficient at both and had established a real online social presence. He tweeted regularly about product developments and 'Linked up' with hundreds of people in his industry. He was also able to 'listen in' on what was happening in the industry with some of his competitors.

Brett found his sales numbers growing again. Because of his new online presence, he found that prospects started to reach out to him and he was also able to find and nurture prospects that he hadn't been able to before. He had recently received a call from a customer who said to him, "I had just stumbled upon one of your postings where you were discussing the benefits of the new electrical service panels your company was producing and I would like to meet with you to discuss a possible purchase."

Brett realized that these new techniques were not cutting into his "socializing," the part of his job that he enjoyed so much. He found that he was just socializing in a slightly different way. The next time he ran into Eva, he thanked her for her wonderful advice. She simply said, "Welcome to the modern sales world."

textbook you will become more effective in each of the above situations. Your ability to communicate effectively is crucial to your success in life.

Sales courses are full of people who not only want to improve their professional selling skills for increased success in their business lives, but also want to enhance their personal communication skills. Learning how to communicate to others how your ideas or products can satisfy their needs will be invaluable throughout your life.

Many may be trained as professional purchasing agents or buyers, but they also see the value of learning effective sales skills. Some might believe that they are simply trying to learn the "tricks" of the trade to arm themselves for the onslaught of sales representatives. Most simply want to enhance their performance by gaining an understanding of the salesperson's perspective, which leads to more effective purchasing, negotiation, and selling. The skills and knowledge gained from a selling course can be used by a student who plans to go into virtually any field, such as law, financial services, medicine, or journalism, or by those who start their own business.

In today's competitive environment, where good interpersonal skills are so valued, people are at a disadvantage when they lack selling capability. As you read this book and progress through the course, think about how you can use the material both personally and in business.

Exhibit 1.1 shows a simplified organizational chart for a marketing-oriented organization. Although research departments can study markets to determine

EXHIBIT 1.1

Where selling fits in.

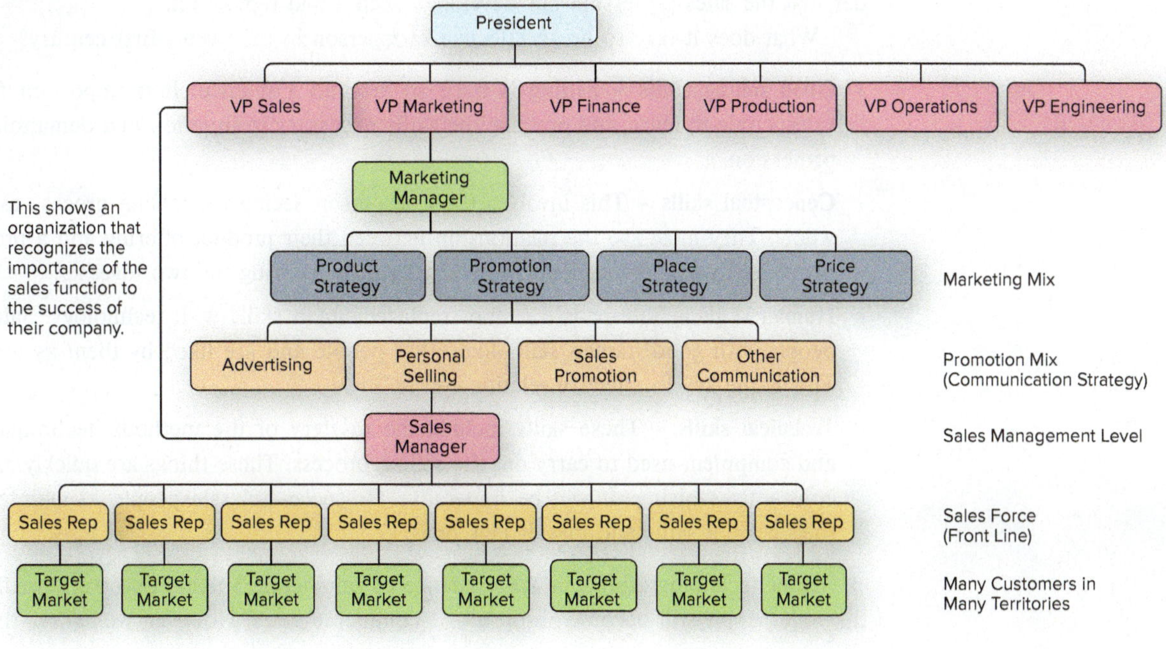

their buying habits and needs, it is the sales force that acts as front-line representatives for companies. Part of the selling job entails learning about market needs, relaying that information to company strategists, and communicating to the market how the company's products can satisfy their needs. Although personal selling is only one part of the promotional element, which in turn is only one part of the marketing mix, today's companies understand the importance of using well trained and effective salespeople–and the contribution that they make to the bottom line.

LO3 Why Choose a Sales Career?

The major reasons for choosing a sales career include:

1. The wide variety of sales jobs available - Check out www.indeed.ca and review various sales jobs available to college graduates in your area. Selling is one of the largest employment categories in Canada.
2. The excitement and freedom of working independently.
3. The challenge of selling - At the beginning of this chapter, Ryan Eddy referred to his sense of competitiveness. Many athletes go into sales because they seek out competitive environments.
4. The opportunity for advancement in a company - Many presidents and vice-presidents in large corporations worked in sales at some point in their career.
5. The financial and other rewards of a sales career.
6. Service to others - Selling allows you the opportunity to help customers solve problems or challenges in their world.
7. The tremendous sense of accomplishment - Achieving your sales goals can lead to financial gain as well as a personal sense of esteem and achievement.

The Sales Force of the Future

Historically, due to the attitudes and philosophies of business owners, salespeople have developed a reputation for being fast talking, aggressive, and slick. Salespeople were expected to "hustle" business and "push" their products on people. It's no wonder that the sales profession has developed such a bad reputation.

What does it take to be an effective salesperson in the twenty-first century?

- **Good selling skills** - Selling is both an art and a science. It is important for salespeople to learn and practise the skills necessary to function in a demanding profession.
- **Conceptual skills** - This involves the salesperson seeing the selling process as a whole. They must see the relationship between their product offering and a prospect's needs and then develop a selling strategy to bring the two together.
- **Human skills** - Salespeople cannot replace human skills with technology. Salespeople with good human skills like other people and are liked by them as well. This is the key to effective relationship selling.
- **Technical skills** - These skills include the mastery of the methods, techniques, and equipment used to carry out the selling process. These things are quickly and constantly evolving. It will be imperative for successful salespeople to maintain their current skills and master new ones.

Does technology threaten the existence of salespeople? Some observers predict that salespeople will become obsolete as e-commerce soars. However, we believe that salespeople will always be needed, although their role may change slightly; salespeople will evolve into "business success coaches." For example, prospective customers may have access via the Internet to information about your products and those of your competitors. However, they will still need your personal contact and expertise to help them diagnose their specific needs and to communicate the best solution to satisfy them. Sales professionals will still be needed to establish and cultivate relationships with their customers.

MAKING THE SALE

A CAREER IN SALES

IF YOU WANT:	IDEAL CAREER	REASON
Flexibility	Sales	Can often set your own agenda and schedule
High income potential	Sales	Salaries, commissions, bonuses, etc.
Pride and accomplishment	Sales	You make it happen; you get to help others
Excitement and variety	Sales	Meeting different people, travel, conventions, etc.
To be your own boss	Sales	You run your territory like it's your business
Challenge	Sales	Quotas, bonuses, constant desire to improve

Social Media in Selling

In addition to the smart phones and other modern communication methods, salespeople are increasingly making use of social media to enhance their selling power. **Social media** refers to technology that allows social interaction and communication over the Internet. Social media such as Facebook, LinkedIn, Instagram, and Twitter are being used more and more by salespeople to prospect for new customers, communicate with potential and existing customers, and provide customer service to their ongoing client base. Later in the text, we will examine ways in which salespeople can use these social media to build and maintain their business.

social media: Technology that allows social interaction and communication over the World Wide Web (for example, Facebook, LinkedIn, and Twitter).

Types of Sales Employment

LO4

Sales positions vary by customer focus, educational and experience requirements, duties and responsibilities, and position in a company's hierarchy. In retail selling, salespeople focus on selling directly to the consumer of a product either from a traditional retail store, or through door-to-door selling, home demonstrations, and so on. In most types of selling, salespeople are selling in a business-to-business setting. These positions can involve selling products to an intermediary for resale or further processing or selling products to companies that will then use them to run their business.

You will note that as the type of sales job becomes more complex and better paying, the education requirements become higher. Many higher-paying sales positions today are filled by people who combine formal educational background with some product-related education.

Careers in Selling

The following sales positions are representative of the sales profession in Canada. Brief job descriptions originate from Monster.ca, a leading online global careers network.[1] The salary figures listed below are from www.salaryexpert.com, and look at data from the Toronto, Ontario area.

Sales clerks typically sell merchandise in a retail store, assisting customers with sales, returns, exchanges, and product knowledge. This type of sales job requires a high school diploma and up to two years of related experience. A sales clerk should possess knowledge of common practices and procedures relating to a particular product field. Sales clerks average approximately $33,000 annually, depending on location, type of company, and experience.

Order desk clerks are often referred to as inside sales reps in that they process and review orders received by mail, by telephone, or online. This position requires a high school diploma and up to two years of related experience. Strict guidelines are followed and clerks should have a working knowledge of the products and procedures of their company. Annual salaries in this field average approximately $41,000.

Customer service representatives are responsible for processing orders, preparing correspondence, and ensuring customer satisfaction in a variety of businesses. A bachelor's degree or college diploma is typically required, along with a general understanding of the tasks necessary to achieve sales and customer service goals. In this position salespeople have some latitude to attain their goals. Customer service reps (CSRs) average approximately $50,000 annually.

Source: © Image Source/Getty Images RF

Merchandisers are not your typical salesperson. They are often referred to as support salespeople and are responsible for setting up displays and providing product literature in a customer's premises. Merchandisers usually have good knowledge of the field in which they are working and often have a college diploma or associated degree. Merchandisers earn approximately $58,000 annually. Many merchandisers work flexible hours, including part-time, and this is a great entry level place for college graduates to start their selling career.

Sales representatives are responsible for developing new business and interacting with existing customers to increase sales of an organization's products and/or services. Sales reps typically have several years of experience in a particular field. Sales reps are more independent and are expected to use their own judgment and experience to plan and achieve sales goals. Sales reps earn approximately $70,000 annually.

Senior sales representatives have duties similar to a sales representative's, with the difference being that they are required to perform more complicated tasks and are often expected to lead and direct others. A great degree of latitude and creativity is expected here, and senior reps typically report to a manager. The higher complexity of the job allows them to earn from $70,000 to $110,000 per year.

Business solutions (development) specialists collaborate with customers and use their education and experience to develop product enhancements or alterations necessary for a sale. These reps normally have extensive experience and must understand and perform a variety of tasks related to their field. They often must direct the work of others, and for these skills they earn approximately $77,000 annually.

Technical sales representatives (Senior) average approximately $102,000 per year depending on their level of expertise and the nature of the products they deal with. These sales reps typically have at least a college diploma and possibly an undergraduate or graduate degree. Technical sales reps are typically responsible for increasing sales to accounts by interacting with customers and providing them with technical knowledge and solutions.

Key account representatives oversee the customer relationships within a designated territory. These reps identify key accounts and develop ongoing relationships with them to increase sales. This popular job requires a college diploma or university degree and, in most cases, several years of experience in the field. These reps require good judgment and creativity to help them establish and achieve goals. These account reps earn from approximately $87,000 to more than $150,000 annually.

Top sales executives can earn salaries from $207,000 to over $394,000 per year. Reporting to top management, these sales executives plan and direct all aspects of an organization's sales policies, objectives, and initiatives. This position typically requires a bachelor's degree and several years of experience.

Many sales job show significant salary increases with years of experience. The graph below comes from www.salestalentagency.com. They surveyed almost 5,000 sales professionals in Canada to understand the average base salary by years of experience. Exhibit 1.2 shows the average base salary for salespeople by years of experience.

EXHIBIT 1.2

Average base salary by years of experience.

Source: Used with the permission of Jamie Scarborough.

Order Takers versus Order Getters

Order takers may ask what the customer wants or even wait for the customer to order. They do not have a sales strategy and do not use creative sales presentations. Order takers seldom attempt to close a sale. Although they do perform many useful services, few truly *create* sales.

Order getters, on the other hand, are responsible for generating new business through many different means. Companies strive to employ the most effective order getters as these people drive the success of the company through creative sales strategies and effective sales presentations. Order getters face an infinitely more difficult task; therefore, they usually earn much more than the order taker.

Exhibit 1.3 shows a continuum of sales jobs and compares their complexity and salaries.

order taker:
An individual who asks what the customer wants or waits for the customer to order.

order getter:
An individual who gets new and repeat business using a creative sales strategy and a well-executed sales presentation.

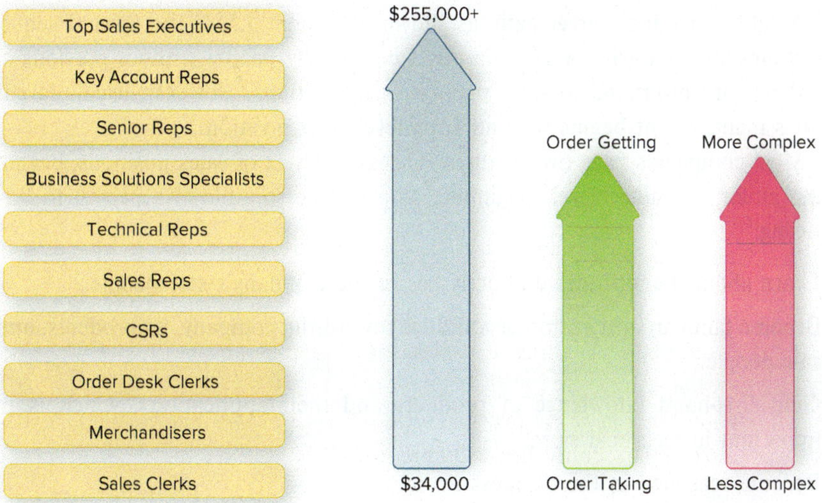

EXHIBIT 1.3

A continuum of sales jobs, comparing complexity and salary.

EXHIBIT 1.4

Selling services offers excellent career opportunities; banks, hotels, airlines, and travel agencies are industries that need professional salespeople.

Source: © Rob Daly/age fotostock

Freedom of Action: You're on Your Own

A second reason that people choose a sales career is the freedom it offers. A sales job provides possibly the greatest relative freedom of any career. Experienced employees in outside sales usually receive little direct supervision and may go for days, even weeks, without seeing their bosses. The term *outside sales* refers to selling activities external to the employer's premises. These contracts involve person-to-person contact between the sales representative and customer or prospective customer. By contrast, *inside sales* occur on the premises, as in retail selling or telemarketing.

Although duties and sales goals are explained by a boss, salespeople are expected to carry out their job duties and achieve goals with minimum guidance. They usually leave home to contact customers around the corner or around the world. As long as you perform your assigned duties, are reliable and, of course, meet your quotas, you likely won't have someone breathing down your neck expecting you to be at work at 7:00 a.m. every morning.

Job Challenge Is Always There

Working alone with the responsibility of a territory capable of generating thousands (sometimes millions) of dollars in revenue for a company is a personal challenge. Salespeople often deal with hundreds of different people and firms. It is much like operating your own business, without the burdens of true ownership.

Opportunities for Advancement Are Great

Successful salespeople have many opportunities to move into top management positions, and, in many instances, this advancement comes quickly (see Exhibit 1.4). For example, General Mills and Quaker Oats may promote successful salespeople to managerial positions, such as district sales managers, after they have been with the company for only two years.

career path: The upward sequence of job movements during a sales career.

A sales personnel **career path**, as shown in Exhibit 1.5, is the upward sequence of job movements during a sales career. Occasionally people without previous sales experience are promoted to sales management positions. However, usually a career in sales management begins with an entry-level sales position.

Most companies have two or three successive levels of sales positions, beginning at the junior or trainee level. Beginning as a salesperson allows a person to do the following:

- Learn about the attitudes and activities of the company's salespeople.
- Become familiar with customer attitudes toward the company, its products, and its salespeople.
- Gain first-hand knowledge of products and their applications, which is most important in technical sales.
- Become seasoned in the business world.

EXHIBIT 1.5

A sales personnel career path.

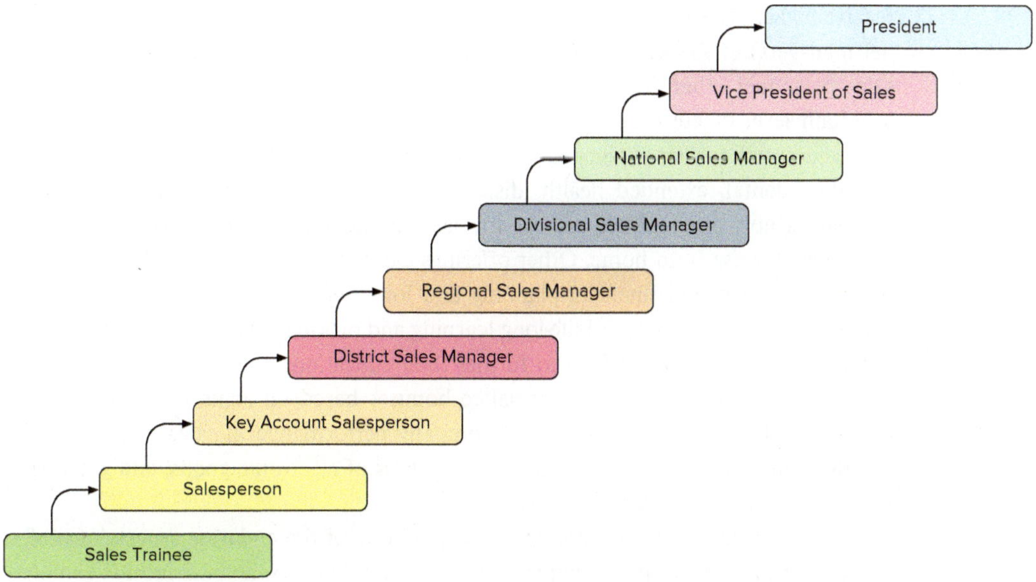

Sales managers frequently mention that this position represents their first major step toward the top; they are on the management team. Instead of being responsible for $1 million in sales as a salesperson, the manager is responsible for $10 million.

Success opens many jobs throughout the sales force and in the corporate marketing department. These jobs can include sales training, sales analysis, advertising, and product management.

Two Career Paths Don't let Exhibit 1.5 mislead you–many salespeople prefer selling to managing people. They want to take care of themselves rather than others. In some companies, a salesperson may even earn more money than the manager.

Many companies have recognized the value of keeping some salespeople in the field for their entire sales career. They do a good job, know their customers, and love what they are doing–so why promote them if they do not want to move up within the organization?

Rewards: The Sky's the Limit

LO5

As a salesperson, you can look forward to two types of rewards: *nonfinancial* and *financial.*

Nonfinancial Rewards

Sometimes called psychological income or intrinsic rewards, **nonfinancial rewards** are generated by the individual, not given by the company. Successfully meeting the challenges of the job produces a feeling of self-worth: You realize that your job is important. Everyone wants to feel good about a job, and a selling career allows you to experience these good feelings and intrinsic rewards daily. Salespeople often report that the nonfinancial rewards of their jobs are just as important to them as the financial rewards.

nonfinancial rewards: Rewards that are generated by the individual, not given by the company; also called psychological income or intrinsic rewards.

For example, some companies offer their top performers foreign postings in exotic locations. In other companies, management attempts to motivate salespeople by providing recognition in the form of public advertising and internal promotion of top performers. How often in a company do you see the top administrators recognized? For the sales department, this is a common practice, whereby salespeople are given the recognition they deserve. After all, if it weren't for them, the company probably wouldn't be in operation.

Financial Rewards

financial rewards: Rewards given or compensation given by a company.

Success also brings **financial rewards**. Both corporate and field sales managers typically receive higher salaries than others (such as production, advertising, product, or personnel managers) at the same organizational level. Besides salary, many firms offer their sales personnel other remuneration or perks. For example, recognizing the need for a certain level of customer entertainment, many companies offer club memberships for business use as well as personal memberships for health clubs. Group medical plans, including dental, extended health, disability, and life insurance, are common. Most companies now offer mobile phones for sales representatives, and many offer laptop computers for use from home. Other offerings can range from pension plans and stock purchases to personal financial planning and low-interest personal loans. Many companies embrace the concept of life-long learning and provide educational reimbursement programs for employees seeking to further their education.

incentive: A reward that serves to motivate someone.

Cash **incentives** include performance bonuses based on achievement of sale targets. Other bonuses based on overall company performance in sales or profitability are also common. All-expense-paid vacations, gifts of electronic goods, and gift vouchers can be used as rewards for sales.

Although there is some variation by region, one of the enduring aspects of professional selling is some form of compensation for travel. Many companies provide company cars for use by their sales representatives. In the remaining companies, either a monthly allowance, a per-kilometre allowance, or a combination of the two is provided.

The Canadian sales force is very diversified (see Exhibit 1.6). Many people are attracted to selling because, in a sales career, financial rewards are usually based solely on performance.

EXHIBIT 1.6

The Canadian sales force is very diversified. There is room for everyone in a sales career.

Source: © Phil Date/Dreamstime.com/GetStock.com

You can use the Internet to compare sales jobs. Several websites listed at the end of this chapter have tools for researching sales salaries. The websites www.monster.ca, www.indeed.ca, www.salestalentagency.com, www.salaryexpert.com, and www.payscale.com have very useful tools that allow you to determine salary levels for various jobs requiring different levels of experience and education, and located in different areas of Canada.

Is a Sales Career Right for You?

It may be too early in life to determine whether you really want to be a salesperson. The balance of this book will aid you in investigating sales as a career. Your search for any career begins with *you.* In considering a sales career, be honest and realistic. Ask yourself questions such as:

- What are my past accomplishments?
- What are my future goals?
- Do I want the responsibility of a sales job?
- Do I mind travel? How much travel is acceptable?
- How much freedom do I want in the job?
- Do I have the personality characteristics for the job?
- Am I willing to transfer to another city? Another province?

Your answers to these questions can help you analyze the various types of sales jobs and establish criteria for evaluating job openings. Determine the industries, types of products or services, and specific companies in which you have an interest.

College placement offices, libraries, and business periodicals offer plenty of information on companies as well as sales positions in them. Conversations with friends and acquaintances who are involved in selling or have been in sales can give you realistic insight into what challenges, rewards, and disadvantages the sales vocation offers. Ask yourself: Do I have any relatives who are in sales? Have I ever personally seen a sales rep in action? Experience with salespeople will give you a better understanding of the sales job. To better prepare yourself to obtain a sales job, you must understand what companies look for in salespeople.

SELLING GLOBALLY

CULTURAL SENSITIVITY

Andrew Stevens and his sales team travelled to Japan to begin negotiations with a major Japanese electronics firm in hopes of becoming the sole supplier of a revolutionary new building technology recently developed in Canada. Mr. Stevens recognized that Japan could become a major market for this technology so these negotiations were critical.

Things started out well. The sales team was invited to a formal company reception with senior company executives and government officials in attendance. During a speech by one of the dignitaries, Mr. Stevens leaned over to his Japanese counterpart and made an offhand remark about the Japanese Royal Family. Several minutes later, his counterpart left the room momentarily. For the rest of the evening, it appeared that the hosts were distancing themselves from the Canadian sales team. Over the next few days, despite a congenial front, negotiations turned sour and Stevens's team wasn't able to gain a commitment for anything.

Over the next few weeks, Stevens met with more rejection. The sales team was getting nowhere. Finally, they gave up and returned to Canada. Something had happened and they just couldn't figure out what it was. Upon returning home, they called a postmortem meeting to discuss their failed business trip.

What happened? Can you offer any advice to salespeople who sell internationally?

A Sales Manager's View of the Recruit

The following discussion of what sales managers consider when hiring a salesperson is based on a summary of a talk given by a sales manager to a sales class.

> We look for outstanding applicants who are mature and intelligent. They should be able to handle themselves well in the interview, demonstrating good interpersonal skills. They should have a well-thought-out career plan and be able to discuss it rationally. They should have a friendly, pleasing personality. A clean, neat appearance is a must. They should have a positive attitude, be willing to work hard, be ambitious, and demonstrate a good degree of interest in the employer's business field. They should have good grades and other personal, school, and business accomplishments. Finally, they should have clear goals and objectives in life. The more common characteristics on which applicants for our company are judged are (1) appearance, (2) self-expression, (3) maturity, (4) personality, (5) experience, (6) enthusiasm, and (7) interest in the job.

A sales job has not only high rewards but also many important responsibilities. Let us review the characteristics of a successful salesperson.

LO6 Success in Selling—What Does it Take?

Throughout this book you will read comments from salespeople about their jobs. Over the years, we have asked thousands of salespeople the question, "What makes a salesperson successful?" The nine most frequently mentioned characteristics are:

1. Love of their job
2. Willingness to work hard
3. Need to achieve success
4. Optimistic outlook
5. Knowledge of their job
6. Careful use of selling time
7. Ability to ask questions and listen to customers
8. Customer service
9. Being physically and mentally prepared for life and the job

Some of these characteristics are described more fully below.

Love of Selling

The successful salesperson is an individual who loves selling, finds it exciting, and is strongly convinced that the product being sold offers something of great value. Salespeople quoted throughout this book comment about how their enthusiasm for their work helps them to be successful. They possess an eagerness to do the job well, which causes them to work hard at selling.

Willingness to Work Hard

A positive attitude toward work works wonders! Successful people are often described as lucky. However, they spell luck W-O-R-K. The harder they work, the luckier they get.

Need to Achieve Success

Successful salespeople say that even though they enjoy it, selling requires long hours of hard work, day in and day out, to reach personal goals. A 10- to 12-hour workday is common—including many Saturdays and Sundays. It is their love of work and their need for success that motivate the top sellers. The need to achieve also involves persistence.

MAKING THE SALE

DON'T QUIT

When things go wrong, as they sometimes will,
When the road you're trudging seems all uphill,
When the funds are low and the debts are high,
And you want to smile, but you have to sigh,
When care is pressing you down a bit—
Rest if you must, but don't you quit.

Life is queer with its twists and turns,
As every one of us sometimes learns,
And many a failure turns about
When he might have won had he stuck it out.
Don't give up though the pace seems slow—
You may succeed with another blow.

Often the goal is nearer than,
It seems to a faint and faltering man,
Often the struggler has given up
When he might have captured the victor's cup;
And he learned too late when the night slipped down,
How close he was to the golden crown.

Success is failure turned inside out—
The silver tint of the clouds of doubt
And you never can tell how close you are,
It may be near when it seems so far,
So stick to the fight when you're hardest hit—
It's when things seem worst that you mustn't quit.

AUTHOR UNKNOWN

Have an Optimistic Outlook

Salespeople credit a positive attitude toward their companies, products, customers, themselves, and life as major reasons for their success. Successful salespeople are enthusiastic, confident, and consider themselves successful. Sure, salespeople have times when things do not go as they want, yet their positive attitude helps them through. They continually look for methods to improve their attitude.

Successful salespeople say that their greatest enemy is procrastination. They know that the early bird gets the worm. They are do-it-now people. They pick up the phone, mail a letter, or make a sales call today. In no other career is the need to think positively more important. Make sure you have a positive, enthusiastic attitude toward yourself, your work, and your customers. This involves:

- Believing in yourself
- Thinking of yourself as a success
- Being positive in your outlook on life and the job

Be Knowledgeable

Successful salespeople place great emphasis on being thoroughly knowledgeable in all aspects of their business (see Exhibit 1.7). This helps them to project a professional image and build customer confidence.

Knowledge also includes awareness of the most up-to-date ideas concerning selling skills. Successful salespeople are expert at developing and presenting talks that sell their products. They constantly educate themselves on methods to better determine customers' needs and to effectively communicate the benefits of their products to satisfy those needs.

EXHIBIT 1.7

Salespeople work hard to become experts on their products and those of their competitors. Only then can they effectively use selling skills to provide information that helps customers.

Source: Leaf/Dreamstime.com/GetStock.com

SOCIAL MEDIA INSIGHTS FOR SALESPEOPLE

Salespeople can embrace social media to support their day-to-day selling activities in three ways:

1. Listen – Stay on top of activities in your industry by setting up Google Alerts. Use search phrases related to your company, product, and competition and those phrases that your customers might use to find out information about your company. Use Twitter and LinkedIn to monitor activities in your industry so you can learn and evolve into a subject matter expert.
2. Network – Social media was made for networking. LinkedIn is excellent for identifying and connecting with key contacts. Build quality relationships based on trust and value. Don't just add contacts, connect with them and participate regularly in discussions.
3. Participate – Become a subject matter expert and share your wisdom. Bring value to the online communities while developing your personal brand.

Source: Excerpt from cpsa.com/knowledgecentre/SRCArticleRead.aspx?articleID=446. Canadian Professional Sales Association (CPSA). Used with permission.

Salespeople read books and magazine articles on selling, and attend sales training courses to learn how to sell their products better. This knowledge is incorporated into sales presentations that are rehearsed until they sound like a natural conversation between seller and buyer.

Be Ruthless about Time

The most successful people are ruthless about guarding their time. In daily activities, they instinctively understand the powerful secret to success called the Pareto principle.

The Pareto principle is named after nineteenth-century economist Vilfredo Pareto, who found that in any human activity, the biggest results usually arise from a small number of factors. For example, studies have shown that most people spend 80 percent of their time on the least important 20 percent of their jobs, and only 20 percent doing the work that yields 80 percent of their bottom-line results.

Successful salespeople define the specific results that practically guarantee success. Then they ruthlessly arrange daily priorities to invest 80 percent of their time into the 20 percent of work with the greatest results payout. Since there is only so much time in the day for contacting customers, and there are so many demands on their time, successful salespeople value time and use it wisely by carefully planning their day's activities. Which customer will be called on, what product will be presented, and how to present it must be planned carefully.

CPSA: Canadian Professional Sales Association.

SELLING TIPS

THE CANADIAN PROFESSIONAL SALES ASSOCIATION

The Canadian Professional Sales Association (**CPSA**) is a national association comprising more than 30,000 sales and marketing professionals located in communities of all sizes in every part of Canada.

The CPSA was founded in 1874; today, CPSA members represent the full spectrum of the sales profession, including senior managers, entrepreneurs, sales managers, and sales representatives.

Providing sales professionals with the tools and resources to succeed has remained CPSA's mandate. CPSA members enjoy special rates on travel and hotels, car leasing and rentals, insurance, and financial services. CPSA has an outstanding professional development program that includes an extensive library of sales and marketing materials, national seminar and conference sessions, and sales training courses. This program enhances CPSA's commitment to sales professionals across Canada.

Visit the CPSA website to learn more at www.cpsa.com.

Source: Canadian Professional Sales Association (CPSA). Used with permission.

Ask Questions and Then Listen to Uncover Customer Needs

Joe Gandolfo, who sold more than *$1 billion* of life insurance in a single year, has a sign on his office wall that reads, "God gave you two ears and one mouth, and He meant for you to do twice as much listening as talking."

Good salespeople are good listeners. They ask questions to uncover prospects' needs and then listen as prospects answer the questions and state their needs. Then they show how their products will fulfill these needs. The ability to identify and meet customer needs separates the successful salesperson from the average salesperson.

Empathy is the ability to put yourself in someone else's shoes. In subsequent chapters, you will learn the importance of determining customers' needs and determining the many factors that can influence your prospects in their purchase decision making. Developing your empathy will allow you to feel what your prospect is feeling and be affected by what is affecting your prospect. Empathetic salespeople can be much more effective at satisfying customer needs and hence will become much more successful than those who don't care.

empathy:
The ability to identify and understand another person's feelings, ideas, and circumstances.

Serve Your Customer

The most important characteristic for establishing a lasting sales relationship with a customer is willingness to provide service. Customers must believe that you care about them and their welfare. Successful salespeople respect their customers, treat them fairly, like them, and develop a good working relationship with them that is like a partnership.

MAKING THE SALE

WHAT IS YOUR VALUE?

Top-performing salespeople are always striving to be the best they can be. Each of us has control of our destiny. We will be what we want to be. Consider, for example, a plain bar of iron that is worth about $5. Made into a horseshoe, it's worth about $11; made into screwdrivers, it's worth about $15; made into needles, it's worth about $3,500. The same is true for another kind of material—YOU! Your value is determined by what you decide to make of yourself.

Be Physically and Mentally Prepared

With physical preparedness comes mental strength. Knowing that you are in shape, mentally and physically, to deal with today and tomorrow is important to your success. Ten minutes of aerobic exercise per day will improve cardiovascular fitness if you can't wedge 30- to 60-minute exercise periods into your schedule three to five times per week.

In addition, what we choose to eat and drink and whether we smoke directly influences our physical and mental processes. Learn about the dietary and physical aspects of your body, and commit to sustaining your mental and physical fitness.

Relationship Selling

Salespeople are no longer adversaries who manipulate people for personal gain. They want to be consultants, partners, and problem solvers for customers. Their goal is to build a long-term relationship with clients through **relationship selling**. Salespeople seek to benefit their employer, themselves, and customers.

relationship selling:
Salespeople build a long-term relationship with clients by acting as consultants, partners, and problem solvers.

In recent years, the distinction between a salesperson and a professional has blurred because the salesperson of today is a pro. Many salespeople know more about their field and product than the buyer does. This expertise enables the seller to become the buyer's partner, a counsellor on how to solve problems. Today's salesperson provides information that helps customers make intelligent choices to achieve their short- and long-term objectives. Service and follow-up are then provided to ensure satisfaction with the purchase. This sequence builds *customer loyalty*—a relationship.

Exhibit 1.8 shows the four main elements in the customer relationship process used by salespeople to build relationships. They analyze customers' needs, recommend a solution and gain commitment for the purchase, implement the recommendation, and maintain and grow the relationship.

EXHIBIT 1.8

Main elements in the customer relationship process. This exhibit shows the strategic process that salespeople would use to develop and maintain customer relationships. Refer to Exhibit 1.11 to see the tactical steps that need to be executed by salespeople to make the process work.

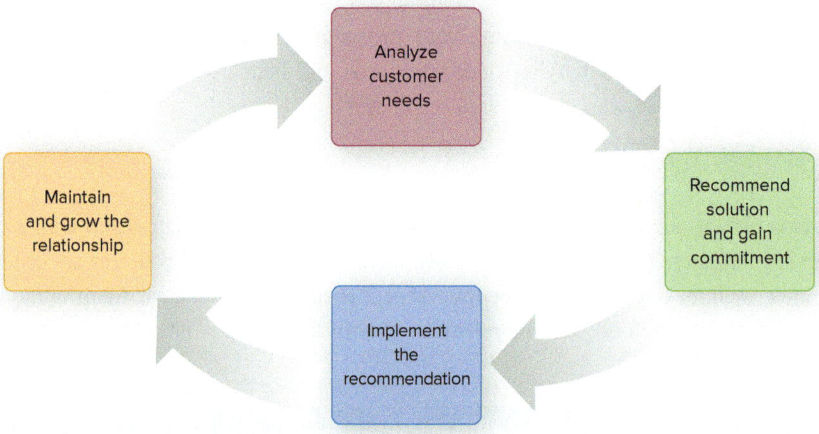

Do You Have What It Takes?

For each of the following statements, rank your agreement level from 1 to 5 with 1 being disagreeable to 5 being most agreeable. Write your score in the right hand column and total this column at the bottom (on the next page).

		1	2	3	4	5
1.	Income is my main priority in my intended profession.					
2.	Job flexibility is very important to me.					
3.	I see myself as an entrepreneur and would like my career to relate to this skill.					
4.	I enjoy being recognized for a job well done.					
5.	I thrive on and am motivated by challenge.					
6.	I am an ambitious person, motivated to advance my career.					
7.	I like to have control over my own time.					
8.	Job security is important to me.					
9.	I enjoy hard work and being rewarded for it.					
10.	I consider myself resilient—able to shrug off failures easily.					

		1	2	3	4	5
11.	I consider myself a creative problem solver and enjoy solving other people's problems.					
12.	I love meeting new people and developing personal and professional relationships.					
13.	I enjoy learning and would be open to continuous personal development.					
14.	I am empathetic and a very good listener.					
15.	I enjoy travel and experiencing new things.					
16	I consider myself to be an excellent communicator.					
17.	I have the physical stamina to put in a hard day's work.					
18.	I am adept with social media and able to learn new platforms quickly.					
19.	I am ruthless about managing my time.					
20.	I love selling.					
	TOTAL					

Results – If you scored:

85 or above – Sales might be a rewarding profession for you, both financially and personally.

70 to 84 – You would probably make a very good salesperson and enjoy the profession, especially if you scored high on statements 1, 3, 11, 12, and 20.

55 to 69 – Sales is not out of the question but try to find the type of sales position that suits your character.

Below 55 – You might not be cut out to be an effective salesperson who loves their job.

Note: This is not a scientific aptitude test but a simple guideline to help you consider whether a selling career may be right for you or not.

Sales Jobs Are Different

As you can see, sales jobs are different from other jobs in several ways. Here are some major differences:

- Salespeople represent their companies to the outside world. Consequently, opinions of a company and its products are often formed from impressions left by the sales force. The public ordinarily does not judge a firm by its office or factory workers.
- Other employees usually work under close supervisory control, whereas the outside salesperson typically operates with little or no direct supervision. Moreover, to be successful, salespeople must often be creative, be persistent, and show great initiative–all of which require a high degree of motivation.
- Salespeople probably need more tact, diplomacy, and social poise than other employees in an organization. Many sales jobs require the salesperson to display considerable emotional and social intelligence in dealing with buyers.
- Salespeople are among the few employees authorized to spend company funds. They spend this money for entertainment, transportation, and other business expenses.
- Sales jobs frequently require considerable travel and time spent away from home and family. At times, salespeople deal with customers who seem determined not to buy the sellers' products. These challenges, coupled with the physical demands of long hours and travelling, require mental toughness and physical stamina rarely demanded in other types of jobs.

Selling is hard work! It requires intelligence, the desire to achieve, and the ability to overcome difficulties.

What Does a Professional Salesperson Do?

The salesperson's roles or activities can vary from company to company, depending on the firm's market characteristics, the location of customers, and whether sales involve goods or services. For example, a salesperson selling Avon products performs similar, but somewhat different, job activities from the industrial salesperson making sales calls for General Electric.

Most people believe that a salesperson only makes sales presentations, but there is much more to the job than person-to-person selling. The salesperson functions as a **territory manager**–planning, organizing, and executing activities that increase sales and profits in a given territory. A sales territory comprises a group of customers assigned within a geographical area. Exhibit 1.9 indicates a few typical activities of a salesperson.

territory manager: A person who plans, organizes, and executes activities that increase sales and profits in a given territory.

EXHIBIT 1.9

A professional salesperson . . .

. . . helps meet the needs and solve the problems of the customer.

Source: © Joshua Hodge Photography/iStockphoto

. . . makes presentations to new and current customers.

Source: Monty Rakusen/Getty Images

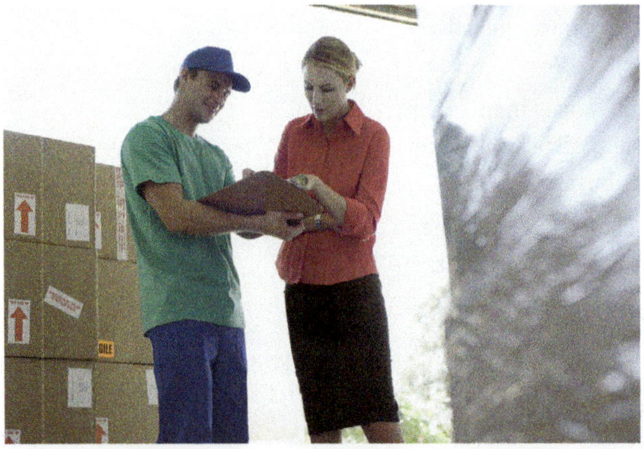

. . . sells to wholesalers and distributors.

Source: © David Schaffer/age fotostock

. . . handles customer complaints.

Source: © Ocean/Corbis

As salespeople essentially manage a territory, they perform the following ten functions:

1. **Create new customers** - To increase sales and replace customers that will be lost over time, many types of sales jobs require a salesperson to prospect. Prospecting is the lifeblood of sales because it identifies potential customers. Salespeople need the ability to *close*, or make the sale.
2. **Sell more to present customers** - Tomorrow's sales come from selling to new customers and selling to present customers again, and again, and again.
3. **Build long-term relationships with customers** - Earning the opportunity to sell more product to current customers means salespeople must have positive, professional business relationships with people and organizations that trust them and the products purchased.
4. **Actively use and manage social media platforms** - The Internet has provided many opportunities for salespeople to interact with potential customers and clients using one or more of the many social media platforms. This is becoming an important duty for salespeople to perform. Sales professionals with knowledge and skills in social media have a huge advantage over ones who don't.
5. **Provide solutions to customers' problems** - Customers have needs that can be met and problems that can be solved by purchasing goods or services. Salespeople seek to uncover potential or existing needs or problems, and show how the use of their products or services can satisfy needs or solve problems.
6. **Provide service to customers** - Salespeople provide a wide range of services, including handling complaints, returning damaged merchandise, providing samples, suggesting business opportunities, and developing recommendations on how the customer can promote products purchased from the salesperson. If necessary, salespeople may occasionally work at the customer's business. For example, a salesperson selling fishing tackle may arrange an in-store demonstration of a manufacturer's products and offer to repair fishing reels as a service to the retailer's customers.
7. **Help customers resell products to their customers** - A major part of many sales jobs is helping wholesalers and retailers resell the products that they have purchased. Salespeople help wholesale customers sell products to retail customers and help retail customers sell products to consumers. Consider a Quaker Oats salesperson selling a product to grocery wholesalers. Not only must they contact the wholesaler, they also must call on grocery retailers, make sales, and write up orders and send them to the wholesaler. In turn, the wholesaler sells and delivers the products to the retailers. The Quaker Oats salesperson also develops promotional programs to help the retailer sell the firm's products. These programs involve supplying advertising materials, conducting store demonstrations, and setting up product displays.
8. **Help customers use products after purchase** - The job is not over after the sale is made. Often, customers must be shown how to obtain full benefit from the product. For example, after a customer buys an IBM computer system, technical specialists help the buyer learn how to operate the equipment.
9. **Build goodwill with customers** - A selling job is people-oriented, entailing face-to-face contact with customers. Many sales are based, to some extent, on friendship and trust. Salespeople need to develop personal, friendly, businesslike relationships with everyone who may

Source: © Marcus Clackson/iStockphoto

influence a buying decision. This ongoing part of the job requires integrity, high ethical standards, and a sincere interest in satisfying customers' needs.

10. **Provide the company with market information** - Salespeople provide information to their companies on such topics as competitors' activities, customers' reactions to new products, complaints about products or policies, market opportunities, and their job activities. This information is so important for many companies that their salespeople are required to send in weekly or monthly reports on activities of the firm's competition in their territory. Salespeople are a vital part of their employers' information retrieval system.

MAKING THE SALE

WHAT IS A CUSTOMER?

- Customers are the most important people in any business. Customers are not dependent on us. We are dependent on them.
- Customers are not an interruption of our work. They are the purpose of it.
- Customers do us a favour in doing business with us. We aren't doing customers a favour by waiting on them.
- Customers are part of our business—not outsiders. Customers are not just money in the cash register.
- Customers are human beings with feelings, and they deserve to be treated with respect.
- Customers are people who come to us with needs and wants. It is our job to fill them.
- Customers deserve the most courteous attention we can give them.
- Customers are the lifeblood of this and every business.
- Customers pay your salary. Without customers we would have to close our doors.
- Don't ever forget it!

Reflect Back

Review the 10 functions shown in Exhibit 1.10 to see whether you could do any or all of them. Carefully think about the second and third functions. To be successful, a salesperson must close sales and build relationships with the same person or organization in order to sell more. To do both is challenging to any person. It requires salespeople to solve problems, provide service, help resell, teach how to use the product, build goodwill, and keep their employer up-to-date on customers' needs and feelings toward the product and service.

EXHIBIT 1.10
What does a professional salesperson do?

1. Creates new customers
2. Sells more to present customers
3. Builds long-term relationships with customers
4. Actively uses and manages social media platforms
5. Provides solutions to customers' problems
6. Provides service to customers
7. Helps customers resell products to their customers
8. Helps customers use products after purchase
9. Builds goodwill with customers
10. Provides the company with market information

This book is about these 10 functions and much more. When combined and properly implemented, these 10 job activities produce increased sales for the organization and more rewards for the salesperson. See the Making the Sale box, "A Typical Job Description for a Professional Salesperson," for an example of how a salesperson integrates these activities.

MAKING THE SALE

A TYPICAL JOB DESCRIPTION FOR A PROFESSIONAL SALESPERSON

Do you/will you have what it takes?

Summary: Within an assigned territory, salespeople are expected to achieve maximum sales profitability and growth.

Functions:

- Promote and secure orders from existing and prospective clients using a relationship based approach.
- Present products and services to both potential and existing clients and ensure that client needs are being satisfied by providing them with the best solution.

Specific Functions:

- Analyze market potential and determine the value of existing and prospective customers to the company.
- Plan personal sales strategy.
- Practise efficient time management in performing the sales function.
- Establish and maintain business relationships with new and current client base.
- Use variety of prospecting tools to grow the customer base.
- Develop effective and accurate written proposals for current and prospective clients.
- Maintain excellent customer relationships by expediting the resolution of client concerns.
- Supply management with effective written and oral reports.
- Promote product and company by participating in trade shows and conventions.
- Keep current with industry trends, product applications, customer trends, and competitive activities.
- Practise excellent ethical decision making in all dealings with clients and the organization.
- Attend yearly professional development activity as determined in consultation with supervisor.

Reporting Structure:

- Salespeople will report directly to the director of sales.

Qualifications:

- Must possess a valid driver's licence
- Minimum of two years' experience in the industry or equivalent. (product knowledge)
- Post-secondary diploma or degree in applicable discipline
- Proficiency in Microsoft Office applications
- Working knowledge of sales force automation and/or CRM software
- Demonstrated aptitude for problem solving
- Both written and oral communication skills
- Ability to work in a team environment and be a team player

Relationship Marketing

Organizations target new and present customers, to ensure that they'll have customers today and tomorrow. **Relationship marketing** creates customer loyalty by paying continuous attention to important customers. Organizations use combinations of products, prices, distribution, promotions, and service to achieve this goal.

relationship marketing: The combination of products, prices, distributions, promotions, and service that organizations use to create customer loyalty.

An organization using relationship marketing is not seeking a simple sale or transaction. It has targeted a major customer that it would like to sell to now and in the future. The company wants to demonstrate to the customer that it can serve the account's needs in a superior way, particularly if a committed relationship can be formed. The type of selling needed to establish a long-term collaborative relationship is complex. General Motors, for example, prefers suppliers that can sell and deliver a coordinated set of goods and services to many locations, quickly solve problems that arise in their different locations, and work closely with GM to improve products and processes.

Most companies, unfortunately, are not set up to meet these requirements. Many organizations still sell customers and then forget them. More progressive organizations, though, develop a close relationship—even a partnership—with their customers.

Levels of Relationship Marketing

What types of relationships should an organization have with its customers? Is keeping a relationship worth the cost? To answer these questions, let's define the three general levels of selling relationships with customers:

- **Transactional selling** - Customers are sold to and not contacted again.
- **Relationship selling** - The seller contacts customers after the purchase to determine whether they are satisfied and have future needs.
- **Partnering** - The seller works continually to improve the customers' operations, sales, and profits.

Most organizations focus solely on the single transaction with each customer. When you go to McDonald's and buy a hamburger, that's it; you never hear from the company again unless you return for another purchase. The same thing happens when you go to a theatre, subscribe to a streaming service, open a bank account, visit a grocery store, or have your clothes cleaned. Each example involves low-priced, low-profit products, and a large number of customers who are geographically dispersed, making it very difficult and quite costly to contact them. The business is forced to use **transactional selling**.

transactional selling: The first level of selling where customers are sold a product or service and not contacted again.

Relationship selling focuses on the transaction—making the sale—along with follow-up and service after the sale. The seller contacts the customer to ensure satisfaction with the purchase. The Cadillac Division of General Motors contacts each buyer of a new Cadillac to determine the customer's satisfaction with the car. If that person is not satisfied, General Motors works with the retailer who sold the car to make sure the customer is happy.

Partnering is a phenomenon of the 1990s and the twenty-first century. Businesses' growing concerns over the competition not only in Canada but also internationally revitalized their need to work closely with important customers. The familiar **80/20 principle** states that 80 percent of sales often come from 20 percent of a company's customers. Organizations now realize the need to identify their most important customers and designate them for their partnering programs. The organization's best salespeople are assigned to sell and service these customers.

partnering: The third level of selling where the seller works continually to improve the customer's operations, sales, and profits.

80/20 principle: 80 percent of sales often come from 20 percent of a company's customers.

LO7

Building Relationships through the Sales Process

Much of your course will revolve around the sales process. The **sales process** refers to a sequence of actions by the salesperson that leads toward the customer taking a desired action and ends with a follow-up to ensure purchase satisfaction. This desired action by a prospect is usually buying, which is the most important action. Such desired actions can also include advertising, displaying, or reducing the price of the product.

sales process: A sequence of actions by the salesperson that leads toward the prospect taking a desired action and ends with a follow-up to ensure purchase satisfaction.

In the course of a normal workweek, many salespeople have to play the role of detective, researcher, listener, educator, entertainer, persuader, negotiator, problem solver and supporter. The many activities that make up a salesperson's day or week may appear haphazard to the casual observer, but they are actually part of a step-by-step process.

The sales process is a logical series of 10 steps that increase the chances of not only making a sale but also creating a customer. These steps are listed in Exhibit 1.11 and are discussed in detail in the following chapters.

1.	**Prospecting** - Locating and qualifying prospects
2.	**Pre-approach** - Obtaining an interview; determining sales call objectives; developing customer profiles, customer benefit programs, and sales presentation strategies
3.	**Approach** - Meeting prospects and beginning a customized sales presentation
4.	**Presentation** - Further uncovering needs; relating product benefits to needs using demonstration, dramatization, visuals, and evidence statements
5.	**Trial close** - Asking the prospect's opinions during and after the presentation
6.	**Objections** - Uncovering objections
7.	**Meet objections** - Satisfactorily answering objections
8.	**Trial close** - Asking the prospect's opinion after overcoming each objection and immediately before the close
9.	**Close** - Bringing the prospect to the logical conclusion to buy
10.	**Follow-up and service** - Serving customers after the sale

EXHIBIT 1.11

Ten important tactical steps in the customer relationship selling process. Refer back to Exhibit 1.8 to see how they relate to relationship selling.

Selling Is for Large and Small Organizations

Many textbook examples are from big business, typically because readers recognize the Ford Motor Company or McDonald's. Even though Canada's large organizations are easily recognizable and extremely important to our prosperity, it is easy to overestimate the importance of big business because of its greater visibility. Small businesses seem dwarfed by corporate giants. Yet small firms, even though less conspicuous, are a vital component of our economy.

Small business contributes significantly to our economy. The Canadian Federation of Independent Business represents approximately 110,000 small and medium-sized enterprises (SMEs) across Canada. Recent statistics indicate that this sector is creating the majority of job growth in Canada. In fact, 9 out of 10 Canadians in the private sector work for small to medium-sized businesses and 70 percent of all Canadian employment is provided by small and medium-sized businesses (companies with fewer than 500 employees).[2] Further, small to medium-sized businesses contribute to 41 percent of the Canadian Gross Domestic Product (GDP). This sector has shown the most employment growth in our economy.

Small enterprises run the gamut from a corner news vendor to a developer of optical fibres. Small-business owners sell gasoline, flowers, and coffee. They publish magazines, haul freight, teach languages, and program computers. They make wines, motion pictures, and high-fashion clothes. They build new homes and restore old ones. They repair plumbing, fix appliances, recycle metals, and sell used cars. They drive taxicabs, run cranes, and fly helicopters. They drill for oil, quarry sand and gravel, and mine exotic ores. They forge, cast, weld, photoengrave, electroplate, and anodize. They also invent antipollution devices, quality control mechanisms, energy- saving techniques, microelectronic systems—the list goes on.

Often, small-business entrepreneurs cannot compete head to head with giant firms. However, most large firms started small and then prospered by using many of the concepts, ideas, and practices discussed in this textbook. Due to this fact, we use many small-business examples throughout the textbook as well.

Summary of Major Selling Issues

Personal selling is an old and honourable profession. It has helped improve much of the world's standard of living and provided benefits to individual buyers through the purchase of products. Millions of people have chosen a sales career because of the availability of sales jobs, the personal freedom sales provides, its challenge, the multitude of opportunities for success, and its nonfinancial and financial rewards. The introduction of new technologies and social media have moved the sales profession forward in a big way in recent years.

ETHICAL DILEMMA

I PROBABLY WON'T SEE HER AGAIN ANYWAY

As you are making your presentation to Julie, you realize that her company is moving in a direction that will probably make her unlikely to buy your product in the future. Her company is moving to a different manufacturing method that will require her to buy smaller, more efficient machinery than what you currently offer. Your company is considering moving in that direction but no decision has been made yet.

Being that she is new in her position, you know that you could convince her to give you the order but you also know that she will have to replace your equipment prematurely to be consistent with her company's strategy. At this point, you doubt that you'll be calling on her much in the future so you are thinking. "Do I just get the order and get out—after all, I do have a family to feed," or do you just bow out and leave without the order?

How do you handle this situation based on what you've learned in this chapter?

A person can become a successful salesperson through company and personal training and by developing skills and abilities that benefit customers. Also important are a belief in the product or service being sold, working hard, wanting to succeed, and maintaining a positive outlook toward both selling and oneself. In addition, a successful salesperson should be knowledgeable, able to plan, and able to use selling time wisely.

En route to success, salespeople develop a range of skills through study and practice, enhancing their ability to think strategically, relate to others, and understand the technical aspects of their business. The remainder of this book expands on these topics to provide you with the background either to improve your present selling ability or to help you decide whether a sales career is right for you.

MEETING A SALES CHALLENGE

In reviewing the example at the start of the chapter, let's compare your advice with Chin Lee's career decision.

Without any formal training in sales and after a very shaky start as a computer technician, Chin was given a transfer to the sales department.

After making the transfer, he said, "I quickly learned that training is essential for success—especially in sales. In retrospect, I wish I had had the opportunity to take a sales course as part of my computer technology studies."

Chin has become one of the top salespeople at his company. His advice: "If you don't have it, get training. Your confidence increases, and when it does, your performance improves. Moving into a sales career is the best move I have made. I highly recommend a career in sales."

PLAYING THE ROLE

Role A: Recently hired salesperson of Canadian Paper Supply, a mid-size paper supply company located in the middle of a major metropolitan city in Alberta. You are unhappy with your job. You are stressed out as you had expected that you would be making a lot more money after three months on the job so you are meeting with your sales manager. Aside from the money and stress, think of three other work-related factors that may be causing your unhappiness. Be prepared to discuss these at your meeting.

Role B: Sales manager of the company in the situation above. You are preparing to meet with a disgruntled employee who was hired just three months ago. You understand that she has some concerns regarding her job. Be prepared to handle any concerns that she may have. Can you motivate her to improve her performance? Should you just ask for her resignation?

Prepare your role for an in-class dramatization of this meeting between salesperson and sales manager.

Key Terms for Selling

career path
CPSA
80/20 principle
empathy
financial rewards
incentive
nonfinancial rewards
order getter
order taker
partnering
personal selling
relationship marketing
relationship selling
sales process
social media
territory manager
transactional selling

Sales Application Questions

1. The term *salesperson* refers to many types of sales jobs. What are the major types of sales jobs available?
2. *a.* If you were the sales manager for a fast-growing mobile phone company and were asked by your boss to hire 15 new salespeople as soon as possible, what would you look for on applicants' resumés to help you develop a short list of those you would like to interview?

   b. What type of compensation and incentive plan would you offer new recruits?
3. People choose a particular career for many reasons. What are some reasons someone might give for choosing a sales career?
4. "A career in sales is a career in dishonesty and crookedness." Formulate a constructive argument against this position, citing information from the chapter.
5. Those new to a sales job often experience some feelings of anxiety and fear. What advice would you give to a sales rookie to help him or her develop a confident attitude?
6. Refer back to the Making the Sale box, "A Typical Job Description for a Professional Salesperson." What steps can you take in the next couple of years to better qualify for this type of sales position?
7. Think of an experience you had with a salesperson who displayed a poor sales image. How did the salesperson's attitude affect your purchase decision?

Sales Online Exercise

Find Out About a Career in Sales!

Are you looking for a job? Would you consider a sales job? Do you want to find out more about a sales career? Here are some examples of useful websites.

www.salestalentagency.com
www.careerbeacon.com
www.careerbuilder.com
www.careers.org
www.cpsa.com
www.hrsdc.gc.ca
www.monster.ca
www.linkedin.com
www.salesexcellence.com
www.indeed.ca
www.salesjobs.com
www.salesrep.ca
www.shsinc.com
www.workopolis.com

In addition, look at your school's home page. Many schools refer you to career opportunities. Also go to the website of a specific company. Many companies have hyperlinks from their home page to their job openings.

Further Exploring the Sales World

1. Interview one or more salespeople and write a brief report on what they like and dislike about their jobs, why they chose a sales career, what activities they perform, and what they believe it takes to succeed at selling their products.
2. Contact your school's placement office and report on what staff there believes firms recruiting people for sales positions look for in applicants.
3. Visit the Canadian Professional Sales Association website (www.cpsa.com). Describe the steps that one would need to take to become certified; that is, to receive the CSP designation.

Selling Experiential Exercise

Are You a Global Traveller?

Our global environment requires that Canadian sales personnel learn to deal effectively with people in other countries. The assumption that foreign business leaders behave and negotiate in the same manner as Canadians is false. How well prepared are you to live with globalization? Consider the following items, writing the numbers reflecting your views on another sheet of paper.

Are you guilty of	Definitely No				Definitely Yes
1. Being impatient? Do you think "Time is money" or "Let's get straight to the point"?	1	2	3	4	5
2. Having a short attention span or bad listening habits, or being uncomfortable with silence?	1	2	3	4	5
3. Being somewhat argumentative, sometimes to the point of belligerence?	1	2	3	4	5
4. Being ignorant about the world beyond your borders?	1	2	3	4	5
5. Having a weakness in foreign languages?	1	2	3	4	5
6. Placing emphasis on short-term success?	1	2	3	4	5
7. Believing that advance preparations are less important than negotiations themselves?	1	2	3	4	5
8. Being legalistic and believing a deal is a deal, regardless of changing circumstances?	1	2	3	4	5
9. Having little interest in seminars on the subject of globalization, failing to browse through international topics in libraries or magazines, or not interacting with foreign students or employees?	1	2	3	4	5
		Total Score_____			

Results – If you scored:

Less than 27 – Congratulations! You have the temperament and interest to do well in a global company.

More than 27 – It's time to consider a change.

Regardless of your score, go back over each item and make a plan of action to correct deficiencies indicated by answers of 4 or 5 to any question.

CASE 1–1

IS A CAREER IN SALES RIGHT FOR YOU?

Janice Jones graduated from a Canadian community college with a diploma in marketing management. At 22, she was an engaging person, an active community volunteer, and heavily involved in extracurricular activities at her college. She played on the varsity basketball team and served in a leadership capacity in her school's student government. While doing this, she maintained high enough grades to remain on the Dean's Honour list throughout her college career. Janice always loved selling. She excelled at it in any of her part-time retail jobs and loved meeting people. She was a true "people person." Janice's short-term goal upon graduation was to make a lot of money so she could settle down and be comfortable before she was 30 years old.

Ishmar Patel was a recruiter for the Canadian division of a major business machine manufacturer. The company's expansion plans created a need for 10 new salespeople so Ishmar was on the recruiting trail at colleges and universities across Canada. When he arrived on campus, he was given a pile of resumés to review in hopes of finding a few candidates to whom he would offer an interview. After a day of reviewing there were a few that caught his eye but in particular, he liked the resumé of Janice Jones. To him, she seemed to have all of the qualities that often lead to success in sales, so he offered her an interview.

During the interview, Janice was outstanding. She presented herself well and was confident in her abilities. Ishmar informed Janice of the responsibilities of the job and the tremendous earnings potential. In fact, he informed her that some of the current salespeople were earning in excess of $200,000 per year. Janice's eyes lit up as she visualized herself being able to reach her short-term financial goals. Ishmar was so impressed by her interview that he offered her the job and, not being known to shy away from challenges, Janice accepted.

Janice immediately purchased a new car and a new wardrobe as her new position would require her to have reliable transportation and always appear professional. She was proud of her new position but over the course of the first few months, she felt overwhelmed. She had a tough time getting appointments and was beginning to take the rejection personally. Her stress levels were increasing each week. She found that even after getting appointments with prospective buyers, only half were actually giving her the order.

If she kept up her current level of sales, she determined that she would earn approximately $60,000 in her first year of sales. She was disappointed with this. After hearing in the interview that many of her colleagues were earning six-figure salaries, she had thought that she could easily reach these figures, if not exceed them. After all, she had always succeeded in anything she put her mind to.

Near the end of the third business quarter, Janice had a particularly poor week of sales. Combined with the fact that she had just received notice of a rent increase, she wondered if she was in the wrong line of work. Janice set up a meeting with her sales manager for the following Monday morning. She spent the weekend depressed about the meeting; she was contemplating quitting her job and moving on to something different. She hated thinking this way as she had always enjoyed selling and had planned a career in it.

QUESTIONS

1. What should Janice do to properly prepare for her meeting?
2. How should Janice's sales manager handle the meeting?
3. Should Janice consider switching careers? Why or why not?
4. What qualities did Janice have that would make her an attractive sales recruit?
5. Were Janice's expectations too high as she entered a sales career?
6. What can professors do to better prepare students for a sales career?

Source: © Hero Images/ Getty Images

CHAPTER 2

Ethics First . . . then Customer Relationships

Meghan Clark
Niagara College, Niagara Falls, Ontario
Source: Courtesy of Meghan Clark

A Sales Success Story

Meghan Julienne Clark graduated from Niagara College in 2002 with a Business Administration: Marketing diploma. Since then, she has worked in a number of sales-related careers and is now a Senior Regional Sales Manager, Higher Education, with McGraw-Hill Ryerson.

There are rarely two days that look the same, Meghan says. "I could be having a conversation about developments in education technology during part of my day, and then learning about physics the next. I never stop learning. As a sales manager, my selling skills continue to grow through coaching and developing talent. Supporting my team with reaching their achievements is a truly valuable experience. Although my day-to-day responsibilities have changed slightly, one important element of the job remains the same: The voice of the customer shapes everything we do. A customer-centric approach is not only the key to success, it also helps make a natural evolution from selling to consulting."

Her least-favourite part of the sales job? Not winning. She adds, "Sales professionals are winners, it's who we are." There have been times that despite great effort, business was lost or not won. Meghan's satisfaction in these cases has come from "being confident that I've done the very best I can do," and ensuring that her customers "know how grateful I am for their time and consideration."

Meghan uses social media extensively. She states, "From my experience, the most successful use of social media is to create a platform that encourages customers to share positive experiences with potential customers, whether on a blog or via social media. Furthermore, sites like LinkedIn can also be a great way to research your customer/company and prove you've prepared yourself for an upcoming call, while also respecting your customer's time by getting to valuable objectives faster."

And for aspiring salespeople, Meghan says, "Knowing who you are is critical. You must have the ability to successfully manage your time, juggle conflicting priorities, and be very adaptive to change. Be genuine and positive with all of your business relationships and show dedication through hard work."

MAIN TOPICS

Management's Social Responsibilities

What Influences Ethical Behaviour?

Management's Ethical Responsibilities

Ethics in Dealing with Salespeople

Salespeople's Ethics in Dealing with Their Employers

Ethics in Dealing with Customers

Managing Sales Ethics

LEARNING OBJECTIVES

This chapter is one of the most important in this text. Social, ethical, and legal issues for sales professionals are often personal and technical in nature, yet they are essential for understanding how to be an outstanding professional. Recent events have stressed the importance of sales personnel keeping up to date on current regulations in their industry. After studying this chapter, you should be able to:

LO1 Describe management's social responsibilities.

LO2 List the principles set forth in the CPSA Code of Ethics.

LO3 Explain how to demonstrate social responsibility.

LO4 Explain what influences ethical behaviour.

LO5 Describe management's role in addressing ethical responsibilities.

LO6 Discuss ethical dealings among salespeople, employers, and customers.

FACING A SALES CHALLENGE

As the sales manager of a printing company, you are about to invest in a car leasing program that involves 18 company cars for your sales staff. Together with your comptroller, you have examined several leasing programs. You have narrowed down your selection to two leasing companies that offer very similar terms. You are meeting with the president of Equilease, a company with which you have never done business before. You know from your own prospect files that one of your sales representatives has tried to call on the purchasing manager of Equilease before to get some of their printing business; however, he could not sell the account.

As you meet with the president for lunch, you gently steer the conversation in the direction of printing services. Since he is very knowledgeable about printing services and prices, you ask him about ballpark prices charged by his existing supplier. You believe you could provide his company with higher-quality service at a better price.

Since the president of Equilease is in a good mood, you think about setting up a win–win situation. You are considering making this offer: Let's make this a double win. I'll give you 100 percent of our leasing business if you'll consider giving us 50 percent of your printing business. Fair enough?

Is there an ethical conflict in this situation? Would it be ethical to propose such a deal?

(Continued at end of chapter.)

Sales personnel are constantly involved with social, ethical, and legal issues. Actually, everyone is–including you. If you found a bag full of $100 bills lying on the side of the road, would you keep it? Would you ever say you were sick to get extra time off work or to get out of a test you weren't prepared for? Would you use the company car to run a personal errand? Have you ever exceeded the speed limit? Have you ever gone home with one of your employer's pens in your pocket?

The Internet, newspapers, radio, and television frequently present news stories of individuals and organizations involved in both good and bad practices. This chapter addresses many of the important social, ethical, and legal issues in selling. It begins by discussing management's social responsibilities. Then it examines ethical behaviour and the ethical issues involved in dealing with salespeople, employers, and consumers. The chapter ends by presenting ways an organization can help its sales personnel follow ethical selling practices.

LO1 Management's Social Responsibilities

In one sense, the concept of corporate social responsibility is easy to understand; it means distinguishing right from wrong and doing right. It means being a good corporate citizen. **Social responsibility** is a business's obligation to maximize its positive impact and minimize its negative impact on society.

social responsibility: A business's obligation to maximize its positive impact and minimize its negative impact on society.

As straightforward as this definition seems, social responsibility can be a difficult concept to grasp, because different people have different opinions as to which actions improve society's welfare. To complicate matters, social responsibility covers a range of issues, many of which have ambiguous boundaries or grey areas between right and wrong.

Organizational Stakeholders

To understand social responsibility, managers determine to whom they are responsible. Enlightened organizations view the internal and external environment as a variety of stakeholders. A **stakeholder** is any individual or group within or outside the organization that has a stake in the organization's performance. Each stakeholder has a different interest in the organization.

stakeholder: Any group within or outside the organization that has a stake in the organization's performance.

Exhibit 2.1 illustrates eight important stakeholders. These are represented by the acronym **CCC GOMES**. The first *C* refers to customers and the last *S* refers to suppliers. Owners', creditors', and suppliers' interests are served by managerial efficiency–that is, the use of resources to achieve profits. Managers and salespeople expect work satisfaction, pay, and good supervision. Customers are concerned with decisions about the quality and availability of goods and services.

CCC GOMES: A stakeholder acronym: customers, creditors, community, government, owners, managers, employees, and suppliers.

Other important stakeholders are the government and the community. Most corporations exist under the proper charter and licences, and operate within the limits of the laws and regulations imposed by the government, including safety laws and environmental protection requirements. The community includes local government, the natural and physical environments, and the quality of life provided for residents. If your school were to look at all of the stakeholders impacted by their decision to double enrolment, who would those stakeholders be? Students, professors, employees, employers, the local hospital, the local Tim Hortons, and Starbucks? There are many stakeholders affected by the decisions of public institutions, and the expectations by the community are for them to be socially responsible. Socially responsible organizations pay attention to all stakeholders.

EXHIBIT 2.1

Major stakeholders in the organization's performance.

An Organization's Main Responsibilities

Once a company is aware of its stakeholders, it has four main types of responsibilities: (1) economic, (2) legal, (3) ethical, and (4) discretionary (see Exhibit 2.2).

Economic Responsibilities

The business institution is, above all, the basic economic unit of society. Its responsibility is to produce the goods and services that society wants and to maximize profits for its owners and shareholders.

Often, corporations are said to operate solely to maximize profits. Certainly, profits are important to a firm, just as an academic average is important to a student. Profit provides the capital to stay in business, expand, and compensate for the risks of conducting business. There is a responsibility to make a profit to serve society. Imagine what would happen to our society if large corporations (e.g., McCain Foods, Postmedia, Telus Mobility) did not make a profit and went out of business. Thousands of people and the Canadian economy would be affected.

Legal Responsibilities

All modern societies lay down ground rules, laws, and regulations that organizations are expected to follow. Legal requirements are imposed by municipal councils and provincial legislators, and define what society deems important with respect to appropriate corporate behaviour. Organizations are expected to fulfill their economic goals within the legal framework.

In Canada, hundreds of sales professionals in the telecommunications industry have complained about intense pressure to mislead and even lie to customers in order to hit unrealistically high sales goals with some employees citing that they targeted mostly older customers in order to get away with the unlawful tactics.[1]

In the financial service industry, salespeople must meet many compliance requirements. These requirements were established to protect buyers from potentially unethical sales practices by financial service sales agents; however, even some of the biggest banks in Canada have been accused of misrepresentation by employees who have suggested they have deceived customers in an attempt to achieve higher sales targets. Although Canadian banks have tried to avoid the consumer scandals that have plagued their American counterparts, some recent whistleblowers in the Canadian banking industry have alluded to similar practices when feeling pressure to achieve their sales quotas, particularly by not advising customers of additional fees.[2]

EXHIBIT 2.2

An organization's main responsibilities.

LO2 Ethical Responsibilities

Ethical responsibility includes behaviours that are not necessarily codified into law and may not serve the corporation's direct economic interests. To be ethical, organizational decision makers should act with equity, fairness, and impartiality; respect the rights of individuals; and provide different treatment of individuals only when relevant to the organization's goals and tasks. Unethical behaviour occurs when decisions enable an individual or company to gain at the expense of society.

In 2018, after a video went viral showing a Starbucks employee mistreating two Black men and kicking them out of the store, Starbucks took the incident so seriously that they shut down all of their stores in the United States to hold a four-hour ethical training exercise with all of their employees. The company also apologized to the victims of the racial discrimination and offered to pay for them to go to college.[3] This incident shows how seriously companies are taking ethical responsibilities.

SELLING TIPS

THE CANADIAN PROFESSIONAL SALES ASSOCIATION'S CODE OF ETHICS

The CPSA Sales Institute Code of Ethics is the set of principles and standards that a certified sales professional will strive to adhere to with customers, organizations, competitors, communities, and colleagues.

The Certified Sales Professional pledges and commits to uphold these standards in all activities.

I will:

1. Maintain honesty and integrity in all relationships with customers, prospective customers, and colleagues and continually work to earn their trust and respect.
2. Accurately represent my products or services to the best of my ability in a manner that places my customer or prospective customer and my company in a position that benefits both.
3. Respect and protect the proprietary and confidential information entrusted to me by my company and my customers and not engage in activities that may conflict with the best interest of my customers or my company.
4. Continually upgrade my knowledge of my products/services, skills and my industry.
5. Use the time and resources available to me only for legitimate business purposes. I will only participate in activities that are ethical and legal, and when in doubt, I will seek counsel.
6. Respect my competitors and their products and services by representing them in a manner which is honest, truthful and based on accurate information that has been substantiated.
7. Endeavour to engage in business and selling practices which contribute to a positive relationship with the community.
8. Assist and counsel my fellow sales professionals where possible in the performance of their duties.
9. Abide by and encourage others to adhere to this Code of Ethics.

As a certified sales professional, I understand that the reputation and professionalism of all salespeople depends on me as well as others engaged in the sales profession, and I will adhere to these standards to strengthen the reputation and integrity for which we will strive. I understand that failure to consistently act according to this Code of Ethics may result in the loss of the privilege of using my professional sales designation.

Source: Reprinted with permission of the Canadian Professional Sales Association, 2008. For more information, see the Sales Professional Competency Framework at https://www.cpsa.com/professional-certification/competency-framework.

discretionary responsibility: Behaviours that are purely voluntary and guided by the desire to make social contributions not mandated by economics, law, or ethics.

Discretionary Responsibilities

Discretionary responsibility is purely voluntary and guided by a company's desire to make social contributions not mandated by economics, law, or ethics. Discretionary activities include generous philanthropic contributions that offer no monetary return to the company and are not expected. We know of companies that have needed to reduce the size of their sales forces because of difficult economic circumstances.

Instead of firing people, they stopped hiring, offered early retirements, and let normal turnover decrease sales force size. In addition, in situations where there has been an acquisition of a company, contractual obligations have been placed on the buyer by the seller to give first right of refusal in hiring the selling company's staff, who might otherwise be forgotten in the acquisition process.

For example, Tim Hortons often partners with non-profit charities in their local communities. In September 2018, Tim Hortons in the Windsor-Essex region in Southwestern Ontario had Smile Cookies week where over $100,000 was raised and donated to the John McGivney Children's Centre to help pay for an accessible playground for children and families. In addition, a portion of the proceeds was given to the Maryvale Adolescent and Family Services. Tim Hortons' actions contributed to the community's welfare and exceeded societal expectations. Discretionary responsibility is the highest criterion of social responsibility because it goes beyond societal expectations to contribute to the community's welfare.

Remember however, that although organizations have much of the responsibility for managing ethical behaviour, it is ultimately the salesperson's responsibility to conduct their own day-to-day activities in an ethical manner.

SELLING TIPS

ETHICSCENTRE CA—CANADIAN CENTRE FOR ETHICS AND CORPORATE POLICY

EthicsCentre CA is a registered charity governed by volunteers and supported by organizations and individuals who share a commitment to ethical values.

Founded in 1988, they are a uniquely Canadian, independent ethics centre dedicated to promoting and maintaining an ethical orientation and culture in Canadian organizations.

Their mission is to champion the application of ethical values in the decision-making process of business and other organizations.

They operate in a non-judgmental and inclusive way to explore and promote the positive role of ethical decision making, serving as a forum and catalyst for constructive discussion and debate.

Visit this site to access articles and other resources on a variety of topics dealing with ethical business practices: www.ethicscentre.ca/EN/index.cfm

How to Demonstrate Social Responsibility

LO3

A corporation can demonstrate social responsibility in numerous ways. Actions that can be taken by all organizations include:

1. Taking corrective action before it is required
2. Working with affected constituents to resolve mutual problems
3. Working to establish industry-wide standards and self-regulation
4. Publicly admitting mistakes
5. Getting involved in appropriate social programs
6. Helping to correct environmental problems
7. Monitoring the changing social environment
8. Establishing and enforcing a corporate code of conduct
9. Taking needed public stands on social issues
10. Striving to make profits on an ongoing basis

Companies that do not maintain ethical standards face tangible costs. For example, in 2015 Amazon was penalized by Canada's Competition Bureau and was forced to pay a $1 million fine due to unfair pricing practices. Amazon relied on their supplier to show "list prices" but never verified their accuracy, which was a misleading claim to customers and resulted in Amazon sometimes appearing to be offering bigger savings than they really were.[4] Amazon has also been under scrutiny for some of their employees deleting poor reviews for some of their products.[5]

Some corporations, however, are using their positions to benefit society. For example, MEC (Mountain Equipment Co-op) fashions its business model on the triple bottom line, an idea that espouses that everything they do leaves its mark: environmentally, socially, and economically. This has led to them being voted one of the 50 best corporate citizens of Canada and has resulted in tremendous success. Their website says: "As a business–and as people–we operate with integrity and show respect for each other and the environment. For over 40 years we've been dreaming big and demonstrating the best of what business can be in our society."

worldview: People's different beliefs about the world around them.

morals: People's adherence to right or wrong behaviour and right or wrong thinking.

LO4

What Influences Ethical Behaviour?

Organizations are composed of individuals. These individuals' morals and ethical values help shape those of the organization. Critical to making decisions in an ethical manner is the individual integrity of the organization's managers, especially those in leadership positions. Thus, two major influences on the ethical behaviour of sales personnel are employees and the organization itself.

preconventional moral development level: The first level of an individual's moral development. At this level, an individual acts in their own best interest and thus follows rules to avoid punishment or receive rewards. This individual would break moral and legal laws.

The Individual's Role

All of us, employees and managers alike, bring certain beliefs about the world to a job. These beliefs direct our daily decisions. This "big picture" view of life that directs our behaviour is based on our core belief system. Personality, religious background, family upbringing, personal experiences, and the situation faced are examples of factors shaping our core belief system. This is why you hear, "no two people are alike." Each one views the world differently than someone else. Your parents probably view many things differently than you do, for example.

EXHIBIT 2.3
What is your level of moral development?

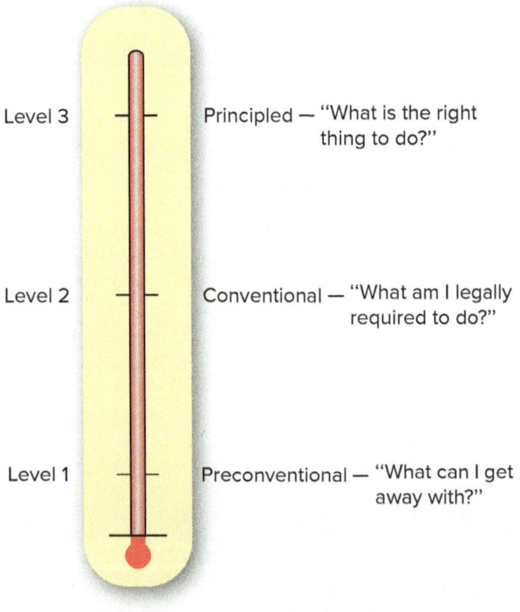

Because people have different beliefs about the world around them, referred to as a person's **worldview**, they tend to have different views on ethics and morality.[6] From an early age, you begin a journey down a road to higher moral development. Research has shown that individuals grow or progress in their ability to understand the "truth" or the ability to know what is right or wrong. People's **morals** are their adherence to right or wrong behaviour.

Over time, moral development gradually matures in many people. With moral maturity many individuals–but not all–adhere to more truthful or stringent moral principles. Often a person's current moral development can be placed into one of the levels shown in Exhibit 2.3.

- **Level 1: Preconventional** - At the **preconventional moral development level**, individuals act in their own best interest and thus follow rules to avoid punishment or receive rewards. These individuals would break moral and legal laws. In making an ethical or moral decision, a salesperson at this level might ask, "What can I get away with?" Some see individuals at this stage as moral infants with little capacity for self-insight because their genetically installed conscience has hardened over time. They do not see wrong in unethical behaviour. If they do, it is rationalized in their favour and quickly forgotten. Whatever happens is someone else's fault.

- **Level 2: Conventional** – At the **conventional moral development level**, individuals conform to the expectations of others, such as family, friends, employer, boss, or society, and uphold moral and legal laws. A salesperson at this level might ask, "What am I legally required to do?" when making an ethical or moral decision.
- **Level 3: Principled** – At the **principled moral development level**, individuals live by an internal set of morals, values, and ethics regardless of punishments or majority opinion. These individuals would disobey orders, laws, and consequences to follow what they believe is right. These people follow the Core Principles. When making an ethical or moral decision, a salesperson at this level might ask, "What is the right thing to do?"[7]

conventional moral development level: The second level of an individual's moral development. At this level, an individual conforms to the expectations of others, such as family, employer, boss, and society, and upholds moral and legal laws.

principled moral development level: The third level of an individual's moral development. At this level, an individual lives by an internal set of morals, values, and ethics, regardless of punishments or majority opinion.

As shown in Exhibit 2.4, the majority (60 to 80 percent) of sales personnel, as well as people in general, behave at the conventional level—level 2. However, approximately 10 to 20 percent of people behave at each of the other two levels—levels 1 and 3. Within each level, there is a lower and higher level of moral development behaviour. Some people at level 2, for example, have behaviour closer to level 1 people or level 3 people.

The Organization's Role

If the vast majority of people in our society are at the preconventional or conventional level, it seems that most employees in an organization would feel they must "go along to get along"; in other words, they acquiesce to questionable ethical standards to keep their jobs. At most, they only follow formal policies and procedures.

How will sales personnel handle ethical dilemmas? What if there are no policies and procedures pertaining to some sales practices and a superior directs the salesperson to do something that appears unethical? It is no wonder that radio, television, newspaper, and online reports frequently feature unethical business practices. Following the hear-no-evil, see-no-evil, speak-no-evil philosophy can create a preconventional or conventional organizational climate.

EXHIBIT 2.4

Levels of moral development.

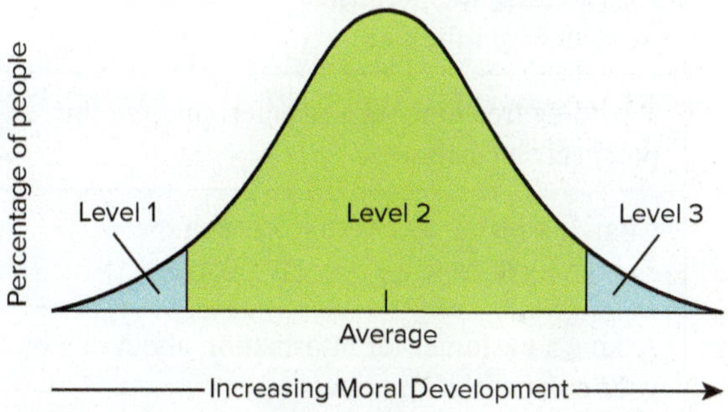

People's levels of moral development differ, as does the number of people at each level of moral development. Where are you on your moral development journey?

Management's Ethical Responsibilities

LO5

The concept of ethics, like social responsibility, is easy to understand. However, ethics are difficult to define in a precise way. In a general sense, **ethics** are the code of moral principles and values that governs the behaviours of a person or a group with respect to what is right or wrong. Ethics set standards as to what is good or bad in conduct and decision making.[8]

ethics: The code of moral principles and values that governs the behaviours of a person or a group with respect to what is right or wrong.

Unethical sales practices aren't new. The words *caveat emptor* (buyer beware) appeared on buildings in ancient Rome. Today, however, it is the sensational cases and lawsuits that heighten the public's perception of dishonesty.

The Conference Board of Canada, within its Canadian Centre for Business in the Community, addresses the issue of business ethics and acts as a resource to Canadian industry in advancing ethics policies and practices as integral parts of a company's corporate culture. In recent research findings, the following notable information surfaced:

1. In one survey, 42 percent of working Canadians said they have witnessed some form of ethical misconduct in their workplace, and 48 percent of those people did not report.
2. An Ipsos-Reid poll determined that one in three working Canadians felt that "delivering results in their workplace was more important than doing the right thing."
3. Seventy-eight percent of investors consider sustainable investing to be more important to them today than five years ago.[9]

ETHICAL DILEMMA

WHERE DO YOU STAND?

Check the boxes in the column that best resembles your attitude in each of the following situations. Add up your score and then rate yourself below. Do any of the questions surprise you?

ACTIVITY	I WOULD DO THIS 4	I MIGHT DO IT 3	NOT SURE 2	NEVER 1
Criticizing your company in front of your customers and/or competitors				
Closing a deal with a colleague's customer without telling anyone				
Exaggerating the performance of an inferior product to get the sale				
Providing free lunches and entertainment for prospective customers				
Charging higher prices to lower volume customers despite no cost differences				
Asking a customer for information about one of your competitor's products				
Helping a customer avoid taxes by "fudging" the numbers on an order				
Snooping around the stock room at a prospective customer's business				
Giving preferential treatment to firms who supply your company				
Providing expensive gifts to an established customer to get a new contract				
TOTAL				

Results – If you scored:

35 to 40 – You will probably get yourself into trouble.

30 to 34 – You should read this chapter again.

20 to 29 – You will have to give some serious thought to how you want to conduct yourself in the world of sales.

10 to 19 – You have a sound understanding of the morality of selling.

Many companies and their sales personnel get into trouble by assuming that if it's not illegal, it must be ethical. Ethics are powerful forces for good that can regulate behaviours both inside and outside the sales force. As principles of ethics and social responsibility become more widely recognized, companies can use codes of ethics and their corporate cultures to govern behaviour, thereby eliminating the need for additional laws governing right and wrong and regaining the trust of the public.

What Is an Ethical Dilemma?

Because ethical standards are not codified, disagreements and dilemmas about "proper" behaviour often occur. An ethical dilemma arises in a situation when each alternative choice or behaviour has undesirable elements due to potentially negative ethical or personal consequences. In ethical dilemmas, right or wrong cannot be clearly identified. Consider the following examples:

- Your boss says he cannot give you a raise this year because of budget constraints; however, because of your good work this past year, he will look the other way if your expense accounts come in a little high.
- You are stationed at the corporate headquarters in Toronto and have 14 salespeople in countries all over the world. A rep living in another country calls to get approval to pay a government official $10,000 to okay an equipment purchase of $5 million. Such payoffs are part of common business practice in that part of the world.
- Your good friend, an industrial engineer, tells you three of your competitors have submitted price bids on her company's proposed new construction project. She suggests a price you should submit and mentions certain construction specifications her boss is looking for on this job.

Now let's turn to the three main ethical areas most frequently faced by sales personnel. These involve:

1. Salespeople
2. Employers
3. Customers

Ethics in Dealing with Salespeople

LO6

Sales managers have both social and ethical responsibilities to sales personnel. Salespeople are a valuable resource; they are recruited, carefully trained, and given important responsibility. They represent a large financial investment and must be treated in a professional manner. Yet, occasionally, a company may place managers or salespeople in positions that force them to choose among compromising their ethics, not doing what is required, or leaving the organization. The decision depends on the magnitude of the situation. At times, situations arise in which it is difficult to say whether a sales practice is ethical or unethical. Sales managers face five ethical considerations:

1. The level of sales pressure to place on a salesperson
2. Decisions concerning a salesperson's territory
3. Whether to be honest with the salesperson
4. What to do with the ill salesperson
5. Employee rights

Level of Sales Pressure

What is an acceptable level of pressure to place on salespeople (Exhibit 2.5)? Should managers establish performance goals that they know a salesperson has only a 50–50 chance of attaining? Should the manager acknowledge that goals were set too high? If circumstances change in the salesperson's territory–for example, a large customer goes out of business–should the manager lower sales goals?

These are questions all managers must consider. There are no right or wrong answers. Managers are responsible for group goals, so there is a natural tendency to pressure salespeople to reach the manager's goals. Some managers motivate their people to produce at high levels without applying pressure while others place tremendous pressure on salespeople to attain sales beyond quotas. However, managers should set realistic and obtainable goals. They must consider individual territory situations. If this is done fairly and sales are still down, then pressure may be applied.

EXHIBIT 2.5

How much pressure should a manager place on salespeople to increase sales?

Source: © Shutterstock/fizkes

Decisions Affecting Territory

Management makes decisions that affect sales territories and salespeople. For example, the company might increase the number of sales territories, which often necessitates splitting a single territory. A salesperson may have spent years building the territory to its current sales volume only to have customers taken away. If the salesperson has worked on commission, this would mean a decrease in earnings.

Consider a situation of reducing the number of sales territories. What procedures would you use? Several years ago, a large manufacturer of health and beauty aids (shaving cream, toothpaste, shampoo) reduced the number of territories to lower selling costs. So, for example, three territories became two. Here is how one of the salespeople described it:

> I made my plane reservation to fly to our annual national meeting. Beforehand, I was told to get my records up to date and bring them to the regional office in Calgary. I drove from Edmonton to Calgary with my bags packed to go to the national meeting. I walked into the office with my records under my arm. My district and regional managers were there. They told me of the reorganization and said I was fired. They asked for my car keys. I called my wife, told her what

> happened, and then caught a bus back home. There were five of us in the region that were called in that day. Oh, they gave us a good job recommendation—it's just the way we were treated. Some people had been with the company for five years or more. They didn't eliminate jobs by tenure but by where territories were located.

Companies must deal with individuals in a fair and straightforward manner. It would have been better for the managers of these salespeople to go to their hometowns and explain the changes personally. Instead, they treated the salespeople unprofessionally.

One decision affecting a territory is what to do with extra-large customers, sometimes called *key accounts.* Are they taken away from the salesperson and made into house accounts? Here, responsibility for contacting the accounts rests with someone from the home office (house) or a key-account salesperson. The local salesperson may not get credit for sales to this customer even though the customer is in the salesperson's territory. A salesperson states the problem:

> I've been with the company 35 years. When I first began, I called on some people who had one grocery store. Today, they have 208. The buyer knows me. He buys all of my regular and special greeting cards. They do whatever I ask. I made $22,000 in commissions from their sales last year. Now, management wants to make it a house account.

Here, the salesperson loses money. It is difficult to treat the salesperson fairly in this situation. The company does not want to pay large commissions, and 90 percent of the 208 stores are located out of the salesperson's territory. The manager should carefully explain this to the salesperson. Instead of taking the full $22,000 away from the salesperson, the company could pay a one-time bonus as a reward for building up the account.

To Tell the Truth?

Should salespeople be told they are not promotable, that they are marginal performers, or that they are being transferred to the poorest territory in the company so that they will quit? Good judgment must prevail. Tell the truth. What happens when you fire a salesperson? If a fired employee has tried and has been honest, many sales managers will tell prospective employers that the person quit voluntarily rather than being fired. One manager put it this way: "I feel he can do a good job for another company. I don't want to hurt his future."

The Ill Salesperson

How much help do you give to an alcoholic, drug-addicted, or physically or mentally ill salesperson? Many companies require salespeople to seek professional help for substance abuse, and, if they improve, offer support and keep them in the field. Yet, there is only so far a company can go. The firm cannot have a salesperson under the influence of drugs or alcohol calling on customers. If the illness has a negative effect on business, the salesperson should be taken out of the territory.

These are difficult decisions, and many organizations are recognizing the extent to which many employees need career-saving help. Employee Assistance Programs (EAPs) or Employee Family Assistance Programs (EFAPs) have been commissioned to provide extraordinary help to employees. These organizations provide counselling and remedial support for employees. The organizations function autonomously and confidentially, with the support of the company's management, to help the organizations retain valuable employees who are experiencing short-term personal problems. Coupled with a sales manager who shows a sincere, personal interest in helping a salesperson in difficulty, these innovative programs greatly contribute to a person's chances of recovery.

Employee Rights

The sales manager must be up to date on ethical and legal considerations regarding employee rights and must develop strategies for the organization in addressing those rights. Here are several important questions that all managers should be able to answer:

- Under what conditions can an organization fire sales personnel without violating the law?
- What rights do and should sales personnel have regarding the privacy of their employment records and access to them?
- What can organizations do to prevent harassment of any type, and other forms of bias in the workplace?

employee rights: Rights desired by employees regarding their job security and the treatment administered by their employer while on the job.

Employee rights are rights desired by employees regarding their job security and the treatment administered by their employers while on the job, irrespective of whether those rights are currently protected by law or collective bargaining agreements of labour unions. Let's briefly examine two employee-rights questions.

Privacy

Canadians may be surprised to discover that we have no specific constitutional right to privacy. We do have some protection against unreasonable privacy invasions through the Canadian *Charter of Rights and Freedoms.* However, the *Charter* does not regulate the practices of private enterprise directly. This situation applies not only to what we would consider confidential information but also to a company's data.[10]

PIPEDA: Personal Information Protection and Electronic Documents Act (PIPEDA) is the federal privacy law for private-sector organizations. It sets out the ground rules for how businesses must handle personal information in the course of commercial activity.

One area of privacy that has been the subject of scrutiny and legal action is the broad area of customer lists. A general rule has been established that an organization's private information is the property of the organization and cannot be used in another enterprise without permission of the originating company. This concept has been legally tested on a number of occasions in Canada, especially in instances where a customer list has been taken from one company to another by an exiting employee and used to compete against the former company. Although courts have been precise about the theft of "physical information," they have been reluctant to apply judicial restraints on information that could reasonably be accumulated in the normal course of performing a job and applied in another organization (even a competitive one). This issue not only relates to the broader issue of business ethics but also provides a hint of the complexity of the subject from the employee's perspective and that of management.

EXHIBIT 2.6

Canadian human rights legislation protects workers from discriminatory hiring practices.

Source: Andresr/Dreamstime.com/GetStock.com

The *Personal Information Protection and Electronic Documents Act* **(PIPEDA)** sets out ground rules for how private sector organizations may collect, use, or disclose personal information in the course of commercial activities. PIPEDA also applies to federal works, undertakings, and businesses in respect of employee personal information. The law gives individuals the right to access and request correction of the personal information these organizations may have collected about them. See the Making the Sale box for the 10 principles of PIPEDA.

Canada's human rights legislation prohibits the denial of employment for a broad range of characteristics (see Exhibit 2.6). These include but are not limited to:

- Race or colour
- Religion
- Physical or mental disability
- Age
- Sex
- Marital status
- Family status
- Sexual orientation
- Language

MAKING THE SALE

PRINCIPLES OF THE PERSONAL INFORMATION PROTECTION AND ELECTRONIC DOCUMENTS ACT (PIPEDA)

An organization is responsible for the protection and fair handling of personal information at all times. This applies throughout its organization and in dealings with third parties. Care in the handling of personal information is essential to continued consumer confidence and good will.

- **Principle 1: Accountability** – An organization is responsible for personal information under its control. It must appoint someone to be accountable for its compliance with these fair information principles.
- **Principle 2: Identifying purposes** – The purposes for which the personal information is being collected must be identified by the organization before or at the time of collection.
- **Principle 3: Consent** – The knowledge and consent of the individual are required for the collection, use, or disclosure of personal information, except where inappropriate.
- **Principle 4: Limiting collection** – The collection of personal information must be limited to that which is needed for the purposes identified by the organization. Information must be collected by fair and lawful means.
- **Principle 5: Limiting use, disclosure, and retention** – Unless the individual consents otherwise or it is required by law, personal information can only be used or disclosed for the purposes for which it was collected. Personal information must only be kept as long as required to serve those purposes.
- **Principle 6: Accuracy** – Personal information must be as accurate, complete, and up-to-date as possible in order to properly satisfy the purposes for which it is to be used.
- **Principle 7: Safeguards** – Personal information must be protected by appropriate security relative to the sensitivity of the information.
- **Principle 8: Openness** – An organization must make detailed information about its policies and practices relating to the management of personal information publicly and readily available.
- **Principle 9: Individual access** – Upon request, an individual must be informed of the existence, use, and disclosure of their personal information and be given access to that information. An individual shall be able to challenge the accuracy and completeness of the information and have it amended as appropriate.
- **Principle 10: Challenging compliance** – An individual shall be able to challenge an organization's compliance with the above principles. Their challenge should be addressed to the person accountable for the organization's compliance with PIPEDA, usually their Chief Privacy Officer.

Source: https://www.priv.gc.ca/en/privacy-topics/privacy-laws-in-canada/the-personal-information-protection-and-electronic-documents-act-pipeda/p_principle/. Used with permission of the Office of the Privacy Commissioner of Canada.

The definition of discrimination has been extended to encompass the topic of sexual harassment. Although the assumption is usually made that this is strictly an issue that arises from traditional superior/subordinate relationships, harassment could arise between a salesperson and a customer. What would you do if harassed by a customer? What would you do if you were the manager of the person who was being harassed? The intent of the legislation targeted at reducing harassment in the workplace is simple—a harassment-free workplace—however, as we will see, the complexity of the subject is a significant management challenge.

What exactly is harassment? The Human Rights Commission defines it in an unequivocal way: "Harassment is a form of discrimination. It includes any unwanted physical or verbal behaviour that offends or humiliates you. Generally, harassment is a behaviour that persists over time. Serious one-time incidents can also sometimes be considered harassment."[11]

The Commission goes on to identify the forms that harassment can take, namely "threats, intimidation, or verbal abuse; unwelcome remarks or jokes about subjects like your race, religion or age, displaying sexist, racist, or other offensive pictures or posters . . ." An act can be deemed harassment not only in a superior/subordinate relationship: "the harasser could be the same or opposite sex, may be a supervisor, co-worker or someone providing you with a service such as a bank officer or a clerk in a government department."[12]

Employers are responsible for preventing racial and sexual discrimination and harassment within their companies and in their relationships with customers and suppliers. Organizations should recognize and value the diversity of Canada's workforce, and work to encourage all employees to respect others.

The attitude of any organization to these complex social issues begins at the top. Effective employee training can establish the required level of expectations for compliance within the organization. Specific training in the areas of objective performance appraisal and compensation policies will ensure a level of compliance. Going a step further, comprehensive inclusion and communication of all human rights and harassment legislation to company employees in company policy manuals, employee handbooks, and information sessions will indicate the company's level of commitment to the process and to its employees. Finally, monitoring and verifying compliance and taking appropriate immediate remedial action for noncompliance will complete the management process.

More recent sexual assault allegations in Canada and the United States have sparked a new viral movement popularly known as the #MeToo movement. This movement was given more power after high-profile cases such as Harvey Weinstein, an entertainment producer who was accused by various actors of many episodes of sexual misconduct in the workplace. Comedian Bill Cosby was also accused of aggravated indecent assault for drugging and sexually assaulting women in his home, and in September 2018 he was convicted and sentenced to 3 to 10 years in prison for one such assault. Although not all of these incidences happened in the workplace, these high-profile cases have shed light on sexual assault and power imbalance and how they can affect the workplace.

Is there a benefit for organizations that embrace these important concepts? Acknowledging and recognizing the necessity of employee rights in any organization will lead to the following:

- A high-quality work environment
- More effective selection and recruitment of new hires; the company will be seen as a good place to work and will attract better-quality people
- Reduced risk of the significant financial penalties associated with noncompliance with the law, but more importantly, reduced risk of negative publicity that could have a negative long-term impact on business
- A match between employer and employee rights, expectations, and obligations

Both organizations and employees benefit from anti-discrimination measures. Organizations benefit from reduced legal costs, since not observing employee rights is illegal, and their image as a good employer increases, resulting in enhanced organizational attractiveness. This makes it easier for the organization to recruit a pool of qualified applicants. And, although critics suggest that expanded employee rights, especially job security, may reduce management flexibility and profitability, expanded employee rights may be an impetus for better planning, resulting in increased profitability.

Increased profitability also may result from the benefits employees receive when their rights are observed: employees may experience feelings of being treated fairly and respectfully, increased self-esteem, and a heightened sense of job security. Employees who have job security may be more productive and committed to the organization than those who do not. As employees begin to see the guarantees of job security as a benefit, organizations also gain through reduced wage-increase demands and greater flexibility in job assignments.

SOCIAL MEDIA INSIGHTS FOR SALESPEOPLE

Are there ethical concerns surrounding a salesperson's use of social media? Here are some of the issues:

- How much time do you spend socializing with friends on Twitter or Facebook when you should be doing business?
- Are you broadcasting too much personal information or are you keeping it strictly business?
- Are you being publicly critical of competitors with the hope of making yourself look better?
- Do you manage your social media time diligently or do you end up wasting valuable selling time?
- Do you ever complain about work on social media (e.g., having to work overtime or weekends)?
- Do you ever boast about work accomplishments or achieving your sales quota? Should you publicize this?

Many companies have strict policies in place that limit the amount of time employees can spend using social media, if any at all. While it is critical today for salespeople to engage with social media to enhance their sales effort, it is imperative that they use it in an ethically responsible way. Some employees have been fired over comments made on social media about their workplace.

One rule of thumb: If you don't want your mother or boss to see it, don't write about it on social media!

Salespeople's Ethics in Dealing with Their Employers

Salespeople, as well as sales managers, may occasionally misuse company assets, moonlight, or cheat. Such unethical practices can affect co-workers and need to be prevented before they occur.[13]

Misusing Company Assets

Company assets most often misused are automobiles, expense accounts, samples, and damaged-merchandise credits. All can be used for personal gain, or as bribes and kickbacks to customers. For example, a credit for damaged merchandise can be given to a customer when there has been no damage, or valuable product samples can be given to a customer.

Moonlighting

Salespeople are not closely supervised, and as a result they may be tempted to take a second job–perhaps on company time. Some salespeople attend university or college on company time. It is imperative for employees to advise their supervisors if they are trying to get a second job or if they are going to school; many companies require employees to request permission before the employee can accept another position on top of their "day job." For example, a salesperson may enrol in an evening MBA program but take off in the early afternoon to prepare for class. Sales positions tend to have a lot of freedom and this should not be abused by employees moonlighting during work hours.

Cheating

A salesperson may not play fair in contests. If a contest starts in July, the salesperson may not turn in sales orders for the end of June and lump them with July sales. A salesperson might arrange, with or without the customer's permission, to ship

merchandise that is not needed or wanted. The merchandise is held until payment is due and then returned to the company after the contest is over. The salesperson also may overload the customer to win the contest.

Affecting Other Salespeople

Often, the unethical practices of one salesperson affect other salespeople within the company. Someone who cheats in winning a contest is taking money and prizes from other salespeople. A salesperson also may not split commissions with co-workers or may take customers from co-workers.

EXHIBIT 2.7
This salesperson can easily download company data and take them with him to his next employer.
Source: © Jacob Wackerhausen/ iStockphoto

Technology Theft

A salesperson or sales manager may quit, or be fired, and take the organization's customer records to use for their own or a future employer's benefit. (See Exhibit 2.7.) How is that possible? Well, it's getting easier to do these days because more and more companies provide their sales personnel with computers, software, and data on their customers. However, employees should be aware of how they handle their customers' data as the The *Personal Information Protection and Electronic Documents Act* (PIPEDA) is increasing in importance and awareness, as is the law that governs how private sector organizations collect, use, and disclose personal information in the course of commercial business.

Ethics in Dealing with Customers

Many ethical questions can arise in the activities of professional salespeople. Companies should develop and implement business conduct guidelines to ensure that their sales personnel will avoid being implicated in an unethical or illegal activity (see Exhibit 2.8).

EXHIBIT 2.8
This salesperson must be careful about the claims made in the sales presentation. If he says, "This equipment will increase production 2 percent," and it doesn't, the salesperson and his company may find themselves in court.
Source: © Jose Luis Pelaez Inc/ Blend Images LLC

SELLING TIPS

VALUES AND ETHICS CODE FOR THE PUBLIC SECTOR

The Government of Canada publishes public sector standards for government employees. The stated values are:

- Respect for democracy
- Respect for people
- Integrity
- Stewardship
- Excellence

Their statement of values reads:

These values are a compass to guide public servants in everything they do. They cannot be considered in isolation from each other as they will often overlap. This Code and respective organizational codes of conduct are important sources of guidance for public servants. Organizations are expected to take steps to integrate these values into their decisions, actions, policies, processes, and systems. Similarly, public servants can expect to be treated in accordance with these values by their organization.

Employment and Social Development Canada expands on this in their Code of Conduct, which reads:

All ministers, parliamentarians, and public servants have a role to play in serving Canadians. You have an obligation to preserve the public trust by being effective, efficient, and courteous in your work and workplaces. By demonstrating the values of the public sector, you not only help raise public confidence in public institutions, but also help departments create and maintain work environments in which employees experience less stress and more satisfaction.

Are there any elements of the public sector code of conduct that you would not include in a corporate sales code of conduct? Explain.

Sources: Government of Canada, Values and Ethics Code for the Public Sector, retrieved from http://www.tbs-sct.gc.ca/pol/doc-eng.aspx?id=25049 on April 25, 2019; and Government of Canada, ESDC Code of Conduct, retrieved from https://www.canada.ca/en/employment-social-development/corporate/code-conduct.html#a3 on April 25, 2019.

Self-Regulation

For many years, companies that sold direct to consumers had a poor reputation. Salespeople were described as pushy, and in some cases used unethical sales practices. Concerned with their future relationships with customers, many professional associations across Canada, such as the Investment Dealers Association of Canada and the Direct Sellers Association, began to practise self-regulation; they created a set of guiding principles that members must abide by to retain their membership. Self-regulation provides salespeople with many professional opportunities as well as intangible benefits. These self-regulating associations allow for the following:

- Professional credibility and increased profile
- Quality standards and accountability
- Increased public trust and confidence
- Ways and means (enforcement of guidelines to prevent unskilled practice or unprofessional conduct)
- Documented proof of membership and practice
- The ability for consumers to make more informed decisions
- Recognition of specialized expertise
- Disciplinary action by peers as opposed to people outside the organization

The Direct Sellers Association website reinforces these principles:

> Under the Code's provisions, consumers may rest assured that salespeople representing DSA member companies will:
>
> - Tell you who they are, why they're approaching you, and what products they're selling

- Explain how to return a product or cancel an order
- Respect your privacy by calling at times that best suit your convenience and wishes
- Respect your right to end a sales call.

When you make a purchase, you can count on DSA member companies to provide you with:

- Accurate and truthful information on the price, quality, performance, quantity and availability of their products or services
- A written receipt in clear language
- Their own name and address and the name and address of the company represented
- A complete description of any warranty or guarantee, limited or full.

You can count on DSA member companies to

- Make sure all testimonials and endorsements are truthful, current, and authorized by the person or organization quoted
- Base any product claims on substantiated facts.

Bribes

bribe:
The process of giving something to somebody to get them to do something.

Occasionally, a salesperson might attempt to **bribe** a buyer.[14] Money, gifts, entertainment, and travel opportunities may be offered. At times, there is a thin line between good business and misusing a bribe or gift. A $10 gift to a $10,000 customer may be merely a gift, but how do we define a $4,000 ski trip for buyers and their spouses? Companies need to give clear direction on what is an appropriate gift for business-to-business gift-giving, or if it is appropriate at all!

SELLING GLOBALLY

INTERNATIONAL GIFT GIVING

Management of West Coast Technologies, a Canadian company, was excited about their upcoming trip to Asia and Europe to drum up business for their new computer networking hardware. They were going in with a management directive to "spend what it takes" to get the job done. Jane Johnson, the sales manager responsible for leading the sales team, felt that it was imperative that they get off on the right foot with each prospect. She thought that bringing gifts for them would certainly accomplish this. She had heard that gift giving in many societies can make the difference in cultivating long-lasting relationships.

Jane went on a shopping spree. Her shopping list included an expensive bottle of fine Canadian whiskey, a beautifully carved stainless steel knife, and a very expensive bottle of Niagara ice wine.

With gifts in hand, Jane and her team headed to China. Their meetings were going well. The Chinese were quite receptive to the sales team and their products, and said they'd make a decision by the end of the week. Near the end of their meeting, Jane presented the stainless steel knife to Sun Hwang, head of the Chinese delegation. Mr. Hwang looked a little bewildered. The sales team never heard back from Mr. Hwang and couldn't understand why.

Off they went to Pakistan. They landed in Islamabad, the nation's capital, and were met by Raj Singh, the president of Pakistan Network Systems, one of the country's largest companies. Mr. Singh hosted his guests for dinner at his home the night before their business meetings. It was a relaxed dinner; Jane got along extremely well with her host and they shared information about each other freely. She found that Raj was a very educated man, extremely friendly, and a devout Muslim. Jane was very impressed by him and thought that they would be doing business soon. Near the end of their meeting the following day, Jane presented Mr. Singh with the bottle of fine Canadian whiskey. Raj opened the gift and smiled politely. The sales team ended up leaving Pakistan without a firm commitment.

Their next stop was France, where they had meetings lined up with one of the country's leading communications companies. Again, they were greeted by their French prospects and invited to a formal dinner reception in the executive dining room at the company headquarters in Paris. As the Canadian sales team arrived at the dinner, Jane made a point of presenting the host with the high-quality ice wine that she had brought. The host, Mr. Losier, appeared a little perplexed but graciously accepted the gift. Mr. Losier then instructed the servers to make sure the ice wine was served at the head table, rather than the wine that had been selected. Losier and the sales team never really hit it off together and, not surprisingly, no deals were signed.

Back at their hotel, Jane and her team were bewildered as to why they were not getting any business. They didn't want to return home empty-handed. Gabe, one of the salespeople, remembered a contact that he had made with a government official in Turkey and fortunately, he was able to contact him and request that he try to line up some contacts in his country on very short notice. The Turkish contact hinted to Gabe that he would expect a "token of appreciation" for his efforts upon their arrival. Gabe passed this message on to Jane. She wondered what she should do. After careful consideration, Jane decided that none of the gift giving so far had any benefit at all, so she decided that there would be no gift giving in this situation.

The team landed in Turkey and were met by the government official, who escorted them to their hotel for the evening. He mentioned that he had set up some key meetings over the next few days and they could expect a call to finalize the details. Gabe found his conversations with his contact that evening a little awkward—something seemed a little odd. The sales team never got their call.

What went wrong with the sales trip? Do some research on the gift-giving for each country Jane visited. Were these gifts appropriate? Why or why not?

What would you suggest to Jane Johnson for future sales trips?

What are the ethical considerations of gift giving? Do they change depending on where you are doing business? Why or why not?

Is it a bribe or simply gift giving? Because it is difficult to make a clear distinction, many companies forbid their buyers from taking gifts of any size from salespeople. The intent of this policy is to encourage employees to make sound, objective purchase decisions. However, bribery does exist. It is estimated that bribes and kickbacks account for approximately 50 percent of white-collar crimes committed annually in North America.

Buyers may ask for cash, merchandise, or travel payments in return for placing an order with the salesperson. Imagine that you are a salesperson working on a 5 percent commission. The buyer says, "I'm ready to place a $20,000 order for office supplies with you. However, another salesperson has offered to pay my expenses for a weekend in Las Vegas in exchange for my business. You know $500 tax-free is a lot of money." You quickly calculate that your commission is $1,000. You'd still make $500. Would it be hard to pass up that $500?

Many large organizations, such as the Northern Alberta Institute of Technology's (NAIT's) purchasing department, publish internal policies for the public. NAIT's policies are available on the Institute's website and describe guidelines within which the purchasing function conducts its business. Sellers to this organization are expected to abide by the policies. Most companies, public or private, have some internal policies; it is important to understand your company's policies as well as the policies of any company you are doing business with.

Misrepresentation

Today, even casual misstatements by salespeople can put a company on the wrong side of the law. Most salespeople are unaware that they assume legal obligations–with accompanying risks and responsibilities–every time they approach a customer. Nevertheless, we all know that salespeople sometimes oversell. They exaggerate the capabilities of their products or services and sometimes make false statements just to close a sale.

misrepresentation: Statements made by salespeople that exaggerate the capabilities of their products or services and false statements made to close a sale.

breach of warranty: A situation in which a product does not perform as promised by the company's representatives.

Often, buyers depend heavily on the technical knowledge and professional integrity of salespeople. Yet sales managers and staff find it difficult to know just how far they can go with well-intentioned sales talk, personal opinion, and promises. They may not realize that, by using certain statements, they can embroil their companies in a lawsuit and ruin the business relationship they are trying to establish.

When a customer relies on a salesperson's statements, purchases the product or service, and then finds that it fails to perform as promised, the supplier can be sued for **misrepresentation** and **breach of warranty**.

You can avoid such mistakes, however, if you're aware of the law of misrepresentation and breach of warranty relative to the selling function, and if you follow strategies that keep you and your company out of trouble. Salespeople must understand the difference between sales puffery (opinions) and statements of fact—and the legal ramifications of each. There are preventive steps to follow; salespeople must work closely with management to avoid time-consuming manufacturing and delivery delays, and costly legal fees.

Food fraud or misrepresentation is a huge issue with seafood; in fact, a recent study by UBC, conducted in Metro Vancouver, found that approximately 25 percent of seafood is mislabelled. The study revealed some of this was unintentional, but by the time the seafood was transported to various parts of the world for processing, it was a complex process to trace where it had originated. Sometimes the fish was incorrectly labelled as well. The next time you order red snapper at a restaurant, be sure it is not tilapia![15]

What the Law Says

The majority of transactions in which a Canadian sales representative participates fall within the scope of the *Sale of Goods Act*. This law separates goods from property and deals with the effect of fraud, misrepresentation, mistake, or other invalidating causes.

MAKING THE SALE

CONFLICT OF INTEREST?

The real estate salesperson assured the young couple that she would work hard to find them the right house. "Consider me your scout," she said. "I'll find you the best house for the least money."

The couple was reassured, and on the way home they talked about their good fortune. They had a salesperson working for them. With prices so high, it was nice to think they had professional help on their side.

The family selling the house felt the same way. They carefully chose the real estate salesperson because, with house prices all over the place these days, they hoped a good salesperson might win them several thousand dollars more. They had another reason to choose carefully: At today's prices, the 6 percent sales commission is a lot of money. "If we have to pay it," they reasoned, "we're better off paying it to the best salesperson."

How can both parties expect the best deal? How can a salesperson promise the seller the most for the money and then make the same promise to the buyer? In the same vein, how can a salesperson whose commission rises or falls with the price of the house being sold be expected to cut into her income? Isn't her total allegiance to the person paying her?

Critics complain that regulators haven't made greater efforts to clarify matters to protect both buyers and sellers. Two explanations are sometimes offered. First, this is more a human than a legal problem; even if warned, buyers will continue to assume that salespeople work solely for them, rather than for the seller, who pays the salesperson a commission.

Second, a good salesperson sometimes can come close to serving the desires of both parties. The point is arguable, but the justification offered is that the salesperson's compromises may be necessary to save a sale from falling through.

A somewhat similar situation exists in the stock market, where many small investors view their stockbroker as a confidant and adviser.

Misrepresentation is a complex legal concept since there is a provision in law that distinguishes between innocent misrepresentation and fraudulent misrepresentation.

Innocent misrepresentation is a misstatement unknown as such by the party making it. In general, a party misled by such statements is not entitled to sue for damages but may be in a position to void a contract.

Fraudulent misrepresentation is a misstatement that was known as such by the party making the statement. If this misrepresentation induced the making of a contract, and the buyer determined that the contract was deficient as a result of the misstatement, the contract could be voided or damages sought.

In addition, a buyer has remedies in law for transactions that fall within the *Sale of Goods Act*. For example, buyers can reject the goods in a transaction for the following reasons:

1. When the seller has been in breach of a condition of a sales contract
2. Where there has been a breach of warranty by the seller; for example:
   - Nondelivery of goods
   - Delayed delivery of goods

Unfortunately, Canadian law books on this subject are filled with cases where the seller overpromised and underdelivered, resulting in financial damages and damage to the selling company's reputation.

The following is an illustration of how Canadian law would likely apply according to the *Sale of Goods Act:*

> An independent sales rep sold heavy industrial equipment. He went to a purchaser's construction site, observed his operations, then told the company president that his proposed equipment would "keep up with any other machine then being used," and that it would "work well in cooperation with the customer's other machines and equipment."
>
> The customer informed the rep that he was not personally knowledgeable about the kind of equipment the rep was selling, and that he needed time to study the rep's report. Several weeks later, he bought the equipment based on the rep's recommendations.
>
> After a few months, he sued the rep's company, claiming that the equipment didn't perform according to the representations in sales literature sent prior to the execution of the contract and to statements made by the rep at the time of sale. The equipment manufacturer defended itself by arguing that the statements made by the rep were nonactionable opinions made innocently by the rep, in good faith, with no intent to deceive the purchaser.
>
> The court would likely favour the customer, because the rep's statements were "predictions" of how the equipment would perform, making them more than mere sales talk. The rep would likely be held responsible for knowing the capabilities of the equipment he was selling, and his assertions would be deemed statements of fact, not opinions. Furthermore, it would likely be found that it was unfair that a knowledgeable salesperson would take advantage of a naive purchaser.[16]

Staying Legal

You don't have to be a lawyer to stay legal. If you are involved in selling long-term, high-cost, sophisticated products and services on a contractual basis, it is likely that one of your primary responsibilities will be to have the sales contracts prepared before closing a deal. This will involve direct involvement with your company's attorneys, who will ensure that these contracts are not only legal but also able to pass the scrutiny of the buyer's legal experts.

The following suggestions provide guidance in avoiding legal disputes:

- Understand the difference between statements of fact and statements of praise made during a sales presentation. If your company has been in business for some time and has a record of serving customers, it may be difficult to separate the two. Honesty is the best policy. If your company has a level of experience and expertise in the industry in which it competes, an honest presentation of the features, advantages, and benefits of your product or service, combined with your professionalism, will keep you out of trouble.
- Be accurate when describing a product's capabilities. Don't make speculative claims, particularly with respect to predictions concerning what a product will do. Here is an opportunity to enhance your sales presentation with the use of objective criteria. These are data about your product, and tests or surveys performed and made available by an outside resource such as an independent market research company or a testing laboratory.
- If your product is a technical product or has a technical component associated with it, you need to know the latest specifications of the product. Although your company usually prepares the official information that is available to customers, it never hurts to review and question any information that you are not comfortable with and that you are asked to accept as true.
- Certain laws vary by province and by municipality. Get acquainted with local laws.
- Don't offer opinions. In the heavy-equipment business involving bulldozers, earth movers, and power shovels, questions regarding capacity and durability factors needed to perform certain types of jobs will already be answered by success stories from current customers. In a new application, it is not unusual for the seller and the potential customer to test out certain equipment for particular applications where no past data exist.
- Beware of libel and slander. **Libel** is a written act of defamation such as in a newsletter, blog, or published announcement. **Slander** is an act of defamation which is verbal or spoken. Be honest, don't act maliciously, and state facts only. Do not tweet that your competitor, Andy Jones, is a lying cheat. You might be safer by saying that you read an article about a potential lawsuit involving his company. Keep yourself out of trouble and keep your own reputation intact.

libel:
A written act of defamation such as in a newsletter, blog, or published announcement.

slander:
An act of defamation that is verbal or spoken.

Price Discrimination

price discrimination:
The act of selling the same quantity of the same product to different buyers at different prices.

Price discrimination is covered by the *Competition Act* and exists when the following conditions can be proven:

- A discount, rebate, allowance, price concession, or other advantage was granted to one customer and not to another.
- The customers are competitors.
- The price discrimination occurred in respect of articles of similar quality and quantity.
- The act of discrimination was part of a practice of discrimination.

An interesting aspect of price discrimination in Canada is that the buyer is seen as liable along with the seller in price discrimination cases. The law was structured intentionally to restrain large-volume buyers from demanding discriminatory pricing. An upstart paintball gaming company in the Toronto area was searching for a supplier of paintballs. They started doing business with a supplier with an initial purchase of 100,000 paintballs at 5 cents each. As other companies entered into the gaming side of the business, one of the larger operators was ordering 1 million at a time for the same 5 cents apiece. When the upstart tried to reorder, they were told that their orders were not large enough and that they would now have to order from the larger operator (their own competitor) and that the price would be 10 cents each. After an argument, the supplier relented and agreed to sell the smaller quantities, but now at 7 cents each. This was price discrimination. It would have put the upstart at a competitive disadvantage. Eventually, after being threatened with legal action, the supplier relented again and reduced the price to 5 cents.

Tied Selling or Tie-in Sales

A firm engages in **tied selling** when it makes the purchase of one or more goods or services conditional on the purchase of others. This can be accomplished either through making the tied selling an overt condition of purchase or through some form of inducement such as a price for the bundle of tied goods lower than the sum of the individual prices of the goods if purchased separately. The two most common types of tied sales are bundling and requirements tying. **Bundling** (or package tie-in) occurs when a product is sold only on the condition that some specified number of units of some other product are purchased from the same supplier (for example, in order to purchase a unit of B from a supplier, a consumer must also purchase two units of A from the same supplier); with a requirements tie, consumers must make all of their purchases of product A from a firm if they want to purchase product B from that firm.

tied selling: Selling in which a buyer is required to buy additional products not wanted when purchasing particular items.

bundling: Offering several products as one combined product.

The law, however, concedes that these requirements can be either anti-competitive or pro-competitive. Tying may be anti-competitive when it shuts out or forecloses on competitors that also supply the tied product(s). Foreclosure leads to a reduction in the choice of suppliers of the tied goods. If the level of foreclosure is such that consumers are adversely affected either through higher prices, less variety, or both, then antitrust intervention is warranted.

However, tying can also be pro-competitive if it allows suppliers to take advantage of economies of scope in production, sale, and distribution, or if it reduces

MAKING THE SALE

DO I REALLY HAVE TO BUY THAT?

Brodie and Carrie were shopping for a new home. They decided to visit their bank to get pre-approved for a mortgage. The CSR informed them that in order to get a mortgage, they would have to also buy life insurance and auto insurance through that bank. They found this odd and were disappointed as they had a good relationship with both the bank and their insurance broker.

WHAT THE LAW SAYS:

Banks in Canada are not allowed to engage in "coercive tied selling" or "forced purchases." This means that banks are not allowed to unduly pressure or coerce you into obtaining a product or service from them or from their affiliates as a condition for obtaining another product or service from them. Coercive tied selling is illegal in Canada. For example, if you apply for a mortgage at a bank, the institution cannot make you buy another product or service as a condition for obtaining the mortgage.

However, banks (and their affiliates) are allowed to offer consumers, in conjunction with one of their products, another product or service on more favourable terms than they normally would provide. This is similar to a company offering a deal or discount to its customers if they purchase more than one item from the company. For example, if you obtain a loan from a bank to purchase a Registered Retirement Savings Plan (RRSP) investment, the bank might offer you a better rate on your loan if you also purchase your RRSP investment from them.

Banks are also required to display, and make available in their branches, a statement that advises customers about the prohibition on coercive tied selling.

transactions costs. The fact that many products supplied in competitive markets are commonly tied together suggests that pro-competitive rationales for tying are pervasive. The Competition Bureau has recommended against an outright ban on tying in any market, unless it is clear that the only motivation for a tie is to foreclose on competition.

Examples of potentially pro-competitive instances of tied selling in financial markets involve the provision of various forms of credit, mortgages, or loans. At some stage in the process of providing a customer with these products, the financial institution must incur the cost of assessing the creditworthiness of the customer. Once an institution has incurred this cost for the provision of one product, it need not incur it again to provide the same customer with other credit-related products. By bundling a group of such products together, the institution provides these services at a lower cost to the customer than if each product had to be purchased separately.[17]

Exclusive Dealing

exclusive dealing: Prohibiting a channel member from carrying competitive products.

In **exclusive dealing**, a manufacturer or marketer prohibits channel members from carrying competitive products. Although this prohibition is not automatically illegal under the *Competition Act,* the usual legal test is whether competition is restricted.

Reciprocity

reciprocity: An agreement whereby a person or organization buys a product if the person or organization selling the product also buys a product from the first party.

Reciprocity refers to buying a product or service from someone if that person or business agrees to buy from you. Once again, if this practice is seen to limit competition, legal action can be taken under the *Competition Act.*

Consumer Protection

The following sections deal primarily with business-to-business situations and provide evidence of the complexities of selling today. We also need to recognize that there is another level of the law that deals with the consumer. For example, in British Columbia, door-to-door selling requires a provincial licence. Although there are some exceptions (real estate salespeople, for example), anyone engaged in direct selling to consumers in their residence must be licensed.

cooling-off period: A period during which the buyer may cancel the contract, return any merchandise, and obtain a full refund.

In addition, extensive consumer protection is contained in the *British Columbia Consumer Protection Act.* Most provinces have enacted similar protective legislation. One protection in the legislation is the **cooling-off period**. In our example of door-to-door selling, if consumers enter into a contract for goods or services valued at more than $50, they have 10 days during which they have the right to cancel that contract without penalty. What is the law in your province?

Further discussion on consumer protection laws is beyond the scope of this textbook. If you are interested in this subject, your local Better Business Bureau is an excellent resource.

Source: © Endostock/Dreamstime.com/GetStock.com

Managing Sales Ethics

Surveys to determine managers' views of business ethics have found the following:

- All managers feel they face ethical problems.
- Most managers feel they and their employers should be more ethical.
- Managers are more ethical with their friends than with people they do not know.
- Even though they want to be more ethical, some managers lower their ethical standards to meet job goals.

- Managers are aware of unethical practices in their industry and company ranging from price discrimination to hiring discrimination.
- Business ethics can be influenced by an employee's superior and company environment.

Organizations now recognize the importance of improving their social responsiveness and ethical climate. Managers must take active steps to ensure that the company stays on ethical ground. Management methods for helping organizations to be more responsive include (1) creating an ethical sales climate, (2) top management taking the lead, (3) carefully selecting leaders, (4) establishing and following a code of ethics, (5) creating ethical structures, (6) formally encouraging whistle- blowing, and (7) establishing control systems.

Source: © Digital Vision RF

Business Ethics

In the past, many have considered business ethics an oxymoron. Today, however, business ethics is a management discipline.

The Canadian Centre for Ethics and Corporate Policy, founded more than 30 years ago, is headquartered in Toronto, and includes Canada's largest and most respected companies among its board of directors and membership. As further evidence of the impact of ethics on Canadian business, recent research indicates that 90 percent of college and university business programs have at least one course in ethics in their curricula.

Historically, the field of ethics has been the focus of philosophers, academics, and social scientists. However, in today's highly complex, increasingly international marketplace, managers constantly face ethical dilemmas such as conflicts of interest, misuse of company resources, and human rights violations.

Create an Ethical Sales Climate

The single most important factor in improving the climate for ethical behaviour in a sales force is the action taken by top-level managers. Sales managers must help develop and support their codes of ethics. They should publicize the code and their opposition to unethical sales practices to their subordinate managers and their salespeople. A stronger level of ethical awareness can be achieved during sales meetings, training sessions, and when contacting customers while working with salespeople (job shadowing).[18]

EXHIBIT 2.9

Top-level management sets the climate for ethical behaviour in the sales force.

Source: © Stockbyte/Getty Images RF

Leader Selection Is Important

Since so few individuals are at the principled level of moral development, it is critical to choose managers carefully. Only people who have the highest level of integrity, standards, and values should assume leadership positions.

Senior Management

An organization's senior managers must develop ethical standards for their businesses and exhibit compliance to these standards. If leadership is shown at this level, the majority of employees will follow that lead (see Exhibit 2-9). Involvement in basic forms of ethical organizations, such as the local Better Business Bureau or an industry or professional association with a code of ethics, is a start. In terms of Canada's larger international companies, involvement in ethical industry associations, and with organizations such as the Centre for Ethics and Corporate Policy and the Conference Board of Canada, will ensure receipt of a flow of current information on ethics.

ETHICAL DILEMMA

THE BOSS MADE ME DO IT

Your prospect insists that her company must have delivery of your product in four weeks to meet a national advertising rollout. The company has made a tremendous investment in its ad campaign. After extensive prodding by you and your managers, the production department cannot do any better than a six-week delivery. Your boss orders you to promise the customer delivery within four weeks. What is the most ethical action to take?

1. Tell your boss that you do not believe that it is right to lie to the customer. State that you will not pass the four-week lead time along but would be more than happy to tell the customer about the true six-week lead time. Tell your boss that you cannot support dishonesty within the company.
2. Do as your boss says and promise the four-week delivery time, even though you know there is no possibility of meeting the deadline.
3. Tell your boss to pass the information to the customer himself. That way, you do not have to actually lie to your customer.
4. Resign your position. Would you resign your position over this type of situation?

Establish a Code of Ethics

code of ethics: A formal statement of the company's values concerning ethics and social issues.

A **code of ethics** is a formal statement of the company's values concerning ethics and social issues. It states those values or behaviours that are expected and those that are not tolerated. These values and behaviours must be backed by management action. Without top management support, there is little assurance that the code will be followed.

The two types of codes of ethics are principle-based statements and policy-based statements. Principle-based statements affect corporate culture, define fundamental values, and contain general language about company responsibilities, quality of products, and treatment of employees. General statements of principle are often called *corporate credos.* Examples of internationally recognized companies with corporate credos are Johnson & Johnson, Starbucks, and Levi Strauss. Canadian companies operating on a global basis and displaying a commitment to ethical standards include Microsoft, with its ethical commitment to "Corporate Citizenship" In addition, Desjardins Group provides statements of "Core Values" that guide the organization in a highly competitive market.

Policy-based statements generally outline the procedures to be used in specific ethical situations. These situations include marketing practice, conflicts of interest, observance of laws, proprietary information, political gifts, and equal opportunities. Examples of policy-based ethics can be found in international companies' policies such as Textron's (makers of Bell helicopters and Cessna aircraft) "Business Conduct Guidelines," Honeywell Inc.'s "Code of Business Conduct," supported further by a corporate ethics officer, and Motorola, whose "Code of Business Conduct" is enhanced by an ethics hotline, a communication line available for all stakeholders.

Create Ethical Structures

ethics committee: A group of executives appointed to oversee company ethics and provide rulings on questionable ethical issues.

ethics ombudsman: An official given the responsibility of corporate conscience who hears and investigates ethical complaints and informs top management of potential ethical issues.

An **ethics committee** is a group of executives appointed to oversee company ethics. The committee provides rulings on questionable ethical issues and assumes responsibility for disciplining wrongdoers. This responsibility is essential if the organization is to directly influence employee behaviour. An **ethics ombudsman** is an official given the responsibility of being the corporate conscience who hears and investigates ethical complaints and informs top management of potential ethical issues. For example, some companies, such as the Royal Bank, have an office of the ombudsman who will "provide an impartial avenue for unresolved concerns and will recommend changes to improve customer and employee experiences."[19]

AN INDUSTRY PERSPECTIVE

HOW TO TELL IF YOU'RE BURNED OUT ON SELLING

Perhaps more than any other profession, selling is a series of highs and lows. One hallmark of potential sales stars is their love of selling and consistently positive outlook. A sour attitude and dishonest selling practices often signal long-term trouble ahead, so take a close look at your thoughts and actions for some insight into your success potential. Your honest, objective answers to the questions below and your attention to the comments that follow will help point you in the right direction on your quest for success.

Instructions: Take a few minutes to answer true or false to the eight statements below. After answering each question, take a look at the comments next to the answer you selected. The comments will help you understand which attitudes help you succeed and which ones hold you back. Keep an open mind and ask yourself if your answers and the comments that accompany them represent your real actions and feelings.

1. The biggest incentive for me to keep selling is personal profit.
2. Sometimes I have to tell a "little white lie" to help prospects stop procrastinating and make a decision.
3. My number-one goal in any selling situation is to see how fast I can close.
4. My product's high price and mediocre quality are holding me back as a salesperson.
5. I find that selling and motivational podcasts, books, and seminars just present the same old message over and over.
6. I think a positive mental attitude is one of the most important keys to sales success.
7. After I've given my presentation, if my prospect tells me they have committed to purchasing from another company, my next step is to go back to my office and research my competitor's product or service.
8. Even when I lose a sale, I still write a note thanking my prospects for their time and for considering my product or service.

Answers and Commentary

Question #1

TRUE: When making money is a salesperson's primary objective, the prospect needs take a backseat to personal greed. Perceptive buyers will often shy away from salespeople who don't make their customers' needs the number-one priority. Putting money before people often saps your work of its meaning, which may lead to burnout.

FALSE: Successful salespeople truly enjoy sharing products or services that they know will improve their customers'lives. To them, happy customers, not money, are selling's greatest reward. The more satisfaction you get from serving your customers, the more you'll find that selling is a joy instead of a burden—an attitude critical to long-lasting success.

Question #2

TRUE: When faced with losing a sale, some salespeople may tell "harmless" white lies—"We only have one left" or "Our prices are about to go up, so you'd better decide quickly"—in an attempt to close fast. If you're frustrated or desperate enough to resort to such tactics, find out why. There's no substitute for sharp selling skills, a motivated attitude, and confidence to ward off burnout.

FALSE: True professionals adhere to a high standard of ethics. They recognize that sales made at the expense of their integrity benefit no one. Repeat business and referrals, not the quick sale, are their goal, and they conduct themselves so that their customers want to do business with them and only them. By using books, videos, podcasts, and seminars to constantly improve their selling skills and motivation, they eliminate any need for lies or other underhanded tactics.

Question #3

TRUE: Salespeople who approach prospects thinking, "Close, close, close!" may face a burnout problem. Reducing the sales process to one result-oriented step also reduces the benefits of each sale. Eventually, close-hungry salespeople may discover that neglecting the important elements of the sales process takes its toll on profits and repeat business.

FALSE: After reaching a qualified prospect, competent salespeople know the sales process is just beginning and that each step demands careful attention. They (1) establish rapport, (2) identify the prospect's needs and expectations, (3) make a benefit-loaded presentation, and (4) decide if the product or service will meet the prospect's needs and create a satisfied customer. If it will, the salesperson (5) closes politely but persistently, answering questions, concerns, and objections, then (6) services the account and asks for referrals. Focusing on each step increases your odds of making the sale and establishes you as a competent professional who deserves your customers'—and their associates'—business.

Question #4

TRUE: To deflect responsibility for low sales and poor attitude away from themselves, burned-out salespeople may blame their product, service, or company. Instead of seeking out ways to improve sales, they may moan about a slow economy. The same low motivation and poor attitude that cause the burnout prevent them from seeing problems as the disguised opportunities that they are.

FALSE: Successful salespeople sell well partly because they have absolute faith in what they sell. They know their products and services are worth their price, and that their buyers won't regret the purchase. If they have a need for it, many salespeople own and use the products they represent and endorse them personally. The best way to sell customers on your product is to sell yourself on it first.

Question #5

TRUE: When you stop learning and growing as a salesperson, you become more vulnerable to burnout. Salespeople who appear to be in a slump have often forgotten the basics that capitalize on the human aspects of selling and that keep it challenging and interesting. The more focused you are on what you stand to gain from a sale, the more out of touch you become with the people who make it worthwhile.

FALSE: Sales superachievers are lifelong students. They constantly and continuously stimulate their minds and invest in education. Education affords them the opportunity to review the all-important sales basics as well as to learn effective new techniques. They take responsibility for keeping themselves informed and motivated.

Question #6

TRUE: Though a positive attitude is critical to sales success, great salespeople know that attitude is a means to an end and not an end in itself. To sell effectively you must team polished selling skills with the right attitude. Confidence is key to motivation, so keep your skills fine tuned, learn all you can about your product or service, and make the customer your top priority. The knowledge that you're well equipped to meet your goals will help you maintain an attitude that maintains profits.

FALSE: A classic symptom of burnout, a poor attitude can be either a cause or an effect of the condition. Either way, once your attitude suffers, it's only a matter of time before your sales and everyone around you suffer as well. If you can't seem to pull yourself out of the depths of despair, you may be facing a serious case of burnout.

Question #7

TRUE: Burnout victims often use rejection to redirect their attention away from making personal contacts. They've lost the motivation required to pursue challenging prospects, and may take rejection personally. Low closing confidence may prevent them from asking for a customer's business to eliminate the risk of possible rejection.

FALSE: Selling is fraught with rejection, but for super salespeople rejection and setbacks are a challenge—an opportunity to test the skills they've worked hard to perfect. They ask themselves, "How can I learn something from this? What did I do right? How can I turn this seemingly negative experience into a personal victory?" Even if a presentation ends with a "no," the winning salesperson appreciates the chance to meet a contact and practise presentation skills.

Question #8

TRUE: Successful salespeople build relationships—they don't burn bridges. A graceful thank-you note in response to a "no" may turn a rejection into a source of referrals. Presentations that end without a sale are often more effective learning experiences than those that end with a sale, so thank your prospects for their time and the chance to learn how to present your product more effectively.

FALSE: Many burnout victims don't bother with thank-you notes because they don't look for the opportunity in every contact. If they don't see an opportunity, they don't feel they owe the contact a thank you. Their gratitude is often prompted only by immediate financial gain instead of appreciation for the prospect's valuable time and attention.

Even those with the highest hopes and the loftiest ambitions can go only as far as their attitudes will take them. Your answers to the quiz above should tell you whether or not you're on the right track. If your responses point to burnout ahead, do what it takes to change your outlook and your direction. Your attitude—and your future—are up to you.

Source: Gregory Lousig-nonthttps://www.sellingpower.com/2010/02/02/4218/how-to-tell-if-youre-burned-out-on-selling. Used with the permission of Personal Selling Power, Inc.

Encourage Whistle-Blowing

Employee disclosure of illegal, immoral, or illegitimate practices on the employer's part is called **whistle-blowing**. Companies can provide a mechanism for whistle-blowing as a matter of policy. All employees who observe or become aware of criminal practices or unethical behaviour should be encouraged to report the incident to their superiors, to a higher level of management, or to an appropriate unit of the organization, such as an ethics committee. Formalized procedures for complaining can encourage honest employees to report questionable incidents. For example, a company could provide its employees with a toll-free number to report unethical activities to top management. This silent-witness program may encourage employees to report incidents because they do not have to confront personnel. This program is especially valuable if the employee's own manager is involved in unethical practices. However, with such programs, careful verification is necessary to guard against vindictive employees.

whistle-blowing: Employee disclosure of illegal, immoral, or illegitimate practices on the employer's part.

The Toronto Transit Commission (TTC) developed a whistleblower hotline to encourage employees to speak up if they see fraud or waste in their company. Workers can call a 1-800 number to report any fraudulent behaviours about their peers.[20]

Establish Control Systems

Establish control systems. Employ methods to determine whether salespeople give bribes, falsify reports, or pad expenses. For example, check sales made from low bids to determine whether procedures have been followed correctly. Dismissal, demotion, suspension, reprimand, and withholding of sales commissions are possible penalties for unethical sales practices.

Summary of Major Selling Issues

Ethics and social responsibility are hot topics. Ethical behaviour pertains to values of right and wrong, and ethical decisions and behaviour are typically guided by a value system. For individual managers, the ability to make correct ethical choices will depend on both individual and organizational characteristics, including the individual's own level of moral development and the corporate culture in which they work.

Corporate social responsibility concerns a company's values toward society. Organizations can be good corporate citizens by evaluating their social performance through four criteria: economic, legal, ethical, and discretionary. Social responsibility in business means profitably serving employees and customers in an ethical and lawful manner. Extra costs can accrue because a firm takes socially responsible action, but this is a part of doing business in today's society, and it pays in the long run. Companies such as MEC and Tim Hortons have shown that practising corporate social responsibility can pay off, as evidenced by their success and by the fact that they pay attention to the triple bottom line–that is, understanding that everything they do has an impact environmentally, socially, and economically.

Salespeople and managers must be ethical in dealing with salespeople, employers, and customers. Ethical standards and guidelines for sales personnel must be developed, supported, and policed. In the future, ethical selling practices will be even more important to conducting business profitably. Techniques for improving social responsiveness include leadership, codes of ethics, ethical structures, whistle-blowing, and establishing control systems. Finally, research suggests that socially responsible organizations perform as well as–and often better than–organizations that are not socially responsible.

MEETING A SALES CHALLENGE

In essence, the sales manager was seeking reciprocity. The contemplated deal is clearly unethical. In some cases, such a deal may even be unlawful. Companies that are aware of their legal and ethical responsibilities protect themselves and their employees from unnecessary exposure to illegal activity like this.

For example, IBM marketing representatives are urged to follow the specific steps set forth in IBM's "Business Conduct Guideline"—a policy-based code of ethics—which states, "You may not do business with a supplier of goods or services." Reasonable? Yes. Important? *Absolutely.*

Remember that your career and the future of your company depend on creating values that last. This objective depends on making decisions we can live with tomorrow, not on what we might get away with today.

PLAYING THE ROLE

Role A: Sales rep for Canadian Paper Supply. Your conscience is finally getting to you. You've been overcharging some of your loyal customers over the past few months to increase your commissions. In fact, you've even double-billed one customer, knowing that its accounts payable department is disorganized and would likely pay you twice. The guilt has caused you to become depressed and you've been drinking more heavily recently and then hiding your hangovers with painkillers. Your overall performance has been slipping, so you arrange a meeting with your superiors to discuss your situation.

Role B: Sales manager and/or general manager of Canadian Paper Supply. A troubled employee is meeting with you to discuss some personal problems he has been experiencing and that he feels are affecting his job performance. After listening to his problems, what should you do? How do you handle employees in these situations? What are your options?

Prepare your role for an in-class dramatization of this situation.

Key Terms for Selling

breach of warranty
bribe
bundling
CCC GOMES
code of ethics
conventional moral development level
cooling-off period
discretionary responsibility
employee rights
ethics
ethics committee
ethics ombudsman
exclusive dealing
libel
misrepresentation
morals
PIPEDA
preconventional moral developmental level
price discrimination
principled moral development level
reciprocity
slander
social responsibility
stakeholder
tied selling
whistle-blowing
worldview

Sales Application Questions

1. Which of the following situations represent socially responsible actions by firms?
   a. Creating recreation facilities for sales personnel
   b. Paying for university courses for your employees in an MBA program
   c. Allowing sales personnel to buy company products at a discount
2. How should sales managers promote and enforce ethical practices? Describe some ethical situations that sales managers may face in dealing with salespeople.
3. Imagine that you were being encouraged to inflate your expense account. Do you think your choice would be most affected by your individual moral development or by the cultural values of the company for which you worked? Explain.

4. Have you ever experienced an ethical dilemma? Evaluate the dilemma with respect to its impact on other people. Who were the stakeholders in your dilemma?
5. Do you think a code of ethics combined with an ethics committee would be more effective than leadership alone for implementing ethical behaviour? Discuss.
6. Discuss the difference between sales "exaggeration" and "misrepresentation." How can you avoid mistakes that could prove costly to the firm?
7. Some companies consider customers and employees to be more important stakeholders than shareholders are. Is it appropriate for management to define some stakeholders as more important than others? Should all stakeholders be considered equal?
8. For each of the following situations, indicate how you would respond in each situation with *Yes*, *No*, *It depends*, or *I just don't know*. Prepare a justification for each response.
   a. Providing free entertainment (professional hockey game tickets) to prospective clients
   b. Asking a buyer for information regarding a competitor
   c. Selling an inferior quality product to an unsuspecting buyer
   d. Complaining about your company to a customer or competitor
   e. Overstating the performance of a product to secure an order

Sales Online Exercise

Corporate Ethics Research

If you had to guess which corporations in the world deserve to be called the best corporate citizens, which companies would you choose? To make this job easier, The Ethisphere Institute conducts an annual survey that ranks the top 100 corporations on ethical measures pertaining to treatment of stakeholders including customers and employees. Go to the Ethisphere website, www.ethisphere.com/worlds-most-ethical/wme-honorees, and review the leaders in this unique survey. Research these companies by going to their websites, and determine each organization's commitment to ethical business practices and social responsibility.

Further Exploring the Sales World

1. Contact your local Better Business Bureau and prepare a report on local laws regulating the activities of salespeople.
2. The Office of the Privacy Commissioner of Canada website has a section called "Commissioner's Findings." Report on several of the summaries in this section that are related to a firm's marketing activities.
3. Talk to a sales manager about the social, ethical, and legal issues involved in the job. Does the manager's firm have
   a. A code of ethics?
   b. An ethics committee?
   c. An ethical ombudsman?
   d. Procedures for whistle-blowing? Get copies of any Internet, magazine, or newspaper articles relating to topics discussed in this chapter. Report your findings.
4. Visit the *Competition Act* website at https://laws.justice.gc.ca/eng/acts/C-34/page-17.html#h-89169. Describe at least two marketing practices that could tempt some unethical salespeople. What are the implications for salespeople of using these practices?

Selling Experiential Exercise

Ethical Work Climates

On a separate sheet of paper, answer the following questions by writing down the number that best describes an organization for which you have worked.

	Disagree				Agree
1. Whatever is best for everyone in the company is the major consideration here.	1	2	3	4	5
2. Our major concern is always what is best for the other person.	1	2	3	4	5
3. People are expected to comply with the law and professional standards over and above other considerations.	1	2	3	4	5
4. In this company, the first consideration is whether a decision violates any law.	1	2	3	4	5
5. It is very important to follow company rules and procedures here.	1	2	3	4	5
6. People in this company strictly obey company policies.	1	2	3	4	5
7. In this company, people are mostly out for themselves.	1	2	3	4	5
8. People are expected to do anything to further the company's interests, regardless of the consequences.	1	2	3	4	5
9. In this company, people are guided by their own personal ethics.	1	2	3	4	5
10. Each person in this company decides for himself or herself what is right and wrong.	1	2	3	4	5
		Total Score ________			

Total your score. These questions measure the dimensions of an organization's ethical climate:

- Questions 1 and 2 measure caring for people.
- Questions 3 and 4 measure lawfulness.
- Questions 5 and 6 measure rules adherence.
- Questions 7 and 8 measure emphasis on financial and company performance.
- Questions 9 and 10 measure individual independence.
- Questions 7 and 8 are reverse scored. (That is, if you answered "5," your actual score to write down is "1"; a "4" is really a "2," etc.).

Results - If you scored:
Above 40 - The organization has a very positive ethical climate.
30 to 40 - The organization has an above-average ethical climate.
20 to 30 - The organization has a below-average ethical climate.
Below 20 - The organization has a very poor ethical climate.

Go back over the questions and think about changes that you could have made to improve the ethical climate in the organization. Discuss with other students what you could do as a manager to improve ethics in future companies you work for.

CASE 2–1

FANCY FROZEN FOODS*

Last Friday, Bill Wilkerson of Fancy Frozen Foods (FFF) was confronted with a situation that he has not resolved successfully. Grady Bryan, a purchasing agent for Smith Supermarket Chain, Inc., made it apparent to Bill that if he wanted to retain the company's business in frozen food sales, special action would be necessary. In a telephone conversation, Grady suddenly got onto the subject of his new fishing boat and how much better it would perform with an 80-horsepower, inboard-outboard Evinrude motor. Bill and Grady have been fairly friendly, having done business together for the past four years. However, a conversation of this kind seemed out of the ordinary to Bill, especially during a long-distance call for which he was paying. What got Bill's attention was Grady's subtle mention of a competitor, Specialty Frozen Foods, whose territorial sales representative had stopped in to price some outboard motors after lunch with Grady. This alerted Bill to the complicated situation he faced. He realized it would take some thought to enable his company to retain Smith's exclusive business.

Fancy Frozen Foods

Fancy Frozen Foods operates in Manitoba and Saskatchewan, with Brandon and Regina being the two largest markets. FFF carries a complete line of frozen foods that it manufactures and wholesales, enabling it to undercut most wholesalers' prices. The company currently employs 20 salespeople. Their territories are divided according to geographic size, keeping salespeople's travel time to a minimum. Salespeople are paid a set salary of $12,000 yearly and commission of 3 percent for everything above a designated quota. Quotas differ by territory. They are set according to the relative potential of each market.

The company has no formal written policy regarding gift giving and entertainment. However, in the past, the president emphasized that customers may not receive gifts worth more than $25. In addition to this, FFF owns a ranch in Saskatchewan. The company invites each of its customers for a three-day vacation, involving hunting and other outdoor activities.

Smith Supermarket Chain

Smith has 15 supermarkets in Saskatchewan and 13 outlets in Manitoba. All of these accounts are currently serviced exclusively by FFF. Grady Bryan, in one of his various duties as warehouse ordering agent in the Brandon area for Smith, selects sellers of frozen foods. The 13 store managers call in their weekly frozen food orders to Grady, who then compiles the orders and calls in the order to Bill Wilkerson of FFF. This type of system is used to obtain lower prices than if each individual outlet made an order. The order is sent to the central warehouse, where it is broken down for individual outlets and scheduled for delivery in an efficient fashion.

What to Do?

Bill is confronted with a situation that he has never faced. He has, in the past, given Grady modest gifts in line with the president's wishes, and occasionally taken Grady to lunch. The company-sponsored hunting trips are another form of entertainment. However, none of these things, at least to Bill, indicated that Bill would succumb to a suggested bribe of this proportion. The crux of the matter is not that Bill's previous practices have indicated he would comply with this request, but that Bill's competition has shown a blatant willingness to employ unethical tactics to gain Smith's frozen food sales. The question is, should Bill take the chance of losing the 13 accounts by not offering the bribe, or should he succumb to the bribe and avoid the risk?

QUESTIONS

1. What is the main problem presented in this case?
2. What must Bill do?

*This case is adapted from a case prepared by Bill A. Wilkerson, a salesperson, as a basis for classroom discussion and not to illustrate either effective or ineffective handling of an administrative position. Company names have been changed.

CASE 2–2

ETHICAL SELLING AT PERFECT SOLUTIONS: THE CASE OF THE DELAYED PRODUCT

VIDEO CASE

Scott Patterson is a salesperson for Perfect Solutions, a chemical manufacturing firm. He sells to distributors, sometimes called wholesalers. Distributors buy in large quantities from various manufacturers and sell in smaller quantities to other businesses. Larry Ingram, the CEO of one of Scott's best distributors, called Scott into his office to discuss some concerns he has regarding their business relationship.

Ingram's company has been distributing Perfect Solutions products for over 10 years. In addition, Ingram's company has been the top seller for Perfect Solutions products two of the past three years. However, Scott seems to be doing things that may affect Ingram's sales. Ingram is very upset!

Scott Signs Competitor

Scott recently signed up Barber Distributing to distribute and sell his company's products. Barber Distributing is a competitor of Ingram's. Ingram found out about this relationship when Scott's new client, Barber Distributing, sold to one of Ingram's customers at a price 10 percent under Ingram's normal list price to get the DIS project. Ingram had cut their prices to the bone and still did not win the bid. "Did PS give Barber special price deals?" asks Ingram. Scott says, "No." Ingram wants to know if Barber will bid for the "plant" business coming up. He wants Scott to get him their bid price. Ingram places pressure on Scott to get him the best price for the bid or lose his business.

Ingram feels that his company has been very valuable to Perfect Solutions and demands that Patterson reveal the prices at which he sold products to Barber Distributors. Patterson then promises Ingram that Perfect Solutions has fixed prices that are never altered. Scott told Ingram that he and Barber pay the same price for a particular product.

The Customer Is Upset!

This does not satisfy Ingram and he lets Patterson know that the Dymotzue Company, a competitor of Scott and Perfect Solutions, has quoted Ingram better prices. The price sheets are on Ingram's desk. Ingram says he will not hesitate to leave Patterson for Dymotzue if Scott does not take care of him. Scott asks Ingram what he could do to help ease Ingram's frustration. Ingram says he wants to buy about two truckloads of Bond-do-Perm that Scott promised him but has not yet delivered.

While the Cat Is Away

Ingram is called out of the office. While Ingram is out of his office Patterson calls his manufacturing plant and talks with Jack, the manager. Jack tells him the Bond-do-Perm has some manufacturing problems and will not be available for two months. The company does not want to ship a bad product. Scott gets off the phone as Ingram walks back into his office. Patterson promises Ingram one truckload of the Bond-do-Perm within a few weeks knowing it cannot be delivered at that time. Ingram says he can sell one truckload to his customers as soon as the Bond-do-Perm arrives.

About this time, one of Ingram's salespeople comes into the distribution centre's main office and says that Barber Distributing, Ingram's competitor, has just made an offer to sell LubeExcel to one of Ingram's customers at a price 5 percent lower than that of Ingram's price. Ingram is furious, yelling at Scott to do something about this! To help Ingram meet the price, Patterson offers a free drum of LubeExcel to Ingram. Scott is authorized to give free samples only to new customers.

When Ingram leaves the office, Scott decides to look at the Dymotzue price list on Ingram's desk.

QUESTIONS

1. Describe the situation faced by both Scott Patterson and Larry Ingram.
2. What would you do if you were Scott Patterson?
3. What would you do if you were Larry Ingram?
4. What are the ethical considerations, if any, in this case?
5. What level of moral development are Patterson and Ingram operating at in this business relationship?

PART TWO

Preparation for Relationship Selling

In today's sales world, it is imperative that sales people be knowledgeable. Gone are the days when salespeople could fluff their way through a sales presentation. With the available technology, buyers are often highly educated about a product before even speaking with a salesperson.

This part of the book examines just what types of knowledge salespeople are expected to have as they begin their sales jobs. To achieve great success, it is critical that salespeople be knowledgeable about buyer behaviour, communication skills, products, prices, distribution, promotion, and competition.

In addition, it is important for modern salespeople to remain competent in the many technologies available today that complement the sales function. Mobile phones, tablets, customer relationship management software, and social media are all tools that can be used effectively by professional salespeople.

This part includes:

Source: © Juice Images/Getty Images

CHAPTER 3

The Psychology of Selling: Why People Buy

Matthew Sfetkidis
St. Clair College, Zekelman School of Business and IT, Windsor, Ontario.
Source: Courtesy of Matthew Sfetkidis

A Sales Success Story

Matthew Sfetkidis always knew he wanted to work in sports. As a human kinetics student in university, Matthew soon realized his future in sports was more likely on the business side. Matthew is a graduate of the St. Clair College Business Administration Marketing program and is now the coordinator of fan development for the Windsor Spitfires. While studying marketing at St. Clair, Matthew worked part-time as a retail salesperson and eventually as the retail manager for Lids, a sports store in the local mall. He applied much of his marketing learning to his experience working in the mall, but had aspirations to move out of retail and into a more professional sales setting.

After winning gold in the retail event at the Ontario Colleges Marketing Competition, Matthew knows hard work and dedication to continual learning about marketing bring great rewards. His commitment to staying on top of trends in marketing sets him apart as a competitor and helped him achieve his dream of working in sports. Understanding why people go to games and focusing on the fan experience have allowed him to stay on the forefront of fan development.

Matthew understands the need to use any and every way to get the Windsor Spitfires' name out there. "Facebook, Twitter, Instagram, SnapChat, and LinkedIn seem to be the most popular for social media," he explains, "and having fans and clients post photos for their family or friends to like is the best source of customers you can have."

Matthew encourages students to set high goals and focus on a path to achieve their dreams. He would love to continue to work for the Spitfires, and aspires one day to work for an NHL team. "You are selling the experience in sports. Every fan comes to the games wanting their team to win, but the key to success in sports is in selling a unique experience that, regardless of the game outcome, makes them want to return to see more games."

MAIN TOPICS

Why People Buy—The Black Box Approach

Psychological Influences on Buying

Consumer versus Organizational Buying

How to Determine Important Buying Needs—A Key to Success

Classifying Buying Situations

The Organizational Buying Decision Process

Social Style Theory

Difficult Customers

LEARNING OBJECTIVES

What do people really buy? They buy the benefits of a product. This chapter examines why and how individuals buy. It emphasizes the need for salespeople to stress benefits in their presentations. After studying this chapter, you should be able to:

- **LO1** Explain why people buy.
- **LO2** Recognize the importance of the psychological factors that influence buyer behaviour.
- **LO3** Explain the differences between consumer and organizational buying.
- **LO4** Describe how to determine important buying needs.
- **LO5** Classify various buying situations in the decision-making process.
- **LO6** Describe the organizational buying decision process.
- **LO7** Recognize the importance of social style theory and how it applies to the buyer and customer relationship.
- **LO8** Examine various ways to deal with difficult customers and recognize why satisfied customers are easier to sell.

FACING A SALES CHALLENGE

Seven years ago John Salley graduated with a computer science degree from Western University. One year later, he earned his MBA from the University of Windsor with an A average. John was on every campus recruiter's list as an outstanding applicant. He had the brains, personality, looks, and motivation of a winner. IBM convinced him to take a sales job.

John was at the top of his class in the IBM sales-training program. However, his results during his first two years in sales were just average. He could not understand why, because his knowledge of the products was outstanding. John could discuss in great depth the most technical aspects of his products. John loved sales but felt things had to change.

If you were in John's position, what would you do?

(Continued at end of chapter.)

Like many people, John Salley has done everything it takes to be successful in sales, yet for some reason has never reached his maximum potential. To be successful, salespeople need to be knowledgeable, even expert, on everything we discuss in this part of the book, "Preparation for Relationship Selling."

Chapter 3 examines why and how an individual buys. We discuss the influences on a purchase and connect them to the various steps in the customer's buying process. This chapter presents selling techniques that will aid you later in developing your sales presentation. These techniques can also help John Salley in his efforts to improve his sales performance. He needs to know why people buy.

LO1 Why People Buy—The Black Box Approach

The question of why people buy has interested salespeople for years. Salespeople know that some customers buy their product after the presentation, yet they wonder what thought process resulted in the decision to buy or not to buy. Prospective buyers are usually exposed to various sales presentations. In some manner, a person internalizes or considers this information and then makes a buying decision. This process of internalization is referred to as a **black box** because we cannot see into the buyer's mind–meaning the salesperson can apply the stimuli (a sales presentation) and observe the behaviour of the prospect but cannot witness the prospect's actual decision-making process.

black box: The unobservable, internal process taking place within the mind of prospects as they reach a decision whether or not to buy.

The classic model of buyer behaviour shown in Exhibit 3.1 is called a **stimulus-response model**. A stimulus (sales presentation) is applied, resulting in a response (purchase decision). This model assumes that prospects respond in some predictable manner to the sales presentation. Unfortunately, it does not tell us why they buy or do not buy the product. This information is concealed in the black box.

stimulus–response model: A model of behaviour that describes the process of applying a stimulus (sales presentation) that results in a response (purchase decision).

Salespeople seek to understand as much as they can about the mental processes that yield the prospects' responses. We know the following about buyer behaviour:

- People buy for both practical (rational) and psychological (emotional) reasons.
- Salespeople can use specific methods to help determine prospects' thoughts during sales presentations.
- Buyers consider certain factors in making purchase decisions.

This chapter introduces these three important topics. Each topic emphasizes the salesperson's need to understand human behaviour.

EXHIBIT 3.1

Stimulus–response model of buyer behaviour.

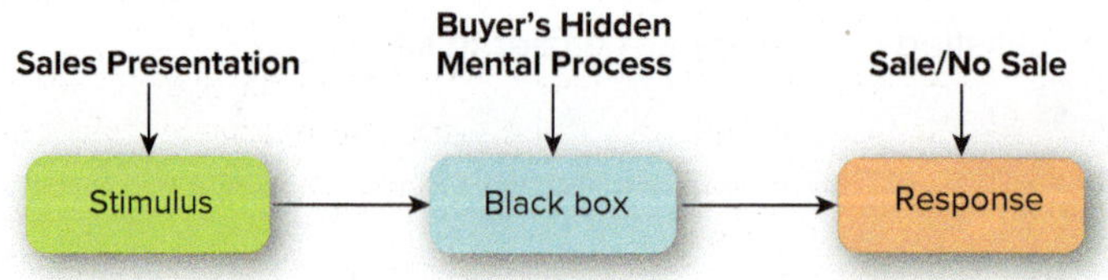

Psychological Influences on Buying

LO2

Since personal selling requires understanding human behaviour, each salesperson must determine a prospective customer's motivations, perceptions, learning, attitudes, and personality. Furthermore, the salesperson should know how each type of behaviour might influence a customer's purchase decision.

Motivation to Buy Must Be Present

Human beings are motivated by needs and wants, which build up internally, creating a desire to buy products or services (e.g., a new computer or transportation to another city). Because people buy things to satisfy needs and wants, it is important to differentiate between the two.

Needs are the basic requirements of human life–food and water, shelter, clothing, security, interaction with others, and self-fulfillment. We are all born with needs that must–to a greater or lesser degree–be satisfied throughout our lives. Needs are at the "must have" level.

needs:
The basic requirements of human life—food and water, shelter, clothing, security, interaction with others, and self-fulfillment.

Wants are not required to sustain life. They are discretionary items on the "would like to have" level–gourmet meals and fine wine, a spacious home in a prestigious neighbourhood, designer fashions, and so on. We are not born with wants–we learn them. Our knowledge, experiences, culture, and personality all influence what we want.

wants:
Not required to sustain life. Discretionary items on the "would like to have" level—gourmet meals and fine wine, a spacious home in a prestigious neighbourhood, designer fashions, and so on. We are not born with wants—we learn them. Our knowledge, experiences, culture, and personality all influence what we want.

Given that we live in a developed country where basic needs are often easily met, wants are more powerful motivators than needs. As consumers, satisfying wants becomes essential to achieving and sustaining the lifestyle we desire. For example, people need transportation, but some want a Porsche while others prefer a Ford Mustang. So, in essence, when a person wants something badly enough that they begin seeking satisfaction, it becomes a need. It may not be considered a rational need by some (Porsche versus Ford) but to the individual, it's a need nevertheless.

This example illustrates that both practical or rational reasons (e.g., the need for transportation) and emotional or psychological reasons (e.g., the desire for the prestige of owning a Porsche) influence buying behaviour (see Exhibit 3.2). One buyer might have only rational, logical reasons for buying, while another might have only emotional reasons. Yet another buyer may have a blend of both rational and emotional reasons for buying a product. A salesperson must determine a prospect's reasons in order to tailor the presentation for maximum impact.

Another way to look at it is this: Both businesses and people have wants. Although a want may not be necessary to sustain a life, if it becomes powerful enough to cause that business or person to seek satisfaction, it can essentially become a need. Do people "need" designer jeans? Absolutely. It may not appear to be a rational need but it is a need to them nevertheless. Does a business need a fancy office building in an upscale part of town? A pragmatist may say that functionality is all that is necessary. However, that business may want to project a certain image just like consumers do with their designer jeans.

EXHIBIT 3.2
Customers are motivated to buy by both practical and emotional needs.
Source: © Mangostock/Dreamstime.com/GetStock.com

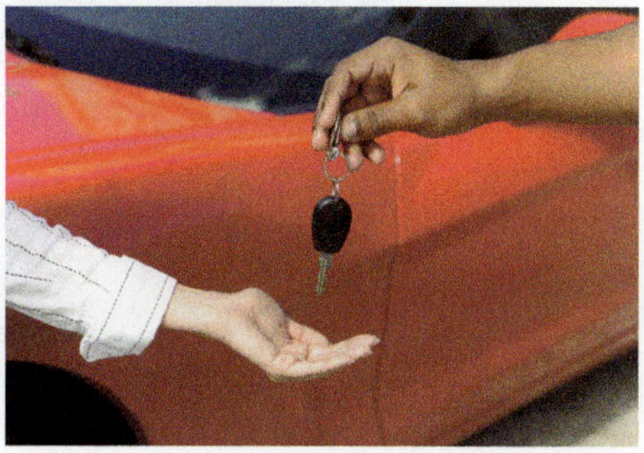

Keep in mind that, although people buy to satisfy their own personal needs and wants, sometimes they buy to satisfy the needs and wants of others. If you are selling footwear to a retail shoe store chain, for example, the buyer's decision may be based on a need to impress his superiors with profitability, or to meet the warehouse manager's demand for a better delivery schedule, or to please store managers with attractive packaging. Meeting the needs of the buyer may also involve satisfying the needs of those whom the buyer represents.

Awareness of Needs: Some Buyers Are Unsure

Buyers are not always fully aware of their needs. For example, a business owner who is experiencing some inventory management problems is thinking she'll have to hire two new employees just to manage her inventory. Then an inventory specialist calls on her business one day to evaluate and recommend a software solution customized to her business, all without having to increase her payroll expenses.

It is important that both buyer and salesperson have a clear understanding of why a purchase is being made and what results the customer hopes to achieve by buying. A high level of need awareness enables the salesperson to focus on the most appropriate product for the buyer's situation, and helps the buyer to make the best purchase decisions.

Let's say you are ill and pay a visit to your doctor. "What's the trouble?" she asks. "I feel terrible," you reply. "Okay, take this for a week, then come and see me," she says, while hastily writing a prescription on a small pad of paper. Astonished, you accept the piece of paper from your doctor and leave the office. The visit lasted 30 seconds. What is wrong with this picture? The doctor does not know enough about your discomfort. She cannot possibly recommend effective treatment without having more information about your problem. How confident would you be about swallowing the medication prescribed? Not very! This same principle is true in selling.

Sometimes buyers with limited needs awareness think they know what product they should buy. This can prove risky because the product they purchase may not satisfy their needs. For example, a prospect might begin by saying, "I'd like to buy a new car, and I want a Cadillac sedan loaded with accessories." During a brief needs analysis by the salesperson, however, the buyer divulges, "I take my family camping on weekends during the spring, summer, and fall." In this case, buying the Cadillac sedan may be a mistake because a station wagon or sport utility vehicle would better fit the buyer's situation (see Exhibit 3.3).

EXHIBIT 3.3

Product plus: A product is more than a product.

economic need: The buyer's need to purchase the most satisfying product for the money.

Economic Needs: The Best Value for the Money

An **economic need** is the buyer's need to purchase the most satisfying product for the money. Economic needs include price, quality (performance, dependability, durability), convenience of buying, and service. Many salespeople mistakenly assume that people base their buying decisions solely on price. This is not always correct. A higher product price relative to competing goods often can be offset by such factors as service, quality, better performance, friendliness of the salesperson, or convenience of purchase.

Consumer versus Organizational Buying

LO3

Consumer buying refers to the purchasing activities of individuals and households for their personal use, consumption, or to meet the collective needs of the household unit such as a family or individual.[1] When salespeople (representing a business) sell to consumers (i.e., the end user), this is called B2C, or business-to-consumer selling. **B2C selling** examples include a salesperson selling financial services, such as life insurance and retirement plans, to individuals, and home security systems firms selling a system to homeowners. In B2C selling, the salesperson may only interact or discuss the opportunity with one or two individuals before a decision is made.

consumer buying: The purchasing activities of individuals and households for their personal use or consumption or to meet the collective needs of the household unit, such as a family or individual.

B2C selling: Business-to-consumer selling, occurs when salespeople (representing a business) sell to consumers (i.e., the end user).

Organizational buying includes all of the activities of organizational members as they define a buying situation and identify, evaluate, and choose among alternative brands and suppliers.[2] When salespeople, representing a business, sell to other businesses, this is called B2B, or business-to-business selling. **B2B selling** examples include apparel manufacturers such as Under Armour® representatives selling the firm's spring apparel line to a sporting goods distributor, or a healthcare technology company selling its newest MRI scanner to a hospital system.

organizational buying: All of the activities of organizational members as they define a buying situation and identify, evaluate, and choose among alternative brands and suppliers.

Although organizational buying is different from individual buying as shown in Exhibit 3.4,[3] effective salespeople recognize that it is the "human touch" that shapes and maintains relationships between buying and selling organizations.[4] While the B2B salesperson must understand the customer's processes, the customer's business objectives, the customer's culture, and the buying centre's roles and responsibilities, the salesperson also recognizes that buying is an interpersonal process. Regardless of whether the buying situation is your parent purchasing a $10,000 life insurance policy or a chief information officer procuring a multi-million dollar server system, an effective salesperson understands that sales requires interpersonal skills, trust, and adaptability.

B2B selling: Business-to-business selling, occurs when salespeople (representing a business) sell to other businesses.

Buying Characteristics	Consumer Context	Organizational Context
Motive	Purposes of the consumer/household	Purposes of the organization
People	Typically an individual	Group of people (e.g., buying center)
Expertise	Decision-maker(s) not expected to possess expertise	Decision-maker(s) expected to possess expertise
Process	Process often impacted by individual's emotions and formal guidelines not necessarily followed	Rationality often recommended as a goal and decision making process may involve formal rules and guidelines
Complexity	Decision tasks more routine in nature and relatively less complex	Decision tasks often complex and significant
Time	Relatively quick decision making	Time-consuming process

EXHIBIT 3.4
Comparison between consumer and organizational buying contexts.

Applying your Understanding of Needs

Why is it important to understand your customers' needs? By understanding their needs, you begin to recognize how you can help the customers and their firms. For example, a salesperson may visit a manufacturing firm where the firm's operations manager is dissatisfied with the number of items produced every hour by the manufacturing process. The operations manager is unhappy with the firm's current situation (i.e., the quantity of units produced). The operations manager is already aware better options exists. As a salesperson, your goal is to help them reach an improved future situation–the ability to produce more. Therefore, you may discuss a range of options that will help the buyer meet the company's production goals.

In other instances, a buyer may not be aware of a better solution, or may be so busy with responsibilities they have not considered new approaches, processes, or solutions. The customer is not aware of a better future situation. For example, a salesperson may meet with the buyer of the pickles category for a chain of grocery stores. The buyer expresses they are happy with the annual sales growth of pickles in the store (around 3 percent). However, the salesperson knows that other grocery stores are stocking a new type of pickle that has captured the interest of grocery consumers. By distributing this new type of pickle, many retailers have increased the sales of the pickle category by another 2 percent. The salesperson's goal is to help the grocery buyer understand that an opportunity exists to increase the sales of pickles by discussing the opportunity of an improved future situation.

As you can see from our examples, understanding the background of needs and how the needs process works is very important for the salesperson. In some instances, the customer may be aware of their needs and is seeking to improve the future situation. However, in other instances, the salesperson will need to create awareness of the opportunity and teach the customer that a better future situation is available. Exhibit 3.5 provides examples of how salespeople help buyers understand a better situation is available.

EXHIBIT 3.5

Examples of how salespeople help buyers understand a better situation is available.

Salesperson Helps the Buyer Understand the Possibility of a Better Situation

Current Situation		Future Situation
We are doing okay. I think we are comfortable with sales growth of 3%.	Did You Know That You Could...	You mean we could increase sales rates by 6%?
I think our company's manufacturing process is doing okay with our current level of production (100 units per day).		Gee, I never knew that we could increase our production so substantially (300 units per day).
Our margins are decreasing slightly. But I think all of our competitor's margins are dipping as well.	Did You Know That You Could...	Selling more of your product could really result in overall margins increasing two (2) points?
Our pickle customers appear to be happy with our current assortment. Our sales are increasing 3% each year.	Did You Know That You Could...	I never knew that our grocery customers would want sliced pickles for hamburgers. Can we really generate 2% in additional sales by stocking this new type of pickle?

SELLING GLOBALLY

ARE YOU READY FOR YOUR INTERNATIONAL SALES TRIP?

You're leaving Canada—be ready for it.

1. Read about the geography, history, and politics of the country or region you are visiting. (Check out *The World Factbook* website: www.cia.gov/library/publications/the-world-factbook/index.html)
2. Gain an understanding of the ethnic and social makeup of your destination.
3. Become familiar with the country or region's religious and cultural nuances.
4. Familiarize yourself with any recent news and developments.
5. Find local interpreters or guides who can help you get around.
6. Research whether the business ethics of the country are consistent with your own standards. If not, how will you handle it?
7. Become familiar with local currencies.
8. Explore whether typical local cuisine will provide for your dietary needs.
9. Familiarize yourself with local transportation methods, schedules, and costs.
10. Develop an appreciation for cultural diversity.
11. Research, research, research.

How to Determine Important Buying Needs—A Key to Success

LO4

Your initial task when first meeting the customer is to differentiate between important buying needs and needs of lesser or no importance. Exhibit 3.6 illustrates the concept that buyers have both important needs and needs that are not major reasons for buying a product (relatively unimportant buying needs).

Start by determining the buyer's important needs and concentrate on emphasizing product benefits that will satisfy those needs. Benefits that would satisfy the buyer's unimportant needs should be de-emphasized in the sales presentation. Suppose your product has benefits involving service, delivery, time savings, and cost reductions. Is the buyer interested in all four benefits? Maybe not. If you determine that delivery is not important, concentrate on discussing service, time savings, and cost reductions. This selling strategy is important to your success in helping the buyer.

The buyer's needs may be economic or psychological.

Elmer Wheeler, a famous sales speaker, said, "Sell the sizzle, not the steak!" Wheeler is saying that people buy for reasons other than what the product will actually do or its price. They have both practical (rational) and psychological

EXHIBIT 3.6

Match the buyer's needs to the product's benefits and emphasize them in the sales presentation.

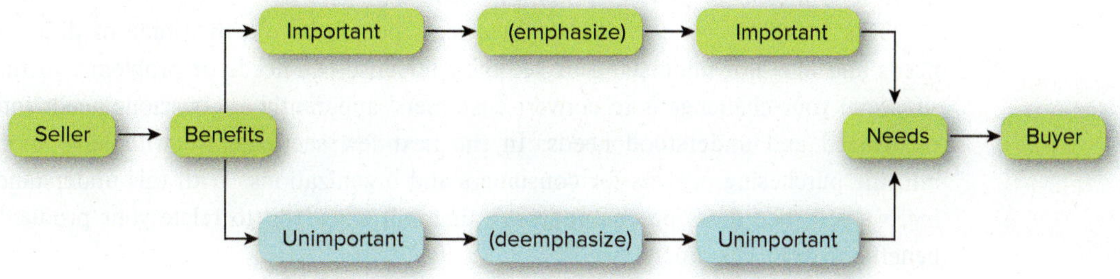

(emotional) reasons for buying. Customers may not buy the product to solve the rational need that the salesperson perceives as important. They may buy to satisfy an emotional need not easily recognized. It is important to understand this sales concept and learn to determine the buyer's important buying needs. Common psychological buying needs include:

- Fear
- Vanity (keeping up with the Jones's)
- Desire for gain
- Security
- Love of family
- Personal pleasure
- Desire to succeed
- Comfort or luxury
- Self-preservation
- Prevention of loss
- Relationships
- Internal image

There are several ways through which a salesperson can uncover important needs of prospects. For example, salespeople can pinpoint the important needs through in-depth conversation with prospects. The success of such endeavours, however, would be highly dependent on salespeople's ability to ask good questions and actively listen to prospects' responses to those questions. It is equally imperative for a salesperson to observe a prospect's surroundings and non-verbal expressions to determine the important need. Apart from talking to prospects, a salesperson should also hold interactions with others who are working with the prospect as well as talk to their own colleagues within the organization who may have information about the prospect's important needs.

Once you determine the major buying need, you are ready to relate the person's needs to your product's benefits. Like the television camera that transmits images to the television receiver, buyers picture desired products in their minds. Before they focus the picture, buyers often need to be turned on and tuned in. Once you find their real reasons for wanting a particular product or identify major problems that they want to solve, you have uncovered the key to helping them.

Determine your customers' needs and then propose a solution to help them.

Uncovering these important buying needs is pushing the button that turns on a machine. You have just pushed the customer's hot button. You have awakened a need, and customers realize that you understand their problems. *Basically, this is what selling is all about—determining the customer's needs and skillfully relating your product's benefits to show how its purchase will fulfill their needs.*

This is not always easy. As we have seen, people have a multitude of different needs and may not understand or see their unconscious needs or problems. In this situation, your challenge is to convert customers' apparently unconscious needs into recognized and understood needs. In the next few sections, we will delve more into the purchasing process for consumers and organizations. With this understanding, we will then describe one approach that will allow you to relate your product's benefits to your customers' needs.

SOCIAL MEDIA INSIGHTS FOR SALESPEOPLE

THE EFFECT SOCIAL MEDIA HAS ON BUYER BEHAVIOUR

In today's world, social connection is a must, especially for businesses. Businesses that do not use social media will have little to no success in growing. According to Chadwick Martin Bailey, a Boston-based marketing research company, 51 percent of Facebook fans and 67 percent of Twitter followers are more likely to buy from specific companies after they start following them. Also, 60 percent of Facebook fans and 79 percent of Twitter followers were found to recommend the company or brand that they are now following. Connecting your company to social media allows consumers to talk to each other and recommend friends and other buyers to your company. This is especially important since consumers trust other consumers more than any other source of information.

Red Bull does a great job when it comes to using Facebook and Twitter to connect with and inform its customers. Red Bull has 36,576,552 Facebook fans, 924,946 Twitter fans, and 1,811,951 YouTube subscribers. Having 36+ million fans on Facebook gives your company the opportunity to market and advertise directly to your audience. Your customers could recommend their friends to your page and share your content to other consumers, resulting in reaching an audience much larger than 36+ million. But in order to be successful at doing this you must be creative and understand your audience.

Red Bull's Facebook page advertises their product, but they also understand that their audience is into extreme sports, so they upload extreme pictures and videos to grab their audience's attention and cause them to spend more time on the page. Having these pictures on their Facebook newsfeed will promote people to share these ads with friends and attract new customers. Red Bull's Facebook page is filled with pictures and videos of every extreme sport they sponsor. They are doing a great job using social media to their advantage.

How Does This Control Buyer Behaviour?

Having interesting and attention grabbing pictures on your Facebook page, posting continuously on Twitter about current trends and topics related to your product, and posting cool, extreme videos on YouTube will get consumers to follow your company religiously and share your pictures, videos, and posts to friends, family, and other fans. This causes a strong consumer/company relationship, which results in loyalty and ultimately profits. Constantly maintaining and updating your company's social content is extremely important in keeping and attracting customers. Social media is currently (and will be for a long time) the centre of attention, and not being involved will have an adverse effect on buyer behaviour. Companies not on social media will be ignored and trusted less than companies using social media.

If you used social media to the extreme that companies like Red Bull, Old Spice, and Coca-Cola do, where could your company be? Using social media isn't an option, if you want your company to experience growth, customer loyalty, and word of mouth then you must join the world of social media!

Source: http://mikedelanegreen.wordpress.com/2013/03/11/the-effect-social-media-has-on-buyer-behavior; Reprinted by permission of the author; Mike Green.

Classifying Buying Situations

LO5

Some people may appear to make up their minds quickly and easily either to buy or not to buy. The speed and ease of deciding which product to buy typically depend on the buying situation. People have more difficulty selecting, organizing, and interpreting information when purchasing an automobile than when buying a litre of milk. Also, their attitudes and beliefs toward the automobile may not be well formed.

Although a few people have the type of personality (and resources) that allow them to quickly purchase an expensive product like an automobile, this is unusual. When purchasing some types of products, most people carefully compare competing brands and talk to salespeople. As information is collected, attitudes and beliefs are formed toward each product. People must decide which product has the most desirable features, advantages, and benefits. When considering several brands, people may seek information on each one. The more information collected, the greater the difficulty they may have in deciding which product to buy.

The purchase decision is viewed as a problem-solving activity falling into one of three classifications shown in Exhibit 3.7. These situations are routine decision making, limited decision making, and extensive decision making.

EXHIBIT 3.7

The three classes of buying situations.

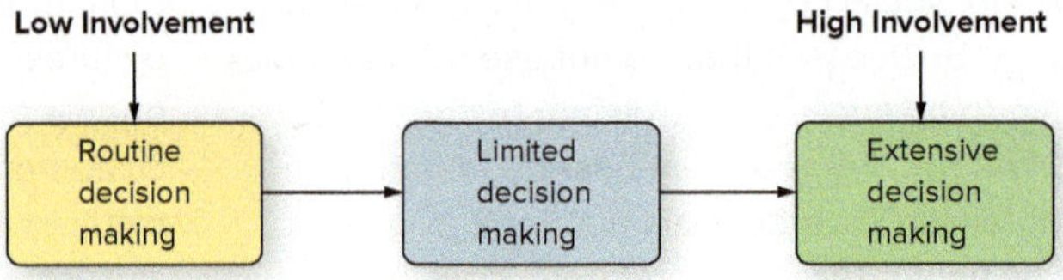

Routine Decisions

Many products are purchased repeatedly. People give little thought or time to the routine purchase; they fully realize the product's benefits. These are called low-involvement goods. Milk, cold drinks, and many grocery items often are purchased through **routine decision making**.

routine decision making: The process of being in the habit of buying a particular product, so attitudes and beliefs toward the product are already formed and are usually positive.

For a customer making a routine purchase decision, reinforce that this is a correct buying decision. It is important to have the product in stock. If you do not have it, the customer may go to another supplier.

For someone not currently using your product, the challenge is to change this person's product loyalty or normal buying habits. The features, advantages, and benefits of your product should be directly compared to the buyer's preferred brand.

Limited Decisions

When buyers are unfamiliar with a particular product brand, they seek more information when making a purchase decision. In this case, there is **limited decision making**–a moderate level of buyer involvement in the decision. The general qualities of goods in the product class are known to the buyer; however, buyers are not familiar with each brand's features, advantages, and benefits. For example, they may perceive that Xerox, 3M, and Canon copiers are the same in performance.

limited decision making: Decision making characteristic of a buyer who invests a moderate level of energy in making the decision to buy because, although the buyer is not familiar with each brand's features, advantages, and benefits, they know about the general quality of the good.

These buyers have more involvement in buying decisions in terms of shopping time, money, and potential dissatisfaction with the purchase than in the routine purchase decision. They seek information to aid them in making the correct decision. Develop a sales presentation to provide buyers with the necessary knowledge to make brand comparisons and to increase their confidence that the purchase of your product is the correct decision. Occasionally, the purchase of some products requires prospective buyers to go one step further and apply extensive decision making.

Extensive Decisions

Buyers seeking to purchase products such as insurance, a home, or an automobile are highly involved in making the buying decision. They may be unfamiliar with a specific brand or type of product, and have difficulty making the purchase decision. This kind of purchase requires more of an investment in time and money than the limited decision. This situation demands **extensive decision making** and problem-solving activities.

extensive decision making: Decision making characteristic of buyers who are unfamiliar with a specific product and who must therefore become highly involved in the decision-making process.

In making extensive decisions, buyers believe that much more is at stake relative to other buying decisions. They may become frustrated during the decision-making process, especially if a large amount of information is available. They may become confused–not knowing what product features they are interested in because of unfamiliarity with the products. Buying an automobile or a life insurance policy, for example, entails potentially confusing purchase decisions.

Determine all possible reasons for the buyer's interest in a product. Then, in a simple, straightforward manner, present only enough information to allow the buyer to make a decision. At this time, product comparisons can be made, if necessary. You also can help the buyer evaluate alternative products.

In summary, your job is to *provide buyers with product knowledge that allows them to develop positive beliefs that your products fulfill their needs.* Determining the type of decision process a buyer is engaged in is critical to you as a salesperson.

Viewing Buyers as Decision-Makers

Earlier in this chapter we explored *why* people buy. Now we will examine *how* they buy. Buyers, whether private consumers or industrial purchasing agents, are constantly exposed to information about various products. What steps do people go through in making a purchase decision?

Typically, buying involves the five basic steps shown in Exhibit 3.8. Buyers recognize a need, collect information provided by the salesperson, evaluate that information, decide to buy, and after the purchase determine whether they are satisfied with the purchase. This sequence reveals that several events occur before and after the purchase, all of which should be considered by the salesperson.

Source: © Dmitriy Shironosov/ Shutterstock.com

During this five-step sequence, the prospective customer makes several decisions leading up to—and after—the decision to buy. The purchase decision step is just one of these decisions—the "I will buy" decision. As discussed earlier, a salesperson uses trial closes to encourage buyers to make the series of minor decisions leading up to the purchase decision step. A close is used to prompt the buyer to make the "I will buy" decision.

As shown in Exhibit 3.8, numerous forces influence a consumer's buying behaviour. Wealthy people or older people, for example, often view purchases differently than lower-income or younger consumers. Psychological factors such as past experience with a salesperson—good or bad—certainly influence buying decisions. In addition, we all have had a friend or family member convince us to buy one product rather than another. Thus, whether we realize it or not, numerous factors influence why someone buys something.

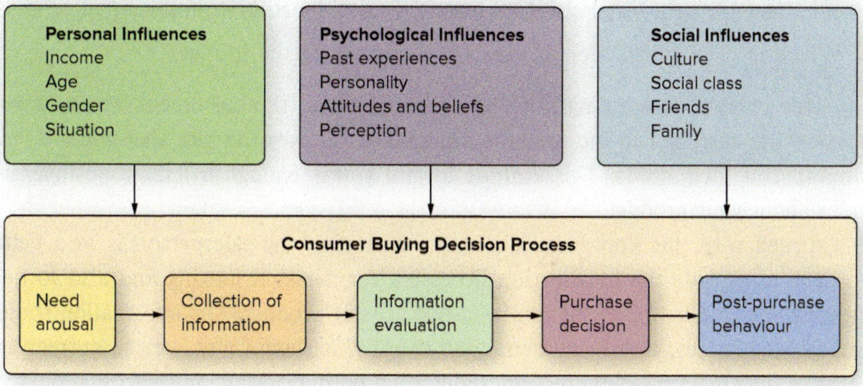

EXHIBIT 3.8

Personal, psychological, and social forces influence consumers' buying behaviour.

Need Arousal

Remember from the first part of this chapter that buyers may experience a need, or the need can be triggered by the salesperson: this is called **need arousal**. It could be

need arousal: A situation in which a salesperson triggers a psychological, social, or economic need in the buyer.

psychological, social, or economic; it could be a need for safety, self-actualization, or ego fulfillment. You must determine a person's needs to know what product information to provide. This information should relate the product's benefits to the person's needs.

Collection of Information

If buyers know which product satisfies a need, they buy quickly. The salesperson may need only to approach them; they already want to buy the product. However, when buyers are faced with limited or extensive problem solving, they may want to **collect information** about the product. They might visit several retail stores and contact several potential suppliers. They may talk with a number of salespeople about a product's price, advantage, size, and warranty. They will likely search the Internet and social media before making a decision.

collect information: The process by which buyers visit retail stores, contact potential suppliers, or talk with salespeople about a product's price, size, advantage, and warranty before making a decision regarding buying.

Information Evaluation

A person's product **information evaluation** determines what will be purchased. After mentally processing all the information about products that will satisfy a need–and this may or may not include your product–a buyer matches this information with needs, attitudes, and beliefs. Only then will a **purchase decision** be made. This evaluation process includes rating preferences on factors such as price, quality, and brand reputation. Attitudes on different products are based on either psychological or rational reasons.

information evaluation: A process that determines what will be purchased as the buyer matches this information with needs, attitudes, and beliefs in making a decision.

purchase decision: A buyer's decision to purchase something.

At this stage, a salesperson can be effective. Providing information that matches product features, advantages, and benefits with a buyer's needs, attitudes, and beliefs increases the chances of a favourable product evaluation. So, the salesperson is responsible for uncovering the person's needs, attitudes, and beliefs early in the discussion to match the product with the person's needs.

One way to get such information is to determine not only needs, beliefs, and attitudes, but also the type of information a person needs before making the purchase decision. Here are some questions you have to answer:

- Which product attributes are important in this decision–price, quality, service?
- Of these attributes, which are most important?
- What are the prospect's attitudes toward your products?
- What are the prospect's attitudes toward your competitor's products?
- Which level of satisfaction is expected from buying the product?

This type of questioning not only tells you about the customer's needs, it also involves the customer in the presentation and will convey the idea that you are truly interested in their needs. This attitude toward you is enough to create positive attitudes about your product.

Armed with this knowledge about the customer, the salesperson is in a better position to provide the information necessary for decision making and also to help the customer evaluate information in favour of your product. The information should be provided simply, clearly, and straightforwardly. It should also seek to correct any negative information or impression about your product. Matching information with a customer's needs may enable you to do the following:

- Alter the person's beliefs about your product (e.g., by convincing the customer that your product is priced higher than the competition's because it is a quality product).
- Alter the person's beliefs about your competitor's products.

- Change the amount of importance a person attaches to a particular product attribute (e.g., by having the customer consider quality and service rather than price alone).
- Show unnoticed attributes of your product.
- Change the search for the ideal product into a more realistic pursuit, such as by substituting a $200,000 home for a $400,000 home, or showing a very tall prospect a mid-size car rather than a compact.

A company has no better promotional device than having its sales force help prospects and customers evaluate products on the market–and not merely its own products. The two-way communication between buyer and seller is exceptionally effective in providing the information needed to make the sale on the one hand, and to evaluate the product on the other. In many respects, salespeople are teachers (professors, if you will) who provide helpful information.

EXHIBIT 3.9

Other people can influence the prospect's decision to purchase. This pharmaceutical rep must service and meet the needs of technicians, physicians, and buyers in hospitals that use his company's products.

Source: © Jon Feingersh/Blend Images LLC RF

Purchase Decision

Is the sale made once the prospect states an intention to buy? No. Do not consider the sale final until the contract is signed or until you have the buyer's money, because there is still a chance for a change of mind. Even after a customer has selected a product, purchase intentions can be changed by these four basic factors:

1. The attitude of significant others, such as a relative, spouse, friend, or boss, or even some negative comments made online within a product review. Consideration should be given to both the intensity of another person's attitude and the level of motivation the buyer has to comply with or to resist this other person's attitude (see Exhibit 3.9).
2. The perceived risk of buying the product–will the seller give a return on the money?
3. Uncontrollable circumstances, such as not being able to finance the purchase of a house or to pass the physical examination for a life insurance policy.
4. The salesperson's actions after the decision has been reached–sometimes it is unwise to continue to talk about a product after this point; something could change the customer's mind.

Post-purchase

The decision process does *not* end with the purchase–not for the buyer at least! A product, once purchased, yields satisfaction and dissatisfaction. **Purchase satisfaction** comes from receiving benefits expected, or greater than expected, from a product.

purchase satisfaction: Gratification based upon a product that supplies expected, or greater than expected, benefits.

The buyer can experience **cognitive dissonance** after the product's purchase. Dissonance causes tension over whether the right decision was made in buying the product. Some people refer to this as *buyer's remorse.* Dissonance increases with the importance of the decision and the difficulty of choosing between products. If dissonance occurs, buyers may get rid of a product by returning it or by selling it to someone else. Alternatively, they may seek assurance from the salesperson or friends that the product is a good one and that they made the correct purchase decision (positively reinforcing their beliefs).

cognitive dissonance: Tension on the part of a buyer regarding whether the right decision was made in purchasing a product.

This salesperson should sell to both people in the discussion. Otherwise, one person could talk the other out of buying the product.

Source: © Arne9001/Dreamstime.com/ GetStock.com

You can help the buyer be satisfied with the product and lower the level of dissonance in several ways. First, if necessary, show the buyer how to use the product properly. Second, be realistic in claims made for the product. Exaggerated claims may create dissatisfaction. Third, continually reinforce buyers' decisions by reminding them how well the product actually performs and fulfills their needs. Remember, in some situations buyers can return the product to the seller after purchase; this cancels your sale and hurts your chances of making future sales to this customer. Fourth, follow up after the sale to determine whether a problem exists. If so, help correct it. This follow-up is a great way to increase the likelihood of repeat business.

In summary, seek to sell a product that satisfies the buyer's needs. In doing so, remember that the sale is made only when the purchase is complete, and that you should continue to reinforce the buyer's attitudes about the product at all times, even after the sale.

LO6 The Organizational Buying Decision Process

Every buying decision aims to satisfy a need or solve a problem. However, the underlying decision process differs when it is made by consumers (i.e., individuals) and firms (i.e., organizations). Earlier in the chapter (see Exhibit 3.4) we discussed the distinctions between the consumer and organizational buying contexts. Salespeople offering products and services to organizations (such as industrial buyers) need to understand how organizations make buying decisions.

Organizational buyers tend to focus on very rational goals, such as reducing expenses or increasing sales, and therefore their decision-making process usually incorporates more formal rules, guidelines, and steps. The **organizational buying process** describes the problem-solving procedure the firm uses to meet its goals and objectives, as it relates to making purchases. When the salesperson sells to organizations, they will probably notice that the buying process involves many individuals, multiple goals, and potentially conflicting decision criteria.[5] Generally, firms use a five-step process when making a buying decision:

organizational buying process: The problem-solving procedure the firm uses to meet its goals and objectives as it relates to making purchases.

1. Define the problem.
2. Establish the decision criteria.
3. Identify alternatives.
4. Evaluate alternatives.
5. Select appropriate solution.

organizational buying situation: The firm's perception of a business problem (also called a need).

An **organizational buying situation** begins when the firm perceives a business problem (also called a need). This is very similar to any type of need. The firm perceives that a gap exists between their actual situation and a desired state (or outcome). In order to resolve the business problem (i.e., the need), the firm begins the activities associated with its buying process. As a salesperson, your goal is to work with organizations to help identify and define their gap (i.e., need) and develop a solution that helps the firm meets its objective.

One of the major ways an organizational buying situation differs from the buying process of an individual consumer lies in the number of people involved in the process. In organizational buying situations, a group of employees is usually involved in the decision-making process (establishing the decision criteria, evaluating alternatives, etc.). This group, often called the **buying centre**, comprises all of the people performing different roles in the buying process (e.g., user, buyer, decider, influencer, gatekeeper) based on their expertise and responsibilities within their firm. For example, a salesperson representing a healthcare technology company and selling a new MRI scanner to a hospital system may have to deal with a group of employees in the buying centre. The buying centre may comprise the doctor that reviews the MRI results (the user), the director of the supply chain (the decider), the chief financial officer (the buyer), the medical technicians that administer the MRI to patients (the influencers), and departmental staff that are responsible for setting meetings and accepting appointments for the doctors and directors (the gatekeepers).

buying centre: A group composed of all the people performing different roles in the buying process (e.g., user, buyer, decider, influencer, gatekeeper) based on their expertise and responsibilities within their firm.

SELLING TIPS

DISCOVERING NEEDS IN ORGANIZATIONAL BUYING

Because the organizational buying process differs from the buying process of individuals, the types of questions that the salesperson uses may also be distinct. While this is not a comprehensive list, we provide a few examples of questions that a salesperson may ask members of a buying centre in order to understand the firm's needs.

- What are the steps in the buying process for your firm (or for this project)?
- Who are the members of the buying team? What are their specific roles and responsibilities?
- What current challenges is your firm experiencing in this area?
- What are the goals for this project (or product or solution)?
- Can you describe for me your timeline for this project (or decision)?
- What budgets or other resources have been identified for this project?
- What have previous partners (or vendors or other companies) accomplished for you that made them valued partners?
- What are your expectations of the company that you chose to work with on this project?

Factors Influencing Organizational Buying Process

When selling to a business customer or an organization, salespeople must recognize that the organizational buying process is impacted by a variety of factors, including individual, social, and organizational factors. For instance, the individual influences describe the people in the buying centre and their personality characteristics, their roles and responsibilities, and their beliefs and attitudes. Salespeople should consider all of these characteristics as they will be interacting with different members of the buying centre and will need to adapt to each individual.

Social influences describe the interpersonal relationships and interactions among and between the members of the buying centre. Sometimes employees within the same firm disagree, possess varying levels of trust between one another, and hold different goals for the buying process. Successful salespeople often study the way the group functions and understand these relational dynamics.

ETHICAL DILEMMA

WHAT WOULD YOU DO?

Selling new cars often is difficult, but Linda Martin feels she has a new Cadillac sold. A woman called and said she wants to buy a new Cadillac exactly like the one parked outside of Linda's office. Linda has another one the same colour, but it is fully loaded with the latest high-tech equipment and costs $16,000 more.

The buyer, a 68-year-old widow, listens as Linda describes both cars, emphasizing the higher-priced Cadillac. The buyer seems to become confused over how to work a lot of the technology options. Suddenly the buyer says, "Linda, you seem like a nice person. Which car do you think I should buy?"

What would be the most ethical action to take?

1. Tell the customer to buy the more expensive model. She probably has enough money and you will get more commission.
2. Advise the customer that you think she would be happier with the less expensive model—she does not seem to need or want all of the high-tech gadgets in the more expensive car. Offer to call other dealers in town to see if they have one in stock. You might lose the commission, but at least you have a satisfied customer.
3. Advise the customer that both are equally good options and let her make the decision herself. But do tell her that you only have the more expensive model in stock and that the other car would take six to eight weeks to deliver.

Finally, the organizational buying process is affected by the organization's climate, its goals, and its working environment. Thus, understanding elements, such as the firm's culture and its expectations of its employees as well as the firm's financial objectives is important to understanding the firm's buying process.

LO7 Social Style Theory

Successful sales professionals should have a firm grasp of the negotiating process and a good understanding of people. Accomplished sales professionals know not only their own personal negotiating style but also their buyer's preferred style–and they use this knowledge to build a stronger relationship that will help them accomplish their goals (see Exhibit 3.10).

EXHIBIT 3.10
What's YOUR Social Style?

ASSERTIVENESS I SEE MYSELF AS: (CIRCLE THE APPROPRIATE RATING.)		RESPONSIVENESS I SEE MYSELF AS: (CIRCLE THE APPROPRIATE RATING.)	
Quiet	Talkative	Closed	Open
1 2 3	4	1 2 3	4
Slow to Decide	Quick to Decide	Deliberate	Impulsive
1 2 3	4	1 2 3	4
Going Along	Taking Charge	Using Facts	Using Opinions
1 2 3	4	1 2 3	4
Supportive	Challenging	Formal	Informal
1 2 3	4	1 2 3	4
Compliant	Dominant	Unemotional	Emotional
1 2 3	4	1 2 3	4

ASSERTIVENESS I SEE MYSELF AS: (CIRCLE THE APPROPRIATE RATING.)		RESPONSIVENESS I SEE MYSELF AS: (CIRCLE THE APPROPRIATE RATING.)	
Deliberate	Quick to Decide	Hard to Know	Easy to Know
1 2 3 4		1 2 3 4	
Asking Questions	Making Statements	Cool	Warm
1 2 3 4		1 2 3 4	
Cooperative	Competitive	Calm	Excitable
1 2 3 4		1 2 3 4	
Risk Averse	Taking Risks	Straight-faced	Animated
1 2 3 4		1 2 3 4	
Slow, Studied	Fast-paced	Task oriented	People oriented
1 2 3 4		1 2 3 4	
Cautious	Carefree	Cautious	Carefree
1 2 3 4		1 2 3 4	
Indulgent	Firm	Nonresponsive	Responsive
1 2 3 4		1 2 3 4	
Non-Assertive	Assertive	Serious	Humorous
1 2 3 4		1 2 3 4	
Mellow	Matter-of-Fact	Methodical	Impulsive
1 2 3 4		1 2 3 4	
Reserved	Outgoing	Intense	Light-hearted
1 2 3 4		1 2 3 4	
Add up your assertiveness ratings then divide by 15. Your assertiveness rating is __________		Add up your responsiveness ratings then divide by 15. Your responsiveness rating is __________	
Plot your assertiveness rating on the graph that accompanies the section called "Amiables" below.		Plot your responsiveness rating on the graph that accompanies the section called "Amiables" below.	

Many sales professionals don't pay enough attention to the effects of behavioural styles on a negotiation. Many use the same approach in every negotiation and are surprised when they do not get consistently good results. But everyone is different and every negotiation is different. Salespeople who understand these differences and vary their approach to negotiations have a higher likelihood of successfully negotiating. Successful sales professionals tailor their approach to the behavioural style and needs of their buyers–it's a matter of empathy.

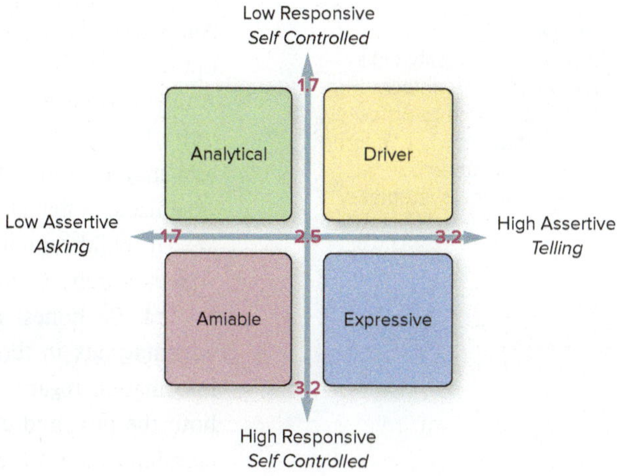

Being able to identify a buyer's preferred style and adapt your own style accordingly can be incredibly helpful in building long-term relationships. With this in mind, let's examine the characteristics that will help you identify your buyer's preferred style as shown in the figure below, and consider some tips to building relationships that lead to win-win outcomes.

Amiables

Amiables:
A buyer personality type focused more on relationships and less on facts; amiables have a strong need to feel recognized and valued and they tend to be trusting, friendly, and optimistic negotiators.

Amiables are one of the easiest buyers to get an appointment with, yet one of the most difficult buyers to close. Buyers who use the Amiable style have a strong need to feel recognized and valued in the negotiating partnership. They place a great emphasis on relationships; therefore, they tend to focus more on feelings and less on facts. They will often begin a negotiation with social conversation that is unrelated to the negotiation. They are trusting, friendly, optimistic, and generally committed to outcomes that benefit both parties.

To build rapport with your Amiable buyer, show genuine respect and care for the prospect and their problems. Be sincere, and don't discount personal feelings. Remain positive and solution-oriented. Do not argue or engage in any "head to head" confrontation, which will most likely cause the Amiable to shy away and end the negotiation. Negotiate in a manner that builds trust, and understand that for your Amiable buyer negotiation is more than just business–it is personal. Never say to an Amiable, "Don't take it personally." Use testimonials, stories, and analogies. If you can help your prospect solve a problem they have with others, you will have a higher likelihood of success.

Drivers

Drivers:
A buyer personality type focused on results and the bottom line; Drivers have a strong concern for positive outcomes and are quick to decide, even with minimal detail; winning is important for Drivers, who tend to be impatient, self-confident, and assertive.

Drivers and Amiables are often noted to be at opposite ends of the behavioural style continuum. While Amiables are focused on the relationship, **Drivers** are results-oriented and focused primarily on the bottom line. Drivers have a strong concern for positive outcomes and can be ruthless. They tend to be impatient, have little need for detailed information, and want to close the negotiation quickly. Drivers are self-confident, are assertive, and can be aggressive. While both the Amiable and the Driver have a need to achieve a positive outcome, for the Driver, winning is all-important.

Be prepared with a Driver. Know your bottom line. Keep your interactions focused on business. This will help you remain confident, focused, and concise. Remember: "You can tell a Driver, but you can't tell them much, so don't try." Instead, ask questions that allow Drivers to discover solutions and suggest acceptable alternatives. Understand that when negotiating with a Driver, however ruthless your counterpart becomes, from the Driver's perspective it's not personal; it's just business.

Analyticals

Analyticals:
A buyer personality type focused on the details; analyticals tend to process information slowly and to be methodical, unemotional, organized and systematic.

Analyticals appear cautious and reserved. True Analyticals methodically explore all options, leaving no stone unturned in their quest for a fair and economical outcome. Analyticals have a strong need for facts, figures, and details, and won't move forward until they carefully analyze all available data. They tend to process information slowly and may be somewhat withdrawn or unemotional during the negotiation. They are organized, systematic, and approach the negotiation pragmatically, one step at a time.

To build rapport and gain respect from the Analytical, be prepared. Ensure that your research is complete and accurate. Keep your discussions factual and business related. Be honest and ethical, and demonstrate ways in which outcomes will be advantageous in terms of money, time, or resources conserved. When you present information regarding your product or service to an analytical buyer, always present both the pros and cons. Finally, be patient and respect the Analytical's need to process information methodically.

Expressives

Expressives care most about perceptions. Status and approval are important to them. How they perceive things and how other people perceive them take precedence. They are mostly impulsive, colourful, egocentric, undisciplined, and spontaneous.

Actors, teachers, musicians, artists, art lovers, graphic designers, directors, and comedians often fall into the Expressive category. As an example, these people are often the ones who buy mostly for the sake of prestige of ownership, or to boost their standing in their organization or peer group. They may intentionally flaunt their purchases so that people will notice them.

Ultimately, your presentation or negotiation should show the prospect exactly how your product will make them look good.

Expressives: A buyer personality type focused on perceptions, status, and gaining approval; Expressives tend to be impulsive, colourful, and egocentric, with spontaneous perconalltles, and they often buy for the sake of status or prestige.

How Do You Know?

Now that you have a general understanding of the different styles buyers use when negotiating, you may be wondering how to identify *your* buyer's specific style. There are four main ways: (1) research, (2) general observation, (3) listening, and (4) asking questions.

Use Your Head!

To learn about your buyer's personality before even meeting, do some research. Speak with other people who may know this prospect; read company literature. It is not always possible, but do your best to be prepared before you meet them for the first time.

Use Your Eyes!

You will get clues about your buyer's style through general observation. When you walk into your buyer's office, look around. The types of things that are displayed on the walls or desk can provide insight into what your buyer feels is important. Are family pictures or company photos displayed, indicating that relationships are important? If so, you may be negotiating with an Amiable. Are the walls covered with plaques and certificates noting achievements and displaying a pride in accomplishment? This may indicate that your buyer is a Driver. Is the office neat and organized, or are stacks of files and papers lying around? The neater and more organized the office is, the greater the likelihood that you are negotiating with an Analytical. Does the office have fine artwork and does the buyer wear stylish brand name clothes? This may indicate an Expressive. It is important to note that you cannot determine your buyer's style by observation alone, but you can certainly gain some initial insights.

Use Your Ears!

Another important tool to help identify your buyer's style is listening. For example, consider an executive who visits a custom tailor for a consultation for some wardrobe additions.

If they are an Analytical, during the meeting they will be preoccupied mostly with the details of the manufacturing process. Knowing precisely what type of material is used, how strong the stitching is, and whether the clothes are hand sewn or machine manufactured will all be of enormous interest. On the other hand, a Driver will want to know how long the clothes will take, and how much they will cost.

The Amiable is mostly concerned with any disruption to their routine that might occur, their happiness with the new look, and their ability to please family, friends, or boss with an improved appearance. Finally, the Expressive will be mostly interested with how good their new clothes will look, how the clothes change their appearance, and how attractive the clothes will make them to other people. They can't wait to wear them.

Use Your Mouth!

A third way to determine your buyer's behavioural style is by asking questions and listening carefully to the responses. For example, to determine if your buyer is a Driver or an Analytical, you could ask, "We have a 50-page document that supports our position. Would you like me to review the complete document with you, or would you like to see the two-page summary?" An Analytical will almost always want to review the entire document, while a Driver will usually want to see the two-page summary.

Other good questions to help you determine your buyer's style might be, "How are you doing today?" or "How was your weekend?" In response, Amiables will typically give some personal information. In fact, Amiables will often provide far more information than Drivers or Analyticals want to know! Drivers may respond with, "Fine," and quickly switch the topic to the business at hand.

Applying Your Knowledge of Behavioural Science

The ability to identify, understand, and respect your buyers' negotiating styles—and adapt your style accordingly—can help you build productive relationships that lead to win-win outcomes. Remembering one of the most important characteristics for salespeople to have—*empathy*—will serve you well in every negotiation.

LO8 Difficult Customers

The personality theories discussed so far have been developed through research and provide some very good insights into the minds of buyers. However, over the years many salespeople have reported several variations of these theories and have developed suggestions for dealing with these people.

Source: © FK PHOTO/CORBIS

Angry People

Angry types may be power strugglers looking for a way to get the edge. They may also be intimidators—people who use anger to throw others off guard. These two types are usually rewarded for their behaviour by people who want to avoid confrontations with them. You probably can't deflate their anger, but you can stop taking it personally. Remember that angry people generally have self-esteem issues that underlie their hostility.

Complainers

Complainers will never be happy with any solution. Try to turn the complaint around by asking, "If this solution won't work, what would?" Before you know it, complainers may be solving their own problems.

Know-It-Alls

These people like it when someone makes them feel important by asking questions that acknowledge their experience and qualifications. You might say, "You've been in this business a long time. Tell me how the business has changed over the years. What's the greatest challenge you face now?" That way, you can get lots of valuable information while making them feel appreciated. You'll also be able to offer an intelligent solution that makes sense to them.

MAKING THE SALE

COMMUNICATING WITH DIFFERENT SOCIAL STYLES

DRIVERS	AMIABLES	ANALYTICALS	EXPRESSIVES
Reduce "idle chatter."	Be personable.	Be prepared!	Be prepared to listen as they like to express.
Discover what "drives them," then tailor your message to that drive.	Use more "idle chatter."	Back up your pitch with facts and figures.	Relationship comes first, then your presentation.
Be conceptual–discuss in terms of the big picture.	Use reference groups–they care what people think.	Don't rush–they need time to analyze.	Show how your product will make them shine.
Keep it brief and to the point. An efficient presentation is good.	Product benefits should relate to benefiting them socially.	Use logical reasoning.	Benefits are critical–what's in it for them?

Silent Types

These shy and reserved customers don't like to open up to strangers. Use some common ground to break the ice. Ask these customers open-ended questions, then be quiet and let them do the talking. You could also say, "If we had to present this to others in your company, what would you suggest we do?" When they're actively involved, they'll open up more.

Indecisive Prospects

When customers are undecided, take a direct approach. Do some research so you can say, "I've been thinking about your concerns and doing some homework. What if we went this way as our next step?" Many times, these customers need someone to hold their hand during the process and make the decision for them. You can also share customer testimonials–when they see that other people have put their trust in you, they will, too.

Greedy Customers

These are people who try to take advantage of your business relationship by demanding that you cut your prices or add more services without increasing price. Try saying something like, "We will, as always, give you a fair price and the service we've promised. But we have a business just like you do and for us to remain in business, we have to stay within this price range. I'm sure you can understand." Stand your ground and remind them how your product or service adds value to their company. If they still don't see the value you offer, perhaps it's time to end the relationship.

What's the best tool for dealing with tough customers? Empathy. Be sure to listen to their concerns without interruption. Don't argue with them or get angry or frustrated. Get as much information as you can to understand each customer as an individual, and then adjust your selling techniques to each situation accordingly. It's the only way to turn tough customers into your best customers.

Satisfied Customers Are Easier to Sell

It is easier to sell to a customer than a stranger–especially a satisfied customer! That's why building a relationship–keeping in touch after the sale–is so

EXHIBIT 3.11

A salesperson works remotely on his tablet computer while between sales calls.

Source: © goodluz/Fotolia.com

important to a salesperson's success (see Exhibit 3.11). Sales representative Sally Fields says:

> It took me five tough years to build up my customer base. Now selling is easy and fun. But the first months were terrible. Calling only on strangers got old, but I hung in there. I was going to succeed—no matter how hard I had to work.
>
> The more strangers I sold to, the more friends (customers) I had. It is easy to sell a friend. So in the mornings I contacted possible new customers and in the afternoons I visited customers to make sure they were happy with their purchases and sell them more office supplies. Today, 80 percent of my monthly sales comes from [repeat] customers. I still make cold calls to keep sharp. By next year my goal is to have 95 percent sales come from [repeat] customers. To do that I must do all I can to make sure customers are happy and find new customers. The relationships I build today will take care of my tomorrow!

Fields owes her success to doing everything she can to ensure that her customers are happy with their purchases and her organization's service. Her yearly income is now more than $100,000. She has built her business through hard work, selling, and service. We'll discuss follow-up and service again later in the book.

Summary of Major Selling Issues

As a salesperson, be knowledgeable about factors that influence your buyer's purchase decision. You can obtain this knowledge, which increases your self-confidence and the buyer's confidence in you, through training and practice.

Psychological factors include the buyer's motives, perceptions, learning, attitudes, beliefs, and personality—all of which influence the individual's needs. To determine these buying needs, you can ask questions, observe prospects, listen to them, and talk to their associates about their needs. Established relationships strongly influence buying decisions, making satisfied customers easier to sell to than new prospects. Salespeople should understand the characteristics of the target market (consumer or organizational) and how these characteristics relate to the buyer's behaviour to better serve and sell to customers.

Individuals go through various steps or stages in the three buying situations (routine decision making, limited decision making, and extensive decision making). Find out who is involved in the buying decision and the main factors that influence the decision, including various psychological and practical buying influences.

Realize that not all prospects will buy your products, at least not all of the time, due to the many factors influencing their buying decisions. You need to uncover buyers' needs, solve buyers' problems, and provide the knowledge that allows them to develop personal attitudes toward the product. These attitudes result in positive beliefs that your products will fulfill their needs. Uncovering prospects' needs is often difficult, since they may be reluctant to tell you their true needs or may not really know what and why they want to buy. People usually buy to satisfy a need, fulfill a desire, and obtain a value.

ETHICAL DILEMMA

DO THE RIGHT THING—CREATING A NEED?

Samantha was leery about door-to-door selling but saw some tremendous income potential when she joined the Good Health Filter Company (GHFC). She thought, "With all the hullabaloo about air pollution and its contribution to ill health, these filters should be a cinch to sell." GHFC manufactured furnace air filters and claimed that they would reduce indoor air pollution by 90 percent. The company chose to distribute its products directly to homeowners so salespeople could deliver a standardized sales presentation.

During her training, Samantha was given a sales kit that included sales literature and an actual filter that was loaded with contaminants that no homeowner would like to see in their home. The demonstration filter had been exposed to conditions that would not be found in most normal homes and was left in place longer than the recommended replacement interval. The idea was that people would see the filter and perceive it as being effective at improving their health. When combined with the "scary" sales literature, it would be tough for people to say no. In reality, the filter was less effective than most of the air filters that could be purchased at any home improvement store.

Samantha couldn't miss. Each time she made a presentation, she emphasized how the home's occupants would enjoy healthier air. At twice the cost of regular air filters, she was making some healthy commissions.

Is she doing anything wrong? Is she creating a need that in reality may not be present? Are "scare tactics" a legitimate selling technique?

AN INDUSTRY PERSPECTIVE

HOW THE INTERNET IS IMPACTING THE BUYING DECISION PROCESS

BY DON MORGAN

As marketers, we know that the Internet has dramatically affected the buying process for many products as online purchasing continues to grow at a dramatic pace. But we should also understand that the Internet and Web 2.0 have also had a major influence on the buying decision process as well.

A recent study by McKinsey concludes that consumers no longer proceed in a linear "purchasing funnel" process when deciding to make a purchase. The funnel analogy has been a basic guideline for marketing thinking and planning for many years—consumers start with a number of potential brands in mind (the wide end of the funnel) and then systematically move through linear stages of familiarity, consideration and purchase by narrowing the choices along the way to get to the one brand they ultimately purchase. It sounds logical, and has been until now.

The explosion of products, media alternatives and access to word-of-mouth experiences through social media and other Web 2.0 access points has created a radically new decision process. Marketers and their agencies must acknowledge this new "consumer decision journey," as McKinsey describes it, and revise the focus of their marketing to be in the right place at the right time to reach consumers when their message is most likely to influence their purchases.

The McKinsey research examined the purchase decisions of almost 20,000 consumers across five industries and three continents, and identified four critical stages of the decision buying process—initial consideration, active evaluation, moment of purchase, and post-purchase experience. Rather than moving in a systematic straight line, the McKinsey study found that today the decision process is more circular than linear and the subsequent stages often produce a broader consideration set than those initially considered.

The first step in the buying decision is the same. The consumer considers an initial set of brands based on brand perceptions and exposure to recent touch points. It should be noted, however, that other research has confirmed that the initial consideration set is typically much larger than it might have been in previous buying decision based on the greater number of products and a decline in brand loyalty from a preferred brand to a preferred set of brands.

It's the second step in the buying decision that has been most affected by the web. Rather than narrowing the choices, the consumer enters an active evaluation phase where the number of choices may be dramatically expanded. Internet access to information from a variety of social media and other word-of-mouth touch points can have a dramatic effect on the brands that were initially considered, and those original choices can be easily replaced with more informed choices based on trusted input and evaluation.

This active evaluation phase shows a profound change in consumer response and requires much more consideration by marketers if they want to be successful. The traditional "push" marketing elements, that most likely affected the initial consideration set, can be easily modified by an empowered consumer who now takes control of the decision process. Today's empowered consumer actively seeks corroboration of previous brand impressions and new input from Internet reviews and other information sites as well as word-of-mouth recommendations from friends and family and other trusted sources. The McKinsey report concludes that traditional marketing remains important, but argues that marketers must move aggressively to learn to also find ways to influence these consumer-driven touch points in order to remain in the consideration set.

Ultimately, the consumer selects a brand to close the purchase, but the McKinsey study shows that even this stage has seen changes. Their study places much greater closure importance on the impact of the in-store (or online store) experience as well as recollections of past experiences. They conclude that many purchases become a last minute decision.

Another important finding from this study is that the post-purchase experience has changed dramatically as well. Many consumers go online to conduct further research after the purchase, a stage never considered in the original funnel model. This post-purchase research can either confirm the wisdom of their decision, or have a significant impact on future purchases by exposing the consumer to new, previously unknown, alternatives.

This new knowledge on the "consumer decision journey" requires that all marketers re-evaluate their marketing programs to ensure that they are influencing and impacting consumers at every stage of the process. It certainly tells us that we must do everything we can to develop touch points during the consumer-driven stage of the decision process. For many marketers, this will require a mind-set shift from a reliance on buying media to more balanced program that supports developing assets such as interactive web sites, social media properties, and rich media applications that provide a way for consumer to learn more about their products and services.

This also presents a new challenge, and a new opportunity, for agencies to help their clients navigate these new alternatives to find the best solution for their brand. As I have said in previous posts, clients are not just looking for an agency to develop an ad or design a web site, they are looking for someone to help them build a bridge between the brand and their customer. Helping them understand how their customer reaches the ultimate purchase decision is an crucial ingredient in finding that bridge.

Built any bridges lately?

Source: blogger.com/profile/07133875908630987282

Don Morgan—Raindance Consulting; Reprinted by permission of Dan Morgan, Raindance Consulting.

MEETING A SALES CHALLENGE

John Salley takes the advice of Joe Gandolfo, who has reportedly sold more life insurance than any other person in the world. Joe's philosophy is that "selling is 98 percent understanding human beings and 2 percent product knowledge." But don't let that statement mislead you. Joe is extremely knowledgeable about insurance, tax shelters, and pension plans. In fact, he spends several hours a day studying recent changes to pensions and taxation. "But," Joe says, "I still maintain that it's not product knowledge but understanding of human beings that makes a salesperson effective."

John has his sales region's training director work with him two days a week for a month. John's sales presentations were analyzed and found to concentrate almost entirely on the technical features and advantages of the products. The training director contacts six of John's customers. Each say they often do not understand him because he is too technical.

John immediately begins emphasizing *benefits* and discussing *features* and *advantages* in nontechnical terms. Slowly, his sales begin to improve. Today, John Salley is a true believer of the phrase, "It's not what you say, but how you say it."

PLAYING THE ROLE

The situation: You are the salesperson for Canadian Paper Supply and you have four appointments scheduled for today. Each prospect represents a relatively large order of your paper products. You expect that you will be dealing with four different types of social styles so you must be prepared for each one.

Role A: The salesperson. Be prepared to recognize and deal properly with each style of buyer.
Role B: An Amiable buyer. Be prepared to present yourself as this type of buyer.
Role C: An Expressive buyer. Be prepared to present yourself as this type of buyer.
Role D: An Analytical buyer. Be prepared to present yourself as this type of buyer.
Role E: A Driver buyer. Be prepared to present yourself as this type of buyer.

Prepare your role for an in-class dramatization of a sales meeting. Note: It would be ideal if the salesperson did not have prior knowledge of the prospect. It is up to each salesperson to recognize which type of personality they are dealing with.

Key Terms for Selling

Amiables
Analyticals
B2B selling
B2C Selling
black box
buying centre
cognitive dissonance
collect information
consumer buying
Drivers
economic need
Expressives
extensive decision making
information evaluation
limited decision making
need arousal
needs
organizational buying
organizational buying process
organizational buying situation
purchase decision
purchase satisfaction
routine decision making
stimulus-response model
wants

Sales Application Questions

1. What three types of buying situations may the buyer be in when contacted by a salesperson? Briefly describe each type.
2. What are the psychological factors that may influence the prospect's buying decision?
3. Although you do not have to be a psychologist or understand exactly how the buyer's mind works, you do need to uncover the buyer's motives.
   a. Why?
   b. What techniques can be used to uncover the buyer's motives?
4. Try to remember a significant purchase that you've made recently. How did you proceed through the decision-making process? What were the major factors that influenced your decision?
5. It is obvious that people in the consumer market are subject to many influences in their decision-making process. Does the same hold true for professional purchasing agents who purchase for their companies?
6. For each of the different types of social styles, highlight two techniques that a salesperson could use to help them "get along."

Sales Online Exercises

What Is Your Personality?

Communication skills help customers do a better job of relating product benefits to customer needs, which increases the salesperson's productivity. An essential part of having good communication skills is to better understand your own personality.

To better understand yourself, first complete the selling Experiential Exercise at the end of this chapter, entitled "What's Your Style–Senser, Intuitor, Thinker, Feeler?" This exercise uses an adaptation of the Myers-Briggs Temperament Indicator. The Keirsey Temperament Sorter URL below has you complete a more comprehensive Myers-Briggs type indicator.

To further your understanding of the real you, go to these sites and complete several of the personality exercises you feel are important for salespeople:

www.humanmetrics.com/cgi-win/JTypes2.asp
www.keirsey.com/sorter/instruments2.aspx?partid=0, the Keirsey Temperament Sorter
www.strategicbusinessinsights.com/vals/
www.yahoo.com, type in *emotional intelligence*

Write a short report summarizing what the personality tests uncovered about you. Do you believe the tests accurately assessed your personality and the real you?

Further Exploring the Sales World

1. Keep a diary of your purchases for two weeks. Select five or more of the products you purchased during that period and write a short report on why you purchased each product and what you believe are the features, advantages, and benefits of each product.
2. Shop for a product costing more than $100. Report on your experience. Find out whether the salesperson is on a commission-pay plan. Do you think it affected the way in which they treated you?

Student Application Learning Exercises (SALES)

At the end of appropriate chapters, beginning with this chapter, you will find Student Application Learning Exercises (SALES). SALES are meant to help you construct the various segments of your sales presentation by building on one another.

Part 1

1. State the product that you plan to sell.
2. Briefly describe the individual or organization to which you will sell.
3. From this chapter, identify and list the factors that are most likely to influence the purchase of your product. Pay particular attention to your buyers' needs.
4. Identify the information that you will have to uncover before you start planning your sales presentation.

Selling Experiential Exercise

You have learned much about selling in this course. Let's find out how much, and at the same time better understand your attitude toward selling. Three of the following 10 statements are false. Which are the false statements? Please first cover the answers.

Is Organizational Selling for You?

1. Dealing with customers is less exciting than the work involved in most other jobs.
2. Selling brings out the best in your personality.
3. Salespeople are made, not born; if you don't plan and work hard, you'll never be exceptional at selling.
4. Attitude is more important in selling positions than in most other jobs.
5. Those good at selling often can improve their income quickly.
6. Learning to sell now will help you to succeed in any job in the future.
7. In your first sales job, what you learn can be more important than what you earn.
8. Selling is less demanding than other jobs.
9. You have less freedom in most selling positions.
10. A smile uses fewer muscles than a frown.[6]

False statements: 1, 8, and 9.

CASE 3–1

TOP-LINE TABLET COMPUTERS

As a salesperson for Top-Line Tablet Computers, you have been asked to research customers' attitudes and beliefs toward your brand of tablets. With this information, you will determine whether your company has the correct product line and suggest selling points for the company's salespeople when discussing computer tablets with customers who come into the retail stores.

You decide to hold an open house on a Sunday in one of your typical stores located in an upper-income neighbourhood, and advertise your special prices. During the open house you ask everyone to be seated, thank them for coming, and ask them to discuss their attitudes toward your company's computer tablets.

Some people believe that tablet style computers should be shopped for without considering brands; once a brand is selected, they go to the stores that carry the particular brand and buy from the store with the best price. Most people collect information on tablets from personal sources (such as friends), commercial sources (such as advertising, salespeople, and product literature), and public sources (such as *Consumer Reports* and *Online Reports*). Sixty percent had narrowed their choice to tablets from Samsung, Sony, and Top-Line, and they seem to look for three things: price, quality, and style.

QUESTIONS

1. Given this information on why people buy computer tablets, what should salespeople be instructed to do when a customer enters their store?
2. If you were a salesperson representing Top-Line Computer Tablets, and calling on purchasing agents from different retail chains, briefly describe what you might do if faced with the following type of buyer personalities:
   a. Driver
   b. Amiable
   c. Expressive
   d. Analytical

CASE 3–2

SUPERIOR OFFICE FURNITURE MANUFACTURERS (SOFM)

Luca Alexander sold a full line of high-end office furniture for SOFM. He called on all types of businesses to show his product line of finely crafted office goods. While he had a tremendous knowledge of his product line, he was having great difficulty relating to some of his prospects. He made four presentations last week that he thought he would close but somehow he left each without securing the sale. This is his account of each case.

Monday: Arrived at Friendly Jim's Glass Repair Company at 8:00 a.m. Friendly Jim himself greeted me at the door with a warm handshake and invited me to join him for breakfast. We sat down and Jim started discussing his wonderful weekend of golfing. Having already eaten breakfast and knowing I had a busy day ahead of me, I asked Jim if we could just get down to business and I started talking about our product. I stayed for an hour and haven't heard anything from him since.

Tuesday: Arrived at Gentleman James Electronics on Tuesday morning; I was about 10 minutes late due to heavy traffic and a little dishevelled due to the poor weather. I asked James if he would like to discuss the product over a coffee in the staff lounge. He didn't seem too sociable and seemed to want to rush the whole meeting, thus I felt a little uncomfortable during my presentation. I did most of the talking and told him how much his staff would appreciate him for purchasing this new high-end office furniture. He didn't buy.

Wednesday: Arrived at Top Notch Solutions, a technical consulting firm that wanted to furnish its new office high-rise. I met with Sally Smith—who was impeccably dressed—in her office, which was kept as tidy as any office I had ever seen. It was a bit overwhelming and I had forgotten some of my presentation materials in my office so I tried to improvise. I couldn't remember exact figures so often had to ballpark some of my estimates to her. I had really hoped to get this contract but haven't heard anything yet.

Thursday: Met with Sam Chang of Acme Importing at a downtown restaurant for breakfast. While waiting for him, I noticed him pull up in his brand new Jaguar convertible and park it right in front of the restaurant. I couldn't help but notice the expensive jewellery he was wearing—in fact, it appeared like he was showing it off. I spoke with him about the high-quality manufacturing process of our office furniture line and, for some reason, he seemed a little uninterested.

QUESTIONS

1. Can you see any possible causes for Luca's failure in these situations?
2. How might you have handled each situation differently?

Source: © Purestock/Superstock

CHAPTER 4

Communication for Successful Selling: How to Build Relationships

Selena Ujj
St. Clair College, Zekelman School of Business and IT, Windsor, Ontario.
Source: Courtesy of Selena Ujj

A Sales Success Story

Selena Ujj graduated from the Business Marketing program at St. Clair College, Zekelman School of Business and IT, in 2018. The program has helped her get to where she is in her career: Security Adviser and Investment Representative for London Life and Quadrus. Even in her early twenties, Selena knew building relationships would be essential to her success.

Selena did not initially consider the financial investment field after graduation, but a recruiter introduced her to it after contacting her on LinkedIn. After hearing about the position and the kind of work she would be doing, Selena was intrigued. She investigated further and spoke to her mother's adviser, a representative of Freedom 55 Financial, a branch of London Life. Her mother's adviser discussed all the pros and cons of the job with Selena. The rest is history, and Selena now works in a field that she loves and that challenges her on a daily basis.

"I have always been an easy-going person, well spoken, friendly to talk to, and good at keeping things conversational," explains Selena. "The directors at Freedom 55 Financial also saw those traits in me and believed my bright personality would be a great asset to their team."

Selena also recognizes how her education played into their decision to hire her. "They viewed my background in business marketing as a major advantage that I could bring to the table. Every day, I can relate what I've learned and am thankful for what I was taught in those classrooms. It has truly helped develop my skills in marketing and presenting. I have gained much confidence in my ability to speak in front of others, which is something I do several times a day." Selena speaks fondly of her selling and social media classes at St. Clair College, and she says she even kept the books and still references them weekly.

"Being able to present myself with confidence and knowledge in what I am communicating are major key factors in being successful and having people not only listen, but respond," Selena explains. The relationships she is building allow her to feel secure that her future in financial investments is bright. "A sale is a sale, but a relationship is what builds on that sale. Providing a great experience and showing potential clients I actually care about helping them achieve their goals rather than just making a sale is everything. You want to provide value and you want to provide a solution to their problem."

She also has been able to incorporate social media into the work that she does. Not only has it allowed her to provide others with information, it has been a great way for her to meet new people and share the type of work she does. Growing her list of contacts and receiving referrals is a crucial part of business. "I was taught in college how to position social media platforms and how to properly make my reach-out to people," she explains. "It has been a useful tool that I have been able to rely on in my daily activities."

"The support I have from my directors and the education I have received are with me every day and at every meeting. This is a field of constant learning and constant challenges, but with my background, I feel extremely prepared and motivated to be successful in this career. Every meeting is different and everyone's needs are different, but my goal remains the same: to help small businesses and families live out the lives they have envisioned for themselves and set them up for a future of success."

MAIN TOPICS

Communication: It Takes Two

Nonverbal Communication: Watch for It

Barriers to Communication

Master Persuasive Communication to Maintain Control

Communication Style

Netiquette for Sales Professionals

Text Messaging for Sales Professionals

Social Media in Sales

Listening: The Key to Unlocking Buyers' Needs

LEARNING OBJECTIVES

The ability to communicate effectively, both verbally and nonverbally, is crucial to sales success. This chapter introduces this important sales skill. After studying this chapter, you should be able to:

LO1 Discuss the salesperson's communication process.

LO2 Define and demonstrate the importance of recognizing and using different types of nonverbal communication when selling.

LO3 Discuss how appearance and handshaking can enhance communication.

LO4 Recognize potential barriers to communication.

LO5 Recognize the importance of empathy and listening to communication.

LO6 Discuss the different types of communication styles that people use.

LO7 Discuss and demonstrate the essentials of professional email netiquette.

LO8 Recognize and demonstrate proper texting etiquette.

LO9 Recognize the popular social media tools available to salespeople.

LO10 Discuss the steps that lead to better listening.

FACING A SALES CHALLENGE

Amos Skaggs, purchasing agent, stands as a salesperson enters his office. "Hi, Mr. Skaggs," the salesperson says, offering his hand. Skaggs returns a limp, one-second handshake and sits down behind his desk. He begins to open his afternoon mail, almost as though no one else were in the room.

The salesperson sits down and begins his canned sales talk by saying, "Mr. Skaggs, I'm here to show you how your company can lower manufacturing costs by 10 percent."

Skaggs lays his mail down on his desk, leans back in his chair, crosses his arms, and says with a growl, "I'm glad to hear that. You know something, young fellow, pretty soon it won't cost us anything to manufacture our products."

"Why is that?" the salesman mumbles, looking at the floor.

"Well, you are the ninth person I've seen today who has offered to save us 10 percent on our costs." Skaggs stands up, leans over the table, and says slowly, "I believe I've heard enough sales pitches for one day."

The initially enthusiastic salesperson now apologetically says, "If this is not a good time for you, sir, I can come back at a later date."

The problem facing this salesperson is common. The buyer has been seeing salespeople all day. Basically, they say the same thing: "Buy from me and I'll save you money."

What message has Skaggs sent to the salesperson? If you were the salesperson, what might you do now?

(Continued at end of chapter.)

While many factors are crucial to sales success, the ability to communicate effectively is critical. This chapter describes several factors influencing communication, along with barriers to effective communication. We will also examine the often ignored—though always critical—topic of nonverbal communication. The balance of this chapter provides techniques to improve sales communication.

Communication: It Takes Two

LO1

communication: The act of transmitting verbal and nonverbal information and understanding between seller and buyer.

Communication, in a sales context, is the act of transmitting verbal and nonverbal information and understanding between seller and buyer. This definition presents communication as an exchange of messages with some type of response expected between seller and buyer.

This sounds simple, right? But have you ever had someone talk to you and afterwards realize you did not hear what they said? "You have eyes but do not see; you have ears but do not hear" is a saying that dates back thousands of years. This wise saying is important to all of us, including salespeople, in our daily living. Salespeople have to understand the many ways people communicate with them. Exhibit 4.1 expands on this point by illustrating the psychological thought processes of both the speaker and the listener.

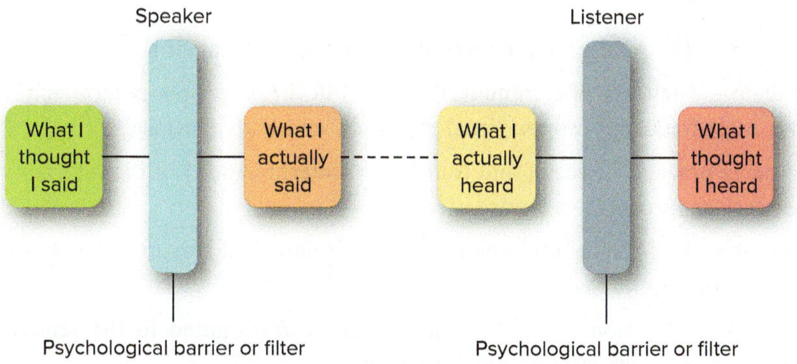

EXHIBIT 4.1

What you say verbally is not always what your listener hears.

Research has found that face-to-face communication is composed of *verbal, vocal,* and *facial* communication messages. One equation presents the total impact of communicated messages as equal to 7 percent verbal, 38 percent tone of voice, and 55 percent nonverbal expressions.[1] If we recognize these findings as a reasonable approximation of the total communicative process, then uninformed salespeople actually ignore a major part of the communication process that occurs during buyer–seller interaction: How the sales message is given can be as important to making the sale as what is said. Thus, nonverbal communications are important in communication between buyer and seller. An awareness of nonverbal communication is a valuable tool in successfully making a sale.

Vocal communication includes such factors as voice quality, pitch, inflection, and pauses. A salesperson's use of vocal factors can aid in sales presentation, too. Along with verbal, vocal, and nonverbal communication, many other elements also are involved in sales communication.

Salesperson–Buyer Communication Process Requires Feedback

Exhibit 4.2 (on the next page) shows a basic communication model of the salesperson-buyer communication process. Communication occurs when a sender transmits a message through some type of medium to a receiver who responds to that message.

The eight major communication elements are defined as follows:

- **Source** - The origin of communication (also called the communicator); in our case, it's the salesperson.
- **Encoding process** - The conversion by the salesperson of ideas and concepts into the language and materials used in the sales presentation.

source: The origin of a communication.

encoding process: Conversion of ideas and concepts into information.

EXHIBIT 4.2

The basic communication model has several elements.

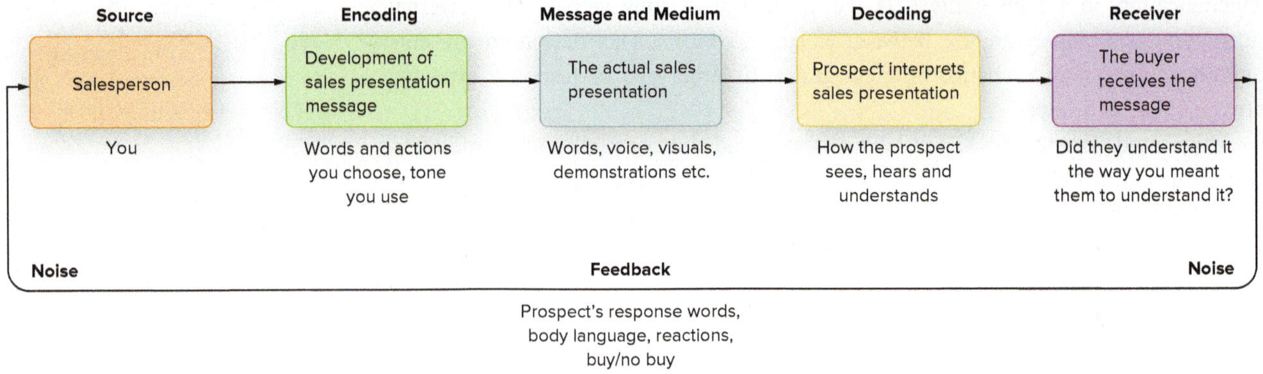

message: Information conveyed in the sales presentation.

medium: The form of communication used in the sales presentation and discussion, most frequently words, visual materials, and body language.

decoding process: Receipt and translation of information by the receiver.

receiver: The person a communication is intended for.

feedback: Verbal or nonverbal reaction to communication as transmitted to the sender.

noise: Factors that distort communication between buyer and seller, including barriers to communication.

- **Message** - The information conveyed in the sales presentation.
- **Medium** - The form of communication used in the sales presentation and discussion; most frequently words, visual materials, and body language.
- **Decoding process** - Receipt and translation (interpretation) of the information by the receiver (prospective buyer).
- **Receiver** - The person the communication is intended for; in our case, it's the prospect or buyer.
- **Feedback** - Reaction to the communication as transmitted to the sender. This reaction may be verbal, nonverbal, or both.
- **Noise** - Factors that distort communication between buyer and seller. Noise includes barriers to communication, which we discuss later.

A salesperson should develop a sales presentation (encoding) so that the buyer has maximum understanding of the message (decoding). Clear verbal discussion, use of visual aids such as pictures or diagrams, and development of models or samples of the product are several ways a salesperson might communicate a sales message.

Studies have shown that people retain 10 percent of what they read, 20 percent of what they see, 30 percent of what they hear, and 50 percent of what they hear and see. If possible, it is important to incorporate into your presentation communication that appeals to all five senses (sight, hearing, smell, feel, taste). This is challenging to do!

One-way communication occurs when the salesperson talks and the buyer only listens. The salesperson needs a response or feedback from the buyer to know whether the buyer understands the message. Once feedback or interaction and understanding between buyer and seller exists, two-way communication has been established.

Two-way communication is essential to make the sale; the buyer must understand your message to make a buying decision. Two-way communication gives the salesperson the ability to present a product's benefits, instantly receive buyer reactions, and answer questions. Buyers usually react both verbally and nonverbally to sales presentations.

LO2 Nonverbal Communication: Watch for It

Recognition and analysis of nonverbal communication in sales transactions is relatively new. However, the presence and use of nonverbal communication has been acknowledged for years. In the early 1900s, Sigmund Freud noted that people cannot keep a secret even if they do not speak; their gestures and actions reveal their hidden feelings.

People communicate nonverbally in several ways. Four major **nonverbal communication** channels are the physical space between buyer and seller, appearance, handshake, and body language.

nonverbal communication: Unspoken communication such as physical space, appearance, handshake, and body movement.

Physical Space

The concept of **territorial space** refers to the area around oneself that a person will not allow another person to enter without consent.

territorial space: The area around oneself that a person will not allow another person to enter without consent.

Salespeople should be careful not to violate territorial space; to do so may set off the customer's defence mechanisms and create a barrier to communications. Most North Americans have four main types of distances to consider: intimate (up to 0.5 metres), personal (0.5–1.5 metres), social (1.5–3.5 metres), and public (greater than 3.5 metres).

Intimate space of up to a half metre, or about an arm's length, is the most sensitive zone, since it is reserved for close friends and loved ones. To enter intimate space in the buyer–seller relationship, for some prospects, could be socially unacceptable—possibly offensive.

intimate space: A spatial zone up to 0.5 metres, about an arm's length from a person's body, that is reserved for close friends and loved ones.

During the presentation, a salesperson should carefully listen and look for signs that the buyer feels uncomfortable, perhaps that the salesperson is too close. A buyer may deduce from such closeness that the salesperson is attempting to dominate or overpower, resulting in buyer resistance. If such uneasiness is detected, the salesperson should move back to reassure the customer.

Personal space is the closest zone a stranger or business acquaintance is normally allowed to enter. Even in this zone, a prospect may be uncomfortable. Barriers, such as a desk, often reduce the threat implied when someone enters this zone.

personal space: An area 0.5 to 1.5 metres from a person; it is the closest zone a stranger or business acquaintance is normally allowed to enter.

SELLING TIPS

SAY WHAT YOU MEAN

There are at least six messages involved in the communication process:

1. What you mean to say
2. What you really say
3. What the other person hears
4. What the other person thinks is heard
5. What the other person says about what you said
6. What you think the other person said about what you said

It gets complicated, doesn't it? Consider two people holding hands while looking at a gorgeous moon together. While sharing the moment, one person is feeling romantic. If we follow the six messages, the incident looks something like this:

1. What the person means to say	"The moon puts me in a romantic mood."
2. What the person really says	"Isn't that a brilliant moon?"
3. What the other person hears	"The moon is bright."
4. What the other person thinks is heard	"Yes, it's bright enough for a walk."
5. What the other person says about what the first person said	"Yes, it's bright enough to hit a golf ball by."
6. What the first person thinks the other person said about what they said	"I don't feel romantic."

We can miss each other's meanings altogether by the time the six messages are completed, without realizing what has happened. Because all of us are constantly in the process of encoding and decoding messages, we need to learn to ask questions, or restate the point for clarification of meaning. Our goal is to say what we mean straightforwardly so listeners do not have to decode—and perhaps misconstrue—our meaning.

EXHIBIT 4.3
Office arrangements and territorial space.

Social space is the area normally used for a sales presentation. Again, the buyer often uses a desk to maintain a distance of 1.5 metres or more between buyer and seller. A salesperson standing while facing a seated prospect may seem too dominating to the buyer. Thus, the salesperson should normally stay seated to convey a relaxed manner. A salesperson should consider beginning a presentation in the middle of the social distance zone (2–2.5 metres).

Public space can be used by a salesperson making a presentation to a group of people. It is similar to the distance between teacher and student in a classroom. People are at ease and thus easy to communicate with at this distance, since they do not feel threatened.

Space Threats

Territoriality causes people to feel that they should defend their space or territory against **space threats**. The salesperson who pulls up a chair too close, takes over all or part of the prospect's desk, leans on or over the desk, or touches the objects on the desk runs the risk of invading a prospect's territory. Be careful not to create defensive barriers.

Space Invasion

The prospect who allows you to enter personal and intimate space is saying, "Come on into my space; let's be friends." In this case you can use space to your advantage.

In most offices, the salesperson sits directly across the desk from the prospect; this defensive barrier allows the prospect to control much of the conversation and remain safe from **space invasion**. Often, seating is prearranged, and some prospects might consider it a space threat if you moved your chair when calling for the first time.

However, if you have a choice between a chair across the desk or beside the desk, take the latter seat, as shown in Exhibit 4.3. Sitting beside the prospect lowers the desk communication barrier. If you are friends with the buyer, move your chair to the side of the desk. This helps create a friendly, cooperative environment between you and the buyer.

social space:
A zone that is 1.5 to 3.5 metres from a person and is the area normally used for sales presentations.

LO3

Communication Through Appearance

Common types of nonverbal communication are signals conveyed by a person's physical appearance and handshake. Once territorial space has been established, general appearance is the next medium of nonverbal communication conveyed to a customer by a salesperson. Appearance not only conveys information such as age, sex, height, weight, and physical characteristics, but also provides clues to personality. Remember the old adage, "You only have one chance to make a good first impression."

public space:
Distances greater than 3.5 metres from a person.

space threats:
Situations in which a person threatens to invade another's spatial territory.

space invasion:
A situation in which one person enters another person's personal or intimate space.

Style Hair Carefully

According to many image and communication consultants, a person's hairstyle is one of the first things people notice. It is often the basis of our image, and can communicate how we think of ourselves and our stage in life. Hairstyles can take many forms, from classic looks to trend-setting new styles. Your style should depend on your personal characteristics and possibly the industry in which you are working. Many experts suggest that Canadian business style is mainly about being neat, appropriate, and non-distracting. Correct hairstyles enhance a person's personality, face, and dress.

Regardless of personal preference, successful salespeople often practise "mirroring," whereby they consciously try to appear similar to their prospects and/or meet their expectations in order to open the lines of communication more easily.

Look the Part—Dress as a Professional

You get only one chance to make a first impression, and your appearance plays a large role. Always look professional (see Exhibit 4.4). Although "business casual" dress is sweeping the business world, people who rely on face-to-face contact with clients must adhere to different rules. Mirroring, as mentioned above, is a good strategy.

The following basic guidelines will help you project professionalism through your appearance. These will not apply to every situation; appearance standards vary between industries, so it is best to rely on a company dress code–or, at the very least, your own common sense. Observing senior people in your own company might be a wise strategy until you learn the industry norm.

General Appearance and Personal Care Tips

- It is always better to be a little overdressed than underdressed.
- Always have neatly combed and styled hair.
- Shoes should always be clean and polished.
- Don't apply cologne or perfume before going to meet a customer. Strong scents can be offensive, and some people can have allergic reactions. Deodorant is fine and is, in fact, encouraged.
- Keep jewellery to a minimum.
- Tattoos are still frowned upon by some, so highly visible ones should be avoided.
- Always wear neatly pressed clothes.

EXHIBIT 4.4

To look sharp, be sharp, and feel sharp, the correct clothes, grooming, attitude, and physical conditioning are required. This applies to your career, to interviewing, and to your life.

Natural fibres, a good fit, and current styles are important.

Source: © Zhudifeng/Dreamstime.com/GetStock.com

Physical conditioning produces the stamina and positive mental attitude necessary to be a success.

Source: © Comstock Images/Jupiterimages RF

First impressions are crucial. Remember that you are representing your organization—and your customer's perception of that organization begins with you.

Source: © Shutterstock/ Stephen Coburn

- Always keep your vehicle clean in case you have to provide transportation.
- Avoid smoking in front of a customer. Avoid carrying the smell of smoke on your clothes or your breath.
- It is best not to drink alcohol during business hours.
- Wear minimal make-up and ensure your nails are trimmed and neat.
- Do not chew gum.
- Brush your teeth and keep your breath fresh–use breath mints or sprays if you're unsure.

Remember, these tips are designed to keep sales presentations professional. You want your prospect to focus on what you're presenting rather than be distracted by you.

Special Tips for Men

- Traditional suit colours are blue, grey, and black; avoid brown, green, and bright colours. Solids or light patterns (pinstripe, tweed, light plaid, herringbone) are best.
- White or light, solid colours or simple prints for shirts are best. Choose a button-down collar if you're not wearing a tie.
- Choose medium-width ties, which according to several fashion publications means from 7.5 to 10 centimetres wide. Knot it tightly, with the length extending to your belt buckle.
- Avoid sweatshirts, T-shirts, tight polo shirts, blue jeans, and athletic shoes.

Special Tips for Women

- Suits are best, either with skirt or pants, as they add credibility.
- Dark suits and solid colours are best. Avoid open-toed shoes and shoes that hinder walking fast.
- Stick with classic styles and avoid trends.
- Long, wool coats are best in winter. Good colours are camel, navy, charcoal, and black.

Even when you are away from work, be conscious of how you look; carry the professional image everywhere you go.

Business Casual

Many business environments today find it acceptable to dress in "business casual," which is a more relaxed and informal look. Business casual clothes should be comfortable but should not compromise professionalism. Examples include an Oxford or polo shirt with button-down collar, or a nice blouse, with a sweater and dress slacks. Blazers and jackets can be worn over blouses and polo shirts. Business casual does not include items like jogging pants, tank tops, jeans, loud prints, or low-cut shirts.

Shoe style should still reflect professionalism. For women, closed toe or closed heel are generally acceptable, while basic walking shoes or leather shoes are appropriate for men. No sport shoes or sandals should be worn.

Make sure accessories do not cause a distraction. For men, neutral watches, one or two rings, and possibly a bracelet could be worn, while women may get by with a little more. Scarves, earrings, and bracelets are appropriate in reasonable styles and quantities.

Even though business casual is a slight "dress down," professional grooming standards should still be maintained.

Choose a suit that means business.

Source: © Monkeybusinessimages/Dreamstime.com/GetStock.com

Communication Through the Handshake

There are three parts to the handshake:

1. How you extend your hand
2. How you apply pressure
3. The length of engagement

Although handshakes have nothing to do with a person's character, sometimes people on the receiving end will base their perception of you on the quality of your handshake (see Exhibit 4.5).

1. **How you extend your hand -** When you extend your hand, you have three choices:
   a. Palm down may be a power play. If you feel strong and are trying to exude confidence then you automatically will offer your hand palm down. This forces the other person to offer palm up, and they may feel subservient. Take time to research the controversial handshakes of U.S. President Donald Trump.[2] He has been known to offer his palm down when shaking hands with world leaders, thereby trying to express U.S. dominance in the world. This is not a great relationship builder.
   b. Palm vertical means "Let's work together". This may be the best way to offer a handshake. It sends the signal of cooperation: "I want to work with you." This technique is excellent to establish a trusting relationship.
   c. Palm up means "I am fully at your service". Salespeople often offer a handshake palm up. This is a subtle way of indicating that you're there to please. While this may appear to be a good technique, the desired outcome should be that you are partners, with neither party dominating the other.

   Extend your hand slowly; suddenly extending your hand may startle your prospect and appear unnatural. It is best to maintain eye contact during the handshake, which will send a message of confidence to the prospect. Also, be sensitive to the fact that your prospect may, in fact, not want to

EXHIBIT 4.5

People on the receiving end may base their entire perception of you on the quality of your handshake.

Source: © Monkeybusinessimages/Dreamstime.com/GetStock.com

shake your hand. Don't take offence, they may have a cold or not want to catch one from you. Don't force the issue if this situation arises.

2. **How you apply pressure -** In the Western world, people sometimes form their opinion of someone based on the strength of their grip. Therefore, it is important for salespeople to ensure that they engage in a handshake properly. Ideally, offer a palm-vertical hand and ensure that your hand is fully engaged with the other person. Letting someone get hold of your fingers may inadvertently send the signal that you are weak and lack confidence. With full engagement, it is difficult for either party to fully "control" the handshake. Aim for making contact between the base of your prospect's thumb and the base of yours.

   Remember that the handshake is often a cultural issue. In other parts of the world, to apply pressure is regarded as impolite. If a North American woman with a good firm hand grip goes to the Far East, she should be warned that taking a man's hand and giving it a firm press signals to him that the woman has a sexual interest.

3. **The length of engagement -** This aspect of handshaking also has many implications. If you ask people how long a good handshake should last, they often say three or four seconds. Try it—this is a long handshake and could send unwanted signals. In Canada, a professional handshake should be two to three shakes. If it's any longer, you may appear to be making a power play; if it's any shorter, you may appear uninterested. To return to U.S. President Donald Trump, when he met Prime Minister Shinzo Abe, it was noted that their handshake lasted 19 seconds, whereas a November 2016 handshake between Trump and his predecessor, President Barack Obama, lasted less than two seconds and included little eye contact. Consider this guideline: Shake for as long as it takes to determine the colour of your prospect's eyes. This will both limit your engagement and ensure eye contact. Note, though, that in some cultures—those of South America, for example—a short engagement is regarded as rude. You should pump about a dozen times, and hold for much longer!

Other Tips

- Watch for sweaty palms, which occur due to nervousness or stress. Often, an individual's stress level is measured by the temperature of the fingertips: the more stressed they are, the colder the fingertips (the body reacts with sweating palms). Learn from this—when you shake hands with a customer whose hand feels warm to the touch, the individual is probably more relaxed than you are. Conversely, if the hand feels cold and clammy, the individual is probably more stressed and nervous than you. If you have habitually sweaty palms, try to relax so you can enter the handshake stage with confidence. Failing this, use a handkerchief or wash your hands in warm water as you're waiting for the meeting.
- Make eye contact. When shaking hands, you are attempting to establish a warm and caring relationship with your prospect. Making eye contact will prove your sincerity and get the relationship off to a good start.

See Exhibit 4.6 for some cultural nuances regarding the handshake.

Body Language

From birth, people learn to communicate their needs, likes, and dislikes through nonverbal means. The salesperson can learn much from a prospect's raised eyebrow,

1. International protocol dictates that you shake hands with everyone in a room—omissions are noticed and are considered a rejection.
2. Women should initiate handshakes and shake hands with other women and men. Not extending her hand to a European male will cause a North American businesswoman to lose credibility.
3. Western and Eastern Europeans re-shake hands whenever they're apart for even a short period of time (e.g., lunch).
4. French and Japanese businesspeople shake hands with one firm gesture. In Japan, the handshake may be combined with a slight bow, which should be returned.
5. In Arab countries, handshakes are a bit limp and last longer than typical North American handshakes. Latin Americans also tend to use a lighter, lingering handshake. In all cases, don't pull your hand away too soon; such a gesture will be interpreted as a rejection.

EXHIBIT 4.6
Five tips for international handshaking.

smile, touch, scowl, or reluctance to make eye contact during a sales presentation. The prospect can communicate with you without uttering a word. An ability to interpret these signals is an invaluable tool to the successful sales professional. The salesperson's skilful use and control of physical actions, gestures, and overall body position also are helpful.

Acceptance signals indicate that your buyer is favourably inclined toward you and your presentation. These signals give you the green light to proceed. While this may not end in a sale, at the least the prospect is saying, "I am willing to listen." Common acceptance signals include:

acceptance signals: Signs that your buyer is favourably inclined toward you and your presentation.

- **Body angle** - Leaning forward or upright at attention
- **Face** - Smiling, pleasant expression, relaxed, eyes examining visual aids, direct eye contact, positive voice tones
- **Hands** - Relaxed and generally open, perhaps performing business calculations on paper, holding on as you attempt to withdraw a product sample or sales materials, firm handshake
- **Arms** - Relaxed and generally open
- **Legs** - Crossed and pointed toward you or uncrossed

Salespeople frequently rely only on facial expressions as indicators of acceptance. This practice may be misleading since buyers may consciously control their facial expressions. Scan each of the five key body areas to verify your interpretation of facial signals. A buyer who increases eye contact, maintains a relaxed position, and exhibits positive facial expressions gives excellent acceptance signals. (See Exhibit 4.7.)

Acceptance signals indicate that buyers perceive that your product might meet their needs. You have obtained their attention and interest. You are free to continue with your planned sales presentation.

EXHIBIT 4.7
Which elements of nonverbal communication can a salesperson look for with these individuals?
Source: © Arne9001/Dreamstime.com/GetStock.com

caution signals: Signs that a buyer is neutral or skeptical toward what the salesperson says.

Caution signals should alert you that buyers are either neutral to or skeptical about what you say. Caution signals are indicated by the following:

- **Body angle** - Leaning away from you
- **Face** - Puzzled, little or no expression, averted eyes or little eye contact, neutral or questioning voice tone, saying little, and then only asking a few questions
- **Arms** - Crossed, tense
- **Hands** - Moving, fidgeting with something, clasped, weak handshake
- **Legs** - Moving, crossed away from you

It is important to recognize and adjust to caution signals. First, they indicate blocked communication. Buyers' perceptions, attitudes, and beliefs regarding your presentation may cause them to be skeptical, judgmental, or uninterested in your product. They may not recognize that they need your product or that it can benefit them. Even though you may have their attention, they show little interest in or desire for your product.

Second, if caution signals are not handled properly, they may evolve into disagreement signals, which cause a communication breakdown and make a sale difficult. Proper handling of caution signals requires that you to do the following:

- Adjust to the situation by slowing down or departing from your planned presentation.
- Use open-ended questions to encourage your buyers to talk and express their attitudes and beliefs: "Have you ever needed to measure the efficiency of your workers?" and "What do you think about this benefit?" are examples of open-ended questions.
- Listen carefully to what buyers say, and respond directly.
- Project acceptance signals. Be positive, enthusiastic, and smile. Remember, you are glad to be there to help buyers satisfy their needs. Refrain from projecting caution signals even if a buyer does so. If you project a positive image in this situation, there is greater probability that you will change the situation and make the sale.

disagreement signals: Signs that the prospect does not agree with the presentation or does not think the product is beneficial.

Disagreement signals tell you to stop the planned presentation immediately and quickly adjust to the situation. Disagreements, or red-light signals, indicate that you are dealing with a person who is becoming uninterested in your product. Anger or hostility may develop if you continue the presentation. Your continuation can cause a buyer to feel an unacceptable level of sales pressure resulting in a complete communication breakdown. Disagreement signals may be indicated by:

- **Body angle** - Retracted shoulders, leaning away from you, moving the entire body back from you, or wanting to move away
- **Face** - Tense, showing anger, wrinkled face and brow, little eye contact, negative voice tones, or suddenly silent
- **Arms** - Tense, crossed over chest
- **Hands** - Motions of rejection or disapproval, tense and clenched, weak handshake
- **Legs** - Crossed and away from you

Handle disagreement signals by trying the following four techniques. First, stop your planned presentation. There is no use in continuing until you have changed disagreement signals into caution or acceptance signals. Second, temporarily reduce or eliminate any pressure on the person to buy or to participate in the conversation. Let the buyer relax as you slowly move back to your presentation. Third, let your buyer know you are aware that something upsetting has occurred. Show that you are there to help, not to sell at any cost. Finally, use direct questions to determine a buyer's attitudes and beliefs, such as, "What do you think of . . . ?" or "Have I said something you do not agree with?"

Remember to pay attention to nonverbal communication:

- Recognize nonverbal signals.
- Be able to interpret them correctly.
- Be prepared to alter a selling strategy by slowing, changing, or stopping a planned presentation.
- Respond nonverbally and verbally to a buyer's nonverbal signals.

See Exhibit 4.8 to test your skill at assessing nonverbal signals.

EXHIBIT 4.8

What nonverbal signals are these buyers giving you?

When you mention your price, this purchasing agent tilts his head back, raises his hands, and assumes a rigid body posture. What nonverbal signals is he communicating, and how would you move on with the sale?

Source: © Digital Vision RF

As you explain your sales features, this buyer looks away. What nonverbal signals is he communicating, and how would you move on with the sale?

Source: © wavebreakmedia ltd/ Shutterstock.com

As you explain the quality of your product, this company president opens his arms and leans toward you. What nonverbal signals is he communicating, and how would you move on with the sale?

Source: © racorn/123 RF

Answers

1. **Your buyer is sending negative, defensive signals. That means you are facing nearly insurmountable barriers. You've got to stop what you are doing, express understanding, and redirect your approach.**
2. **This buyer is sending cautionary signals that warn you to make adjustments to your presentation. Your own words and gestures must be aimed at relaxing the buyer or the prospect may soon communicate negative signals.**
3. **This buyer is sending positive, accepting signals that say everything is "go." With no obstacles to your selling strategy, simply move to the close.**

Barriers to Communication

LO4

Salespeople often lose sales by failing to recognize communication barriers between buyer and seller. Communication breaks down in the sales situation for eight main reasons.

1. **Differences in perception** - If the buyer and seller do not share a common understanding of information contained in the presentation, communication breaks down. The closer a buyer's and seller's perceptions, attitudes, and beliefs, the stronger communication will be between them. Cultural differences are easily misperceived by buyers and sellers. See, for example, the Selling Globally box, "Cross-Cultural Communication" later in this chapter.
2. **Buyer does not recognize a need for product** -Communication barriers exist if the salesperson is unable to convince the buyer of a need or that the salesperson represents the best supplier to buy from.

3. **Selling pressure** - There is a fine line between what is acceptable sales pressure or enthusiasm and what the buyer perceives as a high-pressure sales technique. A pushy, arrogant selling style can quickly cause the prospect to erect a communication barrier.
4. **Information overload** - You may present the buyer with an excess of information. This overload may cause confusion or perhaps offend, and the buyer will stop listening. The engineer making a presentation to a buyer who is not an engineer may concentrate on the technical aspects of a product, but the buyer may want only a small amount of information.
5. **Disorganized sales presentation** - Sales presentations that seem unorganized to the buyer tend to cause frustration or anger. Buyers commonly expect you to understand their needs or problems, and to customize your sales presentation to their individual situation. If you fail to do this, communication can fall apart.
6. **Distractions** - When a buyer receives a telephone call or someone walks into the office, these are distractions. A buyer's thoughts may become sidetracked, and it may be difficult to regain attention and interest.
7. **Poor listening** - At times, the buyer may not listen to you. This result often occurs if you do all or most of the talking, not allowing the buyer to participate in the conversation.
8. **Not adapting to buyer's style** - Salespeople who prefer talking to showing should keep in mind that clients may instead prefer to see the product. It is critical for salespeople to use different communication styles for different clients, as discussed in Chapter 3. Most successful salespeople have learned to match their customers' communication styles.

SELLING TIPS

THE POWER LUNCH: 11 TIPS

1. Choose the right place. It's best not to choose a fast-paced, busy eating establishment. There will be too many distractions.
2. Choose the best seat. Ask for a table that is away from traffic and distractions so that you can communicate more clearly.
3. Make reservations and inform your client that reservations have been made under your name.
4. Arrive before your prospect to ensure everything is in order, and then turn OFF your cell phone.
5. Stand (women included) to greet your prospect with a handshake when they arrive.
6. Do not talk business until after you've ordered. Engage in small talk until then.
7. Let your guest order first—you may suggest something or ask the waiter for a recommendation.
8. Only if your prospect orders an alcoholic drink, should you. Even then, have only one.
9. Be engaged and engaging. Pay careful attention to your prospect and don't be distracted.
10. Make sure you're familiar with proper dining etiquette.
11. Pick up the tab and remember to leave a tip.

LO5 Master Persuasive Communication to Maintain Control

persuasion: The ability to change a person's belief, position, or course of action.

Salespeople want to be good communicators to persuade people to purchase their products. **Persuasion** means the ability to change a person's belief, position, or course of action.

Chapters 6 to 12, on the selling process, go into greater detail on specific persuasion techniques. For now, let's review several factors that help to develop persuasive communication skills.

Communication: Improve Your Encoding and Decoding

To become a better communicator, consider two major elements of communication. First, always strive to improve the message and its delivery in the sales presentation. You need to be a capable encoder. Second, improve your ability to determine what the buyer is communicating to you. To do so, you need to be a good listener or decoder. A good sales communicator knows how to effectively encode and decode during a presentation.

Encoding: The Sender's Professional Communication

As you learned earlier, the communication process includes the sender encoding the message properly. Encoding describes the salesperson converting ideas into language. In the following section, we introduce a few best practices to ensure your sales communication is encoded effectively.

1. **Reduce vocalized pauses.** Vocalized pauses are the words and phrases that speakers inject between words when they speak.[3] You may have heard speakers place words such as "umm," "uhh," "like," "awesome," "great," or "and" throughout a conversation. In some instances, vocalized pauses may be so rampant in a conversation that the listener's attention focuses on the number of vocalized pauses rather than the content of the message. To enable effective, professional communication, a salesperson should aim to reduce the use of vocalized pauses. How can you do this? Consider watching a video of your sales role play. Many students become more aware of their vocalized pauses when they watch their video role play. You may also want to join professional development organizations, such as Toastmasters International, to hone your communication skills.
2. **Use positive, specific, professional language.** Using professional language is important for building your credibility and communication effectiveness. By using *specific language,* you create the opportunity for greater understanding by your buyer. By using *positive language,* you potentially create greater levels of enthusiasm and interest within the buyer; and by using *professional language,* you help create a perception of credibility and expertise. Exhibit 4.9 (on the next page) provides a few common areas that entry-level salespeople often confront in enhancing their positive, specific, professional language. Please note that we use a little hyperbole in the exhibit to demonstrate our point.
3. **Use transitions to maintain conversational flow.** Sales conversations should have a natural flow. Transitions help relate or link two ideas or sections of the conversation in a natural way. One easy method to create transitions within a sales conversation is by replaying the buyer's needs. You will learn that during the approach section, the buyer will communicate their needs. In order to transition between the sections in your sales presentation, you could reiterate a need. By reiterating the need, you foreshadow the value of the upcoming information. For instance, a transition between the product section and the marketing plan section might start with, "And Mr. Jones, you mentioned that all new products introduced into your store require incremental promotional support *[replaying the need].* I'm happy to report that our multitiered marketing plan provides over $3 million in consumer promotions. . . ."

EXHIBIT 4.9

The use of professional language is an important element of your professional credibility.

INSTEAD OF STATING	CONSIDER USING THE WORD(S)
Cost	Expenses or investment or value
Loss	Opportunity cost
What were you thinking?	Share with me your decision process?
Why would you do that?	Can you explain to me what led to those actions?
Worries or problems?	Concerns?
What should we do now.	How would you like to proceed? What might the next steps be?
We are absolutely the cheapest.	We are pleased to offer you an investment that requires a minimal financial commitment.
I have two ways we could go.	May I submit two potential solutions for you to consider?
I'd like to throw a couple of ideas your way.	May I suggest three ideas for you to consider?
I will need you to okay this.	Would you be comfortable reviewing and approving this?
Are you ready to do the deal?	Could we please move forward with the purchase agreement?
Yep or You Bet	Yes. Absolutely. We can move forward.

proof statements: Statements that substantiate claims made by the salesperson; also called *evidence statements.*

enthusiasm: A state of mind wherein a person is filled with excitement toward something.

empathy: The ability to identify and understand another person's feelings, ideas, and circumstances.

4. **Use proof statements to create credibility in your communication.** Salespeople have known for years that using highly credible sources can improve the effectiveness of the sales presentation message. **Proof statements** substantiate the salesperson's claims. For example, pharmaceutical companies often quote research studies performed by outstanding physicians at prestigious medical schools to validate claims of product benefits. These proof statements add credibility to a sales message.
5. **Express enthusiasm through vocal tone and vocal inflection.** Great salespeople use various forms of **enthusiasm** to show their excitement toward helping their customer. Demonstrating a positive, willing attitude can create genuine interest in other people.
6. **Express empathy when appropriate. Empathy** is the ability to identify and understand the other person's feelings, ideas, and situation. As a salesperson, you need to be interested in what the buyer is saying–not just in giving a sales presentation. Many of the barriers to communication mentioned earlier can be overcome when you place yourself in the buyer's shoes. Empathy is saying to a prospect, "I'm here to help you," or "Tell me your problems and needs so I can help *you.*" Empathy is also evidenced by a salesperson's display of sincerity and interest in the buyer's situation. This may mean acknowledging at times that a prospect may not need your product.
7. **Keep the message simple.** Simplicity in communication often demonstrates the speaker's discipline. That is, great speakers invest a great deal of time and effort to distill complex subjects into readily understandable elements. You may hear the acronym KISS. This stands for the old sell philosophy of **K**eep **I**t **S**imple, **S**alesperson. The story is told of an elderly woman who went into a hardware store. The clerk greeted her and offered her some help. She replied that she was

looking for a heater. So the clerk said, "Gee, are you lucky! We have a big sale on these heaters, and a tremendous selection. Let me show you." So after maybe 30 or 45 minutes of discussing duothermic controls, heat induction, and all the factors involved with how a heater operates, including the features and advantages of each of the 12 models, he turned to the woman and said, "Now, do you have any questions?" To which she replied, "Yes, just one, sonny. Which one of these things will keep a little old lady warm?"

> *"Try honestly to see things from the other person's point of view."*
>
> *DALE CARNEGIE*

An overly complex, technical presentation should be avoided when it is unnecessary. Be specific and concise, but use words and materials that the buyer can understand easily. The skilled salesperson can make a prospect feel comfortable with a new product or complex technology through the subtle use of nontechnical information and a respectful attitude.

8. **Use feedback to guide your communication.** Learn how to generate feedback to determine whether your listener has received your intended message. Feedback does not refer to any specific type of listening behaviour by the buyer, but rather to a recognizable response. A shake of the head, a frown, or an effort to say something are all signals to the salesperson. If the salesperson fails to notice or respond to these signals, no feedback can occur, which means faulty or incomplete communication.

Often, feedback must be sought openly because the prospect does not always give it voluntarily. By interjecting into the presentation questions that require the customer to give a particular response, you can stimulate feedback. Questioning, sometimes called *probing,* allows the salesperson to determine the buyer's attitude toward the sales presentation. **Probing** refers to gathering information and uncovering customer needs using one or more questions. For example, a telecommunications company included this type of feedback in their sales training sessions. Their sales trainers suggested to their salespeople that they use questions in their presentations, such as:

probing:
The act of gathering information and uncovering customer needs using one or more questions.

- Would you be willing to share your thoughts on your current investment in your firm's telecommunications equipment?
- On a scale of 1 to 100, how would you rate the level of service your firm is being provided?
- What is your current satisfaction level with the equipment you presently have installed and use?

These questions were intended to draw responses from the customers concerning the relationship with their present supplier. They provided the salespeople with a method of determining how the prospect felt about the current provider. The responses allowed the salesperson to discuss the specific features, advantages, and benefits of the salesperson's products relative to the products the prospect used at that time. Future chapters will fully discuss questioning techniques to use during your presentation.

9. **Generate feedback on your communicated benefits through a trial close.** In planning your presentation, it is important to predetermine when and what feedback-producing questions to ask. The use of a question after discussing a benefit is a great method of obtaining feedback and can help you with your trial close.

SELLING GLOBALLY

CROSS-CULTURAL COMMUNICATION

Earlier in the text, we discussed the necessity of being sensitive to cultural diversity. Consider these guidelines to enhance your cross-cultural communication effectiveness.

1. For those whose native language is not English, use simple, concise, and clear language.
2. Be perfectly clear while avoiding exaggerations.
3. Be careful to avoid slang and figures of speech. They may mean nothing at all to the listener or cause confusion.
4. Avoid sales "puffery" ("This is the best product in the world.") This could be interpreted literally and create problems down the road.
5. Use caution when using humour. It can be useful in building rapport but may inadvertently offend someone.
6. Avoid even minor profanity. What may be acceptable in our culture might be highly offensive in other cultures, so don't use it.
7. Be aware of cultural body language; in some cultures, if you were to give the buyer two thumbs up, he or she might throw you out of the office.
8. Watch the tone of your voice. Although some cultures see a loud, expressive tone as a sign of your excitement and enthusiasm, others may see it as rude and forceful.

Creating Mutual Trust Develops Friendship

Salespeople who develop a mutual, trusting relationship with their customers cannot help being successful. This type of relationship eventually results in high credibility for the salesperson and even friendship. The buyer appreciates being sold products that perform to expectations and were worth their price, and that the salesperson did everything promised. Building mutual trust is important to effective long-run communication.

LO6 Communication Style

Our communication skill determines how successfully we interact with others, whether one-on-one or in a large group. Imagine three people placed in a buying group are listening to your sales presentation:

- The visual person says, "I can't see how your product will meet our needs. Just show me what you see as the outcome."
- The kinesthetic person may respond, "He has touched on all the heavy issues. Why can't you grasp his meaning?"
- The auditory person then says, "It doesn't sound like either of you knows what you're talking about." They've each explained their ideas in their own language and can't understand why the others don't get it.

Salespeople must be sensitive to the learning or sensory systems of their prospects to maximize their communication effectiveness. Visual learners like to see things. Providing a simple graph outlining the performance results of your product versus the competition would be far more useful than simply saying, "Ours is better." Kinesthetic learners prefer to touch and do things. Bringing in a product sample and allowing them to handle it and use it would be a very effective way of proving your product's benefits. Auditory learners like to listen. A simple verbal presentation will communicate your message.

SELLING TIPS

CANADA IS A DIVERSE COUNTRY

Below is some advice from the Indigenous Corporate Training, Inc. website. Check out their site for more tips to consider when doing business with Indigenous Peoples In Canada at www.ictinc.ca

1. **Research.** Learn about their culture and ask about their business goals. There are over 600 Indigenous communities in Canada and each one has its own unique culture. A successful working relationship will be based on a solid foundation of respect.
2. **Practise consistent, open communication.** Have regular, face-to-face meetings with open and respectful communication. Don't just have a meeting when a document has to be signed or when an issue has arisen. Plan to visit the community frequently and even attend and support cultural events. If and when an issue does arise, the conversation is going to go a lot more smoothly if you have an established, respectful relationship.
3. **Practise respectful communication.** Ensure the speaker has finished speaking before jumping in. A silence at the end of a statement does not necessarily indicate the person has finished speaking. Always wait for what might be considered an uncomfortable length of time before speaking.
   - Some issues are emotionally charged. Don't take it personally but listen respectfully
   - Indigenous Peoples are NOT stakeholders—do not refer to them as such.
   - Constant eye contact as practised in European culture is not comfortable for some Indigenous Peoples who avoid direct eye contact.
   - Try to keep it light and expect to be the brunt of jokes. In fact, if you are the brunt, it could be a sign that you are being accepted, so take it as a compliment.
4. **Don't always rely on written documents sent in the mail or electronically.** Indigenous culture is oral. Meet and discuss documents in-depth.
5. **Have realistic expectations.** Details of your business agreement cannot be dealt with in one meeting. Allow for an adequate time frame to work out the details of the agreement. Keep in mind that while economic developments are important to the community, Chief and Council have other pressing community matters that must be attended to and can take precedence over yours. Additionally, they are often inundated with requests for meetings, so keep that in mind while trying to book a meeting. Also realize that meetings can be cancelled at very short notice if a community matter arises.
6. **Don't use top-down approaches.** Indigenous Peoples have endured hundreds of years of top-down approaches via the *Indian Act*. Avoid authoritative attitudes and approaches to issues. Use a consensus building approach.
7. **Promise less, deliver more.** Don't fill the air with empty promises—your word is taken seriously. If you make a promise that you find you can't deliver on, expect to feel some shame. Treat your Indigenous partner with the same respect you would like shown to yourself. Be trustworthy and respectful.
8. **Long-term planning means LONG TERM.** Keep in mind that Indigenous Peoples have a completely different view on the meaning of "long term" than do non-Indigenous. When they make a decision they weigh the impact on seven generations into the future and respect those who are no longer here.
9. **Decision making requires consultation.** Individuals can become uncomfortable if asked to make decisions for the group. Oftentimes, community consultation, collective decision making, and permission to make decisions must occur—this can be time consuming, so again, check your watch at the door and go with the flow.

Source: Adapted from "9 Tips for Doing Business with First Nations," Indigenous Corporate Training Inc., blog. April 27, 2015. Updated February 2018, at http://www.ictinc.ca/blog/9-tips-for-doing-business-with-first-nations. Used with permission of the Indigeneous Corporate Training, Inc.

Communication Style Flexing

Communication style flexing occurs when a salesperson adapts their own communication style to the needs of others. As shown in Exhibit 4.10 (on the next page), when making presentations, it is imperative that you make an effort to determine the communication style of the person or people you are presenting to by observing and

EXHIBIT 4.10

Buyers are reached best through their own preferred learning style.

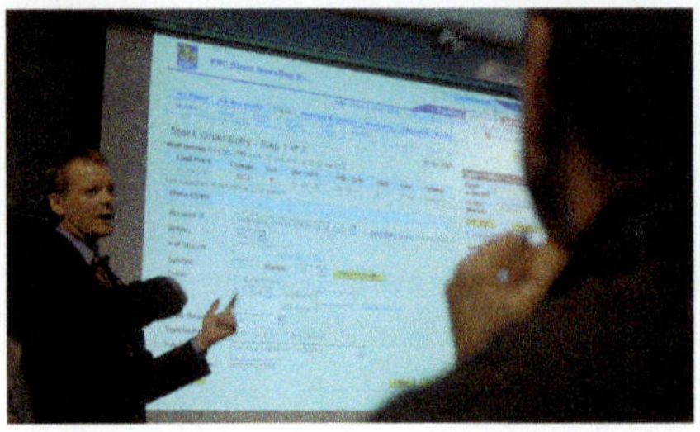

Visual learner

Source: Toronto Star/GetStock.com

Auditory learner

Source: © gstockstudio/123RF

Kinesthetic learner

Source: © Christopher Bissell/Getty Images

listening carefully. Be prepared to communicate using a variety of communication tools. Visuals, demonstrations, prospect involvement, and clear, concise language will ensure that you meet the needs of all buyers in a group.

LO7

Netiquette for Sales Professionals

Because email doesn't allow the reader to interpret body gestures and facial expressions or tone qualities in the voice, it is imperative that email communication be constructed carefully to achieve the desired effect. Services available online can allow you to have an email message checked for unintended negative emotion or tone before you send it to an unsuspecting prospect or customer. For example, Tone Analyzer (www.tone-analyzer-demo.ng.bluemix.net) allows you to enter your email text and then it analyzes your tone. When salespeople communicate by letter, they typically follow certain rules of etiquette, including guidelines for formatting the letter and addressing the recipient. When communicating by email, you need to follow a similar set of rules, often referred to as "netiquette." **Netiquette** can enhance the effectiveness of your email communication—just as not following it can result in very poor customer perception and relationships.

netiquette: Proper rules and manners for communicating over the Internet.

When you compose an email message, you control three elements of that communication:

1. **Subject line** - Describes the content of the message.
2. **Message body** - The text that makes up the main part of the message.
3. **Signature** - The equivalent of a business card that tells the reader who you are, what you do, and where to find you.

The Subject Line

The subject line is scanned by recipients to determine whether they will open, delete, or forward your email. Composing effective subject lines is an imperative skill for salespeople. Your subject line should:

- Accurately convey what the message is about
- Be no more than four to six words
- Not "shout" by using all capital letters
- Not seem too aggressive or obviously sales oriented ("Super offer just for you!")
- Be worded so the message is not perceived as spam
- Be inviting ("Can we meet on Thursday?" or "Some thoughts on improving your productivity")

The Message Body

If you're contacting someone cold, you may want to include some identification early in the message body so that the recipient has an understanding of the context of the message. Your message body should:

- Include a greeting or salutation that is friendly but businesslike
- Convey information effectively and concisely
- Not take too much of the recipient's time or technical resources due to excessive length or file size
- Be sent in plain text, which is most universal (HTML formatting may result in the recipient's not being able to read the message)
- Not include information that would be better communicated using a different medium, such as a phone call or a link to a web page
- Not offend the reader
- Address all the points or answer all the questions in the original message, if it is a reply

The Signature

Your signature line should:

- Be included in every message
- Contain all the information the reader needs about you: your name, title, company name, company URL, mailing address, telephone and fax numbers; you may want to consider using a tag-line that is part of your company's brand, such as, "Service is Job One"
- Be complete and up to date (see Exhibit 4.11)

Salespeople must construct their email communication carefully and manage it effectively. For example:

- Respond promptly to messages to confirm that the email was received.
- Organize your email system so that information can be retrieved quickly.
- Declutter your mailboxes periodically so that important emails don't get lost in your inbox.
- Don't confuse personal with business emails. In fact, it is often better to use your business email address strictly for business so that you don't inadvertently send out jokes or other inappropriate communications to business associates. Remember these rules when emailing your professors as well. Your professional image and reputation start in your academic life and poorly written emails do not reflect the image you will want to convey.

****

Irene Koehler

Almost Savvy

Social Media News, Views, and How-To's

Featured on CNN: How Undersharing Online Can Hurt You

Facebook: facebook.com/AlmostSavvy

LinkedIn: linkedin.com/in/irenekoehler

Twitter: http://twitter.com/irenekoehler

About.me: http://about.me/irenekoehler

Phone: (555) 555-5555

EXHIBIT 4.11

This signature is effective, and shows all kinds of contact information.

Sales Netiquette–A Brief Checklist

1. When sending a first-time email, state where you obtained the recipient's email address.
2. Put something meaningful in the subject line.
3. Ensure your name appears professionally in the "from" box.
4. Do not send unsolicited attachments; wait for permission.
5. Use an email letterhead for highly formal correspondence.
6. Create a professional-looking signature for consistency.
7. Use correct grammar and spelling.
8. Don't be the first to use first names. Use formal salutations (Mrs. Smith or Mr. Jones) until your correspondent does otherwise.
9. Stay formal with international emailing until your correspondent indicates otherwise.
10. Be concise!
11. Don't use smileys or emoticons.
12. Don't send junk or include business clients on your "joke" list.
13. Don't send impersonal mass emails (spam).
14. If replying to a message, include in your reply just the section you're replying to, not the entire original.
15. Remember to use empathy; consider how you would feel if you received the email.

LO8 Text Messaging for Sales Professionals

Imagine receiving this message on your cell phone:

> Hello Jane, DRIB. FYI, AFAIC, I think your company is LOPSOD. IANOL but I think your response to the RFP was way out of whack. Next time KISS. If you want to STD, please respond and tell me WIIFM. I always thought that GMTA; obviously, I was wrong. So . . . let's try to STD and get this done ASAP. MTFBWY.

text messaging: Short message service (SMS) communications sent between cell phones.

Text messaging (texting) is a tremendous sales and communication tool. It allows us to keep in touch with prospects and clients at times when using the telephone may simply not work out. It is sometimes referred to as SMS for short message service, a form of communication that is used trillions of times per year around the world. However, when salespeople use it, they must be careful to distinguish between personal and business text messaging. As many of you know, personal texting takes on a language of its own that is not acceptable in business communications. Use good judgment regarding acronyms and emoticons when texting in business.

Some Simple Texting Guidelines

textiquette: Etiquette for text messaging.

Just as you follow certain rules of etiquette when meeting with someone in person, there are rules of "**textiquette**" that should be followed when texting. For example:

1. **Never text and drive.** It is illegal in many jurisdictions but also just plain dangerous.
2. **Be careful of timing.** Don't send a text message late at night or early in the morning. Also, avoid times when you know for sure that the client may be tied up at a meeting or unavailable.
3. **Communicate succinctly.** Text messages shouldn't be long winded–they are meant for brief conversations, not detailed and important communications.

4. **Be aware of where you are.** It is considered impolite to text while in a movie theatre, at a meeting, during meals, or whenever your attention is needed for the task at hand.
5. **Avoid texting to multiple people simultaneously.** You will waste too much of other people's time by doing this.
6. **Take the time to text properly.** The quality of your text messaging will reflect on your credibility, and on your company's.
7. **Manage your texting time wisely.** It is easy to get caught up in constant texting, so you have to determine if this is the best use of your time.

Social Media in Sales

LO9

According to *Forbes* magazine, 78 percent of sales people using social media as part of their sales strategy outperformed those who weren't using social media.[4]

> *"Why use social media? Marketing is no longer about the stuff that you make, but about the stories you tell."*
>
> *SETH GODIN*

Social media is growing in importance every day in our society and selling on social media is no different. *Forbes* magazine also reports that "more than 40 percent of salespeople say they've closed between two and five deals as a result of social media."[5] These numbers are hard to ignore. Given that salespeople can get a lot done on social media with relatively little investment of time, the ROI is very attractive.

Using Social Media to Communicate

Everybody seems to be using social media these days, which is precisely why salespeople should consider using it as part of their sales strategy. Salespeople can use social media to search for new customers, research prospects, network, communicate, and provide customer service. Salespeople are limited only by their own creativity in finding ways to use social media in their sales strategy. There are many social media applications available to salespeople but this text will limit its discussion to some of those that are more commonly used today.

According to the **LinkedIn** web page, "LinkedIn strengthens and extends your existing network of trusted contacts." In 2017, Fortune.com attributed over 500 million subscribers to this professional networking service in over 200 countries, with a new member being added approximately every second.[6] This service is the ultimate in staying connected. It can be used to do the following:

LinkedIn: A social networking site that facilitates professional networking.

- Manage the information that's publicly available about you as a professional.
- Find and introduce you to potential clients, service providers, and subject experts who come recommended.
- Help you create and collaborate on projects, gather data, share files, and solve problems.
- Help you find and be found by business opportunities and potential partners.
- Give you new insights from discussions with like-minded professionals in private group settings.
- Make available inside connections that can help you land jobs and close deals.
- Post and distribute job listings to find the best talent for your company.

YouTube:
A worldwide video-sharing community that salespeople can use to enhance their sales.

Twitter:
A social media microblogging service that lets users send "tweets" up to a maximum of 280 characters.

Facebook:
A social networking site that facilitates building relationships, communicating with clients, and prospecting for new customers.

Skype:
A software application that uses the internet for voice calling, video calling, group calling, video conferencing, text messaging, and more.

EXHIBIT 4.12

Skype lets you meet face to face although you're half a world apart.

Source: © AVAVA/iStockphoto

Little explanation is needed to make apparent the usefulness of this service to professional salespeople.

YouTube is a worldwide video-sharing community that salespeople can use to enhance their sales. It is possible to make a virtual sales presentation that can be broadcast to millions of people, or to offer only select customers a product walk-through to demonstrate the functions and benefits of your product. YouTube can be both a major company promotional tool and a salesperson's personal tool to communicate directly to prospects and customers.

Twitter connects businesses to customers in real time. This microblogging service, which allows people to send "tweets" of up to a maximum of 280 characters, can be used by salespeople to share product information, provide customer service, and stay in touch with many prospects and customers easily. Businesses use Twitter to quickly share information with people interested in their products and services, to gather real-time market intelligence and feedback, and to build relationships with customers, partners, and influential people. From brand lift to CRM to direct sales, Twitter offers businesses a chance to reach an engaged audience.

EXHIBIT 4.13

Computers help you to remember. Computers and mobile devices are great tools for recording what was discussed in the sales call.

Source: © Darrenbaker/Dreamstime.com/GetStock.com

On the **Facebook** Newsroom website, the company mission is stated as follows: "Facebook's mission is to give people the power to build community and bring the world closer together. People use Facebook to stay connected with friends and family, to discover what's going on in the world, and to share and express what matters to them." As a salesperson, you can use Facebook to connect and share information with the prospects and customers in your life. Salespeople use this service to build relationships, communicate with clients, and prospect for new customers. Facebook's optimization tools allow salespeople to connect to a very targeted group that may have an interest in their product. As of September 2018, there were 2.27 billion users on Facebook worldwide, making it the world's largest social media site.[7]

Skype, now owned by Microsoft, is a software application allowing 1.33 billion people and businesses around the world to stay in touch, and is projected to reach 2.1 billion users by 2023.[8] Its features include voice calling, video calls, group calling, video conferencing, text messaging, and others, all over the Internet. Salespeople use Skype to work with colleagues and build relationships with customers and clients from around the globe. For example, a salesperson sitting in an airport in Calgary can have a face-to-face meeting with a client halfway around the world or attend a virtual sales department meeting by using a cell phone or notebook computer (see Exhibits 4.12 and 4.13). Imagine the reductions in travel time and expenses and the increases in productivity for those who use this service.

SOCIAL MEDIA INSIGHTS FOR SALES PEOPLE

COMMUNICATING WITH CUSTOMERS THROUGH SOCIAL MEDIA

According to the online statistics portal, Statista, social media now has a global penetration rate of 45 percent. Think about that: Almost half the world's population is now on social media. It is amazing to see how quickly the world has adapted to the evolving platform of social media. Some recent statistics stress the importance for companies to stay on top of social media with their customers. According to a recent article on Dreamgrow:

- 71 percent of consumers who have had a good social media service experience with a brand are likely to recommend it to others.
- 63 percent of customers actually expect companies to offer customer service via their social media channels, and 90 percent of social media users have already used social media as a way to communicate with a brand or business.
- 95 percent of online adults aged 18 to 34 are more likely follow a brand via social networking, over other forms of promotion.
- Visual content is more than 40 times more likely to get shared on social media than other types of content.

What Does This Mean to You?

Does your business have a social media strategy? If not, then you should definitely start planning and preparing to have one in the very near future, as you are already missing the boat. Companies that understand their online customers and their social media habits realize the importance and influence of social media content. These tools have been particularly important for small and medium-sized companies that, in the past, couldn't compete for the share of media with larger companies. Social media levels the playing field somewhat in the world of media, and companies must learn to become adept at targeting these new media habits.

Instagram is a video and photo sharing site owned by Facebook that has been increasing in popularity with businesses and consumers alike. There are now over 1 billion users on Instagram who love its simplicity and ease of use.[9] Anne's on the Avenue, a women's fashion store in Windsor, Ontario, frequently posts photos of customers in various new outfits purchased at the store. This is an easy way for Anne to show off her latest fashions to her Instagram followers. This quick advertisement on the "Gram" often leads to immediate sales when customers view the items on Anne's post.

Instagram: A video and photo sharing site popular with business and consumers alike due to its simplicity.

Snapchat is another social media platform, with roughly 186 million users. The application allows you to text and send photos easily to your friends and those photos are then deleted by default.[10] While popular with the younger generations, this may not be welcomed in a professional setting as much, as the application is very informal and may not reach a professional audience.

Snapchat: A popular social media platform that allows users to text and send photos easily; photos and videos are deleted by default; while this app is popular with younger generations, it is not as suitable for a professional audience.

Listening: The Key to Unlocking Buyers' Needs

LO10

Hearing refers to being able to detect sounds. **Listening** means deriving meaning from sounds that are heard. Not everything you hear is worth your undivided attention; however, listening is a communication skill critical to success.

hearing: The ability to detect sounds.

listening: Ability to derive meaning from sounds that are heard.

Salespeople often believe that their job is to talk rather than to listen. Nevertheless, if they talk *and* listen, their persuasive powers increase. Since people can listen roughly twice as fast (about 400 words per minute) as the average rate of speech, it is understandable that a person's mind may wander while listening to a salesperson's presentation or that the salesperson may tune out a prospect. To keep the buyer listening, ask questions, get the buyer involved in the conversation, and use visual aids. If you ask a question, carefully listen to the answer.

Listen to Words, Feelings, and Thoughts

When someone speaks, they are expressing thoughts and feelings. However, most of us listen to only the words.

Listen *behind* the words for the emotional content of the message, which is conveyed in the nuances of voice and body language. Some people, such as Analyticals and Drivers (discussed in Chapter 3), give you little emotional information. That's all right, because you deal with them in a factual, business-only style. Amiables and Expressives, on the other hand, reveal their emotions and, in turn, they appreciate your acknowledgement of their feelings. It is appropriate to discuss their feelings and treat them more as friends than as strictly business associates.

You can hear the emotions behind the words in several ways. First, look for changes in eye contact. After establishing a comfortable and natural level of eye contact, any sudden deviations from the norm tip you off to emotional content in the message. People tend to look away from you when they talk about something embarrassing. When this happens, make a quick mental note of what it pertained to and treat that subject delicately. Also, give a person the courtesy of looking away momentarily yourself—as if you are saying, "I respect your privacy."

Listen *between* the words for what is not said. Some people reveal more by what they don't say. A salesperson was talking to the president of a large paper mill. "I simply asked him what kind of training he had for his salespeople. He went into a long discourse on all the seminars, training films, videotapes, and cassettes they had from the parent company, suppliers, industry associations, and in-house programs. I sat, listened, and took notes. At the end of his speech I said to him, 'I noticed you didn't mention anything about time management for salespeople.' He raised his voice and emphatically said, 'You know, just this morning I was talking to a guy and I told him we have to have some time-management training for our salespeople.'"

The lesson here is to get the prospect talking-so you can listen actively. Take notes, look for clues to emotions, and don't interrupt or start thinking about your next question (see Exhibit 4.14).

EXHIBIT 4.14

Active listening is important to your sales success. Concentrate, take notes, look for clues, and don't interrupt!

Source: © Nyul/Dreamstime.com/GetStock.com

The Three Levels of Listening

Whenever people listen, they are at one of three basic levels of listening. Each requires various degrees of concentration by the listener. As you move from the first to the third level, the potential for understanding and clear communication increases.

Marginal Listening

Marginal listening, the first and lowest level, involves the least concentration, and typically listeners are easily distracted by their thoughts. During periods of marginal listening, a listener exhibits blank stares, nervous mannerisms, and gestures that annoy the speaker and cause communication barriers. The salesperson hears the message, but it doesn't sink in. There is enormous room for misunderstanding when a salesperson is not concentrating on what is said. Moreover, the prospect cannot help but feel the lack of attention, which may be insulting and diminish trust. It may be funny when family members continually patronize each other with, "Yes, dear," regardless of what is said. In real life, however, it is not funny:

Prospect: What I need, really, is a way to reduce the time lost due to equipment breakdowns.

Salesperson: Yeah, OK. Let's see, uh, the third feature of our product is the convenient sizes you can get.

SELLING TIPS

CONFERENCE CALL ETIQUETTE

When presented with the opportunity to participate in a **conference call** or teleconference, make sure you're prepared by following these simple tips.

1. Be in the right place. Don't be in an environment with lots of background noise and distractions.
2. If there is background noise, use the mute button until you're ready to speak. Get comfortable with the mute button so you don't leave it on while you're speaking.
3. Use a sound-activated headset so you don't have to worry about distractions, but try to use a higher quality one so you can hear and be heard properly.
4. Identify yourself before you speak so others will know who's speaking—you can't expect everyone to recognize your voice unless, of course, there are only a few people involved in the call.
5. Pre-arrange the start time and start on time. Don't establish a reputation for tardiness here. Be sensitive to time-zone differences in your planning.
6. Have a notepad ready. Be ready to take good notes. If your microphone is muted, you can take notes using the keyboard of your computer.
7. Remember, you can't read body language here and neither can the other participants. Use your voice carefully and listen carefully for emotions evident in others' voices.
8. Avoid annoying behaviour. Don't tap your pen, or shuffle your papers, etc. It's a big distraction when people are relying on sound alone.
9. When asking a question, identify which person you are addressing. "Jim, can you give me your thoughts on the situation?"
10. End the call formally. Thank everyone for their time and effort. Remind everyone of any next steps so you don't have to make individual calls to remind them later.

conference call: A teleconference or meeting conducted from multiple locations using the telephone.

Salespeople of all experience levels may be guilty of marginal listening. Beginners who lack confidence and experience may concentrate so intensely on what they are supposed to say next that they stop listening. Old pros, by contrast, have heard it all before. They have their presentations memorized and want the prospect to hurry and finish talking so the important business can continue. These traditional salespeople forget that the truly important information lies in what the prospect says.

Evaluative Listening

Evaluative listening, the second level of listening, requires more concentration and attention to the speaker's words. At this level, the listener actively tries to hear what the prospect says but isn't making an effort to understand the intent. Instead of accepting and trying to understand a prospect's message, the evaluative listener categorizes the statement and concentrates on preparing a response.

The evaluative listening phenomenon is a result of the tremendous speed at which a human can listen and think. It is no surprise that evaluative listening is the level of listening used most of the time. While it is a difficult habit to break, it can be done with practice.

Prospect: What I need, really, is a way to reduce the time lost due to equipment breakdown.

Salesperson (defensively): We have tested our machines in the field, and they don't break down often.

In this example, the salesperson reacted to one aspect of the prospect's statement. Had the salesperson withheld judgment until the end of the statement, he could have responded more objectively and informatively.

In evaluative listening, it is easy to be distracted by emotion-laden words. At that point, you aren't listening to the prospect. Instead, you are obsessed with the offensive word and wondering what to do about it. This practice is a waste of time for both you and the prospect. It increases personal and relationship tension and throws your communication off course. To avoid the problems of marginal and evaluative listening, practise active listening.

MAKING THE SALE

DO YOU HAVE ANY OF THESE LISTENING HABITS?

No one is perfect. We all have some bad listening habits that we get away with when we talk to our family and friends. In a business context, however, leave these bad habits behind and practise active listening. To gain insight into your listening habits, read through this list of common irritating listening habits and be honest with yourself; notice what you are guilty of and use this awareness to begin eliminating them.

- You do all the talking.
- You interrupt when people talk.
- You never look at the person talking or indicate that you are listening.
- You start to argue before the other person has a chance to finish.
- You constantly feel obligated to digress with a story, since everything that is said reminds you of an experience you've had.
- You finish sentences for people if they pause too long.
- You wait impatiently for people to finish so that you can interject something.
- You work too hard at maintaining eye contact and make people uncomfortable.
- You look as if you are appraising the person talking to you, looking him or her up and down.
- You overdo the feedback you give—too many nods of your head and "uh-huhs."

Active Listening

Active listening is the third and most effective level of listening. The active listener refrains from evaluating the message and tries to see the other person's point of view. Attention is on not only the words spoken but also the thoughts, feelings, and meaning conveyed. Listening in this way means the listener puts herself into someone else's shoes. It requires the listener to give the other person verbal and nonverbal feedback.

Prospect: What I need is a way to reduce the time lost due to equipment breakdowns.

Salesperson: Could you tell me what kinds of breakdowns you have experienced?

In this example, the salesperson spoke directly to the prospect's concerns, not around them. Her desire to make a presentation was deferred so she could accomplish a more important task: effectively communicating with the prospect.

Active listening is a skill that takes practice in the beginning, but after a while becomes second nature. The logic behind active listening is based on courtesy and concentration.

Active listening is sometimes difficult to do, especially for the novice salesperson. The novice may continue to talk about a particular situation or problem. However, the salesperson must ***learn to listen.*** It is a key to sales success. People like and appreciate a listener, as this poem says so well:

His thoughts were slow,
His words were few,
And never made to glisten,
But he was a joy
Wherever he went.
You should have heard him listen.

–Author Unknown

Your Attitude Makes the Difference

enthusiasm:
A state of mind wherein a person is filled with excitement toward something.

While a variety of methods and techniques exist in selling, truly effective sales persuasion is based on the salesperson's attitude toward the sales job and customers. **Enthusiasm** is a condition in which an individual is filled with excitement about solving the customer's problems.

SELLING TIPS

NINE STEPS TO BECOMING A BETTER LISTENER

- Stop talking, to show the prospect that you want to listen.
- Watch carefully for nonverbal signals, and be sure to project positive nonverbal signals. Simple head nods and lively facial expressions can encourage your prospect to continue to provide you with information.
- Learn to "listen ahead." Trying to anticipate where a discussion is heading during a dialogue allows you to determine the conclusion in advance of your required response, which allows you to relax and improve information absorption.
- Learn to periodically validate communicated information. By mentally and even verbally validating the accuracy and completeness of information points made by the prospect, especially during pauses, you can allow yourself to absorb more information more easily, especially information forthcoming in the continued dialogue.
- Utilize active listening techniques. By periodically mentally summarizing and restating the major points communicated by the prospect, you add tremendous clarity to the information exchanged thus far.
- Strive for understanding versus judging. Working to consciously understand what the prospect is saying versus the natural tendency to judge will allow you to absorb what is actually said more than any other listening development technique.
- Use your eyes to get "the rest of the story." By paying attention to the prospect's body language and nonverbal facial and body movements or hand gestures, you can see what the whole body, not just the mouth, is trying to tell you. (See Exhibit 4.15.)
- Mentally prepare common responses. By mentally developing and rehearsing in advance of a sales call how you are going to respond to, for example, common sales prospect purchase objections, you can then listen more effectively. A comprehensive mental inventory of common responses will also give you more confidence in any selling situation.
- Ask questions to clarify meaning. This will allow you to remove any ambiguity and will lead to the best possible solution to the prospect's problem.

EXHIBIT 4.15

Use your eyes to get "the rest of the story." Pay attention to the prospect's body language and nonverbal facial and body movements to get the full meaning of what they are say.

Source: © Yuri Arcurs/Dreamstime.com/GetStock.com

SELLING TIPS

SALES ETIQUETTE TIPS: MAKING CALLS

It seems these days that, all too often, people are forgetting simple manners, and social interaction skills are a lost art for many. While young salespeople, with their youthful enthusiasm and ability to adapt to rapidly changing technology, may have a great advantage in a modern sales force, not all business is done through emails and text messaging. Therefore, they must learn the minutiae of effective social interaction and good old-fashioned sales etiquette. Watch throughout the text for Sales Etiquette Tips on proper manners in sales situations.

1. Watch your timing. Don't call when you might be interrupting something like a meal, a vacation, or a meeting.
2. Ensure that the person you're calling has the time to speak, otherwise, ask them to suggest a better time.
3. Do not accept a call or a text message when you are meeting with a customer or in a meeting.
4. Don't try to hide the fact that you are reading a text message by holding your phone in your lap, below table level. Simply keep your phone off.
5. Speak in a normal tone of voice and smile while you're speaking.

The highly successful salesperson goes all out to help customers. Strive to make the buyer feel important, and show that you are there solely as a problem solver. Do this by expressing sincere interest, such as by asking questions instead of talking at the buyer.

credibility: A salesperson's believability, established through empathy, willingness to listen to specific needs, and continual enthusiasm toward his or her work and the customer's business.

Salespeople who have established **credibility** with their customers through continued empathy, willingness to listen to specific needs, and continual enthusiasm toward their work and their customers' business can make claims that their customers treat as absolute truth in some cases. Combining enthusiasm with evidence statements greatly improves a salesperson's persuasion.

Salespeople sometimes quote acknowledged experts in a field on the use of products. Demonstrating that other customers or respected individuals use the products encourages customer belief in the validity of information presented in a sales presentation. People place greater confidence in a trustworthy, objective source (particularly one not associated with the salesperson's firm) and are therefore more receptive to what is said by the salesperson.

Summary of Major Selling Issues

Communication is a transmission of verbal and nonverbal information and understanding between salesperson and prospect. The communication process comprises a sender (encoder) who transmits a specific message to a receiver (decoder) who responds to that message. The effectiveness of this communication process can be hampered by noise that distorts the message as it travels. A sender can judge the effectiveness of a message and media choice by monitoring the feedback from the receiver.

Barriers to constructive communication result from the perceptional differences between the sender and receiver, cultural differences, outside distractions, or how sales information is conveyed. Regardless of their source, barriers must be recognized and either overcome or eliminated if communication is to succeed.

Social media is growing in popularity among salespeople by leaps and bounds. It is critical for salespeople to stay at the cutting edge of emerging social media platforms to ensure maximum sales performance.

Nonverbal communication has emerged within the past 10 or 15 years as a critical component of the overall communication process. Recognition of nonverbal communication is essential for sales success in today's business environment.

Awareness of the prospect's territorial space, a firm and confident handshake, and accurate interpretation of body language are critical to a salesperson's success.

Overall persuasive power is enhanced through development of several key characteristics. The salesperson who creates a relationship based on mutual trust with a customer by displaying empathy (desire to understand the customer's situation and environment), a willing ear (more listening, less talking), and a positive attitude of enthusiastic pursuit of lasting solutions for the customer's needs and problems increases the likelihood of making the sale.

ETHICAL DILEMMA

HIGH PRESSURE OR GOOD SELLING?

Nico is a large man. He was a star football player at university and measures six and a half feet tall and 280 pounds. He works out regularly to retain his muscular stature. He has chiselled facial features and a shaved head. Nico has tremendous self-confidence, almost to the point of arrogance. He always dresses impeccably, but he can come across as an extremely intimidating person.

Nico works as a salesperson for a major manufacturer of photocopiers. He is a fierce competitor and works hard to close every sale. During some presentations, if things aren't going well, Nico will often change his communication style. He has found that if he sits more upright, sometimes even leaning over the prospect's desk, and raises the volume of his voice slightly, prospects sometimes became more cooperative.

What seems to be happening here? Is this behaviour ethical? Can you suggest a better way of dealing with these situations?

MEETING A SALES CHALLENGE

In this imaginary sales call, buyer and seller communicated both verbal and nonverbal messages. Here, nonverbal messages conveyed both parties' attitudes better than the actual verbal exchange. The salesperson's negative reactions served to increase Amos Skaggs's hostile attitude. He could sense that the salesperson did not understand his problem and was there only to sell him something—not to solve his problem. This impression caused a rapid breakdown in communication. The end result, as in this case, is usually no sale.

The salesperson may have reacted correctly to Skaggs. Since Skaggs is in a bad mood, coming back another day may be best. If the salesperson cannot come another day, then the salesperson needs to stop the planned presentation and let the buyer know he understands. He should show that he is there to help. But most of all, he must project a positive attitude and not be frightened by Skaggs.

PLAYING THE ROLE

The situations:

1. **B is meeting with A** to make a presentation about his/her paper products. B hopes to land A's account, which will result in a tremendous increase in sales volume.
2. **Same situation as above** except that C is making the sales call.

Role A: **Purchasing agent for Halton Print Works.** Being a talkative type, after your initial greeting, you want to tell the salesperson all the details of the wonderful weekend that you've had.

Role B: **Salesperson for Canadian Paper Supply.** As an impatient type, you are to play the role of a poor listener. Read about all the poor listening habits in this chapter and dramatize them during your conversation with your prospect.

Role C: **Salesperson for Canadian Paper Supply.** You are a patient person. Read about the habits of effective (active) listeners and listen properly to the same story about the wonderful weekend your prospect had.

Prepare your roles for an in-class dramatization of both good and bad listening techniques.

Key Terms for Selling

acceptance signals
caution signals
communication
conference call
credibility
decoding process
disagreement signals
encoding process
enthusiasm
Facebook
feedback
hearing
Instagram
intimate space
LinkedIn
listening
medium
message
netiquette
noise
nonverbal communication
personal space
persuasion
public space
receiver
Skype
Snapchat
social space
source
space invasion
space threats
territorial space
textiquette
text messaging
Twitter
YouTube

Sales Application Questions

1. Draw the salesperson-buyer communication process. Describe each step in the process. Why is two-way communication important in this process?
2. This chapter outlined several forms of nonverbal communication.
   a. Give an example of a salesperson making a good first impression through the proper use of an introductory handshake.
   b. What signals should the salesperson look for in a buyer's body language? Give several examples of these signals.
3. A salesperson may spend hours developing a sales presentation and yet the buyer does not buy. One reason for losing a sale is that the salesperson and the buyer do not communicate. What barriers to communication may be present between seller and buyer during a sales presentation?
4. When two people are talking, each wants the listener to understand. What can a salesperson do to help ensure that the buyer is listening?
5. You arrive at the industrial purchasing agent's office on time. This is your first meeting. After you have waited five minutes, the agent's secretary says, "She will see you." After the initial greeting, the purchasing agent asks you to sit down. For each of these three situations determine:
   a. What nonverbal signals is she communicating?
   b. How would you respond nonverbally?
   c. What would you say to her?
      i. She sits up straight in her chair behind her desk. She clasps her hands together and with little expression on her face says, "What can I do for you?"
      ii. She sits down behind her desk. She moves slightly backward in her chair, crosses her arms and, while looking around the room, says, "What can I do for you?"
      iii. She sits down behind her desk. She moves slightly forward in her chair. She seems hurried, yet she is relaxed toward your presence. Her arms are uncrossed. She looks you squarely in the eye, and with a pleasant look on her face says, "What can I do for you?"
6. In each of the following selling situations:
   a. What nonverbal signals is the buyer communicating?
   b. How would you respond nonverbally?
   c. What would you say?
      i. The buyer seems happy to see you. Because you have been calling on him for several years, the two of you have become business friends. In the middle of

your presentation, you notice the buyer slowly lean back in his chair. As you continue to talk, a puzzled look comes over his face.

ii. As you begin the main part of your presentation, the buyer reaches for the telephone and says, "Keep going; I need to tell my secretary something."

iii. As a salesperson with only six months' experience, you are somewhat nervous about calling on an important buyer who has been a purchasing agent for almost 20 years. Three minutes after you have begun your presentation, he rapidly raises his arms straight up into the air and slowly clasps his hands behind his head. He leans so far back in his chair that you think he is going to fall backward on the floor. At the same time, he crosses his legs away from you and slowly closes his eyes. You keep on talking. Slowly the buyer opens his eyes, uncrosses his legs, and sits up in his chair. He leans forward, placing his elbows on the desk top, propping his head up with his hands. He seems relaxed as he says, "Let me see what you have here." He reaches his hand out for you to give him the presentation materials you have developed.

iv. At the end of your presentation, the buyer leans forward, his arms open, and he smiles as he says, "You really don't expect me to buy that piece of junk, do you?"

Sales Online Exercise

Dress to Get a Job!

This chapter discusses verbal and nonverbal communication. One of the key nonverbal communication tools is your attire.

Review each of the following websites. Note that continual review of sites such as these will keep you abreast of appropriate dress codes for job interviews and when you join the workforce.

www.ask.com, Type in *how to dress for success*

www.dresscodeguide.com

www.managementhelp.org/career/dress.htm

Further Exploring the Sales World

Using questions is an effective method for a salesperson to obtain feedback from a buyer. For the next two days, try using questions in your conversations with other people, and report on your results. These questions should reflect an interest in the person you are talking to as well as the topic being discussed. Using the words *you* and *your* should increase feedback and create an atmosphere of trust.

For example, questions such as "What do you mean?," "What do you think?," and "How does that sound?" can be used in your conversation to encourage listeners to participate and to help determine how they feel about the topic of conversation.

Asking people's opinions also can result in a positive response, since they may feel flattered that you care about their opinion. Questions can help you guide the direction of topics discussed in conversation. Try to determine people's reactions to your questions and report your findings in class.

Student Application Learning Exercises (SALES)

SALES are meant to help construct the various segments of your sales presentation. SALES build on one another so that as you complete each exercise, you are constructing more of your sales presentation.

In Part 1, you identified the information that you would need to help you tailor your sales presentation.

Part 2

1. Summarize the needs that you plan to satisfy with your product proposal.
2. Review the discussion in this chapter on the importance of nonverbal communication. Develop a checklist to help you prepare your presentation. Be sure to include things such as dress, grooming, the handshake, body language, and so on.
3. Review the listening techniques discussed in this chapter and list ways in which you can enhance your listening effectiveness with your prospect.

Selling Experiential Exercise

Listening Self-Inventory

Instructions: Read the following questions and write *yes* or *no* for each statement on a separate sheet of paper. Mark each answer as truthfully as you can in light of your behaviour in the last few meetings or gatherings you attended.

	Yes	No
1. I frequently attempt to listen to several conversations at the same time.	_____	_____
2. I like people to give me only the facts and then let me make my own interpretation.	_____	_____
3. I sometimes pretend to pay attention to people.	_____	_____
4. I consider myself a good judge of nonverbal communications.	_____	_____
5. I usually know what another person is going to say before he or she says it.	_____	_____
6. I usually end conversations that don't interest me by diverting my attention from the speaker.	_____	_____
7. I frequently nod or frown to let the speaker know how I feel about what he or she is saying.	_____	_____
8. I usually respond immediately when someone has finished talking.	_____	_____
9. I evaluate what is being said while it is being said.	_____	_____
10. I usually formulate a response while the other person is still talking.	_____	_____
11. The speaker's delivery style frequently keeps me from listening to content.	_____	_____
12. I usually ask for people's points of view.	_____	_____
13. I make a concerted effort to understand other people's points of view.	_____	_____
14. I frequently hear what I expect to hear rather than what is said.	_____	_____
15. Most people believe that I have understood their points of view when we disagree.	_____	_____

According to communication theory, effective communicators answer as follows: No for questions 1, 2, 3, 5, 6, 7, 8, 9, 10, 11, and 14; and Yes for questions 4, 12, 13, and 15. If you missed only one or two questions, you strongly approve of your own listening habits, and you are on the right track to becoming an effective listener in your role as a salesperson. If you missed three or four questions, you have uncovered some doubts about your listening effectiveness, and your knowledge of how to listen has some gaps. If you missed five or more questions, you probably are not satisfied with the way you listen, and your friends and co-workers may feel you are not a good listener either. Work on improving your active listening skills.[11]

CASE 4–1

SKAGGS MANUFACTURING

John Alvez arrived promptly for his 10:00 a.m. meeting with Martha Gillespie, the buyer for Skaggs Manufacturing. At 10:15, when she hadn't arrived, John asked her secretary if she was out of the office for the morning. The secretary smiled and said, "She'll probably be a few minutes late." John resented this delay and was convinced that Martha had forgotten the appointment.

Finally, at 10:20, Martha entered her office, walked over to John, said hello, and promptly excused herself to talk to the secretary about a tennis game scheduled for that afternoon. Ten minutes later, Martha led John into her office. At the same time, a competing salesperson entered the office for a 10:30 appointment. With the door open, Martha asked John, "What's new today?" As John began to talk, Martha began reading letters on her desk and signing them. Shortly after that, the telephone began to ring, whereupon Martha talked to her husband for 10 minutes.

As she hung up, Martha looked at John and suddenly realized his frustration. She promptly buzzed her secretary and said, "Hold all calls." She got up and shut the door. John again began his presentation when Martha leaned backward in her chair, pulled her golf shoes out of a desk drawer, and began to brush them.

About that time, the secretary entered the office and said, "Martha, your 10:30 appointment is about to leave. What should I tell him?" Martha replied, "Tell him to wait; I need to see him." Then she said, "John, I wish we had more time. Look, I think I have enough of your product to last until your next visit. I'll see you then. Thanks for coming by."

John quickly rose to his feet, did not shake hands, said "OK," and left.

QUESTIONS

1. What nonverbal cues did the salesperson, John Alvez, experience when contacting Martha Gillespie?
2. If you were John Alvez, how would you have handled the situation?

CASE 4–2

WESTERN OFFICE SUPPLY

Judy Picard sells scanners for Western Office Supply in Winnipeg. Today she is calling on Bill Taylor, purchasing agent for a large manufacturing firm. Two weeks earlier, she had made her first sales call to Western, and had left a demonstrator for the company executives to try out. The previous evening, Bill had called Judy and asked her to come in so he could give her an order. After their initial hellos, the conversation continued:

Bill: Judy, thanks for coming by today. Our executives really like your equipment. Here is an order for four scanners. When can you deliver them?

Judy: Is tomorrow too soon?

Bill: That is perfect. Leave them with Mei, my secretary. [Bill says over the intercom] Mei, Judy will deliver the scanners tomorrow. Mei, I want you to go ahead and take them to Sally, Anita, and Salisha. Women sure understand the use of modern equipment.

Judy: Bill, thanks for your help.

Bill: Forget it Judy, I wish I could have helped more. Your scanners can reduce the faxes we send with private customer data. Customers are leaving us because they can't fax their orders to our salespeople and get frustrated when the faxes are too busy.

Judy: You're right; many of my customers use them for that very reason.

Bill: I know, but some executives still feel they don't want them. They have serious concerns about private consumer data going to the cloud when it is scanned. Plus, the technology has them confused about using it and they have serious confidentiality and security concerns about customer information. I wish the men in our company felt the same way the women do about using these things.

QUESTIONS

1. Analyze and describe the conversation between Judy Picard and Bill Taylor.
2. What should Judy do now?

© Uber Images/Shutterstock

CHAPTER 5

Sales Knowledge: Customers, Products, Technologies

Kade Kirkham
Algonquin College, Ottawa, Ontario.
Source: Courtesy of Kade Kirkham

A Sales Success Story

Kade Kirkham had a great opportunity to start his sales career in a B2B software company prior to attending Sheridan College for his post-secondary education. This job offer came on one condition: the pursuit of further education would be required. Kade began working at DynaSCAPE Software in 2014, focusing entirely on lead generation (cold calling). He blew past the three-month probation period and spent the following two years mastering his prospecting craft before starting his journey at Sheridan College in the Business Marketing program.

From 2016 to 2018, while Kade completed his diploma, he was also highly active in additional extracurricular activities such as growing from a lead-generation role to an account management role in his career, becoming president of the Sheridan chapter of DECA U, and doing significant prep work for the OCMC sales case competition. After graduating with a diploma from Sheridan, he decided to continue his educational journey by bridging into the degree program.

Kade's natural inclination to pursue sales really comes from his desire to help people solve their business problems. He has a very outgoing personality, but has always tried to maintain the persona of a consultative salesperson rather than a high-pressure salesperson. Kade says, "If you can manage to listen, truly listen, to your customer and build enough rapport with them, at that point they will trust that your recommendations are in their best interest, rather than for your personal gain."

After being with DynaSCAPE for over four years and being part of a large company acquisition, Kade advises that the bare-minimum expectation is to do your job to the best of your ability. As either a part-time employee or a student just graduating from school, he advises that you go above expectations and do your best to become a "yes guy," or someone who can be relied on when management requires something extra. "Naturally, over time, management will feel they can rely on you and will be inclined to ask you before others."

MAIN TOPICS

Sources of Sales Knowledge

Knowledge Builds Relationships

Know Your Customers

Know Your Company

Know Your Product

Know Your Channels of Distribution

Know Your Product's Pricing and Discount Policies

Know Your Competition, Industry, and Economy

A FABulous Approach to Buyer Need Satisfaction

Position Your Product with a Unique Selling Proposition

Advertising Aids Salespeople

Sales Promotion Generates Sales

Technology and Selling

Knowledge of Technology Enhances Sales and Customer Service

LEARNING OBJECTIVES

Successful salespeople are knowledgeable individuals. Many salespeople are experts in their field. After studying this chapter, you should be able to:

LO1 Explain the importance of knowledge to sales professionals and determine various sources of sales knowledge.

LO2 Discuss the general areas of knowledge needed for increased sales success.

LO3 Understand the importance of features, advantages, and benefits.

LO4 Develop a FAB worksheet.

LO5 Develop and use a unique selling proposition.

LO6 Explain the purpose of planogram software for many types of salespeople.

LO7 Explain the main technologies used by salespeople.

FACING A SALES CHALLENGE

You are proud of the products you sell and tell everyone they are the top-line of the industry, the best on the market, light years ahead of the competition. Of course you have worked for the company for only two weeks. But the sales training course you took last week clearly convinced you that your products are much better than any others. During one presentation on a new detergent for washing machines, you concentrated on discussing the quality of the product: how well it cleans, its environmental safety, how much users like its pleasant scent. The grocery store buyer said, "I couldn't care less about the quality of your products."[1]

Why did the buyer respond in a negative way? What is the buyer interested in?

(Continued at end of chapter.)

Salespeople need to know many things. It's important to discuss features, advantages, and benefits (FABs)–but which FABs interest the buyer? What about a retailer, wholesaler, manufacturer, or consumer? Each is likely interested in similar, but different, FABs.

This chapter examines the basic body of knowledge essential for a salesperson's success. Knowing about products and customers is only part of it. The professional salesperson must also know about his company's policies, procedures, marketing efforts, distribution channel, and competitors; the industry; and the economy. Of course, the salesperson must also keep current with computers, software applications, and other technologies as new advances occur.

LO1 Sources of Sales Knowledge

Knowledge for selling is obtained in two ways: First, most companies provide some formal sales training that teaches information through preliminary training programs and sales meetings. Second, the salesperson learns by being on the job. Experience is the best teacher for the beginning salesperson.

sales training: The effort put forth by an employer to provide the opportunity for the salesperson to acquire job-related culture, skills, knowledge, and attitudes that result in improved performance in the selling environment.

Sales training is the effort an employer puts forth to provide the opportunity for the salesperson to receive job-related culture, skills, knowledge, and attitudes that result in improved performance in the selling environment. Successful companies thoroughly train new salespeople and maintain ongoing training programs for their experienced sales personnel. Companies are interested in training primarily to increase sales volume, salesperson productivity, and profitability.

Like many professional careers, selling is a skill that is truly developed only through *experience.* Sales knowledge obtained through education, reading, formalized sales training, and word-of-mouth is helpful in enhancing overall sales ability, but actual experience is the critical source of sales knowledge. Some sales managers hire only experienced people to fill entry-level selling slots. Indeed, some corporations do not allow people to fill marketing staff positions unless they have had field sales experience with the company or a major competitor.

Sales experience improves a salesperson's abilities by:

- Showing how buyers perceive a product or product line
- Revealing unrecognized or undervalued product benefits or shortcomings
- Voicing a multitude of unanticipated protests and objections
- Showing a great number of prospect moods and attitudes over a short period
- Providing a challenge that makes selling a skill that is never mastered, only improved

No author or sales trainer can simulate the variety of situations that a salesperson confronts over the span of a career. Authors and trainers can only provide general guidelines as a framework for action. Actual selling experience alone gives a person direct feedback on how to function in a specific selling situation. The sales knowledge gained through periodic sales training and actual experience benefits the salesperson, the firm, and the customers.

> *"I am still learning."*
>
> *MICHELANGELO*

Only through possessing a high level of knowledge can the salesperson provide excellent service. Knowledge based upon wisdom and truthfully conveyed to the buyer builds relationships.

Knowledge Builds Relationships

LO2

Selling knowledge will increase the salesperson's self-confidence and build the buyer's confidence in the salesperson, as well as build their relationship.

Knowledge Increases Confidence of Salespeople and Buyers

Salespeople who call on, for example, computer systems engineers, university professors, or aerospace experts may be at a disadvantage. In some cases, they have less education and experience than prospects in their fields of expertise.

Imagine making a sales call on a distinguished heart surgeon. Can you educate her in the use of your company's synthetic heart valves? Not really, but you can offer help in supplying product information from your firm's medical department. This personal service, your product knowledge, and her specific needs will make the sale. Knowledge about your company, its market, and your buyer enables you to build your self-confidence, which results in increased sales.

Furthermore, prospects want to do business with salespeople who know their business and the products they sell. When a prospect has confidence in the salesperson's expertise, a sales presentation becomes more acceptable and believable.

SELLING TIPS

STRENGTHEN THESE AREAS

Salespeople need strength in the following four areas of selling.

1. **Product knowledge** – Know how to communicate both the technical and emotional components of your products.
2. **Sales techniques** – Understand the process. From prospecting onward, salespeople must stay up-to-date on best practices and industry developments in terms of technology and technique.
3. **Procedural knowledge** – Know how to write up sales reports and contracts, how to arrange for service calls and returned goods, and what your company's policies and procedures are.
4. **Customer service skills** – Know how to thank a customer, service their account, and invite them back. Stay current in exceptional customer service practices.

Strive to be an expert on all aspects of your product, which will allow you to answer questions confidently and to field objections raised by prospects. Often, within minutes, buyers can tell whether salespeople know what they are talking about. They ask questions and quickly form an impression of the salesperson; a relationship begins. Typically, the more knowledge you have, the higher your sales.

Know Your Customers

How can you match your product's benefits with a buyer's needs if you don't know your customers? If you are selling to someone you've never met before–such as in a retail store–you have to ask about the buyer's needs. Business-to-business selling also requires asking numerous questions, sometimes spending weeks with a customer before a sale. We offer a few questions in Exhibit 5.1 (i.e., what, who, and when/how) that salespeople commonly ask themselves to better understand their customers. Refer also to Chapter 3 for details about conducting a customer needs analysis.

EXHIBIT 5.1

Questions that salespeople should ask to better understand their customers.

WHAT	WHO	WHEN AND HOW
What are the key needs of your buyer?	Who has a role in the purchasing process? What are their respective roles in the process?	How might the buyer prioritize needs? Which need(s) is absolutely essential to meet? Which need(s) might not be required to be met exactly?
What are your customer's personal objectives or goals?	Who is the buyer (i.e., who purchases the product) versus who is the user of the product? Are they the same individual(s)? What influence do they have on the decision?	When does your customer make decisions (e.g., seasonal, specific buying times, during certain life transitions, anytime)?
What are your customer's roles and responsibilities? How does each impact the buying decision?	Who makes the final decision for the purchase?	How often does your customer expect contact or progress updates from you?
What is the buying process? What are the stages in the buying process? Who plays a role in each stage?	Who currently serves the customer's needs (i.e., competitors)?	When might key dynamics in your customer's industry impact your customer's firm? Which of these trends offer opportunities and challenges?
What is your customer's perception of your firm and its products or services?	Who might be able to provide you with a referral or recommendation that the customer would perceive as credible?	How would the customer pay for your solution (financing terms, cash terms, etc.)?
What policies and procedures do salespeople have to follow in order to sell to the customer?	Who does the customer seek for guidance (formally or informally)?	How long does the buying process last (hours, days, months, years)?
What specific information is required in order for the buyer to make a decision?	If a purchase is made, who will be your key daily contact(s)?	When are the key deadlines for meeting with your customer or providing proposals?
What are key concerns or risks that the customer considers when making this type of purchase?	Who will need to be aware of any implementation steps or play a role in the implementation process?	How should you communicate with your customer (i.e., e-mail, text, instant message, phone call, face-to-face)? When should you use each type of communication media?

Know Your Company

Knowledge of your firm usually helps you project an expert image to the prospect. Company knowledge includes information about the history, policies, procedures, distribution systems, promotional activities, pricing practices, and technology that have guided the firm to its current position.

The type and extent of company knowledge to use depends on the company, its product lines, and the industry (see Exhibit 5.2). In general, consumer-goods salespeople require less information about the technical nature of their products; however, selling high-technology products (computers, rocket-engine components, complex machinery, etc.) to highly knowledgeable industrial buyers requires extensive knowledge.

EXHIBIT 5.2

What would you need to know for selling . . .

tablets to consumers?. . .

Source: © Frank Gaertner/Shutterstock.com

. . . industrial equipment to an engineer?

Source: © Monty Rakusen/Getty Images RF

General Company Information

All salespeople need to know the background and current operating policies of their companies. These policies are your guidelines, and you must understand them to do your job effectively. Information on company growth, policies, procedures, production, and service facilities is often used in sales presentations.

Company Growth and Accomplishment

Knowledge of your firm's development since its origin provides you with promotional material and builds your confidence in the company. A technology salesperson might say to a buyer:

> In 1952, our firm placed its first commercial electronic computer on the market. That year, our sales were $342 million. Currently, our sales are projected to be over $95 billion. We have reached these high sales figures because our advanced, technological office equipment and information processors are the best available at any price. Our newest product, the "I-Execution and Artificial Intelligence" system I am showing you, is the most advanced piece of equipment on the market today. It is five years ahead of any other technology on the market.

Policies and Procedures

Effective salespeople are always enhancing their knowledge.

To give good service, you should be able to tell a customer about policies: how an order is processed, how long it takes for orders to be filled, your firm's returned goods policy, how to open a new account, and what to do in the event of a shipping error.

When you handle these situations quickly and fairly, your buyer gains confidence in you and the firm.

Production Facilities

Many companies require their new salespeople to tour their production facilities to give them a firsthand look at the company's operations. This is a good opportunity to gain product knowledge. For example, the Bigelow-Sanford Carpet Company salesperson can say, "When I was visiting our production plant, I viewed each step of the carpet-production process. The research and development department allowed us to watch comparison tests between our carpets and competitors' carpets. Our carpets did everything but fly . . . and they are working on that!"

Service Facilities

Many companies, such as Intel, Xerox, and 3M, have both service facilities and service representatives to help customers. Being able to say, "We can have a service representative there the same day you call our service centre," strengthens a sales presentation, especially if service is important for the customer (as it is in the office copier and technology industries).

Know Your Product

Knowledge about your company's product and your competitors' product is a major component of sales knowledge. Become an expert on your company's products. Understand how they are produced and their level of quality. Product knowledge may include such technical details as:

- Performance data
- Physical size and characteristics
- How the product operates
- Specific features, advantages, and benefits of the product
- How well the product is selling in the marketplace

Many companies have their new salespeople work in the manufacturing plant (e.g., on the assembly line) or in the warehouse (filling orders and receiving stock). This hands-on experience may cost the salesperson sweat and sore muscles for a couple of weeks or months, but the payoff is a world of product knowledge and help in future selling that could not be earned any other way. Often, new salespeople in the oil and gas industry roughneck and drive trucks during the first few months on the job. At Finning International, one of the largest Caterpillar dealers in the world, new salespeople work in sales administration positions for six months, learning the features, advantages, and benefits of all the pieces of heavy equipment before dealing directly with customers.

Much is learned at periodic company sales meetings. At sales meetings, a consumer-goods manufacturer may concentrate on developing sales presentations for the products to receive special emphasis during the company sales period. Company advertising programs, price discounts, and promotional allowances for these products are discussed. Although little time may be spent on the technical aspects of consumer products, much time is devoted to discussing the marketing mix for these products (product type, promotion, distribution, and price).

A complete understanding of your product is not enough in itself to fully satisfy the needs of prospects; understanding how your product relates to the prospect's needs is critical.

SELLING GLOBALLY

TECHNOLOGY—CURSE OR SAVIOUR?

Another business trip? Bernie Dougall hated the thought of travelling to Asia for another sales meeting with his colleagues from around the globe but a problem had arisen with one of his company's Eastern European customers. Senior management for his international hardware company preferred that sales managers meet in person to discuss important issues, so Bernie felt obliged to attend.

In his conversation with Lauren Mathews, his company's communications consultant, he learned the following: Personal meetings won't become obsolete because most people still prefer to meet face to face—bad news for Bernie. However, technologies such as Skype, Facetime WiFi, and interactive video conferencing have changed the way people meet and exchange information. These technologies won't reduce the number of meetings; in fact, by encouraging "virtual" meetings, they could facilitate even more global management meetings or brainstorming sessions. The good news is that many of these meetings would require no travel.

Now Bernie was listening. The technology for effective virtual meetings is already here. High-quality video capability over the Internet allows for higher-resolution video feeds from several users. Now Lauren really had Bernie's attention. He made a note to speak to his managers about this.

Bernie told Lauren about the meetings he had recently attended and complained that many were interrupted by people receiving mobile phone calls, text messages, or emails on their smartphones. It was a tough audience, he complained. Lauren agreed and pointed out that this phenomenon put pressure on speakers to keep the audience's attention.

She explained that good speakers use wireless connectivity to conduct more effective meetings by forcing involvement and participation. Some bring their wireless PCs to the podium and invite real-time questions on game applications such as Kahoot!.

Other technologies revolutionizing meetings and conferences include the following:

- **Social networking** – Self-serve registration kiosks can help you determine who is attending which sessions, which will help you arrange to "run into" them.
- **Audience response** – This technology lets speakers survey the audience. The electronic key pads can be used to build consensus and set agendas. The technology is getting cheaper, more reliable, and easier to use.
- **Blogs** – Conference organizers are starting to generate **blogs**, online diaries in which participants write about the day's activities. Following these blogs will help you keep track of what's going on at the conference, and perhaps revise session selections and identify new prospects.
- **Digital pens** – Rather than leave meetings with pages of notes you can barely read, you can buy a digital pen that converts your handwritten notes into Word documents, making them much more accessible.
- **Infinite audiences** – Not able to attend? Technology allows you to buy "live" access to meetings, through video-conferencing software.

At the conclusion of his conversation with Lauren, Bernie pondered these technologies and wondered how they could be implemented into his sales job. He definitely saw less travel in his future.

blog:
A frequently updated personal journal using the Internet; intended for people to read.

Know Your Channels of Distribution

It is essential to understand the channel of distribution used by your company to move its products to the final consumer. Knowledge of each channel member (also called reseller or intermediary) is vital. Wholesalers and retailers often stock thousands of products, and each may have hundreds of salespeople calling on its buyers. Know as much about each channel member as possible. Some important information you will need includes:

- The likes and dislikes of each channel member's customers
- Product lines and the assortment each one carries
- When each member sees salespeople

- Distribution, promotion, and pricing policies
- What quantity of which product each channel member has purchased in the past

While most channel members will have similar policies concerning salespeople, keep abreast of the differences.

In summary, salespeople today must be knowledgeable to be effective in their jobs. Four important reasons for the salesperson to have selling knowledge are to:

1. Increase the salesperson's self-confidence.
2. Build the buyer's confidence in the salesperson.
3. Build relationships through truly caring about the needs of others.
4. Meet the buyer's expectations.

Know Your Product's Pricing and Discount Policies

price:
The value or worth of a product.

An important part of a comprehensive marketing strategy for a product is establishing its price. **Price** refers to the value or worth of a product that attracts the buyer to exchange money or something of value for the product. A product has some want-satisfying attributes for which the prospect is willing to exchange something of value. The person's wants assign a value to the item offered for sale. For instance, a golfer who wants to purchase a dozen golf balls already has conceived some estimated measure of the product's value. Of course, the sporting goods store may have set a price higher than estimated. This could diminish *want* somewhat, depending on the difference between the two. Should the golfer then find the same brand of golf balls on sale at a discount store, at a price more in line with a preconceived idea of the product's value, the want may be strong enough to stimulate a purchase.

Many companies offer customers various types of discounts from normal prices to entice them to buy. These discounts become an important part of the firm's marketing effort (see Exhibit 5.3). They are usually developed at the corporate level by the firm's marketing managers. Immediately before the sales period when the product's promotion begins, the sales force is informed of special discounts that they may offer to customers. This discount information becomes an important part of the sales presentation. It is important for salespeople to familiarize themselves with the company's price, discount, and credit policies so that they can use them as a competitive advantage and enhance their professional image with the buyer.[2]

Salespeople must know the selling price of each of their products along with any discounts that may be offered to the customer. Often, management will determine that certain price discounts may be given under certain circumstances to buyers. Detailed knowledge of these discounts can become part of a sales presentation and a price negotiation.

markup:
The dollar amount added to the product cost to determine its selling price.

Salespeople should have a thorough understanding of the arithmetic in **markup** and discount structures for different types of product. This will allow them to explain pricing mechanisms and profitability for their customers.

Further discussion of the various pricing issues salespeople must be able to explain to buyers is provided at the end of this text. Appendix A, "Sales Arithmetic and Pricing," has information useful for developing a sales presentation for the class project role-play.

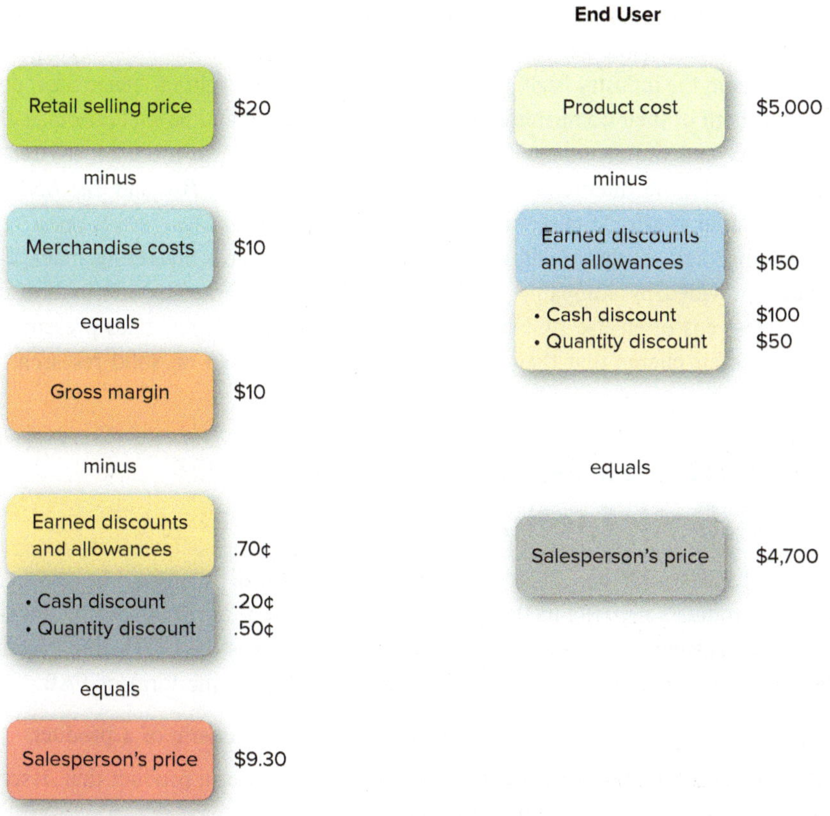

EXHIBIT 5.3
Examples of prices and discounts salespeople discuss in their sales presentations.

Know Your Competition, Industry, and Economy

Today's successful salespeople understand their competitors' products, policies, and practices as well as their own. It is common for a buyer to ask a salesperson, "How does your product compare to the one I'm currently using?" If unable to confidently answer such a question, a salesperson will lose ground in selling (see Exhibit 5.4).

One way to obtain information on competitors is through advertisements. From a competitor's advertising, Joe Mitchell, a salesperson representing a small business machines firm, developed a chart for comparing the sales points of his machines against the competition. Joe does not name the competitive equipment on the chart. Instead, he calls them Machine A, Machine B, and Machine C. When he finds a claimed benefit in one of the other machines that his product does not have, he works to find a better benefit to balance it.

> Maybe the chart isn't always useful, but it certainly has prepared me to face a customer. I know just what other machines have—and what they do not have—that my prospect might be interested in. I know the principal sales arguments used in selling these machines and the benefits I must bring up to offset and surpass competition. Many times a prospect will mention an advertisement of another company and ask about some statement or other. Because I've studied those ads and taken the time to find out what's behind the claims, I can give an honest answer and I can demonstrate how my machine has the same feature or quality and then offer additional benefits. Of course, I never run down a competitor's product. I just try to run ahead of it.

EXHIBIT 5.4
What does this automotive salesperson need to know about his products and competition?
Source: © Tatagatta/Dreamstime.com/GetStock.com

An industrial-goods salesperson and an industrial buyer work for different companies but are in the same industry. The industrial buyer often seeks information from salespeople on the industry itself, and how economic trends might influence the industry as well as both of their companies. Thus, the salesperson should be well informed about the industry and the economy. This information is available in the company records, television, radio, the Internet, newspapers such as the *National Post* and *The Globe and Mail,* industrial and trade periodicals, and magazines such as *Canadian Business.*

Another key source of information for salespeople and marketing managers is research provided by companies such as ACNielsen, a marketing information company. Sales reps often use ACNielsen's analysis to augment their sales presentations and show their clients that their recommendations are based on solid research.

LO3

A FABulous Approach to Buyer Need Satisfaction

benefit selling: A method of selling whereby a salesperson relates a product's benefits to the customer's needs using the product's features and advantages as support.

FAB selling technique: A technique stressing features, advantages, and benefits of a product.

feature: Any tangible or intangible characteristic of a product.

advantage: The performance characteristic of a product that describes how it can be used or how it will help the buyer.

benefit: A favourable result the buyer receives from the product because of a particular advantage that has the ability to satisfy a buyer's need.

Successful salespeople use a powerful technique called **benefit selling**; the salesperson relates a product's benefits to the customer's needs, using the product's features and advantages as support. This technique is often referred to as the **FAB selling technique** (**F**eature, **A**dvantage, and **B**enefit). Most companies use some form of FAB.

- A product **Feature** is any tangible or intangible characteristic of a product.
- A product **Advantage** is the performance characteristic of a product that describes how it can be used or will help the buyer.
- A product **Benefit** is a favourable result the buyer receives from the product because of a particular advantage that has the ability to satisfy the buyer's need.

The Product's Features: "So What?"

Products have features (tangible or intangible characteristics) such as the following:

• Size	• Terms	• Packaging
• Colour	• Quantity	• Flavour
• Taste	• Price	• Service
• Quality	• Shape	• Uses
• Delivery	• Ingredients	• Technology

Descriptions of a product's features answer the question, "What is it?" When used alone in the sales presentation, features have little persuasive power.

The Product's Advantages: "Prove It!"

Once a product feature is presented to the customer, the salesperson usually begins to discuss the advantages provided by that product's characteristics. The chances of making a sale are increased by describing the product's advantages, how a product can be used, or how it will help the buyer. Examples of product advantages (performance characteristics) include:

- It is the fastest-selling soap on the market.
- You can store more information and retrieve it more rapidly with our computer.
- This machine will copy on both sides of the page instead of only one.

How does the prospective customer know that your claims for a product are true? Imagine that a prospect is thinking, "Prove it!" Be prepared to substantiate any claims you make.

Although your chances of making a sale increase when you discuss both the features and the advantages of your product, you must learn how to stress product benefits in your presentation that are important to the prospect. Once you have mastered this selling technique, your sales will increase.

The Product's Benefits: "What's In It for Me?"

People are interested in what results they will receive by buying and using the product or service. Emphasizing benefits appeals to the customer's personal motives by answering the question, "What's in it for me?" In your presentation, stress how the prospect will benefit from the purchase rather than stressing the features and advantages of your product, as shown in Exhibit 5.5.

To illustrate the idea of buying benefits instead of only features or advantages, consider four items: (1) a new high-speed photocopier, (2) a new software application, (3) video-conferencing capability, and (4) an ethical mutual fund. Do people buy these products or services for their features or advantages? No. Instead, people buy the product's benefits, such as:

- A new high-speed photocopier - increased office productivity and profits
- A new software application - improved efficiency and happier employees
- Video-conferencing capability - enhanced communication capability
- An ethical mutual fund - peace of mind knowing that you're investing in ecologically and environmentally responsible companies

As you can see, people buy benefits—not features or advantages. These benefits can be both practical, such as an investment, and psychological, such as an image of success. The salesperson needs to discuss benefits to answer the prospect's question, "What's in it for me?"

> **Vacuum cleaner salesperson to householder:** "This vacuum cleaner's high-speed motor (feature) works twice as fast (advantage) with less effort (advantage), which saves you 15 to 30 minutes in cleaning time (benefit) and the aches and pains of pushing a heavy machine (benefit).

EXHIBIT 5.5

Discuss benefits to fulfill people's needs and to increase sales.

B2B salespeople work closely with customers to design products and systems that fit their needs.

Source: © Dean Mitchell/Shutterstock.com

Consumer-goods salespeople can show customers how to increase sales by setting up strategic merchandise displays.

Source: © Bloomberg via Getty Images

Notice that the benefit specifically states the favourable results of buying the vacuum cleaner, which answers the buyer's question, "What's in it for *me?*" You can see that the benefits are specific statements and not generalizations. Instead of saying, "This vacuum cleaner will save you time," say, "You will save 15 to 30 minutes."

Notice also that a benefit can result in a further benefit to the prospect. For example, "By saving cleaning time (a benefit), you reduce the aches and pains of pushing a heavier machine (a benefit of a benefit) because the high-speed motor (advantage) pulls it (advantage)." Examples of general product benefits include:

• Greater profit	• Cost reductions
• Time savings	• More customers drawn into retail store
• Increased sales	• Elimination of out-of-stock merchandise

LO4 Order Can Be Important

Some salespeople prefer to state the benefit and then state that the feature or advantage makes the benefit possible, such as, "The high-speed processor (feature) will bring you *additional profits* (benefits) because it is 70 percent faster at making photocopies (advantage)." In this example, the advantage supports the statement of benefits.

Although stating the benefit first is preferable, you can discuss the FAB in any particular order:

Air conditioning salesperson to customer: "This air conditioner has a high energy-efficiency rating (feature) that will save you 10 percent on your energy costs and improve your bottom line (benefits) because it uses less electricity (advantage)."

Sporting goods salesperson to retail store manager: "With this ball, players will get an extra 5 to 10 metres on their drives (advantage), making them happier customers and more willing to recommend your shop to their friends, thus increasing sales (benefit) all because of this ball's new solid core (feature)."

Salesperson to buyer of grocery store health and beauty aids: "Our economy size (feature) sells the best of all brands (advantage) in stores like yours. You can increase store traffic 10 to 20 percent (benefit) and build your sales volume by at least 5 percent (benefit) by advertising and reducing its normal price (feature) in next Wednesday's ad."

New salespeople should practise using feature, advantage, and benefit phrases in their sales conversation:

The . . . *(feature)* . . . means you . . . *(advantage)* . . . with the real benefit to you being . . . *(benefit)* . . . .

This FAB sequence allows you to easily remember to state the product's benefit in a natural, conversational manner. For example:

The *new solid-core centre of the Gunshot Golf Ball* means players *will have an extra 5 to 10 metres on their drives,* with the real benefits to you being *happier customers and increased business.*

Substitute any features, advantages, and benefits among a variety of transition phrases to develop FAB sequences. Several sequences can be used one after another to emphasize your product's benefits.

Try it. Read the golf ball FAB sequence aloud. Then do it again, using your own phrasing. Create several variations of transition language that you feel comfortable using.

Matching FABs to Buyer Needs

Exhibit 5.6 illustrates the concept that buyers have important needs as well as relatively unimportant buying needs. When presenting FABs, emphasize product benefits that satisfy important buyer needs. De-emphasize benefits that would satisfy unimportant needs. Suppose your product had benefits involving service, delivery, time savings, and cost reductions. Let us also suppose that, during needs analysis, you discover that delivery is not important to the buyer. In this case, concentrate on discussing service, time savings, and cost reductions.

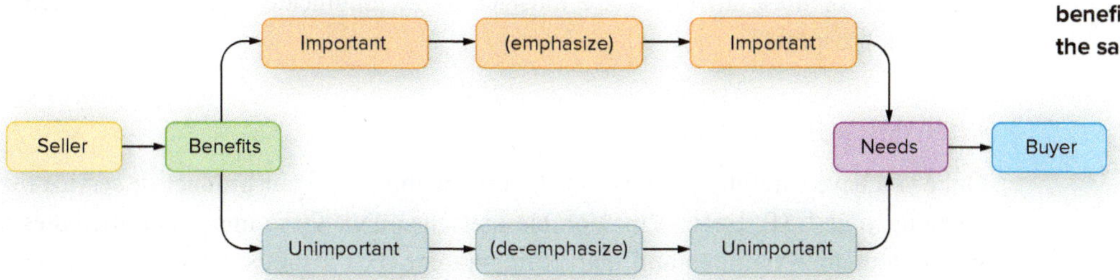

EXHIBIT 5.6

Match buyer's needs to product's benefits and emphasize them in the sales presentation.

This selling strategy is important; low-performance salespeople often discuss features and benefits of little or no interest to the prospect–often because they didn't take the time to determine what the buyer's real needs were.

The Three Realms—Selling the Whole Package

Buyers are not interested in only products or services. **Three realms** of selling actually make up the complete package customers get when they buy. As a skilled salesperson, you must sell:

- Yourself
- Your company
- Your products and services

three realms: The three aspects involved in selling; salespeople must have the ability to sell the company, the company's products, and themselves.

You may be selling the greatest products at the lowest prices, made by the most respected company around, but the prospect will not buy from you if they do not believe you and trust your word. Buyers want to deal with salespeople who are reliable, honest, and knowledgeable and who will be there for them should they need help. You are also part of the sales package. Sell yourself as part of the value the buyer will receive by buying from you.

Position Your Product with a Unique Selling Proposition

LO5

A **unique selling proposition** (USP) clearly answers the question, "Why should I buy from you?" Let's face it–in most selling situations it is this question going through a prospect's mind, so you should answer it clearly.

unique selling proposition (USP): A statement about why a prospect should buy from you—it offers a reason why your product or company is both different and better than your competition's.

If you have competition, you should develop at least one USP and possibly several. The more you have, the easier it is to position your product in your prospect's mind.

Developing a USP

To develop a successful USP, ask yourself several questions about your product or business:

1. What attributes set your product or business apart from direct competitors? You will not necessarily use all of these, but the following questions will help you decide what to focus on.
2. Which of these attributes are most important to your prospects?
3. Which of these attributes are truly unique and would be difficult for your competition to imitate?
4. Which of these attributes are most easily communicated and demonstrated to your prospects?

Using Your USP

Once you have carefully thought out the key attributes of your product or service that make up your USP, create a memorable message about these important attributes to use in your presentations and marketing strategy. For instance, guaranteed next-day delivery could become a unique selling proposition for you providing that (1) it's true, and (2) none of your competitors offer it. Examples may include:

- Delivery overnight–guaranteed
- Guaranteed inventory on all parts
- Live operators, all the time
- Free returns–no questions asked

Remember, though, that seldom are two customers exactly alike–so using the same USP for every prospect will not get the same result. You must understand your prospect's buying motives and develop a USP to best suit them. Emphasize your USP. You may want to "brand" your USP by including it on your presentation slides, your business card, and/or your email signature line.

Advertising Aids Salespeople

Personal selling, advertising, publicity, and sales promotion are the main factors of a firm's promotional effort. Companies sometimes coordinate these promotional tools in a promotional campaign. A sales force may be asked by the corporate marketing manager to concentrate on selling Product A for April and May. Product A is simultaneously promoted on television and in magazines, and direct-mail samples or coupons for Product A are sent to consumers.

Keeping abreast of your company's advertising and sales promotion activities is critical. By incorporating these data into your sales presentation, you can provide customers with a world of information that they probably know little about–and that information can secure the sale. Knowing your company's advertising budget, schedule, and messages can be a terrific aid in your sales presentation. When asked, "Can you guarantee that this product will sell in my store?" you can explain the advertising support that the product will be given by your company.

There's no longer any excuse for the marketing and sales departments to be disconnected. Company intranets and wireless technology make it very easy for company departments to share and coordinate their activities across all functional areas.

Sales Promotion Generates Sales

Sales promotion involves activities or materials other than personal selling, advertising, and publicity used to create sales. Sales promotion can be divided into consumer and trade sales promotion. **Consumer sales promotion** includes samples, coupons, contests, and demonstrations to consumers. **Trade sales promotion** encourages resellers to purchase and aggressively sell a manufacturer's products by offering incentives such as sales contests, displays, special purchase prices, and free merchandise (for example, buy ten cases of a product and get one case free).

These promotions, along with things like point-of-purchase (POP) displays, can be very useful sales tools for an enterprising salesperson. Sales promotion offers may prove to the retailer or wholesaler that the selling firm will assist actively in creating consumer demand. This, in turn, improves the salesperson's probability of making the sale.

consumer sales promotion: A promotion that includes free samples, coupons, contests, and demonstrations to consumers.

trade sales promotion: A promotion that encourages resellers to purchase and aggressively sell a manufacturer's products by offering incentives such as sales contests, displays, special purchase prices, and free merchandise.

Shelf Positioning Is Important to Your Success

Another important sales stimulator is the shelf positioning of products. **Shelf positioning** refers to the physical placement of the product within the retailer's store. **Shelf facings** are the number of individual products placed beside each other on the shelf. Determine where a store's customers can easily find and examine your company's products, and place products in that space or position them with as many shelf facings as the store allows (see Exhibit 5.7).

shelf positioning: The physical placement of the product within the retailer's store.

shelf facings: The number of individual products placed beside each other on the shelf.

LO6

Planogram Software

Recognizing the importance of shelf positioning and point-of-purchase displays, companies such as Shelf Logic, PlanoGraphics, and Spaceman have developed *planogram software* to help sales reps, buyers, and merchandisers make the best use of selling space.

A planogram is a blueprint of where products should be placed on display shelves. The software usually stores the width, depth, and height of each product and its SKU, along with an electronically stored visual of the product. The software user can then automatically create a planogram by dragging and dropping products on different shelves while estimating stock turnover and optimal restocking times. Shelf designs can be done in colour, which helps retailers determine how the colours will work together.

The software can further automate the process of calculating the product layout range of the entire category before the layout is produced. This allows the category manager or buyer to determine space allocation for different products while considering sales and margins, and keeping decisions in line with the company's marketing objectives.

For further information, check out the following websites, some of which show the software in action:

- www.shelflogic.com
- www.planographics.com
- www.nielsen.com/intl-campaigns/us/planograms.html

EXHIBIT 5.7

Sales reps know that good shelf positioning and shelf facings boost sales.

Source: © Viorel Dudau/Dreamstime.com/GetStock.com

Premiums

The premium has come a long way from being just a trinket in a Cracker Jack box; today, it is a major marketing tool. Canadian businesses spend millions of dollars on consumer and trade premiums and incentives because premiums create sales.

premium: An article of merchandise offered as an incentive to the user to take some action.

A **premium** is an article of merchandise offered as an incentive for the user to take some action. The premium may act as an incentive to buy, to sample the product, to come into the retail store, or to request further information. Premiums include contests, consumer premiums, and dealer premiums.

LO7

Technology and Selling

For most college and university graduates these days, computers and other sales technologies are not at all intimidating. However, the nontechnical person may be apprehensive about being able to use a computer and its software properly. However, computer manufacturers, software suppliers, and company training programs quickly and effectively train people and provide easy-to-use computer software. The top 10 uses of technology applications by salespeople are shown in Exhibit 5.8.

EXHIBIT 5.8
Here are the top 10 technology applications by salespeople.

TOP 10 TECHNOLOGY APPLICATIONS FOR SALESPEOPLE	
1. Customer/prospect profile	6. Sales presentation
2. Lead tracking	7. Time/territory management
3. Call reports	8. Order entry
4. Sales forecasts	9. Travel and expense reports
5. Sales data analysis	10. Checking inventory/shipping status

If you have little knowledge of technology, start learning! Take an introductory computer course through a local college or university's continuing education program. It is never too late, and since the technology is continuing to evolve, salespeople need to be continuing to learn.

Technology Enhances Sales and Customer Service

Technology is at the heart of salespeople's ability to provide top-quality customer service by receiving and sending out information. Technology is advancing at a rapid pace, and affecting people–including salespeople–in all aspects of their lives (see Exhibit 5.9).

Technology helps salespeople increase their productivity and effectiveness, and allows them to gather and access information more efficiently. You can use computer technology to improve communication to the home office, with others on your sales force, and with customers. Salespeople also use technology to create better strategies for targeting and tracking clients. Sales force automation can be broken down into three broad areas of functionality covering (1) personal productivity, (2) communications, and (3) order processing and customer service.[3]

Personal Productivity

personal productivity: Improvement of an individual's performance through more efficient data storage and retrieval, better time management, and enhanced presentations.

Many programs can help a salesperson increase **personal productivity** through more efficient data storage and retrieval, better time management, and enhanced presentations. Remember that you do business with the one you trust and you trust the one you know. So keep in touch with customers. Let's discuss some of the more popular uses of technology.

EXHIBIT 5.9

By using technology, this salesperson can sell and serve customers no matter what her location.

Source: © Dougal Waters/Getty Images

You do business with the one you trust and you trust the one you know. So keep in touch with your customers.

Customer Relationship Management (CRM) Technology

Customer relationship management (CRM) is a technology system that helps companies manage information about existing and potential customers. Many CRM systems include contact management technology, a listing of all the customer contacts that a salesperson makes in the course of conducting business. The form of the technology is like an electronic collection of business cards and includes such information as the contact's name, title, company, address, phone number, fax number, and email address. It also may include additional information such as the particular industry, date of last order, name of administrative assistant, other key decision makers, and so on (see Exhibit 5.10).

customer relationship management (CRM): A technology system that helps companies manage information about existing and potential customers.

EXHIBIT 5.10

Her cell phone provides information needed about a prospect.

Source: © Ariel Skelley/Blend Images LLC

CUSTOMER RELATIONSHIP MANAGEMENT TECHNOLOGY

You may not be acquainted with the term CRM, but you may be aware of many of the leading providers of CRM technology systems. CRM is the combination of a customer-centred philosophy in the organization supported by technology that often combines sales, marketing, and customer service into one. Common vendors of CRM software include:

- Salesforce
- Microsoft dynamics
- Netsuite

The value of a CRM system lies in its ability to manage knowledge. CRM software often combines sales, marketing, and customer service data into one information technology platform.[4] For example, the CRM system may include insight from the salesperson's colleagues. In some firms, the customer service department may have had interactions with a customer and documented the communication, or the marketing department may have sent the customer an invitation to a webinar and captured this information within the CRM system. CRM technology not only provides a tracking mechanism, it also allows salespeople and their colleagues to share critical information throughout their organization and collaborate more effectively.

Calendar Management

calendar management: Scheduling appointments, telephone calls, or "to-do" lists.

As a salesperson, the most vulnerable asset you have to manage is time. Improvement of time management directly increases productivity. Electronic **calendar management**, as a part of sales force automation, can make time management easier and less prone to errors or oversights.

When a salesperson schedules appointments, telephone calls, or to-do lists on an electronic calendar, the system automatically checks for conflicts, eliminating the need for rescheduling. An electronic calendar can assign a relative priority to each item. It also can create an electronic link between a scheduled event and a particular contact or account so the appointment or call information is accessible as part of the salesperson's calendar, and as part of the contact or account history. Once it can be viewed from different perspectives, the information contained in the calendar becomes much more useful.

For the sales manager, electronic calendar management automatically consolidates information concerning the whereabouts of the entire sales force. Weekly or monthly calendars, which quickly become outdated, have been improved. Now information can be automatically generated when salespeople schedule their appointments. The system also allows salespeople to instantly update their appointments and schedules directly from the field.

Automated Sales Plans, Tactics, and Ticklers

Sales strategies often fall in a sequence of events that can be identified and plotted. A traditional example involves a thank-you letter sent immediately after an initial sales call and a follow-up telephone call three days later. In the sales world, it may be difficult for busy salespeople to track all the details. As a result, important follow-up items sometimes get overlooked. If this happens, a salesperson's diligent prospecting efforts become wasted and valuable prospects are squandered. Today, many sales cycles begin with opportunity alerts that may originate with different social media tools. It could be a response from someone who has read one of your tweets or blogs, or perhaps a contact is made through LinkedIn or Facebook. Regardless of origin, once a contact is identified, technology will allow you to follow through with these contacts to ensure you don't waste time or lose any valuable prospects. For example, a tickler is an automatic reminder to ensure the sales professional sends out a follow-up with a particular prospect.

A sales force automation system begins working as soon as the initial meeting is entered into the system. A few simple commands tell it to remind you to send a thank-you letter and schedule a follow-up phone call. It also can notify the sales manager if these follow-ups are not completed.

Another sales situation might call for a regular follow-up every year or two after the sale, depending on the sales cycle associated with your product. It is particularly easy for follow-up calls like this to be neglected because of the long lead time involved. The problem becomes more apparent if the salesperson who made the original sale leaves the company or is promoted. When that happens, the customer often falls through the cracks, becoming an orphan. Automated sales tactics and ticklers (or reminders) prevent this from happening.

Geographic Information Systems

A **geographic information system (GIS)** allows salespeople to view and analyze customer and/or prospect information on an electronic map. This may be extremely useful if you are visiting an area for the first time. It also can be helpful in a familiar area. Customer information can be accessed directly from contact-management data and sorted accordingly, allowing you to plan sales calls geographically and make the most efficient use of your time. Also, a GIS may reveal customer buying patterns that otherwise may not be apparent.

geographic information system (GIS): Allows salespeople to view and manipulate customer or prospect information on an electronic map.

Computer-Based Presentations

Computer-based presentations can be a powerful presentation tool. PowerPoint presentations with short product video clips provide a means of creating a customized dynamic video and sound discussion of the product.

computer-based presentations: Dramatic and interactive presentations created at relatively low cost with the help of sales force automation using a computer.

Tablets Improve Sales

Tablets allow salespeople to show data and videos about specific products in their presentations to buyers. Likewise, podcasts and other forms of e-learning modules are an excellent way to train salespeople on product knowledge and selling skills. They can provide coaching and practical advice at a moment's notice.[5] Imagine a salesperson preparing to call on a major customer. The video clip enables the seller, while sitting in the customer's waiting room, to review such things as objection handling and closing techniques, as well as a video sales presentation role-play of the product being presented to the buyer. It provides a great way for getting mentally prepared to help someone minutes before being called into the buyer's office.

Communications with Customers and Employer

In the twenty-first century, a company's success hinges on its ability to deliver information quickly to customers and employees. Today's most popular sales force automation systems involve written communication and email.

Written Communication

Written communication plays a large role in the lives of most salespeople. Particularly important is the need for written communication with customers. A thank-you letter or email sent immediately after an initial sales call can often mean the difference between a favourable impression and one that is not as favourable. Sometimes it can even make or break a sale. In spite of its potential impact, salespeople frequently overlook this simple task because they lack an easy way to get it done. There always seem to be other, more pressing things to do.

written communication: A thank-you letter or email mailed immediately after an initial call.

electronic mail (email): Messages sent electronically through a computer system that delivers them immediately to any number of recipients.

Electronic Mail (Email)

Electronic mail (email) allows messages to be sent electronically through a system that delivers them immediately to any number of recipients worldwide. When creating an email to customers, use the same professional writing skills you would in a business letter. Correct grammar, sentence structure, spelling, and content are extremely important in building customer relationships. Also, make sure you send the email to the correct person. An email sent to the wrong customer may surprise and upset the customer. Take care in writing and sending emails.

virtual office: A venue (home, vehicle, hotel room, or even local coffee shop) where salespeople are able to conduct business with the help of technology.

tablet: A general-purpose computer contained in a single panel that uses a touch screen as the input device.

smartphone: A cell phone that also has computer functions including Internet access, calendar management, GPS, email, customer account information, and other advanced functionality.

Customer Order Processing and Service Support

The process of obtaining, generating, and completing an order is much more complicated than it may actually sound. The many steps involved in a manual system may take several days or even weeks to complete and confirm. Automated systems shorten the sales-and-delivery cycle. While in the office with your customer, you can use the Internet to access information and make things happen more efficiently. For example, you can check the inventory status of merchandise on the sales order, receive approval for your client's credit status, and begin the shipping process immediately. Salespeople's automated order entries directly update the company computer without having to be re-entered at the home office.

Salespeople's Virtual Offices

Due to the availability, processing speeds, and expanding reach of technology, salespeople are able to conduct business in a variety of venues that effectively serve as **virtual offices**. For salespeople who need to be constantly in touch with their clients, technology allows a functioning virtual office in the salesperson's home, vehicle, hotel room, or even local coffee shop. Laptops, tablets, cell phones, printers, data services, and WiFi allow salespeople to stay in constant contact with their customers, even when driving between cities or provinces.

Source: © Dave and Les Jacobs/Blend Images LLC

The Value of Mobile Technology

Technology has enabled mobility for salespeople. The average salesperson's cell phone often includes mapping/GPS technology, CRM technology, capabilities for phone and web conferencing, and access to marketing and sales collaterals, such as online brochures or other marketing materials.

Sales force technology and automation come in a variety of sizes and applications. In addition to desktop and laptop computers, **tablets** and **smartphones** are used by salespeople to improve their productivity and connectivity (Exhibit 5.11). The salesperson has immediate access to their appointment schedule, to-do list, opportunity alerts, account information, sales order status, and inventory availability, and contacts are always close at hand in a pocket, purse, or briefcase. Plus their data—including email, important files, and documents—can be transferred or quickly and easily synched between the hand-held device and a laptop or desktop computer.

EXHIBIT 5.11

The tablet has numerous applications.

Source: © Monty Rakusen/Image Source

MAKING THE SALE

THE MODERN BUSINESS CARD—WHAT SHOULD YOU INCLUDE?

Today's business cards often show multiple pieces of contact information. They are, in fact, contact cards. Look at this sample two-sided business card design. Some new design considerations include:

- QR codes that prospects can scan with a smart phone to be linked directly to a company's website
- Links to your social networking sites so your prospects/customers can follow you
- Links to company or other personal blog sites.

Remember, make it easy for your customers to keep in touch.

Your Business Name Here

Logo and/or Tag Line Here

www.mheducation.ca

Your Name

YOUR TITLE

NUMBER AND STREET
CITY, PROVINCE
POSTAL CODE

Company Phone: 555-555-5555
Cell Phone: 444-444-4444
Fax: 333-333-3333
Email: someone@example.ca

Follow me on:

linkdin.com/csrep

twitter.com/csrep

facebook.com/csrep

youtube.com/csrep

Cell Phone Considerations

Millions of people subscribe to wireless service in Canada; it has become an essential tool in sales. Although cellular phones bring significant convenience—such as checking your email, reading and writing your text messages, and **surfing the Internet** from your phone—cell phone etiquette should be practised to avoid interrupting or ruining sales calls and meetings.

surfing the Internet: Exploring the different websites found within the web of links on the Internet.

1. Remember that the person you are with is the most important person to talk to. Whether you are with a customer, a potential buyer, or a supervisor, program

your ringer to vibrate or turn your phone off. You may even decide to let your voicemail take a message or your phone can text the caller to advise them you will return the call at a more convenient time.

2. Use text messaging to simplify your life. If you are expecting important information from a colleague but need to be in a public area, ask her to text you instead.
3. Turn off your phone during meetings, sales calls, and presentations. Talking on the phone during any of these can be disruptive and violates basic courtesy. Just the ring tone or vibration of your phone is enough to interrupt a speaker, so if you are expecting an important call, switch to silent mode and use text messaging.
4. Don't engage in **cell yell**. Yelling on a mobile phone can be offensive to anyone around you. There is no need to speak louder on your mobile phone than you would on any other phone.

cell yell:
Yelling into a cell phone thinking that yelling is necessary to be heard.

SOCIAL MEDIA INSIGHTS FOR SALES PEOPLE

5 MOBILE APPS TO KEEP YOUR SALES TEAM PRODUCTIVE

Sales is a fast moving part of business and it does not let up. For many sales teams, they are in front of customers and prospects and use mobile apps to get things done quickly and conveniently. Thus, it is important for salespeople to remain productive when they are not in front of a computer. Otherwise, there can be a lot of forgotten tasks and missed opportunities to further relationships and close deals.

Here are five mobile apps that can help your sales efforts and ways to use them strategically.

1. **Evernote** – When you have an idea or find resources, you need a place to put these notes. Evernote is a digital notebook that syncs between all of your devices. A salesperson can quickly take notes with their own texting. Furthermore, documents can be scanned and the image can be digitized for convenient searching later. This is a quick and easy way to catalogue meeting notes and resources to make the sale.
2. **Reeder** – This is an easy-to-use RSS (Really Simple Syndication) reader for blogs. Salespeople need to be tuned into industry news and use this as part of their follow-up and customer engagements. Reeder allows for quick reading of relevant industry publications and blogs. Sharing is easy and your team can read their personal daily news and easily share this with prospects they are trying to touch base with and customers they are maintaining relationships with. It allows you to be current and continually be a resource of information.
3. **Dropbox** – Your sales documents and files need to be easy to access and easy to store. Dropbox is one of the simplest and most user friendly applications that syncs your computer, tablet and mobile devices without any management. When you are trying to get out marketing materials or sales presentations to prospective customers, you can send or share these files without any headaches.
4. **Recorder** – So many things happen in conversation quickly. A salesperson can use this mobile app to record important conversations, get customer testimonials to use for future sales opportunities or record thoughts while in the car. The audio files can be shared, saved or used later in a variety of ways for marketing projects. Being top of mind and in real-time can create the authentic connection and build trust in a sales engagement with strangers that need proof of your success.
5. **SlideRocket** – You want to be ready with your sales presentations any time anywhere. SlideRocket syncs with an online account where your slide presentations exist. You can create a slide deck explaining your company, product and services and then share them out easily or present right from your mobile device. You are then positioned to give a visual presentation at any time and share it with people that are interested in what you do. Keep a library of presentations to explain and clarify what you do with this integrated application.

We can always become more productive. These five mobile apps can become quick, convenient, and reliable tools that help your team sell more without having to spend cycles on their computers. The power of using mobile apps in a natural sales process can equip your salespeople to remain plugged in while they work on the go. Once you get these installed, continue exploring how to collaborate, share, and drive sales by using the apps creatively.

5. Consider using a lock code on your phone. This will not only make data more secure but also will prevent incidents of "pocket dialling," in which your phone places an unintended call that you are unaware of, which can lead to potentially embarrassing situations with important clients.
6. Do not use your cell phone while driving. In many jurisdictions, distracted driving laws prohibit people from using hand-held technological devices while driving. Most cars now have hands-free services that can help you to stay safe if it is truly necessary to use your phone while driving.

Technology Essentials for the Modern Salesperson

There is so much technology and so many software applications available to modern salespeople that it is difficult to keep up with it. In Chapter 4, we discussed some of the tools available to enhance the communication between salespeople, their companies, and their customers. We will continue discussion of these applications throughout the text to highlight where they can be used throughout the sales cycle.

Some of the top technological areas that modern salespeople should be well versed in are social networking, blogging, customer relationship management, smart phones, and presentation technology.

Social Networking

social networking: Meeting and communicating with different people, often done using the Internet.

Social networking is becoming a very important tool for salespeople. No longer must you attend endless social and business engagements just for the purpose of prospecting. With social networking, you can accomplish better results in far less time. For example, you exchange contacts with your LinkedIn network. You may then discover that someone you've been trying to reach is in a friend's network, in which case you're a little closer to establishing that first communication.

Facebook is a very popular social networking site that is used by many salespeople in different ways. It can be used to create awareness and supply information about you, your product, your company, and your industry. You can engage your contacts by encouraging discussion and comments and having them rate ("like") your products. You can often build a relationship with visitors which may provide you with many opportunities to encourage a purchase. If these things are done well, you may develop long-term relationships with your followers.

Instagram, Twitter, and Snapchat can also be used to build a relationship with your customers. It is essential to understand your customer's social media habits in order to use the best social media platform. With any of these social media tools, it is important to drive people to your website(s). Include these tools on any of your marketing communication to increase the likelihood that they will drop in for a visit.

Blogging

Using sites like Twitter or even your own company-sponsored site, you can share your thoughts with anyone who will listen by blogging. For example, some salespeople use Twitter to respond quickly to customer complaints and/or to answer customer questions. They use it to communicate upcoming promotions or introduce new products. Salespeople can use corporate blogs to provide expertise in a particular business field, build an email subscriber list, or provide testimonials from satisfied customers. All of these techniques can help to start and to maintain business relationships.

Customer Relationship Management

There are many customer relationship management (CRM) options available to salespeople today, whether online, stand-alone, or proprietary. The functionality of most of these tools is phenomenal. It is imperative that modern salespeople not shy away from these tools as they can lead to huge increases in productivity and efficiency. They allow salespeople to stay in touch, stay organized, and have access to all the information they need to help them close more sales. With an effective CRM tool, it will never be necessary to respond to a customer with, "I'll have to let you know!"

The Cloud

Cloud:
A technology approach that enables a more mobile, portable opportunity for salespeople by allowing access to software anywhere, as long as the individual is connected to the Internet.

What is the **cloud?** You are probably already using it. Do you use Google docs, Dropbox, or Office 365? These are all online, cloud-based applications.

Previously, firms and their employees needed to have software downloaded on their computers, or firms managed their own servers. Now, firms contract with companies that are responsible for the software applications and hardware technology. Thus, employees only need to access the Internet, enter their username and password, and open the appropriate software application.

The cloud has enabled a more mobile, portable opportunity for salespeople. The cloud allows access to software anywhere, as long as the individual is connected to the Internet. Today's salesperson can access CRM technology, order processing, and other important purchasing and background data from their tablet, smartphone, or other computing device.

Smartphones

As you have already read and probably already know, with the number of applications available today there are not many things that you can't do with a smartphone. Applications include GPS, calendar managers, Internet access, video conferencing, instant messaging, weather forecasts, and a plethora of other applications. They are an invaluable tool for salespeople to have today.

Presentation Technology

PowerPoint, by Microsoft, is the norm these days, but several other vendors have developed applications to make your presentations much more engaging. You can incorporate voice-overs, motion, animations, and other touches that will make your presentation stand out.

Prezi:
A cloud-based presentation software package that allows salespeople to design engaging presentations.

Prezi is another presentation package that is becoming popular. Their USP is: *Present anywhere, anytime.* Prezi is cloud-based, meaning you can present from your browser, desktop, tablet or smartphone and always have the latest version of your work at your fingertips. Create or edit on the go, then auto-sync across all your devices with ease.

Summary of Major Selling Issues

Company knowledge includes information on a firm's history, development policies, procedures, products, distribution, promotion, and pricing. A salesperson also must know the competition, the industry, and the economy. This knowledge can build self-confidence.

Wholesalers and retailers stock thousands of products, which often makes it difficult to support any one manufacturer's products the way the manufacturer wants. To aid channel members in selling products, manufacturers offer assistance in advertising, sales promotion aids, and pricing allowances. In addition, many manufacturers spend millions of dollars to compel consumers and industrial buyers to purchase from channel members and the manufacturer.

National, retail, trade, industrial, and direct-mail advertising create demand for products and are powerful selling tools for the salesperson during sales presentations. Sales promotion activities and materials are another potential selling tool for the salesperson to use when selling to consumer and industrial buyers. Samples, coupons, contests, premiums, demonstrations, and displays are effective sales promotion techniques employed to help sell merchandise.

The salesperson should be able to discuss price, discounts, and credit policies confidently with customers. Customers want to know the salesperson's list and net price, and whether there are any transportation charges. Discounts (quantity, cash, trade, or consumer) represent important buying incentives for the buyer. The buyer also wants to know the terms of payment. The salesperson needs to understand company credit policies to open new accounts, see that customers pay on time, and collect overdue bills. See Appendix A for additional discussions on pricing.

Finally, success in sales requires knowledge of the many technologies used to sell and service customers. Computers, texting, email, cell phones, smartphones, social media, the Internet, and the cloud have quickly become part of the professional's sales kit.

ETHICAL DILEMMA

USING "TWEETS" IN SALES

Alex Serpino works as a manufacturer's agent representing three different food producers in a large Western Canadian market. He prides himself on keeping abreast of everything going on in his industry so he can relay that information to his customers. Having recently upgraded his computer literacy, Alex has been introduced to the world of Twitter. He thinks this will be a wonderful tool for him to share his industry knowledge and educate readers about the food business. This has been working well, and Alex has come up with a new idea. He thinks that if he carefully mentions some of the shortcomings of his competitors in his tweets, it might attract more customers to him.

Is this something Alex should consider? After all, it could improve his business.

MEETING A SALES CHALLENGE

To be successful, salespeople need to be knowledgeable. However, being an expert on the product is only part of what it takes to be a top performer. You also need to know how to use good communication and selling skills.

We now know that empathy is a critical skill for relationship building and effective selling.

It's all about benefits. Sure, this seller wants to sell her customers a good product, but the reseller is possibly more interested in whether she can sell the product once she buys it, and how much money she will make. Resellers are "bottom-line" oriented; because they want to know what's in it for them, they concentrate on discussing return on investment. If you empathized with her, you would have realized this and probably changed your presentation to make these very valid points.

PLAYING THE ROLE

The situation: Two salespeople are debating the issue of modern technology and its use in selling. Assume the role of one of them and prepare arguments to support their position. Then, informally debate the issue using your supporting arguments.

Role A: "Old-World Sales Rep." Your feelings are that technology is taking the personal touch out of selling and is turning off too many customers.

Role B: "Modern Sales Rep." You feel that technology has too many benefits **not** to be used by the professional salesperson.

Key Terms for Selling

advantage
benefit
benefit selling
blogs
calendar management
cell yell
cloud
computer-based presentations
consumer sales promotion
customer relationship management (CRM)
electronic mail (email)
FAB selling technique
feature
geographic information system
markup
personal productivity
premium
Prezi
price
sales training
shelf facings
shelf positioning
smartphones
social networking
surfing the Internet
tablets
three realms
trade sales promotion
unique selling proposition (USP)
virtual office
written communication

Sales Application Questions

1. A salesperson's knowledge needs to extend into many areas such as knowledge about the company; product; upcoming advertising and promotional campaigns; company price, discount, and credit policies; the competition; the industry; and the economy. These are all vital for sales success. For each of these categories, explain how a salesperson's knowledge can lay the groundwork for successful selling.
2. How do salespeople generally acquire their sales knowledge?
3. Explain how a salesperson's knowledge can be converted into selling points used in the sales presentation. Give two examples.
4. A salesperson must have a good understanding of the competition, customers, and everything connected with the company. Why should a salesperson take time to be up-to-date on facts about the economy and the industry?
5. What is the difference between a product's shelf positioning and its shelf facings? How can a salesperson maximize both shelf positioning and shelf facings? Why is this important?
6. Companies use numerous premiums in their efforts to market products. Why? What types of premiums do they use? How can a salesperson use a premium offer in a sales presentation to a wholesaler or a retailer?
7. In the following statements, write down each idea that is a benefit:
   a. Counsellor talking to a student: "To improve your science grade, Susie, you must establish better study habits."
   b. Construction supervisor talking to a worker: "That job will be a great deal easier, Joe, and you won't be as tired when you go home nights if you use that little truck over there."
   c. Father talking to his son: "You will make a lot of friends, Johnny, and be respected at school if you learn how to play the piano."
   d. Banker talking to customer: "If you open this special checking account, Ms. Brown, paying your bills will be much easier."
8. In the following statements, determine what parts of each statement are features, advantages, or benefits:
   a. Hardware sales representative to homeowner: "Blade changing is quick and easy with this saw because it has a push-button blade release."
   b. Consumer sales representative to grocery store buyer: "The king-size package of Tide will bring in additional profits because it is the fastest selling, most economical size."

c. Clothing salesperson to customer: "For long wear and savings on your clothing costs, you can't beat these slacks. All the seams are double-stitched and the material is 100 percent Dacron."

9. Indicate which of the following statements is a feature, advantage, or benefit:
   a. Made of pure vinyl.
   b. Lasts twice as long as competing brands.
   c. It's quick-frozen at 30 °C below zero.
   d. Available in small, medium, and large sizes.
   e. New.
   f. No unpleasant aftertaste.
   g. Saves time, work, and money.
   h. Approved by Underwriters Laboratories (UL).
   i. Gives 20 percent more kilometres to the litre.
   j. Contains XR-10.
   k. Baked fresh daily.
   l. Includes a one-year guarantee on parts and labour.
   m. Is packed 48 units, or eight six-packs, to the case.
   n. Guaranteed to increase your sales by 10 percent.
   o. Adds variety to your meal planning.
10. Consider the following information:

    The DESKTOP XEROX 2300 copier is a versatile model that delivers the first copy in six seconds. It is also the lowest-priced new Xerox copier available. The 2300 is designed as a general purpose office copier and occupies less than half the top of a standard desk. The new unit copies on a full range of office materials as large as 8½ by 14 inches. A special feature is its ability to reproduce 5½ by 8½-inch billing statements from the same tray used for letter-size or legal-size paper. Selling price of the 2300 will be as low as $3,495 and rentals as low as $60 a month on a two-year contract without a copy allowance.

    What are the features, advantages, and benefits of the DESKTOP XEROX 2300 copier? List two additional features, advantages, and benefits that a Xerox salesperson could use in presenting the new copier to a prospective buyer.
11. Several features of a car are listed below. Match each feature with its corresponding benefit(s):
    a. Low hoodline:
       I. Better visibility
       II. Economy
       III. Quick start-up
    b. Tinted glass:
       I. Reflects sunlight
       II. Reduces eyestrain
       III. Reduces glare from sun
    c. Rear window defroster:
       I. Clears rear windshield and thus reduces the danger of driving on a cold, foggy day
       II. Rear windshield can be deiced or defogged automatically so you do not have to do it yourself
       III. Increases the cost of the car by $250
    d. Whitewall tires:
       I. Provide better handling and a more stable ride
       II. More appealing to the eye
       III. Increase the life of your tires
12. Consumer sales promotion and trade sales promotion try to increase sales to consumers and resellers, respectively. Several promotional techniques follow; classify each item as a consumer or trade promotional technique and give an example for each one. Can any of the promotions be used for both consumers and the trade?
    a. Coupons on or inside packages
    b. Free installation (premium)
    c. Displays
    d. Sales contests
    e. Drawings for gifts
    f. Demonstrations
    g. Samples

Sales Online Exercise

Business Intelligence: Can the Web Help?

A few clicks of the mouse can provide an avalanche of free—but priceless—information about competitors, or you can use these links to access other useful information, Useful websites include:

www.news.excite.com	www.fuld.com	www.scip.org
www.canada411.com	www.hoovers.com	www.sedar.com
www.linkedin.com	www.individual.com	www.theweathernetwork.com
www.411.ca	www.mapquest.ca	www.viamichelin.com

Research one or more companies you have an interest in working for or that you know or have worked for in the past.

Further Exploring the Sales World

Choose one of the following products:

- GPS
- iPod
- Cell phone

Now, let's practise **uncovering relevant benefits**. Start by considering the product's attributes:

- **Features** - What does the product offer? "This application handles multiple users concurrently."
- **Advantages** - What do the features do? "This application provides essential information in real time."
- **Benefits** - What do the features mean? "This information will allow your managers to keep their fingers on the company's financial pulse at all times."
- **Needs** - What do the features satisfy? "This feature will provide cost savings, control, and efficiency."
  1. Develop a FAB worksheet for your selected product as you would present it to a fellow student working in a retail store.
  2. Develop a FAB worksheet for your selected product as you would present it to a purchasing agent for an electronics store if you were representing a manufacturer.

feature:
Any tangible or intangible characteristic of a product.

advantage:
The performance characteristic of a product that describes how it can be used or how it will help the buyer.

benefit:
A favourable result the buyer receives from the product because of a particular advantage that has the ability to satisfy a buyer's need.

needs:
The basic requirements of human life—food and water, shelter, clothing, security, interaction with others, and self-fulfillment .

Student Application Learning Exercises (SALES)

SALES are meant to help you construct the various segments of your sales presentation. SALES build on one another so that as you complete each exercise you are constructing more of your sales presentation.

Part 3

A. Develop a feature/advantage/benefit worksheet for the product that you have selected to sell.

After reviewing Parts 1 and 2 of this SALES exercise in Chapters 3 and 4, for each FAB package that you list, identify the prospect need that you are attempting to satisfy. Use four columns as shown.

Sample Worksheet for Photocopier Prospect

Need	Feature	Advantage	Benefit
Increased productivity	High-speed processing	Will produce 100 copies per minute	Less time wasted at photocopier—higher productivity
Improve company's image	High-resolution, full-colour capability	Produces crisp, high-quality colour photocopies	Customers who look at your copied material will be impressed by its high quality

B. Review the section of the chapter dealing with developing a USP. Based on this information and the highlights of your FAB worksheet, develop an appropriate USP for your presentation.

Selling Experiential Exercise

Many people think that because they use a computer to email their friends and surf the net, that they are technological geniuses. Modern salespeople have all kinds of technology at their disposal that can enhance their selling effectiveness greatly. Take the following informal test by reading each statement then rating your level of agreement from 10 (fully agree) to 1 (disagree). On a separate sheet of paper, write the number that best describes you for each statement.

How technologically savvy are you?	Fully Agree 10	Disagree 1
1. I use email extensively to stay in touch with acquaintances.		
2. I use social media to communicate my daily activities.		
3. My cell phone is of the very latest technology.		
4. I have a LinkedIn account and update it frequently.		
5. I keep track of my social contacts daily using Facebook.		
6. I tweet regularly and follow others' tweets.		
7. I regularly use a tablet.		
8. I use technology to help keep my life organized.		
9. I use social media technology for research (weather, movie listings, etc.)		
10. If I had no access to technology, I would feel lost.		
	Total your score	

Results - If you scored:

- 80 to 100 - You would likely have no trouble adapting to the many technology based sales tools available today.
- 60 to 79 - You get by but could probably use a little more exposure to newer technologies.
- Less than 60 - You could certainly update your technical skills for the modern world. Perhaps you just prefer to communicate the old-fashioned way. To be an effective salesperson, you will likely have to modernize.

While not a scientific exercise, this will serve to get you thinking about where you stand in the world of Sales 2.0 relative to many of your peers.

CASE 5–1

TECHNOPHOBIA

Alyssia Perri had always been considered a top-notch sales rep and had been a top performer in her company for many years. She had a wonderful personality and was a terrific conversationalist. She always went out of her way to provide outstanding service to her many customers in the office furniture industry. She was thought of as a typical old-style sales rep. Her kids were all grown now and Alyssia planned to retire in about 10 years. She was ready to put in 10 solid years of selling to build her retirement nest-egg.

Alyssia made it her job to keep up to date on all of her company's product lines. She was often seen at her desk flipping through furniture catalogues. As good as she was, her sales numbers had been pretty steady over the last few years. It was strange, though, that many of the newer salespeople, with much less product knowledge, were able to sell more product than Alyssia was able to. She was becoming a little worried about this, so she approached Jim, her sales manager, to seek some advice. After a good discussion, Jim suggested that he shadow Alyssia for a day and observe her in action–she agreed and they decided that Tuesday would be the best day.

Tuesday

8:00 a.m. Alyssia arrived a little early to go over her appointments for the day.

8:30 a.m. Alyssia and her manager departed for her 9:00 appointment, which was in the neighbouring town. This was a first-time meeting. She had checked the address on her map before she left but then ran into a detour just outside of town. It meant a short delay but then Alyssia got disoriented and had trouble finding her destination. Luckily, Jim had brought his smartphone and was able to use the GPS feature to help navigate her to her customer's business. However, they still arrived about 10 minutes late. She apologized, then continued with the presentation.

9:45 a.m. Off to the next appointment. She had to backtrack back to near her office, then head off in a different direction to arrive at her 10:30 appointment. This one seemed to go a little better. Alyssia was showing her prospect some catalogues to gain an understanding of what he might be interested in. The customer mentioned that he had seen some pictures of some very nice furniture on one of Alyssia's competitors' Facebook pages, and wondered if Alyssia had anything like it. She didn't have that information with her so promised the prospect that she would get back to him as soon as possible.

10:45 a.m. Alyssia flipped through her appointment book to check on the address of her next customer. She then pored over her city map to get an idea of just where it was. They headed off, hoping to arrive on time for her 11:30 appointment. They just made it on time but upon check-in, the secretary informed Alyssia that the meeting had had to be cancelled and that they hadn't been able to contact her before she arrived.

11:00 a.m. Jim and Alyssia were sitting in the car and decided that they should take an early lunch, given that the appointment had been cancelled. They weren't familiar with the area and didn't know what was good there, so they simply went to a local fast food establishment.

1:00 p.m. After a long lunch, they headed off to Alyssia's last appointment of the day. This one had promise. Near the end of her conversation with the buyer, the buyer simply said, "Alyssia, if you can have 100 desks and chairs delivered by Friday, we've got a deal." Alyssia wasn't sure of her inventory status so promised the customer that she would call him as soon as she returned to head office later in the day, Her sales manager said, "Hold on there, Alyssia, give me a moment." He pulled out his smartphone, logged into the company's intranet, found 147 desk and office sets in inventory, then assigned them to this particular account. He simply stated that "The deal is done–they'll be here." Alyssia looked dumbfounded and appreciative at the same time.

On the way back to the office, Jim had the following conversation with Alyssia:

Jim: "Alyssia, do you have a cell phone?"

Alyssia: "Yes I do, but I don't use it that much–it seems too impersonal."

Jim: "What about a GPS unit?"

Alyssia: "Well I've heard of them but didn't think I'd be able to figure out how to use one."

Jim was sensing a pattern here so decided that he'd like to meet with her the following day regarding some tips he could give her to help her increase her sales. She agreed.

QUESTIONS

1. What do you think Jim is going to tell Alyssia?
2. Can you recommend some technologies that would help Alyssia to increase her sales? List as many ideas as you can. How would she use them?
3. Do you think she'll "buy in" to using this technology? Why or why not?

PART THREE

The Relationship Selling Process

This section of the text explores the fundamental elements of the selling process. It provides step-by-step coverage of how a professional salesperson would perform the sales function. It all begins with finding prospects that you can sell to. It then describes the steps necessary to turn these prospects into long-term customers.

Within the process, you will learn how to: plan your sales call, make an effective presentation, deal with resistance, close the sale, follow up, and provide service after the sale.

This part includes:

Source: © Pressmaster | Dreamstime.com

CHAPTER 6

Prospecting—The Lifeblood of Selling

Erik van Ees
University of Waterloo,
Waterloo, Ontario.
Source: Courtesy of Erik van Ees

A Sales Success Story

Erik van Ees started his career in sales during university by founding and co-founding start-ups and creating sales processes from scratch. While completing his studies in psychology and business at the University of Waterloo, he worked part-time selling his start-up's mental health kits to post-secondary institutions throughout Canada and the United States (mostly online).

Instead of a typical sales route involving formal training, Erik developed his sales knowledge through reading books, finding mentors, taking sales courses where he could, and hard-earned experience: cold calling, in-person meetings, crafting emails, and building and understanding sales processes. Erik moved from one role to the next while carefully crafting his sales experience until he gained enough for a full-time position upon graduation from the business program at the University of Waterloo in 2018. Now Erik works in business development, selling SaaS software to some of the largest financial, professional services, and tech companies at PostBeyond, a tech start-up in downtown Toronto.

Erik's passion for psychology led him to discover his passion for sales. Like psychology, sales is both a science and an art. Understanding people, what their pain is and how to solve it, how to build trust and relationships, and how to challenge people's beliefs and do it effectively require data and experimentation, along with smooth execution. According to Erik, "You earn the right to be excellent at what you do. It's true in sports, in politics, in music, and business, and it's true in sales."

MAIN TOPICS

The Sales Process Has 10 Steps

Steps before the Sales Presentation

Prospecting—The Lifeblood of Selling

How to Qualify a Prospect

Prospecting Methods

Prospecting Using Social Media

Prospecting Guidelines

Referrals

Applying CRM Technology to Prospecting

How Is Prospecting Changing?

LEARNING OBJECTIVES

In this chapter, we examine the first step in the sales process—prospecting. After studying this chapter, you should be able to:

LO1 Define and describe the 10 steps in the sales process.

LO2 Explain why prospecting can be considered the "lifeblood of selling."

LO3 Defend the importance of prospecting.

LO4 Demonstrate how to properly qualify a prospect.

LO5 Describe the various methods of prospecting.

LO6 Describe how social networking can be used as a prospecting tool.

LO7 Explain some guidelines for prospecting.

LO8 Describe the importance of referrals to a salesperson's success.

LO9 Explain how to apply CRM technology to prospecting.

LO10 Describe how prospecting is changing.

FACING A SALES CHALLENGE

Joe, a business graduate, and two of his friends, Alex and Kathryn, engineering graduates, participated in a university innovation competition during their last semester in college. Building on the applications of IOT (Internet of Things), they pitched an idea for a home security system. The idea met with such positive feedback, the team started the business the following summer. With much excitement they started developing the business plan. The product is suitable for people who are not ready for an expensive dedicated security system. Their proposed system lets people monitor their homes with indoor and outdoor security cameras, video doorbells, and smart locks from anywhere using routine gadgets such as a phone or tablet. However, as they moved forward, things were not looking as simple anymore!

On a fine Thursday afternoon, all three partners sat down for their weekly business planning meeting. Joe said, "Selling a new technology-enabled home security system in our market will not be easy for us. The city has only 45,000 households; the county has 55,000. Yet there are eight or more companies offering home security systems in the area. I'm not sure where to begin."

Kathryn joined in the conversation, saying, "Moreover, many homes in the area already have home security systems in place. So, I'm not sure we can count on promoting to them. We're going to have to explore new territories, knock on doors, and dial-for-dollars to even come up with leads."

Alex broke in with, "Let's go after the market leader. They have the biggest market share in our area. We need to hit them head-on."

"No way," replied Joe. "We could get creamed if we got into a war by attacking the biggest competitor or any of our other competitors. But with easy-to-use features," Joe continued, "excellent service and support, and our fair price on a state-of-the-art home security system, we can develop our market share."

"Hold it, hold it," Kathryn said. "Let's start over and develop a plan that will allow us to uncover as many prospects as quickly as we can. After all, we need to push this new product and get the competitive edge before the competition knows what hit 'em."

If you were one of these young entrepreneurs, how would you respond? What would be your sales plan?

(Continued at end of chapter.)

EXHIBIT 6.1

The selling process has 10 important steps.

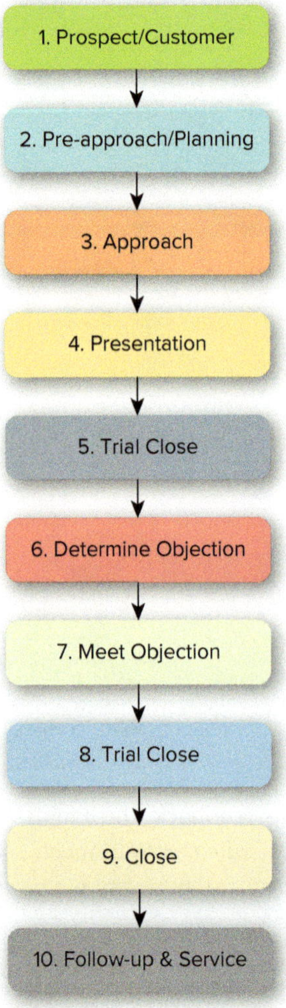

The first two parts of this book give much of the background a salesperson needs for making an actual presentation. However, you can be the most knowledgeable person on topics such as buyer behaviour, competitors, and product information, yet still have difficulty being a successful salesperson unless you are thoroughly prepared for each part of the sales call. In Part 3, we begin by reviewing the sales process and discussing methods of prospecting that can help salespeople plan their sales program.

LO1 The Sales Process Has 10 Steps

As discussed in Chapter 1, the sales process refers to a sequence of actions by the salesperson that leads toward the customer taking a desired action and ends with a follow-up to ensure purchase satisfaction. Although many factors may influence how a salesperson makes a presentation in a particular situation, a logical sequence of steps can greatly increase the chances of a sale. These 10 steps are listed in Exhibit 6.1. Step 1 is discussed in this chapter, and the others are discussed in greater detail in upcoming chapters. Steps 3 through 9 make up the sales presentation itself. Before a sales presentation can be attempted, several important preparatory activities should be carried out.

Many types of selling require prospecting. Without previous knowledge of who might purchase a product, the salesperson locates individuals and/or organizations that have the money, authority, and the desire to buy. Because people tend to do business with the people they know and who they feel are honest and ethical, prospecting is not easy. Buying from a stranger is getting harder and harder. People want to trust the person they buy from and they buy from people they know.

All salespeople who begin their sales careers prospecting look forward to the day when most of their sales come from existing customers. Frequently, these salespeople gain new customers through referrals from customers. Referrals are earned by demonstrating your integrity, trustfulness, and character to the customer who eventually provides you with the referral. Ethical service builds relationships and is based upon the truth.

Steps before the Sales Presentation

As indicated in Exhibit 6.2, successful salespeople prospect; this involves obtaining an appointment with the prospect and planning the sales interview before the meeting. Like a successful lawyer, the salesperson does a great deal of background work before meeting the judge–the prospect. A general rule states that a good sales process involves 40 percent preparation, 20 percent presentation, and 40 percent follow-up, especially when selling large accounts. At Xerox, the national account manager will spend up to 18 months preparing a detailed description of a potential national account. This report, which can easily end up being 50 pages long, is basically a business plan for selling the prospect. Thus preparation time for this sales call would be greater than the 40 percent general rule.[1]

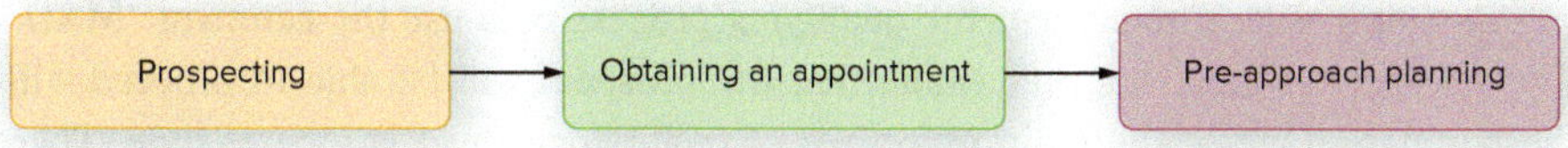

EXHIBIT 6.2
Before the sales presentation.

Prospecting—The Lifeblood of Selling

LO2

Why Prospect?

Prospecting is the first step in the selling process. A **prospect** is a qualified person or organization that has the potential to buy your good or service. **Prospecting** is the lifeblood of sales because it identifies potential customers. A salesperson must look constantly for new prospects for two reasons:

1. To increase sales
2. To replace customers that will be lost over time

prospect: A qualified person or organization that has the potential to buy a salesperson's product or service.

prospecting: The process of identifying potential customers.

Exhibit 6.3 illustrates the importance of prospecting by using the analogy of a Ferris wheel. The **Ferris-wheel concept** compares prospecting to the management of a Ferris wheel; as riders (customers) exit the Ferris wheel, the attendant (salesperson) must replace them in order to keep the ride profitable. Look closely at the many reasons that customers may be lost each year.

EXHIBIT 6.3
The Ferris-wheel concept.

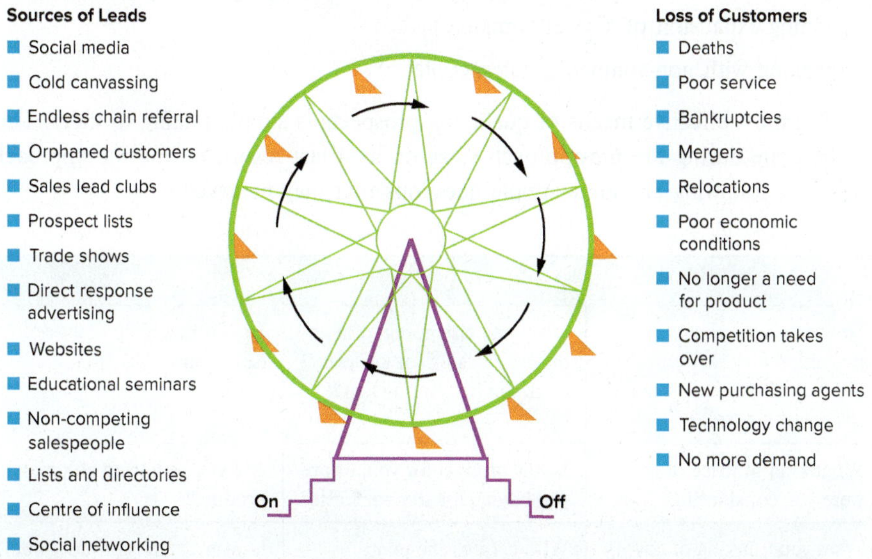

This diagram illustrates the **"Ferris-wheel" concept** of prospecting. Notice that there are nearly as many opportunities for prospects to get off the Ferris wheel as there are for getting on. If salespeople do not work diligently to keep the wheel full, there will be few customers left after a while.

"Ferris wheel" concept: An analogy that compares prospecting to the management of a ferris wheel; as riders (customers) exit the ferris wheel, the attendant (salesperson) must replace them in order to keep the ride profitable.

LO3

The Importance of Prospecting

lead:
A person or organization that might be a prospect.

qualified prospect:
A prospect who has the financial resources to pay, the authority to make the buying decision, and a desire for the product.

MAD:
An acronym for the three questions that determine whether a prospect is a qualified one; a qualified prospect needs the money, authority, and desire to buy.

Prospecting is the first step in the selling process. Salespeople are usually able to obtain **leads**, which are simply the names of individuals who may have a need for the salesperson's product. For some types of salespeople, effective prospecting is the key to their livelihood as salespeople; for others, leads are simply provided for them to follow up on. To be a prospect, a lead must be a qualified person or company that has the potential to buy a salesperson's product or service. To become a **qualified prospect** then, the following must be determined:

1. Does the prospect have the **M**oney to buy?
2. Does the prospect have the **A**uthority to buy?
3. Does the prospect have the **D**esire to buy?

A simple way to remember the qualifying process is to use the acronym "**MAD**." The salesperson must first determine that the prospect will be able to proceed with the purchase. One of the main objectives of qualifying a lead is to save time. There is no point preparing and planning a major presentation to a prospect who has no money or doesn't have the authority to make a decision.

To understand prospecting, remember old westerns. After equipping themselves with the knowledge and resources needed, gold prospectors stake out a claim (establishes a sales territory) on a piece of land where the likelihood of finding gold (customers) is high. The process may involve scraping the bed of a stream with a pan to lift out silt (leads). By sifting the silt (leads), prospectors are eliminating the debris (unqualified) and ideally are left with real gold (qualified prospects) that they can cash in.

LO4

How to Qualify a Prospect

To save time and effort, all leads should be subjected to the qualification process. Necessary information can be obtained using several means:

- Asking the referral for information
- Researching the company prospectus and other materials
- Keeping your industry knowledge up to date (perhaps you have read about a pending expansion of a local company)
- Speaking with non-competing salespeople

The most effective means of qualifying prospects is simply talking to them. This can be done during the pre-approach stage or, as a last resort, during the approach stage. The following are some simple questions that may be asked.

MONEY	AUTHORITY	DESIRE
How much were you budgeting for this type of purchase? Are you prepared to spend this budget?	Is anyone else going to be in on the decision, or are you the main decision maker?	How urgently do you need this product?
What kind of price range were you considering?	Is this product for you, or are you buying for someone else?	Are you replacing an older product?
Were you thinking of paying cash for this or financing it?	Who is (are) the main decision maker(s) for this purchase?	Is your current product not satisfying you anymore?

If the lead cannot be qualified, you may waste a great deal of time pursuing leads that will not or cannot become customers. Do not make assumptions about MAD–ask.

Motive, Means, and Opportunity: Another Way of Looking at Qualifying

As discussed, a primary reason for proper qualification is to allocate your resources (time) efficiently. Ultimately, salespeople need to find out *why* someone would buy something in the first place, and *how* they could buy it if they wanted to.

Motives

In Chapter 3, we discussed why people buy. In terms of qualifying, a salesperson needs to have an understanding of the prospect's business, its goals and objectives, and its performance relative to these goals. If there is a discrepancy between where the business is or is heading and where it should be, then a solution is needed. This is where salespeople often come in, asking qualifying questions:

- Why does this discrepancy create a problem?
- Why did it occur?
- Why haven't you acted before?
- What would happen if we solved this problem?
- Why invest in this problem rather than other investments?
- Are there any risks in solving this problem?
- Can someone else in the company solve this problem?
- Is it really important that you do something about it?

The answers to these questions will reveal many different types of buying motives, both corporate and personal.

Means

Once the motive is established, you need to qualify for means, or ability to buy. Qualifying questions include the following:

- Can you afford my proposed solution?
- How will you justify the purchase?
- Will it ultimately be approved? How?
- How will you pay for it or finance it?
- Is there a third party involved (lender, etc.)?
- Who will ultimately give approval?
- Are all resources in place to use my solution?
- Will you get good value and will you provide us with referrals?

Opportunity

Once the motive and means are identified, it is up to you to provide the opportunity to buy. If the motives and means are present, it is certainly worth your effort to get the solution implemented. However, if the prospect's means and motives are not entirely present then you will have to weigh your efforts carefully. Perhaps you could consider ending your efforts here to avoid wasting time.

Salespeople may be tempted to leave the tough questions–such as "How will the purchase be financed?"–until the end of the sales process; however, these details should be handled as early as possible because tension and the perception of risk will increase toward the end of the sales cycle.

Where to Find Prospects

Prospecting requires both creativity and diligence on the part of the salesperson. Sources of prospects can be many and varied or few and similar, depending on the service or good sold. Naturally, people selling different services and goods might not use the same sources for prospects. A salesperson of oil-field pipe supplies would make extensive use of various industry directories in a search for names of drilling companies. A life insurance salesperson would use personal acquaintances and current customers as sources of prospects. A pharmaceutical salesperson would scan the local newspaper looking for announcements of new physicians and hospital, medical office, and clinical laboratory openings. A sales representative for a company such as General Mills or Quaker Oats would watch for announcements of the construction of new grocery stores and shopping centres.

MAKING THE SALE

SHIFT PROSPECTING INTO A HIGHER GEAR

Many salespeople feel the pressure to manage their own lead generation and increase sales levels, which often involves having to regroup and rethink current prospecting practices. This is not always an easy task for salespeople, so they may need to shift into the next gear. They need not radically depart from current prospecting methods, but should rethink how these methods could be made more efficient. Ask these questions:

- Are you concentrating on leads with the best potential?
- Are you being empathetic and looking at your prospects through their eyes with an understanding of their critical needs and issues?
- Have you defined your ideal customer—those consistent with your current best customers, thus creating a better close ratio?
- Have you improved the timing of your call by researching your prospects' buying cycles? (How and when do they purchase products? Is there a buying centre? What time(s) of the year do they evaluate and/or buy?)
- Are you calling on the right people—those decision makers whose approval will improve your odds?
- Have you created a strong business proposition so that prospects in higher levels of an organization will give you the time of day?

Planning a Prospecting Strategy

Frequently, salespeople, especially new ones, have difficulty prospecting. Meeting strangers and asking them to buy something can be uncomfortable. To be successful, prospecting requires a strategy. Like most skills, prospecting can constantly be improved by a dedicated salesperson. Some salespeople charge themselves with finding X number of prospects per week. Indeed, in many companies the sales force is asked to allocate a portion of each working day to finding and contacting new prospects. A successful salesperson continually evaluates prospecting methods, comparing results to find a prospecting strategy that will result in the most effective contact rate.[2]

LO5 Prospecting Methods

Salespeople use various methods to obtain prospects. Exhibit 6.4 shows several of the more popular prospecting methods.

EXHIBIT 6.4

Prospecting methods that work!

Prospecting is the lifeblood of selling. While some salespeople don't have to prospect, most rely on prospecting to increase sales and make money. Here are 13 popular methods:

- Prospecting on the Web
- Cold canvassing
- Endless chain customer referrals
- Orphaned customers
- Sales lead clubs
- Prospect lists
- Getting published
- Public exhibitions and demonstrations
- Center of influence
- Direct mail
- Telemarketing
- Observation
- Networking

Which methods use referrals from customers and other people?

Prospecting on the Web

The most recent advancement in prospecting is the use of the Internet to find and learn about potential buyers. This is a fast and easy way to find information about individuals or businesses by using technology.

Email Marketing

In order to generate leads, firms may purchase lists of potential contacts, including their email addresses. Then, the firm emails opportunities, offers, and invitations to potential customers. If the email garners interest, the customer may respond to the firm. The salesperson then contacts the lead.

Social Media Platforms

The most recent advancement in prospecting is the use of social media tools and platforms such as LinkedIn, Facebook, and others to find potential buyers. Social media platforms provide great opportunities to learn about potential customers, their firms, and their decision makers. For example, a salesperson working in the construction industry can learn that a civil engineering company has secured a large account via the search updates feature in LinkedIn. At this point, the salesperson may decide to send a congratulatory note to the engineering firm and also initiate a communication regarding a new product line for the construction industry that the company may find useful. In another instance, a salesperson working at a pharmaceutical firm can reach out to social network connections and promote business by tweeting deals and promotions that may generate some interest among connections.

Also, salespeople could use social media to communicate product and service reviews and showcase testimonials to enhance their credibility. Salespeople should join LinkedIn groups that have a common interest within an industry or area of interest. In this way, they may start a discussion topic that is pertinent to the group or join an existing discussion. In some instances, the salesperson may have information that can assist in the discussion and therefore post a pertinent link to access the firm's website, a white paper, or recent content. When the interested group members visit the information and download it, they complete a form to access the data. This form provides you with their respective contact information.

Online Events

To generate interest and create awareness of their products and services, many firms offer online events. This may include webinars, demonstrations, insight on trends, or easily accessible on-demand videos. It is important to note that such events may create a variety and depth of customer information on the leads. However, the key for the salesperson is to prioritize the information in a method that can be readily acted upon.

When developing online events such as a webinar, it's important to be customer focused and work diligently to make sure the webinar is perceived as valuable to the attendees. For example, a salesperson working for a company that sells technology services may use webinars to generate leads. That being said, the salesperson should be well versed in the technology and its application in a customer setting. To demonstrate credibility, the salesperson should be able to answer questions that may get asked during the webinar. It is also a smart move to make yourself available via social media platforms and email after the webinar to answer additional questions. This way, a salesperson could continue the conversation with webinar attendees. However, it's probably not advisable to sell the product during the webinar. Instead, view the webinar as an opportunity to focus on issues and solutions that are important to your prospects.

Cold Canvassing

cold canvass prospecting method:
A method whereby the salesperson contacts as many leads as possible with no prior knowledge of the business or individual called upon.

The **cold canvass prospecting method** is tough! Also known as cold calling, contacting strangers day after day is challenging even for the most motivated individuals. By using online resources, most salespeople will gain valuable information about most prospects before making contact—therefore it seldom is a true "cold" call. Yet there are still some sales jobs where new salespeople have to begin their sales careers by cold calling to get customers. If past experience reveals that one person out of 10 will buy a product, then 50 sales calls could result in five sales. Thus, the salesperson contacts as many leads as possible in person, by phone, by email, and/or by mail, recognizing that a certain percentage of people approached will buy. There is generally no knowledge about the individual or business the salesperson calls on. This form of prospecting relies solely on the volume of cold calls made.

Salespeople building a new customer base often employ cold canvass prospecting. For example, home security salespeople may be given responsibility for a new geographic area. In this instance, canvassing may mean visiting neighborhoods and introducing themselves and their firm's services. In industries such as third party logistics providers, salespeople may cold-call small and medium-sized businesses to introduce the firm and its shipping services. Many office supply salespeople do the same thing, going from one business to another. Real estate, insurance, and stock brokerage firms are other businesses that use cold calls.

Endless Chain Customer Referral

endless chain referral method:
A method of prospecting whereby a salesperson asks each buyer for a list of friends or colleagues who might also be interested in buying the product.

referral:
A person or organization recommended to you by someone who feels that this person could benefit from you or your product.

First, satisfied customers are likely to buy again from the salesperson. That is why we stress the importance of building a relationship with the customer. It is critical to your success. Second, the customer often refers the salesperson to someone she knows. This is known as the **endless chain referral method** of prospecting. This is a very effective method for finding customers. *Repeat sales* and *customer referrals* are the two best sources of future sales, with repeat sales from customers being better. A **referral** is a person or organization recommended to you by someone who feels that this person or organization could benefit from you or your product.

Don't ask current customers, "Do you know anyone else who could use my product?" Rarely are clients eager to judge whether colleagues are prepared to make a purchase. Instead, ask whether your customer knows any other individuals or organizations that might be interested in finding out about your product.

Customers and customer referrals are your future.

If you sense hesitation from customers to give out referrals, it's probably because they are afraid that their associates may not want to be pestered. Say, "Let me tell you what I'm going to do with any names you give me. I will make one phone call to each party, indicate that you were nice enough to give me their names, and give them a brief outline of what we do. If they express an interest, we will get together and I will give them the same professional service I've given you. If, on the other hand, they express no interest, I will thank them for their time and never call them again." This approach puts your customers at ease and moves solid, new prospects onto your lead list.

Don't forget that your prospects are friends, neighbours, relatives–anyone and everyone you know or come into contact with. They may know people who are looking for your product and the great service you provide your customers. Everyone is a prospect!

Orphaned Customers

Orphaned customers are customers whose salesperson has left the company. Salespeople often leave their employers to take other jobs; when they do, their customers are orphaned. These orphans are great prospects. A salesperson should quickly contact such customers to begin developing relationships. You can turn orphans into a lead-generating gold mine.

orphaned customers: customers who are abandoned as a result of a salesperson's leaving the company.

In addition, if you've been selling for a while, you've surely built up a backlog of inactive accounts. Weed out the names who for whatever reason will never buy. The rest are solid prospects. Call them again and find out why they're not buying from you anymore. What would it take to change that? They may have stopped ordering your type of product altogether, or they may have gone with a competitor because of a special one-time offer, or there may have been a management change and therefore a change in buying patterns. You have to determine why the customer stopped buying from you. After you do that, re-establishing contact and turning that prospect into a customer again is *standard sales procedure.*

Sales Lead Clubs

Organize a group of salespeople in related but non-competitive fields to meet twice a month to share leads and prospecting tips. To get started, write a formal mission statement, charge dues to ensure commitment, and grant membership to only one salesperson from each specific field. Next, set up administrative procedures and duties to keep the club on track and committed to its stated mission.

Finally, establish guidelines for what constitutes a good lead, and track prospect information and effectiveness. Group the leads by effectiveness so members can better understand which leads can help the rest. You may even have every member who closes a lead contribute to a kitty. Each month the winner can be the member who provided the most closed leads.

Many North American cities have organizations called "executive associations" (such as the Ottawa Executives Association, for example) that local businesses form to foster the success of members through sales leads and networking. There are also Chamber of Commerce organizations and Business Improvement Associations in many Canadian cities, which are great avenues for salespeople to begin networking in their community.

Become an Expert—Get Published

Although you may give away your services as a writer for free, the residual benefits make your efforts well worth the time. Submit articles about your field or industry to journals, trade magazines, newspapers, and social media sites, such as LinkedIn. You, or a team of your colleagues, can develop and maintain a blog in the format of an online journal. Such blogs are useful for writing opinions, educating prospects, and initiating discussions regarding your product and its usefulness. Your submissions or blogs don't have to be glossy and expensive; just fill them with information that people can genuinely use, then make sure you have no spelling or grammatical mistakes. Instead of getting paid, ask the publication to include your address and telephone number at the end of the article and to write a little blurb about your expertise.

By demonstrating your knowledge and expertise in your field, you can enhance your credibility in your potential prospects' eyes. Once prospects think of you as a credible expert, you may be the one they contact when they're ready to buy. In addition, prospects who call you for advice can come to depend on you and your product. Thus, you attract prospects without having to go out prospecting.

Research Publications and Insights

In some industries, firms create e-books, white papers, executive summaries, or research overviews that provide useful and timely insights into the customers' industries, consumers, processes, and technology. In this area, the firm and salesperson's goal is to develop credibility, disseminate knowledge, and position the firm as a resource and knowledge broker for potential customers.

SELLING TIPS

WHY IS QUALIFYING LEADS IMPORTANT?

The short answer: Customers often have distinct needs.

For the salesperson, this means that your solution may not always be suitable for every business or every industry. It is important to remember that a greater number of leads may not always be better for the company. The time that a salesperson invests with an ill-qualified lead—that does not convert into a customer—consumes financial resources. Unqualified leads also result in frustration and missed opportunities for salespeople. In addition, a highly qualified lead means an opportunity for revenue for the firm and a greater return on the salesperson's time investment.

As a salesperson, your goal is to find the segments, or groups of prospects, that you can best help. Simply put, salespeople must ask themselves, "Which group of customers can I provide the most value for?" As such, a reliable method to qualify leads into prospects is an important step in this process.

Public Exhibitions and Demonstrations

exhibitions and demonstrations: A situation in which a firm operates a booth at a trade show or other special-interest gathering staffed by salespeople.

Exhibitions and demonstrations frequently take place at trade shows and other types of special-interest gatherings. Many times, related firms sponsor a booth at such shows and staff it with one or more salespeople.[3] As people walk up to the booth to examine the products, a salesperson has only a few minutes to qualify leads and get names and addresses in order to contact them later at their homes or offices for demonstrations. Although salesperson–buyer contact is usually brief, this type of gathering gives a salesperson extensive contact with a large number of potential buyers over a brief time. Remember, however, that success at trade shows stems from preparation. Here are several things to do:

- Set up an interesting display to get people's attention. A popcorn machine, local celebrity, or inexpensive giveaway are good ideas.
- Write down your message so that it fits on the back of a business card.
- Practise communicating two or three key points that get your message across succinctly. Get it down pat but don't memorize your sales pitch to make it sound overly canned.

SELLING TIPS

USE PROPER ETIQUETTE AT THE TRADE SHOW

1. Be courteous to all vendors—don't monopolize their time.
2. Don't walk around grabbing giveaways for your kids.
3. Don't eat while attending to your booth—it's unprofessional.
4. Be friendly with all vendors—a simple smile and hello will prove this.
5. Do not converse with people while standing in front of another vendor's booth.
6. Do not let personal chatting take the place of business conversations.
7. Keep personal belongings out of sight—you're there for business.
8. Keep conversations private—don't draw attention to your discussions.
9. Be available for information—don't wander around aimlessly.
10. Watch your posture and body language. Make sure you appear approachable.
11. Don't be distracted by the hustle and bustle of pedestrian traffic—deal with one prospect at a time.

- Make a list of the major buyers at the show you want to pursue for contacts.
- Set up to maximize your display's visibility based on the flow of traffic.
- Be assertive in approaching passersby. Instead of the common "Hello" or "How are you?" try "Do you use [product or service] in your operations?" or "Have you seen [product or service]? If I can show you how to be more profitable, would you be interested?" Next offer them a sample to handle, but not to keep. Don't let them take the item and move on without talking to you.
- Use lead cards to write down prospect information for efficient and effective post-show follow-up.
- Be prepared for rejection. Some buyers will ignore you. Don't take it personally. Be brief but professional. Your time is too valuable to waste on non-prospects.
- Become part of an expert panel or deliver a presentation during the trade show, as these can give a salesperson credibility and exposure to an even broader audience. An effective participation in a trade show may create a buzz for the salesperson's product but that interest could fade away in a short time as your prospect gets in touch with many suppliers and sales reps during the trade show. Therefore, it is critical for you to follow up quickly to reap the benefits.

Centre of Influence

Prospecting via the **centre of influence method** involves finding and cultivating people in a community or territory who are willing to cooperate in helping to find prospects. They typically have a particular position that includes some form of influence over other people, as well as information that allows the salesperson to identify good prospects. For example, a person who graduates from college and begins work for a local real estate firm might contact professors and administrators at their alma mater to obtain the names of teachers who have taken a job at another university and are moving out of town. The salesperson wants to help them sell their homes.

centre of influence method: A method whereby the salesperson finds and cultivates people in a community or territory who are willing to cooperate in helping to find prospects.

Clergy, salespeople who are selling noncompeting products, officers of community organizations like the chamber of commerce, and members of organizations such as the Lions Club or a country club are other individuals who may function as a centre of influence. Be sure to show your appreciation for this person's assistance. Keeping such influential persons informed on the outcome of your contact with the prospect helps to secure future aid.

SELLING GLOBALLY

PROSPECTING IN HONG KONG?

Try to make appointments as far in advance as possible—even months before.

Be punctual—it shows respect. Plan your travel times to take into account the often-heavy traffic conditions. A sincere and humble apology is necessary if you're late.

Generally there is a six-day workweek. Business hours are usually 9:00 a.m. to 5:00 p.m.; however, offices may be open only during the morning hours on Saturdays.

Business trips are best scheduled during the late fall or from March to June to avoid vacation and celebration times. Chinese New Year is a major holiday period, so avoid this time.

Watch what you wear. Dark-coloured business suits for men and subdued colours for women are best. Avoid wearing blue or white at social events; these colours are associated with death and mourning.

Direct Mail

direct-mail prospecting: The process of mailing advertisements to a large number of people over an extended geographical area.

In cases where there are a large number of prospects for a product, **direct-mail prospecting** is sometimes an effective way to contact individuals and businesses. Direct-mail advertisements have the advantage of contacting large numbers of people, who may be spread across an extended geographical area, at a relatively low cost when compared to the cost of using salespeople. People who request more information from the company subsequently are contacted by a salesperson.

Telemarketing

telemarketing: A marketing communication system using telecommunication technology and trained personnel to conduct planned, measurable marketing activities directed at targeted groups of consumers.

Telemarketing is a marketing communication system using telecommunication technology and trained personnel to conduct planned, measurable marketing activities directed at targeted groups of consumers. The internal process of a telemarketing centre is shown in Exhibit 6.5. For some telemarketing campaigns, the salesperson makes outbound calls. The salesperson is provided a list of potential prospects or uses dialling technology, in which a computer and telephony system are integrated. The system provides a list of prospects and begins dialling them. Once someone answers, the system alerts the salesperson. The salesperson takes the call. After the call, the system allows the salesperson to track the results.

In other instances, firms attempt to incentivize consumers to call into their call centre. Potential customers may also take it upon themselves to call your firm. How might this happen? Firms often place their phone numbers on their websites, emails, or white papers. As the customer reads this information, they become more and more

EXHIBIT 6.5

The processing system within a telemarketing centre.

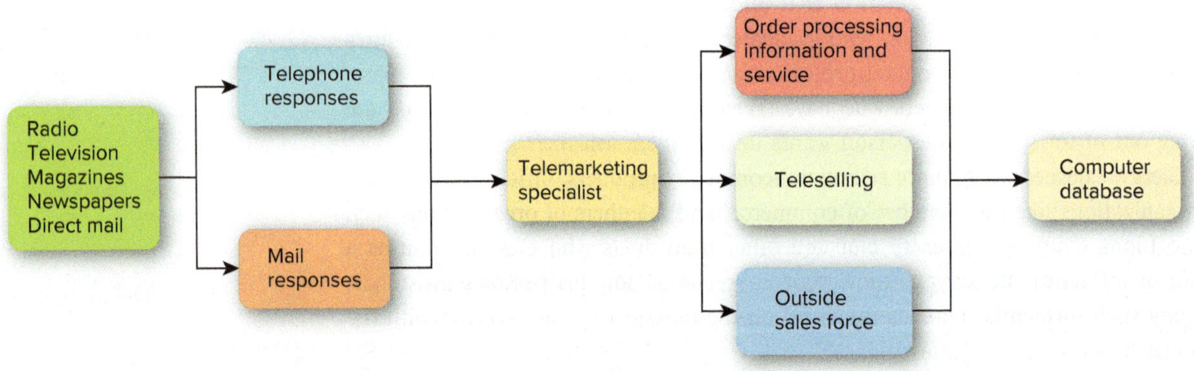

interested and seek out additional information. Firms are also enabling their mobile apps with click-to-call abilities; and phone numbers are being placed on advertisements using Google AdWords. This allows quick access to a live information source and expertise and enables the lead generation process.

Another means by which to initiate telemarketing ventures is by featuring an 800 phone number in print, Internet, or television advertisements. When the viewer or reader responds, the call comes into a call centre and a trained specialist handles it. This person may take an order (in the case of a telephone call) or transfer the person to a telephone selling or teleselling unit. The specialist may provide information or service. The specialist also can determine whether the customer has sufficient potential to warrant a face-to-face sales call.

The duties of a telemarketing specialist are based on the type of product being sold and to whom it is sold. As you probably have experienced, telemarketers tend to rely on memorized or formula selling, which tends to be a much more structured conversation in which the buyer does 70 percent or more of the talking. You will learn more about the types of sales presentation in Chapter 7.

Teleprospecting

As relational selling continues to evolve, many firms are adopting an approach named teleprospecting, as an element within their lead generation process. **Teleprospecting** could be described as a process to qualify a prospect and to determine if an organization is the right fit for their product. Hence, it often involves a number of calls and discussions with the lead. Unlike telemarketing, teleprospecting applies critical sales behaviours, such as listening and attempting to diagnose customer needs rather than using a script.[4] In many instances, teleprospecting requires more sales training than what is traditionally provided to a telemarketer, as the assessment of business needs and the communication of potential options is required for success.

teleprospecting: The process of reaching potential customers over the phone. The process tends to use a greater range of traditional selling elements, including needs discovery and solution provision.

Like direct marketing, use of **telephone prospecting** to contact a large number of prospects across a vast area is far less costly than use of a canvassing sales force, though usually more costly than mailouts.[5] This person-to-person contact afforded by the telephone allows for interaction between the lead and the caller—enabling a lead to be quickly qualified or rejected.

telephone prospecting: The process of reaching potential customers over the phone.

A firm's marketing and sales departments may collaborate to develop a list of targeted leads. While the potential customers may not be expecting a call from the teleprospector, the background research assists the teleprospector in generating greater levels of customer interest and attention than conventional telemarketing processes. In other instances, the lead may have requested more information or made direct contact with the selling firm through a website or other response method. In this example, the teleprospector generates a "warm-call" because the prospect is already aware of the product and has demonstrated interest in learning more about it.

Inside Sales

Due to the cost of face-to-face interactions, many firms are seeking more cost-effective means of enabling the customer-salesperson interaction. As such, firms are centralizing many elements of their sales force. Rather than have a national canvassing sales force, firms introduce inside sales centres that focus on working remotely with customers from a regional or national headquarters.[6]

This trend continues to increase due to the enhanced quality of technology such as telephony, web conferencing, and webinars. As such, the salesperson's skill sets must expand beyond simply using the phone. Today's inside sales representatives must be able to leverage a wide range of technology—whether it is the phone, webinars, web conferencing, or video demonstrations.

While many inside sales centres have salespeople with the full range of sales skills, some also employ lead specialists who qualify prospects and determine if the customer and her organization are the right fit for the salesperson's solution. If the prospect is deemed viable, the lead specialist transfers the customer to an inside sales account specialist. Other sales organizations start the sales conversation through an inside sales rep to make the process more efficient (and less costly) for the buyer as well as the selling firm.

Observation

observation method: The process of finding prospects by a salesperson constantly watching what is happening in the sales area.

A salesperson often can find prospects by constantly watching what is happening in the sales area—the **observation method**. Office furniture, computer, and copier salespeople look for new business construction in their territories. New families moving into town are excellent leads for real estate and insurance salespeople. No matter what prospecting method you use, you must always keep your eyes and ears open for information on who needs your product.

Networking

networking: The continuous prospecting method of making and utilizing contacts.

For many salespeople, prospecting never ends. They are always on the lookout for customers. Everyone they meet may be a prospect, or that person may provide a name that could lead to a sale. The term given to making and using contacts is **networking**.

Of the many ways to find new prospects, networking can be the most reliable and effective. People want to do business with, and refer business to, people they know, like, and trust. The days of the one-shot salesperson are over; the name of the game today is relationship building.

Building a network is important, but cultivating that network brings sales. The key is positioning, not exposure. The goal of cultivating your network is to fill a niche in the mind of each of your contacts so when one of those contacts, or someone they know, needs your type of product or service, you are the *only* possible resource that would come to mind.

Here are several tips for cultivating your network to dramatically increase your referral business:

1. Focus on meeting *centre-of-influence* people. These people have established a good reputation and have many valuable contacts. A few places to find the key people in your industry are trade association meetings, trade shows, or any business-related social event.
2. Ninety-nine percent of your first conversation with a networking prospect should be about their business. People want to talk about *their* business, not yours.
3. Ask open-ended, feel-good questions like "What do you enjoy most about your industry?"
4. Be sure to ask, "How would I know if someone I'm speaking with would be a good prospect for you?" If you're on the lookout to find this person new business, they will be more inclined to do the same for you.
5. Get a networking prospect's business card. It's the easiest way to follow up with your new contact.
6. Send a handwritten thank-you note that day: "It was nice meeting you this morning. If I can ever refer business your way, I certainly will."
7. When you read newspapers and magazines, keep the people in your network in mind. If you find an article one of your contacts could use or would enjoy, email it.

8. Stay on your contacts' minds by sending them something every month; notepads with your name and picture are perfect. They will keep these pads on their desks and be constantly reminded of you and your product or service.
9. Send leads. The best way to get business and referrals is to give business and referrals.
10. Send a handwritten thank-you note whenever you receive a lead, regardless of whether it results in a sale.

When meeting someone, tell them what you sell and ask what they do. Exchange business cards and periodically contact the person. Eventually, you may build a network of people talking to each other, sharing ideas, and exchanging information. Also, you can use several of the previously discussed methods of prospecting, such as the endless chain and centre of influence methods, to build your network.

Prospect Lists

Make a list of what your ideal prospect looks like. This may differ depending whether you are targeting individuals (households) or businesses. Ask yourself the following questions:

- Who are my ideal prospects?
- What is their economic bracket (household) or business size (revenue, profits, or employees)?
- What kinds of organizations (household) or industries (business) do they belong to?
- What characteristics do most of my existing customers share?
- What changes, transitions, or trends are they potentially confronting?
- Do they have children (household) or how many employees do they employ (businesses)?
- Do they use certain technologies, systems, or processes?
- Do they have similar occupations, educations, hobbies, illnesses, transportation needs, or family concerns (household) or belong to certain trade organizations and groups (businesses)?

And the key question:

- Where am I most likely to find the greatest conglomeration of people or businesses who fit my prospect's profile?

List #1. Take the information you have accumulated and apply it. Go to the library or use the Internet and look up the North American Industry Classification System (NAICS) for your ideal prospects' businesses. Ask a librarian for help if you need it. Every type of business has a specific NAICS code. Related industries have similar numbers; scan the directory to locate the numbers that fit the profile. This should provide you with an excellent prospect list. In addition, literally hundreds of other business directories can help you generate lists based on corporate profiles.

List #2. What kinds of publications do your ideal prospects likely read? Find out whether these publications sell lists of subscribers. If a publication's readership matches your prospect profile well enough, this list should be well worth the cost.

List #3. A number of firms sell lists. These companies offer a variety of criteria that you can use to generate a quality prospect list. Dun & Bradstreet is an example of such a company. This information may also be available online.

> *Don't wait for your ship to come in . . . swim out to it.*

LO6 Prospecting Using Social Media

Companies today have caught on to the popularity of social media and use it effectively in many areas of their business, including prospecting. Social media networks such as Facebook, Twitter, and LinkedIn can be used to research, identify, engage, and follow up with sales leads. Remember, each time you communicate with someone on a social media network, there is the opportunity that you'll be exposed to many other people or businesses that are acquaintances or business associates of that person. Careful monitoring of these networks can lead to several good leads provided that you remain tuned in and follow up with the prospects that you identify.

Facebook. Develop a Facebook page for yourself and a separate one for your company. Use it to establish an online image for your company. Don't push, push, push here. Make yourself and your company seem approachable. Provide some product information. Include pictures of yourself and your company in positive situations. You can include positive customer testimonials. Of course, provide complete contact information should someone want to contact you regarding your product. You can also use it to search key words or find relevant conversations taking place on pages or public groups.

Twitter. Set up a Twitter account. You can start posting content or search for some keywords relative to your product or industry. You can begin following people who follow that topic and they may start following you. You can include links to your company Facebook page, and post links to sites that would be of interest to your followers. From this, you may be able to engage some prospective customers. If you tweet regularly, you can even use tools such as Twuffer, which will allow you to have tweets automatically released to your account at a future time. Irene Koehler of Almost Savvy asserts that Twitter is an "excellent way to listen in on conversations, organizational news, and updates." She goes on to say that it's a "phenomenal research tool. You can find those potentially interested in your product and those unhappy with a competitor."

Here are the top features of ***LinkedIn*** and why salespeople should use them.

1. **Profile** - Your profile can serve as your extended business card, and will have maximum impact when it's 100 percent complete. You can enhance your credibility by asking your past employers and clients to add a recommendation to your profile. Recommendations are one of the top features people look at when first viewing your profile. LinkedIn also allows you to add a photo, making you immediately recognizable to your connections at events and conferences you might both attend.
2. **Search** - LinkedIn's Search tools enable you to find an individual person, or a whole range of people you might be looking for. Use their name—or other

MAKING THE SALE

SOCIAL MEDIA IN SALES

Karen Emanuelson of Reciprocate LLC in Minnesota suggests that each of these social media can be searched using keywords, targeted companies, and targeted individuals. As Karen tells it, "I had one gentleman find my company on Facebook—he was searching for a social media speaker to present to his group. Because of the keywords I have in my Facebook business page name and that I use in my Facebook posts, he found me, reviewed my information on my website and reached out to me. Since speaking at his meeting, I have met with several prospects, sent out proposals and have already landed at least one of his group members as a client! Pretty cool."

distinguishing characteristics such as location, company, or title–to find the person. Or, use LinkedIn's Advanced Search to target specific skill sets or subject-matter experts. Employers can also conduct reference searches on potential job candidates and business partners. Using the search bar in the top right-hand corner of the website, you can search for people, groups, answers, jobs, or messages within your inbox.

3. **Applications** - LinkedIn's applications can boost your profile, credibility, and potential for finding a new job or business partner. The Application Directory is the best place to find all the applications LinkedIn has to offer, including *Tweets* for your Twitter account, *Blog Link*, *TripIt* for your travels, *SlideShare* for your presentations, and *Events* and *Company Buzz* to find out what people are saying about your company.

4. **Jobs** - Employees can use this feature and their inside connections with potential employers to land their dream job. Using the advanced job search, find your new role with keywords and by specifying an experience level or job title. You can also refine your search by defining your location, industry, and company. Once you've found a job you like, you can apply directly through LinkedIn. LinkedIn lets you see who in your network can assist you with the position, and allows you to ask them for a referral or introduction to the person who posted the job. LinkedIn Jobs is also useful for employers, allowing you to recruit from professionals worldwide. The LinkedIn tool gives you unique job listings, candidate searches, and trusted referrals to ensure that your selections are from the highest quality candidates. LinkedIn allows employers to tap into a pool of passive candidates, who could be the best candidates for the job, but are hard to reach because they are rarely actively seeking new jobs.

5. **Groups** - LinkedIn Groups are the best way to meet like-minded individuals and engage in discussions on topics of importance to your industry and expertise. Joining groups relevant to your field is a way to make new connections and find potential clients or business partners. For small business members, groups are a great place to test new ideas with potential clients and a community that is supportive and critically helpful. You can also follow influential people by checking the Top Influencers board. If you can't find a group that suits your needs, you can create your own.

6. **Company pages** - Company profiles feature overviews of the company, who you know at the company, and unique data from the LinkedIn network, and these are a powerful way to find companies you might want to work for or do business with. Company pages also give key statistics on the demographics of the company's current employees, as well as tell you who in your network is currently employed in the company.

7. **Mobile** - Download the LinkedIn application to your Smartphone to access your connections, profiles, network updates and inbox wherever you go. The application also allows you to search for professionals you might have met at events or conferences and instantly find out more about them, or invite them to be part of your network. You can also integrate your contacts, messages, and calendar from your phone with your LinkedIn network, so that you can view profiles of meeting attendees and integrate your connections with your existing address book.

8. **Settings and personalization** - LinkedIn allows you to control who can see your profile, and even control the type of information certain members can see. You can hide your photo, recommendations, and

Source: © franckreporter/iStockphot

personal information from different groups of people to maintain your privacy but still engage with your existing connections and make new ones.

9. **Follow company** - By activating the Follow Company tab, you can easily track companies you're interested in, as well as your competitors. That way, you can be the first to see developments at the world's largest companies, as well as possible business development opportunities. The tool also gives you insight into the hiring styles and rates of your competitors, and new directions companies might be taking based on unusual new hires.

Why not broadcast a public sales presentation? YouTube videos usually get high search engine rankings and are an excellent means of building a presence on the web. You can provide information, positive customer testimonials, and contact information should someone want to follow up with you regarding your product.

These are a few of the social media tools that are used broadly in the selling field. You can also use many other tools to help you become even more effective with your online presence. For example, TweetBeep allows you to receive alerts when a specific word or phrase is tweeted. Hootsuite is a social media management system that helps you keep track of and manage different social network channels associated with your brand. It enables you to keep track of the comments posted online about your organization, giving you the opportunity to respond quickly. It is clear that there are myriad social media tools at your disposal. What's key is that you find tools that you're comfortable with, and then use them regularly.

When using social media, there should be no overt pitching or sales talk. This goes against the etiquette of social networking. Still, there are important opportunities to attract the right people–in groups or question-and-answer (Q&A) forums, for example.

Lists and Directories

There are several sources of lists and directories that are fruitful for salespeople selling in Canada. Some are free; however, many charge for their services. In addition to the sites profiled below, other possible information sources include Innovation, Science, and Economic Development Canada, at www.ic.gc.ca, and the Canadian Business Directory at CanadaOne (www.canadaone.com/business/index.html).

Scott's Directories: www.scottsdirectories.com

Scott's provides access to accurate business contact information and has been one of the most respected business information databases for over 60 years. Updated monthly, an annual online account allows users to:

- download the Scott's Directories data
- use Geocode Mapping to pinpoint where each contact is located
- take advantage of unlimited viewing and printing
- insert their own notes, contact names, titles, and other details
- use unlimited mailing labels via 12 Avery templates–no formatting required

Users can click on one of several search modes. For example, a sales rep selling group insurance to companies employing over 50 people could click Demographic, then Number of Employees, then enter search criteria that will result in a list of companies meeting these criteria.

For each company selected, users are provided with information on the company including the full company name, address, executives, business type, parent company, and other important information, which could prove invaluable to many types of salespeople. The company recently added a Search Engine Optimization feature where subscribers can target specific industries with more ease of use. The database is available to businesses in print, or online formats and online subscriptions are available to customize as well.

411.ca: www.411.ca

411.ca is another example of an online directory. This site could prove useful to salespeople as it allows searches for people and businesses by geographic area with links to company websites. Using this one tool, a salesperson could find the name of a particular type of business in a particular geographic area along with the company's phone number and link to its website, research the company, and then get specific directions and a map to that company's location. The site will even suggest the top restaurants located near you in case you're hungry.

Prospecting Guidelines

LO7

Although prospecting will vary depending on the product or good, generalizations can be made. Use three criteria to develop the best prospecting method:

1. *Customize* a prospecting method to fit the specific needs of your individual firm. Do not copy another company's method; however, it's all right to adapt someone's method.
2. Concentrate on *high-potential* customers first.
3. Always call back on prospects who did not buy. If you have a new product, do not restrict yourself to present customers only. A business may not have purchased your present products because they did not fit the business's present needs; your new product may be exactly what they need.

Keep knocking on your prospects' and customers' doors to help them solve problems through the purchase of your product. Only in this way can you maximize your long-term sales and income. See Exhibit 6.6 for an illustration of the "sales funnel" approach to thinking about prospecting.

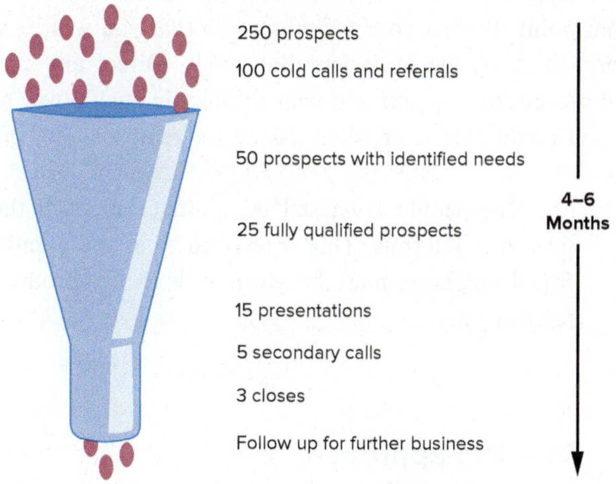

EXHIBIT 6.6

The sales funnel. Note that the funnel can take up to six months to clear itself. If salespeople don't work diligently to keep it full, then dry spells will certainly ensue.

Referrals

LO8

Many salespeople are reluctant to ask for referrals. Yet referrals create business and sales.

Objections

Some clients may not want to give referrals for the following reasons:

- Clients are afraid of upsetting friends, relatives, or business associates.

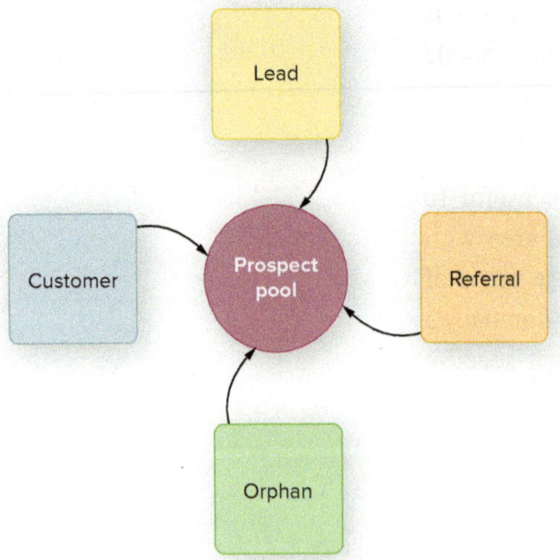

EXHIBIT 6.7
Components of the prospect pool.

- Clients do not want friends to think they're being talked about.
- Clients may believe in the product but not in the salesperson.
- Clients fear the salesperson may not be around in the future.
- Clients do not feel they can benefit from giving the salesperson referrals.

It is absolutely essential to address these objections when asking for referrals. By doing so, you will obtain more referrals, get more appointments, and make more sales. When asking for referrals, reassure your clients that you will approach these referrals with courtesy and professionalism. If they are truly reluctant, don't push too hard–you don't want to damage the relationship with your client. Perhaps a good technique to use here is to ask your client for a recommendation or an introduction to the referral. This will break the ice and perhaps ease any tension that your client may be feeling.

As shown in Exhibit 6.7, a prospect pool is usually created from the four sources discussed earlier: leads, referrals, orphaned customers, and current customers.[7]

Most salespeople do not like to cold call. Their goal is to have a prospect pool of customers, referrals, and, when available, orphans. The secret to reaching this goal is the referral cycle.

The Referral Cycle

referral cycle: The process that provides guidelines for a salesperson to ask for referrals in four commonly faced situations experienced by salespeople.

parallel referral sale: A method of selling that makes the sale and gains referrals.

Obtaining referrals is a continuous process; salespeople should always be looking for the right opportunity to find a referral. The **referral cycle** provides guidelines for a salesperson to ask for referrals in four situations commonly experienced by salespeople, as shown in Exhibit 6.8.

You can begin the referral cycle in the presentation, product delivery, pre-approach, or service phase. However, wherever you are in the referral cycle, you can begin at that point. Perfect your techniques so that you will be working to get referrals at every phase of the cycle simultaneously. Direct any contact with the prospect toward presenting yourself and your product in such a way as to overcome any objections you could face later when asking for referrals and, of course, when making a sale.

EXHIBIT 6.8
The referral cycle: when to ask for referrals.

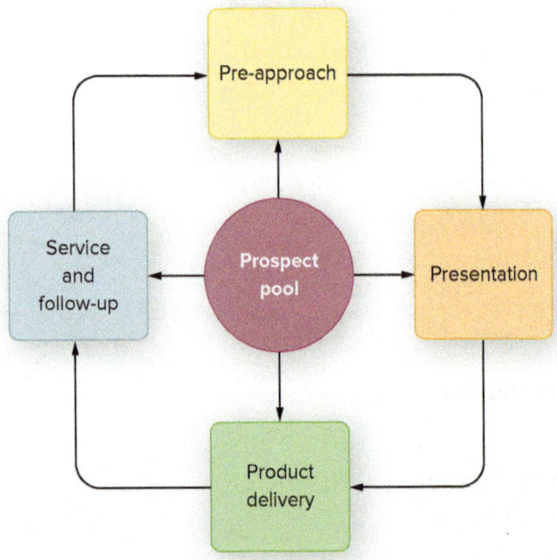

Salespeople must sell the product and sell the prospect on providing referrals. This is referred to as the **parallel referral sale.** Equal emphasis must be given to both the product sale and the referral sale.

When to Ask

The Pre-approach

Take great care during the pre-approach phase of the referral cycle. Whether the initial contact is face to face or via telephone, the effectiveness of your approach will determine whether you are given the opportunity to make a sales presentation.

Many prospects will hang up the phone as soon as they suspect that an attempt is being made to sell them something. If, in the first several seconds, you fail to overcome their initial feelings of discomfort and intrusion, your chances of developing a relationship are slim.

Mentioning that a firm or business acquaintance of theirs recommended that you call helps alleviate some of their initial anxiety. This is one reason that working on referrals is so effective. Certainly, people are willing to listen a bit longer if they know a person they trust has initiated this personal contact. Here's an example:

> Hello, is this John? . . . Hi, John, my name is Kim Lee from Merrill Lynch. George and Barbara Smith are clients of mine. I met with them last week and helped them set up their retirement program. They were really pleased with both my products and service. *And since I work primarily through referrals,* they were kind enough to mention that you might be interested in learning about the value I have to offer.
>
> I'd like to set up a time to stop by your home or office and share some ideas that you may find of great benefit. *It's not really important to me that we do business;* all I ask is that if you appreciate the time we share together, if you feel that you benefit from the time we spend together, and, most importantly, if you respect my integrity, *you would be willing to pass my name on to a friend or business associate who may also benefit from my services,* just as George and Barbara did. Is that fair enough?

We have begun the process of selling the prospect–and, we hope, customer–on giving us one or more referrals. We are telling John that it is not important for us to make a sale. We are asking if he feels it is reasonable, if and only if he is happy with us, that he pass our name on just as his friends did. It is easy for John to answer yes. We have presented our offer in a non-threatening manner that was endorsed by his friends George and Barbara.

SELLING TIPS

GET MOTIVATED. BREAK OUT OF THAT SLUMP.

Salespeople often find themselves in a bit of a prospecting slump, which adversely affects morale. What can you do?

1. Stay calm. Don't become paralyzed by panic! If you feel desperate, you may resort to desperate measures that may become counterproductive.
2. Focus on what you're trying to accomplish and stay positive.
3. Keep trying. Don't give up. Keep your sense of humour.
4. Get back to basics. Think of the things that have worked well for you, and reconnect to them.
5. Work a little harder. Commit to a few days of stronger effort. Good things happen to those who work hard.
6. Ask for help. Have a colleague or sales manager review some of your tactics with you.
7. Avoid negative events and people. To stay on top of your game, don't let external events or people drag you down.
8. Change your pace. Try a different environment. Sometimes change can lift your mood.

To say "it's not really important to me that we do business" is very unusual. People are not accustomed to hearing a salesperson say that it is not important to make a sale.

The Presentation

Depending on your particular industry, the situation in which you present your product for sale may be called by a variety of names: meeting, appointment, interview, or presentation. Throughout this book we refer to it as the presentation.

During the presentation you have the greatest opportunity to influence your prospect. Remember that your prospect will scrutinize everything you say and do. The presentation phase of the referral cycle actually begins when you sit down with your prospect for the purpose of making a sales presentation. As naturally as possible, you should make a conscious effort to mention the referring person. This may be a remark as simple as: "George told me that you like to golf. Did you get a chance to get out this week?" or "Barbara mentioned that you like to garden. Did the last frost we had affect your plants at all?"

This initial contact plants the seed for the beginning of the parallel referral sale. During the next 10 or 15 minutes, there should be no discussion about the product or service being offered. This time is best used to build rapport and help break down any barriers between the prospect and their perception of you as a salesperson. To accelerate this process, you should mention the referring person as often as possible. The walls of resistance have fallen when you begin to feel comfortable with your prospects. If you do not feel comfortable with your prospects, they certainly will not feel comfortable with you.

Once you establish rapport, take a moment to explain to your prospects what will occur during the time you will be together. Then, when appropriate, mention the referrals. Here are two examples:

> John and Nonnie, if you're happy with my service, I hope you will be willing to pass my name on to other people who would appreciate the same honesty and integrity I have extended to you. I don't do this because I'm a good person; I do it because it makes good business sense. If I take care of you, you'll take care of me. And my livelihood depends on getting referrals.
>
> My success and the success of my business are totally dependent on getting quality referrals from my clients. I realize that you will introduce me to your friends, family, and business associates only if the quality and integrity of the service I provide surpasses that to which you've grown accustomed.

Product Delivery

Almost every selling profession has some type of product delivery phase, although the phase is more obvious with some products than others. For example, in the life insurance industry it involves the agent physically handing the policy to the client. In real estate, it is the day the sale closes on the home or property. With computers, it is the day that the system is installed and usable. Whatever your product, identify the precise moment that your product becomes of value to your customer, and at this point the product delivery phase begins. Here's an example of how to ask for a referral at this point:

> I'm sure that by now, John, you realize that I work strictly through referrals. I am constantly striving to bring my clients even greater service by improving my business. I have a very important question for you and would appreciate your giving this some thought. Is there any one thing that you would like to see me change or improve that would increase the likelihood of my getting referrals from you in the future?

Service and Follow-up

customer service:
The activities and programs provided by the seller to make the relationship a satisfying one for the customer.

Customer service is the performance of any helpful or professional work or activity for a customer. The service and follow-up phase of the referral cycle provides you with ongoing opportunities to maintain contact with your clients. Whenever you have contact with your clients, it may be possible to get more referrals. High-quality service creates a professional and caring image that clients are more eager to share with their friends, family, and business associates; high-quantity service helps keep you and your product fresh in the minds of clients.

For many salespeople, the product delivery phase represents the end of the relationship with their clients. First, the nature of the business may not require any additional service. Second, although there may be a need for continued service, salespeople are so preoccupied with prospecting or selling that they cannot devote adequate time to providing good service. Third, salespeople may not realize that providing quality customer service will result in more business. Here is an example of what might be said during a typical annual follow-up:

> Hello, John. This is Kim Lee. As I promised when we first did business, this is my "official" once-a-year call to let you know that I am thinking about you. Do you have any questions? Is there anything I can do for you? . . . I also want to make sure you and Nonnie have received your birthday cards and quarterly newsletters. What do you think of my newsletters? . . . Terrific. I'll let you go now. Don't forget, you've got my number if you need any help. Please keep me in mind when talking to your friends and business associates. As you know, John, I depend on quality clients like you and Nonnie to keep me in business. One of the reasons I work so hard to help my customers is because of the people you refer to me. Your referrals are really appreciated. *(Pause)* John, is there anyone you or Nonnie feel I should help? . . . Thank you very much! I look forward to seeing you soon. Goodbye.

Don't Mistreat the Referral

One final thought on referrals–don't mistreat them! The salesperson who mistreats a referral can lose both the referring customer and the prospect.

Once you have sold the referral, and gotten more referrals, ask the *new* customer to contact the *referring* customer on their experience with you. Now you have two customers giving you referrals. This interaction can create the endless chain of referrals, helping to quickly fill your prospect pool with only customers and referrals.

Tracking Referrals

Keeping track of referrals is just as important as staying in contact with customers. Whether you use index cards or a computerized contact system, it's important to keep detailed records on all information you collect on the prospect/customer. (See the review of computerized customer contact programs in Chapter 5 and the discussion of the customer profile in Chapter 7.)

ETHICAL DILEMMA

DO I PAY A COMMISSION FOR LEADS?

You are a salesperson of mutual funds and other financial services. The person who manages your personal and business finances is also your best friend and a chartered accountant. Over lunch one day, you are discussing your decreasing sales levels and your accountant friend mentions that as a key centre of influence, he could provide you with the names of some key people he knows who have money to invest. In exchange for these names, he mentions that he expects you to pay him 25 percent of your commissions resulting from the leads he provides.

What do you tell him?

Is it ethical for him to make this request?

What should you consider here?

LO9 Applying CRM Technology to Prospecting

As you learned about the CRM system and its ability to manage knowledge in Chapter 5, now you will learn how it can assist the firm and its salesforce in the prospecting process. The system serves as a repository for varying information about potential leads, provides tools to segment this pool of potential customers, and enables scoring of these prospects to help salespeople prioritize their efforts.

Lead Generation and Tracking via Marketing Automation

In some CRM systems, you can develop a marketing campaign (i.e., you automate it within the CRM system). The campaigns can involve a number of marketing tactics, including trials of products and services, direct mail, email, and other promotions. For instance, a marketing campaign could target a set of potential customers in the hopes of generating sales leads. Additionally, the CRM technology allows the firm to track the behaviour of leads. For instance, CRM technology can examine how much time prospects spent on the firm's websites, blogs, or social media. Then, the marketing automation technology allows the firm to customize and target each prospect with customized communication strategies, such as emails, e-newsletters, invitations to webinars, and other social events to assist the prospect in learning more about the firm's solution. Finally, the technology allows the firm to measure the results and activities of the campaigns. This type of information allows the salesperson and the firm to allocate resources more efficiently.

Contact Management

Imagine your phone's address and email list, the business cards of prospects you recently met, notes about potential customers, and any additional information about leads. The CRM system combines all of this information. A CRM system allows the salesperson to create a central storage area for each prospect's information. This accessibility allows each salesperson to learn about the prospect.

ETHICAL DILEMMA

WHAT AN OFFER! OR IS IT?

You are a new life insurance agent and have just made a sale to an old family friend who is the personnel manager for a large manufacturing company in your town. To help you in your prospecting, he offers you a large file of personnel data on the employees of the company, including income, family size, phone numbers, and addresses.

This information would be very valuable. You are sure to make five to 10 sales from this excellent prospect list. As he hands you the material, you notice it is stamped, "Not for Publication, Company Use Only!"

What would be the most ethical action to take?

1. Take the information. It could really help you get started.
2. Thank your friend for the offer but refuse the information. It would not be right to accept something that is marked confidential.
3. Refuse the information and tell your friend that it was not good practice for him to offer it. Let him know that if anything like this were to happen again, you would have to report him to the proper people in his company.

Lead Scoring

The CRM system allows the selling firm to input qualifying criteria for the lead scoring process. Then, the CRM system can automatically calculate each lead's score. This allows the sales team to prioritize their efforts and resources quickly and efficiently.

Data Integration and Learning

Not only can a CRM system integrate all of the information about leads, it can also integrate best practices for prospecting and nurturing relations, and it can share this learning across the organization.

Pipeline Management

Firms consider the pipeline as the number of prospects and customers in each stage of the sales process. The goal of pipeline management is to understand the potential for business in the immediate term (current customers) and future term (prospects). A CRM technology's pipeline management function helps salespeople generate reports to better understand the movement of prospects through the sales process. This information is critical to helping salespeople plan their time.

How Is Prospecting Changing?

LO10

Social Selling

You are undoubtedly aware of the term social media. Social media has also impacted sales. **Social sales technology** is defined as any social interaction-enhancing technology that can be deployed by sales professionals to generate content (e.g., blogs, microblogs, wikis) and develop networks (e.g., social networks, online communities).[8]

social sales technology: Any social interaction-enhancing technology that can be deployed by sales professionals to generate content and develop networks.

The use of social sales technology has impacted the interactions of buyers and sellers on a daily basis. For instance, the seller's organization communicates a wide range of information about their firm's company, their products, services, and capabilities on websites; social media posts, such as Twitter, LinkedIn, and Facebook; blogs; white papers; etc. Buyers often initiate their own search for product and service information. They visit websites, join LinkedIn groups and follow perceived thought leaders in their industries, and download information and documents to enhance their understanding of potential solutions.

As we have discussed, LinkedIn, a popular social networking website for businesses and their employees, has emerged as a method to assist in the prospecting process. InMail, LinkedIn's internal email system, makes it possible for a sales representative to email any LinkedIn user without an introduction. LinkedIn also assists salespeople, as it tracks the users who view your profile–including potential leads. But most importantly, LinkedIn allows the salesperson to learn about the needs and of prospects and their firms. Salespeople are able to access comments and posts of prospects, download documents and white papers, and learn background information about their potential customers.

Social Listening

With LinkedIn and other social media, salespeople can better understand buyers and their activities. Further, a salesperson has an opportunity to monitor new and existing customers who are accessing the seller's information, posting comments, and downloading documents. In some industries, the monitoring, interpreting, and seeking understanding of buyer-based actions and communication is called **social listening**. Social listening provides one means of understanding customer needs and is becoming increasingly important to integrate into the selling process.

social listening: The monitoring, interpreting and seeking understanding of buyer-based action and communication.

Summary of Major Selling Issues

The sales process involves a series of actions, beginning with prospecting for customers. In the first step, the salesperson must find prospects to contact. Prospecting involves locating and qualifying the individuals or businesses that have the potential to buy a product. A person or business that might become a prospect is a *lead.* This question can determine whether someone is qualified: Does the prospect have the money, the authority, and the desire to buy my product or service?

Several of the more popular prospecting methods are cold calling and endless-chain referrals, attending public exhibitions and demonstrations, locating centres of influence, sending direct mailouts, conducting observation, and the newer form using social media. To obtain a continuous supply of prospects, the salesperson should develop a prospecting method suitable for their particular situation.

Once a lead has been located and qualified as a prospect, the salesperson can start the referral cycle, with the goal of increasing referrals. Various types of new technology are making the prospecting function much easier, including Customer Relationship Management software. Additionally, social media has allowed salespeople to review and monitor potential leads' opinions, attitudes, and interests by using social listening through the use of social media. Prospecting is evolving as a sales step and salespeople should be aware of all the tools available to make the prospecting function smoother.

MEETING A SALES CHALLENGE

Joe, Alex, and Kathryn analyzed the proposed prospecting systems fairly well. Finding customers is difficult for startups, however. You need a customer base and prospecting is the only way to get there. You can't stay in business for long by just coming up with an innovative and cost-effective product.

Just because a customer buys one thing from a company does not mean that the customer would not be open to learn about the innovations happening in the field. Remember, there is always room for improvement when it comes to serving customers! Moreover, big companies often are fooled by their corporate egos into thinking that their existing customers will keep buying from them forever.

Going after the market leader seems to scare Joe for some reason. However, think a minute: Exactly what will big companies do that they won't do competitively anyway? Competition exists on all sides by many firms. If the company has a good cost story to tell, then go after the big users for whom the cost savings will be significant.

In short, all the systems have virtues and none should be excluded from consideration. Much depends, however, on the particular territory. Some territories may have more young families—those who are more willing to explore high-tech security systems and would want more control compared to others. Salespeople must adapt to the characteristics of the territory.

PLAYING THE ROLE

The situation: As a new sales rep (one of four) selling advertising for a local radio station, you have been cold calling on businesses for two weeks, trying to drum up some business. You've been pretty successful but six prospects just weren't ready to commit. You've been working hard so you book off a Monday to enjoy a long weekend. On that Monday, three of these prospects phone in and ask for you. Because you're not there, the prospects get clarification on some issues from your colleagues, each of whom spends about 20 minutes with a prospect. Over the phone, each prospect commits to some advertising time. Because your colleagues spent time with these people and wrote up the order, they felt entitled to the commission.

Role A: You. You feel entitled to the commission.

Role B: A sales colleague. This person feels entitled to the commission.

Role C: A sales colleague. This person feels entitled to the commission.

Role D: A sales colleague. This person feels entitled to the commission.

Prepare an argument as to why you should get credit for the sales. Your colleagues feel entitled to the commission as they had to spend time with the customers; they will defend their choice to take the credit. *Play out these roles in an attempt to resolve the situation.*

Key Terms for Selling

centre-of-influence method	**MAD**	**referral**
cold canvass prospecting method	**networking**	**referral cycle**
customer service	**observation method**	**social sales technology**
direct-mail prospecting	**orphaned customers**	**social listening**
endless chain referral method	**parallel referral sale**	**telemarketing**
exhibitions and demonstrations	**prospect**	**telephone prospecting**
"Ferris-wheel" concept	**prospecting**	**teleprospecting**
lead	**qualified prospect**	

Sales Application Questions

1. What is the difference between a lead and a prospect? What should you do to qualify a potential customer?
2. This chapter defined prospecting as the lifeblood of selling.
   a. Where do salespeople find prospects?
   b. List and briefly explain the prospecting methods discussed in this chapter. Can you think of other ways to find prospects?
3. Assume that you have started a business to manufacture and market a simple inventory management system selling for between $5,000 and $10,000. Your primary customers are small retailers. How would you uncover leads and convert them into prospects without personally contacting them?
4. Assume you have determined that John Firestone, vice president of Pierce Chemicals, is a prospect for your paper and metal containers. You call Mr. Firestone to see whether he can see you this week. When his secretary answers the telephone, you say, "May I speak to Mr. Firestone, please?" and she says, "What is it you wish to talk to him about?" How will you answer her question? What will you say if you are told, "I'm sorry, but Mr. Firestone is too busy to talk with you"?

5. You are a new salesperson. Next week, your regional sales manager will be in town to check your progress in searching for new clients for your line of industrial chemicals. You have learned that Big Industries, Inc., a high-technology company, needs a supplier of your product. Also, a friend has told you about 12 local manufacturing firms that could use your product. The sales potential of each of these firms is about one-tenth of Big Industries. Knowing that your sales manager expects results, explain how you will qualify each lead (assuming the 12 smaller firms are similar).
6. *a.* Assume you are a salesperson for the manufacturer of each of the following products:

    - Photocopiers
    - LED projection systems
    - Energy-saving fluorescent light bulbs

    Develop a prospect list of 10 organizations in your area that would qualify as potential customers.

    b. Describe how you would make contact with each organization.

    c. Assume that you have made contact, and discuss how you would qualify your prospect.

    d. Develop a script that you might use if using the telephone in an attempt to get an appointment with the appropriate person in the company.

Sales Online Exercise

PizzaMunch and Social Listening

Part 1

Because social listening and social selling continue to evolve, we believe the best way to understand it is by examining an example of how it may occur in the marketplace.

You are a salesperson for an entrepreneurial, emerging company in the consumer packaged goods world, Ag-Kru Foods. Your flagship product is called the PizzaMunch, a portable, healthy pizza product. Because the product is new, your sales team has worked with the marketing department to provide a whole portfolio of online marketing materials including the following:

- An e-book on the changing needs of the pizza category
- A series of white papers on the evolution of American eating habits
- A contact form for a webinar presentation of how to merchandise the PizzaMunch in different channels of retail, including grocery stores, convenience stores, and retail warehouses
- A weekly podcast of retail and consumer trends that impact retail food categories

Your analytics department sends a message to you. A potential prospect, Shari Karkin, just downloaded a number of white papers and has signed up for a webinar—all last night. It appears that Shari may have an interest in PizzaMunch. Now your objective is to take action to assist Shari. But what should you do?

Questions

1. What are your options to contact Shari? What communication mode would you use to contact her (i.e., phone, email, instant message, LinkedIn)? Explain why you chose this mode of communication. Defend using online research.
2. What would be your communications goals in the message to Shari? Write down the actual communication message that you would use.

Social Listening

Part 2

Your firm offers the PizzaMunch. Because this product is new, your sales team is trying to discover prospects that may be interested in the product. The sales team believes a primary target customer is involved in the convenience store industry. As such, your sales team has been following a number of groups on LinkedIn, including the following:

- One group involved in the purchasing of pre-made food for convenience stores
- One group involved in the understanding business trends for convenience stores
- One group involved in understanding food consumption trends in convenience stores
- One group made up of individuals who own convenience stores (i.e., three or fewer convenience stores)

You notice that Jane Sterling, a participant in one of these groups, occasionally posts a question about selling pizza within convenience stores. Jane operates a convenience store outside a strip mall. The strip mall contains a major gym and a national retailer that specializes in workout clothing. Therefore, Jane's store receives a great deal of customer traffic from those who frequent the gym and the retailer. In one of her posts, sent to the group made up of individuals who own convenience stores, she relays that one of her consistent frustrations lies in her inability to find a pizza option that would cater to her customers. Many of her customers have asked her if she can provide a more healthy pizza. She wonders if any other convenience store owners face the same type of customer requests.

Questions

1. What are two specific options that you could use to respond to Jane? How would you use social listening to better understand customers? Defend using your online research.
2. Write down the communication you would send Jane. What specific results would you want to achieve by sending this communication to Jane?

Further Exploring the Sales World

Contact several salespeople in your community and ask them to discuss their prospecting system and the steps they use in planning their sales calls. Write a short paper on your results and be prepared to discuss it in class.

Selling Experiential Exercise

To measure your attitude toward selling, complete this exercise; 5 indicates strong agreement and 1 means strong disagreement.

Your Attitude Toward Selling

		Disagree			Agree	
1.	There is nothing demeaning about selling a good or service to a prospect.	1	2	3	4	5
2.	I would be proud to tell friends that selling is my career.	1	2	3	4	5
3.	I can approach customers, regardless of age, appearance, or behaviour, with a positive attitude.	1	2	3	4	5
4.	On bad days—when nothing goes right—I can still be positive.	1	2	3	4	5
5.	I am enthusiastic about selling.	1	2	3	4	5
6.	Having customers turn me down does not cause me to be negative.	1	2	3	4	5
7.	The idea of selling challenges me.	1	2	3	4	5
8.	I consider selling to be a profession.	1	2	3	4	5
9.	Approaching strangers (customers) is interesting and usually enjoyable.	1	2	3	4	5
10.	I can always find something good in a customer.	1	2	3	4	5
		Total Score ________				

Results - If you scored:

- More than 40 - You have an excellent attitude toward selling as a profession.
- 25 to 40 - You appear to have serious reservations about selling as a profession.
- Under 25 - Another type of job is probably best for you.

CASE 6–1

CANADIAN EQUIPMENT CORPORATION

You work for the Canadian Equipment Corporation selling office equipment. You enter the reception room of a small manufacturing company. You hand the receptionist your business card and ask to see the purchasing agent. "What is this in reference to?" the receptionist asks, as two other salespeople approach.

QUESTION

Which of the following alternatives would you use and why?

a. Give a quick explanation of your equipment, ask whether the receptionist has heard of your company or used your equipment, and again ask to see the purchasing agent.

b. Say, "I would like to discuss our office equipment."

c. Say, "I sell office equipment designed to save your company money and provide greater efficiency. Companies like yours really like our products. Could you help me get in to see your purchasing agent?"

d. Give a complete presentation and demonstration.

CASE 6–2

MONTREAL SATELLITES

As a salesperson for Montreal Satellites, you sell television satellite dishes for homes and businesses. After installing a satellite in Jeff Sager's home, you ask him for a referral. Jeff suggests you contact Tom Butler, his brother-in-law.

Mr. Butler is a well-known architect who designs and constructs unique residential homes. Your objective is to sell Mr. Butler a satellite for his office and one for his home in the hope that he will install them in the homes he builds. Certainly, he is a centre of influence and a good word from him to his customers could result in numerous sales. Thus, another objective is to obtain referrals from Mr. Butler.

QUESTIONS

1. After eight attempts, you now have Mr. Butler on the telephone. What do you say in order to get an appointment and set the stage for getting referrals?
2. You get the appointment and are now in Mr. Butler's office trying to get him to buy a satellite for his home and office. Sometime during the presentation you will ask for a referral. What will you say?
3. Mr. Butler buys a satellite for his home but not his office. You install the system yourself and then spend 15 minutes showing Mr. and Mrs. Butler and their two teenagers how to use it. Before you leave, how do you ask for a referral?
4. Three months after the installation you are talking to Mr. Butler. How do you ask for a referral?

Source: © Antoniodiaz | Dreamstime.com

CHAPTER 7

The Pre-Approach—Planning Your Sales Call and Presentation

Kyle Kirkpatrick
Algonquin College,
Ottawa, Ontario

Source: Courtesy of Kyle Kirkpatrick

A Sales Success Story

Kyle Kirkpatrick graduated from the two-year marketing program at Algonquin College in 2014. For his entire life, Kyle has been well-spoken and relatable, and he attributes his successes to his outgoing personality and up-for-the-challenge mentality. He has had the opportunity to put these soft skills into action as an account executive for Bradley's Insurance.

Algonquin College was a huge factor in developing Kyle's marketing and sales skill set. He believes that the structure of the marketing program, along with opportunities the college offers students to set themselves apart by participating in events like the Ontario Colleges' Marketing Competition (OCMC) and BDC Vanier National Case competition, were huge building blocks in the core foundation of the sales techniques that he relies on every day.

Kyle attributes his sales success to a lifelong enjoyment of seeing effort translate into results. In a sales environment, especially with a commissioned pay structure, every moment that you spend interacting with a client has a direct impact on your financial and professional success. Kyle finds this both extremely rewarding and helpful, as it motivates him to treat every conversation and every interaction as an opportunity to hone his soft skills and further develop his knowledge base.

When asked what he believes is the key to being a successful salesperson, Kyle responds, "It is about being confident and knowledgeable in the product or service that you are providing to your client . . . having a real conversation, listening, and responding to your potential client in a way that makes them want to work with you. The real art to selling is engaging a person so completely that it doesn't feel like you are providing them with a sales pitch or just looking for that transition to the close, but rather that they came to the decision to take the next step forward."

Kyle has this advice for aspiring salespeople:

- Drop the entitlement. The client is choosing to work with you; it is up to you to make the deal.
- Drop the clichés, the canned statements, and the scripts.
- Every conversation is a sale of one type or another. Be open to discussions.
- Never fear rejection. A "no" is an opportunity to learn.

MAIN TOPICS

The Core Principles: Planning

Strategic Customer Sales Planning—the Pre-Approach

The Customer Relationship Model

The Prospect's Mental Steps

Call Reluctance

LEARNING OBJECTIVES

The pre-approach (or planning the sales call) is the second step in the selling process. It is extremely important to spend time planning all aspects of your sales presentation. After studying this chapter, you should be able to

LO1 Explain the importance of sales call planning.

LO2 List the four planning steps in order and understand them.

LO3 Develop a customer benefit plan.

LO4 Describe the prospect's five mental steps in buying.

FACING A SALES CHALLENGE

After being hired, trained, and given a sales territory, you have been assigned by your boss to work with three of your company's salespeople. You immediately notice they are not doing what you've been trained to do. They walk into an office, introduce themselves, and ask whether the customer needs anything today. Prospects rarely buy, and customers tell them what they need. This doesn't seem like selling to you; it's order taking, and that type of job is not for you.

The problem is—how do you get someone to listen to you? How do you know what they think of your product? How do you know when they're ready to buy? Next Monday, you will call on your first customer. What will you do differently?

(Continued at end of chapter.)

Your job as a salesperson is to find prospects who need your product and convince them your product will satisfy their need. Now that you've completed your hard work in finding these prospects, let's not waste it. It is vitally important that you prepare properly to make contact with this prospect. This chapter introduces you to the importance of planning each sales call. It often takes hours to plan a sales presentation and only minutes to present it; however, without proper preparation, your sales will suffer.

LO1 The Core Principles: Planning

A sales manager was working with a new salesperson one day. The boss asked, "What is your purpose for calling on this prospect today?" The salesperson replied, "To sell them something?" The sales manager said, "That's great, but what is your purpose?"

Begin Your Plan with Purpose and Passion Will Follow

The sales manager's question is forcing the new salesperson to create a broad philosophical statement toward a business meeting with a customer or prospect. Purpose is broad in scope. Purpose is not a list of plans, goals, or objectives that differ from one sales call to another. Purpose is a constant truth that guides your business life. Purpose directs how you approach each sales call. It defines success for you. Purpose classifies your relationships. It helps define who you are as a sales professional.

Knowing your purpose focuses your sales efforts to serve others. It concentrates your effort and energy on what is important. Knowing your purpose motivates your life and is your reason to get out of bed in the morning. Purpose produces passion. Nothing energizes like a clear purpose. Conversely, passion evaporates like smoke in the wind without purpose.

sales call purpose: Sales call purpose is to make a contribution to the welfare of a person or organization.

Hopefully your **sales call purpose** is to make a contribution to the welfare of the person or organization. You want to help someone reach their goals or solve their business problems. Could you be enthusiastic and passionate about asking someone to buy something that would help them? You want to make a contribution to the welfare of others–don't you? So how do you help someone? You need a plan that is related to your purpose.

Plan to Achieve Your Purpose

Your tomorrow is today! Your today was yesterday's tomorrow! Concentrate on today. Do not worry about tomorrow. There are enough worries for today.

What does that mean? How you think, how you act, what you accomplish today will determine your future–your tomorrow. To an overwhelming degree, you can control your future by what you do today.[1] Today's test score is based upon yesterday's studying. What you sell today is based on preparation done yesterday. Does that make sense to you?

> *A plan is a method of achieving an end. A plan involves what you want to accomplish and how you will do it.*

Plan each day, do the best you can to carry out your plan and adjust to circumstances as you go, and then at the end of each day evaluate your day to ensure you are on your way toward a successful tomorrow. Everyone knows this, yet the difference between successful and less successful people is that successful people plan, implement their plans, and evaluate the day's sales results in order to know what to do tomorrow. Less successful people think about planning but seldom do it.

Do you plan how to prepare for a test? Once you have taken the test (implemented your plan), do you evaluate how and what you studied versus your test results? Few students do, but the ones who plan, work their plan, and then evaluate their results do much better on the next test. Try it! It works in a class, just as it does in sales.

What Is a Plan?

A **plan** is a method of achieving an end. A plan involves what you want to accomplish and how you will do it. Before ever making the sales call, the salesperson reviews the purpose for the meeting. The salesperson plans how to help solve problems and fulfill the needs of the person or organization. Careful planning of every aspect of the sales call helps the salesperson be organized and prepared to interact with the customer. For each prospect or customer, a salesperson is often faced with a specific, unique set of problems to solve or needs to fulfill. As a result, each sales call requires a specific solution from the salesperson. You plan in order to help. Planning is part of ethical service, which leads to building relationships with the customer. The foundation of your plan must be based upon building a trust-based business relationship.

plan:
A method of achieving an end.

What is the importance of truth? From your honesty (integrity), people realize you can be trusted. Your honesty and trustworthiness form your character or who you are to others. Your use of facts (truth) without distortion by personal feelings or prejudices makes you like a superhero, a super salesperson. How?

You want to help someone in need. How? Sell them something. Why? It will help them meet their need. You can do that!

What Is Success?

With purpose comes a plan; with a plan comes success. What does a successful sales call look like? How do you define success? For example:

- A baseball coach might define success as winning more games than losing. Their boss might define success as winning the national championship or the World Series.
- You might define success as making an A or just passing this course.
- A salesperson might define success as making sales quota this year or being the top salesperson in the company.

But what about calling on the individual customer? What is a success for you? It goes back to purpose. **Success** is setting a goal and accomplishing it. You are meeting with someone with the purpose of helping them. Your purpose, plan, and goal do not centre on selling, but rather on helping. Can you fail?

success:
Setting a goal and accomplishing it.

Statistics show that individuals who establish goals tend to achieve them more than those who don't. In fact, a 2015 study showed that individuals who wrote down their goals were 33 percent more successful in achieving them that those who did not write them down.[2] That is an impressive statistic and one that highlights the importance of having a plan.

Successful but No Sale

How could you *not* make a sale and still have a successful sales call? What if your customer did not have a need? You did not fail. What if your product would not help meet the person's needs? How could you say you were not successful?

Trust serves as the glue that enables relationships. Without trust, it is difficult to develop and maintain a relationship.

Now consider this. Although there are reasons you may not make a sale, there should never be a reason that you do not meet the "purpose" of your business meeting. Why? What is your purpose? To help someone!

The Gap: Trust Building in a Sales Relationship

Many people do not trust salespeople. Some salespeople are self-centred, only wanting to make a sale for their own benefit. However, you can help eliminate this negative stereotype of salespeople by exhibiting honesty and trust-building actions and communication.

There can be no long-term relationships between two parties without trust based upon truth. One lie or one misrepresentation can lead to separation, even divorce, between seller and buyer. Has that ever happened to you?

Why Is Trust Important?

Some suggest that trust serves as the glue that enables relationships. Without trust, it is difficult to develop a relationship. Without trust, your buyers may not confide in you and may not disclose key details regarding their needs. By not revealing this important information, your ability to develop a worthy solution may be hindered.

A secret of successful people: plan, implement, evaluate.

For instance, you probably experience a lack of trust on a consistent basis with certain salespeople. Consider the last time you entered a retail store. Did the retail associate ask, "Is there anything I can help you with?" If so, what was your answer? Perhaps you stated, "No, I'm just looking" or "No thanks." If this was your response, it appears that you communicated an objection to the salesperson in the hopes they would leave you alone.

But, what if you visited the store for a specific reason? Perhaps you needed to find a daring piece of fashion that you were sensitive to ask about. Or, perhaps you visited a hardware store, but you weren't sure of the name of the product. You didn't want to look silly, so you chose to meander the aisles and look for the product rather than ask for help. Why didn't you accept the retail associate's assistance? It may have been due to a lack of trust. You chose to not share your needs because you did not trust that person.

As you can see from our example, trust is an important facet in a business relationship. As a salesperson, your goal is to develop a trusting relationship with the buyer. But what builds trust? According to research, trust building elements include:[3]

- Communication
- Similarity and compatibility
- Expertise
- Investing resources into the relationship, such as time and effort
- Providing benefits such as saving the buyer time or helping to make a decision(s)
- Reducing conflict or opportunities for conflict

Salespeople who want to build trusting relationships with their clients should develop their personal communication and interaction skills; enhance their ability to adapt to the buyers in order to create compatibility; work to develop their knowledge of their own business and the buyers' business; diligently serve their customers; and ensure that customers are able to attain their goals and objectives. You should also note that conflict is often detrimental to a trusting relationship.

Exhibit 7.1 presents a number of ideas to build trust, including specific actions that a salesperson could use to enhance key trust-building elements.

EXHIBIT 7.1

A salesperson can take specific actions to build trust.

How could the salesperson build trust in the following areas?	The salesperson could ask, "Do I...?"
Communication	Do I listen well? Do I express myself clearly? Do I use specific, professional language? Do I work to reduce my vocalized pauses (i.e., umm, uhh)? Do I practise my presentations before I speak to a group? Do I summarize my buyer's needs to ensure I understand the individual?
Similarity and compatibility	Do I build similarity during rapport (i.e., find common values, topics, interests etc.)? Do I use customer-oriented language (you or we vs. me or I)? Do I mirror the buyer when appropriate?
Expertise	Do I share my knowledge with the buyer? Do I study my industry? Do I learn about the intricacies of my customers' businesses? Do I continually learn about my firm, my customers, and my industry (i.e., am I a lifelong learner)? Do I try to help my buyer by sharing my understanding of their business or industry?
Investing resources into relationship	Do I prepare adequately (i.e., invest the needed time) for my meetings? Do I work diligently to find resources and solutions for my customers? Do I seek and find other internal resources (i.e., colleagues) that can also assist my buyer?
Providing benefits, such as time savings or decision making	Do I attempt to understand my buyer's problems and help them solve them? Do I understand my buyer's personal goals, career goals, and business goals? Do I provide multiple solutions to my buyer? Do I work to understand my buyer's industry and how they can become more effective? Do I follow up with my buyer and ensure high-quality post-sales service?

EXHIBIT 7.2

The pre-approach involves planning the sales presentation.

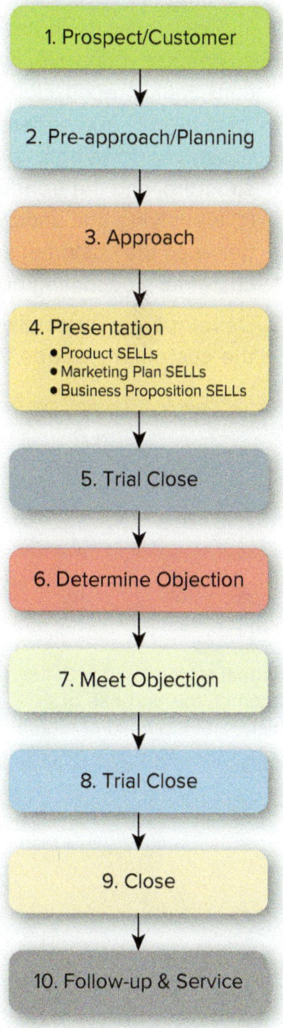

Strategic Customer Sales Planning—The Pre-approach

Once the prospect has been located, or the salesperson determines which customer to call on, the salesperson is ready to plan the sales call. Planning is often referred to as the pre-approach (see Exhibit 7.2). This chapter discusses the many aspects of planning a sales call. Let's begin by learning why salespeople should consider the customer's needs in order to recommend a creative solution that will benefit both the buyer and the seller.

strategic: Programs, goals, and problems of great importance to customers.

High-performing salespeople tend to be strategic problem solvers for their customers. **Strategic** refers to programs, goals, and problems of great importance to customers. The top salespeople who are effective strategic problem solvers have the skills and knowledge to be able to do the following:

- Uncover and understand the customer's strategic needs by gaining in-depth knowledge of the customer's organization.
- Possess the needed knowledge about the customer's organization, the customer's industry, and the firm's product or service.
- Develop solutions that demonstrate a creative approach to addressing the customer's strategic needs in the most efficient and effective manner possible.
- Arrive at a mutually beneficial agreement.
- Create value–as perceived by the customer.

SELLING TIPS

WHAT IS A SOLUTION?

Buyer expectations are increasing, especially when it comes to solutions. But how should we think about a solution? Sales research suggests the following four key elements comprise a solution:

1. Defining the customer's needs and must-haves: This includes (a) a strong needs inquiry to understand the customer's needs (i.e., needs that lay at the conscious, preconscious, and unconscious levels); (b) familiarity and understanding of the customer's business, including its business and operating structure, and the trends in its industry; and (c) identifying and understanding the difference between the customer's present-day needs and the customer's upcoming needs.
2. Developing a customized solution that (a) meets the customer's needs and will align with the customer's circumstances (marketplace, business model, facilities, etc.); and (b) is made of a number of well-organized elements that work well together.
3. Being able to integrate, set up, and implement the solution within the customer's environment (facilities, locations, operational processes, etc.). This might mean modifying the solution during its implementation and providing training to ensure the customer can fully use the solution.
4. Providing support after the solution has been implemented within the customer's business. In this stage, the salesperson's firm may need to provide consistent support and assistance (i.e., post-sales service, training, trouble-shooting, and recognition of ongoing opportunities for enhancement).

Source: Capil R., Tuli, Ajay K. Kohli, and Sundar G. Bharadwaj, "Rethinking Customer Solutions: From Product Bundles to Relational Processes," *Journal of Marketing*, 71, no. 3 (July 2007), 1–17.

strategic customer relationship: A formal relationship with the customer, the purpose of which is joint pursuit of mutual goals.

Strategic needs, creative solutions, and mutually beneficial agreements are critical to strategic problem solving. When properly executed by the salesperson, they create a **strategic customer relationship** or a formal relationship with the customer, the purpose of which is joint pursuit of mutual goals. Strategic goals for a customer typically include reducing costs and/or increasing productivity, responsiveness, sales, and profits. The sales organization has goals of increasing sales and profits.

The purpose of a strategic customer relationship is joint pursuit of mutual goals.

Strategic Needs

The salesperson who understands the full range of the customer's needs is in a much better position to provide a product solution that helps the customer progress more efficiently and effectively toward achieving his or her organization's strategic goal.

"The top salespeople have an in-depth understanding of our needs," said one business purchasing professional. "They can match up their products with these needs to help us reach our goals."

Needs of the Buyer

A critical element of the salesperson's knowledge lies in understanding the buyer's strategic needs. However, needs may be elusive. As we discussed in Chapter 3, many buyers may or may not be totally aware of their needs. Therefore, we provide a list of needs that are commonly associated with buyers. The table includes needs for business-to-business markets (i.e., very economic-based and important to a firm), the human needs of the business buyer (i.e., the needs of humans that are responsible for buying in a business-to-business environment), and business-to-consumer markets (i.e., the needs of the everyday consumer).

The following table provides you with a tool for your pre-approach document. As you begin to forecast your buyer's needs, you can ask yourself whether the buyer possesses any of the following needs.

BUSINESS-TO-BUSINESS NEEDS	PERSONAL NEEDS OF THE BUSINESS-TO-BUSINESS BUYER	BUSINESS-TO-CONSUMER NEEDS
Help increase my firm's revenues (sales)	Help me reach my business objectives and other responsibilities	Help me reach my personal and/or professional goals and objectives
Help increase my firm's net profits	Help me feel competent with my team, colleagues, and supervisors	Help me feel secure (financially, emotionally, relationally)
Help increase my firm's gross margins (price–cost of goods sold)	Help me with my relationships with my team, colleagues, and supervisors	Help me reduce my perceived risk regarding a change
Help increase the speed with which my firm sells its product(s) (i.e., inventory turnover)	Help me reduce my concerns about a change in my business, business plans, or responsibilities	Help me take care of those I love or who are important to me
Help increase the pace of my firm's production processes	Help me become more insightful about my industry	Help me feel secure about my actions
Help increase the satisfaction of my firm's or my business unit's customers	Help me become more insightful about my competition	Help me feel competent in front of others whom I perceive are important
Help reduce my firm's or business unit's expenses (costs)	Help me understand key trends that will impact my firm or my responsibilities	Help me with my personal personal responsibilities
Help my firm's ability to retain customers or develop new customers	Help me generate influence within my organization	Help me enjoy certain aspects of my life that I perceive are important

Creative Solutions

For each customer, a salesperson is often faced with a specific, unique set of problems to solve. As a result, each customer requires a specific solution from the sales organization. The ability of a salesperson to tailor a "custom" solution for each customer is critical today. The salesperson needs to follow a three-stage creative problem solving process: (1) finding the problem, (2) solving the problem, and (3) implementing the solution. Instead of one product, the salesperson often must create the solution from a mix of goods and services. Usually, the solution represents one of two options:

1. A customized version or application of a product and/or service that efficiently addresses the customer's specific strategic needs.
2. A mix of goods and services–including, if appropriate, competitors' products and services–that offers the best possible solution in light of the customer's strategic needs.

creative problem solvers: Individuals who have the ability to develop and combine nontraditional alternatives to meet the specific needs of the customer.

The better a salesperson is at creatively marshalling all available resources to address a customer's strategic needs, the stronger the customer relationship becomes. Today's salespeople need to be **creative problem solvers** who have the ability to develop and combine nontraditional alternatives to meet the specific needs of the customer. In order to become a creative problem solver, the salesperson must invest a significant amount of effort into delving into the buyer's true needs, interpreting the needs, and creating a meaningful solution.

But what is a meaningful solution? A meaningful solution solves the buyer's problems and creates value for the buyer. Value occurs when the buyer perceives that what they have received from the salesperson's solution is greater than what they invested in order to attain the solution (i.e., time, effort, money, or other resources). However, value is perceptual–it is defined by the buyer. The buyer determines the elements, processes, efforts, products, and services that they appreciate. For instance, a buyer may believe a salesperson is extremely valuable because they always input orders correctly and communicate when they have finished key actions (i.e., follow-up). The buyer may believe the salesperson's company provides exactly the same product as does their competition. However, the competitive firm does not create value because its salesperson always makes mistakes during the ordering process.

Let's review another example. A buyer for a sporting goods firm may believe that one of its manufacturers creates value because it is very innovative. While the manufacturing firm may not always introduce the best-selling products, the manufacturer is always introducing new products in an attempt to garner increased sales for its sporting good distributors. Hence, the buyer may believe that the absolute sales numbers for each new product are not is as important as the manufacturer's consistent effort to introduce new products and bring new sales to its sporting goods distributors. As you can see, the perception of value may not always be tied directly to the price of the product. Each buyer will perceive value differently.

As the examples suggest, the salesperson needs to understand how to create value for the customer–through understanding the customer's needs and developing meaningful solutions tied directly to those needs.

Mutually Beneficial Agreements

Salespeople and customers say that a significant shift has occurred in their expectations of the outcome of sales agreements–from the adversarial win-lose to the more collaborative win-win arrangement. To achieve a mutually beneficial agreement, salespeople and customers must work together to develop a common understanding of the issues and challenges at hand.

The Customer Relationship Model

The customer relationship model shown in Exhibit 7.3 brings together the main elements of consultative selling. It shows that customers have strategic needs that salespeople must meet through creative solutions. In doing so, both buyer and seller benefit. The customer reaches their goal, as does the seller. This results in the seller being able to sell the

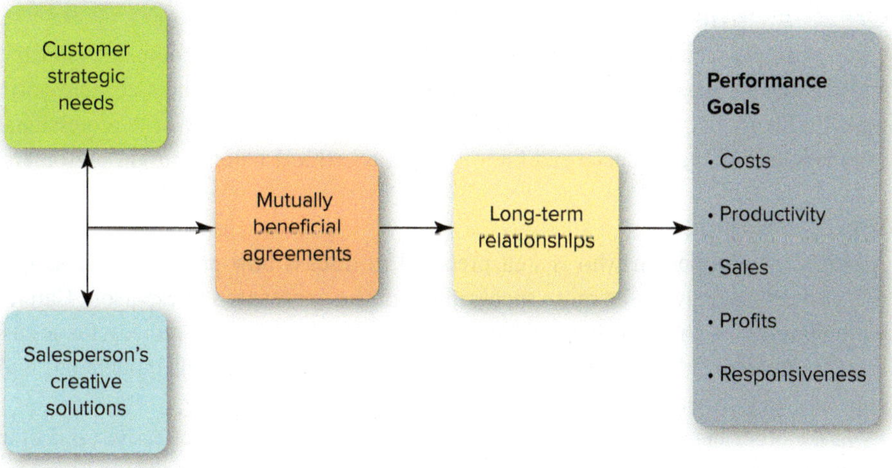

EXHIBIT 7.3
Consultative selling—customer relationship model.

customer again and again and again—building a long-term relationship. Strategic customer sales planning is extremely important to the success of today's salespeople. Let's examine the important aspects of the second step in our customer relationship process, called the pre-approach. The **pre-approach** refers to *planning the sales call* on a customer or prospect.

pre-approach: Planning the sales call on a customer or prospect.

Why Does Preparation Matter?

Planning the sales call is the key to success (see Exhibit 7.4). Salespeople say there are numerous reasons for planning the sales call, and four of the most frequently mentioned reasons are:

1. It helps build confidence.
2. It develops an atmosphere of goodwill between the buyer and seller.
3. It reflects professionalism.
4. It generally increases sales because the salesperson better understands the buyer's needs.

EXHIBIT 7.4
Planning is the key to success. The sales team rehearses an upcoming sales call.
Source: ©Yuri_Acurs/Getty Images

Builds Self-Confidence

In giving a speech before a large group, most people are nervous. You can greatly reduce this nervousness and increase self-confidence by planning what to say and practising your talk. The same is true in making a sales presentation. By carefully planning your presentation, you increase confidence in yourself and your ability as a salesperson. This is why planning the sales call is especially important.

Develops an Atmosphere of Goodwill

Customers appreciate and respect salespeople who understand their needs and are prepared to discuss how a product will benefit them. Knowledge of a customer and concern for their needs demonstrate a sincere interest that generally is rewarded with an attitude of goodwill from the customer. This goodwill gradually builds the customer's confidence and results in a belief that the salesperson can be trusted to fulfill obligations.

Creates Professionalism and Credibility

Good business relationships are built on your knowledge of your company, industry, and customer's needs. Show customers that you are calling on them to help solve their problems or satisfy their needs. These factors are the mark of a professional salesperson, who uses specialized knowledge in an ethical manner to aid customers.

Increases Sales

A confident salesperson who is well prepared to discuss how products address particular needs will always be more successful than the unprepared salesperson. Careful planning ensures that you have diagnosed a situation and have a remedy for a customer's problem. Planning ensures that a sales presentation is well thought-out and appropriately presented.

Like other beneficial pre-sales call activities, planning is most effective (and time efficient) when done logically and methodically. Some salespeople try what they consider planning, later discarding the process because it took too much time. In many cases, these individuals were not aware of the basic elements of sales planning.

LO2

Elements of Sales Call Planning

Exhibit 7.5 depicts the four steps to sales call planning:

1. Determining the sales call objective
2. Developing or reviewing the customer profile
3. Developing a customer benefit plan
4. Developing the individual sales presentation based on the sales call objective, customer profile, and customer benefit plan

EXHIBIT 7.5

Steps in the pre-approach: planning the sale.

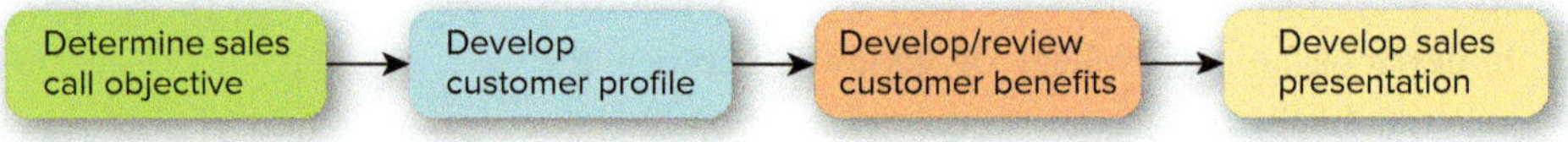

sales call purpose: Sales call purpose is to make a contribution to the welfare of a person or organization.

Always Have a Sales Call Objective

The **sales call objective** is the main purpose of a salesperson's contact with a prospect or customer. Is it possible to make a sales call without having a sales call objective in mind? Why can't salespeople just go in and see what develops? They can; in fact, a survey call is a legitimate sales technique. However, when all the calls that salespeople make are survey calls, they should be working exclusively for the market research department.

The Pre-call Objective Selling is not a very complex process. It's just difficult to do on a consistent basis. That's why, whether you regard it as an art or a science, the discipline of selling starts with setting a pre-call objective.

If anyone doubts this, remember that, by definition, a sales call must move systematically toward a sale or the next step toward a decision to purchase. Often, we're not talking about elaborate planning. Sometimes it takes only a few seconds before a call. But on every occasion, it's vital for the sales representative to answer one simple question: "If this call is successful, what will result?"

Taking the time to do this starts the selling process in motion. Before every sales call, ask yourself, "What am I going in here for? What is the result I'm trying to make happen? If they give me the opportunity, what am I going to recommend?"

Focus and Flexibility Writing down your pre-call objective increases the focus of your efforts. Given today's rising costs and the investment made in the sales force, this focus is essential. If salespeople are just going around visiting customers to see what develops, they are merely well-paid tourists. If they are professional sales representatives, they should be moving their customers toward a predetermined goal.

Knowing where you are going definitely increases the likelihood of getting there. Obviously, if the pre-call objective turns out to be inappropriate as the sales call develops, it's easy to switch tactics. Often, such changes involve a simple redirection.

Making the Goal Specific When asked the purpose of a call, some salespeople say enthusiastically, "It's to get an order!" However, this is too broad of a goal. Goals are much more attainable when they provide concrete direction. While everyone's in favour of getting orders, it is more likely to happen if salespeople stop and ask themselves questions such as these: What customer need can I serve? Which good or service is best for this account? How large an order should I suggest? The more specific the objective, the better.

> *The more specific the objective of each sales meeting, the greater the likelihood of success.*

Moving toward Your Objective Just because a salesperson isn't making a formal presentation doesn't mean that the call shouldn't be planned. Sometimes the sales call has a limited objective. Guiding the customer in the direction of that pre-planned outcome is what is experienced salespeople do on most sales calls. They do it with such simple questions as these:

- If we can meet the spec, can you set up a trial?
- How soon will the vice president be available to make a decision?
- Can you schedule a demonstration before the end of the month?

How to Set a Sales Call Objective Don't let anyone tell you that selling is so repetitive that the next step becomes a matter of rote. Knowing where you are going may be rote, but getting there requires thinking and skill. Set a **SMART** call objective that is:

SMART: A technique to set the sales call objectives by making sure the objectives are specific, measurable, achievable, realistic, and timed.

Specific - to get an order is *not* specific
Measurable - quantifiable (number, size, etc.)
Achievable - not too difficult to fulfill
Realistic - not too easy to fulfill
Timed - at this call or before the end of the financial year

It's amazing how often even veteran salespeople skip the pre-call objective step in favour of just seizing whatever opportunities present themselves. As a professional, it's your responsibility to avoid this kind of behaviour. Commit to having an objective for every call, and after each call check your results against that objective. This is a simple truth that the best sales professionals have always known. Often the most important step in a sale takes place without the customer even being there.

In addition, the sales call objective should be directly beneficial to the customer. A Colgate salesperson might call on a chain store manager with the multiple objectives of making sure that Colgate products are placed where they sell most rapidly, replenishing the store's stock of Colgate products so that customers will not leave the store disgruntled due to stockouts, and helping the manager decide how much promotional Colgate toothpaste and Rapid Shave shaving cream should be displayed.

Industrial salespeople develop similar objectives to determine if customers need to reorder or to sell new products. We provide a few examples of effective SMART objectives and a few examples of less effective SMART objectives below.

Examples of an Effective SMART Call Objective

To meet with the Joe's Retail Grocery buyer with responsibilities in the cleaning category on March 15, 2020 and sign an agreement on March 15, 2020 (specific) to purchase 55 cases of the new Kragni product solution (measurable) and distribute it within 50 of their 100 stores (achievable and realistic) by June 1, 2020 (realistic and time-based).

To present XMZ Electrical Distribution with two specific solutions that provide long-term cost reductions based on their stated needs of reducing their annual energy expenses (specific). The goal of each solution is to meet XMZ Electrical Distribution's stated objective of a payback period less than three years (measurable). My goal is to gain approval by the buyer of both solutions at the August 12, 2020, meeting (achievable and realistic) and begin implementing the solution in XMZ's 10 largest distribution centres by December 1, 2020 (specific and time-based).

Example of an Ineffective SMART Call Objective

To set a meeting with the customer sometime in the next few months (not very specific) and talk to them about some of our products (not measurable) with the hopes they will buy many of the products from our product line (hard to determine if this is realistic or achievable) in the next year or so (not time-based).

To meet with John S. of Alley Grocery in January or February (not very specific) and discuss a few ideas on a promotional plan (not measurable). My goal is to have John S. consider the opportunities and potentially get back to me sometime soon (may not be very realistic or timely).

Customer Profile Provides Insight

A customer profile sheet, as shown in Exhibit 7.6, can be a guide for determining the appropriate strategy to use in contacting each customer. The salesperson should review as much relevant information as possible regarding the firm, the buyer, and the individuals who influence the buying decision–before making a sales call–to properly develop a customized presentation. The salesperson also must consider the material discussed previously concerning why the customer is buying at this time.

A **customer profile** should tell you such things as these:

customer profile: An outline that gives relevant information regarding the firm, the buyer, and individuals who influence the buying decision.

- Who makes the buying decisions in the organization–an individual or committee?
- What is the buyer's background? The background of the buyer's company? The buyer's expectations of you?
- What are the desired business terms and requirements of the account, such as delivery, credit, technical service?
- What competitors successfully do business with the account? Why?
- What are the purchasing policies and practices of the account? For example, does the customer buy special price offer promotions, or only see salespeople on Tuesdays and Thursdays?
- What is the history of the account? For example, past purchases of our products, inventory turnover, profit per shelf foot, our brand's volume sales growth, payment practices, and attitude toward resale prices.
- What are the buyer's critical needs?
- What pressure(s) is the buyer facing within their organization and their competitive environment?

EXHIBIT 7.6

Information used in a profile and for planning.

Customer Profile and Planning Sheet

1. Name: ____________________

Address: ____________________

2. Type of business: ____________________

Name of buyer: ____________________

3. People who influence buying decisions or aid in using or selling our product: ____________________

What mode of communication does the buyer prefer (face-to-face, email, text, phone, instant message, etc.)

4. Buying hours and best time to see buyer: ____________________

5. Mode of communication the buyer prefers (face-to-face, email, text, phone, instant message, etc.): ____________________

6. Administrative assistant's name: ____________________

7. Buyer's profile: ____________________

8. Buyer's personality style: ____________________

9. Sales call objectives: ____________________

10. What are customer's important buying needs:

____

11. Maj or industry pressures faced by the buyer's firm:

____

12. Sales presentation: ____________________

a) Sales approach: ____________________

b) Features, advantages, benefits: ____________________

c) Method of demonstrating *FAB*: ____________________

d) How to relate benefits to customer's needs:

____

e) Trial close to use: ____________________

f) Anticipated objections: ____________________

g) Trial close to use: ____________________

h) How to close this customer: ____________________

i) Hard or soft close: ____________________

13. Sales made—product use/promotional plan agreed on:

____

14. Post-sales call comments (reason did/did not buy, what to do on next call; follow-up promised): ____________________

Determine this information from a review of records on the company or through personal contact with the company.

How Do I Find the Information for a Customer Profile? The available amount of customer information will vary based on the salesperson's firm and industry. For example, some firms have integrated their customer relationship management software into their sales process. In these firms, salespeople can access a range of information about the customer or prospect including the history of the customer account, industry information, social media trends, contact history, and overviews of key discussions.

However, other firms may be limited in their resources. Therefore, the sales force must be able to efficiently find information about prospects and customers on their own.

In these cases, the salesperson can use a range of online sources. A number of resources are widely available to salespeople and their firms. Access may be free or may require some level of an investment. We only highlight a few examples (without endorsement) to provide you with an idea of the variety of information available to you:

- *LinkedIn* is one of the premier social networks for business. It provides an opportunity for individuals and businesses to network. A salesperson can learn an organization's background as well as its decision-makers' background, such as employment history, educational background, educational experience, training, and general interests.
- *D&B Hoovers* provides a range of information about businesses, industries, and markets. While this is a paid service, it provides opportunities to better understand firms, decision makers, and their market environment.
- *Bizstats.com* provides a quick financial overview of companies that operate within a certain industry. For instance, a salesperson could use this information to understand the average industry performance on metrics such as net income, balance sheet metrics, return on sales, and inventory turnover.

Place Yourself in the Buyer's Shoes Great preparation means that a salesperson conducts research in order to better understand the buyer's potential needs. One method to understand the buyer's perspective is to imagine yourself in their role. Based on your understanding of the buyer's firm and industry, you could ask yourself, "Which of the following areas are placing pressure on the buyer?" and "Which of the following areas might be causing the buyer to seek a solution?" Salespeople can use the following questions to better understand the professional buyer and the buying organization:

- Is the buyer under pressure to meet certain personal goals (i.e., on the performance evaluation)? What might be the key challenges facing the buyer in meeting personal performance objectives?
- Is the buyer under pressure to meet certain financial objectives or obligations? What specific financial metrics does the buyer need to assist the firm in meeting?
- Is the buyer and their firm impacted by the competition? In what specific ways is the competition creating challenges to the buyer and their firm?
- Is the buyer confronting technological challenges or trends that are impacting their firm? What are the specific challenges tied to technology? What specific type of assistance might the buyer be seeking?
- Is the buyer confronting certain internal challenges, such as a manufacturing constraint or departmental conflicts? In what specific areas might the buyer be seeking assistance to overcome such internal challenges?
- Are regulations or political challenges impacting the buyer's firm? What type of assistance might the buyer be seeking to confront or overcome such challenges?
- Is the buyer experiencing challenges in serving their customers? What types of assistance might the buyer be seeking?

Salespeople could use a similar approach to understand the buyer's personal or psychological needs. They could ask themselves if it is possible that the buyer is facing any of the following situations:

- Is the buyer attempting to meet certain personal goals related to family matters or pressures?
- Is the buyer attempting to change the perceptions that others have of them?
- Is the buyer attempting to change their personal perception of something in their life or career?
- Is the buyer attempting to avoid a topic or situation that may negatively impact them?

- Is the buyer attempting to meet certain personal financial goals?
- Is the buyer confronting some type of challenge based on the economy or some sort of public policy?

Creating a Foundation for Your Customer Benefit Plan

Earlier you placed yourself in the buyer's role, and you asked a range of questions related to the pressures confronting the buyer. This exercise provided insight into the buyer's potential needs.

The next step combines your understanding of the potential pressures and needs confronting the buyer with an overview of potential solutions. This summary creates a brief outline for developing the Customer Benefit Plan. The following example provides one approach for developing this summary:

"Based on the buyer's key challenges that include (*insert the specific key challenges*), the buyer will need help finding solutions for the following needs including: (*insert needs*). I can assist the customer by providing a solution that will (*insert your benefits that are directly tied to the buyer's needs*). My buyer will undoubtedly want to discuss areas that are important to them. Therefore, I need to specifically discuss metrics or topics such as (*insert key metrics or key topics*). The buyer may also be somewhat leery of change. In fact, many of the common concerns that the buyer might express as objections may include (*insert potential areas of concern, risk or worries regarding a change*)."

Customer Benefit Plan: What It's All About

LO3

Beginning with your sales call objectives and what you know about your prospect, you are ready to develop a **customer benefit plan.** The customer benefit plan contains the nucleus of the information used in your sales presentation; thus it should be developed to the best of your ability. The customer benefit plan incorporates this four-step process:

customer benefit plan: A plan that contains the nucleus of information used in the sales presentation.

Step 1. Once you have outlined the potential needs of your prospect, select the features, advantages, and benefits of your product to present to your customer. This addresses the issue of why the customer should purchase your product: its benefits fulfill certain needs or solve certain problems. Carefully determine the benefits you wish to present. Again, we would like to stress that the benefits you select should align with the customer's most important needs.

Step 2. Develop your marketing plan. If selling to wholesalers or retailers, your marketing plan should include how they will sell your product to their customers. An effective marketing plan includes suggestions on how a retailer, for example, should "promote" the product through displays, advertising, proper shelf space and positioning, and pricing.

Did you hear the story of the guy who went into a small grocery store and asked the owner if he had any salt? "Do I have salt!?" shouted the grocer. He showed the shopper shelves full of salt and then took him to the storeroom and showed him boxes of salt, saying, "Do I have salt!?" Next they went to the basement to see more boxes, where the grocer again exclaimed, "Do I have salt!?"

Do you think the grocer will buy more salt when the salesperson returns? Chances are he will want to return salt, not buy it. To help this grocer generate revenue to pay his rent and employees, the salt salesperson must help him sell salt. How? Well, maybe give away a box of 39¢ salt with each purchase over $5. This might draw more customers into the store. It is often easy enough to sell to national companies, but if they cannot in turn sell what you sold them, you will not sell anything to them again. Provide strategies on selling through to the reseller's customers.

For an end-user of the product, such as the company that buys your manufacturing equipment, computer, or customer relationship management software, develop a program showing how your product is most effectively used or coordinated with existing equipment.

Exhibit 7.7 has other examples of topics often discussed in the marketing plan segment of your sales presentation.

Step 3. Develop your business proposition. The business proposition provides the buyer with an understanding of the important financial metrics. The business proposition includes items such as price, percent markup, forecasted profit per square foot of shelf

EXHIBIT 7.7

What topics should I consider in my planning?

In your Customer Profile and Planning Sheet, you develop a sales presentation strategy as part of the fourth step (developing your sales presentation). However, the question for many entry-level salespeople is "What do I include in each section?" In this exhibit, we provide potential topics that you might discuss with the buyer. Please remember, you will focus your presentation on the elements that will solve the buyer's problems and help them with their needs. Therefore, you will need to be selective with your planned presentation topics.

Marketing Plan Topics		**Business Proposition Topics**	
For Resellers: Helps the reseller understand how you will support them in reselling your product or solution)	**For End-Users: Helps the end-user understand how you will help them integrate the solution into their company, products, and processes)**	**For Resellers: Helps the reseller understand "what is in it for them" by reselling your product or solution**	**For End-Users: Helps the end-user understand "what is in it for them" by integrating the solution into their company, products, and processes**
1. Investment and implementation of awareness activities including: • Geographic reach: National advertising, regional, local, or co-op advertising • Types of advertising, including (social media, television, radio, outdoor, other internet initiatives) 2. Investment and implementation of sales promotion strategies including: • Samples • Point of Purchase displays • In-store signage • Contests • Coupons • Demonstrations • In-store promotions and initiatives 3. Investment and implementation of training the reseller's salesforce or personnel • Online training seminars • In-person training seminars • Training manuals or online reference materials • Training videos • Webinars • Timing of training 4. Investment in trade shows 5. Investment in trade promotion • Promotions in sales circulars • Displays • On-shelf price reductions • End-cap displays	1. Availability • Timelines • Seasonality 2. Delivery • Timelines • Locations 3. Installation • Who does it • When • How • Timelines 4. Training on use or integration • Online training sessions • In-person training seminars • Training manuals or online reference materials • Training videos • Webinars • Timing of training 5. Integration timelines 6. Ongoing service • Monitoring • Evaluation 7. Guarantees 8. Warranty • Length • Terms 9. Maintenance and Service agreements	1. Projected Sales • Units • Dollars 2. Projected Profits • Annual • Reseller's Fiscal Year 3. List price 4. Margins: • Gross margin (percentage and absolute amount) • Markup on cost (percentage and absolute amount • Markup on price (percentage and absolute amount) 5. Discounts • Cash • Consumer • Quantity • Trade 6. Financing • Payment plans • Interest rates • Terms 7. Incremental sales growth of product category due to your product 8. Potential inventory turnover 9. Projected market share 10. Slotting allowances	1. List price 2. ROI 3. Payback period 4. Discounts • Cash • Quantity 5. Shipping costs • Terms • Timelines • Mode (rail, long-haul truck, etc.) 5. Financing terms • Payment plans • Terms • Interest rate 6. Value analysis 7. Cost of ownership (long term) 8. Expected carrying cost • Day of inventory 9. Working capital investment 10. Reduction in expenses 11. Increased productivity • Units • Personnel (hours) • Personnel (sales rates) 12. Projected impact on quality levels • Reduced defects

space, return on investment, and payment plan. Value analysis is an example of a business proposition for an industrial product. Other examples of topics discussed in the business proposition segment of your sales presentation are shown in Exhibit 7.6.

Step 4. Develop a suggested purchase order based on a customer benefit plan. The suggested purchase order and implementation plan provide a recommendation to the buyer. In effect, this section helps the buyer understand the potential action steps that are required. A proper presentation of your customer needs analysis and your product's ability to fulfill these needs, along with a satisfactory business proposition and marketing plan, allows you to justify to the customer what product and/or how much to purchase. This suggestion may include, depending on your product, such things as what to buy, how much to buy, what assortment to buy, and when to ship the product to the customer.

You should also develop visual aids to effectively communicate the information developed in these four steps. The visuals should be organized in the order you discuss them. Your next step is to plan all aspects of the sales presentation. Finally, you will want to plan the steps for implementation. For instance, you will need to consider how often you contact the buyer and provide progress updates.

The Sales Presentation: An Overview of the Process

It is now time to plan your **sales presentation** from beginning to end. This process involves developing Steps 3 to 9 of the sales presentation described in Exhibit 7.2: the approach, presentation, and trial close method to uncover objections; ways to overcome objections; additional trial closes; and the close of the sales presentation. Each step is discussed in the following chapters.

sales presentation: The actual presentation of the sales pitch to the prospect.

New salespeople often ask their sales trainers to be more specific about how to construct the sales presentation. In addition to the 10 steps in the selling process shown in Exhibit 7.2, they ask, "What's involved in the presentation itself?" Exhibit 7.8 (on the next page) summarizes the major phases within the sales presentation. Before briefly discussing them, let's review a few things.

Before developing your presentation, you need to determine the prospect or customer to call on, make an appointment, and then plan the sales call. This process is shown in Exhibit 7.2, and the steps in planning the call are shown in Exhibit 7.5. Now that you know who you will call on and what our objective will be, it's time to plan out and prepare the sales presentation itself.

The major phases within the presentation are provided in Exhibit 7.8, which shows the selling process steps in more detail than Exhibit 7.2. You should plan out everything that is included in Exhibit 7.8 and do each phase in the exact order shown to create a well-organized presentation.

Here's how to create the presentation. Based on the homework you have done on the prospect or customer, create the opening (approach) of the presentation. This section usually comprises a rapport-building opportunity, an agenda, and a discovery section that helps you learn about the buyer's needs. This section is further discussed in Chapter 8. Then prepare your product's FABs, marketing plan, and business proposition. They were discussed earlier in this chapter and in previous chapters. Next, consider the solution that best meets the buyer's needs. Prepare a suggested purchase order and choose a closing method that feels natural for you to use when asking for the business. Should you make the sale or not make the sale, it is important to know how to exit the buyer's office. Thanking the customer for the order and discussing the key next steps in the process are two of the critical areas in this section. Closing the sale and the exit are discussed in Chapter 11.

You should use visual aids and demonstrations to help create an informative and persuasive sales presentation. As mentioned earlier, the *last step* in planning your sales call is the development and rehearsal of the sales presentation.

EXHIBIT 7.8

Major phases in your presentation: a sequence of events to complete in developing a presentation.

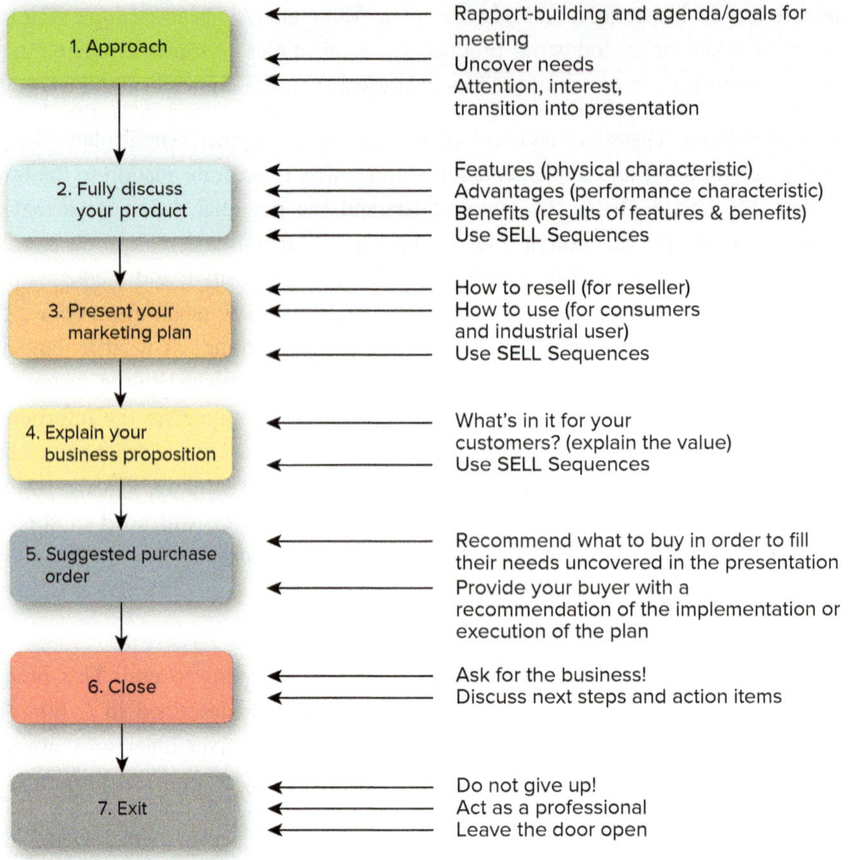

In developing the sales presentation, think of leading the prospect through the five steps or phases that salespeople believe constitute a purchase decision. These phases are referred to as the prospect's mental steps.

LO4

The Prospect's Mental Steps

prospect's mental steps: The five steps or phases that salespeople believe constitute a purchase decision.

In making a sales presentation, consider the **prospect's mental steps**: quickly obtain the prospect's full attention, develop interest in your product, create a desire to fulfill a need, establish the prospect's conviction that the product fills a need, and, finally, promote action by having the prospect purchase the product. As shown in Exhibit 7.9, these steps occur in order.

EXHIBIT 7.9

The prospect's five mental steps in buying.

attention: The first mental step in the buying process. From the moment the salesperson begins to talk, he or she should try to quickly capture and maintain the prospect's attention.

Attention

From the moment you begin to talk, quickly capture and maintain the prospect's **attention.** This may be difficult at times because of distractions, pressing demands on the prospect's time, or lack of interest. Carefully plan what to say and how to say it. Since attention-getters have only a temporary effect, be ready to quickly move to Step 2, sustaining the prospect's interest.

Interest

Before meeting with prospects, determine their important buying motives. These can be used in capturing **interest.** If you don't do this ahead of time, you may have to determine them at the beginning of your presentation by asking questions. Prospects enter the interest stage if they listen to and enter into a discussion with you. Quickly strive to link your product's benefits to prospects' needs. If this link is completed, prospects usually express a desire for the product.

interest:
The second mental step in the buying process. It is important for the salesperson to capture the prospect's interest in their product. If this link is completed, prospects usually express a desire for the product.

Desire

Using the FAB formula, strive to bring prospects from lukewarm interest to a boiling **desire** for your product. Desire is created when prospects express a wish or wanting for a product like yours.

desire:
The third mental step in the buying process. It is created when prospects express a wish or wanting for a product.

> *Attempt to gain the prospect's full attention, develop interest in your product, create a desire to fulfill a need, establish the prospect's conviction that the product fills a need, and, finally, promote action by having the prospect purchase the product.*

To better determine if they should purchase the product, prospects may have questions for you and may present objections to your product. Anticipate prospects' objections and provide information to maintain their desire.

conviction:
The fourth mental step in the buying process. In the conviction step of the prospect's mental buying process, the salesperson should strive to develop a strong belief that the product is best suited to the prospect's specific needs. It is established when no doubts remain about purchasing the product.

Conviction

While prospects may desire a product, they still have to be convinced that your product is best for their needs and that you are the best supplier of the product. In the **conviction** step, strive to develop a strong *belief* that the product is best suited to prospects' specific needs. Conviction is established when no doubts remain about purchasing the product from you.

purchase:
The fifth and last step in the mental buying process. Once the prospect is convinced, the salesperson should plan the most appropriate method of asking the prospect to buy or act.

Purchase or Action

Once the prospect is convinced, plan the most appropriate method of asking the prospect to make a **purchase** or take some **action.** If each of the preceding steps has been implemented correctly, closing the sale is the easiest step in the sales presentation.

action:
The last of the prospect's mental steps—when the prospect buys your product.

ETHICAL DILEMMA

TO CHECK OR NOT TO CHECK . . .

You have been working part-time for a large national department store chain for the past year. Your store, like others in the mall, has been experiencing a higher than normal amount of shoplifting. Store management has hired off-duty police wearing street clothes to walk around the store as if shopping and arrest thieves. The store manager strongly enforces the store policy that all people caught will be arrested.

For several months, you have suspected a fellow salesperson of frequently taking office supplies. You have overlooked these discrepancies because she helped you learn the ropes when you started, and you believe that everyone takes a supply or two on occasion. Today, you saw the person take a damaged jogging suit, give the customer credit, and then put it in a store bag and place it under the counter. That night, as you were both leaving, the person had the bag with something in it. It could have been the jogging suit or just something that your co-worker purchased earlier. You want to know if the jogging suit is in the bag, but you also know that if it is the jogging suit, the store manager will prosecute her.

What would be the most ethical action to take?

1. Take your manager aside and tell them what you witnessed. Let your manager handle the situation from there since it is potentially dangerous.
2. Do nothing. It is not your responsibility to investigate the situation. Let your manager find out on their own.
3. Pull the person aside and explain that you thought you saw her put something in the bag. Let your co-worker know that you aren't going to tell anyone if it is true, but that the person should really stop to avoid jeopardizing her job.

SELLING TIPS

MANAGE GATEKEEPERS

Gatekeepers are plentiful in today's business world. They control the flow of information into and out of corporate offices, which can make them a significant hurdle for many salespeople.

Good technique and manners go a long way. Treating gatekeepers as "lowly" assistants would be a big mistake. They have been assigned this job by their bosses to prevent unnecessary distractions. All calls will be screened unless the buyer is very familiar with the calling salesperson. If you are unfamiliar, then it's up to you to prove that you deserve to speak to the buyer, or get an email address or voice mail, etc.

The gatekeeper has been assigned to evaluate your call. If you pass the test, you're in. So how you speak and what you say to the gatekeeper counts.

1. Begin with a friendly, yet professional, introduction. Be clear and concise. Try to address the gatekeeper by name. Ask if the gatekeeper can give you a few moments; if not, then ask for a more convenient time to call.
2. To capture attention, ensure that what you have to offer is a large reward with little risk. Your proposition should be captivating enough so that the gatekeeper will feel obliged to give you an appointment. "Our product has been proven to save companies like yours 25 percent of their operating costs."
3. Engage gatekeepers. They hold the power in this situation. The more time they invest in you, the more attention they will pay, and therefore will feel more responsibility. They want to do what's best for their boss and their company—so speak in those terms.
4. Listen carefully to any follow-up instructions that you may receive. It would be unfortunate if you secured an appointment then showed up on the wrong day with the wrong material in hand.
5. Try to get gatekeepers on your side both before and after the call. They may become your working partners in dealings with the company. Their experience will help you tremendously in your future dealings with this company. Don't be afraid to ask for their help. It's better if they work with you rather than against you.

ETHICAL DILEMMA

WHAT WOULD YOU DO TO GET THE APPOINTMENT?

Dennis worked as an insurance and financial service salesperson. One of his markets was small to medium-sized businesses for group insurance and benefit plans. In a competitive field with many salespeople, he often found it difficult to get by the gatekeepers. The response often seemed to be, "Oh no, another insurance rep."

He started to resort to the following technique:

Gatekeeper: "Good morning. Innovative Construction Company, how can I help you?"

Dennis: "Good morning, I would like to speak with [name of purchasing agent].

Gatekeeper: "What is the purpose of your call, please?"

Dennis: "It's a personal call."

What do you think? Would this work and solve the problem of getting by the gatekeeper?

SELLING TIPS

AVOID CUSTOMER CALL RELUCTANCE®—YOUR WORST ENEMY

According to a study by Behavioral Sciences Research Press, the problem of call reluctance in sales is widespread and costly. Among the findings of the Dallas research and sales training firm:

- The call-reluctant salesperson loses more than 15 new accounts per month to competitors.
- Call-reluctant stockbrokers acquire 48 fewer new accounts per year than brokers who have learned to manage their fear.
- In some cases, the call-reluctant salesperson loses $10,800 per month in gross sales.
- In others, call reluctance costs the salesperson $10,000 in lost commissions per year.

Call Reluctance*

All salespeople experience call reluctance periodically; however, an estimated 40 percent of salespeople suffer a career-threatening bout of **call reluctance**™ (not wanting to contact a prospect or customer) at some point. In its milder forms, call reluctance keeps countless salespeople from achieving their potential. Research indicates that 80 percent of all first-year salespeople who don't make the grade fail because of call reluctance.[4]

call reluctance: A feeling of not wanting to contact a prospect or customer.

See Exhibit 7.10 (on the next page) for the 12 classic types of call reluctance.

Countermeasures are numerous and depend on the type of call reluctance. But the initial step is always the same: "You must admit you have call reluctance and that your call reluctance is keeping you from earning what you're worth." For many salespeople, owning up to call reluctance is the most difficult part of combating it.

Voice Mail: The Dreaded Mechanical Gatekeeper

What do you do when you hear the voice mail greeting of the prospect? Many will panic and simply hang up. Voice mail can work–follow these tips for more effective voice mail messages:

1. Be prepared - Make sure you've reviewed your notes (customer relationship management file) before you call.
2. Smile when you start speaking and sound enthusiastic - Your good nature and enthusiasm will come through.
3. Plan to be brief - Talk for 25-40 seconds maximum.
4. Discuss benefits that are most attractive to the prospect - Customize your message to the prospect.
5. If there is time, talk about a success story.
6. Leave your phone numbers (office and cell) and email address - Say them slowly and twice if possible.
7. Make a call to action - Ask them to call you or mention that you'll call them at a later date.

Should you force the issue? A successful salesperson once told this author that at the end of a voice mail message, he would say something like this, "I'd like to meet with you next Monday at 10:00 a.m.–if that's not a good time for you, please call me back and let me know." Then he would show up if he hadn't received a call. What do you think?

*Sales Call Reluctance® is a registered trademark of Behavioral Sciences Research Press, Inc. Dallas, Texas. Used with permission. ALL RIGHTS RESERVED.

EXHIBIT 7.10

The 12 faces of call reluctance.

Think you might suffer from call reluctance? See if you fit one of the 12 classic types identified by researchers George Dudley and Shannon Goodson. They're listed in order from most common to least common.

1. **Yielder Sales CR™**

   Fears intruding on others or being pushy
2. **Over-Preparer Sales CR™**

   Overanalyzes, underacts
3. **Emotionally Unemancipated Sales CR™**

   Fears loss of family approval, resists mixing business and family
4. **Separationist Sales CR™**

   Fears loss of friends, resists prospecting among personal friends
5. **Hyper-Pro Sales CR™**

   Obsessed with image, fears being humiliated
6. **Role Rejection Sales CR™**

   Ashamed to be in sales
7. **Social Self-Consciousness Sales CR™**

   Fears intruding on others or being pushy, intimidated by upmarket customers
8. **Doomsayer Sales CR™**

   Worries, won't take risks
9. **Telephobia Sales CR™**

   Fears using the telephone for prospecting or selling
10. **Stage Fright Sales CR™**

    Fears group presentations
11. **Referral Aversion Sales CR™**

    Fears disturbing existing business or client relationships
12. **Oppositional Reflex Sales CR™**

    Rebuffs attempts to be coached

How to Conquer the Fear

- First and foremost, you must admit to having call reluctance. Acknowledgement is a major step toward recovery, but it's not an easy move. Denial is the most frequent companion of call reluctance, and the problem is sometimes hard to identify. Salespeople "typically know something is wrong, but they may not know what it is," says behavioural scientist and call reluctance expert George Dudley. "Many who do know they are experiencing sales call reluctance® don't feel secure admitting it to management, because many sales organizations still tend to feature cultlike, unrealistic emphasis on maintaining a positive attitude," Dudley explains.
- Second, determine your call reluctance type and adopt appropriate countermeasures. The numerous prescriptions often involve clearly and specifically identifying your fears or negative thoughts. Then you can tackle them head-on, one at a time. In a sense, curbing call reluctance is like breaking a bad habit. Some salespeople find token reward systems helpful; others use relaxation techniques. In one countermeasure known as thought zapping, you place a rubber band around your wrist. When a negative thought intrudes, you snap the rubber band sharply and immediately conjure up a positive mental image of yourself–recalling, for example, a time when you did well in a similar situation.
- Third, follow up, keep plugging, make calls. Taming call reluctance is work, and for many salespeople it takes continual effort. "Don't confuse a change in your outlook with a change in the number of contacts you initiate with prospective buyers," Dudley warns. If you're call reluctant, take heart in the knowledge that your problem actually may be a sign of commitment to selling. "Salespeople who are not motivated or goal-focused can never be considered call reluctant," says Dudley. Salespeople with authentic call reluctance care very much about meeting prospecting goals. "You simply cannot be reluctant to get something you don't want in the first place."

SELLING TIPS

MAKE "SNAIL MAIL" WORK!

1. Every letter should look customized for a particular prospect.
2. Personalize the heading and the salutation.
3. Sign the letter with a pen.
4. Avoid the look of junk mail by not using standard issue company envelopes.
5. Go for the personal look—use a handwriting font for their address.
6. Try not to use the standard size and style of envelope. It's also preferable to use something other than the standard white colour.
7. Avoid the look of mass mailings—there should be no metred stamping. Use a real stamp.
8. Provide all contact information for yourself. Don't make it difficult for the reader to reach you.

Summary of Major Selling Issues

Most salespeople agree that careful planning of the sales call is essential to success in selling. Among many reasons why planning is so important, four of the most frequently mentioned are that planning builds self-confidence, develops an atmosphere of goodwill, creates professionalism, and increases sales. By having a logical and methodical plan, you can decide what to accomplish and then later measure your accomplishments with your plan.

There are four basic elements of sales call planning. First, you must always have a sales call objective–one that is specific, measurable, and beneficial to the customer. Second, you must also develop or review the customer profile. By having relevant information about your customer, you can properly develop a customized presentation. You can find information on the background, needs, and competitors of your potential buyer by reviewing your company's records or by personally contacting the buyer and the company.

The third step in planning your sales call involves developing your customer benefit plan. To do this, look at why the prospect should purchase your product and develop a marketing plan to convey those reasons and the benefits to your prospect. Then, develop a *business proposition* by listing your price, percent markup, return on investment, and other quantitative data about your product in relation to your prospect. Last, develop a *suggested purchase order* and present your analysis, which might include suggestions on what to buy, how much to buy, what assortment to buy, and when to ship the product.

Finally, plan your whole sales presentation. Visual aids can help make your presentation informative and creative. In making your call, think in terms of the phases that make up a purchase decision–the mental steps (capturing the prospect's attention, determining buying motives, creating desire, convincing the person that your product is best suited to their needs, and then closing the sale).

By adhering to these guidelines for planning your sales presentation, you may spend more time planning than on the actual sales call. However, it will be well worth it.

MEETING A SALES CHALLENGE

The purpose of your sales presentation is to provide information so the prospect can make a rational, informed buying decision. You provide this information using your FABs, marketing plan, and business proposal.

The information you provide allows the buyer to develop positive personal *beliefs* toward your product. The beliefs result in *desire* (or *need*) for the type of product you sell. Your job is to convert that need into a want and into the *attitude* that your product is the best product to fulfill a certain need. Furthermore, you must convince the buyer not only that your product is the best but also that you are the best source. When this occurs, your prospect has moved into the *conviction* stage of the mental buying process.

When a real need is established, the buyer will want to fulfill that need, and there is a high probability that she will choose your product. Whether to buy is a "choice decision," and you provide the necessary information so that the customer chooses to buy from you.

When you are prepared, the prospect or customer recognizes it. This recognition gives you a better chance of giving and completing your presentations without being cut off, and therefore increases your sales, because the more presentations you give, the more people you sell. Veteran salespeople have a tendency not to prepare; many get lazy and fall into a bad habit of "winging it." Top sales professionals rarely are unprepared. Do you want to be an order taker or an order getter? Your success is entirely up to you!

PLAYING THE ROLE

The situation: You are a salesperson who wants an appointment with the head purchasing manager of your college. You sell a new software program that you know would improve the productivity of the administrators of your college.

Role A: The salesperson. Prepare to make a call to your college to get an appointment with the purchasing agent.

Role B: The gatekeeper. Prepare to screen the call; your boss is a busy person. You should eventually let the salesperson speak to the purchasing agent.

Role C: The purchasing agent. You speak to salespeople all the time; does this one deserve an appointment?

Dramatize this situation in class, having prepared your roles.

Key Terms for Selling

action
attention
call reluctance
conviction
creative problem solvers
customer benefit plan
customer profile
desire
interest
plan
pre-approach
prospect's mental steps
purchase
sales call objective
sales call purpose
sales presentation
SMART
strategic
strategic customer relationship
success

Sales Application Questions

1. What are the elements to consider when planning a sales call? Explain each one.
2. An important part of planning a sales call is the development of a customer benefit plan. What are the major components of the customer benefit plan? What is the difference in developing a customer benefit plan for a Procter & Gamble salesperson selling consumer products versus an industrial salesperson selling products for a company such as IBM?
3. Outline and discuss the sequence of events in developing a sales presentation.
4. Define the term *selling process.* List the major steps in the selling process on the left side of a page of paper. Beside each step of the selling process, write the corresponding mental step that a prospect should experience.
5. Think of a product sold through one of your local supermarkets. Assume you were recently hired by the product's manufacturer to contact the store's buyer to purchase a promotional quantity of your product and to arrange for display and advertising. What information do you need for planning the sales call, and what features, advantages, and benefits would be appropriate in your sales presentation?

6. What is your purpose for going to school? What are your goals for this semester? This year? The next five years? Reflect on why setting goals is important and determine your own personal goals both in your academic career and personal life.

Sales Online Exercise

1. Can You Improve Your Presentation?

The most challenging, rewarding, and enjoyable aspect of the sales job is the sales presentation. An effective presentation completely and clearly explains all aspects of a salesperson's proposition as it relates to a buyer's needs. To learn more about effective presentations, use your favourite search engine to search for sites to improve your presentation skills. Share your tips with the class.

2. Researching Prospects

The more information you have about a potential customer, the better. If your prospect is a large, internationally recognized organization, you can retrieve information from many sources, including the following:

Google: www.google.com

The *Globe and Mail* Report on Business: www.globeandmail.com/business

The Financial Post: www.nationalpost.com/financialpost

Bloomberg Businessweek: www.businessweek.com

LinkedIn: www.linkedin.com

Facebook: www.facebook.com

Twitter: www.twitter.com

Forbes: www.forbes.com

Fortune: www.fortune.com

Fast Company: www.fastcompany.com

The business section of your local newspaper also can be a valuable resource for local companies.

For detailed information on organizations in Canada and the United States, two sites are worth investigating:

- **www.sedar.com** This is Canada's electronic securities documentation filing system. The database is massive and contains current and historical annual reports for Canadian companies that are registered on any of Canada's stock exchanges.
- **www.edgar-online.com** This is a similar site to SEDAR, but is based in the United States. It uses the Securities and Exchange Commission database, provides recent activities within the SEC, and provides current and historical annual report information.

Further Exploring the Sales World

1. Ask a buyer for a business in your community about what salespeople should do when calling on a buyer. Find out whether the salespeople that this buyer sees are prepared for each sales call. Ask why something was or was not purchased. Do salespeople use the FAB method? Does the buyer think privately, "So what?," "Prove it!," and "What's in it for me?" Finally, ask what superiors expect of a buyer in the buyer's dealings with salespeople.

Selling Experiential Exercise

Do you set objectives for each of your classes? Are your course objectives SMART–specific, measurable, achievable, realistic, and timed? Salespeople set objectives for each customer. Would you consider setting objectives for each class, constantly measuring your performance, and reevaluating your progress toward the objective? You can do this by answering the questions in Exhibit 7.11.

EXHIBIT 7.11
SMART course objective setting.

- What grade do you want to make in this course? Write on this line ______
- How many points do you have to earn in this class to reach your objective?______
  (Total points multiplied by 0.9. See your syllabus for total course points.)
- How many points do you now have in the course? ______
- How many points do you need to earn to reach your objective? ______
- Can you reach your objective? ______Yes ______ No
- On a scale of 1 to 10—with 10 being the maximum effort—how hard are you willing to work in this course to reach your objective? Be honest with yourself. My "effort score" will be______.
- In your class notes, write a statement explaining how you will reach your grade objective.

SMART Course Objective Setting

Enough time has passed in your selling course that you have received one or more grades. Let's assume you want to make an A in the class. Ask your instructor or see your class syllabus for the total points you can earn in your sales course. Assuming no curve, multiply the maximum points by 0.9. If you can earn a maximum of 1,000 points, then you need 900 points for an A. Your goal now becomes a total score of 900 points on all graded activities.

Subtract the total points you have earned so far from the number of points needed to reach your objective–900 points. How many remaining test(s) and assignment(s) are ahead? Determine if you can reach your course grade objective by making an 80, 90, or 95 percent average on all remaining test(s) and assignment(s). Each time you receive a grade for a major assignment, recalculate your progress toward scoring 900 points and making your A.

As in sales, usually a person's class performance is a function of their ability and motivation. This is why class performance is a function (f) of an individual's ability times motivation, or

$$\text{Class performance} = f(\text{Ability} \times \text{Motivation})$$

Now for the most important question of all. The answer to this question will determine your future grade in this or any class: "How hard are you willing to work in reaching your course grade objective?" On a scale of 1 to 10–with 10 being the maximum effort–how hard are you willing to work in this course to reach your objective?

Be honest with yourself. Write it down! This is important; write it down, please.

My effort score is ______________________ (1 to 10).

Each time you recalculate your progress toward your goal of making an A in this class, reconsider your "effort score." Write down all future "effort scores." See if, over time, your effort score begins to decline or increase, or stays the same.

Selling Experiential Exercise

Plan Your Appearance—It Projects Your Image!

The most successful people in customer contact jobs claim that being sharp mentally means communicating a positive self-image. Like an actor, you are on stage at all times when interacting with others. Creating a good first impression is essential. Also important is understanding the direct connection between your attitude and your self-confidence. The better your self-image when you encounter customers, clients, or guests, the more positive you are.

On a separate sheet of paper, rate yourself on each of the following grooming areas. If you write 5, you are saying that improvement is not necessary. If you write a 1, or 2, you need considerable improvement. Be honest.[5]

	Excellent	Good	Fair	Weak	Poor
• Hairstyle, hair grooming (appropriate length and cleanliness)	5	4	3	2	1
• Personal cleanliness habits (body)	5	4	3	2	1
• Clothing and jewellery (appropriate to the situation)	5	4	3	2	1
• Neatness (shoes shined, clothes clean, well pressed, etc.)	5	4	3	2	1
• General grooming: Does your appearance reflect professionalism on the job?	5	4	3	2	1
When it comes to appearance on the job, I rate myself:					
☐ Excellent ☐ Good ☐ Need improvement					

Selling Experiential Exercise

You have learned much about selling so far in this course. Let's find out how much, and, at the same time, better understand your attitude toward selling. Three of the following ten statements are false. Can you find them? (Cover the answers!)

Is Selling for You?

1. Dealing with customers is less exciting than the work involved in most other jobs.
2. Selling brings out the best in your personality.
3. Salespeople are made, not born; if you don't plan and work hard, you'll never be exceptional at selling.
4. Attitude is more important in selling positions than in most other jobs.
5. Good salespeople often can improve their income quickly.
6. Learning to sell now will help you succeed in any job in the future.
7. In your first sales job, what you learn can be more important than what you earn.
8. Selling is less demanding than other jobs.
9. You have little freedom in most selling positions.
10. A smile uses fewer muscles than a frown.[6]

False statements: 1, 8, and 9.

CASE 7–1

MS. HANSEN'S MENTAL STEPS IN BUYING YOUR PRODUCT

Picture yourself as a Procter & Gamble salesperson who plans to call on Ms. Hansen, a buyer for your largest independent grocery store. Your sales call objective is to convince Ms. Hansen that she should buy the family-size Tide detergent. The store now carries the three smaller sizes. You believe your marketing plan will help convince her that she is losing sales and profits by not stocking Tide's family size.

You enter the grocery store, check your present merchandise, and quickly develop a suggested order. As Ms. Hansen walks down the aisle toward you, she appears to be in her normal grumpy mood. After your initial greeting and handshake, your conversation continues:

Salesperson: Your sales are really up! I've checked your stock in the warehouse and on the shelf. This is what it looks like you need. [You discuss sales of each of your products and their various sizes, suggesting a quantity she should purchase based on her past sales and present inventory.]

Buyer: Okay, that looks good. Go ahead and ship it.

Salesperson: Thank you. Say, Ms. Hansen, you've said before that the shortage of shelf space prevents you from stocking our family-size Tide–though you admit you may be losing some sales as a result. If we could determine how much volume you're missing, I think you'd be willing to make space for it, wouldn't you?

Buyer: Yes, but I don't see how that can be done.

Salesperson: Well, I'd like to suggest a test–a weekend display of all four sizes of Tide.

Buyer: What do you mean?

Salesperson: My thought was to run all sizes at regular shelf price without any ad support. This would give us a pure test. Six cases of each size should let us compare sales of the various sizes and see what you're missing by regularly stocking only the smaller sizes. I think the additional sales and profits you'll get on the family size will convince you to start stocking it regularly. What do you think?

Buyer: Well, maybe.

QUESTIONS

1. Examine each item you mentioned to Ms. Hansen, stating what part of the customer benefit plan each of your comments addresses.
2. What are the features, advantages, and benefits in your sales presentation?
3. Examine each of Ms. Hansen's replies, stating the mental buying step she is in at that particular time during your sales presentation.
4. At the end of the conversation, Ms. Hansen said, "Well, maybe." Which of the following should you do now?
   a. Continue to explain your features, advantages, and benefits.
   b. Ask a trial close question.
   c. Ask for the order.
   d. Back off and try again on the next sales call.
   e. Wait for Ms. Hansen to say, "Okay, ship it."

CASE 7–2

MACHINERY LUBRICANTS, INC.

Rami Semchuk sells industrial lubricants for machinery to manufacturing plants. Tomorrow, Rami plans to call on the purchasing agent for Acme Manufacturing Company.

For the past two years, Rami has been selling Hydraulic Oil 65 in drums to Acme. Rami's sales call objective is to persuade Acme to switch from purchasing oil in drums to a bulk oil system. Last year, Acme bought approximately 364 drums or 20,000 litres at a cost of $1.39 a litre or $27,800. A deposit of $20 was made for each drum. Traditionally, many drums are lost, and one to two litres of oil may be left in each drum when returned by customers. This is a loss to Acme.

Rami wants to sell Acme two 3,000-litre storage tanks at a cost of $1700. He has arranged with Pump Supply Company to install the tanks for $1,095. Thus, the total cost of the system would be $2795. This system reduces the cost of the oil from $1.39 to $1.25 per litre, which would allow it to pay for itself over time. Other advantages include having fewer orders to process each year, reducing the amount of storage space needed, and having workers handle the oil less.

QUESTION

If you were Rami, how would you plan the sales call?

CASE 7–3

CASCADE SOAP

Syed Alam sells soap products to grocery wholesalers and large retail grocery chains. The following presentation occurred during a call he made on Bill Reese, the soap buyer for a grocery store.

Salesperson: Bill, you have stated several times that the types of promotions or brands that really interest you are ones that carry the best profit. Is that right?

Buyer: Yes, it is. I'm under pressure to increase my profit per square metre in my department.

Salesperson: Bill, I recommend that you begin carrying the king-size box of Cascade. Let's review the benefits and economics of this proposal. King-size Cascade would cost you 86.8¢ a box. The average resale in this market is 99¢. That means that you would make 12.2¢ every time you sold a box of king-size Cascade. Based on my estimated volume for your store of $40,000 per week, you would sell approximately two cases of king-size Cascade per week. That is $19.80 in new sales and $2.44 in new profits per week for your store. As you can see, the addition of king-size Cascade to your automatic dishwashing detergent department will increase your sales and, even more importantly, increase your profits–and this is what you said you wanted to do, right?

Buyer: Yes, I am interested in increasing profits.

Salesperson: Do you want me to give this information to the head stock clerk so that she can make arrangements to put king-size Cascade on the shelf? Or would you like me to put it on the shelf on my next call?

QUESTIONS

1. What sales presentation method is Syed using?
2. Evaluate Syed's handling of this situation.

CASE 7–4

A RETAIL SALES PRESENTATION

A customer is looking at a display of Cross gold pens and pencils.

Customer: I'm looking for a graduation gift for my brother, but I'm not necessarily looking for a pen and pencil set.

Salesperson: Is your brother graduating from college or high school?

Customer: He is graduating from college this spring.

Salesperson: I can show you quite a few items that would be appropriate gifts. Let's start by taking a look at this elegant Cross pen and pencil set. Don't they look impressive?

Customer: They look too expensive. Besides, a pen and pencil set doesn't seem like an appropriate gift for a college graduate.

Salesperson: You're right, a Cross pen and pencil set *does* look expensive. Just imagine how impressed your brother will be when he opens your gift package and finds these beautiful writing instruments. Even though Cross pen and pencil sets look expensive, they are actually quite reasonably priced, considering the total value you are getting.

Customer: How much does this set cost?

Salesperson: You can buy a Cross pen and pencil set for anywhere from $15 to $300. The one I am showing you is gold-plated and costs only $58. For this modest amount you can purchase a gift for your brother that will be attractive and useful, will last a lifetime, and will show him that you truly think he is deserving of the very best. Don't you think that is what a graduation gift should be?

Customer: You make it sound pretty good, but frankly I hadn't intended to spend that much money.

Salesperson: Naturally, I can show you something else. However, before I do that, pick up this Cross pen and write your name on this pad of paper. Notice that in addition to good looks, Cross pens offer good writing. Cross is acclaimed as one of the best ballpoint pens on the market. It is nicely balanced, has a point that allows the ink to flow onto the paper smoothly, and rides over the paper with ease.

Customer: You're right; the pen writes really well.

Salesperson: Each time your brother writes with this pen, he will remember that you gave him this fine writing instrument for graduation. In addition, Cross offers prestige. Many customers tell us that Cross is one of the few pens they have used that is so outstanding that people often comment on it by brand name. Your brother will enjoy having others notice that the pen he uses is high in quality.

Customer: You're right. I do tend to notice when someone is using a Cross pen.

Salesperson: You can't go wrong with a Cross pen and pencil set for a gift. Shall I wrap it for you?

Customer: It's a hard decision.

Salesperson: Your brother will be very happy with this gift.

Customer: Okay. Go ahead and wrap it for me.

Salesperson: Fine. Would you like me to wrap up another set for you to give yourself?

Customer: No, one is enough. Maybe someone will buy one for me someday.

QUESTIONS

1. Describe the selling techniques being used by the retail salesperson.
2. Evaluate the salesperson's handling of this situation.

CASE 7–5

NEGOTIATING WITH A FRIEND

Barney spotted a high-quality used car on a dealer's lot over the weekend. He would have bought it immediately if he had had more cash. The dealer will give him only $1,200 on a trade-in for his current automobile. The car Barney wants is really great, and chances are good it will be sold shortly. Barney has planned carefully and decided he can swing the deal if he can sell his present vehicle to a private party for around $2,000. This would give him $1,500 for a down payment and $500 for accessories he wants to add. The car is in good condition except for a couple of minor dents in the fender. The snow tires for his current car won't fit the new one but can probably be sold; that will help. Barney can remove the new stereo system he installed last month and place it in the new car.

Billie, one of Barney's co-workers, heard that Barney wants to sell his car and plans to talk to him about it. Her daughter is graduating from college in three months and will need a car to drive to work. Billie can afford only about $1,800 including any repairs that might be required, and she needs to reserve enough money for snow tires. Her daughter has seen the car and thinks it's sporty, especially with the stereo. Billie checked the blue book price for the model of Barney's car, and she knows the average wholesale price is $1,200 and the average retail price is $1,950.

QUESTIONS

1. What are Barney's objectives?
2. What are Billie's objectives?
3. What are likely to be the points of conflict?
4. What power does Barney have?
5. What power does Billie have?
6. How important is time to Barney?
7. How important is time to Billie?
8. What are some possible points of compromise?

Source: © Fizkes | Dreamstime.com

CHAPTER 8

The Approach—Begin Your Presentation Strategically

Troy Hutchinson
Douglas College
New Westminster, British Columbia

Source: Courtesy of Troy Hutchinson

A Sales Success Story

Even before he graduated with a Marketing Management Diploma from Douglas College in 2003, Troy Hutchinson knew his career path was always going to be in sales. Today he is territory manager for Associated Health Systems, a medical equipment distributor and manufacturer in Vancouver, British Columbia.

Starting as a part-time sales person in a local bicycle store while in high school, Troy learned the value of customer relationships and good customer service. After he completed his education, Troy landed a business development position at Coca-Cola, where he gained valuable experience in packaged goods sales. He was lucky enough to be in the role when Coca-Cola was a major sponsor for the 2010 Winter Olympics, hosted in Vancouver. This was a terrific opportunity to see how big brands engage with customers and sports organizations.

Using that sporting event experience, Troy moved into a more focused sports marketing role with Nestlé, where he was responsible for sales and sports marketing of the PowerBar brand in Western Canada. Here he gained experience in developing key partnerships with retailers and marquis sports events across the region, regularly providing insights on market trends to help them build their businesses.

In 2015, looking to stretch his skills, Troy transitioned to his current role. At Associated Health Systems, he is expanding his sales skills by serving hospitals and medical professionals with innovative products. Troy finds maintaining customer relationships continues to be essential. Given the complex needs in health care, it often takes having conversations with a variety of people in the hospital to unveil multi-faceted solutions. Listening skills have helped him succeed. Sometimes a conversation with a customer may point him to a new sales opportunity without them even realizing it. Time management is also essential. Every customer is busy. Troy maintains that it is vital to do his homework before a sales call to ensure he has something of value to offer the customer, every time.

Not all of those conversations yield sales, at least not in the short term. Recently, Troy secured a sale that had a two-year closing cycle. "I was approaching a clinical-buyer about a surgical product that other hospitals use successfully. The buyer, confident with their current methods, felt they did not have a use for our product. Regardless, I would periodically send him research on the product, outlining how it would benefit them. One evening I got an urgent call from that buyer—a situation had arisen that required our product, the *next day*. I was able to get them the product in time for their procedure, and it's now a regularly stocked item at the hospital."

From bicycle shop to hospital surgical suite, when asked what has contributed to his success in sales, Troy believes that "sales is a long game," and making every decision with that lens is key. When guiding his customers in their buying decisions, he looks for the best solution for them. And if he doesn't think he has the best solution for his customer at that time, he will say so. Even though the immediate sale is lost, the credibility earned in the customer relationship over the long run will more than make up for it.

For aspiring salespeople, Troy advises researching the industry and roles you are interested in. Prospect the field of sales! Set up informational interviews with salespeople in the field and find out about those "hunter" and "farmer" sales roles. Uncover your preference. Identify which role fits your style. And make sure you can hold a conversation. Regardless of the role, people in sales have to be able to talk to customers. Email and other electronic communication are important tools, but at some point in the sales cycle, you will need to be able to talk to someone, and poor communication skills can make or break a sale. In fact, that in-person selling starts with the job interview.

MAIN TOPICS

Importance of a Strategic Approach

The Approach—Opening the Sales Presentation

The First Impression You Make Is Critical to Success

Rapport—The Relationship Builder

Technology in the Approach

Using Questions Results in Sales Success

Is the Prospect Still Not Listening?

Needs Analysis—A Key to Success

Be Flexible in Your Approach

Group Presentation

LEARNING OBJECTIVES

You have selected your prospect, planned the sales call, and determined how best to approach your customer. Now, you must determine how to begin the sales presentation. This step in the selling process is called the approach. After studying this chapter, you should be able to:

LO1 Explain the importance of using a strategic approach.

LO2 Develop an approach strategy that will effectively make a good first impression and provide examples of approaches.

LO3 Develop an effective rapport.

LO4 Identify and discuss the importance of different types of questioning.

LO5 Explain the importance of effective needs analysis.

LO6 Demonstrate your understanding of multiple-question approaches such as SPIN.

FACING A SALES CHALLENGE

You are making a cold call on the office manager of a local company. You assume that one of the manager's responsibilities involves ordering office supplies. Based on your experience with other companies, you suspect the volume of orders would be small but steady throughout the year.

As a salesperson for University Office Supplies, you especially want to sell your new equipment for mailing out invoices, along with the forms and other products associated with the service. Since this is a small company, you decide to go in cold, relying on your questioning ability to uncover potential problems and make the prospect aware of them.

You are now face to face with the manager. You have introduced yourself, and after some small talk you feel it is time to begin your presentation. Many salespeople face this situation several times each day.

What would you do? What type of presentation would you use? How would you begin the presentation?

(Continued at end of chapter.)

Have you ever been told, "You get only one opportunity to make a good first impression"? If the first minute of talking with a prospect creates a bad impression, it can take hours to overcome it–if you ever do. Many times, salespeople get only one chance to sell a prospect.

The approach–or beginning–of your presentation is essential to the prospect allowing you to discuss your product any further. If done incorrectly, the prospect may stop you from telling your sales story.

This chapter introduces you to the *dos* and *don'ts* of beginning your sales presentation. Many salespeople are nervous about contacting prospects, so let's begin our discussion of the approach by seeing why you have the right to talk with a prospect.

LO1 Importance of a Strategic Approach

You have the right (or duty) to present your product if you can show that it will definitely benefit the prospect. In essence, you have to prove *you* are worthy of the prospect's time and serious attention. You may earn the right to this attention in a number of ways:

- By exhibiting specific product or business knowledge
- By expressing a sincere desire to solve a buyer's problem and satisfy a need

- By stating or implying that your product will save money or increase the firm's profit margin
- By displaying an "at your service" attitude

Prospects want to know how you and your product will benefit *them* and *the company* they represent. Your sales approach should initially establish, and then concentrate on, your product's key benefits for each prospect.

This strategy is especially important during the approach stage of a presentation because it aids in securing the prospect's interest in you and your product. At this point, you want this unspoken reaction from the prospect: "Well, I'd better hear this salesperson out. I may hear something that will be of use to me." Now that you have justified your right to sell to a prospect, determine how to present your product.

EXHIBIT 8.1

The third step in the sales process is the first step in the sales presentation.

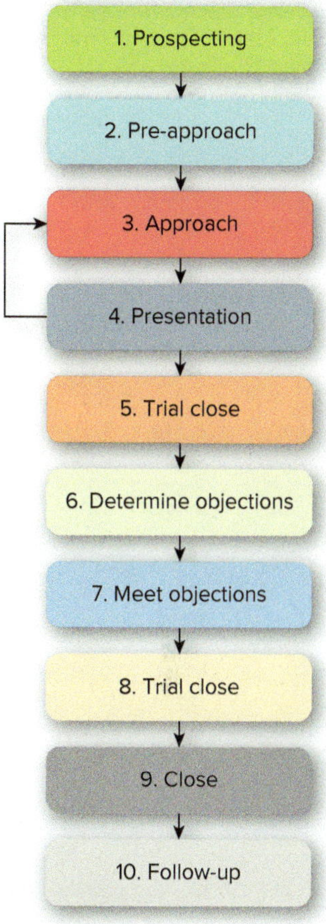

The Approach—Opening the Sales Presentation

Jorge Chavez spent days qualifying the prospect, arranging for an appointment, and planning every aspect of the sales presentation. In the first 60 seconds of the sales presentation, he realized that his chances of selling were excellent. He quickly determined the prospect's needs and evoked attention and interest in his product because of the technique he used to begin the sales presentation.

A buyer's reactions to the salesperson in the early minutes of the sales presentation are critical to a successful sale. This short period is so important that it is treated as an individual step in selling (see Exhibit 8.1), and is referred to as the **approach**. Part of any approach is the prospect's first impression of you (see Exhibit 8.2).

Your Attitude during the Approach

It is common for a salesperson to experience tension when contacting a prospect. Often this stress is brought on when the salesperson has preconceived ideas that things may go wrong during the sale. Prospects may be viewed as having negative characteristics that make the sales call difficult.

EXHIBIT 8.2

You only get one chance to make a first impression, so make sure that it is positive.

Source: Wavebreakmediamicro/Dreamstime.com/GetStock.com

approach: Opening of the presentation from first talk with the prospect to discussion of the product or service.

creative imagery: A relaxation and concentration technique that aids in stress management in which a salesperson envisions successful coping in various sales situations.

All salespeople experience some degree of stress at times. Successful salespeople have often learned a relaxation and concentration technique called **creative imagery**, which allows them to cope with stress. The salesperson envisions the worst that can happen. Then he or she prepares how to react to it and even accept it if necessary. The best that can happen is also envisioned, as portrayed in Exhibit 8.2. Then contingency plans are prepared in case the planned sales talk must be abandoned.

Salespeople should ask themselves, "What are the chances that things will go wrong?" Usually, the answer involves a low probability, particularly when careful planning has taken place before the sales call. A greater than 99 percent probability that things will go as planned should dim the fears of the most worry-prone salespeople.

Sales Presentation Methods—Select One Carefully

The sales presentation involves a persuasive verbal and visual explanation of a business proposition. We present four methods here to highlight some of the alternatives available to help sell your products.

As shown on the continuum in Exhibit 8.3, the four sales presentation methods are (1) memorized, (2) formula, (3) need-satisfaction, and (4) problem-solution selling methods.[1] The basic difference in the four methods is the percentage of the conversation controlled by the salesperson. In the more structured memorized and formula-selling techniques, the salesperson normally has a monopoly on the conversation, whereas the less structured methods allow for greater buyer-seller interaction; both parties participate equally in the conversation. Transactional selling generally is more structured, whereas partnering requires a more customized presentation, with relationship selling typically somewhere in between (see Exhibit 8.3).

EXHIBIT 8.3

The structure of sales presentations.

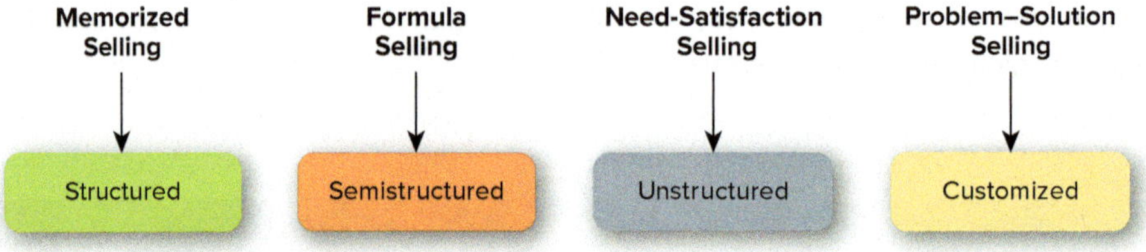

The Memorized Sales Presentation

memorized presentation: A type of presentation in which the salesperson does 80 to 90 percent of the talking, focusing on the product and its benefits rather than attempting to determine the prospect's needs.

The **memorized presentation** is based on either of two assumptions: a prospect's needs can be stimulated by direct exposure to the product via the sales presentation, or these needs have already been stimulated because the prospect has made the effort to seek out the product. In either case, the salesperson's role is to develop this initial stimulus into an affirmative response to an eventual purchase request.

The memorized sales presentation would not be appropriate for more relational or consultative selling.

The salesperson does 80-90 percent of the talking during a memorized sales presentation, only occasionally allowing the prospect to respond to predetermined questions. Notably, the salesperson does not attempt to determine the prospect's needs during the interview, but gives the same canned sales talk to all prospects. Since no attempt is made at this point to learn what goes on in the consumer's mind, the salesperson concentrates on discussing the product and its benefits, concluding the pitch with a purchase request. The seller hopes that a convincing presentation of product benefits will cause the prospect to buy.

In fact, parts of any presentation may be canned, yet linked with free-form conversation. Over time, most salespeople develop proven selling sentences, phrases, and sequences for discussing information. They tend to use these in all presentations.

Despite its impersonal aura, the canned or memorized sales presentation has distinct advantages, as seen in Exhibit 8.4.

EXHIBIT 8.4

Dyno Electric Cart memorized presentation.

Situation: You call on a purchasing manager to elicit an order for some electric carts (like a golf cart). The carts would be used as transportation around the buildings and grounds of a manufacturing plant. The major benefit to emphasize in your presentation is that the carts save time (i.e., reduce transit time between buildings for personnel); you incorporate this concept in your approach. You have chosen to use the memorized stimulus–response presentation for this product.[2]

Salesperson: Hello, Mr. Pride, my name is Abbey Pierce, and I'd like to talk with you about how to save your company executives' time. By the way, thanks for taking the time to talk with me.

Buyer: What's on your mind?

Salesperson: As a busy executive, you know time is a valuable commodity. Nearly everyone would like to have a few extra minutes each day and that is the business I'm in, selling time. While I can't actually sell you time, I do have a product that is the next best thing . . . a Dyno Electric Cart—a real time-saver for your executives.

Buyer: Yeah, well, everyone would like to have extra time. However, I don't think we need any golf carts. [First objection.]

Salesperson: Dyno Electric Cart is more than a golf cart. It is an electric cart designed for use in industrial plants. It has been engineered to give comfortable, rapid transportation in warehouses, plants, and across open areas.

Buyer: They probably cost too much for us to use. [Positive buying signal phrased as an objection.]

Salesperson: First of all, they cost only $2,200 each. With a five-year normal life, that is only $400 per year plus a few cents for electricity and a few dollars for maintenance. Under normal use and care, these carts require only about $100 of service in their five-year life. Thus, for about $50 a month, you can save key people a lot of time. [Creative pricing—show photographs of carts in use.]

Buyer: It would be nice to save time, but I don't think management would go for the idea. [Third objection, but still showing interest.]

Salesperson: This is exactly why I am here. Your executives will appreciate what you have done for them. You will look good in their eyes if you give them an opportunity to look at a product that will save time and energy. But saving time is only part of our story. Dyno carts also save energy and thus keep you sharper toward the end of the day. Would you want a demonstration today or Tuesday? [Alternative close.]

Buyer: How long would your demonstration take? [Positive buying signal.]

Salesperson: I only need one hour. When would it be convenient for me to bring the cart in for your executives to try out?

Buyer: There really isn't any good time. [Objection.]

Salesperson: That's true. Therefore, the sooner we get to show you a Dyno cart, the sooner your management group can see its benefits. How about next Tuesday? I could be here at 8:00 a.m. and we could go over this item just before your weekly management group meeting. I know you usually have a meeting Tuesdays at 9:00 because I tried to call on you a few weeks ago and your secretary told me you were in the weekly management meeting. [Close of the sale.]

Buyer: Well, we could do it then.

Salesperson: Fine, I'll be here. Your executives will really be happy! [Positive reinforcement.]

The benefits of a memorized sales presentation include:

- It ensures the salesperson gives a well-planned presentation and that all of the company's salespeople discuss the same information.
- It both helps and lends confidence to the inexperienced salesperson.
- It is effective when selling time is short, as in door-to-door or telephone selling.
- It is effective when the product is non-technical–such as books, cooking utensils, and cosmetics.

As may be apparent, the memorized method has several major drawbacks:

- It presents features, advantages, and benefits that may not be important to the buyer.
- It allows for little prospect participation.
- It is impractical to use when selling technical products that require prospect input and discussion.
- It proceeds quickly through the sales presentation to the close, requiring the salesperson to close or ask for the order several times, which may be interpreted by the prospect as high-pressure selling.

The story is often told of the new salesperson who was halfway through a canned presentation when the prospect had to answer the telephone. When the prospect finished the telephone conversation, the salesperson had forgotten the stopping point and started over again. The prospect naturally became angry.

In telling of his early selling experiences, salesperson John Anderson remembers that he was once so intent on presenting his memorized presentation that halfway through it the prospect yelled, "Enough, John, I've been waiting for you to see me. I'm ready to buy. I know all about your products." Anderson was so intent on giving his canned presentation, and listening to himself talk, that he did not recognize the prospect's buying signals.

For some selling situations, a highly structured presentation can be used successfully. Examine its advantages and disadvantages to determine if this presentation is appropriate for your prospects and products. Some situations may seem partially appropriate for the memorized approach but require a more personal touch. Such circumstances warrant the examination and use of formula selling.

The Formula Presentation

formula presentation: A presentation by which the salesperson follows a general outline that allows more flexibility and tries to determine prospect needs.

The **formula presentation**, often referred to as the *persuasive selling presentation*, is akin to the memorized method: It is based on the assumption that similar prospects in similar situations can be approached with similar presentations. However, for the formula method to apply, the salesperson must first know something about the prospective buyer. The salesperson follows a less structured, general outline in making a presentation, allowing more flexibility and less direction.

The salesperson generally controls the conversation during the sales talk, especially at the beginning. Exhibit 8.5 illustrates how a salesperson should take charge during a formula selling situation.[3] For example, the salesperson might make a sales opener (approach), discuss the product's features, advantages, and benefits, and then start to solicit comments from the buyer using trial closes, answering questions, and handling objections. At the end of the participation curve, the salesperson regains control over the discussion and moves in to close the sale.

The formula selling approach obtains its name from the salesperson using the attention, interest, desire, and action (AIDA) procedure of developing and giving the sales

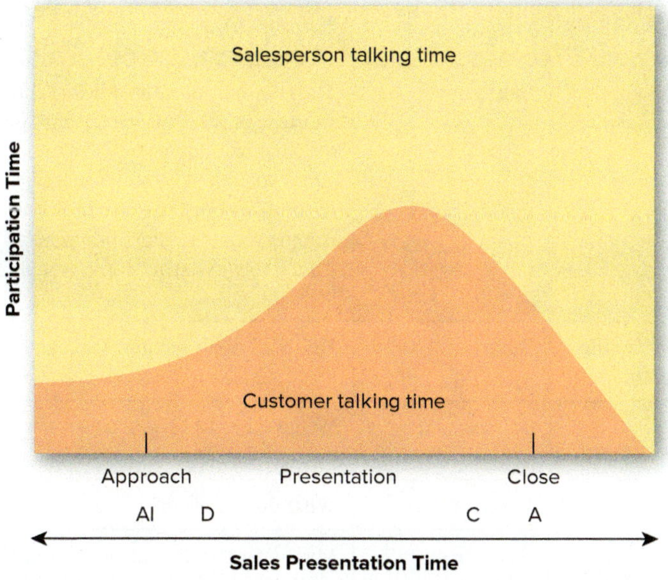

EXHIBIT 8.5

Participation time by a customer and salesperson during a formula sales presentation.

presentation. Straight re-buy situations, especially with consumer goods, lend themselves to this method. Many prospects or customers buy because they are familiar with the salesperson's company. The question is, how can a salesperson for Quaker Oats, Revlon, Gillette, Procter & Gamble, or any other well-known manufacturer develop a presentation that convinces a customer to purchase promotional quantities of a product, participate in a local advertising campaign, or stock a new, untried product?

Formula selling is effective for calling on customers who currently buy and for prospects about whose operations the salesperson has learned a great deal. In such situations, formula selling offers significant advantages, including:

- It ensures that all information is presented logically.
- It allows for a reasonable amount of buyer-seller interaction.
- It allows for smooth handling of *anticipated* questions and objections.

When executed in a smooth, conversational manner, the formula method of selling has no major flaws, as long as the salesperson has correctly identified the prospect's needs and wants. The Procter & Gamble formula sales presentation, given as an example in Exhibit 8.6 (on the next page), can be given to any retailer that is not selling all available sizes of Tide (or of any other product). In this situation, a formula approach is used in calling on a customer to whom the salesperson has previously sold. If, on the other hand, the salesperson does not know a customer's needs and uses this Tide presentation, chances are customer objections would arise early in the presentation—as they sometimes do with the memorized sales presentation method. The formula technique is not adaptable to all complex selling situations; a number of them require other sales presentations.

The Need-Satisfaction Presentation

The television remote is a powerful tool in many homes. It determines which show is watched, how high the sound is, and whether a program plays or stops. The person who holds it has control.[4]

In a similar way, salespeople like to be in charge of the sales presentation—determining the starts, stops, pauses, and rewinds. A sales presentation requiring questions, comments, and long discussions by the buyer challenges the seller to set aside the

EXHIBIT 8.6
A formula approach sales presentation.

FORMULA STEPS	BUYER-SELLER ROLES	SALES PRESENTATION
Summarize the situation for *attention and interest.*	**Salesperson:**	Ms. Hansen, you've said before that the shortage of shelf space prevents you from stocking our family-size Tide—though you admit you may be losing some sales as a result. If we could determine *how much* volume you're missing, I think you'd be willing to *make* space for it, wouldn't you? [Trial close.]
State your marketing plan for *interest.*	**Buyer:**	Yes, but I don't see how that can be done.
	Salesperson:	Well, I'd like to suggest a test—a weekend display of all four sizes of Tide.
	Buyer:	What do you mean?
Explain your marketing plan for *interest* and *desire.*	**Salesperson:**	My thought was to run all sizes at regular shelf price *without* any ad support. This would give us a pure test. Six cases of each size should let us compare sales of the various sizes and see what you're missing by regularly stocking only the smaller sizes. I think the additional sales and profits you'll get on the family size will convince you to start stocking regularly. [Reinforce key benefits.] What do you think? [Trial close.]
Buyer appears to be in *conviction* stage.	**Buyer:**	Well, maybe. [Positive reaction to trial close.]
Suggest an easy next step or *action.*	**Salesperson:**	May I enter the six cases of family-size Tide in the order book now? [Close.]

planned presentation to allow conversational interaction. The rookie salesperson finds this situation nerve-racking, while the seasoned veteran finds this an exhilarating experience. The need-satisfaction and problem-solution presentation methods share the control between buyer and seller.

need-satisfaction presentation: A flexible, interactive type of sales presentation in which a prospect's needs are thoroughly discussed.

The **need-satisfaction presentation** is different from the memorized and the formalized approach; it is designed as a flexible, interactive sales presentation. It is the most challenging and creative form of selling. The salesperson typically starts the presentation with a probing question such as, "What are you looking for in an investment property?" or "What type of technology needs does your company have?" This opening starts a discussion of the prospect's needs and also gives the salesperson an opportunity to determine whether any of the products being offered might be beneficial. When the prospect says something that the salesperson does not understand, the salesperson can clarify by asking a question or restating what the buyer said. The need-satisfaction format is especially suited to the sale of industrial and technical goods with stringent specifications and high price tags.

A common goal: Structure the sales conversation to allow the buyer to talk 80 percent of the time.

Often, as shown in Exhibit 8.7, the first 50–60 percent of conversation time is devoted to a discussion of the buyer's needs.[5] Once aware of the prospect's needs, the salesperson begins to take control of the conversation by restating the prospect's

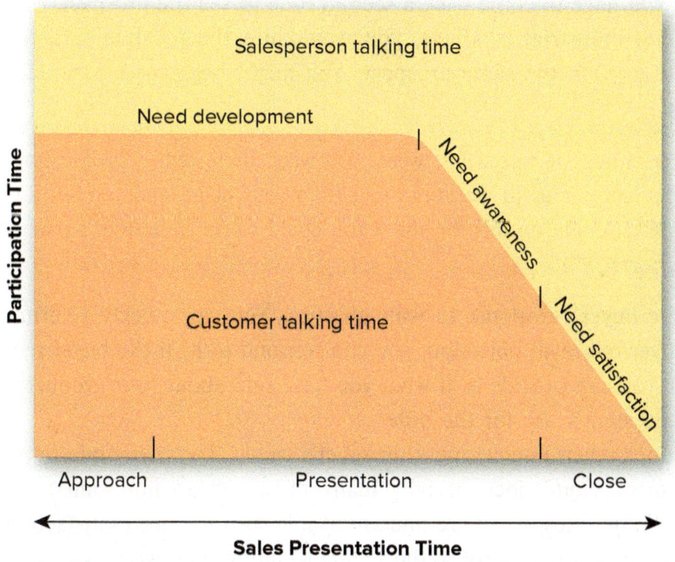

EXHIBIT 8.7
Participation time by customer and salesperson during need-satisfaction and problem—solution sales presentations.

needs to clarify the situation. During the last stage of the presentation, the salesperson shows how the product will satisfy mutual needs. As seen in Exhibit 8.8, the salesperson selling the Dyno Electric Cart begins the interview with the prospect by using the planned series of questions to uncover problems and to determine whether the prospect is interested in solving them.[6]

EXHIBIT 8.8
A need-satisfaction presentation.

Salesperson: Mr. Pride, you really have a large manufacturing facility. How large is it?

Buyer: We have approximately 50 acres under roof, with our main production building almost 25 acres under one roof. We use six buildings for production.

Salesperson: How far is it from your executives' offices to your plant area? It looks like it must be two miles over to there.

Buyer: Well, it does, but it's only one mile.

Salesperson: How do your executives get to the plant area?

Buyer: They walk through our underground tunnel. Some walk on the road when we have good weather.

Salesperson: When they get to the plant area, how do they get around in the plant?

Buyer: Well, they walk or catch a ride on one of the small tractors the workers use in the plant.

Salesperson: Have your executives ever complained about having to do all that walking?

Buyer: All the time!

Salesperson: What don't they like about the long walk?

Buyer: Well, I hear everything from "It wears out my shoe leather" to "It's hard on my pacemaker." The main complaints are the time it takes them and that some older executives are exhausted by the time they get back to their offices. Many people need to go to the plant but don't.

Salesperson: It sounds as if your executives are interested in reducing their travel time and not having to exert so much energy. By doing so, doesn't it seem they would get to the plant as they need to, saving them time and energy and saving the company money?

Buyer: I guess so.

Salesperson: Mr. Pride, on the average, how much money do your executives make an hour?

Buyer: Maybe $65 an hour.

Salesperson: If I could show you how to save your executives time in getting to and from the plant, would you be interested?

Buyer: Yes, I would. [Now the salesperson moves into the presentation.]

Should you have to come back a second time to see the prospect, as is often the case in selling industrial products, you would use the formula sales presentation method in calling on the same prospect. You might begin with a benefit statement such as this:

> Mr. Pride, when we talked last week, you were interested in saving your executives time and energy in getting to and from your plant, and you felt the Dyno Electric Cart could do this for you. (You could pause to let him answer or say, "Is that correct?")

From the buyer's response to your question, you can quickly determine what to do. If the buyer raises an objection, you can respond to it. If the buyer requests more information, you can provide it. If what you have said about your product has pleased the buyer, you simply ask for the order.

Be cautious when uncovering a prospect's needs. Too many questions can alienate the prospect. Remember, initially many prospects do not want to open up to salespeople. Some salespeople are uncomfortable with the need-satisfaction approach because they feel less in control of the selling situation than with a canned or formula presentation. A good point to remember is that you are not there to perform on a stage, but rather to *learn about your prospect's needs–not your own*. Eventually, you can learn to anticipate customer reactions to this presentation and learn to welcome the challenge of the interaction between you and the buyer.

The Problem–Solution Presentation

In selling highly complex or technical products such as insurance, industrial equipment, accounting systems, manufacturing equipment, and technology, salespeople often are required to make several sales calls to develop a detailed analysis of a prospect's needs. After completing this analysis, the salesperson arrives at a solution to the prospect's problems and usually uses both a written analysis and an oral presentation. The **problem-solution presentation** usually consists of six steps:

problem–solution presentation: A flexible, customized approach involving an in-depth study of a prospect's needs, requiring a well-planned presentation.

1. Convincing the prospect to allow the salesperson to conduct the analysis.
2. Making the actual analysis.
3. Agreeing on the problems and determining that the buyer wants to solve them.
4. Preparing the proposal for a solution to the prospect's needs.
5. Preparing the sales presentation based on the analysis and proposal.
6. Making the sales presentation.

The problem-solution presentation is a flexible, customized approach involving an in-depth study of a prospect's needs, and it requires a well-planned presentation. Often, both the need-satisfaction and problem-solution presentations are used when it is necessary to present the proposal to a group of individuals.

Comparison of Presentation Methods

Exhibit 8.9 illustrates differences in the four sales presentation methods. It also shows the wide variety of sales jobs available to choose from if you are seeking a career in this field. Hopefully you will see that selling different products in different industries has similarities but many differences in salespeople's job activities.[7]

Learn about your customer's needs . . . always.

EXHIBIT 8.9

Important characteristics of types of sales calls.

CHARACTERISTICS	MEMORIZED (STRUCTURED)	FORMULA (SEMISTRUCTURED)	NEED-SATISFACTION (UNSTRUCTURED)	PROBLEM-SOLUTION (CUSTOMIZED)
Relationship	Transactional	Relationship	Partnering	Partnering
When Used	New customer door-to-door; telesales	Repeat customer	New customer; new opportunity	New customer; new opportunity
Opening	Canned	Reminder of past status	Questions	Request for study
Presentation Time	Minutes	Half hour(s)	Day(s)	Week(s)
Multiple Calls?	No	Sometimes	Frequently	Always
Type of Negotiations	None	Several variables	Multiple variables	Complex
Script Flexibility	None	Modest	No script	No script
Assumed Interest Level	Already established, or can be generated	Already established	Not established, or not known	Not known
Prior Contact with Buyer?	Not usually	Usually	Not necessarily	Not necessarily
Type of Product	Trivial; simple	Simple; previously sold	Industrial/technical	Complex
Sample Product	Vegetable dicer; vacuum cleaner; cosmetics	Premium cable channel; consumer goods; cars	Home entertainment center	Information technology solutions warehouse system
			Computer real estate	Company insurance
Salary ($)	30-50K	40-70K	50-90K	80-200K

Some of the students in our professional selling classes say, "I do not want to have a sales career." We ask "Why?" They might respond, "I don't want to do any cold-call type of prospecting or work on straight commission." When we describe sales jobs with straight salaries and bonuses with no cold calling and then ask, "What about working for these companies?," they often respond, "That sounds fine." What are the main things you are looking for in a job? Keep in mind that there is a sales job somewhere that has what you are looking for.

What Is the Best Presentation Method?

Each of these sales presentation methods is the best one when the method is properly matched with the *situation*. For example, the memorized presentation method can be used when time is short and the product is simple. Formula selling is effective in repeat purchases or when you know or have already determined the needs of the prospect. The need-satisfaction method is most appropriate when you must gather information from the prospect, as is often the case in selling industrial products. Finally, the problem-solution presentation is excellent for selling high-cost technical products or services, and especially for system selling involving several sales calls and a business proposition. To help improve sales, the salesperson should understand and be able to use each method based on each situation.

LO2 The First Impression You Make Is Critical to Success

When you meet your prospect, initial impressions are based on appearance. If you make a good impression, your prospect is more likely to listen to you; if not, you may face communication barriers that are difficult to overcome.

The first impression is centred on the image projected by your (1) appearance and (2) attitude. Here are some suggestions for making a favourable first impression:

- Wear business clothes that are suitable and fairly conservative.
- Be neat in dress and grooming.
- Refrain from smoking, chewing gum, or drinking when in your prospect's office.
- Stand tall to project confidence.
- Leave all unnecessary materials (overcoat, umbrella, or newspaper) outside the office.
- Remain standing until the prospect offers a chair.
- Be enthusiastic and positive toward the interview.
- Smile, always smile! (Be sincere with your smile; it helps you stay enthusiastic and positive toward your prospect.)
- Do not apologize for taking the prospect's time.
- Do not imply that you were just passing by and that the sales call was not planned.
- Maintain eye contact with the prospect.
- If the prospect offers to shake hands, do so with a firm, positive grip while maintaining eye contact.
- If possible, before the interview, learn how to pronounce your prospect's name correctly, and use it throughout the interview. Should the prospect introduce you to other people, remember their names by using the five ways to remember names listed in Exhibit 8.10.

Source: © Nruboc/Dreamstime.com/GetStock.com

During the approach stage of the presentation, the salesperson must project and maintain a positive, confident, and enthusiastic attitude no matter the prospect's mood when first encountered by the salesperson.

Approach Techniques and Objectives

Approach techniques are grouped into three general categories: (1) opening with a statement, (2) opening with a demonstration, and (3) opening with a question or questions.

Your choice of approach technique depends on which of the four sales presentation methods you have selected based on your situation and sales presentation plan. Using questions in a sales approach is feasible with any of the four presentation methods, whereas statements and demonstrations typically are reserved for either the memorized or the formula sales presentation methods. Because of their customer-oriented nature, the need-satisfaction and problem-solving sales presentation methods always

EXHIBIT 8.10

Five ways to remember a prospect's name.

1. Be sure to hear the person's name and use it: "It's good to meet you, Mr. Firestone."
2. Spell it out in your mind, or if it is an unusual name, ask the person to spell the name.
3. Relate the name to something you are familiar with, such as relating the name Firestone to Firestone automobile tires or a hot rock/stone.
4. Use the name in the conversation.
5. Repeat the name at the end of the conversation, such as "Goodbye, Mr. Firestone."

SOCIAL MEDIA INSIGHTS FOR SALESPEOPLE

YOUR SOCIAL MEDIA PROFILE

Is your prospect expecting you? What are they expecting?

You've made an appointment with your prospect and are preparing to meet them. Hopefully, you've done your research and have a good understanding of both your prospect and their company. If the prospect is considering doing business with you, they may have done their own research. What will they find if they research you?

It is critical for professional salespeople to develop and maintain a professional social media profile. Here are some tips:

- Use your name – You want to make it easy to be "found," so use the name that people would be looking for without nicknames, abbreviations, or credentials.
- Include a photo – It's worth having a professional headshot taken that is optimized for online usage. Don't have a profile picture that includes your pet or you lying on the beach.
- Stay active – Make sure to regularly update your social media presence.
- Check personal information – Ensure that your personal information doesn't dominate your biography. Include business accomplishments and other information that is relevant to your business. Provide information that speaks to your character such as volunteer experience, etc.
- Provide content – Show people that you like to stay current. Post links to articles, videos, product information, etc.
- Get recommended – Testimonials and recommendations from business associates and past customers go a long way in establishing credibility.
- Be present – Make it a point to establish a presence on the popular sites like LinkedIn, Twitter, Facebook, etc.

Your online profile is invaluable. Manage it carefully. There are too many examples of professionals losing their credibility, and in some cases their jobs, because they were irresponsible when it came to managing their online presence.

involve questions at the outset. This section reviews each of the approach techniques with examples of their uses and benefits.

Both the statement and demonstration approach techniques have three basic objectives:

1. To capture the *attention* of the prospect
2. To stimulate the prospect's *interest*
3. To provide a *transition* into the sales presentation

Imagine the prospect silently asking three questions:

1. "Should I see this person?"
2. "Should I listen to, talk with, and devote more time to this person?"
3. "What's in it for me?"

The answers to these questions help determine the outcome of the sale. If you choose to use either of these two approaches, create a statement or demonstration approach that causes the prospect to answer each of these three questions positively.

Rapport—The Relationship Builder

LO3

The approach technique will vary depending on the type of sales call. In a retail environment, for example, a friendly greeting and an offer to help the customer find what they're looking for is short and to the point but nonetheless important for establishing that initial positive relationship and creating a positive sales environment.

In more complex selling situations, especially in business-to-business selling, the initial rapport building will set the pattern for the remainder of the call. It this situation the knowledge of the social style types discussed in Chapter 3 will be important in determining the type of approach to use.

Rapport building can range from small talk to more formal discussions. In the case of business-to-business sales where your call is on the purchasing agent for the company, you will want to ensure that your approach is professional at all times. Your prospect planning can be helpful in providing you with information from which you can create some positive and powerful introductory comments. For example, in doing your customer and prospect research, you scan the business pages of your local newspaper and notice that your customer or prospect company has just won a prestigious business award. There is no better way to start a selling situation than with a congratulatory comment regarding an award recently won. It also indicates that you keep abreast of your customers' or prospects' businesses.

Source: © Nyul/Dreamstime.com/ GetStock.com

We recommend that rapport building be based on safe, relevant topics. Topics of politics, sex, and irrelevant subjects of small talk such as the weather are best replaced with a lead-in that is relevant to the business. Social networking sites like LinkedIn, Facebook, and Twitter are good for uncovering some possible common interests that could be used to facilitate your small talk.

The second part of the approach is the planned, formal selling technique used as the introduction to your presentation. This aspect of the approach will also vary with the situation, and can be a simple statement, a demonstration, or a series of questions. For example, if you are planning a needs-based (questions) selling approach where a formal needs analysis is required (see Chapter 3), you will want to bridge your rapport building smoothly to the next phase. If you create a rapport that is based on relevancy to the prospect company, the transition to the needs analysis is simplified. In many cases, you can use a simple transition comment such as, "Well, it appears that the prospects for your company are very positive, Mr. Hughes. I'm certainly hoping that my company can contribute to that bright future. However, before we determine how my company can help, do you mind if I ask some specific questions about your business to ensure that I can provide the products [or services] you need?"

The Situation Determines the Approach

The situation you face determines which approach technique you use to begin your sales presentation. The situation is dictated by a number of variables that only you can identify. Some of the more common situational variables include the following:

- The type of *product* you are selling
- Whether this is a *repeat call* on the same person
- Your degree of knowledge about the *customer's needs*
- The *time* you have for making the sales presentation
- Whether the customer is *aware of a problem*

The sales approach can be a frightening, lonely experience. It can easily lead to ego-bruising rejection. Your challenge is to move the prospect from an often cold, indifferent, or sometimes even hostile frame of mind to an aroused excitement about the product. By quickly obtaining the prospect's attention and interest, you can make a smooth transition into the presentation that greatly improves the probability of making the sale (see Exhibit 8.11).

EXHIBIT 8.11

The approach leads quickly into the sales presentation.

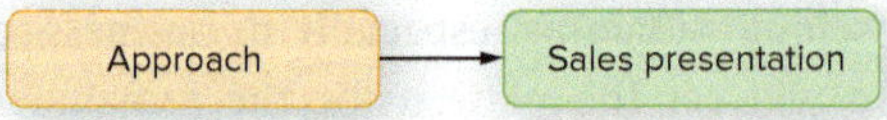

In addition to creating attention, stimulating interest, and providing for transition, using questions in your approach has the following objectives:

1. To *uncover* the needs or problems *important* to the prospect
2. To determine whether the prospect wants to *fulfill* those needs or *solve* those problems
3. To have the prospect *tell you* about these needs or problems and about the intention to do something about them

Since people buy to fulfill needs or solve problems, using questions in your approach is preferable to using statements or demonstrations. Questions allow you to uncover needs, whereas statements and demonstrations are used when you assume knowledge of the prospect's needs. However, any of the three approach techniques can be used by the salesperson in the appropriate situation. Exhibit 8.12 shows the three basic approach techniques and examples of each technique you will study.

STATEMENTS	DEMONSTRATIONS	QUESTIONS
• Introductory	• Product	• Customer benefit
• Complimentary		• Curiosity
• Referral		• Opinion
• Premium		• Shock

EXHIBIT 8.12
Approach techniques for opening the presentation.

Opening with Statements

Opening statements are effective if properly planned, especially if the salesperson has uncovered the prospect's needs before entering the office. Four statement approaches frequently used are (1) the introductory approach, (2) the complimentary approach, (3) the referral approach, and (4) the premium approach.

Introductory Approach

The **introductory approach** is the most common and the least powerful because it does little to capture the prospect's attention and interest. It opens with the salesperson's name and business: "Hello, Ms. Aronovitch, my name is John Gladstone, and I represent the Pierce Chemical Company."

The introductory approach is needed when meeting a prospect for the first time. In most cases, though, the introductory approach should be used in conjunction with another approach. This additional approach could be the complimentary approach.

introductory approach: The most common but least powerful approach; it does little to capture the prospect's attention.

Complimentary Approach

Everyone likes a compliment. If the **complimentary approach** is sincere (and it *must* be sincere), it is an effective beginning to a sales interview. For example:

- "Ms. Rosenburg, you certainly have a thriving restaurant business. I have enjoyed many lunches here. While doing so, I have thought of several products that could make your business even better and make things easier for you and your employees."
- "Mr. Ahermaa, I was just visiting with your boss, who commented that you were doing a good job in keeping your company's printing costs down. I have a couple of ideas that may help you to further reduce your costs."
- "Mrs. Jaggard, I was impressed by the fact that your company has announced plans to develop a philanthropy initiative. I think you'll be very interested in what my foundation has to offer."

complimentary approach: An approach that opens with a compliment that is sincere and therefore effective.

Referral Approach

Sometimes a suitable compliment is not in order or cannot be generated. Another way to get the buyer's attention is to mention a mutual acquaintance as a reference. The use of another person's name, the **referral approach**, is effective if the prospect respects that person; it is important to remember, however, that the referral approach can have a negative effect if the prospect does not like the person. For example:

referral approach: An approach that uses a third person's name as a reference to approach the buyer.

- "Ms. Kessler, my name is Carlos Ramirez, and I'm with the Restaurant Supply Corporation. When I spoke to your brother last week, he asked me to give you a chance to see Restaurant Supply's line of paper products for your restaurant."
- "Hello, Mr. Gillespie. Linda Crawford with the Ramada Inn suggested that I contact you concerning our new Xerox copier."

One salesperson tells of asking the customer to tape-record a brief introduction to a friend. When calling on the friend, the salesperson placed the recorder on the desk and said, "Amos McDonald has a message for you, Ms. James...let's listen."

Few people can obtain a reference for every prospect they intend to contact (this may especially be true for a beginning salesperson). Even if you don't know all the right people, you can still get on track by offering the buyer something for nothing–a premium.

Premium Approach

A **premium approach** is effective because everyone likes to receive something free. When appropriate, use free samples and novelty items in a premium approach. For example:

premium approach: An approach in which the salesperson offers a prospect something as an inducement to buy.

- Early on the morning of her first day on a new campus, one textbook salesperson makes a practice of leaving a dozen doughnuts in the faculty lounge with her card stapled to the box. She claims that prospects actually come looking for her!
- A sales representative of corporate promotional clothing often closed his appointment-getting call with, "By the way Mr. Prospect, can you tell me what size you wear?" Then of course, he would show up to the sales call with a customized golf shirt for that prospect.
- "Mr. Jones, here is a new desk calendar holder with your name engraved on it. Each month I will provide a new calendar for the holder that, by the way, will feature one of our products. This month's calendar, for example, features our lubricating oil."
- "Ms. Flores [handing her the product to examine], I want to leave samples for you, your cosmetic representative, and your best customers, of Revlon's newest addition to our perfume line."

Source: © Shiningcolors/Dreamstime .com/GetStock.com

Creative use of premiums is an effective sales approach. Demonstrations also leave a favourable impression with a prospect.

Demonstration Openings

Openings using demonstrations are effective because they require the prospect to participate in the interview. The product approach is often used by itself or in combination with statements and questions.

Product Approach

In the **product approach**, the salesperson places the product on the counter or hands it to the customer, saying nothing. The salesperson waits for the prospect to begin the conversation. The product approach is useful if the product is new, unique, or colourful, or is an existing product that has changed noticeably.

product approach: An approach in which the salesperson places the product on the counter or hands it to the customer, saying nothing.

If, for example, Pepsi-Cola completely changed the shape of its bottle and label, the salesperson would simply hand the new product to the retail buyer and wait for a reaction. In marketing a new pocket calculator for college students, a Texas Instruments salesperson might simply lay the product on the buyer's desk and wait.

Opening with Questions

Questions are the most common openers because they allow the salesperson to better determine the prospect's needs and require the prospect to participate in the sales interview. The salesperson should use only questions that, as experience and pre-planning have proven, receive a positive reaction from the buyer, since a negative reaction is hard to overcome.

Like opening statements, opening questions can be prepared to suit a number of selling situations. The following sections introduce several basic questioning approaches. This listing is by no means exhaustive, but rather introduces you to a selection of questioning frameworks. With experience, salespeople develop a knack for determining what question to ask which prospect.

Customer Benefit Approach

In this approach, the salesperson asks a question that implies the product will benefit the prospect. If it is their initial meeting, the salesperson can include both their name and the company's name:

- "Hi. I'm Cy Szakos of ABC Shipping and Storage Company. Mr. McDaniel, would you be interested in a new storage and shipping container that will reduce your transfer costs by 10 to 20 percent?"
- "Would you be interested in saving 20 percent on the purchase of our IBM computers?"
- "Ms. Frisini, did you know that several thousand companies–like yours–have saved 10 to 20 percent of their manufacturing cost as described in a recent *BusinessWeek* article? [Continue, not waiting for a response.] They did it by installing our computerized assembly system. Is that of interest to you?"

Your **customer benefit approach** question should be carefully constructed to anticipate the buyer's response. However, always be prepared for the unexpected, as when the salesperson said, "This office machine will pay for itself in no time at all" and the buyer replied, "Fine. As soon as it does, send it to us."

customer benefit approach: An approach whereby the salesperson asks a question that implies that the product will benefit the prospect.

You can also use a direct statement of product benefits to implement a customer benefit approach. The three customer benefit questions shown earlier can be converted into benefit statements:

- "Mr. McDaniel, I want to talk with you about our new storage and shipping container, which will reduce your costs by 10 to 20 percent."
- "I'm here to show you how to save 20 percent on the purchase of our IBM computers."
- "Ms. Frisini, several thousand companies–like yours–have saved 10 to 20 percent on their manufacturing cost by installing our computerized assembly system. I'd like 15 minutes of your time to show how we can reduce your manufacturing costs."

Benefit statements are useful in situations where you know the prospect's or customer's critical needs and have a short time to make your presentation. However, to ensure a positive atmosphere, statements can be followed by a short question–"Is that of interest to you?"–to verify that the benefits are important to the buyer. Even if you know of the buyer's interest, a positive response–"Yes"–to your question is a commitment: The buyer will listen to your presentation because of the possible benefits offered by your product.

Furthermore, you can use the buyer's response to this question as a reference point throughout your presentation. A continuation of an earlier example illustrates the use of a reference point:

- "Mr. McDaniel, earlier you mentioned an interest in reducing your shipping costs. The [now mention your product's feature] enables you to [now discuss your product's advantages]. And the benefit to you is reduced shipping costs."

Curiosity Approach

curiosity approach: An approach whereby the salesperson asks a question or does something to make the prospect curious about the product or service.

Sometimes salespeople prepare an approach that temporarily baffles a prospect. One common method of baffling piques human curiosity. In the **curiosity approach**, the salesperson asks a question or does something to make the prospect curious about the product or service (see Exhibit 8.13).

For example, a salesperson for McGraw-Hill Ryerson, the company that publishes this text, might use the curiosity approach by saying:

- "Do you know why professors such as yourself have made this textbook [as she hands the book to the prospect] the top seller in the market?"

Similarly, a salesperson in manufacturing might ask:

- "Do you know why a recent *BusinessWeek* article described our new computerized assembly system as revolutionary?" [The salesperson briefly displays the *BusinessWeek* issue, then puts it away before the customer can ask to look at the article. Interrupting a sales presentation by urging a prospect to review an article would cause the prospect's attention to be lost for the rest of the interview.]

One manufacturer's salesperson sent an email message to a customer, saying, "Tomorrow is a big day for you and your company." When the salesperson arrived for the interview, the prospect could not wait to find out what the salesperson's message meant. Of course, this could also be done using different social media.

In another example, when calling on a buyer who liked to smoke cigars, a salesperson set a cigar box on the buyer's desk. After some chatting, the buyer said, "What's in the box?" The salesperson handed the box to the buyer and said, "Open it." Inside was a product he wanted to sell. After he bought, the salesperson gave the buyer the cigars. Selling can be fun, especially if the salesperson enjoys being creative.

EXHIBIT 8.13

The curiosity approach. "Mr. Chan, do you know why 300 banks use our customer information system?"

Source: © Pali Rao/iStockphoto

Opinion Approach

People are usually flattered when asked their opinion on a subject. Most prospects are happy to discuss their needs if asked correctly. Here are some examples:

- "I'm new at this business, so would you help me? My company says our Model 100 copier is the best on the market for the money. What do you think?"
- "Mr. Jackson, I've been trying to sell you for months on using our products. What is your honest opinion about our line of electric motors?"

The **opinion approach** is especially good for the new salesperson because it shows that you value the buyer's opinion. Opinion questioning also shows that you will not challenge a potential buyer's expertise by spouting a memorized pitch.

opinion approach: An approach whereby a salesperson shows that the buyer's opinion is valued.

Shock Approach

As its title implies, the **shock approach** uses a question designed to make the prospect think seriously about a subject related to the salesperson's product. It should not be considered an approach that, perhaps unethically, frightens a prospect. For example:

shock approach: an approach that uses a question designed to make the prospect think seriously about a subject related to the salesperson's product.

- "Did you know that 50 percent of start-up businesses in your industry fail within their first year due to improper cash flow management?" said a seller of accounting software.
- "Did you know that employee pilferage has increased this year by 15 percent over last year, according to the local police?" said a seller of video surveillance systems.
- "Shoplifting costs store owners millions of dollars each year! Did you know that there is a good chance you have a shoplifter in your store right now?" said a seller of product sensor security systems.

This type of approach is often used in transactional-type selling and must be used carefully, since some prospects may feel you are merely trying to pressure them into a purchase by making alarming remarks.

Technology in the Approach

A salesperson can quickly capture a prospect's attention and interest by using technology. Technology can be a wonderful means of creatively and professionally beginning a sales presentation. Sounds, visuals, and touch cause the prospect's mind to instantly focus on the salesperson's words and actions. Depending on the product or service you're selling, this may be an opportune time to make use of a notebook, a tablet, or even a cell phone projector to get the prospect's attention. Imagine opening with a YouTube broadcast of yourself or of testimonials from satisfied clients of yours.

However, salespeople should never rely on technology alone in case the technology does not perform at that given moment. As well, some buyers are still somewhat hesitant when it comes to technological advances.

An Approach Checklist

We know that first impressions will often make or break the success of a sales presentation; therefore, preparation for the approach is essential.

1. Ensure that you're meeting the right person (the "qualified" kind).
2. Confirm your appointment (as mentioned during the pre-approach).
3. Familiarize yourself with the structure of your prospect's company.

4. Prepare your sales aids and visuals and have a backup plan. Many salespeople find it useful to have an electronic presentation stored in their email account or on their company's website so they can access it if there are technical difficulties.
5. Ensure that you have directions and maps and anticipate traffic and driving time.
6. Arrive 10–20 minutes early in most situations to allow time for setup.
7. Organize all materials, and know exactly where they are so you can easily retrieve them. Customized materials are a nice touch.
8. Prepare a list of questions that you may need to ask to uncover problems.
9. Don't fret! Anticipate success and a positive experience.
10. Relax and enjoy it. Don't be too aggressive, and pay attention to your audience's reactions.

Proper planning and attention to detail will not go unnoticed by your prospects. Many salespeople have lost sales due to a lack of planning and preparation.

SELLING GLOBALLY

APPRECIATING OUR MULTICULTURAL COUNTRY

In Canada, people from many different cultural backgrounds present a tremendous opportunity for salespeople to increase their sales.

Salespeople should work to develop a diverse customer base. Salespeople who educate themselves on the differences in buying behaviour may see their investment pay off handsomely.

The general manager for a large construction company once had to make last-minute design changes to certain gambling rooms in a new casino because a potential high-stakes gambler, visiting the construction site, complained that the "energy" in the room was just not right. This is just one of many ways in which different cultures may vary in the way they do business.

Some Tips

1. Remember that not all cultures are comfortable being greeted in the same way. You might assume that everyone wants to be met with a firm handshake; however, a handshake can actually be offensive to some people.
2. Don't assume that you know how prospects want to be greeted. Let them determine the most comfortable greeting by hesitating before extending your hand and seeing what they do first. Most men in Canada, regardless of cultural background, will offer a handshake and may even nod as they do so. Simply do the same.
3. Use caution between the genders. In some Middle Eastern and Asian cultures, women are very uncomfortable with the idea of touching an opposite-gender person other than their spouse, and may even be culturally forbidden to do so.
4. Be sensitive to the fact that some cultures are used to hugging and even kissing people on one or both cheeks. If this happens, take it as a sign that they are comfortable with you and return the gesture. Men from the Middle East often shake hands with a slight nod and then exchange kisses on both cheeks. Traditional Muslim men may shake hands and then touch the palm of their right hand to their heart as a sign of friendship. Men from this part of the world usually do not shake hands with women. They often do not introduce women who accompany them nor is it expected that you shake hands with women. This may appear very awkward—but it's business. The rule of thumb in international greeting, then, is: do your research and never assume anything!
5. Personal space varies among cultures. In Canada, we are used to shaking hands and then standing about a metre apart. However, Japanese people may bow or shake hands and then take a step back. This may seem awkward to a Canadian trying to communicate from a greater distance. Don't step forward to bridge the gap as this will be a violation of their personal space. Some cultures prefer a smaller distance. These include people from the Middle East who may hug you and stay at that distance. Don't step back.
6. Some cultures avoid lots of direct eye contact. Don't be alarmed by this; it may be a sign of respect. On the other hand, certain cultures believe that "the eyes are the window to the soul," and hence will maintain complete eye contact. This can be just as uncomfortable for westerners. Be prepared for it.

Using Questions Results in Sales Success

LO4

Asking questions, sometimes called **probes**, is an excellent technique for (1) obtaining information from the prospect, (2) developing two-way communication, and (3) increasing prospect participation.

probes: Questions that help salespeople obtain information from the prospect, develop two-way communication, and increase prospect participation.

When using questions in selling, you need to know or anticipate the answer you want. Once you know the answer you want, you can develop the question. This procedure can be used not only to request information you do not have, but also to confirm information you already know. Only questions that help make the sale should be asked, so use questions wisely.

You can use four basic categories of questions at any point during the presentation: (1) direct, (2) open-ended, (3) rephrasing, and (4) redirect questions.

The Direct Question

The **direct question** or **closed-ended question** is answered in very few words. A simple yes or no answers most direct questions. They are especially useful in moving a customer toward a specific topic. Examples the salesperson might use are: "Mr. Glatter, are you interested in saving 20 percent on your manufacturing costs?" or, "Reducing manufacturing costs is important, isn't it?" You can anticipate a yes response to these questions.

direct question: A question that usually can be answered with yes or no or by a very short response; also known as a *closed-ended question*.

closed-ended questions: Questions that can usually be answered with yes or no or by a very short response. Also known as *direct questions*.

Never phrase the direct question as a direct negative–no question. A *direct negative–no question* is any question that can be answered in a manner that cuts you off completely. The retail salesperson says, "May I help you?" and the reply usually is, "No, I'm just looking." You are completely cut off.

Other types of direct questions ask "What kind?" or "How many?" The questions also ask for a limited, short answer from the prospect. The implication and need-payoff questions used in SPIN (discussed later in this chapter) are examples of direct questions used for the approach.

However, the answer to a direct question does not really tell you much, because little feedback is provided. You may need more information to determine the buyer's needs and problems, especially if you could not determine them before the sales call.

The Open-Ended Question

To open up two-way communication, the salesperson can use an **open-ended question** by beginning the question with one of six words: *Who*, *what*, *where*, *when*, *how*, or *why*. Examples include the following:

open-ended question: A question that opens up two-way communication by beginning the question with who, what, where, when, how, or why.

- Who will use this product?
- What features are you looking for in a product like this?
- Where will you use this product?
- When will you need the product?
- How often will you use the product?
- Why do you need or want to buy this type of product?

One-word questions such as "Oh?" and "Really?" can also be useful in some situations. One-word questions should be said so that the customer is prompted to continue talking. Try it–it works.

To practise using the open-ended questioning technique, ask a friend a question–any question–beginning with one of these six words, or use a one-word question, and see what answer you get. Chances are, the response will consist of several sentences. In a selling situation, this type of response allows the salesperson to better determine the prospect's needs.

The Rephrasing Question

rephrasing question: A question whereby the salesperson rephrases what the prospect has said in order to clarify meaning and determine the prospect's needs.

The third type of question is the **rephrasing question**. At times, the prospect's meaning is not clearly stated. In this situation, if appropriate, the salesperson might say:

- "Are you saying that price is most important to you?" [said sincerely, not too aggressively]
- "Then what you are saying is, if I can improve the delivery time, you would be interested in buying?"

This form of restatement allows you to clarify meaning and determine the prospect's needs. If the prospect answers yes to the second question, you would find a way to improve delivery. If the answer is no, you know delivery time is not an important buying motive; continue to probe for the real problem.

The Redirect Question

redirect question: a question that guides the prospect back to selling points that both parties agree on.

The fourth type of question is the **redirect question**. It is used to redirect the prospect to selling points that both parties agree on. There are always areas of agreement between buyer and seller, even if the prospect is opposed to purchasing the product. The redirect question is an excellent alternative or backup opener. The following example clarifies the concept of redirective questioning.

Imagine you walk into a prospect's office, introduce yourself, and get this response, "I'm sorry, but there is no use in talking. We are satisfied with our present suppliers. Thanks for coming by." Respond by replacing your planned opener with a redirect question. You might say:

- "Can we agree that having a supplier who can reduce your costs is an asset to your company?"
- "You would agree that manufacturers must use the most cost-efficient equipment to stay competitive these days, wouldn't you?"
- "Wouldn't you agree that you continually need to find new ways to increase your company's sales?"

Using a redirect question moves the conversation from a negative position to a positive or neutral one while re-establishing communication. The ability to redirect a

MAKING THE SALE

BE PATIENT!

In selling, the person who asks the questions controls the situation. The information obtained from asking questions is necessary to determine the prospect's likes, dislikes, and topics to avoid. This valuable information also informs the salesperson whether the customer is ready to buy or whether the salesperson should continue selling.

Some salespeople are good at asking questions, but they tend to be impatient and don't offer the buyer an opportunity to answer. Remember—it doesn't matter how long it takes for a buyer's response. Be patient!

seemingly terminated conversation using a question may impress the prospect simply by showing that you are not a run-of-the-mill order taker but a professional salesperson who sincerely believes in the benefits of the product.

Source: © Goodshoot/Punchstock

Three Rules for Using Questions

1. **Use only questions that can easily be answered by the prospect.** Avoid asking questions that are complicated or those that a prospect may not be able to answer. Salespeople are working to build a positive rapport at this stage of the process, so putting prospects on the defensive or intimidating them may prove harmful to this budding relationship.
2. **Pause after a question to allow the prospect time to respond.** Waiting for an answer to a well-planned question is sometimes an excruciating process–seconds may seem like minutes. A salesperson must allow the prospect time to consider the question and must hope for a response. Failing to allow a prospect enough time defeats the major purpose of questioning, which is to establish two-way communication between the prospect and the salesperson.
3. **Listen.** Many salespeople are so intent on talking that they forget to listen to what the prospect says (or they disregard nonverbal signals). Salespeople need to listen consciously to prospects so they can ask intelligent, meaningful questions to determine their prospects' needs and how to solve them. Prospects appreciate a good listener and view a willingness to listen as an indication that the salesperson is truly interested in their situation.

Is the Prospect Still Not Listening?

What happens when, while using your best opening approach, you realize that the prospect is not listening? What about prospects who open mail, who fold their arms while looking at the wall or beyond you into the hallway, who make telephone calls in your presence, or who may even doze off?

This is the time to use one of your alternative openers. Perhaps the prospect might participate in the sales conversation if you use either a question or demonstration approach. By handing the person something, showing something, or asking a question, attention can be briefly recaptured, no matter how indifferent a prospect is to your presence. If you can overcome such preoccupation or indifference, the probability of your making a sale will greatly improve. This is why the approach is so important to the success of a sales call.

Never become flustered or confused when a communication problem arises during your approach. As mentioned earlier, the salesperson who can deftly capture another person's imagination earns the right to a prospect's full attention and interest.

Needs Analysis—A Key to Success

LO5

During the first few minutes of the approach stage, salespeople will attempt to set the stage for the interview by establishing a rapport, getting the prospect's attention, and arousing his or her desire to listen to the presentation. Before getting into the presentation, it is very useful for salespeople to perform a needs analysis.

Learning the buyer's needs and wants and determining which are the most important is a key part of effective selling. It is accomplished through research, skilful questioning, listening, and observation. In business-to-business selling, research begins during prospecting (Chapter 6) and expands during the pre-approach stage (Chapter 7), before you communicate with the buyer. Questioning, listening, and observing are particularly important once you are in contact with the buyer.

Needs analysis enables you as the salesperson to diagnose the buyer's situation before prescribing a product or service solution. Ideally, complete your analysis of buyer needs before starting to provide product information. Sometimes, however, buyers want you to start talking about your product right away because they are impatient or unaware of the value of exploring needs. Avoid the temptation to skip needs analysis altogether. At the very least, convince the prospect that it is worthwhile to spend a few minutes exploring key needs.

It is helpful to prevent potential buyer resistance to needs analysis. You can do this by sharing with the prospect your reasons for conducting needs analysis and then obtaining their agreement to participate before you begin asking needs analysis questions.

Needs Questions Should Focus on Results

What should a salesperson ask about during needs analysis? While the purpose is to discover important needs and wants, a question such as, "Do you need my product?" is likely to draw a negative response. Instead, needs analysis questions should focus on what *results* the buyer is seeking–what he or she desires to be different from the present.

Let's say a person walks into a hardware store and says to a salesperson, "I need a drill." How should the salesperson respond? A poor salesperson might point to the aisle and say, "Over there, in aisle three." Another might lead the person to the display of drills and begin describing the various makes and models available. Both of these employees would be making the mistake of omitting needs analysis.

A third salesperson might pose several questions such as, "What size of motor do you want?" and "Do you want the metal casing or the plastic?" and "Do you need one with a reverse gear?" This salesperson deserves credit for attempting to conduct needs analysis; however, the questions should be results focused, not product focused. Better questions would be, "What do you intend to use the drill for?" and "What types of holes do you need?" and "How many holes are you planning to drill?" and "What material will you be drilling through?" These types of questions delve into the results sought by the buyer and provide valuable information for the salesperson.

Although buyers have more product knowledge today than at any time in the past, the salesperson has the most product knowledge and is in the best position to help the buyer make decisions that will yield a satisfied customer in the long term.

LO6 Structure Needs Analysis Using Multiple-Question Approaches

Needs analysis is best done by using open-ended questions. One strategy is to begin by asking general questions and gradually move to more specific questions. For example, a photocopier salesperson might begin with, "How much do you expect your company to grow over the next two years?" and conclude with, "What would be the best timing for your staff to receive training on new equipment?"

SPIN:
An acronym describing a sequential questioning approach used by salespeople; situation, problem, implication, needs payoff.

Another method of organizing needs analysis questions is called **SPIN**. It involves using a series of four types of questions in a specific sequence.[8] SPIN stands for (1) ***Situation***, (2) ***Problem***, (3) ***Implication***, and (4) *Need payoff*. Let's look at each step in the sequence.

In Step 1, the salesperson uses one or more questions to find out about the prospect's current general ***situation***. These probes need to be related to the salesperson's product or service. For example, an electric cart salesperson might ask a prospect, "How large are your manufacturing plant facilities?"

The salesperson then moves to Step 2 by asking about specific ***problems***, dissatisfactions, or difficulties perceived by the prospect relative to the current situation.

Problem questions can raise the level of needs awareness. For example, "How often do your executives complain about having to do so much walking around the plant?" The goal is to have the prospect realize that she does, in fact, have a problem.

For Step 3, the salesperson explores the ***implications*** of the problems for the prospect. Implication questions reveal the true dimensions of the problems, and how they affect the prospect or the organization. An example used by the electric cart salesperson might be "What impact is the time and energy of this walking around the plant having on the efficiency of your executives?"

In Step 4, the salesperson poses ***need-payoff*** questions that determine how motivated the prospect is to solve the problems. Need-payoff questions reveal what needs the prospect perceives to be important. For example, the electric cart salesperson may ask, "How important is reducing your executives' travel time getting around the plant?"

Although the SPIN sequence is designed to move the conversation logically from one step to the next, situation, problem, and implication questions do not have to be asked strictly in order. You will generally begin with a situation question and follow with a problem question. However, you could ask a situation question, a problem question, and another situation question, for example. As well, you can ask more than one of each type. The need-payoff question is always last.

To demonstrate the SPIN technique, imagine you are approaching a prospect about buying your new models of high-speed photocopiers. From your research of the company, you know that this prospect requires high-volume equipment and also high-quality reproduction capability. A SPIN sequence might go something like this:

Situation	• What type of equipment are you using now? • How many people use the photocopiers? • Approximately how many copies do you need produced in the average month?
Problem	• Have you had any service issues with your current equipment? • How long does the average repair take? • Regarding quality–have you had print jobs that weren't quite up to your high standards?
Implications	• When one of your photocopiers breaks down, how does it affect your productivity? • If you sent out a print job of inferior quality, what would happen?
Need payoff	• If I could show you a copy system that would virtually eliminate some of these problems, is it something you would be interested in?

If your questions thus far were structured properly and were based on some prior knowledge of the prospect's needs, you would be very well positioned to lead into your presentation now–with a very attentive and interested prospect. What features would you open with after this SPIN exchange? You can start by talking about features dealing with reliability and print quality.

Needs Analysis by Email

Most salespeople conduct needs analysis while meeting face to face with the prospect or talking with him or her on the telephone. It is also possible to uncover needs and wants by sending the prospect a questionnaire by email. This may be more appropriate than a face-to-face interview because of factors such as the distance between the salesperson and prospect, scheduling challenges, or the need for the prospect to consult with others to answer the questions. The form in Exhibit 8.14 (on the next page) can be used to help develop a thorough solution for Maritime Shredding. This form can be used in person or sent by email. If email is used, a complete solution can be planned and presented with all the necessary details at the sales interview.

EXHIBIT 8.14

Example of a B2B needs analysis form.

MARITIME SHREDDING LTD.

Company information:

Company name: ____________________

Contact person: ____________________

Company address:

Street address: ____________________

City: ____________ Province: ____________

Postal code: ____________

Phone: ____________ Email: ____________

Fax: ____________ Web: ____________

Materials to be shredded. Check all that apply:

☐ Confidential documents ☐ DVDs/CDs

☐ Heavy stock literature ☐ Videotapes

☐ Envelopes ☐ Stapled documents

Daily shredding requirements:

☐ Up to 200 sheets per day ☐ 2,000–15,000 sheets per day

☐ 200–500 sheets per day ☐ More than 15,000 sheets per day

☐ 500–2000 sheets per day

How secure do you need your shredding to be?

☐ Level 1-daily internal office documents ☐ Level 4-secret documents

☐ Level 2-sensitive internal documents ☐ Level 5-top secret financial documents

☐ Level 3-confidential documents

Cutting option preference:

☐ Strip cut (general security) ☐ Multi-cut (greatest security)

☐ Cross-cut (greater security)

How many shredders would you require?

☐ 1–3

☐ 4–5

☐ More than 5

How often will you be shredding?

☐ Daily ☐ Other ____________

☐ Weekly ☐ Varies

Please estimate the number of boxes of material that you would likely shred over the next 5 years.

Number of boxes: ____________________

Comments or questions: ____________________

____

____

Be Flexible in Your Approach

Picture yourself as a salesperson getting ready to come face to face with an important prospect, Ellen Myerson. You have planned exactly what you are to say in the sales presentation, but how can you be sure Myerson will listen to your sales presentation? You realize she is busy and may be indifferent to your being in the office; she is probably preoccupied with her own business-related situation, and several of your competitors may already have seen her today.

You have planned to open your presentation with a statement about how successful your laptop computer has been in helping office workers save time and eliminate errors in their keyboarding. When you enter the office, Myerson comments on how efficient her office workers are and how they produce error-free work. From her remarks, you quickly determine that your planned statement approach is inappropriate. What do you do now?

You might begin by remarking how lucky she is to have such conscientious office workers, and then proceed into the SPIN question approach, first asking questions to determine general problems that she may have, and then using further questions to uncover specific problem areas she might like to solve. Once you have determined specific problems, you can ascertain whether they are important enough for her to want to solve them in the near future. If so, you can make a statement that summarizes how your product's benefits will solve her critical needs, and test for a positive response. A positive response allows you to conditionally move into the sales presentation.

Practice and Time

Both new and experienced salespeople go through a learning process consisting of three phases of usage before true behavioural changes occur as a result of sales training. Many salespeople feel awkward at first. In the second phase of training usage, the salesperson consciously uses the training more and more, slowly becoming better at its application on the job. In the third phase of training usage, the new techniques become a natural part of the day-to-day job (see Exhibit 8.15).

Habits are difficult to change. It takes regular, on-the-job reinforcement to change a salesperson's habits. As the new training begins to produce more sales, people master the sales techniques and they become natural to use. This may relate to what you are experiencing in your sales class. It is very common!

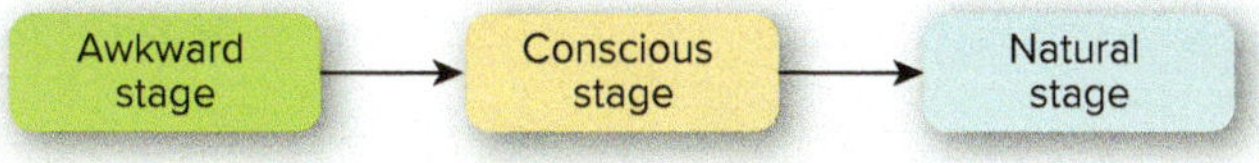

EXHIBIT 8.15

Training usage phases over time.

Source: ©Kelly Redinger/Design Pics

ETHICAL DILEMMA

IS A HALF-TRUTH THE SAME AS A LIE?

You enjoy selling but often find it difficult to get the ball rolling during sales interviews. You try to get the prospects' attention but they never seem to get turned on to your product. You know your product is good—in fact, previous customers have saved an average of 10 percent in their fuel costs while using it. One of your previous customers purchased your product at the same time as they bought a new fleet of smaller, fuel-efficient vehicles, which resulted in that company using 50 percent less fuel in the following year.

With this information, you try a different approach to capture the attention of your next prospect. Read this dialogue:

Seller: "Mr. Buyer, the reason I'm here today is to introduce to you our fuel-saving device, which has been found to save 50 percent of fuel costs in some delivery fleets. Does this sound like it may be useful in your company?"

Buyer: "Fifty percent? That sounds fantastic—let me clear my desk here—I'd love to hear more."

Finally, you have a prospect who is truly interested in what you have to say. It worked!

Have you done the right thing?

What other techniques might you consider using?

The Group Presentation

At times you will meet with more than one decision maker for a group presentation.[9] Many group presentation elements are similar to other types of presentations. The primary difference is that either you or your team presents the proposal to a group of decision makers.

The group presentation, depending on size, may be less flexible than a one-on-one meeting. The larger the group, the more structured your presentation. It would not work if everyone jumped in with feedback and ideas simultaneously, so a semblance of order has to be arranged. As the salesperson in charge, you can structure the presentation and provide a question-and-answer period at the end of or during the presentation.

The ideal situation is to talk with most or all of the decision makers involved during the analysis phase. That way, they will have contributed to determining what is needed. The points you discuss will hit on thoughts they have expressed regarding the problems at hand. In the initial part of the presentation, you should accomplish the following steps:

Give a Proper Introduction

State your name and company name, and explain in a clear, concise sentence the premise of your proposal. For example, your statement might sound like this: "Good morning. I'm Jeff Baxter from International Hospitality Consultants. I'm here to share my findings, based on research of your company and discussions with Mary Farley, that suggest my company can help increase your convention bookings by 15 to 30 percent."

Establish Credibility

Give a brief history of your company that includes the reason the business was started, the company philosophy, its development, and its success rate. Mention a few companies that you have worked with in the past, especially if they are big names. This reassures the client by letting the group know who you are and the extent of your experience and credibility.

Provide an Account List

Have copies of an account list available for everyone in attendance. Hand out copies either in advance or while you talk. This list shows the various sizes, locations, and types of companies you've helped in the past.

State Your Competitive Advantages

Right up front you can succinctly tell the group where your company stands relative to the competition. Don't get into a detailed analysis of comparative strengths and weaknesses; just make it clear that you can do better than the competition.

Give Quality Assurances and Qualifications

Get the group on your side by stating guarantees in the beginning. This shows pride in your product and that you don't skirt the issue of guarantees. Also, give your company's qualifications and credentials. For example, "We are certified by the Canadian Government and licensed in 10 provinces to treat or move toxic waste," or "I have copies of the test reports from an independent lab." If your company has an impressive money-back guarantee or an extended warranty, mention it.

Cater to the Group's Behavioural Style

Every group comprises individuals with personal styles. However, a group also exhibits an overall or dominant style; that is, it has a decision-making mode that characterizes one of the four behavioural styles (see Chapter 3). If you can quickly determine the group style, you will hold their attention and give them what they want more effectively. Some people are more impatient than others. If you don't address their needs, you will lose their attention.

Get People Involved

After establishing the credibility of your company, involve the group in the presentation. The first thing to do is go around the room asking for everyone's input into the decision-making criteria for making the purchase. Preface this with, "I spoke to David, Elizabeth, and Christine and learned their views on what your company would like to see changed in this area. In my research, I discovered it would also benefit you to have X, Y, and Z improved. I'd like to hear all of your thoughts on this matter." Ask each person to add to the list of benefits and the decision-making criteria. Take notes, perhaps on a flip chart, of what everyone says to help shape your presentation.

> *"The only place where success comes before work is in a dictionary."*
>
> *VIDAL SASSOON*

After everyone has had a chance to speak, go through your presentation exactly as in a one-on-one presentation. The primary difference is that you want to answer all the questions, fears, and concerns in the group. Meet each person's specific needs with a specific proposal.

When using this method, it is essential during your preparation to brainstorm all possible concerns and questions the decision makers may have. This information comes from talking to people within the company, other salespeople, and people in the industry. Be so well prepared that there is nothing they could come up with as decision-making criteria that you haven't already thought of and answered.

The Proposal

When you prepare for a group, write a proposal document that ranges from one page to an entire notebook with data, specifications, reports, and solutions to specific problems. The proposal document is a reference source that tells your customer what she bought if she said yes and what she didn't buy if the answer was no. This document addresses everything you and your prospect discussed in the analysis phase: problems, success criteria, decision-making criteria, and how your product or service answers each. At the end, include relevant documents and copies of testimonial letters from satisfied customers.

During your presentation, do not read from the document. It is not the presentation; it is strictly a resource of facts to give your prospect after a decision is made.

In addition, when making your presentation, do not expect to cover every point in the proposal unless you are brief. Your presentation will focus on the issues that relate to the customer's specific need gap; detailed excessive information should be left in the document. Remember that proposal documents don't sell products; people sell products. The document is no substitute for a first-rate presentation.

No Prices

The best way to present a proposal document is without prices. There are several reasons for this. First, some people will go directly to the prices without reading through the document. Second, prices tend to prejudice non-decision makers—who should not be concerned with prices. If the decision maker asks why the prices are missing, tell him, "I thought you would prefer the flexibility of showing the document to other people without their knowing prices. It's a matter of confidentiality." The third reason is politics. Imagine a board of directors that has not had a raise in two years looking at a document that proposes a $2 million computer for the company. This may stir up problems.

Make it clear that you are not trying to hide the prices and that you would be more than happy to talk about them with the appropriate people, the decision makers. It is important to present prices in the proper perspective and context.

When you share the proposal, address each problem and give specific information about your solutions. Make sure you discuss features, advantages, and benefits—and get feedback from the group. Ask trial closes like these:

- "Can you see any other advantages to this?"
- "How do you feel about that? Do you think that would solve the problem?"

Summarize Benefits

At the end, summarize your proposal by giving a benefits summary: "Here is what benefits your firm will receive if you accept my proposal." Talk about how the benefits will address their specific problems.

Before your presentation, find out from your primary contact in the company if the group will make a decision while you are there or if they will discuss it and inform you later. You also should know if they are responsible for dealing with the financial aspects of the purchase. If so, you will have to talk about the costs and the benefits

SELLING TIPS

NEGOTIATION

- When you give up something, try to gain something in return. When you give something for nothing, there is a tendency for people to want more. In all fairness to you and your prospect, balance what you give and receive. For example, "I'll lower the price if you pay in full within 30 days," or "I'll give you 10 percent off, but you will be charged for additional services such as training."
- Look for items other than price to negotiate. For example, gain some flexibility by offering better terms, payment plans, return policies, and delivery schedules; lower deposits or cancellation fees; or implementation and training programs. Often these items are provided for less than your company would lose if you lowered the price.
- Do not attack your prospect's demand; look for the motive behind it. Never tell a prospect their demand is ridiculous or unreasonable. Remain calm and ask for the reason behind the desire.
- Do not defend your position; ask for feedback and advice from the prospect. If you meet resistance to an offer, don't be defensive. Say something like, "This is my thinking. What would you do if you were in my position?"

they will receive in relation to the costs. If they will not be concerned with prices, don't discuss them.

When you have completed the benefits summary, solicit impressions from the group. Ask if they agree that the solution you proposed would solve their problem or meet their needs. Without asking for it, get a feeling for the disposition of the group. If you are working with one person, it is easier to ask for an impression.

At the end of your summary, ask if there are any questions. At this point, you are close to the end of your allotted time. When someone asks a question that is answered in your proposal document, refer them to the appropriate section of the document and assure them that a complete answer is provided.

SELLING TIPS

GROUP PRESENTATION CHECKLIST

✓ Monitor your voice – How you say it is as important as what you say.
✓ Watch your body language – Give the right message.
✓ Pay attention to your appearance – Dress appropriately.
✓ Progress logically – Remember your objectives.
✓ Practise – This will improve your skills.
✓ Focus on the details – Know who and how many will attend and their titles.
✓ Bring handouts – Prepare enough handouts for everyone.
✓ Develop a script – Improvising makes the presentation awkward.
✓ Prepare note cards – Use cards if necessary, and number them.
✓ Use visual aids – Have a backup plan in case you cannot use your visual aids.
✓ Devise a pleasant and professional greeting – Identify yourself and your organization.
✓ Introduce your objectives – Give the group an idea of what you plan to present.
✓ Summarize key selling points
✓ Encourage interaction – Maintain control of the group but let others speak.
✓ Stay within a planned time limit – Finishing early is better than finishing late.

Negotiating So Everyone Wins

No matter what type of presentation method you use, or whether you talk to one person or a group of people, be prepared to negotiate. Many salespeople negotiate during the confirming phase of the sale. Their products or services are big-ticket items with many negotiable details. The negotiating process during the sale confirmation becomes a critical point that can affect the business relationship.

There are many negotiating styles with various names. For example, there are cooperative, competitive, attitudinal, organizational, and personal modes of negotiating. Most inexperienced negotiators operate in the competitive mode because they mistakenly think the shrewd businessperson is one who wins at the other's expense. With a win-lose attitude in mind, they "don't show all their cards" and use other strategies to gain the upper hand. Often this is done at the expense of the business relationship.

If you see prospects as adversaries rather than business partners, you will have short-term, adversarial relationships. The tension, mistrust, and buyer's remorse created are not worth the small gains you may win using this negotiating style. There is a better way.

Professional salespeople negotiate in a way that achieves satisfaction for both parties. They rely on trust, openness, credibility, integrity, and fairness. Their attitude is not "How can I get what I want out of this person?" It's "There are many options to explore that will make both of us happy. If two people want to do business, the details will not stand in the way." It is important *not* to negotiate the details before your customer has made a commitment to your solution.

Phases of Negotiation

If your product or service requires negotiating on a regular basis, set the stage for negotiation early in the sales process. There are things you can do to prepare for negotiation from the beginning.

Planning

The number one asset of a strong negotiator is preparation. During the planning phase, after completing a competition analysis, you know how your company compares with the competition for price, service, quality, reputation, and so on. This knowledge is important at negotiation time. You may be able to offer things the competition cannot. It is advantageous to point out these advantages to your prospect when the time is right.

Before you make a proposal to a client, search your company's sales records to find any reports of previous sales to your prospect or similar businesses. If these records documented the successes and failures of negotiating, you will learn from other salespeople's experience. For this reason, your call reports should include details of what transpired during any negotiation. The knowledge gained from these records is not a strategy per se, but insight into the priorities of this market segment. For example, businesses in a certain industry segment may value service more than price, or they may care more about help in training and implementation than a discount.

During your preparation, review the various bargaining chips available to you. Some of the questions to answer include these:

- What extra services can you offer?
- How flexible is the price or the payment plan?
- Are deposits and cancellation fees negotiable?
- Is there optional equipment you can throw in for free?
- Can you provide free training?
- What items in the negotiation will be inflexible for you?
- How can you compensate for these items?

Meeting

When you meet a prospect, you start building the relationship by proving you are someone who is credible, trustworthy, and, it is hoped, the type of person your prospect likes to do business with. If you are all these things, you will eliminate tension from the relationship and thereby ease the negotiation process.

As proof of this concept, imagine selling your car to a friend. Now imagine selling it to a stranger. Who would be easier to negotiate with? The friend, of course. For both of you, the top priority is the relationship; the secondary priority is the car deal.

Studying

When you study a prospect's business, look at the big picture. As mentioned earlier in the book, don't focus on features; look for benefits you can provide. Look behind a prospect's demands for reasons. You can ask, "What are you trying to accomplish by asking for this?" After the prospect answers, you may be able to say, "We can accomplish that another way. Consider this alternative . . ." The more options for providing benefits, the more flexible the negotiation.

> *"Do not fear going forward slowly; fear only to stand still."*
>
> *CHINESE PROVERB*

During this phase, you must find out what other competitors' products or services your prospect is considering. This gives insight into what they are looking for and willing to pay. If you are selling a half-million-dollar CAT scanner and your prospect is also considering a three-quarter-million-dollar CAT scanner, you know your product is not priced too high. If, however, your prospect is looking at a lot of lower-priced units, it may be an uphill struggle to get the prospect to spend what you're asking. Knowing who your competitors are will help you assess bargaining strengths and weaknesses.

Every purchase is made with decision-making criteria in mind, either consciously or subconsciously. Find out what they are for your prospect and the prospect's company. Within those criteria, there are usually three levels of desire: must have, should have, and would be nice to have. Be clear about these levels and how they create limits for negotiations. Obviously, "must haves" are much less flexible than "would be nice to haves."

Proposing

Proposing is another phase that indirectly affects subsequent negotiations. What you do in the presentation sets the stage for what may come later. During your presentation, tie features and advantages to benefits and emphasize unique benefits. In this way, your product or service and company are positioned above the competition. It is important to position yourself as well. Don't be afraid to let your prospect know they are getting you and everything you have promised to do after the sale.

The successful resolution of a negotiation starts with a commitment to do business together. It is then necessary for both parties to maintain common interests and resolve any conflicts cooperatively.

The key to selling and negotiating is to always seek a win-win solution in which both buyer and seller are happy.

Summary of Major Selling Issues

As the first step in your sales presentation, the approach is a critical factor. To ensure your prospects' attention and interest during a memorized or formula mode of presentation, you may want to use a statement or demonstration approach. In more technically oriented situations where you and the prospects must agree on needs and problems, a questioning approach (SPIN, for instance) is in order. Generally, in developing your approach, imagine your prospects asking themselves, "Do I have time to listen to, talk with, or devote to this person? What's in it for me?"

Words alone will not ensure that you are heard. The first impression that you make on a prospect can negate your otherwise positive and sincere opening. To ensure a favourable impression in most selling situations, dress conservatively, be well groomed, and be truly glad to meet the prospect. Remember that your prospect may have researched you before meeting you. It is imperative that you manage your online profile to maintain a professional image.

Your approach statement should be customized for each prospect. You can choose to open with a statement, question, or demonstration by using any one of the techniques. Several alternative approaches should be ready in case you need to alter your plans for a specific situation.

Carefully phrased questions are useful at any point in a sales presentation. Questions should display a sincere interest in prospects and their situations. Skilfully handled questions employed in a sales approach can wrest a prospect's attention from distractions and centre it on you and your presentation. Questions are generally used to determine prospects' wants and needs, thereby increasing prospect participation in the sales presentation. Four basic types of questions discussed in this chapter are direct, open-ended, rephrasing, and redirect questions.

In using questions, ask questions whose answers you can anticipate. Also, remember to allow prospects time to completely answer the question. Listen carefully to their answers as a guide to how well you are progressing toward selling to them. Should you determine that your prospect is not listening, regain their attention. Techniques such as offering something or asking questions can refocus the prospect's attention.

MEETING A SALES CHALLENGE

Questions are important tools for salespeople. They help uncover needs and problems, obtain valuable selling information, and qualify the prospect's interest and buying authority. So it pays to ask good ones.

Since you may need to first develop an analysis of the company operation, begin with questions that are direct, are well aimed, and, most importantly, force the prospect to talk about a specific problem. Questions that cannot be answered *yes* or *no* provide the most information. A multiple-question approach, such as SPIN, would be appropriate for this situation.

PLAYING THE ROLE

The situation: You are a salesperson for a hockey stick manufacturer. Your company has just developed a revolutionary new hockey stick that is lighter. Its flexibility allows for better stickhandling and a harder shot. You have an appointment with the general manager of a professional hockey team and want them to purchase your sticks for the organization.

Role A: Sales Rep 1. Prepare an effective curiosity approach.

Role B: Sales Rep 2. Prepare an effective shock approach.

Role C: Sales Rep 3. Prepare an effective benefit approach.

Role D: Sales Rep 4. Prepare an effective complimentary approach.

Role E: General manager for the pro hockey team.

Each rep should dramatize a prepared approach to the general manager. Observers can judge and defend which is the most effective.

Key Terms for Selling

approach
closed-ended questions
complimentary approach
creative imagery
curiosity approach
customer benefit approach
direct question
formula sales presentation
introductory approach
memorized presentation
need-satisfaction presentation
open-ended question
opinion approach
premium approach
probes
problem-solution presentation
product approach
redirect question
referral approach
rephrasing question
shock approach
SPIN

Sales Application Questions

1. Explain the reasons for using questions when making a sales presentation. Discuss the rules for questioning that should be followed by the salesperson.
2. What are three general categories of the approach? Give an example of each.

3. In each of the following instances, determine whether a direct, open-ended, rephrasing, or redirect question is being used. Discuss the benefits of each of the four types of questions.
   a. "Now let's see whether I have this right; you are looking for a high-quality product and price is no object?"
   b. "What type of clothing are you looking for?"
   c. "Are you interested in Model 101 or Model 921?"
   d. "Well, I can appreciate your beliefs, but you would agree that price is not the only thing to consider when buying a copier, wouldn't you?"
   e. "When would you like to have your new Xerox 9000 installed?"
   f. "Are you saying that *where* you go for vacation is more important than the cost of getting there?"
   g. "You would agree that saving time is important to a busy executive like you, wouldn't you?"
4. Which of the following approaches do you think is the best? Why? Can you suggest how each could be improved?
   a. "Ms. Silva, in the past, you've made it a practice to reduce the facings on heavy-duty household detergents in the winter months because of slower movement."
   b. "Mr. Galdanzo, you'll recall that last time I was in, you expressed concern over the fact that your store labour was running higher than the industry average of 8 percent of sales."
   c. "Hi! I'm Jeanette Smith of Procter & Gamble, and I'd like to talk to you about Cheer. How's it selling?"
5. Assume you are a salesperson for POS Systems Corporation and you want to sell Mr. Malik, the owner/manager of a large independent supermarket, your computerized customer checkout system. You have just met Mr. Malik inside the front door of the supermarket. After your initial introduction, the conversation continues:

   Salesperson: Mr. Malik, your customers are really backed up at your cash registers, aren't they?

   Buyer: Yeah, it's a real problem.

   Salesperson: Do your cashiers ever make mistakes when they are in a rush?

   Buyer: They sure do!

   Salesperson: Have you ever thought about shortening checkout time while reducing cashier errors?

   Buyer: Yes, but those methods are too expensive!

   Salesperson: Does your supermarket generate more than $1 million in sales each month?

   Buyer: Yes, why?

   Salesperson: Would you be interested in discussing a method of decreasing customer checkout time by 50 percent and greatly lessening the number of errors made by your cashiers, if I can show you that the costs of solving your problems will be more than offset by your savings?

   a. Using the framework of the SPIN approach technique, determine whether each of the above questions asked by the salesperson is a *s*ituation, *p*roblem, *i*mplication, or *n*eed-payoff question.
   b. If Mr. Malik says yes to your last question, what should you do next?
   c. If Mr. Malik says no to your last question, what should you do next?
6. As a salesperson for Gatti's Electric Company, Cliff Defee is interested in selling John Bonham more of his portable electric generators. John is a construction supervisor for a firm specializing in constructing large buildings such as shopping centres, office buildings, and manufacturing plants. He currently uses three of Cliff's newest models. Cliff

just learned that John will be building a new manufacturing plant. As Cliff examines the specifications for the new plant, he believes John will require several additional generators. Two types of approaches Cliff might make are depicted in the following situations:

Situation A:

Salesperson: I see you got the Jonesville job.

Buyer: Sure did.

Salesperson: Are the specs OK?

Buyer: Yes.

Salesperson: Will you need more machines?

Buyer: Yes, but not yours!

Situation B:

Salesperson: I understand you have three of our electric sets.

Buyer: Yes, I do.

Salesperson: I'm sure you'll need additional units on your next job.

Buyer: You're right, I will.

Salesperson: Well, I've gone over your plant specifications and put together the products you will need.

Buyer: What I don't *need* are any of your lousy generators.

Salesperson: Well, that's impossible. It's a brand-new design.

Buyer: Sorry, I've got to go.

a. Briefly describe both approaches in situations A and B. In both situations, Cliff is in a tough spot. What should he do now?

b. What type of approach could Cliff have made that would have allowed him to uncover John's dissatisfaction? Would the approach you are suggesting also be appropriate if John were satisfied with the generators?

7. You are making a cold call on the warehouse manager for Coats Western Wear, a retailer with four stores. You know most of the manager's work consists of deliveries from the warehouse to the four stores. Based on your experience, you suspect that the volume of shipments to the warehouse fluctuates; certain seasons of the year are extremely busy.

   As a salesperson for Hercules Shelving, you want to sell the manager your heavy-duty-gauge steel shelving for use in the warehouse. Since this is a relatively small sale, you decide to go in cold, relying only on your questioning ability to uncover potential problems and make the prospect aware of them.

   You are now face to face with the warehouse manager. You have introduced yourself and after some small talk it is time to begin your approach. Which of the following questions would be best? Rank the questions from best to worst.

   a. "Have you had any recent storage problems?"

   b. "How do you take care of your extra storage needs during busy seasons?"

   c. "Can you tell me a little about your storage problems?"

Sales Online Exercise

Can the Internet Help Build Relationships?

The ultimate outcome of relationship selling is the building of a partnership between the seller and the buyer. More and more companies are using the Web to stay in touch with customers.

1. Look for documents, such as annual reports, that describe a company's sales, profits, markets, and customers. Check to see whether the company is collecting information

from you, such as by having you complete a questionnaire. Then write a report to your boss discussing your findings. Include your suggestions on how an organization can use the Web to build long-term relationships with its customers and attract new customers.

2. Advertisements are developed to capture your attention and interest to sell a product or service quickly. Examine at least five commercials on television or on the Internet and report on the method each used to get your attention, stimulate your interest, and move you from this attention-interest phase into discussing the product. Determine whether the first few seconds of the commercial related to the product's features, advantages, or benefits, and if so, how?
3. Assume that you have a 30-minute job interview next week with a representative of a company you are really interested in. How would you prepare for the interview, and what could you do during the first few minutes of the interview to get the recruiter interested in hiring you? Can you see any differences between this interview situation and the environment of a salesperson making a sales call?

Student Application Learning Exercises (SALES)

For this part of your SALES, first select the method that you will use for your presentation (see Chapter 7). Next, write down the name of the approach technique you will use for this presentation method (Chapter 8).

Presentation method:

Approach technique:

Part 4

Prepare statements that you will actually use in your approach, including what the buyer would likely say. Relate your approach to the FABs developed earlier in your FAB worksheet.

Seller:

Buyer:

Imagine that you have finished your approach. Write out the buyer–seller dialogue for two SELL sequences. A SELL Sequence is an acronym: Show feature, Explain advantage, Lead into benefit, and Let customer talk. Create responses that your buyer will likely use to reply to each of the SELL sequences.

SEQUENCE 1

Seller:

Buyer:

SEQUENCE 2

Seller:

Buyer:

With a partner, role-play your approach and SELL sequences to see whether you are satisfied. If available, use a voice memo recorder to listen to your speed, voice inflections, phrases, and any other unwanted mannerisms such as slang, or repeating the words "uh," "okay," "like," or "I see." Videotape your role-play to look for any physical mannerisms that could affect the quality of your approach such as a prolonged handshake, poor posture, loss of eye contact, or fidgeting. Upon completion, ask your partner if you and your approach strategy would have impressed them.

CASE 8–1

THE THOMPSON COMPANY

Before making a cold call on the Thompson Company, you did some research on the account. Barbara Thompson is both president and chief purchasing officer. In this dual capacity, she often is so rushed that she is impatient with salespeople. She is known for her habit of quickly turning down a salesperson and ending the discussion by turning and walking away. In looking over Thompson's operation, you notice that the inefficient metal shelving she uses in her warehouse is starting to collapse. Warehouse employees have attempted to remedy the situation by building wooden shelves and reinforcing the weakened metal shelves with lumber. They also have begun stacking boxes on the floor, requiring much more space.

You recognize the importance of getting off to a fast start with Thompson. You must capture her attention and interest quickly or she may not talk with you.

QUESTION

Which of the following attention-getters would you choose? Explain your thinking.

a. "Ms. Thompson, I'd like to show you how Hercules Shelving can save you both time and money."

b. "Ms. Thompson, can you spare a few minutes of your time to talk about new shelving for your warehouse?"

c. "Ms. Thompson, how would you like to double your storage space?"

CASE 8–2

THE COPY CORPORATION

Assume you are contacting the purchasing agent for office supplies of a large chain of retail department stores. After hearing that the company is opening 10 new stores, you determine that it will need a copier for each store. Three months earlier, you had sold this purchasing agent a lease agreement on two large machines. The buyer wanted to try your machines in the company's new stores. If they liked them, you would get the account. Unknown to you, one of the machines is now causing the purchasing agent to experience pressure from a store manager to replace it immediately. As you walk into the purchasing agent's office, you say:

Salesperson: I understand you are opening 10 new stores in the next six months.

Buyer: I don't know who told you!

Salesperson: If you'll let me know when you want a copier at each store, I'll arrange for it to be there.

Buyer: Look, I don't want any more of your lousy copiers! When the leases expire, I want you here to pick them up, or I'll throw them out in the street. I've got a meeting now. I want to see you in three months.

QUESTIONS

1. Describe this situation, commenting on what the salesperson did correctly and incorrectly.
2. Develop another approach the salesperson could use to uncover the problems experienced by the purchasing agent.

CASE 8–3

ELECTRONIC OFFICE SECURITY CORPORATION

Ann Saroyan is a salesperson for the Electronic Office Security Corporation. She sells industrial security systems that detect intruders and activate an alarm. When Ann first began selling, she used to make brief opening remarks to her prospects and then move quickly into her presentation. Although this resulted in selling many of her security systems, she felt there must be a better method.

Ann began to analyze the reasons that prospects would not buy. Her conclusion was that even after her presentation, prospects still did not believe they needed a security alarm system. She decided to develop a multiple-question approach that would allow her to determine the prospect's attitude toward a need for a security system. If the prospect does not initially feel a need for her product, she wants her approach to help convince the prospect of a need for a security system.

Ann developed and carefully rehearsed her new sales presentation. Her first sales call using her multiple-question approach was with a large accounting firm. She asked the receptionist whom she should see and was referred to Joe Bell. After she had waited 20 minutes, Bell asked her to come into his office. The conversation went like this:

Salesperson: This is a beautiful old building, Mr. Bell. Have you been here long?

Buyer: About 10 years. Before we moved here, we were in one of those ugly glass and concrete towers. Now, you wanted to talk to me about office security.

Salesperson: Yes, Mr. Bell. Tell me, do you have a burglar alarm system at present?

Buyer: No, we don't. We've never had a break-in here.

Salesperson: I see. Could you tell me what are the most valuable items in your building?

Buyer: Probably the computers in the office.

Salesperson: And are they fairly small, so easy to remove?

Buyer: Yes.

Salesperson: Would it be difficult to run your business without them—if they were stolen for example?

Buyer: Oh, yes, that would be quite awkward.

Salesperson: Could you tell me a bit more about the problem you would face without your computers?

Buyer: It would be inconvenient in the short term for our accounts and records people, but I suppose we could manage until our insurance gave us replacements.

Salesperson: But without computers, wouldn't your billing to customers suffer?

Buyer: Not if we got the replacements quickly.

Salesperson: You said the computers are insured. Do you happen to know if the software—the programs, your customer files—is also insured?

Buyer: I don't believe so; our insurance covers the equipment only.

Salesperson: And do you keep backup records somewhere else—in the bank, for example?

Buyer: No, we don't.

Salesperson: Mr. Bell, in my experience, software isn't left behind after a theft. Wouldn't it be a serious problem to you if that software were taken?

Buyer: Yes, you're right, I suppose. Redevelopment would certainly cost a lot. The original programs were expensive.

Salesperson: And even worse, because software development can take a long time, wouldn't that hold up your billings to customers?

Buyer: We could always do that manually.

Salesperson: What effect would that have on your processing costs?

Buyer: I see your point. It would certainly be expensive to run a manual system, as well as inconvenient.

Salesperson: And if you lost your software, wouldn't it also make it harder to process customer orders?

Buyer: Yes. I don't have much contact with that part of the business, but without order processing and stock control I'm sure we would grind to a halt in a matter of days.

Salesperson: Are there any other items in the building that would be hard to replace if stolen?

Buyer: Some of the furnishings. I would hate to lose this antique clock, for example. In fact, most of our furnishings would be very hard to replace in the same style.

Salesperson: So, if you lost them, wouldn't it hurt the character of your office?

Buyer: Yes, it would be damaging. We've built a gracious, civilized image here, and without it we would be like dozens of other people in our business—the glass and concrete image.

Salesperson: This may sound like an odd question, but how many doors do you have at ground level?

Buyer: Let me see . . . uh . . . six.

Salesperson: And ground-level windows?

Buyer: About 10 or a dozen.

Salesperson: So there are 16 or 18 points where a thief could break in, compared with 1 or 2 points in the average glass and concrete office. Doesn't that concern you?

Buyer: Put that way, it does. I suppose we're not very secure.

QUESTIONS

1. Did the dialogue between buyer and seller seem natural to you?
2. Did the salesperson use too many questions in her approach?
3. Analyze each of the salesperson's questions and state whether it is a situation, problem, implication, or need–payoff type of question.
4. Analyze each of the buyer's responses to the salesperson's questions and state what type of need the salesperson's question uncovered. Was it an implied or minor need response, or was it an explicit or important need response? Why?
5. How would you improve on this salesperson's approach?
6. After the buyer's last statement, which of the following would you do?
   a. Move into the presentation.
   b. Ask a problem question.
   c. Ask a need–payoff question.
   d. Ask for an appointment to fully discuss your system.

Source: © Rawpixel.com/Shutterstock

CHAPTER 9

The Presentation—Elements of Effective Persuasion

Billy Lister,
St. Clair College,
Zekelman School of Business and IT, Windsor, Ontario
Source: Courtesy of Billy Lister

A Sales Success Story

Billy Lister graduated from the Business Administration Marketing program at St. Clair College, Zekelman School of Business and IT, in 2017. After graduation, he decided to pursue his degree in Ireland at IT-Carlow in 2018 and began looking for work upon his return. This risky adventure proved to be a winning move for the ambitious graduate. With years of retail customer sales under his belt, Billy's experience helped land him an inside sales assistant position at Atlas Tube. He feels the key strengths that helped him attain the position were his drive to achieve, resourcefulness, and outgoing personality.

Billy says new graduates should keep these things in mind:

- Be ready for some growing pains—it is hard to be number one right off the bat!
- Focus on your strengths but address your shortcomings and keep a student mentality of continual learning.

- Don't be afraid to ask questions. Everybody had a first day once! Seek mentors in your organization, and listen to their advice.

Billy's least favourite part of his job is the administrative tasks that come along with all sales positions. However, for Billy, sales is a very exciting career that has allowed him to travel, continue his post-graduate studies, and build confidence in his career endeavours. For instance, after his promotion to the position of inside sales representative, Billy travelled to Western Canada to meet his customers. Billy has this advice for new sales representatives:

- Make strong personal connections and relationships with co-workers, who share mutual trust and goals.
- Pay attention to details—this is critical in a fast-paced environment.
- Learn from your mistakes and strive to improve.
- Keep learning about your customers and your products.

MAIN TOPICS

The Purpose of the Presentation

Three Essential Steps within the Presentation

The Sales Presentation Mix

Visual Aids Help Tell the Story

A Checklist for Visuals

Dramatization Improves Your Chances

Demonstrations Prove It

Technology Can Help

The Ideal Presentation

Be Prepared for Presentation Difficulties

The Sales Presentation Goal Model

The fourth step in the selling process is the presentation. Here, you discuss with the buyer the product's features, advantages, and benefits; your marketing plan; and the business proposition. After studying this chapter, you should be able to:

LO1 Discuss the purpose and essential steps of the sales presentation.

LO2 Give examples of the six sales presentation mix elements.

LO3 Understand the importance of the trial close.

LO4 Describe difficulties that may arise during the sales presentation and explain how to handle them.

LO5 Explain how to handle discussion of the competition.

FACING A SALES CHALLENGE

You are a mill salesperson for Far North Carpets. You have been talking to a retailer about several of your new carpet's features, advantages, and benefits. You have just told your customer that because of Far North's new technology, the synthetic fibres in your new product will not fade even if exposed to direct sunlight. Your customer then says, "That sounds great, but I don't know. I've had too many customers complain about fading."

What do you do in this situation? As you see, the customer doubts whether your carpet will resist fading. How do you prove the carpet will not fade? What if the customer will not take your word?

(Continued at end of chapter)

The presentation part of the selling process is a persuasive explanation of a proposition that the client can both see and hear. In developing your presentation, consider the elements you will use to provide the information a buyer needs to make a buying decision. At any time a customer may mention a concern, as described in "Facing a Sales Challenge" above, and a proper response is needed to make the sale.

This chapter discusses the elements of the presentation–the fourth step in the sales process (see Exhibit 9.1). We begin by examining the purpose and essential steps in the presentation. Next, we review and expand on the presentation techniques used by salespeople and how to handle the customer in the sales challenge. The chapter ends by discussing the importance of the proper use of trial closes and difficulties that may arise in the presentation, along with the need to customize your presentation for each individual situation and buyer.

EXHIBIT 9.1

The presentation is the heart of the sale. An effective approach allows a smooth transition into discussing your product's features, advantages, and benefits.

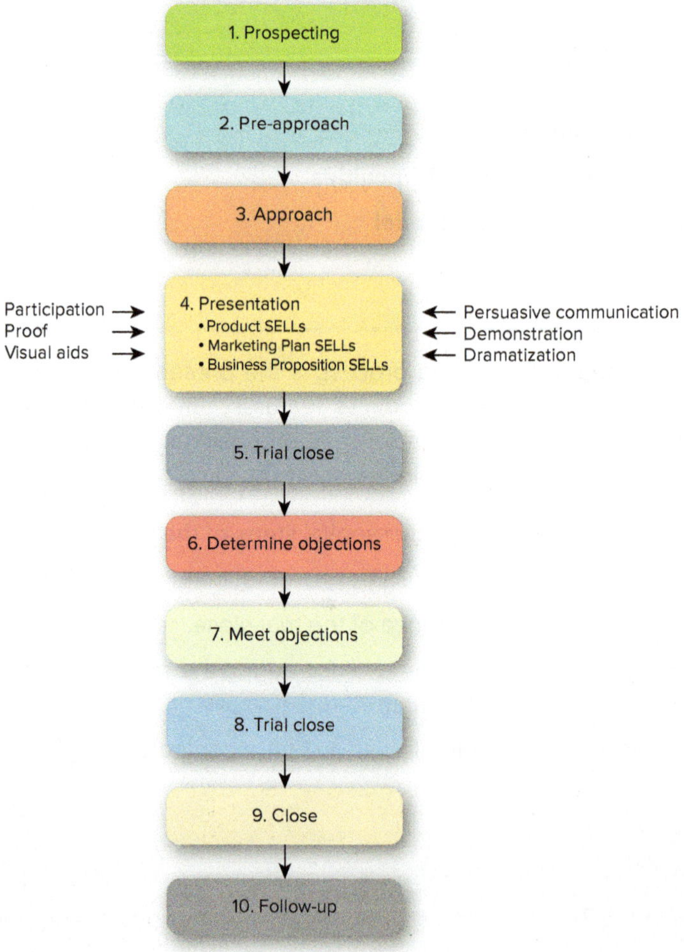

The Purpose of the Presentation

LO1

The main goal of your presentation is to sell your product to your customer. However, we know that a prospective buyer considers many things before making a decision about what product to buy. As we have seen, the approach or first few minutes of the interview should be focused to determine the prospect's need, capture attention and interest, and allow for a smooth transition into the presentation.

The presentation provides knowledge via the features, advantages, and benefits of your product, marketing plan, and business proposal. This *knowledge* allows the buyer to develop positive personal beliefs toward your product. The *beliefs* result in a *desire* (or *need*) for the type of product you sell. Your job, as a salesperson, is to convert that need into a want and into the *attitude* that your product is the best product to fulfill a certain need. Furthermore, you must convince the buyer that not only is your product the best but also that you are the best source from which to buy. When this occurs, your prospect has moved into the *conviction* stage of the mental buying process.

This sequence results in your making a sale, as shown in Exhibit 9.2. Whether to buy or not is a choice decision, and you have provided the necessary information so that the customer chooses to buy from you.

Assume, for example, that you are a salesperson for Dell and you want to sell 10 of your new personal computers that cost $2,000 each to a company. The prospect's company uses your competitor's products, which cost $1,500 each. How should you conceptualize the prospect's thought processes regarding whether or not to buy from you (as shown in Exhibit 9.1) to develop your presentation?

Begin by realizing that the prospect has certain attitudes toward the present personal computers. Next, appreciate that your prospect's job performance is judged by their management of certain responsibilities. Thus, improving the performance of company employees is important. However, the prospect knows nothing about you, your product, or your product's benefits. The prospect may feel that Dell products are good, high-quality, expensive products–or they may not.

Develop a SPIN approach to determine the buyer's attitudes toward personal computers in general and your personal computer specifically. Address each of the four SPIN questions (situation, problem, implications, and needs payoff; see Chapter 8). When you have done this, and you feel that more information about your product is needed, begin the presentation.

Present the product information that allows the buyer to develop a positive attitude toward your product. Next, possibly using a value-analysis proposal, show how your product can increase efficiency, reduce costs, and pay for itself in one year, using a return-on-investment (ROI) technique. A positive reaction from your prospect indicates that the desire stage of the mental buying process has been reached. There is a need for some brand of personal computer.

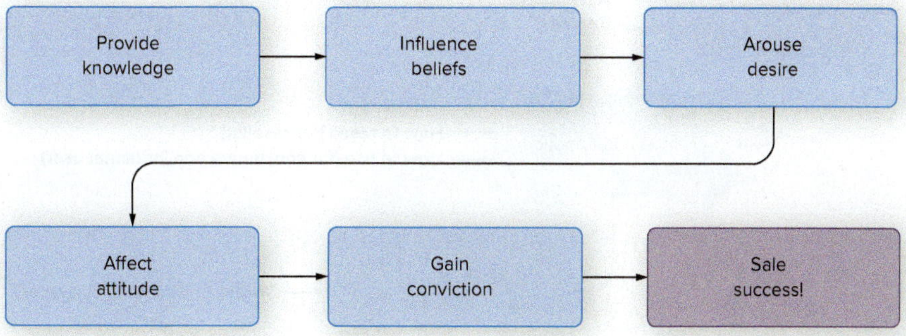

EXHIBIT 9.2
The five purposes of the presentation.

Now, show why your Dell personal computer is the best solution to the buyer's need and show that you will provide service after the sale. A positive response on these two items indicates that the prospect believes your product is best and that the conviction stage has been reached. The prospect wants to buy the Dell personal computer.

Up to this point, you have discussed your product's features, advantages, and benefits; your marketing or promotion plan; and your business proposition. You have *not* asked the prospect to buy. Rather, you have developed a presentation to lead the prospect through four of the five mental buying steps: the attention, interest, desire, and conviction steps. It may take you five minutes, two hours, or several weeks of repeat calls to move the prospect into the conviction stage.

You must move the prospect into the conviction stage before a sale is made. So hold off asking the prospect to buy until the conviction stage; doing otherwise usually results in objections, failure to listen to your whole story, and fewer sales. The sales presentation has seven major steps. Each step is taken in order to logically and sequentially move the prospect into the conviction stage of the buying process.

When a person buys something, they are actually buying a mental picture of the future in which your product helps to fulfill some expectation. The buyer has mentally conceived certain needs. Your presentation must create mental images that move your prospect into the conviction stage.

Three Essential Steps within the Presentation

Recall that the four common sales presentation methods are the memorized (canned) approach, the formula (persuasive selling) approach, the interactive need-satisfaction approach, and the problem-solving approach. No matter which of the four sales presentation methods is used, your presentation must follow these three essential steps, also shown in Exhibit 9.3. The three steps are discussed in Chapter 7 under "Customer Benefit Plan: What It's All About!"

Step 1

Fully discuss the relevant *features, advantages,* and *benefits* of your product. Tell the whole story.

Step 2

Present your marketing or promotion plan. For wholesalers and retailers, this is your suggestion on how they should *resell* the product. For end users, it is your suggestion on how they can *use* the product.

EXHIBIT 9.3

Three essential steps within the presentation.

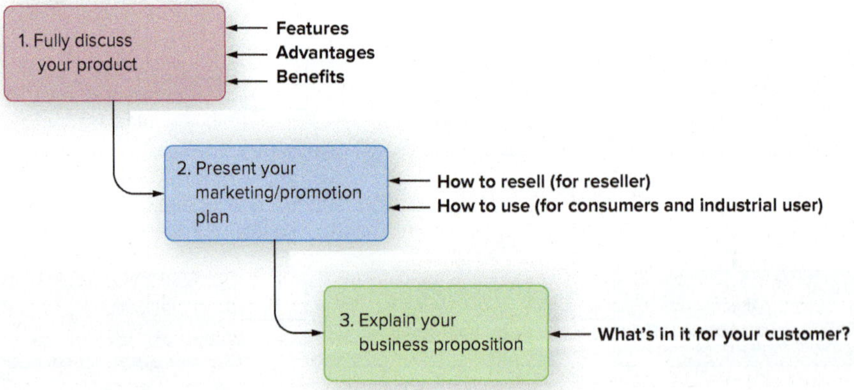

Step 3

Explain your business proposition. This step relates the *value* of your product to its *cost*. It should be discussed last, since you always want to present your product's benefits and marketing plan relative to your product's price.

Remember Your FABs!

It is extremely important to emphasize benefits throughout the presentation. Using the SELL sequence communication technique when discussing the product, marketing plan, and business proposition greatly improves your chances of making the sale. However, limit the discussion to relevant FABs. It might be possible for your product to have a great number of FABs but many of them may not be useful for a particular buyer so keep them relevant to your particular buyer's needs.

Exhibit 9.4 is a table used in a training program for a large restaurant supply distributor. This product is a pancake mix sold to hotels and food retail chains. Notice the FABs for each of the three essential steps within the presentation. Even for a product like pancake mix, salespeople must use benefits to paint a picture in the mind of the buyers of how this product will fulfill their needs. This is what **consultative selling** is all about–relating the product's benefits to the customer's needs.

consultative selling: The process of professionally providing information to help customers make intelligent actions to achieve short- and long-term objectives.

Ideally, information in each of the steps shown in Exhibit 9.3 should be presented to create a picture in the prospect's mind of the benefits of the purchase. To do this,

EXHIBIT 9.4

Salespeople use these FABs in their presentations.

FEATURES, ADVANTAGES, AND BENEFITS OF BIX BUCKWHEAT PANCAKE MIX		
FEATURES	ADVANTAGES	BENEFITS
PRODUCT		
1. Traditional "farmhouse" recipe, with freshest ingredients; fortified with vitamins A, B, C, and D; no preservatives	1. Great tasting, fluffy, and light; highly nutritious	1. Provides an appealing item; expands breakfast menu; increases breakfast business leading to higher profits
2. User needs only to add water, stir, and cook	2. Quick and easy to prepare	2. Requires minimal kitchen time and labour which is attractive to busy people leading to increased sales
MARKETING PLAN		
3. Just-in-time delivery	3. No need to store large quantities	3. Requires minimal inventory space; keeps inventory costs low
4. Local distribution centre	4. Additional orders can be filled quickly	4. Prevents out-of-stock situations
5. An experienced sales representative to serve account	5. Knowledge and background in food-service industry	5. Provides assistance for meeting changing needs and solving business problems
BUSINESS PROPOSITION		
6. Quantity discounts	6. Reduces costs	6. Increases your profits
7. Extended payment plans	7. Reduces interest costs	7. Increases your profits
8. Automated assembly system	8. Improves productivity	8. Improves ROI

use persuasive communication and participation techniques, evidence statements, visual aids, dramatization, and demonstrations as you move through each of the three steps during the presentation.

LO2

The Sales Presentation Mix

Salespeople sell different products in different ways, but all salespeople use six classes of presentation elements to some degree in their presentations to provide meaningful information to the customer. These elements are called the *presentation mix.*

sales presentation mix: The elements the salesperson assembles to sell to prospects.

The **sales presentation mix** refers to the elements the salesperson assembles to sell to prospects and customers. Although all elements should be part of the presentation, it is up to the individual to determine how much each element is emphasized. This determination is primarily based on the sales call objective, customer profile, and customer benefit plan. Let's examine each of the six elements, as shown in Exhibit 9.5.

Persuasive Communication

To be a successful salesperson, do you need to be a smooth talker? No, but you do need to consider and use factors that aid the clear communication of your messages. The following seven factors can help you be a better communicator:

1. Use questions.
2. Be empathetic.
3. Keep the message simple.
4. Create mutual trust.
5. Listen.
6. Have a positive attitude and enthusiasm.
7. Be believable.

LO3

The Trial Close and SELL Sequence

In today's sales world, there are a variety of reasons that prospects do not buy. Lack of trust, failure of the prospect to understand what's in it for them, and difficulty in seeing the pros and cons of buying are just a few. Because of this, it is imperative that salespeople have a test they can use during a presentation to determine if they're on track or not.

The trial close is that very test. It can help you gauge your prospect's reactions at any time during the sales presentation (see Exhibit 9.1). It can help you understand how your prospect is thinking and feeling about your product or service. From this information, you can adjust your presentation to enhance your chances of making the sale. The trial close is often underused in selling, as salespeople are anxious about putting too much pressure on the prospect.

A trial close can be defined as any attempt to start closing the sale before completion of the sales presentation. It is just a test. It will help determine just how close the prospect is to buying. During a trial close, salespeople are really just asking for an opinion as opposed to a specific decision. There is little risk of a final "no" during a trial close, so salespeople shouldn't feel uncomfortable using them.

EXHIBIT 9.5

The salesperson's presentation mix.

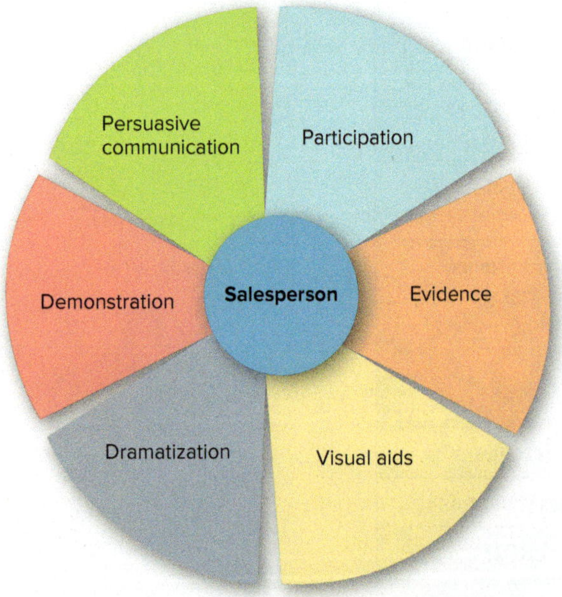

SELLING TIPS

USING TRIAL CLOSES

The trial close is an important part of the sales presentation. It asks for the buyer's feedback about what you have just said (e.g., FAB) or shown (e.g., testimonial letter). The trial close does not ask the prospect to commit or to buy. Here are some examples:

- How does our delivery schedule sound to you?
- What do you think of our money-back guarantee?
- Can you see how our moulded chair will enhance your employees' comfort level?
- Do these independent test results address your concerns about quality?
- How do you like our 24-hour technical support hotline?
- What is your impression of the capacity of our new pump?
- On a scale of 1 to 10, how do you feel our product will fit your needs?
- Are these the types of features you had in mind?
- Do you think your employees would see the benefits of this system?
- Is there anything preventing you from buying now?

As you can see, we've never directly asked the prospect to buy—we're just measuring their level of interest.

Salespeople often experience objections when trying to close a sale because the prospect wasn't encouraged to express their feelings or opinions about the product during the presentation. Simply asking things like, "What do you think so far?" or, "Can you see how this might improve your bottom line?" can help you elicit comments that can draw out your prospect's feelings.

So when should you attempt a trial close? Do it when the prospect gives you a signal that they are interested in your product. This is known as a buying signal. Buying signals can take the form of questions, actions, comments, or expressions. For example, if the prospect straightens up and looks alert after you've just presented a FAB package, use a trial close. If the prospect has an inquisitive look on their face when you show them a return-on-investment visual, use a trial close. If the prospect's eyes light up when you show them a picture of your proposed solution, use a trial close. You get the idea.

Trial close early and often. Remember, you are just asking for an opinion, not the order. You have little to lose and much to gain. You will gain insight into how to proceed with your presentation. When a trial close is used in conjunction with a FAB or major selling point, this forms a SELL sequence. The SELL sequence is a good means of determining a buyer's interest and is an effective form of persuasive communication.

Additional persuasive factors to consider in the presentation are logical reasoning, persuasive suggestions, a sense of fun, personalized relationships, trust, empathy, body language, a controlled presentation, diplomacy, and using words as selling tools.

Logical Reasoning

The application of logic through reasoning is an effective persuasive technique that appeals to prospects' common sense by requiring them to think about the proposition and to compare alternative solutions to problems. This is especially true when selling complicated proposals involving comparative cost data, when price versus benefits must be judged, and when the product is a radically new concept.

Logical reasoning involves a presentation constructed around three parts: a major premise, a minor premise, and a conclusion. Here is an example:

> **logical reasoning:** Persuasive techniques that appeal to the prospect's common sense by applying logic through reason.

1. **Major premise** - All manufacturers want to reduce costs and increase efficiency.
2. **Minor premise** - My equipment will reduce your costs and increase your efficiency.
3. **Conclusion** - Therefore, you should buy my equipment.

Source: © Andreypopov/Dreamstime.com/GetStock.com

If presented exactly in this straightforward manner, the logical formula may be too blunt; the prospect may raise defences. However, you can develop the framework or presentation outline to determine whether the prospect is interested in reducing costs and increasing manufacturing efficiency. If so, then present a value analysis that shows the benefits of your product over alternatives. Information such as performance data, costs, and service and delivery policies can be presented in a persuasive manner using various elements of the presentation mix.

Persuasion through Suggestion

Suggestion, like logical reasoning, is used effectively to persuade prospects. The skilled use of suggestions can arouse attention, interest, desire, conviction, and action. The following types of suggestions may be considered for the presentation:

suggestive proposition: A proposition that implies that the prospect should act now.

prestige suggestions: A technique in which the salesperson has the prospect visualize using products that are used by people whom the prospect trusts.

autosuggestion: A kind of suggestion that attempts to have prospects imagine themselves using the product.

direct suggestion: An approach that suggests prospects buy rather than tells them to buy.

indirect suggestion: A statement by the salesperson recommending that the prospect undertake some action while making it seem that the idea to do so is the prospect's.

countersuggestion: A suggestion that evokes an opposite response from the prospect.

1. **Suggestive propositions** imply that the prospect should act now, such as, "Shouldn't you go ahead and buy now before the price goes up next month?" Prospects often like to postpone their buying decisions, so the suggestive approach can help overcome this problem.
2. **Prestige suggestions** ask the prospect to visualize using products that famous people, companies, or individuals the prospect trusts use, such as, "The National Professional Engineers Association has endorsed our equipment. That's why several hundred Fortune 500 manufacturers are using our products. This elite group of manufacturers finds the equipment helps increase their profits, sales, and market share. Is this of interest to you?"
3. **Autosuggestion** attempts to have prospects imagine themselves using the product. Television advertisements frequently use this form of suggestion. The salesperson visualizes the product, saying, "Just imagine how this equipment will look and operate in your store. Your employees will perform much better and they will thank you."
4. The **direct suggestion** is used widely by professional salespeople in all industries because it does not "tell" but suggests buying, which does not offend the buyer. Such a suggestion might state: "Based on our survey of your needs, I suggest you purchase . . ." or "Let's consider this: We ship you three train carloads of Whirlpool washers and dryers in the following colours and models . . ."
5. The **indirect suggestion** is used for some prospects when it is best to be indirect in suggesting a recommended course of action. Indirect suggestions help instill in prospects' minds factors such as doubt about a competitor's products or desire for your product. The indirect suggestion makes it seem as if it is their idea: "Should you buy 50 or 75 dozen 350-mL cans of Revlon hairspray for your promotion?" or "Have you talked with anyone who has used that product?"
6. The **countersuggestion** evokes an opposite response from the prospect: "Do you really want such a high-quality product?" Often, the buyer will begin expanding on why a high-quality product is needed. This suggestion is an especially effective technique to include in the presentation if you have already determined that the prospect wants a high-quality product.

Make the Presentation Fun

Selling is fun, not a battle between the prospect and salesperson, so loosen up and enjoy the presentation. This is easy to do once you believe in yourself and what you are selling–so sound like it! Have the right mental attitude and you will be successful.

Personalize Your Relationship

One of the authors of this text worked for a large national consumer products manufacturer. The sales manager trained all sales reps to personalize their presentation. He would say, "You are enthusiastic; you believe in yourself, your products, your company; you give a very good presentation. To improve, however, you need to personalize your relationship with each of your customers. In some manner, let them know during your presentation that you have their best interests at heart." He would always say, "Show 'em that you love 'em."

The sales reps came up with the short phrase, "You have me." Once this phrase was incorporated into retailer presentations at the appropriate time, they saw a significant increase in total sales and sales-to-customer call ratio by saying something like: "You are not only buying my products but me as well. You have me on call 24 hours a day to help you in any way I can."

Yes, it sounds corny, but it helped show customers that the company and the sales rep cared for them. This helped build trust. You might choose a different way, but be sure to demonstrate that you look out for their interests.

Build Trust

Two of the best and easiest ways to build your persuasive powers with prospects are *being honest* and *doing what you say you will do.* This builds trust, which increases sales. Most professional buyers have long memories that can be used to your advantage if you follow through after the sale as you said you would when presenting the proposal.

Honesty is always the best policy, and being honest is an effective way to build trust. The salesperson should never claim more than the product can accomplish. If the product does not live up to expectations, apologize, return the product for credit, or trade for another product. This action is important in obtaining repeat sales. It builds trust; the next time the prospect is reluctant to buy, you say, "Haven't I always taken care of you? Trust me, this product is what you need. I guarantee it!"[1]

SELLING TIPS

TRUST DEVELOPS OVER TIME

Salespeople should have the following personal characteristics in order to help build trust with customers:

1. Caring for customers
2. Joy in your work
3. Harmony in relationships
4. Patience in closing the sale
5. Kindness to all you contact
6. Morally ethical
7. Faithful to your word
8. Fairness
9. Self-control

Be Empathetic

Many salespeople who have the task of dealing with purchasing agents at companies across Canada will tell you that regional differences exist in personalities and in buying styles. Marty Legein of Cetec, who has done extensive selling in all areas of Canada, says "I have to use a different approach to my sales presentations depending on which region I am in." For example, it appears that buyers in the Maritimes are often laid back and friendly. With this type of buyer, relationship building is critical—once a positive rapport is established, these buyers will likely respond well to the need-satisfaction presentation strategy.

In Quebec, it is important to acknowledge and recognize the province's distinct cultural differences, since relationships are often built around this principle. Ignoring this fact may isolate a salesperson, which would make any sales presentation very difficult.

In Ontario, which is often fast-paced, competitive, and impersonal, salespeople are often competing with many other salespeople for a company's business. Buyers don't always have the time for relationship building and are very interested in salespeople "getting to the point." Salespeople in these situations therefore should be well prepared to give the facts and figures and outline quickly the major FABs for a particular buyer. A formula strategy often works well in these situations.

The West is similar to the East–relationship selling is very important. Although buyers are still very knowledgeable, an element of trust must be established if salespeople are to be effective here.

Of course, Canada's cultural mosaic is much too diverse to stereotype everyone within a given region. However, knowledge of each region of Canada in terms of economic situation, cultural and ethnic diversity, and any regional difficulties may prove helpful in homing in on your prospect's needs.

Be Aware of Your Body Language

body language: Nonverbal communication that includes facial expression, appearance, handshake, and body movement.

Just as you watch for buying signals from a prospect, the prospect watches your facial expressions and **body language**. Your nonverbal communication must project a positive image to the prospect, one that shows you know what you are taking about and understand the buyer's needs. Your customer will think, "I can trust this person."

The best nonverbal selling technique is the smile. As a sales manager once said, "It's often not what you say but how you say it, and you can say almost anything to anyone if you do it with a smile. So, practise your facial expressions and smile–always smile."

As discussed in Chapter 4, project positive signals. If you are excited about helping the other person, it will show nonverbally. Your whole body will radiate a form of light through your eyes, showing that you care. Your eyes are the lamps of your thoughts. People can tell you care.

Control the Presentation

In making the presentation, direct the conversation to lead the prospect through the presentation and proposal. The salesperson often has to maintain control and know what to do if the prospect takes control of the conversation. For example, what do you do if the prospect likes to talk about hobbies, attacks your company or products for poor service or credit mix-ups, or is a kidder and likes to poke fun at your products?

When this happens, stay with a planned presentation if possible. If there is a complaint, address this first. If the prospect likes to talk about other things, do so briefly. When the prospect's attention and interest are hard to maintain, questions or some manner of eliciting participation in the presentation are the two best methods to rechannel the conversation.

Be sure to control the visual aids and any materials you use in the presentation. New salespeople often make the mistake of handing prospects their catalogue, price list, or brochures showing several products. When buyers are looking through these items, they are probably not listening. So, keep possession of your product materials and discuss the information you want to present while prospects look at and listen to you.

Be a Diplomat

All salespeople face situations where the prospects believe they are right or know it all, and the salesperson has different opinions. For example, the salesperson previously may have sold the prospect's company a machine that always breaks down due to its operator, not the equipment–yet the salesperson's company is blamed. What should you do?

You have to be a diplomat when tempers rise. Retreat may be the best option; otherwise, you risk destroying the relationship. If you challenge the prospect, you could win the battle only to lose the war or you could win the argument only to lose the sale. This is a decision that the salesperson must make based on individual situations.

Dale Carnegie once said that a sure way of not making an enemy is to show respect for the other person's opinions. Never tell people they are wrong.

Simile and Analogy

Words are selling tools. Similes, analogies, pauses, silence, and changes in the rate of speaking, tone, and pitch are effective methods of gaining prospects' attention and capturing their interest in a proposal.

A **simile** is a direct comparison statement using the words *like* or *as:* A poorly manicured lawn is *like* a bad haircut. Our Sylvania Safe light bulbs are *like* a car's shatterproof windshield. Our diet drinks are *like* a chocolate milkshake. The carton folds *as flat as* a pancake for storage. Your production equipment is consuming energy *like* a black hole in space.

simile:
A direct comparison statement using the words like or as.

The **analogy** compares two different situations that have something in common, such as, "Our sun screen for your home will stop the sun's heat and glare before it hits your window. It's like having a shade tree in front of your window without blocking the view." Remember to speak the prospect's language by using familiar terminology and buzzwords in a conversational tone. "These new machines are so quiet that your employees will think they're in a soundproof room."

analogy:
A comparison between two different situations that have something in common.

Participation Is Essential to Success

The second major part of the presentation involves techniques for motivating the prospect to participate in the presentation. Four ways to induce participation are:

1. Questions
2. Product use
3. Visuals
4. Demonstrations

We have already discussed the use of questions and will discuss the use of visuals and demonstrations later, so let's briefly consider having prospects use the product. For example:

- If you sell stereos, let them see, hear, and touch them!
- If you sell food, let them see, smell, and taste it!
- If you sell clothes, let them touch and wear them!

By letting prospects use the product, you appeal to their senses: sight, hearing, touch, smell, and taste. Develop your presentation to appeal to the senses, since people often buy because of emotional needs, and the senses are key to developing emotional appeals.

Evidence Statements Make You Believable

Using highly credible sources can improve the persuasiveness of the sales presentation message. **Evidence statements** substantiate claims made by the salesperson. For example, pharmaceutical companies often quote research studies done by outstanding

evidence statements:
Statements that substantiate claims made by the salesperson; also called *proof statements*.

physicians at prestigious medical schools to validate claims of product benefits. These statements add high credibility to a sales message.

proof statements: Statements that substantiate claims made by the salesperson; also called *evidence statements.*

Evidence statements are sometimes called **proof statements**. While the difference may be subtle, the use of supporting statements as evidence recognizes that it is ultimately the customer who will determine whether the information you have provided is proof enough to accept that information. Remember, what is proof for sales representatives may not have the same relevance to customers. Several useful evidence techniques are the customer's past sales figures, the guarantee, testimonials, company evidence results, and independent research results.

Past Sales Help Predict the Future

Customers' past sales evidence statements are frequently used by salespersons when contacting present customers. Customers keep records of their past purchases from each of their suppliers; the salesperson can use these to suggest what quantities of each product to purchase. For example, the Colgate salesperson checks a customer's present inventory of all products carried, determines the number of products sold in a month, subtracts inventory from forecast sales, and suggests the customer purchase that amount. It is difficult for buyers to refuse when presentations are based on their sales records. If they are offered a price discount and promotional allowances, they might purchase three to ten times the normal amount (a promotional purchase).

Assume, for example, that a food store normally carries 10 dozen of the king-size Colgate toothpaste in inventory with 3 dozen on the shelf, and sells approximately 20 dozen a month. The salesperson produces the buyer's past sales record and says, "You should buy 7 to 10 dozen king-size Colgate toothpaste." If offering promotional allowances, the salesperson might say:

> The Colgate king-size is your most profitable and best-selling item. You normally sell 20 dozen Colgate king-size each month with a 30 percent gross profit. With our 15 percent price reduction this month only, and our advertising allowances, I suggest, based on your normal sales, that you buy 80 to 100 dozen, reduce the price 15 percent, display it, and advertise the discount in your newspaper specials. This sale will attract people to your store, increase store sales, and make your normal profit.

The salesperson stops talking to see the buyer's reaction. A suggested order plus an alternative on the quantity to purchase have been proposed. Does the quantity seem high? It may be high, just right, or low, but it is the buyer's decision. The salesperson is saying that, given your past sales and with my customer benefit plan, I believe you can sell *X* number of units. Be realistic about your suggested increase in order size. Your honesty builds credibility with the buyer.

The Colgate salesperson might suggest purchases not only of toothpaste but also of all Colgate products. That same sales call could involve multiple presentations of several products that have promotional allowances plus the recommended purchase of 10 or more items based on present inventories and the previous month's sales.

The Guarantee

The guarantee is a powerful evidence technique. It assures prospects that if they are dissatisfied with their purchase, the salesperson or the company will stand behind a product. The manufacturer has certain product warranties that the retail salesperson can use in a presentation.

Furthermore, the consumer goods salesperson selling to retailers might say, "I'll guarantee this product will sell for you. If not, we can return what you do not sell." The industrial salesperson may explain the equipment's warranties and service policies, and state, "This is the best equipment for your situation that you can buy.

If you are not 100 percent satisfied after you have used it for three months, I will return it for you."

Testimonials

Testimonials in the presentation as evidence of the product's features, advantages, and benefits are an excellent way to build trust and confidence. Today, manufacturers effectively advertise their consumer products using testimonials, and professional buyers are impressed by testimonials from prominent people, experts, and satisfied customers about a product's features, advantages, and benefits.

testimonial: Using a third-party statement as proof to substantiate a claim.

Company Evidence Results

Companies routinely furnish data concerning their products. Consumer goods salespeople can use sales data such as test-market information and current sales data. Industrial salespeople use performance data and facts based on company research as proof of their product's performance.

A consumer goods manufacturer gave its salespeople test-market sales information to use in their presentations on a new product being introduced nationally. Using this information, a salesperson might say:

> Our new product will sell as soon as you put it on your shelf. The product was a success in our Eastern test market. It had 9.8 percent market share only nine months after the start of advertising. Laboratory tests proved our formula superior to that of the leading competition in our consumer product tests. There was a high repurchase rate of 50 percent after sampling. This means increased sales and profits for you.

Independent Research Results

Evidence furnished by reputable sources outside the company usually has more credibility than company-generated data. Pharmaceutical salespeople frequently tell physicians about medical research findings on their products published in leading medical journals by medical research authorities.

> A sales representative for a large pharmaceutical company explains a typical day:
>
> I see as many physicians as possible and initiate a discussion with them about one of our products that will have importance to them in medicine. I point out advantages that our drugs have in various provinces by using third-party documentation published in current medical journals and texts. The information has much more meaning to a physician who knows that it is not I or my company that has shown our drug to have an advantage but rather a group of researchers who have conducted a scientific study. All of the material that we give to the physicians has been approved for our use by the government.

Publications such as *Straight Goods Online* and *Consumer Reports,* newspaper stories, and government publications may contain information the salesperson can use in the presentation. For an evidence statement referring to independent research results to be most effective, it should contain (1) a restatement of the benefit before proving it, (2) the evidence source and relevant facts or figures about the product, and (3) expansion of the benefit. Consider the following example of a salesperson's evidence statement:

> I'm sure that you want a soundbar that's going to sell and be profitable for you (benefit restatement). Figures in *Consumer Reports* magazine indicate that the Sony XL-100 soundbars, although the newest on the market, are the third largest in sales (source and facts). Therefore, when you handle the Sony XL line, you'll find that soundbar sales and profits will increase, and more customers will come into your store (benefit expansion).

SELLING TIPS

STORYTELLING

Many successful salespeople tell stories—true stories.[2] To use stories successfully, salespeople must combine them with presentations that are interesting, memorable, and persuasive. How? Combine stories with sales objectives. Include narratives, colourful comparisons, metaphors, and similes to help customers understand, believe, and remember what you say—to actually feel your message.

Storytelling in the sales world teaches or persuades your customers because there is a point to the stories that is relevant to the sale. To tell good stories, create a story inventory. First, make a list of all the tough questions, objections, and comments you've heard from customers. Then compile another list of customers who had similar concerns but overcame them, who bought your good or service, and are happy they did. During follow-up, get customers to describe their business now and after their purchase and the lessons they learned from their experience. Match this list to your list of tough questions and objections.

Suppose a prospect asks why your product or service costs more than others on the market. Instead of launching into a general spiel about your product, create a story:

1. Think of a customer who had the same objection but decided to buy your product and is now a very happy and satisfied client.
2. Tell your prospect about this customer's world before making the purchase.
3. Recall the specific event or problem that motivated that customer to seek a solution.
4. Describe the customer's situation now with your product or service.
5. Explain the lesson the customer learned from this experience with your company.
6. Transfer this lesson to the prospect you're currently talking with.

A story can be long or short, but it must blend logic and emotion to make customers want to buy from you:

1. Know what you're telling. The storyteller must clearly understand the objectives illustrated by the story.
2. Reach out. Tell stories that have emotional components that customers can relate to.
3. Weave facts, figures, or other information into your stories to add to your customer's knowledge about the business at hand.
4. Use personal experience. Your stories should have some sort of connection to you personally to have the greatest impact.

Evidence statements must be incorporated into the presentation. They provide a logical answer to the buyer's challenge of "Prove it!"

Exhibit 9.6 shows four examples of using evidence to support what is said about FABs–features, advantages, and benefits. Evidence statements are a great way to help prove that what you have said is true. Often, evidence statements are presented through visual aids.

EXHIBIT 9.6

Evidence statements help to prove what you say.

EVIDENCE STATEMENTS PROVE WHAT YOU SAY

FEATURE	ADVANTAGE	BENEFIT	EVIDENCE
• New consumer product	Early results show it will be a big seller	Drives revenues in comparison to competitors	Test-market results demonstrate sales success versus competitors
• High energy-efficiency rating	Uses less electricity	Saves 10% on energy costs	*Consumer Reports* magazine
• Mobile CRM (customer-relationship management) phone app	Gets information to sales force instantly	Increases closing of sales by 5% and customer retention by 8%	Testimonials from other firms regarding the effects of application on their sales forces
• Buy 100 cases	Reduces out-of-stocks	By enhancing in-stock levels, increases sales, profits, customer satisfaction	Customer's past sales data and research on other customer's success

Show Them the Money—Quantify Your Benefits

If you want to excite your business buyer, you will need to clearly outline the value that they will receive by purchasing your product. As you know, business buyers are bottom-line oriented. More often than not, they will need to see how your product will affect their profitability. Show them!

Rather than talking about yourself, talk to them about their problems and your SOLUTION to their problems. Many buyers worry about whether they will be wasting their money or not getting the best solution for their problems. To assuage their concerns, you will have to make your sales presentation compelling.

Two problems and their solutions are laid out in Exhibit 9.7. With the first problem, by quantifying the proposition, the solution looks like very good value to the prospect.

Numbers don't lie, unless of course you've simply pulled them out of a hat. Testimonials would add further credibility to this solution.

EXHIBIT 9.7

Two problems and quantified proof of their solutions.

<table>
<tr><th>PROBLEM</th><th>SOLUTION</th><th colspan="2">QUANTIFIED PROOF</th></tr>
<tr><td>Unmanageable energy costs of $6,000 per month</td><td>Feature–Roof-mounted photovoltaic cells
Advantage–Can use sun's energy to power your heating and cooling equipment
Benefit–Reduces energy costs</td><td colspan="2">Installed cost $200,000
Energy cost saving per month $6,000
New energy cost per month $1,000
Savings per month $5,000
Payback is $200,000/$5,000 per month = 40 months

After 40 months, energy cost is reduced to $1,000 per month, which is very manageable.</td></tr>
<tr><td rowspan="5">Production machinery breaking down often with heavy maintenance costs</td><td rowspan="5">Feature–Computer controlled robotic replacement
Advantage–Completely automatic
Benefit–Increased productivity
Feature–Automatic lubricating system
Advantage–No need to shut down for maintenance
Benefit–Decreased costs and improved productivity</td><th>NEW SYSTEM</th><th>COST SAVINGS</th></tr>
<tr><td>Cost
$1,000,000</td><td>Maintenance
$150,000/year</td></tr>
<tr><td>Installation
$100,000</td><td>Labour
$175,000/year</td></tr>
<tr><td>Training
$25,000</td><td></td></tr>
<tr><td>Maintenance
$10,000 yearly</td><td></td></tr>
</table>

In the second simplistic example, do you think it's a good value proposition? Examine it. Your prospect has a serious problem with her production machinery. You are proposing a whole new solution to her at a cost of $1,125,000 up front and an ongoing maintenance cost of $10,000 per month. This looks daunting until you quantify it for her. You'll be saving her $325,000 per year, not to mention improving her company's productivity.

How long will it take to recover the initial cost? Given a 10-year expected life span for the product, would you buy it? Quantifying your benefits makes all the difference in the world in terms of your persuasiveness.

Visual Aids Help Tell the Story

In giving a sales presentation, a salesperson does two things: You *show* and *tell* the prospect about a proposal. You *tell* using persuasive communications, participation techniques, and evidence statements. You *show* by using visual aids.

People retain approximately 10 percent of what they hear but 50 percent of what they see. Consequently, you have five times the chance of making a lasting impression with an illustrated sales presentation rather than with words alone.

visuals:
also called visual aids, these are illustrative material that aids a prospect in increasing memory retention of a presentation.

Visuals are most effective when you believe in them and have woven them into your sales presentation message. Use them to:

- Increase retention
- Reduce misunderstanding
- Create a unique and lasting impression
- Show the buyer that you are a professional

The visual presentation (showing) incorporates the three remaining elements of the presentation mix: visual aids, dramatization, and demonstration. Some overlap exists among the three; for example, a demonstration uses visuals and has some dramatics. Let's examine each element to consider how it can be used in a sales presentation.

Visuals, or visual aids, are devices that chiefly appeal to the prospect's vision with the intent of producing mental images of the product's features, advantages, and benefits (see Exhibit 9.8.)

EXHIBIT 9.8

Assuming you are selling a CRM system, which of the following visuals would most effectively demonstrate the improved customer retention that your product has been proven to deliver?

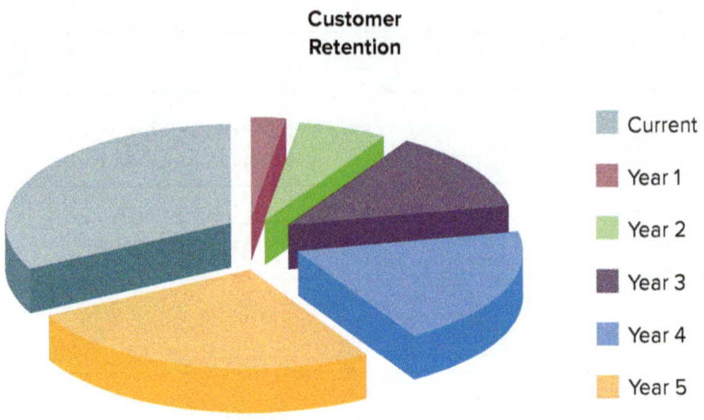

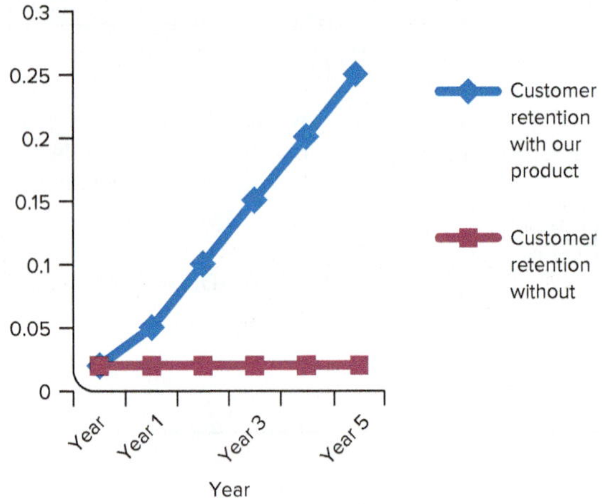

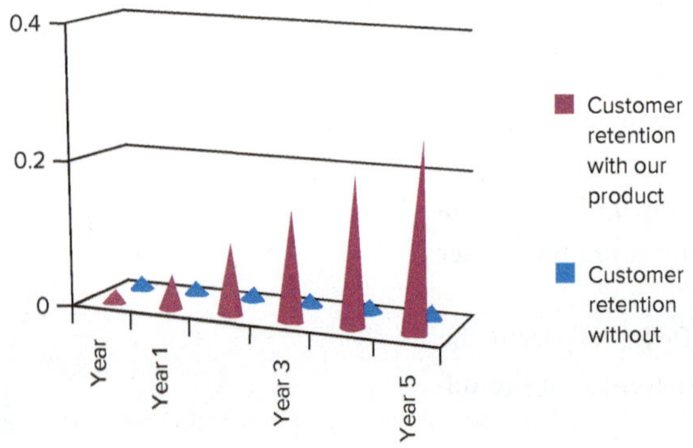

Customer Retention		
Year	With Our Product	Without
Current	2%	2%
Year 1	5%	2%
Year 2	10%	2%
Year 3	15%	2%
Year 4	20%	2%
Year 5	25%	2%

Many companies routinely supply salespeople with visuals for their products. Common visuals include the following:

- Slides, such as those made from Microsoft PowerPoint or Prezi
- The product
- Charts and graphics illustrating product features and advantages such as performance and sales data
- Photographs and videos of the product and its uses
- Models or mock-ups of products, especially for large, bulky products
- Equipment such as videos and computers
- Sales manuals and product catalogues
- Order forms
- Testimonial letters
- A copy of the guarantee
- Flip-boards and posters
- Sample advertisements
- Research whitepapers

Most visual aids are carried in the salesperson's bag (see Exhibit 9.9). Check the sales bag before each sales call to ensure all visuals necessary for the presentation are organized in a manner that allows for easy access to needed materials. Use only new, top-quality, professionally developed visuals. Tattered, torn, or smudged visuals should be routinely discarded. The best visual aid is the actual product.

Review the call plan before seeing the buyer.
Source: © Avava/Dreamstime.com/GetStock.com

This salesperson uses personally developed sales aids customized to the buyer.
Source: © Bloomberg via Getty Images

EXHIBIT 9.9
Visual aids are an important part of a salesperson's presentation. Review the call plan before seeing the buyer. Some visual aids are furnished by the company. This salesperson uses personally developed sales aids customized to the buyer.

A Checklist for Visuals

As a salesperson, you may be called upon to conduct a presentation and need to create visuals, such as slides. Visuals should not only garner attention, but should also have an objective. For instance, a visual's objective could be to:

1. Reinforce a benefit
2. Provide an interpretation of important data and analysis
3. Provide a key take-away (an important point that should be reinforced to the audience)

The following information provides direction regarding best practices for developing a visual.

The Value of Your Visuals To The Buyer

- In some instances, your buyer will use your visuals to sell your product or service to their supervisor or management team. Therefore, your visuals should contain succinct, logical information that will help the customer remember key benefits and the value of your service.

Headlines

- The headline should always communicate the essence of the slide. For example, you may want to ask yourself, "What is the goal of this slide?" You may want to place some form of the answer in the headline.
- Effective headlines use active verbs and clearly communicate a point to the audience. Salespeople use headlines to guide the conversation and communicate important aspects that garner the attention of the customer. For instance, your headline might communicate:
  - **A method or action that may allow the customer to receive a benefit** (By ______, XYZ Increases Revenue by X%)
  - **A critical trend that the customer could take advantage of** (XYZ Leverages Consumer Trend by Stocking 5 Organic Items)
  - **A current situation that the customer can benefit from** if it is lessened or reduced (By Reducing Expenses, XYZ Enhances Profit Margin by 8%)
  - **An approach to reach a new productive state** of their business (Increasing Productivity through Supply Chain Process Enhancement Adds $3 million in Cash Flow)

Data

- Effective visuals interpret data and analysis. As a knowledge broker, the salesperson should present knowledge rather than information. This means that placing a bar chart or line chart without numbers would not be acceptable. Instead, the data should be easy to read and an interpretation of the data should be contained on the slide.

Bullet Points

- Effective bullet points are logical and provide information. If a slide has a bullet point with one or two words, the reader is forced to guess about the information on the slide. Instead, ensure each bullet point communicates something important.
- Logically order bullet points. In this chapter, we discuss the sequence of major premise, minor premise, and conclusion. Consider adapting this approach to order your bullet points to ensure they offer a logical argument to the customer.

Clip-art and Photographs

- Effective visuals tend to reduce the clutter on the slide. While pictures and graphics are a great means of communication, they should be selected to assist in telling the narrative or story that is on the slide rather than distract attention away from the slide's main communication points.

Exhibit 9.10 and Exhibit 9.11 provide two visuals and a few best practices to consider when developing visuals.

EXHIBIT 9.10

Best practices for a slide.

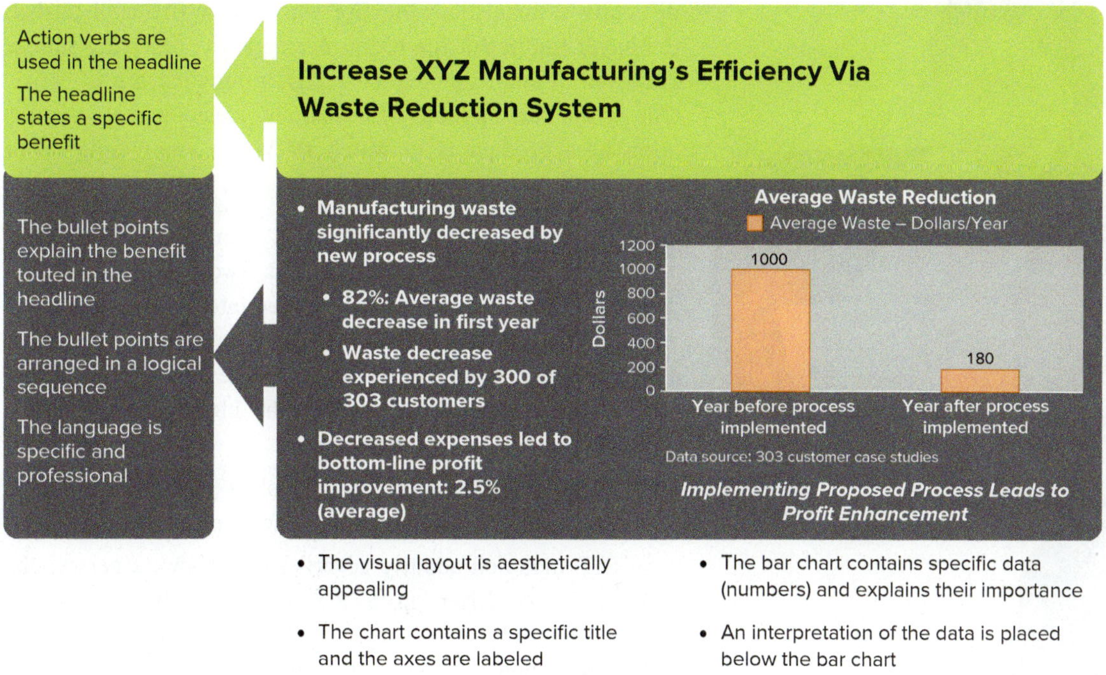

EXHIBIT 9.11

Best practices for a business proposition slide.

Action verbs are used in the headline

The headline states a specific benefit

Margins Per Unit Exceed Annual Goal

The bullet points are arranged in a logical sequence

The language is specific and professional

- **Suggested retail pricing strategy drives incremental profit**
  - **Markup on cost exceeds 65% for product lengths**
- **All product lengths exceed average markup/cost by 10 to 22 points**
- **Using pricing strategy enables penny profit and margin growth**

Suggested Retail Pricing for XYZ Lumber Line

	Pine 2 inch × 4 inch 6 foot	Pine 2 inch × 4 inch 8 foot	Pine 2 inch × 4 inch 10 foot
MSRP (suggested retail price)	$2.89	$3.49	$4.59
Cost of Goods Sold	$1.75	$2.00	$2.60
Penny Profit	$1.14	$1.49	$1.99
Markup/Cost	65%	75%	77%
Your Firm's Average Markup/Cost	55%	55%	55%

- The title of the chart describes the content
- The chart is easy to read and understand
- The chart contains specific titles for the columns and rows

Dramatization Improves Your Chances

Dramatics refers to talking or presenting the product in a striking, showy, or extravagant manner. Thus, sales expertise can involve **dramatization** or a theatrical presentation of products. However, dramatics should be incorporated into the presentation only when you are almost certain that the dramatics will work

dramatization: The theatrical presentation of products.

effectively. This point was not considered by the salesperson who set a buyer's trash can on fire. When the salesperson had difficulty extinguishing the fire with a new fire extinguisher, the buyer ran out of the room to escape the billowing smoke. However, if implemented correctly, dramatics are effective. One of the best methods of developing ideas for the dramatization of a product is to watch television commercials. For example:

- "We challenged the competition . . . and they ran!" says a Heinz tomato ketchup advertisement. Two national brands of ketchup and Heinz ketchup are poured into paper coffee filters held up by tea strainers. The competition's ketchup begins to drip and then runs through the filter. The Heinz ketchup does not drip or run, which indicates the high quality of Heinz ketchup relative to the competition.
- Bounty paper towel advertisements show how quickly Bounty absorbs spilled coffee compared to the competitive paper towel.
- An STP motor-oil additive advertisement shows a person dipping one screwdriver into STP motor-oil additive and another screwdriver into a plain motor oil. The screwdriver covered with plain motor oil can be held with two fingers. The screwdriver covered with STP motor-oil additive slips out of the fingers–indicating that STP provides better lubrication for an automobile engine.

Prepare products and visual aids well in advance.

Source: Tom Wang/Alamy/GetStock.com

Demonstrations Prove It

demonstration: The process of showing a product to a prospect and letting him or her use it, if possible.

One of the best ways to convince a prospect that a product is needed is to show the merits of the product through a **demonstration**. If a picture is worth a thousand words, then a demonstration is worth a thousand pictures. Therefore, it is best to show the product, if possible, and have the prospect use it. If this is not feasible, then pictures, models, or videos are the best alternatives. Whatever the salesperson is attempting to sell, the prospect should be able to see.

Psychological studies have shown that people receive 87 percent of their information on the outside world through their eyes and only 13 percent through the other four senses. What this says to the salesperson is to make a product visible. Also, let the prospect feel, see, hear, smell, and use the product. The dynamic demonstration appeals to human senses by telling, showing, and creating buyer-seller interaction (see Exhibit 9.12).

Demonstrations are part of the dramatization and fun of your presentation. Do not underestimate their ability to make sales for you, no matter how simple they may appear. For example, a glass company once designed a shatterproof glass. This product was not standard equipment in automobiles then, as it is now. They had their salespeople going around the country trying to sell shatterproof glass. One of the salespeople completely outsold the rest of the sales force. When they had their convention, they said, "Joe, how come you sell so much glass?" He replied, "Well, what I've been doing is taking

EXHIBIT 9.12

This prospect experiences how the product actually works. A demonstration is worth a thousand pictures in helping make a sale.

Source: Antonio Jodice Dreamstime.com

little chunks of glass, and a ball-peen hammer along with me on my sales calls. I take the little chunk of glass, and I hit it with the hammer. This demonstration shows that it's shatterproof. It splinters but doesn't shatter and fall all over the ground. This has helped me sell a lot of glass."

So, the next year the company equipped every salesperson with a ball-peen hammer and little chunks of glass. But an interesting thing happened. Joe still far outsold the rest of the sales force. So, when the convention occurred the next year, they asked, "Joe, how is it you're selling so much? You told us what you did last year. What are you doing differently?" He replied, "Well, this year, I gave the glass *and* the hammer to the *customer* to let *him* hit it." You see, the first year Joe used dramatization in his demonstration. The second year, Joe used dramatization and participation in his demonstration. Again, it's often not what you say but how you say it that makes the sale.

A Demonstration Checklist

There are eight points to remember as you prepare your demonstration (see Exhibit 9.13). Ask yourself whether the demonstration is really needed and appropriate for your prospects. Not every sale needs a demonstration, nor will all products lend themselves to a demonstration.

EXHIBIT 9.13
Eight points to remember about demonstrations.

☑ Is the demonstration *needed* and *appropriate?*
☑ Have I developed a specific demonstration *objective?*
☑ Is the demonstration tied to a benefit that is important to the customer?
☑ Have I properly *planned* and *organized* the demonstration?
☑ Have I rehearsed to the point that the demonstration *flows smoothly* and appears to be *natural?*
☑ What is the probability that the demonstration will go as *planned?*
☑ What is the probability that the demonstration will *backfire?*
☑ Does my demonstration present my product in an *ethical* and *professional* manner?

If the demonstration is appropriate, what should the demonstration accomplish? Be sure you have properly planned and organized the demonstration; rehearse it so the demonstration flows smoothly and appears natural. Take your time in talking and going through your demonstration; make it look easy. Remember, if you, the expert, cannot operate a machine, for example, imagine how difficult it will be for the prospect.

The only way to ensure a smooth demonstration is to practise. Be prepared in case something goes wrong. For example, a former student was demonstrating his new Kodak slide projector to a buyer for a large discount chain. Two bulbs in a row burned out as he demonstrated the product. Fortunately, he had anticipated what could go wrong and always carried extra parts in his sales bag. When the first bulb went out, he talked of how easy it was to change bulbs, and when the second one blew, he said, "I want to show you that again," with a smile. He had always carried two spare bulbs, but now he carries three.

Finally, make sure your demonstration presents the product in an ethical and professional manner. You do not want to misrepresent the product or proposal.

Use Participation in Your Demonstration

Confucius, the Chinese philosopher (551-479 BCE), is often credited with saying, "Tell me and I'll forget. Show me and I'll remember. Involve me and I'll understand."

By having the prospect participate in the demonstration, you obtain his or her attention and direct it where you want it. Participation also helps the prospect visualize owning and operating the product. The successful demonstration aids in reducing buying uncertainties and resistance to purchase.

A successful demonstration involves the prospect by:

1. Letting the prospect do something simple
2. Letting the prospect work an important feature
3. Letting the prospect do something routine or frequently repeated
4. Having the prospect answer questions throughout the demonstration

First, ask the prospect to do something simple with a low probability of foul-ups. Second, in planning the demonstration, select the main features that you will stress in the interview and allow the prospect to participate on the feature that relates most to an important buying motive. Again, keep it simple.

A third way to have a successful demonstration is by having the prospect do something with the product that is done frequently. Finally, receive feedback from the prospect throughout the demonstration by asking questions or pausing in your conversation. This is extremely important in order to:

- Determine the prospect's attitude toward the product.
- Allow you to progress in the demonstration or wait and answer any questions or address any objections.
- Aid in moving the prospect into the positive yes mood.
- Set the stage for closing the sale.

Little agreements lead to the big agreement and saying yes. Phrase questions in a positive manner such as "That is really easy to operate, isn't it?" instead of "This isn't hard to operate, is it?" They ask the same thing, yet the response to the first question is positive instead of negative. The best questions force the prospect to place the product in use mentally, such as the question phrased, "Do you feel this could increase your employees' productivity?" This yes answer commits the buyer to the idea that the feature will increase employee productivity. Remember, it is often not what you say but how you say it.

Reasons for Using Visual Aids, Dramatics, and Demonstrations

As we have seen, visual aids, dramatics, and demonstrations are important to the salesperson's success in selling a prospect. Including these features allows you to do the following:

- Capture attention and interest.
- Create two-way communication.
- Involve the prospect through participation.
- Afford a more complete, clear explanation of products and the benefits that are important to the customer.
- Increase a salesperson's persuasive powers by obtaining positive commitments on a product's single benefit.

Guidelines for Using Visual Aids, Dramatics, and Demonstrations

Although visual aids, dramatics, and demonstrations are important, using them properly is critical.

- Rehearse by practising in front of a mirror, or filming yourself selling to a friend. Once you are ready to make the presentation, try it out on less important prospects. This practice allows you time to refine the presentation before contacting more important accounts.
- Customize your presentation to the sales call objective (the prospect's customer profile; the customer benefit plan), concentrating on the prospect's important buying motives and using appropriate multiple appeals to sight, touch, hearing, smell, and taste. See Exhibit 9.14.
- Make your presentation simple and clear.
- Make sure you control the demonstration by not letting the prospect divert you from selling. It can be disastrous to have the prospect not listen or miss major selling points you wanted to present.
- Make visual aids, dramatics, and demonstrations true to life.
- Encourage prospect participation.
- Incorporate trial closes (questions) after showing or demonstrating a major feature, advantage, or benefit to determine whether it is believed and important to the prospect.

EXHIBIT 9.14

Which buyer senses are being appealed to by the seller?

Source: © Yuri Arcurs/Dreamstime.com/GetStock.com

George Wynn the Showman

Use a dramatic demonstration to set yourself apart from the many salespeople whom buyers see each day. Buyers, such as industrial purchasing agents, like to see you, as they know you will have an informative and often entertaining sales presentation. One salesperson known for his effective presentation was George Wynn, who was an industrial salesperson for Exxon. Wynn was responsible for sales of machine lubricating oils and greases in the Ohio region.

George Eats Grease One group of products Wynn sold were oils and greases for the food-processing industry. These lubricants had to be approved by the federal Food and Drug Administration (FDA) for incidental food contact. One of the products was a lubricating grease, Carum 280. He ordered a number of one-pound cans for customer samples. As George started his sales presentation of these FDA-approved products, he would take one of the cans from his sample case, open it, and spread this grease on a slice of bread. After taking a bite of bread spread with the grease, he then offered a bite to the buyer. The buyer generally refused the offer. However, in the mind of the buyer, this dramatic demonstration set George's presentation apart from others. It helped prove to the buyer the product was safe to use in a food-processing plant.

George Lights Up Another of his dramatic demonstrations involved lubricating greases used by the steel industry. Greases that resist high temperatures are desirable for most applications in the steel industry. Exxon developed a line of temperature-resistant greases that used a new thickener that held the oil in suspension better than competitive products. To demonstrate this product attribute, George used a pie tin held at a 45-degree angle centred over a small lighted alcohol lamp. A small glob of the Exxon grease and globs of several better-known competitors were placed on the pie tin. As the pie tin was heated, the oil separated from each of the competitive greases and ran down the pie tin. The oil did not separate from the Exxon product, dramatically demonstrating the high temperature resistance of this steel-mill grease as compared with leading competitive products.

Technology Can Help

Technology provides excellent methods of presenting information to the buyer in a visually attractive and dramatic manner. Using a computer tablet in front of the buyer can be impressive. Today, technology enables the presentation of video clips, sound bites, and beautifully illustrated graphics. Salespeople can also connect it to projection equipment for great presentations. Analytical software can quickly crunch data—providing instant solutions to buyers' questions. Salespeople selling products such as services, real estate, and industrial equipment can quickly show buyers a product's cost when considering different instalment payment schedules at various interest rates. Remember, it's often not what you say but how you say it that makes the sale.

Video Conferencing

Technology has truly expanded and improved video conferencing. For the average person, options like Skype and FaceTime are prevalent. However, a number of other vendors, such as WebEx, GoToMeeting, and Adobe Connect, provide businesses and their salespeople with opportunities to interact over video, share screens, and provide more interactive conversations across the world. Salespeople can hold client meetings, introduce new products, and demonstrate key benefits and features. The increased use of video conferencing also means that many salespeople will need to develop their communication skills specific to the video arena. In the Selling Tips box below, we provide a few considerations for salespeople using video-conferencing technology in the sales process.

SELLING TIPS

CONSIDERATIONS FOR USING VIDEO CONFERENCING TECHNOLOGY

Practise using the video technology. Conduct a practice round and then watch it.

Place yourself in the viewer's shoes. If possible, watch the practice round ahead of time. Take note of the elements that were difficult to understand, hear, or interpret.

Have a contingency plan. Ensure you have established a backup plan in case of a technical glitch.

Plan interaction. Understand how people will interact with you.

- If it's a demonstration, will you use video technology that allows users to electronically signal that they have questions?
- If it's a webinar with multiple attendees, will you use video technology that allows users to be muted to reduce the opportunity for paper ruffling, movement, etc.?

Check the environment. Consider your background. Do the participants see a natural view of you or do you appear scrunched behind a webcam?

Monitor the sound. Is the room you are using quiet? Will your microphone pick up the background noise?

Consider lighting. Where should you place the lighting to ensure the video captures you in an appealing manner?

Check clothing. What types of patterns on your clothing should you wear to create a great impression on video?

Ensure software accessibility. Make sure everyone has the software or access to the software application for the video conference.

SOCIAL MEDIA INSIGHTS FOR SALESPEOPLE

USING YOUTUBE TO PREPARE YOUR PROSPECT

Many buyers today know a great deal about the product they are considering before they even listen to a salesperson's presentation. Where did they get their information from? Social media presents a terrific opportunity for salespeople to be proactive—to present accurate and compelling information to a targeted audience.

Imagine that you are selling a high-tech safety device that, when installed on heavy equipment, prevents injury to workers due to accidents. This would be a tough product to demonstrate during a presentation as you can't very well bring heavy equipment into a prospect's office and a field demo may be difficult to organize. The solution: Before your meeting, send your prospect a link to a YouTube video that shows a real demonstration of your product in action.

Some Tips:

1. Keep it short. One to two minutes should be enough to get the prospect's attention and arouse their interest.
2. Use good quality video and techniques. An amateurish video would not serve to enhance the quality image that you are trying to present. Consider the use of a professional to help you produce a video.
3. Demonstrate clearly but visually the benefits that users can enjoy by using your product.
4. Consider testimonials. A few customer testimonials will go a long way to enhance credibility.
5. Make your video dramatic yet believable; remember, a demonstration is worth a thousand pictures.

Don't provide so much information that your video becomes overly long and the prospect may make a decision before you even get a chance to discuss the product with them.

The Ideal Presentation

In the ideal presentation, your approach technique quickly captures your prospect's interest and immediately finds signals that the prospect has a need for your product and is ready to listen. The ideal prospect is friendly, polite, relaxed, and focused, participates in your demonstration as planned, avoids interruptions, and asks questions. This allows you to move through the presentation skilfully.

The ideal customer cheerfully and positively answers each of your questions, allowing you to anticipate the correct moment to ask for the order. You are completely relaxed and sure of yourself when you come to the close. The customer says yes, and enthusiastically thanks you for your valuable time. Several weeks later, you receive a copy of the letter your customer wrote to your company's president glowing with praise for your professionalism.

MAKING THE SALE

DOS AND DON'TS FOR EFFECTIVE SLIDESHOW PRESENTATIONS

There's nothing worse than a poor slideshow presentation. We've all seen them with too much animation, too much information, and gimmicky sound effects. The main objective of a slideshow presentation is to provide the information you feel will be necessary for your prospect(s) to leave with a clear idea and a favourable impression.

Do:

- Use an introduction slide at the beginning to introduce your purpose and planned agenda. Use a welcoming slide if people will be sitting and waiting for things to begin.
- Add your prospect's logo to your slides; this is a nice touch and personalizes your presentation.

- Construct your slides using a consistent background that pertains to your company.
- Use high-quality pictures but avoid clip art. Make the pictures relevant to your presentation.
- Limit each slide to four or five bullet points. Do not write out full sentences—just summarize your points.
- Proofread. There's nothing worse than having an audience looking at a spelling or grammatical error for an extended period of time.
- Practise, practise, practise.
- Have a backup plan. Technical difficulties may prevent you from using your equipment—so be ready.
- Ensure that your presentation is viewable from all angles and distances.
- Use a wireless remote to keep slide transitions smooth and timely.
- Speak to the audience, not to the slides.
- Summarize charts and graphs for the audience so people know what they're looking at.
- Summarize. Conclude your presentation with a summary slide of the key points you have made.
- Watch your timing. Try to finish a little earlier than expected.

Don't:

- Fill the slide with pictures or animation, which will distract from your message.
- Overuse colour.
- Use silly customized transitions—remember, it's the content that's important.
- Use fancy fonts that may be difficult to read, or colours that may be difficult to see.

LO4

Be Prepared for Presentation Difficulties

Yes, a few sales presentations go incredibly smoothly; most, though, have one or more hurdles. Although all of the difficulties you might face cannot be discussed here, the three main problems encountered during sales presentations are handling an interruption, discussing your competition, and making the presentation in a less-than-ideal situation.

How to Handle Interruptions

It is common for interruptions to occur during the presentation. The secretary comes into the office or the telephone rings, distracting the prospect. What should you do?

First, determine whether the discussion that interrupted your presentation is personal or confidential. If so, by gesture or voice you can offer to leave the room—this is always appreciated by the prospect. Second, while waiting, gather your thoughts and mentally review how to return to the presentation. Once the discussion is over, you can:

1. Wait quietly and patiently until you have regained the prospect's attention completely.
2. Briefly restate the selling points that had interested the prospect; for example, "We were discussing your needs for a product such as ours and you seemed especially interested in knowing about our service, delivery, and installation. Is that right?"
3. Do something to increase the prospect's participation, such as showing the product, using other visuals, or asking questions. Closely watch to determine whether you have regained the prospect's interest.
4. If interest is regained, move deeper into the presentation.

LO5

Should You Discuss the Competition?

Competition is something all salespeople must contend with every day. If you sell a product, you must compete with others selling comparable products. How should you handle competition? Basically, remember four considerations: (1) do not refer to a competitor unless absolutely necessary; (2) acknowledge your competitor only briefly; (3) make a detailed comparison of your product and the competition's product; and (4) be professional.

Do Not Refer to Competition

Reduce any surprises the buyer may present by properly planning for the sales call. In developing your customer profile, try to learn which competing products are used and your prospect's attitude toward your products and competitors' products. Based on your findings, the presentation can be developed without specifically referring to competition.

Acknowledge Competition and Drop It

Many salespeople believe their competition should not be discussed unless the prospect initiates it. Then, acknowledge competition briefly and return to your product. "Yes, I am familiar with that product's features. In fact, the last three of my customers were using that product and have switched over to ours. May I tell you why?"

Here, you do not knock competition, but acknowledge it and in a positive manner move the prospect's attention back to your products. If the prospect continues to discuss a competing product, you should determine the prospect's attitude toward it. You might ask, "What do you think about the IBM 6000 computer system?" The answer will help you mentally determine how you can prove that your product offers the prospect more benefits than your competitor's product.

Make a Detailed Comparison

At times, it is appropriate to make a detailed comparison of your product to a competing one, especially for industrial products. If products are similar, emphasize your company's service, guarantees, and what you do personally for customers.

If your product has features that are lacking in a competitor's product, refer to these advantages. "Our product is the only one on the market with this feature! Is this important to you?" Ask the question and wait for the response. A yes answer takes you one step closer to the sale.

Often the prospect can use both your product and a competitor's product. For example, a pharmaceutical salesperson is selling an antibiotic that functions like penicillin and kills bacteria resistant to penicillin. However, it costs 20 times more than penicillin. This salesperson would say, "Yes, Dr. Jones, penicillin is the drug of choice for this disease. But, do you have patients for whom penicillin is ineffective?" "Yes, I do," says the doctor. "Then, for those patients, I want you to consider my product because . . ."

Be Professional

No matter how you discuss competition with your prospect, always act professionally. If you discuss competition, talk only about information that you know to be accurate, and be straightforward and honest–not belittling and discourteous.

Your prospect may like both your products and the competitor's products. A loyalty to the competitor may have been built over the years; by knocking competition, you may insult and alienate your prospect. However, the advantages and disadvantages of a competitive product can be demonstrated acceptably if done professionally. One salesperson relates this story:

> Several customers I called on were loyal to my competitors; however, just as many were loyal to my company. I will always remember the president of a chain of retail stores who flew 500 kilometres to be at one of our salespeople's retirement dinners. In his talk, he noted how 30 years ago, when he opened his first store, this salesperson extended him company credit and made him a personal loan that helped him get started.

It would be difficult for a competing salesperson to sell to this loyal customer. When contacting customers, especially ones buying competitive products, it is important to uncover why they use competitive products before discussing competition in the presentation.

Making the Presentation in a Less-Than-Ideal Situation

The ideal presentation happens in a quiet room with only the salesperson, the prospect, and no interruptions. However, at times the salesperson may meet the prospect somewhere other than a private office and need to make the presentation under less-than-ideal conditions.

For short presentations, a stand-up situation may be adequate; however, when making a longer presentation, you may want to ask the prospect, "Could we go back to your office?" or make another appointment.

ETHICAL DILEMMA

OVERSTATEMENT VS. UNDERSTATEMENT

You are in the competitive field of selling high-capacity photocopiers. One of your prospects is looking for copiers that will reliably run up to 5,000 copies per day without being overloaded. After doing an analysis of the prospect's paper purchases over the last year, you extrapolate that 90 percent of her copiers ran at only 60 percent (3,000 copies per day) capacity over the last year.

Your dilemma is this: Should you propose your medium-duty copier, which was designed for 3,500 copies per day, knowing that this will handle her needs most of the time based on the usage history? This will allow you to come in with a price about 15 percent below your competitors and will allow you to get this lucrative deal. After all, it is highly unlikely that a problem will ever arise.

What do you do?

SELLING GLOBALLY

MAKING A DEAL IN MEXICO

Typically, Mexicans prefer doing business with people they know, so developing sincere relationships is critical. In business culture, the relationship is probably more important than your competence, knowledge, or experience. In Mexico the family plays a dominant role and often extends into the business, with many companies being family owned.

The business culture in Mexico has a slower pace and warmer, friendlier atmosphere. Don't expect quick results; the relationship must be nurtured. Mexicans like to become involved in finding a solution, so partnership selling can be very useful.

Use visuals in your presentations. They should be of high quality but should not be used as a substitute for a strong relationship. You can expect a longer than normal negotiation and it will appear a little less formal—more like haggling.

Mexican businesspeople are often well informed about who they are doing business with, so be prepared. It helps if you are the one with the authority to act and not just a liaison for your company.

Any literature and correspondence is considered important so should be of high quality. Always handle documents with formality and respect so as not to offend anyone.

When the decision is made, it is important that it be summarized in a written agreement.

PLAYING THE ROLE

Role: You are a salesperson for one of the following products: office chairs, photocopiers, HDTV, iPhone, GPS.

Develop two examples of simile, and analogy that could be used in a presentation of that product. Be prepared to dramatize these to a prospect (classmate).

Observers can listen carefully to determine if the examples had a positive effect. That is, would the prospect find the product more attractive after hearing these techniques used? Have the observers comment on whether the statements sounded phony or realistic.

The Sales Presentation Goal Model

"Wow!" you say. There are many things to consider when creating a sales presentation. Persuasive communication, participation, proof statements, visual aids, dramatization, demonstration that may or may not include technology. How do you decide what elements of the sales presentation mix to use in a sales presentation? It depends on the goal of your presentation and the answers to six questions.

Exhibit 9.15 will help you decide whether to use some or all of the sales presentation mix ingredients.

You need to answer these six questions:

1. What is your objective?
2. Who is your audience?
3. How will you structure your presentation?
4. How will you create impact?
5. How will you design and display visual aids?
6. How will you stage your presentation?

Your sales presentation goal(s) and the answers to these six questions will be your guide to skillfully show and tell your customers how your product will fulfill their needs.

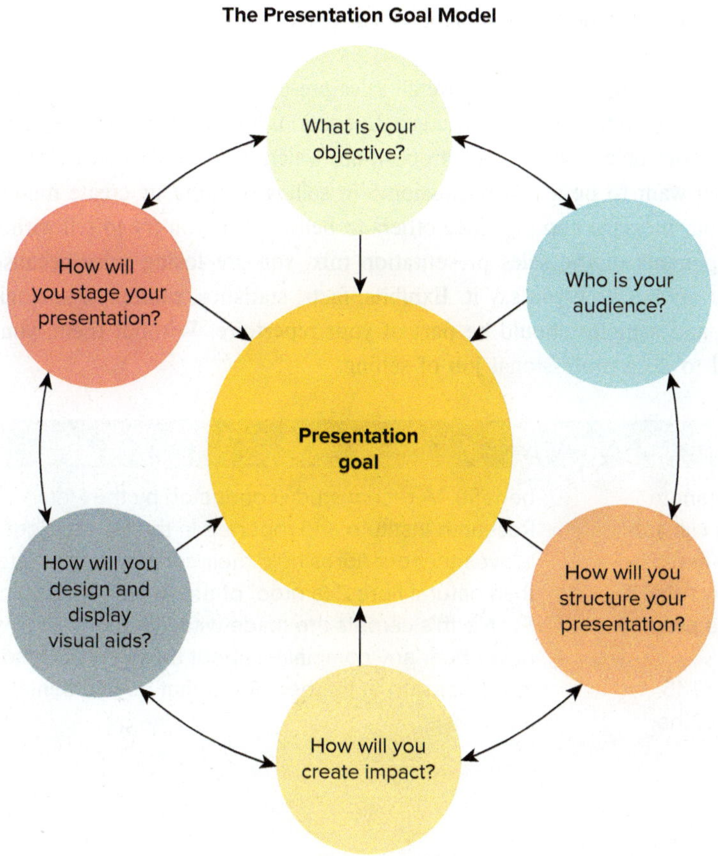

EXHIBIT 9.15

The sales presentation goal model.

Summary of Major Selling Issues

The sales presentation is a persuasive vocal and visual explanation of a proposition. Although there are numerous methods for making a sales presentation, the four common ones are the memorized, formula, interactive need-satisfaction, and problem-solving selling methods. Each method is effective if used for the proper situation.

In developing your presentation, consider the elements of the sales presentation mix that you will use for each prospect. The proper use of persuasive communication techniques, methods to develop prospect participation, evidence statements, visual aids, dramatization, and demonstrations increases your chances of illustrating how your products will satisfy your prospect's needs.

It is often not what we say but how we say it that results in the sale. Persuasive communication techniques (questioning, listening, logical reasoning, suggestion, and the use of trial closes) help to uncover needs, to communicate effectively, and to pull the prospect into the conversation.

Evidence statements are especially useful in showing your prospect that what you say is true and that you can be trusted. When challenged, prove it by incorporating facts on a customer's past sales into your presentation, by guaranteeing that the product will work or sell, or by offering testimonials and company and independent research results.

To both show and tell, visuals must be properly designed to illustrate features, advantages, and benefits of your products through graphics, dramatization, and demonstration. This pairing allows you to capture the prospect's attention and interest; to create two-way communication and participation; to express your proposition in a clearer, more complete manner; and to make more sales. Careful attention to development and rehearsal of the presentation is needed to ensure it occurs smoothly and naturally.

Always prepare for the unexpected, such as a demonstration that falls apart, interruptions, the prospect's questions about the competition, or the necessity to make your presentation in a less-than-ideal place, such as the aisle of a retail store or in the warehouse.

The presentation part of the overall sales presentation is the heart of the sale. It is where you develop the desire, conviction, and action. By giving an effective presentation, you have fewer objections to your proposition, which makes for an easier sale close.

If you want to be a real professional in selling, acquire or create materials that convey your message and convince others to believe it. If you try to sell without using the components of the sales presentation mix, you are losing sales because of not what you say but how you say it. Exhibits, facts, statistics, examples, analogies, testimonials, and samples should be part of your repertoire. Without them, you are not equipped to do a professional job of selling.

MEETING A SALES CHALLENGE

The carpet's ability to resist fading is important to the customer who needs proof your carpet will not fade. In this situation, the proof statement should be authoritative, using independent research results, if possible. Here is an example of an effective proof statement:

"Mr. Jones, a carpet made of our new XT-15 synthetic fibres will not fade" (restatement of the benefit). "A recent study conducted by the Home Research Institute and reported in the Home Digest proves that our fibres hold their colours much better than natural fibres" (a proof of the benefit). "And since Far North's carpets are made with synthetic fibres, you'll never hear any complaints about these carpets fading" (an expansion of the benefit). "What do you think?" (trial close).

Key Terms for Selling

analogy
autosuggestion
body language
consultative selling
countersuggestion
demonstration
direct suggestion
dramatization
evidence statements
indirect suggestion
logical reasoning
prestige suggestions
proof statements
sales presentation mix
simile
suggestive propositions
testimonial
visuals

Sales Application Questions

1. You plan to give a demonstration of a new forklift truck that has a hybrid engine to the purchasing agent of a company with a storage facility that covers 50 hectares. Which of the following is the best technique for your demonstration? Why?
   a. Let your prospect drive the forklift.
   b. You drive the forklift and ask the prospect to ride along so that you can discuss the truck's benefits.
   c. Leave a demonstrator and return a week later to see how many the prospect will buy.
2. When contracting a purchasing agent for your hybrid forklift truck, you plan to use your 10-page visual presenter to guide the prospect through your benefit story. This selling aid is a binder containing photographs of your truck in action along with its various colour options, a guarantee, and a testimonial. Should you:
   a. Hand over the binder? Why?
   b. Hold on to it? Why?
3. Assume you are halfway through your presentation when your prospect has to answer the telephone. The call lasts five minutes. What should you do?
4. Discuss the various elements of the sales presentation mix and indicate why you need to use visuals during your presentation.
5. In your evidence statement of the benefit, cite your evidence source, in addition to relevant facts or figures about your product. Which of the following is a correct evidence of a benefit?
   a. An article in last month's *Appliance Report* stated that the Williams blender is more durable than the other top 10 brands.
   b. You'll get 10 percent more use from the Hanig razor.
   c. *Marathon* is the most widely read magazine among persons with incomes over $25,000 per year.
   d. Figures in *Marathon* magazine indicate that your sales will increase if you stock Majestic housewares in your store.
6. Examine the following conversation:

   Customer: What you say is important, all right, but how do I know that these chairs will take wear and tear the way you say they will?

   Salesperson: The durability of a chair is an important factor to consider. That's why all Crest chairs have reinforced plastic webbing seats. *Furniture Dealer's Weekly* states that the plastic webbing used in Crest chairs is 32 percent more effective in preventing sagging chair seats than fabric webbing. This means that your chairs will last longer and take the wear and tear that your customers are concerned about.

   Look at each sentence in this conversation and state whether it is:
   a. An expansion of the benefit
   b. A restatement of the benefit
   c. An evidence statement
7. After a two-hour drive to see an important new prospect, you stop at a local coffee shop for a bite to eat. As you look over your presentation charts, you spill coffee on a half dozen of them. You don't have substitute presentation charts with you. What should you do?
   a. Phone the prospect and say that you'd like to make another appointment. Say that something came up.
   b. Keep the appointment. At the start of your presentation, tell the prospect about the coffee spill and apologize for it.
   c. Go ahead with your presentation, but don't make excuses. The coffee stains are barely noticeable if you're not on the lookout for them.

Sales Online Exercise

High-Tech Presentations!

Search the following URLs to find information to help you create a presentation enhanced by technology:

www.salesandmarketing.com
www.sellingpower.com
www.prezi.com
www.vidyard.com for video presentations
www.google.com/slides/about/
www.vyond.com

Use search engines to find websites on sales or presentation technology. Salespeople are using more multimedia presentations to convey their message. See what you can find out about methods, equipment, and the effectiveness of using multimedia in a sales presentation.

Further Exploring the Sales World

1. What is one thing in this world on which you are an expert? Yourself! Develop a presentation on yourself for a sales job with a company of your choice. Relate this assignment to each of the 10 steps of the selling process.
2. Visit several retail stores in your community and report on the demonstration techniques, if any, that were used in selling a product. Suggest ways that you would have presented the product.
3. Report on one television advertisement that used each of the following: an evidence statement, a demonstration, unusual visual aids, and a dramatization.
4. Magazines are available online and in your library where companies advertise their products to retail and wholesale customers, along with information about current price discounts. Find at least three advertisements containing current price discounts offered by manufacturers to wholesalers or retailers. How might you use this information in a sales presentation?

Student Application Learning Exercises (SALES)

An important part of consultative selling is the use of questions to uncover the customer's needs. You have planned some of your questions in constructing your SELL sequences. SELL sequences should be contained in your discussion of the product, marketing plan, and business proposition.

Every important sales presentation should contain most–if not all–of the presentation mix ingredients shown in Exhibit 9.5.

Part 5

1. Construct and write out one SELL sequence. After your trial close, the buyer questions what you have just said. The buyer sounds unsure whether what you are saying is true. Create an evidence statement that shows your claim is true.
   SELL sequence: **Buyer's skeptical remark:** **Evidence statement:**
2. Create one analogy and simile to use in your role-play.
   Simile: **Analogy:**
3. Describe a demonstration you could do of one of your product's benefits. If possible, add dramatization. Remember, simply showing the product is not a demonstration.
4. Describe three visual aids you could use in your presentation. Flip-charts and notebooks are easy to develop, or you can place your visuals in a folder and pull one at a time out as you discuss it.
   Visual 1: **Visual 2:** **Visual 3:**

CASE 9–1

DYNO ELECTRIC CART COMPANY

You plan a call-back to the purchasing manager, Mr. Jennings, and the president of his company to sell them several of your electric carts. (Refer to Exhibit 8.4.) The company's manufacturing plant covers some 100 hectares and you have sold up to 10 carts to many companies smaller than this one. Since Jennings allows you to meet with his company's president and maybe other executives, you know that he is interested in your carts.

You are determined to make a spellbinding presentation of your product's benefits using visual aids and a cart demonstration. Mr. Jennings raised several objections during your last presentation that may be restated by other executives. Your challenge is to develop a dramatic, convincing presentation.

QUESTIONS

1. How would you demonstrate the cart to Pride and the president? What would you specifically plan?
2. Consider crafting an evidence statement for Dyno Electric Cart that you would provide to Pride and the president. What would your evidence statement specifically state?
3. Consider crafting a testimonial for Dyno Electric Cart that you would provide to Pride and the president. What would it specifically state?
4. Develop two visuals that you would present Pride and the president. What benefits would they focus on? Ensure your visuals follow the best practices outlined in the chapter.

CASE 9–2

MAJOR OIL, INC.*

Tim Christensen sells industrial lubricants to manufacturing plants. The lubricants are used for the plants' machinery. He is calling on Petar Balogh, a purchasing agent for Acme Manufacturing Company. Petar currently buys Tim's Hydraulic Oil 65 in drums. Tim's sales call objective is to persuade Petar to switch from purchasing his oil in drums to a bulk oil system. The secretary has just admitted him to Petar's office.

Salesperson: Hello, Petar.

Customer: Well, if it isn't Tim Christensen, my lube oil salesperson! How is everything over at Major Oil these days?

Salesperson: Fine! We're adding to our warehouse, so we won't be quite as crowded. Say, I know you like to fly. I was just reading in a magazine about the old Piper Tri-Pacer.

Customer: Yeah! I do enjoy flying and fooling with old airplanes. I just got back this weekend from a fly-in over at Hamilton.

Salesperson: You don't say! What types of planes did they have?

Customer: They had a bunch of homebuilts. You know, many pilots spend from 5 to 15 years just building their own planes.

Salesperson: Would you like to build your own plane someday?

Customer: Yes, I would. But you know, this job takes so much time–and with my schedule here and some travel, I don't know if I'll ever get time to start on a plane, much less finish one.

Salesperson: Well, I don't know that I can save you that much time, but I can save the people in the plant time and reduce your cost of Hydraulic Oil 65. Also, I may even save your office some time and expense by not having to place so many orders.

You know, we talked a couple of weeks ago about the possibility of Acme buying Hydraulic Oil 65 in bulk and thus reducing the cost per litre by buying larger quantities each time you order. In addition, you will save tying your money up in the $20 drum deposit or even losing the deposit by losing or damaging the empty drum.

Customer: Sounds like this is going to cost us some money.

*Case developed by George Wynn, professor of marketing, James Madison University, © 1998.

Salesperson: Well, we might have to spend a little money to save a larger amount, plus make it easier and quicker in the plant. Do you know exactly what you are paying for Hydraulic Oil 65 now?

Customer: I think it's about $1.40 a litre.

Salesperson: That's close. Your delivery cost is $1.39 per litre, not counting drum deposit. You used approximately 20,000 litres of Hydraulic Oil 65 last year at a total cost of $27,800.

Customer: Between what I pay at the gas station and what we pay here, I see why Major Oil is getting bigger and richer all the time. How much money can you save us?

Salesperson: Well, we try to get by and make ends meet. However, I can save your company more than $2,800 per year on oil costs alone.

Customer: That sounds awful big. How are you going to do that?

Salesperson: I am going to show you how you can purchase oil in bulk, save 14¢ per litre on each litre you buy [14¢ times 20,000 litres equals $2,800], and eliminate handling those drums and having your money tied up in deposits. Last year, you purchased about 364 drums–and I'll bet you did not return all the drums to us.

Customer: I know we damaged some drums, and I imagine we ended up with some expensive trash barrels for our employees. I wonder how much of a total deposit we pay?

Salesperson: The total deposit on those drums was $7,280. Are you and your company totally satisfied with the performance of Hydraulic Oil 65?

Customer: It seems so. I have heard nothing to the contrary; and our bearing supplier, Timken, says that the oil is doing a first-class job. You know, this savings sounds good in theory, but will it really work? Besides, where will we put a big bulk system?

Salesperson: Petar, I've already thoroughly checked into what the total equipment and installation will cost. Here's a picture of the installation we made over at the Foundry and Machine Shop. We put the installation above ground to save the expense of digging holes for the tanks. The cover shown here in the picture protects the pump and motor from the weather, and the pipe into the shop goes underground. There's a control switch for the pump motor mounted inside the building next to the nozzle outlet. It looks good, doesn't it?

Customer: It certainly does, Tim, but what about the cost?

Salesperson: We can get two new 3,000-litre tanks delivered here for a cost of $1,700 from our tank supplier. This is about $120 less than what you could buy them for. Our quantity purchases of tanks give us a little better price–and we'll be glad to pass these savings on to you. I have checked with Pump Supply Company, and they have in stock the pump and motor with flexible coupling and built-in pump relief valve, just what we need for handling this oil. The cost is $475. The control switch, pipe, pipe fittings, inside hose, and nozzle come to $120, and the person who does our installation work has given me a commitment to do all the installation work for $500, including furnishing the blocks to make the tank supports.

This totals $2,795, so let's round off to $2,800. And at a savings of 14¢ per litre, based on your present usage of 20,000 litres per year, this would be paid off in about 12 months, during which time you'd pay $1.25 per litre for your oil rather than the $1.39 you now pay. How does that sound to you, Petar?

Customer: That sounds pretty good to me, Tim. Didn't you have an article about this in a recent issue of your company magazine?

Salesperson: We sure did. It was in the March issue. Here it is, right here. The situation was a little different, but the basic idea is the same. Our company has used this idea to considerable advantage and over the past three years I have set up six installations of this type. Do you have any questions regarding the plan I've outlined?

Customer: Just one thing–you know we're short on space behind the warehouse. Have you thought about where we might locate an installation of this type?

Salesperson: Yes, I have, Petar. Recall one of our earlier conversations where you told me about your plans to clean up that old scrap pile near the corner of the warehouse? That would be an ideal location. We could then locate the control switch, filling hose, and nozzle right on the inside at the end of the assembly line so the units could have their initial oil fill just before they come off the assembly line. How would that fit into your plans?

Customer: That's a good idea, Tim. That way we can get that junk pile cleaned up, replace it with a decent looking installation, and then make our initial oil fill the last step in our assembly procedure.

Salesperson: Do you have any other questions, Petar?

Customer: No, I believe I've got the whole picture now.

Salesperson: Good. Now, to sum up our thinking, Petar, the total cost of installation will be about $3,000. Immediately on completion of the installation, and when you receive your first transport truckload shipment of Hydraulic Oil 65, instead of being billed at $1.39 per litre, as you are now paying for barrel deliveries, you will be billed $1.25 per litre. I'll work with Bill Smith, the plant superintendent, and I'll handle all the outside contacts so that we can make the installation with little turmoil.

Customer: That sounds good to me. When can we start the installation?

Salesperson: Tomorrow. I'll bring a contract for you to have your people sign. It should take about three to four weeks after the contract is signed.

Customer: Good. What do I need to do right now?

Salesperson: If you'll arrange to clean the junk out of the corner, then we'll be ready. I'll order the equipment and have it moving so that we can be ready in about four weeks. What would be the best time to see you tomorrow?

Customer: Any time will be okay with me, Tim.

Salesperson: Swell, Petar. Thanks for your help. I know you will be pleased with this new installation and also save money. See you tomorrow.

QUESTIONS

1. Evaluate Tim's sales presentation. Include in your answer comments on his approach, presentation, use of trial closes, handling of objections, and his close.
2. How would you develop visual materials to illustrate Tim's sales presentation, including the arithmetic?
3. Now that Tim has sold to Petar, what should Tim do next?

CASE 9–3

DUMPING INVENTORY: SHOULD THIS BE PART OF YOUR PRESENTATION?

Ron Kapra is sales manager at Electra Toy Company, a retail toy store specializing in electronic games. Ron's brother-in-law, Jerry, works for the company that manufactures the Lasertron electronic game. Jerry mentioned to Ron that the company is coming out with the Lasertron II in three months. However, it will not be announced to retailers for another two months.

Lasertron II will have advanced technology over the present model. The new game cartridges will not be compatible with Lasertron I. Once Lasertron II comes on the market, consumers will want it and not the present model. Jerry explains that for any of the present models the retailer returns after the introduction of Lasertron II, the manufacturer will refund to the retailer the retailer's original cost of Lasertron I.

The Way to Make Extra Sales

Kapra has decided to run a special sale offering 20 percent off the regular price of Lasertron I. With 1,000 cases in stock, Ron wants to sell as many of the current models as possible to his customers. Then when the new model comes out, the same customers will come in and purchase Lasertron II. This will greatly increase sales, Ron feels.

Salesperson Is Unsure

Bill Corrington has been a top salesperson with Electra Toy for about two years. Although excited about the new model, Bill questions Ron's idea. Bill feels his customers trust him. If he sold them Lasertron now and the new model came out in a few months, customers would be upset with him. Bill feels this is no way to treat customers. However, Ron sees nothing wrong. "The loss of a few customers will be offset by the increase in sales," says Ron.

QUESTIONS

1. What are the ethical considerations, if any, in this case?
2. At what level of moral development are Ron and Bill operating in this business situation? Explain your answers.
3. What would you do if you were Ron?
4. What would you do if you were Bill?

Source: © PhotoAlto/Alamy Stock Photo

CHAPTER 10

Objections—Welcome Your Prospect's Concerns

Joseph Potter
Nova Scotia
Community College
Dartmouth, NS.

Source: Courtesy of Joseph Potter

A Sales Success Story

Joseph Potter graduated with a Business Administration and Marketing Diploma from Nova Scotia Community College (NSCC) in 2008. Before this, he had worked for Commercial Tent Rentals and Sales Limited as a part-time summer labourer. Joseph was presented with a career opportunity by the company, so he attended NSCC to earn his diploma. After graduation, he continued to work for Commercial Tent Rentals in sales, management, and operations roles, and is now the general manager in the company, having worked his way through the ranks.

Joseph comments, "I think sometimes in business we get a paper that says we trained in sales, and we become locked into that position and we can feel stuck. It is very evident to me and to my co-workers that I am much better suited for a role in management. I enjoy it more, and I believe being in this role is better not only for myself, but for the company. So I encourage anyone that is in a role, even though may have even studied for it, not to feel bound by that if other opportunities come up. An 18-year-old high school graduate likely doesn't know who they are and what they want to do until they are about 25 years old, and maybe even older." Obviously, starting in sales led to many managerial opportunities that were a great fit for Joseph.

"Interestingly enough," he says, "management and sales are similar in the sense that you're constantly dealing with people. In sales you are trying to please people with a product, and in management you're trying to please people with a positive work environment. In my current role as general manager, I oversee human resources, advise on sales, control expenditures, and give input into the operations of the company."

Joseph was drawn to this career originally by the "thrill of the sale." As he explains, "Sales are always a battle. Either I will win the sale, or the competition will win the sale. It is my competitive side that attracted me to sales."

Joseph's advice for aspiring salespeople?

- Keep in mind that not every day will be a selling day—there will be days with disappointments.
- Understand the importance of "knowing your stuff" and knowing the competition.
- Know how to sell service, not just the product.
- Be willing to go out of your way to meet your clients' requirements.
- Remember your customer's name, and make them remember yours (business cards are essential).
- Make your relationships as personal as possible, while keeping it professional.

MAIN TOPICS

Welcome Objections!

What Are Objections?

When Do Prospects Object?

Objections and the Sales Process

Six Major Categories of Objections

Techniques for Meeting Objections

After Meeting the Objection—What to Do?

Dealing with Difficult Customers

Negotiating a Win–Win Outcome

LEARNING OBJECTIVES

When you learn how to skilfully handle your prospect's questions, resistance, and objections, you are a professional. After studying this chapter, you should be able to:

LO1 Explain why you should welcome a prospect's objections.

LO2 Describe what to do when objections arise.

LO3 Discuss objections and the sales process.

LO4 Explain six major categories of objections.

LO5 List techniques for meeting objections.

LO6 Describe what to do after meeting an objection.

LO7 Understand how to deal with difficult customers.

LO8 Explain the process of negotiating with a win–win outcome.

FACING A SALES CHALLENGE

As you drive up into the parking lot of a top distributor of your home building supplies, you recall how only two years ago the company purchased the largest opening order you ever sold. Last year, their sales doubled, and this year you hope to sell them more than $100,000 worth.

As you wait, the receptionist informs you that since your last visit, your buyer, Mary Smalley, was fired and another buyer, Nonnie Young, was transferred to her position. Mary and you had become good friends over the past two years, and you hate to see her go.

As you enter the new buyer's office, Young asks you to have a seat and then says: "I've got some bad news for you. I'm considering switching suppliers. Your prices are too high."

What would you do in this situation? Salespeople commonly face challenges; in most presentations, they experience objections. How does a professional salesperson handle a difficult situation?

(Continued at end of chapter.)

This chapter examines objections. It discusses how to meet objections, techniques to use in overcoming objections, and how to proceed after addressing an objection. Professionals welcome objections!

LO1 Welcome Objections!

When a prospect first gives an objection, *smile,* because that's when you start earning your salary. You want to receive personal satisfaction from your job and at the same time increase your salary–right? Well, both occur when you accept objections as a challenge that, handled correctly, benefits both your prospect and you. The more effectively you meet customers' needs and solve their problems, the more successful you will be in sales. If you *fear* objections, you will *fumble* your response, which often causes *failure.*

Remember, although people want to buy, they do not want to be exploited. Buyers who cannot see how your offering will fulfill their needs ask questions and raise objections. If you cannot effectively answer the questions or meet the objections, you will not make the sale. It is *your* fault, not the buyer's fault, that the sale was not made if you sincerely believe your offering fulfills a need, but the prospect still will not buy. The salesperson who can overcome objections when they are raised and smoothly return to a presentation will succeed.

objection:
A statement by your buyer indicating resistance to your proposal.

sales objection:
The prospect's opposition or resistance to the sales person's information or request.

What Are Objections?

Interestingly, prospects who present **objections** often are easily sold on your product. They are interested enough to object; they want to know what you have to offer.

Opposition or resistance to information or to the salesperson's request is labelled a **sales objection**. Salespeople should welcome sales objections because they indicate prospect interest and help determine what stage the prospect has reached in the buying cycle–attention, interest, desire, conviction, or readiness to close.

LO2 When do Prospects Object?

The prospect may object at any time during your sales call–from introduction to close. Imagine walking into a retail store, carrying your materials, and the buyer yells out, "Oh no, not another salesperson. I don't even want to see you, let alone buy from you!" What do you say?

> *Objections can occur any time throughout the sales conversation.*

One salesperson said, "I understand. I'm not here to sell you anything, only to check your stock, help stock your shelves, and return any old or damaged merchandise for a refund." As the salesperson turned to walk away, the buyer said, "Come on back here; I want to talk to you."

If the salesperson had simply said OK, he would not have made that sale. The salesperson knew that he could benefit that customer, and his response and attitude showed it. The point is always to be ready to handle a prospect's objections, whether at the approach, during the presentation, after a trial close, after you have already met a previous objection, or during the close of the sale.

Objections and the Sales Process

LO3

Objections can occur at any time. Often, however, the prospect allows you to make a presentation, often asking questions along the way. Inexperienced salespeople traditionally finish their presentation and wait for the prospect's response.

Experienced, successful salespeople have learned to use the system shown in Exhibit 10.1. After the presentation, they use a trial close to determine the prospect's attitude toward the product and assess whether it is time to close.

Remember, the *trial close* asks for the prospect's opinion about what was said in the presentation. Typically, the trial close causes the prospect to ask questions or state objections. The salesperson should be prepared to respond in one of four ways:

1. If there is a positive response to the trial close immediately after the presentation, move to the close as shown in Exhibit 10.1, moving from Step 5 to Step 9.
2. If an objection is raised, understand or clarify it, respond to it, and attempt another trial close to see whether you have met the objection. If you have, then move to the close.
3. After meeting one objection, be prepared to determine whether there are other objections. You may have to move from Step 8 back to Step 6.
4. If, after responding to the objection and attempting a trial close, you have not overcome the objection, return to your presentation (Step 4) and further discuss the product relative to the objection.

To handle an objection effectively, a salesperson must be able to recognize the type, or category, of objection being raised by the buyer.

No matter what type of objections the prospect raises, certain basic points should be considered in order to meet them:

- Plan for objections.
- Anticipate and forestall.
- Handle objections as they arise.
- Be positive.
- Listen–hear them out.
- Understand objections.
- Meet the objection.

The salesperson can plan for each of these basic points for meeting objections.

EXHIBIT 10.1

When objections occur, quickly determine what to do.

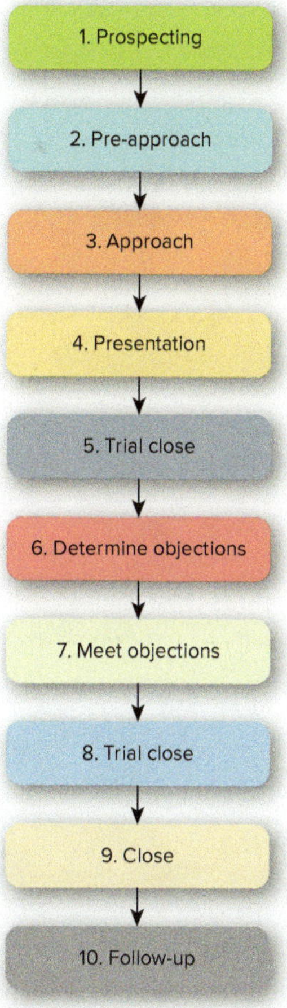

EXHIBIT 10.2

Prepare for objections.

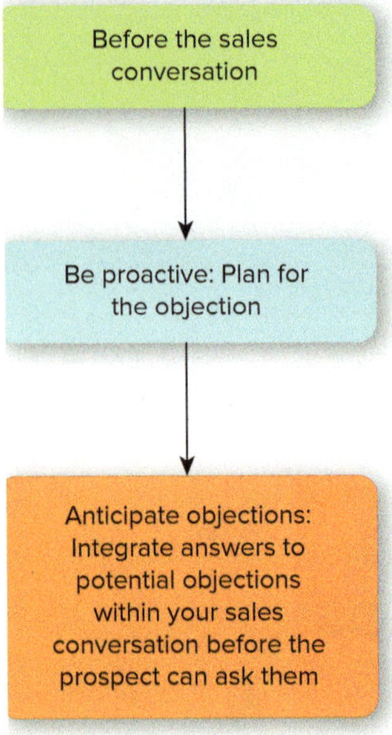

Plan for Objections

Plan for objections that your customer might raise, as shown in Exhibit 10.2. Consider not only the reasons that prospects should buy but why they should *not* buy. Structure your presentation to minimize the disadvantages of your product. Do not discuss disadvantages unless prospects raise them in the conversation.

After each sales call, review the prospect's objections. Divide them into major and minor objections. Then develop ways to overcome them. Your planning for and rehearsal of overcoming objections allows you to respond in a natural and positive manner. Planning for and review of the sales call allows you to anticipate and forestall objections.

> *Proactively plan for potential objections and how you will handle them.*

Anticipate and Forestall

Forestalling the objection has the salesperson discussing an objection before the prospect raises it. It often is better to forestall or discuss objections before they arise. The sales presentation can be developed to address anticipated objections directly.

> *Anticipate the objection: Consider discussing the buyer's potential concerns before they arise.*

For example, take an exterior house paint manufacturer's salesperson who learns that an unethical competitor is telling retail dealers that his paint starts to chip and peel after six months. Realizing the predicament, this salesperson develops a presentation that states, "Three independent testing laboratories have shown that this paint will not chip or peel for eight years after application." The salesperson has forestalled or answered the objection before it is raised by using a proof statement. This technique also can prevent a negative mood from entering the buyer–seller dialogue.

Another way to anticipate objections is to discuss disadvantages before the prospect does. Many products have flaws, and they sometimes surface as you try to make a sale. If you know of an objection that arises consistently, discuss it. If you acknowledge it first, you don't have to defend it.

On the other hand, a customer who has an objection feels compelled to defend that objection. For example, you might be showing real estate property. En route to the location you say, "You know, before we get out there, I just want to mention a couple of things. You're going to notice that it needs a little paint in a few places, and I noticed a couple of shingles on the roof the other day that you may have to replace." When you arrive, your customer may take a look and say, "Well, those shingles aren't so bad and we're going to paint it anyway." Yet, if you reached the house without a little prior warning of small defects, those items are often what a customer first notices.

A third way of using an anticipated objection is to brag about it and turn it into a sales benefit. A salesperson might say, "I want to mention something important before we go any further. Our price is more than our competitors' because our new software provides technology found in no other equipment. It will improve your operation and eliminate the costly repairs you are now experiencing. In just a minute, I want to fully discuss your investment. Let's first discuss the improvements we can provide. Take a look at this."

This takes the sting out of the price objection because you have discussed it. It is difficult for a buyer to come back and say, "It's too high," because you have mentioned that already. So, there are times when you can anticipate objections and use them advantageously.

SELLING TIPS

A STRATEGY FOR HANDLING OBJECTIONS

One of the biggest hurdles to success for salespeople is handling objections. Here is a strategy top salespeople use to draw out, understand, and overcome objections:

1. Plan for objections.
2. Anticipate and forestall objections when needed.
3. Handle objections as they arise.
4. Be positive.
5. Listen to objections—hear them out.
6. Understand objections—ask questions to clarify.
7. Meet the objection by selecting methods or techniques to use in responding to the objection.
8. Confirm that you have met the objection—use a trial close.
9. Where am I? Decide if you need to keep selling, handle another objection, or close the sale.

Handle Objections as They Arise

Very infrequently, situations arise in which it is best to postpone your answer to an objection. When the objection raised will be covered later in your presentation, or when you build to that point, pass over it for a while. However, the best practice is to meet objections as they arise; postponement may cause a negative mental picture or reaction such as these:

- The prospect may stop listening until you address the objection.
- The prospect may feel you are trying to hide something.
- You also feel it's a problem.
- You cannot answer because you do not know the answer or how to deal with this objection.
- It may appear that you are not interested in the prospect's opinion.

The objection could be the only item left before closing the sale. So, meet the objection, determine if you have satisfied the prospect, use another trial close to uncover other objections, and if there are no more objections, move toward closing the sale. Exhibit 10.3 (on the next page) gives some good examples on how to handle objections during the sales conversation.

Be Positive

When responding to an objection, use positive body language such as a smile. Strive to respond in a manner that keeps your prospect friendly and in a positive mood. Do not take the objection personally. Never treat the objection with hostility. Take the objection in stride by responding respectfully and showing sincere interest in your prospect's opinion.

> *Objections are a natural element of the sales process; all solutions will have drawbacks.*

At times, the prospect may raise objections based on incorrect information. Politely deny false objections. Be realistic; all products have drawbacks, even yours. If a competitor's product has a feature your product lacks, demonstrate the overriding benefits of your product.

EXHIBIT 10.3

Process for handling an objection.

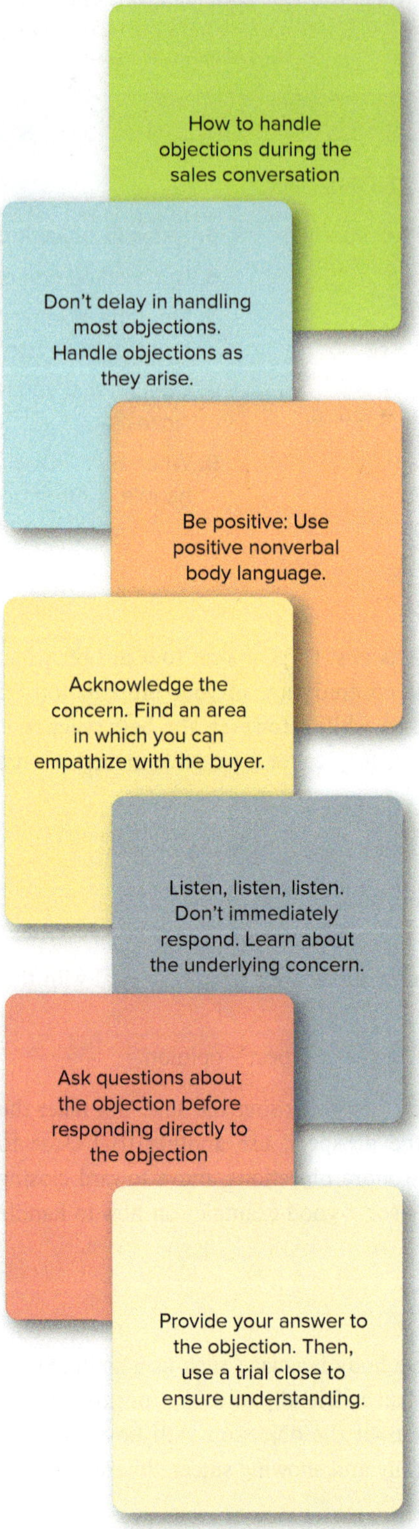

Example:
The buyer states, "Well I'm a little hesitant to stock the quantity you are suggesting, Normally, we sell approximately one-half of that amount of your competitor's product. I just don't feel comfortable in moving forward with this quantity." [Objection]

Example:
The salesperson nods and acknowledges positively the customer's concern. The salesperson's body position is open and emits green signals (i.e., positive nonverbal communication signs). Remember, the objection is a gift. It shows that the buyer is still engaged in the conversation.

Example:
The salesperson states, "I understand it is very important to align your inventory with your sales. It totally makes sound business sense." [Empathize with the buyer.]

Example:
The salesperson asks, "Can you share with me how often the competitor's product is supported with advertising and promotional initiatives?" [Ask question about objection before responding directly.]

Example:
The customer answers, "Actually, very rarely. In fact, only during the holidays." [Customer answer.]

Example:
Now with a better understanding of the concern, the salesperson answers the objection, "That makes sense, as the holidays are an important time. However, I'd like to show you our promotional calendar for our product. As you will note, we have five months of national advertising throughout the year. Additionally, we distribute coupons every four months to drive traffic into your store. As such, we will invest in marketing to ensure our product moves off your shelves and into your customer's shopping carts." [Answer the objective.]

"What are your thoughts on how this type of promotional plan could drive faster turnover of our product?" [Use a trial close to ensure you have reduced the customer's concern.]

Listen—Hear Them Out

Many salespeople leap on an objection before the other person has a chance to finish. The prospect barely says five words–and already the salesperson is hammering away as though the evil thing will multiply unless it's stomped out. "I have to prove he is mistaken, or he won't take the product" is a panicky reaction to the first hint of any objection.

Don't respond immediately. The key to handling objections is to LISTEN and then ASK QUESTIONS to understand the customer's perception.

Not only does the prospect feel irritated at being interrupted, but the prospect also feels pushed and uneasy. Your prospect will ask, "Why's he jumping on that so fast and so hard? I sense something is wrong." Suppose you run south when the prospect heads north, and you answer the wrong objection or even raise one that the prospect hadn't thought of?[1]

Understand Objections

When customers object, they do one of several things, as shown in Exhibit 10.4. They are requesting more information, setting a condition, or giving a genuine objection. The objection can be hopeless or true.

Request for Information

Many times, prospects appear to make objections when they are requesting more information. That is why it is important to listen. If prospects request more information, chances are that they are in the conviction stage. You have created a desire; they want the product, but they are not convinced that you have the best product or you are the best supplier. If you feel this may be the case, supply the requested information indirectly.

A Condition

At times, prospects may raise an objection that turns into a **condition of the sale**. They are saying, "If you can meet my request, I'll buy," or "Under certain conditions, I will buy from you."

condition of the sale: a situation wherein an objection becomes a condition of the sale, such that if the condition is met the prospect will buy.

If you sense that the objection is a condition, quickly determine if you can help the prospect meet it. If you cannot, close the interview politely. Take the following real estate example:

Prospect: It's a nice house, but the price is too high. I can't afford a $2,000-a-month house payment. [You do not know if this is an objection or a condition.]

Salesperson: I know what you mean [acknowledging the prospect's viewpoint]. If you don't mind my asking, what is your monthly salary?

Prospect: My take-home pay is $2,700 a month.

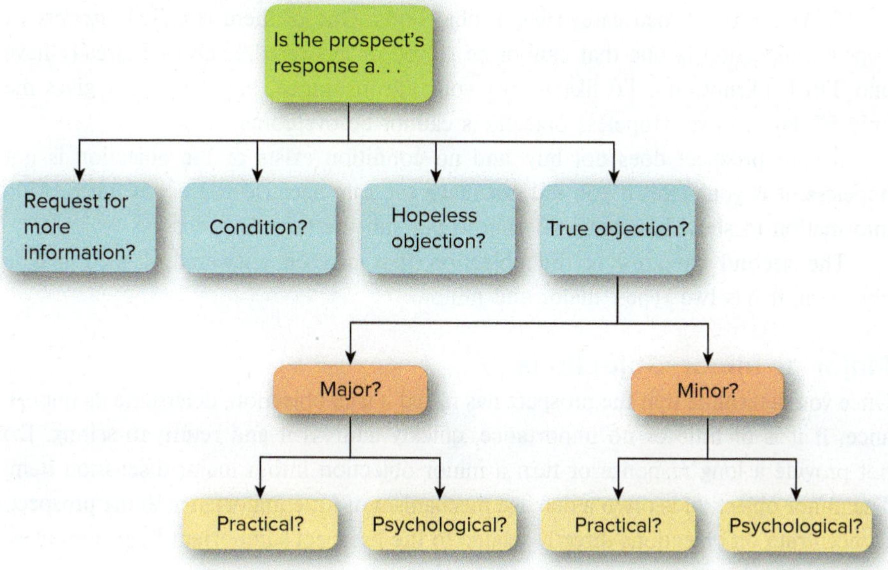

EXHIBIT 10.4
What does a prospect mean by an objection?

In this case, the prospect has set a condition on the purchase that cannot be met by the salesperson realistically; it is not an objection. Continuing the exchange by bargaining would waste time and possibly anger the prospect. Now that the prospect's income is known, the salesperson can show a house in the prospect's price range.

negotiation: The act of reaching an agreement mutually satisfactory to both buyer and seller.

Negotiation can overcome a condition. Often, conditions stated by the prospect are overcome through negotiation between buyer and seller. **Negotiation** refers to reaching an agreement mutually satisfactory to both buyer and seller. Prospects may say things like, "I'll buy your equipment if you can deliver it in one month instead of three," or "If you'll reduce your price by 10 percent, I'll buy."

If you determine that this type of statement is a condition rather than an objection, through negotiation you may make the sale with further discussion and an eventual compromise between you and the buyer. In the example above, you might ask the manufacturing plant if equipment can be shipped to the prospect in two months instead of three. This arrangement may be acceptable to the prospect. You may have a current customer who has that piece of equipment but is not using it. You might arrange for the prospect to lease it from your customer for three months.

> *"Seek first to understand, then to be understood."*
>
> *STEPHEN COVEY*

If the prospect sets a price condition saying, "I will buy your product only if you reduce your price by 10 percent," determine if your company will reduce the price if the buyer will purchase a larger quantity. Consider this example. As a provincially funded school, George Brown College purchased much of its office equipment on a bid system. The Lenovo salesperson could not sell a certain type of computer hardware to the Marketing Department because the cost of a single machine was too high for the department's budget. The department wanted the machine; however, it could not afford it. Instead of giving up, the salesperson went to other departments in the college and found a need for a total of 16 machines (at a lower price of $4,000 per unit, less than the price of one machine). Lenovo could lower the price substantially because of the large number of machines purchased. The salesperson determined that price was a condition, found a way to overcome the condition, and made the sale. Through initiation and inquiry, a potentially lost sale became a multiple victory beneficial to all parties.

There are two broad categories of objections. One of them is called *hopeless.* A hopeless objection is one that cannot be solved or answered, such as I already have one, I'm bankrupt, and I'd like to buy your life insurance, but the doctor gives me only 30 days to live. Hopeless objections cannot be overcome.

If your prospect does not buy, and no condition exists or the objection is not hopeless, it is your fault if you did not make the sale because you could not provide information to show how your offering would suit the buyer's needs.

The second category is the objection that can be answered. Called a true objection, it has two types: major and minor.

Major or Minor Objections

Once you determine that the prospect has raised a true objection, determine its importance. If it is of little or no importance, quickly address it and return to selling. Do not provide a long response or turn a minor objection into a major discussion item. The minor objection is often a defence mechanism of little importance to the prospect. Concentrate on objections directly related to the prospect's important buying motives.

Practical or Psychological Objections

Objections, minor or major, can be **practical (overt) objections** or **psychological (hidden) objections** in nature. Exhibit 10.5 gives some examples. A real objection is tangible, such as a high price. If this is a real objection, and the prospect says so, you can show that your product is of high quality and worth the price, or you might suggest removing some optional features and reducing the price. As long as the prospect states the real objection to purchasing the product clearly, you should be able to answer the objection.

practical objection: An overt objection based on real or concrete causes.

psychological objection: A hidden objection based on the prospect's attitudes.

PRACTICAL	PSYCHOLOGICAL
• Price • Product is not needed • Prospect has an overstock of your or your competitor's products • Delivery schedules • Level of profitability • Ability to integrate the solution into current processes • Ability of solution to meet buyer's goals	• Resistance to spending money • Resistance to domination • Predetermined beliefs • Negative image of salespeople • Dislikes making a buying decision • Resistance to change • Concerned with how others in the organization will perceive the decision

EXHIBIT 10.5
Examples of objections.

However, prospects do not always clearly state their objections. Rather, they often give some excuse why they are not ready to make a purchase, which conceals real objections. Usually, the prospect cannot purchase the product until hidden objections are rectified. You must uncover a prospect's hidden objections and eliminate them.

Meet the Objection

Once you fully understand the objection, you are ready to respond to the prospect. How to respond depends on the objection. Over the course of a year, salespeople will hear hundreds of objections. Prospects object to various items in different ways.

Generally, objections fall into six categories. By grouping objections, you can better plan how to respond. Let's examine these six categories and discuss specific techniques for meeting objections.

Six Major Categories of Objections

LO4

Most objections that salespeople encounter are placed into the six categories shown in Exhibit 10.6. Each category represents a different area of concern or disagreement. When the buyer raises an objection, the salesperson must be able to mentally identify its category. Only then can they respond appropriately to the objection and address the buyer's true reason for resistance. Knowing ahead of time how you will handle these objections will help you become a better salesperson by improving your image as a problem solver.

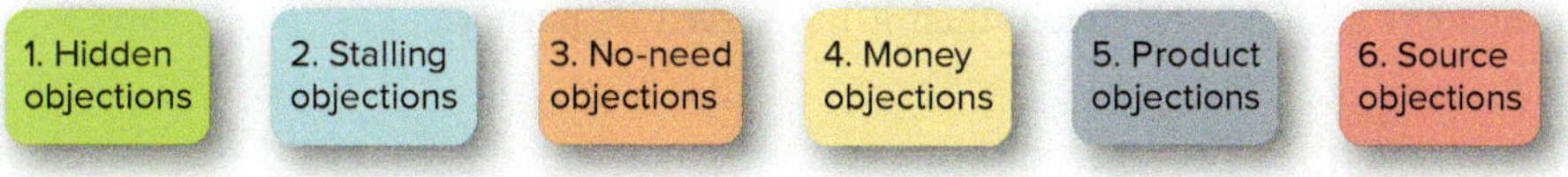

EXHIBIT 10.6
Six major categories of objections.

The Hidden Objection

hidden objection: An objection that disguises the actual objection either with silence or triviality.

Prospects who ask trivial, unimportant questions or conceal their feelings beneath a veil of silence have **hidden objections**. They do not discuss their true objections to a product because they may feel they cannot trust you, they are afraid objections will offend you, or they may not feel your sales call is worthy of their full attention.

Such prospects may have a good conversation with you without revealing their true feelings. You have to ask questions and carefully listen to know which questions to ask in order to reveal their true objections to your product. Learning how to determine what questions to ask a prospect and how to ask them are skills developed by conscious effort over time. Your ability to ask probing questions improves with each sales call if you try to develop this ability.

Smoke Out Hidden Objections

With prospects who are unwilling to discuss their objections or who may not know why they are reluctant to buy, be prepared to smoke out objections by asking questions. Do what you can to reveal the objections. Consider the following questions:

- What are the major benefits you need in order to move forward?
- What causes you to say that?
- Let's consider this, suppose my product would [do what prospect wants] . . . then would you consider it?
- Tell me, what's really on your mind?
- Can you lead me through your decision process?

> *"Every adversity carries with it the seed of an equivalent or greater benefit."*
>
> *NAPOLEON HILL*

Uncovering hidden objections is not always easy. Observe the prospect's tone of voice, facial expressions, and physical movements. Pay close attention to what the prospect is saying. You may have to read between the lines occasionally to find the buyer's true objections. All these factors will help you discover whether objections are real or simply an excuse to cover a hidden objection.

Prospects may not know consciously what their real objections are. Sometimes they claim that the price of a product is too high. In reality, they may be reluctant to spend money on anything. If you attempt to show that your price is competitive, the real objection remains unanswered and no sale results. Remember, you cannot convince anyone to buy until you understand what a prospect needs to be convinced of.

If, after answering all apparent questions, the prospect is still not sold, you might subtly attempt to uncover the hidden objection. Consider asking the prospect what the real objection is. Direct inquiry should be used as a last resort because it indirectly may amount to calling the prospect a liar, but if it is used carefully, it may enable the salesperson to reveal the prospect's true objection. Smoking out hidden objections is an art form skillful salespeople develop over time. Using it successfully can greatly increase sales. This approach should be used carefully, but if it enables the salesperson to uncover a hidden objection, then it has served its purpose.

The Stalling Objection

When your prospect says, "I'll think it over," or "I'll be ready to buy on your next visit," you must determine whether the statement is the truth or whether it is a smokescreen designed to get rid of you. The **stalling objection** is a common tactic.

stalling objection: An objection that delays the presentation or the sale.

What you discovered in developing your customer profile and customer benefit plan can aid you in determining how to handle this type of objection. Suppose that before seeing a certain retail customer, you checked the supply of your merchandise both in the store's stockroom and on the retail shelf and this occurs:

Buyer: I have enough merchandise for now. Thanks for coming by.

Salesperson: Ms. Marcher, you have 50 cases in the warehouse and on display. You sell 50 cases each month, right?

You have legitimately questioned the wisdom of stalling. This buyer either has to order more merchandise from you or tell you why she is allowing her product supply to dwindle. An easily handled stall is illustrated in Exhibit 10.7. When the prospect says, "I'm too busy to see you now," you might ask, "When would be a good time to come back today?"

One of the toughest stalls to overcome arises in selling a new consumer product. Retail buyers are reluctant to stock consumer goods that customers have not yet asked for, even new goods produced by large, established consumer product manufacturers.

Another common stall is the alibi that your prospect must have approval from someone else, such as a boss, buying committee, purchasing agent, or home office. Since the buyer's attitude toward purchasing your product influences the firm's buying decision, it is important to determine the buyer's attitude toward your product.

When the buyer stalls by saying, "I will have to get approval from my boss," you can counter by saying, "If you had the authority, you would go ahead with the purchase, wouldn't you?" If the answer is yes, chances are that the buyer will positively influence the firm's buying decision. If not, you must uncover the real objections. Otherwise, you will not make the sale.

An additional response to the "I've got to think it over" stall is, "What are some of the issues you have to think about?" Or you may focus directly on the prospect's stall by saying, "Would you share with me some things that hold you back?"

Sometimes, the prospect will not answer the question. Instead, the response is, "Oh, I just need to get an opinion." You can follow up with a multiple-choice question such as, "Will you explore whether this is a good purchase in comparison to a competitor's product or do you wonder about the financing?" This helps display an attitude of genuine caring.

As with any response to an objection, communicate a positive attitude. Do not become demanding, defensive, or hostile. Otherwise, your nonverbal expressions may signal a defensive attitude–reinforcing the prospect's defences.

EXHIBIT 10.7

Imagine walking up to your prospect, who says, "I'm too busy to see you now." What would you say?

Source: ©Huntstock.com/Shutterstock

SELLING TIPS

STALLING OBJECTIONS

A. I have to think this over.

1. Let's think about it now while it is fresh in your mind. What are some of the items you need to know more about?
2. I understand that you want more time to think. I would be interested in hearing your thoughts about the reasons for and the reasons against buying now.
3. You and I have been thinking this over since the time we first met. You know that this is a terrific opportunity, you like the product, and you know it will save you money. Right? [If prospect says yes:] Let's go ahead now!

B. I'm too busy.

1. I appreciate how busy you are. When could we visit for just a few minutes? [Stop or add a benefit for seeing you.]

C. I'm too busy. Talk to first.

1. Do they have the authority to approve the purchase? [If prospect says yes:] Thank you. I'll tell them you sent me. [If prospect says no:] Well, then why should I talk with them?
2. We almost never deal with purchasing managers. This is an executive-level decision. I need to talk with you.

D. I plan to wait until [future time].

1. Why?
2. Some of my best customers said that. Once they bought, they were sorry they had waited.
3. You promise me you will buy this fall? [If prospect says yes, then:]
   a. Okay, let's finalize the order today and I'll have it ready to arrive October 1.
   b. Great! Should I call you in September or October so we can set it up?
4. What if I could arrange for it to be shipped to you now but you didn't have to pay for it until the fall?

Your goal in dealing with a stall is to help prospects realistically examine reasons for and against buying now. If you are absolutely sure it is not in their best interest to buy now, tell them so. They will respect you for it. You will feel good about yourself. The next time you see these customers, they will be more trusting and open with you.

However, the main thing to remember is not to be satisfied with a false objection or a stall. Tactfully pursue the issue until you have unearthed the buyer's true feelings about your product. If this does not work, (1) present the benefits of using your product now; (2) if there is a special price deal, mention it; and (3) if there is a penalty for delay, mention it. Bring out any or all of your main selling benefits and keep on selling!

The No-Need Objection

The prospect says, "Sounds good. I really like what you had to say, and I know you have a good product, but I'm not interested now. Our present product (or supply or merchandise) works well. We will stay with it." Standing up to conclude the interview, the prospect says, "Thanks very much for coming by." This type of objection can disarm an unwary salesperson.

no-need objection: An objection in which the prospect declares he or she does not need the product and implies the end of the selling effort but that may actually be either a hidden or a stalling objection.

The **no-need objection** is used widely because it politely gets rid of the salesperson. Some salespeople actually unwittingly encourage it by making a poor sales presentation. They allow prospects to sit and listen to a sales pitch without motivating them to participate by showing true concern and asking questions. Therefore, when the presentation is over, prospects can say quickly, "Sounds good, but . . . ." In essence, they say no, making it difficult for the salesperson to continue the call. Although not always a valid objection, the no-need response strongly implies the end of a sales call.

The no-need objection is especially tricky because it also may include a stall. If your presentation was a solo performance or a monologue, your prospect might be indifferent to you and your product, having tuned out halfway through the second act. Aside from departing with a "Thanks for your time," you might resurrect your presentation by asking questions.

SELLING TIPS

NO-NEED OBJECTIONS

A. I'm not interested.

1. May I ask why?
2. You are not interested now or forever?
3. I wouldn't be interested if I were you, either. However, I know you'll be interested when you hear about. . . . It is very exciting! [If prospect still says no:] When would be a better time to talk?
4. Some of my best customers first said that until they discovered . . . [state benefits].
5. You are not interested? Then who should I talk to who would be interested in . . . [state benefits].

B. The . . . we have is still good.

1. Good compared to what?
2. I understand how you feel. Many of my customers said that before they switched over. However, they saw that this product would . . . [discuss benefits of present product or service versus what you are selling].
3. That's exactly why you should buy—to get a good trade now.
4. What stops you from buying?

C. We are satisfied with what we have now.

1. Satisfied in what way?
2. What do you like most about what you have right now? [Then compare to your product.]
3. I know how you feel. Often we're satisfied with something because we have no chance (or don't have the time) to compare it with something better. I've studied what you are using and would like a few minutes to compare products and show you how to . . . [state benefits].
4. Many of our customers were happy with what they had before they saw our product. There are three reasons they switched . . . [state three product benefits].

The Money Objection

money objection: A price-oriented objection.

The **money objection** encompasses several forms of economic concerns: I have no money, I don't have that much money, it costs too much, or your price is too high. These objections are simple for the buyer to say, especially in a recessionary economy.

Often, prospects want to know the product's price before the presentation, and they will not want you to explain how the product's benefits outweigh its costs. Price is a real consideration and must be discussed, but it is risky to discuss product price until it can be compared to product benefits. If you successfully postpone the price discussion, you must eventually return to it because your prospect seldom forgets it. Some prospects are so preoccupied with price that they give minimal attention to your presentation until the topic re-emerges. Other prospects falsely present price as their main objection to your product, which conceals the true objection.

Many salespeople think that offering the lowest price gives them a greater chance of sales success. Generally, this is not the case. Once you realize this, you can become even more successful. You might even state that your product is not the least expensive one available because of its benefits and advantages and the satisfaction it provides. Once you convey this concept to your buyer, price becomes a secondary factor that usually can be handled successfully.

By observing nonverbal signals, asking questions, listening, and positively responding to the price question when it arises, you can easily handle price-oriented objections. Do not be afraid of price as an objection; be ready for it and welcome it. Quote the price and keep on selling. It is usually the inexperienced salesperson who makes this often minor objection into a major one. If the price objection becomes major, prospects can become excited and overreact to your price. The end result is the loss of the sale. If prospects overreact, slow down the conversation; let them talk it out and slowly present product benefits as related to cost.

One way to view the money objection concerns the price/value formula.

SELLING TIPS

MONEY OBJECTIONS

A. Your price is too high.

1. Compared to what?
2. How much did you think it would cost?
3. We can lower the price right now, but we need to decide what options to cut from our proposal. Is that what you really want to do?
4. Our price is higher than the competition's. However, we have the best value [now explain].
5. How high is too high?
6. If it were cheaper, would you want it?

B. I can't afford it.

1. Why?
2. If I could show you a way to afford this purchase, would you be interested?
3. I sincerely believe that you cannot afford not to buy this. The benefits far outweigh the price. Right?
4. You cannot afford to be without it! The cost of not having it is greater than the cost of having it. Think of all the business you can lose, the productivity you can lose, and that lost income from not having the latest, best, and most reliable technology. You'll love it! You'll wonder how you've done without it! Let's discuss how you can afford it—okay?
5. Do you mean you can't afford it now or forever?

C. Give me a 10 percent discount and I'll give you an order today.

1. I always quote my best price.
2. If you give me an order for 10, 1 can give you a 10 percent discount. Would you like to order 10?
3. [Prospect's name], we build your product up to a certain quality and service standard—not down to a certain price. We could produce a lower-priced item, but our experience shows it isn't worth it. This is a proven product that gives 100 percent satisfaction— not 90 percent.

D. You've got to do better than that.

1. Why?
2. What do you mean by *better?*
3. Do you mean a longer service warranty? A lower price? Extended delivery? Tell me exactly what you want.

The Price/Value Formula

The price objection is a bargaining tool for a savvy buyer who wants to ensure the best, absolutely lowest price. However, often there is more to it than shrewd bargaining.

If the buyer is merely testing to be sure the best possible price is on the table, it's a strong buying signal. But perhaps the prospect sincerely believes the price is too high. Let's define why one buyer might already be convinced the product is a good deal–a fair price–but is just testing to make sure it's the best price, while another buyer may sincerely believe the asking price is more than the goods are worth.

Remember that cost is what concerns the buyer, not just the price. Cost is arrived at in the buyer's mind by considering what is received compared to the money paid. In other words, price divided by value equals cost:

$$\frac{\text{Price}}{\text{Value}} = \text{Cost}$$

In this price/value formula, the value is what the prospects see the product doing for them and/or their company. *Value* is the total package of benefits you have built for the prospect. Value is the solution you provide to the buyer's problems.

The price will not change. The company sets that price at headquarters. The company has arrived at the price–based on costs, competition, and other salient factors. It is a fair price, and it's not going to change. So, the only thing to change is the prospect's perception of the value. For example, assume the buyer viewed the cost as follows:

$$\frac{\text{Price } 100}{\text{Value } 90} = \text{Cost } 1.11$$

The price is too high. You have to solve the prospect's problem with the product by translating product benefits into what it will do for the buyer. You have to build up the value:

$$\frac{\text{Price } 100}{\text{Value } 110} = \text{Cost } 0.90$$

The price/value formula is not the answer to "Your price is too high." It is only a description of the buyer's thinking process and an explanation of why the so-called price objection is heard so often. It tells us what we must do to answer the price objection.

Remember, at one extreme, the buyer may be sold on the product and simply testing to see if there is an extra discount. At the other extreme, the buyer may not see any benefit in the product or service but see only the price. When this is the case, "it costs too much" is a legitimate objection to be overcome by translating features into advantages into benefits for the buyer.

The Product Objection

All salespeople encounter **product objections** that relate directly to the product. Not everyone likes the best-selling product on the market. At times, most buyers have fears over risks associated with buying a product–they are afraid that the product will not

product objection: An objection relating directly to the product.

SELLING TIPS

PRODUCT OBJECTIONS

A. Your competitor's product is better.

1. You're kidding! [Act surprised.]
2. Better in what way? [Have customer list features liked in the other product; then show how your product has the same or better features.]
3. I'm interested in hearing your unbiased opinion of the two products.
4. You've had a chance to look at their product. What did you see that impressed you?
5. Are you referring to quality, service, features, or the product's value after five years of use?

B. The machine we have is still good.

1. I understand how you feel. Many of my customers said that before they switched over. However, they found that the reason a new model makes an old model obsolete is not that the old one is bad but that the new one is so much more efficient and productive. Would you like to take a look at what these businesses found?
2. That's exactly why you should trade now. Since your machine is still good, you still have a high trade-in value. When it breaks down, your trade-in value will go down, too. It's less expensive to trade in a workable machine than to wait for it to fail.

C. I'll buy a used one.

1. When you buy a used product, you take a high risk. You buy something that someone else has used and probably abused. Do you want to pay for other people's mistakes?
2. You may save a few dollars on your monthly payments, but you'll have to pay much more in extra service, more repairs, and downtime. Which price would you rather pay?
3. Many of our customers thought about a used product before they decided to buy a new one. Let me show you why they decided that new equipment is the best buy. The cost comparisons will make it clear.
4. I understand you want to save money. I like to save money. But, you have to draw the line somewhere. Buying a used product in this field is like shopping for a headache. Perhaps you should consider the smaller model for starters. At least you won't have any worries about its reliability!

D. I don't want to take risks.

1. You feel it's too risky? We rarely hear that. What do you mean by *risky*?
2. You feel that this is risky compared to what?
3. What could we do to make you feel more secure?
4. [Prospect's name], it may be more risky for you not to buy. What is the price you may pay for low productivity in your plant?

EXHIBIT 10.8

Imagine that this customer says, "I like your proposal but we are happy with our present supplier." What would you say?

Source: © Yuri Arcurs/Dreamstime.com/GetStock.com

do what the salesperson says it will do, or that the product is not worth either the time and energy required to use it or the actual cost.

You also sell against competition. The prospect either already uses a competitive product, has used one, would like to use one, has heard of one, or knows people who have used one. Your reaction to a product must use a positive tone. The use of guarantees, testimonials, independent research results, and demonstrations helps counter the product objection.

The Source Objection

The **source objection** is the last major category of objections typically faced by salespeople. Source objections relate to loyalty to a present supplier or salesperson (see Exhibit 10.8). Also, the prospect may not like you or your company.

Prospects often discuss their like for a present supplier or salesperson. They may tell you that they do not like your company. Seldom, however, will someone directly say, "I don't want to do business with you."

source objection: A loyalty-related objection by which the prospect states a preference for another company or salesperson, and may specify a dislike for the salesperson's company or the salesperson.

Usually, handling a source objection requires calling on the prospect routinely over a period. It takes time to break this resistance barrier. Get to know the prospect and the prospect's needs. Show your true interest. Do not try to get all the business at once–go for a trial run, a small order. It is important to learn exactly what bothers the prospect.

SELLING TIPS

SOURCE OBJECTIONS

A. I'm sorry; we won't buy from you.

1. Why not?
2. You must have a reason for feeling that way. May I ask what it is?
3. Are you not going to buy from us now or forever?
4. What could we do to win your business in the future?
5. Is there anyone else in your company who might be interested in buying our cost-saving products? Who?
6. I respect the fact you aren't buying from us this one time. However, I suspect that as you hear more about our fantastic products in the news and from customers, you will buy something from us in the future. Do you mind if I stop by periodically to update you on our new products?
7. Would you like to work with someone else in our company?
8. Is there anything about me that prevents you from doing business with our company?

B. I want to work with a more established company. We've done business with . . . for five years. Why should I change?

1. I understand how safe you feel with a relationship that goes back five years. And yet, I saw your eyes light up when you looked at our products. I can see that you're giving serious consideration to diversity. Just out of curiosity, could we compare the pros and cons of the two choices? Let's take a piece of paper and list the reasons for and against buying from us. The first reason against us is that we haven't worked with you for the past five years. What are some reasons for giving us a chance to prove ourselves?
2. I can only say good things about my competitor, and if I were you, I would go with him or her—unless, of course, you want a better product at a better price.

Techniques for Meeting Objections

LO5

Having uncovered all objections, a salesperson must answer them to the prospect's satisfaction. We highly suggest using the technique of empathizing, listening, asking questions, answering the concern, and using a trial close. However, different situations require different techniques; several techniques are presented in the following sections. In some situations you may be able to integrate multiple techniques. Again, it is important to adapt the technique to the situation and the customer. Techniques used by salespeople include:

1. Let a third-party answer.
2. Ask questions to smoke out objections.
3. Rephrase an objection as a question.
4. Compensate for the objection.
5. Boomerang the objection.
6. Postpone the objection.
7. Dodge the objection.
8. Pass up the objection.
9. Indirectly deny the objection.
10. Directly deny the objection.

Let a Third Party Answer

An effective technique for responding to an objection is to answer it by giving a **third-party answer** such as data, evidence statement, or someone else's experience as your proof of testimony. Salespeople use a wide range of evidence statements today. Therefore, it's important to be prepared to present a range of evidence, including case studies, market data, white papers, research from industry thought-leaders, and the customer's sales data. You might respond to a question in this way: "I'm glad you asked. Here is what our research has shown," or, "Government tests have shown," or, "You know, my best customer brought that point up before making the purchase . . . but was completely satisfied." These are examples of evidence statement formats. If you use a person or a company's name, be sure to obtain their approval first.

third-party answer: The technique of responding to an objection with testimony from authoritative sources.

Providing buyers the necessary information to make a decision can frequently overcome objections. A wide range of data can provide information to overcome buyers' objections. For example, Frito-Lay salesperson June Steward frequently uses her laptop to show buyers their past purchases of products and to project future sales. Using his laptop computer while in the buyer's office, Fisher Electronic's salesperson John Berry checks with his warehouse daily on available products and shipment schedules. Merrill Lynch salesperson Sandy Lopez uses software to display her client's present investments, past earnings, and recommendations on how much money should be put into stock and bond mutual funds.

Technology can be incorporated easily into most, if not all, of the techniques for meeting objections. Anytime you need to provide information to buyers, you can create a technological method of presenting data in an accurate and dramatic manner.

Secondary data or experiences, especially from a reliable or reputable source, are successful with the expert or skeptical prospect. If, after hearing secondary testimony, the prospect is still unsure about the product, one successful equipment salesperson asks the buyer to contact a current user directly:

Salesperson: I still haven't answered your entire question, have I?

Buyer: Not really.

Salesperson: Let's do this. Here is a list of several people (or companies and their buying representatives) currently using our product. Would you be willing to contact them *right now* and ask them that same question? They have used our product for several years and are willing to share their candid opinions with you.

A salesperson should use this version of the third-party technique only when certain that the prospect is still unsatisfied with how an objection has been handled, and that positive evidence or proof will probably clinch the sale. This dramatic technique allows the salesperson to impress a prospect. It also shows a flattering willingness to go to great lengths to validate a claim.

Ask Questions to Smoke Out Objections

Intelligent questioning impresses a prospect in several ways. Technical questions show a prospect that a salesperson knows the business. Questions relating to a prospect's particular business show that a salesperson is concerned more with the prospect's needs than with just making a sale. Finally, people who ask **intelligent questions**, whether they know much about the product, the prospect's business, or life in general, are often admired. Buyers are impressed with the sales professional who knows what to ask and when to ask it. Examples of questions are

intelligent questions: Questions relating to a prospect's business that show the salesperson's concern for the prospect's needs.

Prospect: This house is not as nice as the one someone else showed us yesterday.

Salesperson: Would you tell me why?

or

Prospect: This product does not have the [feature].

Salesperson: If it did have [feature], would you be interested?

[This example is an excellent questioning technique to determine if the objection is a smoke screen, a major or minor objection, or a practical or psychological objection. If the prospect says no to the response, you know the feature was not important.]

or

Prospect: I don't like your price.

Salesperson: Will you base your decision on price or on the product offered you . . . at a fair price?

[If the prospect says "Price," show how benefits outweigh costs. If the decision is based on the product, you have eliminated the price objection.]

Five-Question Sequence Method of Overcoming Objections

Buyers state objections for numerous reasons. From time to time, all salespeople sense that a buyer will not buy. As you gain sales experience, you will be able to feel it. It may be the buyer's facial expressions or a tone of voice that tips you off. When this occurs, find out quickly why a prospect doesn't want to buy. To do this, consider using a preplanned series of questions as shown in Exhibit 10.9.

Let's assume you have finished the presentation. You try to close the sale and see that the buyer will not go further in the conversation. What do you do? Consider using the following **five-question sequence**.

five-question sequence: The five-step process of overcoming objections in which facts, logic, and tact are used.

First, use this question: *"There must be some good reason why you're hesitating to go ahead now; do you mind if I ask what it is?"* When the buyer states a reason or an objection, immediately double-check the objection with one more question by using question number two: *"In addition to that, is there any other reason for not going ahead?"* The buyer may give the real reason for not buying, or the buyer may give the original objection. No matter what the customer says, you have created a condition for buying.

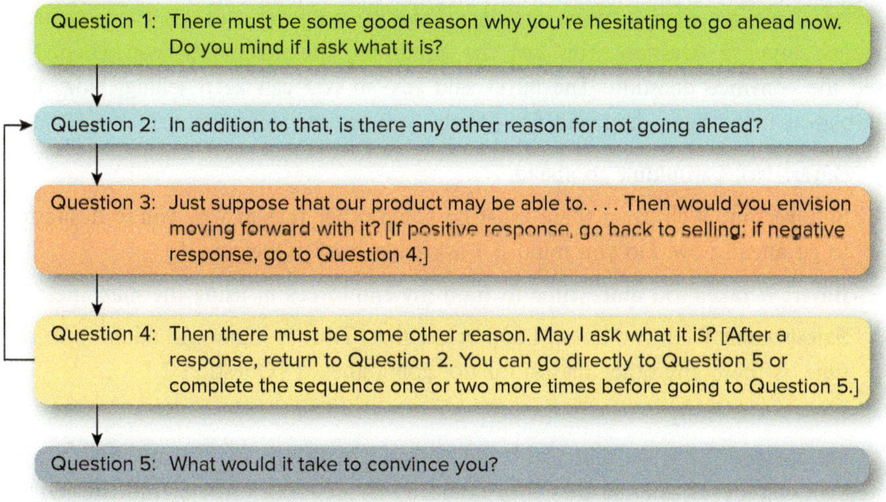

EXHIBIT 10.9

Five-question sequence method to overcome objection.

> *"Just suppose you could convince yourself that. . . . Then would you want to go ahead with it?"*

Now, use question number three, a "just suppose" question: *"Just suppose you could. . . . Then you'd want to go ahead?"* If the answer is yes, discuss how you can do what is needed. If you receive a negative response, use question number four: *"Then there must be some other reason. May I ask what it is?"* Respond with question number two again. Then ask, *"Just suppose. . . . You'd want to go ahead?"* If you receive another negative response, use question number five by saying, *"What would it take to convince you?"*

What often happens will surprise you. The buyer often will say, "Oh, I don't know. I guess I'm convinced. Go ahead and ship it to me." Or, you might be asked to go back over some part of your presentation. The important point is that this series of questions keeps the conversation going and reveals the real objections, which increases your sales. Imagine you are the salesperson in this example:

Salesperson: Should we ship the product to you this week or next?

Buyer: Neither; see me on your next trip. I'll have to think about it.

Salesperson: You know, there must be some good reason why you're hesitating to go ahead now. Would you mind if I asked what it is? [Question 1.]

Buyer: Too much money.

Salesperson: Too much money. Well, you know, I appreciate the fact that you want to get the most for your money. In addition to the money, is there any other reason for not going ahead? [Question 2.]

Buyer: No.

Salesperson: Well, suppose that you could convince yourself that the savings from this machine would mean it pays for itself in just a few months, and that we could fit it into your budget. Then you'd want to go ahead with it? [Question 3.]

Buyer: Yes, I would.

Next, return to selling by discussing the return on investment and affordable payment terms. You went from the first objection to the double-check question.

(*"In addition to the money, is there any other reason for not going ahead?"*) Then, you used the just suppose question. You met the condition, the machine's cost. Then, you used the convince question. The buyer said yes, so you can keep selling. Now, let's role-play as if the buyer had said no. (Again, you are the salesperson.)

Buyer: No, I wouldn't go ahead.

Salesperson: Well, then there must be some other reason why you're hesitating to go ahead now. Do you mind if I ask what it is? [Question 4.]

Buyer: It takes too much time to train my employees in using the machine.

Salesperson: Well, you know, I appreciate that. Time is money. In addition to the time, is there any other reason for not going ahead? [Question 2.]

Buyer: Not really.

Salesperson: Suppose that you could convince yourself that this machine would save employees time so that they could do other things. You'd find the money then, wouldn't you? [Question 3.]

Buyer: I'm not sure. [Another potential negative response.]

Salesperson: Money and time are important to you, right?

Buyer: Yes, they are.

Salesperson: What would it take for me to convince you that this machine will save you time and money? [Question 5.]

Now you have to get a response. The buyer has to set the condition. You, as the salesperson, are uncovering the real needs. The buyer is answering the questions. Remember, you want to help the person buy. When you get an objection, it tells you what you must do to make the sale happen. So do not fear objections; welcome them!

Rephrase an Objection as a Question

rephrasing question: A question whereby the salesperson rephrases what the prospect has said in order to clarify meaning and determine the prospect's needs.

Since it is easier to answer a question than to overcome an objection, counter an objection with a **rephrasing question** when you can do so naturally. Most objections are easily rephrased. Exhibit 10.10 presents examples of several procedures for rephrasing an objection as a question. Each procedure, except when the objection is based on a bad previous experience with the product by the prospect, has the same first three steps: (1) acknowledging the prospect's viewpoint, (2) rephrasing the objection into a question, and (3) obtaining agreement on the question.

EXHIBIT 10.10

Examples of rephrasing objections as questions.

FACTS ARE INCORRECT	FACTS ARE INCOMPLETE	FACTS ARE CORRECT	BASED ON BAD PERSONAL EXPERIENCE
• Acknowledge prospect's viewpoint. • Rephrase objection. • Obtain agreement. • Answer question providing information supported by evidence—a third party. • Ask for prospect's present viewpoint. • Return to selling sequence.	• Acknowledge prospect's viewpoint. • Rephrase objection. • Obtain agreement. • Answer question by providing complete facts. • Ask for prospect's present viewpoint. • Return to selling sequence.	• Acknowledge prospect's viewpoint. • Rephrase objection. • Obtain agreement. • Answer question; outweigh it with benefits. • Ask for a present viewpoint. • Return to selling sequence.	• Thank prospect for telling you. • Acknowledge prospect's viewpoint. • Rephrase objection. • Obtain agreement. • Answer question. • Return to selling sequence.

Here is an example:

Buyer: I don't know—your price is higher than your competitors'.

Salesperson: I can appreciate that. You want to know what particular benefits my product has that make it worth its slightly higher price. [Or, What you're saying is that you want to get the best product for your money.] Is that correct?

Buyer: Yes, that's right.

Now discuss product benefits versus price. After doing so, attempt a trial close by asking for the prospect's viewpoint to see if you have overcome the objection.

Salesperson: Do you see how the benefits of this product make it worth the price? [Trial close.]

A variation of this sequence is sales training consultant Bruce Scagel's Feel-Felt-Found method, where he first acknowledges the prospect's viewpoint, saying, "John, I understand how you *feel.* Bill at XYZ store *felt* the same way, but he *found,* after reviewing our total program of products and services, that he would profit by buying now." Scagel refers to rephrasing the objection to a question as his Isolate and Gain Commitment method. He gives as an example: "Mary, as I understand it, your only objection to our program is the following. . . If I can solve this problem, then I'll assume that you will be prepared to accept our program."

Scagel knows that he can solve the problem or he would not have asked the question. When Mary says yes, he has isolated the main problem. He is not handling an objection; he is answering a question. He now shows her how to overcome the problem and then continues selling. If Mary says no, Bruce knows he has not isolated her main objection. He must start over in uncovering her objections. He might say, "Well, I guess I misunderstood. Exactly what is the question?" And now, when Mary responds, it usually will be a question. "Well, the question was about. . . ." Involve the customer and find out what is happening internally. You can do this with the proper use of questions.

Compensate for the Objection

Sometimes a prospect's objection is valid and calls for the **compensation method**. Several reasons for buying must exist to justify or compensate for a negative aspect of making a purchase. For example, a higher product price is justified by benefits such as better service or higher performance. In the following example, it is true that the prospect can make more profit on each unit of a competing product. You must develop a technique to show how your product has benefits that will bring the prospect more profit in the long run.

compensation method: The method of offsetting negative product aspects with better benefit aspects.

Prospect: I can make 5 percent more profit with the Stainless line of cookware, and it is quality merchandise.

Salesperson: Yes, you are right. The Stainless cookware is quality merchandise. However, you can have an exclusive distributorship on the Supreme cookware line, and still have high-quality merchandise. You don't have to worry about Supreme being discounted by nearby competitors as you do with Stainless. This will be the only store in town carrying Supreme. What do you think? [Trial close.]

If the advantages presented to counterbalance the objection are important to the buyer, you have an opportunity to make the sale.

Boomerang the Objection

Always be ready to turn an objection into a reason to buy. By convincing the prospect that an objection is a benefit, you have turned the buyer immediately in favour of

SELLING TIPS

BE POSITIVE IN DISCUSSING PRICE

All prospects are sensitive to how price is presented. This is a typical list of negative and positive ways to deal with price issues during the business proposition phase:

Negative Words:

- This costs $2,300.
- Your down payment . . .
- Your monthly payment . . .
- You can pay the purchase price over a series of months.
- How much would you like to pay us every month?
- We'll charge you two points above the prime rate.
- We'll take off $6,700 to trade in your used equipment.

Positive Words:

- This is only $2,300.
- Your initial investment . . .
- Your monthly investment . . .
- We would be happy to divide this investment into small monthly shares.
- What monthly investment would you feel comfortable with?
- Your rate will be only prime plus two.
- We are offering you $6,700 to trade your existing equipment.

boomerang method: The process of turning an objection into a reason to buy.

your product. This is the heart of the **boomerang method**. Take, for example, the wholesale drug salesperson working for a pharmaceutical firm, who is selling a pharmacist a new container for prescription medicines. Handling the container, the prospect says:

Prospect: They look nice, but I don't like them as well as my others. The tops seem hard to remove.

Salesperson: Yes, they are hard to remove. We designed them so that children couldn't get into the medicine. Isn't that a great safety measure? [Trial close.]

Or, consider the industrial equipment salesperson who is unaware that a customer is extremely dissatisfied with a present product:

Prospect: I have been using your portable generators and do not want to use them anymore.

Salesperson: Why?

Prospect: Well, the fuses kept blowing out and causing delays in completing this project! So get out of here and take your worthless generators with you.

Salesperson: [with a smile] Thank you for telling me. Say, you and our company's design engineers have a lot in common.

Prospect: Oh yeah? I'll bet! [Sarcastically.]

Salesperson: Suppose you were chief engineer in charge of manufacturing our generators. What would you do if valued customers–like yourself–said your generators had problems?

Prospect: I'd throw them in the trash.

Salesperson: Come on, what would you really do? [With a smile.]

Prospect: Well, I would fix it.

Salesperson: That's why I said you and our design engineers have a lot in common. They acted on your suggestion–don't you think? [Trial close.]

You have used reverse psychology. Now, the prospect is listening, giving you time to explain your product's new features and to make an offer to repair the old units. You are ready to sell more products, if possible.

Another example is the industrial salesperson who responds to the prospect's high price objection by saying, "Well, that's the very reason you should buy it." The prospect was caught off guard and quickly asked, "What do you mean?" "Well," said the salesperson, "for just 10 percent more, you can buy the type of equipment you really want and need. It is dependable, safe, and simple to operate. Your production will increase so that you will pay back the price differential quickly." The prospect said, "Well, I hadn't thought of it quite like that. I guess I'll buy it after all."

Boomeranging an objection requires good timing and quick thinking. Experience in a particular selling field, knowledge of your prospect's needs, a positive attitude, and a willingness to stand up to the objection are necessary attributes for successful use of this technique.

Postpone the Objection

Often, the prospect may skip ahead of you in the sales presentation by asking questions that you address later in the presentation. (See Exhibit 10.11.) If you judge that your customary method will handle the objection to your prospect's satisfaction, and that the prospect is willing to wait until later in the presentation, you politely **postpone the objection**.

postpone the objection: the option of a salesperson to respond to an objection later during the sale presentation.

Five examples of postponing objections include:

Prospect: Your price is too high.

Salesperson: In just a minute, I'll show you why this product is reasonably priced, based on the savings you will receive compared to what you presently do. That's what you're interested in, savings, right? [Trial close.]

or

Salesperson: Well, it may sound like a lot of money. But let's consider the final price when we know the model you need. OK? [Trial close.]

or

Salesperson: There are several ways we can handle your costs. If it's all right, let's discuss them in just a minute. [Pause. This has the same effect as the trial close. If there is no response, continue.] First, I want to show you. . . .

EXHIBIT 10.11

Suppose you show your prospect your business proposition, and the prospect asks, "How much does this software cost?" What would you say?

©Xavier Arnau/Getty Images

or

Salesperson: I'm glad you brought that up [or, I was hoping you would want to know that] because we want to carefully examine the cost in just a minute. OK? [Trial close.]

or

Salesperson: High? Why, in a minute I'll show you why it's the best buy on the market. In fact, I'll bet you a Coke that you will believe it's a great deal for your company! Is it a deal? [Trial close.]

Tactfully used, postponing can leave you in control of the presentation. Normally, respond to the objection immediately. However, occasionally it is not appropriate to address the objection. This is usually true for the price objection. Price is the primary objection to postpone if you have not had the opportunity to discuss product benefits. If you have discussed the product fully, then respond to the price objection immediately.

Dodge the Objection

Central Michigan University students in Professor Dean Kortge's personal selling class created a communication technique for handling a sales objection. Here's how. When the buyer said, "I think your price is a little high," Scott Dodge replied, "Before you decide to buy let me tell you about the value that goes with this product." It is called the **dodge** because the salesperson neither denies, answers, nor ignores the objection, but simply temporarily dodges it.

dodge: Doesn't deny, answer, or ignore the objection, but temporarily dodges it.

Notice how the phrase is structured in a positive manner: "Before you decide to buy. . . ." This positive communication technique now allows the seller to effectively make a smooth transition into a proper response to the buyer. Done in a calm, natural manner it is a very professional technique.

You can use the dodge by itself or in combination with one of the other techniques, such as the pass up, rephrase, postpone, boomerang, or third party. As you study the following objection handling techniques, see if you could first use the phrase "Before you decide to buy. . . ." You would use it only once in a presentation.

Pass Up the Objection

Occasionally, you may have a prospect raise an objection or make a statement that requires not addressing it. After introducing yourself, for example, a prospect may say, "I'm really not interested in a service such as yours."

You have two options. First, you can say, "Well, if you ever do, here is my card. Give me a call." Or second, you could take the **pass up** approach used by top salespeople and say something that allows you to move into your presentation, such as immediately using the customer benefit approach or simply asking "Can you explain to me your concerns?"

pass up: The option of a salesperson not to pursue a presentation or sale or not to respond to an objection.

As you gain selling experience, you will be confident in knowing when to pass or to stop and respond to the objection. If you pass up an objection and the prospect raises it again, then treat this as an important objection. Use your questioning skills to uncover the prospect's concerns.

Indirectly Deny the Objection

indirect denial: An apparent agreement with the prospect used by the salesperson to deny the fundamental issue of the objection.

An **indirect denial** is different from a direct denial in that it initially appears as an agreement with the customer's objection but then moves into a denial of the fundamental issue in the objection. The difference between the direct denial and the indirect denial is that the indirect denial is softer, more tactful, and more courteous. Use the direct denial judiciously, only to disconfirm especially damaging misinformation.

The typical example of indirect denial is the "yes, but" phrase. Here are several examples:

- Yes, but would you agree that it takes information, not time, to make a decision? What kind of information are you really looking for to make a good decision?
- I agree. Our price is a little higher, but so is our quality. Are you interested in saving $1,200 a year on maintenance?
- Sure, it costs a little more. However, you will have the assurance that it will cost much less over its lifetime. Isn't that the way your own products are made?
- Your point is well taken. It does cost more than any other product on the market. But why do you think we sell millions of them at this price?
- I appreciate how you feel. Many of our customers made similar comments prior to buying from me. However, they all asked themselves: "Can I afford not to have the best? Won't it cost me more in the long run?"

The indirect denial begins with an agreement or an acknowledgment of the prospect's position: Yes, but; I agree; Sure; Your point is well taken; and, I appreciate how you feel. These phrases allow the salesperson to tactfully respond to the objection. Done in a natural, conversational way, the salesperson will not offend the prospect.

Try this yourself: when a friend says something you disagree with, instead of saying, "I don't agree," say something like "I see what you mean. However, there's another way to look at it." See if this, as well as the other communication skills you have studied, help you to better sell yourself–and your product.

Directly Deny the Objection

You will face objections that are often incomplete or incorrect. Acknowledge the prospect's viewpoint; then answer the question by providing the complete or correct facts:

Prospect: No, I'm not going to buy any of your lawn mowers for my store. The Bigs-Weaver salesperson said they break down after a few months.

Salesperson: Well, I can understand. No one would buy mowers that don't hold up. Is that the only reason you won't buy?

Prospect: Yes, it is, and that's enough!

Salesperson: The BW salesperson was not aware of the facts, I'm afraid. My company produces the finest lawn mowers in the industry. In fact, we are so sure of our quality that we have a new three-year guarantee on all parts and labour. [Pause.]

Prospect: I didn't know that. [Positive buying signal.]

Salesperson: Are you interested in selling your customers quality lawn mowers like these? [Trial close.]

Prospect: Yes, I am. [Appears that you have overcome the objection.]

Salesperson: Well, I'd like to sell you 100 lawn mowers. If even one breaks down, call me and I'll come over and repair it. [Close.]

As you see by this example, you do not say, "Well, you so-and-so, why do you say a thing like that?" Tact is critical in using a direct denial. A sarcastic or arrogant response can alienate a prospect. However, a **direct denial** based on facts, logic, and politeness can effectively overcome the objection.

direct denial: The method of overcoming objections through the use of facts, logic, and tact.

If I say to you, "You're wrong. Let me tell you why," what happens to your mind? It closes! So, if I tell you that you are wrong and this closes your mind, what would I have to tell you to open your mind? That you are right! But, if what you said was wrong, do I tell you it was right? No, instead, do what the example illustrated by saying, "You know, you're right to be concerned about this. Let me explain." You have made the buyer right and kept the buyer's mind open. Also, you could say, "You know, my best customer had those same feelings until I explained that. . . ." You have made the customer right.

A mind once stretched by a new idea never regains its original dimensions.

LO6 After Meeting the Objection—What to Do?

As shown in Exhibit 10.12, your prospect has raised an objection that you have answered and overcome; now what? First, as shown in Exhibit 10.13, use a trial close; then either return to your presentation or close the sale.

EXHIBIT 10.12

Imagine you are this salesperson and you just answered an objection. What should you do now?

©Amble Design/Shutterstock

EXHIBIT 10.13

The procedure to follow when a prospect raises an objection.

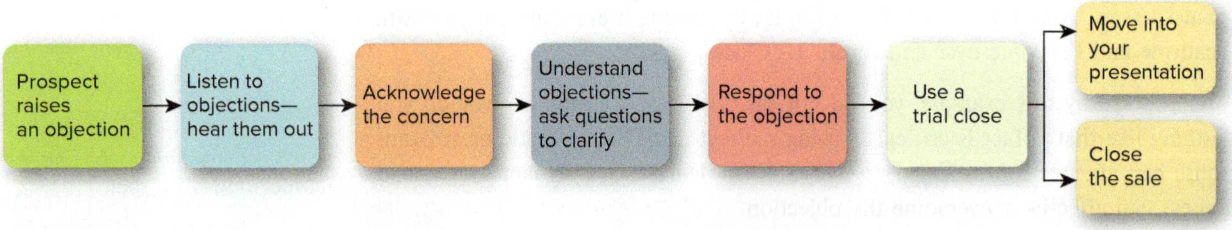

ETHICAL DILEMMA

A UNIVERSITY SETS A CONDITION

You are a salesperson for a large, national company that publishes and sells college and university textbooks. Three days ago you talked with Dr. Bush, the department head, about adopting one of your books in a second-year course of 2,000 students. He said the book is a good one but there are three others that are just as good.

Before leaving, Dr. Bush said the department would use your book if the publisher donates $1,000 and provides a new computer and printer to the English department. You tell your boss about this and she says, "Do it, but keep it quiet so none of your other schools hear of it. This will be a $100,000 sale. The home office will approve this expense if we don't do it for too many schools."

What would be the most ethical action to take?

1. Tell your boss that you do not think that the situation is fair but go ahead and do it anyway—it is ultimately her call in the end.
2. Tell your boss that you are uncomfortable making that type of sale and that you no longer want to be involved. It is not only unfair to your customers, but also unfair to you by asking you to keep it quiet.
3. Go ahead—take the sale and donate the computer and the money.

First, Use a Trial Close—Ask for Opinion

After meeting an objection at any time during the interview, you need to know if you have overcome the objection. If you have not overcome it, your prospect may raise it again. Whether it resurfaces or not, if your prospect believes that an objection was important, your failure to handle it, or your mishandling of it, will probably cost you the sale. Ideally, all objections raised should be met before closing the sale. So, after responding to the objection, use a trial close to determine if you have overcome the objection. Remember, open-ended trial closes provide an opportunity for customer feedback. A few examples are provided:

- Does this help clarify your concern? Are there any other concerns in this area I can address?
- Are there any additional areas that we haven't covered?
- With that question out of the way, would it be acceptable to continue?
- Have we adequately covered the question you raised and given you a way to handle it? Are there any concerns we've missed?
- Now that's settled entirely, isn't it?
- That solves your problem, doesn't it?

Once you have confirmed overcoming an objection, immediately go to the next SELL Sequence step. To signal that the last step is over, and that you are moving on, use body language as you speak. That is, make an appropriate gesture, look in a new direction, turn the page of your proposal, or shift in your chair–make some physical movement. Now, do one of two things (assuming you have handled the objection): either return to your presentation or close the sale.

Move Back into Your Presentation

When you have answered and overcome an objection, make a smooth transition back into your presentation. As you nonverbally signal that the last step is over, let the prospect know you are returning to your presentation with a phrase such as, "As we were discussing earlier." Now, you can continue the presentation.

Move to Close Your Sale

If you had finished your presentation when the prospect raised an objection, and the prospect's response to your trial close indicates that you overcame an objection, your next move is to close the sale. If the objection was raised during your close, then it is time to close again.

As you move on to the close with a gesture, you might summarize benefits discussed previously with a phrase such as, "Well, as we have discussed, you really like. . . ." Then, again ask the prospect for the order. Later chapters will give you other ideas on how to ask for the order.

If You Cannot Overcome the Objection

If you cannot overcome an objection or close a sale because of an objection, be prepared to return to your presentation and concentrate on new or previously discussed features, advantages, and benefits of your product. If you determine that the objection your prospect raises is a major one that cannot be overcome, admit it, and show how your product's benefits outweigh this disadvantage.

If you are 100 percent sure that you cannot overcome the objection and that the prospect will not buy, go ahead and close. *Always ask for the order.* Never be afraid to ask your prospect to buy. The buyer says no to the product–not you. Someone else may walk into the prospect's office after you with a product similar to yours. Your competitor also may not be able to overcome this person's objection, but they may get the sale nonetheless just by asking for it!

LO7 Dealing with Difficult Customers

Most of us have either had or been an angry customer–one thing that most salespeople can live without. On the other hand, taking an angry customer, solving their problem, and converting them to a satisfied customer is a challenge that many salespeople enjoy.

Difficult customers come in many forms. Some are arrogant and their personality rubs you the wrong way. Then there are those who are difficult for everyone: picky people, know-it-alls, condescending egocentrics, fault-finders, and constant whiners. We've all observed these types.

Perhaps the most difficult for everyone is the angry customer. This is someone who feels they have been wronged, and are upset and emotional about it. These customers complain, and they are angry about something you or your company did or–commonly–didn't do.

From a business perspective, it is cheaper to keep customers than it is to find new ones, so companies would prefer not to lose any. Research indicates that as long as they believe they were treated fairly, customers who complain are likely to continue doing business with companies they complain to. It's estimated that as many as 90 percent of customers who perceive themselves as having been wronged never complain; they just take their business elsewhere. So angry, complaining customers care enough to talk to you, and have not yet decided to take their business to the competition. They are customers worth saving.

Some Guidelines for Dealing with Difficult Customers

1. **Respect** - Regardless of their attitude and behaviour, this customer deserves respect. Remember that it is not you (in most cases) who is the target of their anger. You may be just a small part of the situation but yet have the power to solve the problem. Remember, you must stay in control here. *You* are not angry. It is not *your* problem. You are the problem solver, so stay in control. Getting emotionally involved in the issue will not help.
2. **Empathy** - This topic is mentioned several times throughout this text, and it may be here that it is most important. Put yourself in the customer's shoes, and try to see the situation from their perspective. You've likely been there yourself. Your responsibility is to let the customer vent and to listen attentively in order to understand the source of their frustration. When you do this, you are giving a powerful message that you care about them and their situation. Often, as the customer comes to realize that you really *do* care and that you are going to attempt to help them resolve the problem, the customer will calm down on their own and begin to interact with you in a positive way.

The Process

1. **Stop, look, and listen** - Just as when crossing the street, you have to be aware of your surroundings and the situation. When an angry customer begins an emotional tirade of how they were wronged, all you can do is *stop* what you were doing, *pay attention* to them, and *listen*. Don't try and cut them off; don't urge them to calm down. Be interested and listen carefully. As you listen, you can begin to piece together the story. Once the customer has had the chance to vent a little, there may be a good opportunity to step in. Empathize here. "This is not a good situation, so let's see what we can do to solve it for you." You can apologize and let them know that it's not acceptable to you either. Let them know that they are justifiably upset. Get them to look at you as an ally. Importantly, ask what would be the best outcome for them.
2. **Identify the problem** - In a calm fashion, get all the details as the angry customer sees them. Ask questions to get the customer to think about facts. Once the facts are uncovered, restate them to ensure that both parties have full understanding. Acknowledge again that this problem will be dealt with seriously; you can even offer an apology that it happened in the first place, but avoid placing blame.
3. **No blame** - Even if the customer is to blame here, let it go. Don't place the blame on them: "If you had just read the delivery date more carefully on your invoice, you would realize this is your fault–not ours." This approach will get you nowhere. Also, don't blame your suppliers or a delivery service. The customer wants to deal with *you*.
4. **Solve the problem** - This is the satisfying part. If you can solve the problem with a couple of quick calls, do so! If not, you must give the customer the impression that you will do something about the situation. Give a timeline. "I will call you this afternoon to bring you up to date." Now do everything in your power to solve the problem. Keep the customer apprised of everything that is going on. Doing this right will result in a loyal customer who knows that they are being looked out for.
5. **Follow up** - Hopefully, before long the problem has been solved and your customer is happy. This is a great opportunity to follow up with your customer to ensure that things are now running smoothly.

ETHICAL DILEMMA

WHEN ALL ELSE FAILS

As a salesperson for a large Montreal-based robotics company, you have entered into a very complex negotiation with a major machinery manufacturer. The deal is worth millions to your company. You've been sitting across the desk from a very hard-nosed purchasing manager for days now.

You discover that the purchasing manager is just months away from retirement and this will probably be their last major purchase before retirement. During one of your meetings, the prospect tells you about their impending retirement and without coming out and directly asking, they make some subtle overtures regarding what it will take to get the deal done.

The manager strongly hints that if you would make it worth their while personally, they would arrange to get the deal done. Your guess is that the manager is looking for a way to supplement their retirement. Perhaps a personal cash payout or a small cottage in the country would suffice. You figure it would cost your company approximately $150,000 to get the deal done.

What do you do?

LO8 Negotiating a Win–Win Outcome

Negotiation skills help you to resolve situations where what you want conflicts with what someone else wants. The aim of negotiation is to explore the situation to find a solution that is acceptable to both parties.

Depending on circumstances, there are many different styles of negotiation. "Playing hardball" and "confrontation" are some of the connotations that spring to mind when thinking about negotiation. These may seem appropriate when you do not expect to ever have to deal with people again and you do not need to cultivate a relationship. People behave this way when they buy or sell a car or a house, which often makes these experiences unpleasant.

The hardball approach to negotiation is usually highly inappropriate when resolving disputes with people you have, or would like to have, an ongoing relationship with. If one person feels disadvantaged and then feels as though they have lost, they will not likely revisit that situation again. This is counterproductive for the salesperson who wishes to establish and cultivate relationships. Similarly, using tricks and manipulation during a negotiation process will have an adverse effect on trust. While a manipulative salesperson may succeed in the short term, it is certainly not conducive to establishing a relationship where salesperson and client will work together frequently. Honesty and openness are the best policies in this case.

Preparing for Win–Win Negotiation

Depending on the size of the deal or the scale of the disagreement, a certain level of preparation may be appropriate for conducting a successful, **win–win negotiation**.

win–win negotiation: A negotiation result where both parties have gained and neither party perceives that he or she gave up too much.

For small negotiations, excessive preparation can be counterproductive, because it takes time that is better used elsewhere. Overpreparing can be seen as overkill—beating your opponent into submission.

If a major negotiation needs to be resolved, then prepare for it thoroughly. Think through the following points before you start negotiating:

- **Goals** - What do you want to get out of the negotiation? What do you expect the prospect will want?
- **Trades** - What do you and the prospect have that you can trade? What do you each have that the other might want? What might you each be prepared to give away?
- **Alternatives** - If you don't reach agreement with the prospect, what alternatives do you have? Are these good or bad? How much does it matter if you do not

reach agreement? Does failure to reach an agreement cut you out of future opportunities? What alternatives might the prospect have?

- **Relationships** - What is the history of the relationship? Could or should this history impact the negotiation? What is the future of this relationship? Is it something of value? What's in it for you in the long run? Will there be any hidden issues that may influence the negotiation? How will you handle these?
- **What do you expect?** What outcome will people be expecting from this negotiation? What has the outcome been in the past, and what precedents have been set?
- **What could happen?** What are the consequences if you win or lose this negotiation? What are the consequences for the prospect?
- **Who has the power?** Who controls resources? Who stands to lose the most if agreement isn't reached? What power does the other person have to deliver what you hope for?
- **What are the answers?** Based on all of the considerations, what possible compromises might there be?

For a negotiation to be win-win, both parties should feel positive about the situation when the negotiation is concluded. This helps to maintain a good working relationship afterward, and governs the style of the negotiation–drama and displays of emotion are inappropriate, because they introduce personality to the negotiation instead of logical, objective facts. Drama also introduces a competitive nature to the discussion.

MAKING THE SALE

NEGOTIATION CHECKLIST

Pre-Negotiation

- Do not begin negotiations until you've fully presented your proposition.
- Adopt and keep a positive attitude.
- Ensure you're dealing with the decision maker so that the negotiation is not fruitless.
- Be prepared to discuss the value your prospect will receive and to quantify it.
- Pay close attention to the interaction during the presentation to determine the prospect's key motivation.
- Be prepared to move toward a win–win negotiation.
- Predetermine when you'll have to walk away.

During the Negotiation

- Ensure that you understand the prospect's key needs by using questioning skills.
- Remind the prospect of how they will benefit from your offering.
- Don't be swayed by the nonverbal responses by your prospect (flinching, squirming, etc.).
- Employ all of your listening skills.
- Don't let silence worry you—you don't need to fill in the gaps.
- Try to adjust the value of your offering rather than drop price (faster delivery, preferred service etc.).
- Keep track of small agreements and verbalize them occasionally.
- Be sincere—show your commitment to the success of the negotiation.

Post-Negotiation

If Successful

- Provide a summary of agreement.
- Show an appreciation for the prospect's time.
- Reinforce the purchase decision.
- Watch your attitude—it was a win–win, not an "I WON."
- Learn from the experience—what worked well?

If Unsuccessful

- Show appreciation for the prospect's time.
- Don't burn bridges—leave an opening for future business.
- Learn from the experience—what didn't work well?

The negotiation itself is a careful exploration of your position and the prospect's position, with the goal of finding a mutually acceptable compromise that gives you both as much of what you want as possible. People's positions are rarely as opposed as they first appear–the other person quite often has very different goals from the ones you expect! In an ideal situation, you will find that the other person wants what you are prepared to trade, and that you are prepared to give what the other person wants.

If this is not the case and one person must give a bit, then it is fair for that person to try to negotiate some form of compensation for doing so–the amount of this compensation will often depend on many of the factors we discussed above. Ultimately, both sides should feel comfortable with the ultimate solution if the agreement is to be considered win-win.

Summary of Major Selling Issues

People want to buy, but they do not want to be misled, so they often ask questions or raise objections during a sales presentation. Your responsibility is to be prepared to respond logically and clearly to your prospect's objections whenever they arise.

Sales objections indicate a prospect's opposition or resistance to the information or request of the salesperson. Here are the four steps for effectively handling objections:

1. Acknowledge the buyer's viewpoint.
2. Identify the problem and clarify the concern.
3. Meet the objection.
4. Use a trial close.

Before you can successfully meet objections, determine whether the prospect's response to your statement or close is a request for more information, a condition of the sale, or an objection. If it is a real objection, determine whether it is minor or major. Respond to it using a trial close, and if you have answered it successfully, continue your presentation based on where you are in the sales presentation. For example, if you are still in the presentation, then return to your selling sequence. If you have completed the presentation, move to your close. If you are in the close and the prospect voices an objection, then you must decide whether to use another close or return to the presentation and discuss additional benefits.

Be aware of and plan for objections. Objections are classified as hidden, stalling, no-need, money, product, and source objections. Remember, the true category of objection could be hidden from you! Develop several techniques to help overcome each type of objection, such as stalling the objection, turning the objection into a benefit, denying the objection if appropriate, illustrating how product benefits outweigh the objection drawbacks, or developing evidence statements that answer the objection.

Welcome your prospect's objections. They help you determine whether you are on the right track to uncover prospects' needs and whether they believe your product will fulfill those needs. Valid objections are beneficial for you and the customer. A true objection reveals the customer's need, which allows a salesperson to demonstrate how a product can meet that need. Objections also show inadequacies in a salesperson's presentation or product knowledge. Finally, objections make selling a skill that a person can improve constantly. Over time, a dedicated salesperson can learn how to handle every conceivable product objection–tactfully, honestly, and to the customer's benefit.

MEETING A SALES CHALLENGE

Before handling an objection, it's important to find out what the *exact* objection is. Is price a stall or bona fide reason for changing suppliers? Is the competitor's cheaper price attractive, or does the problem exist with the salesperson and a possible inability to sell a high-priced line? There could be many problems, so before you answer the objection, do some probing and find out what the real one is. A good question would be, "Would you mind telling me exactly why you're considering this move?" Then continue to probe until you totally understand the buyer's reasoning for wanting to change suppliers.

Listen carefully to what the buyer says. Nonnie Young may be a tough negotiator wanting to see whether you will lower your prices.

PLAYING THE ROLE

The situation: At the end of one of your courses you decide that you want to sell one of your textbooks to another student (not your ABCs text, of course, because you know it will be a great life-long reference book!). Assume that you paid $90 for your text and you decide that you want to sell it for $80 because you kept it in pristine condition. However, anybody you talk to offers you only $25 for the text.

Role A: Textbook owner wanting to sell it. Plan for a negotiating process to maximize the amount you can charge.

Role B: Interested textbook buyer. Plan for a negotiating process that will minimize what you will pay for the text.

Dramatize your negotiation by demonstrating your understanding of win—win negotiation tactics.

Key Terms for Selling

boomerang method
compensation method
condition of the sale
direct denial
dodge
five-question sequence
hidden objection
indirect denial
intelligent questions
money objection
negotiation
no-need objection
objections
pass up
postpone the objection
practical objection
product objection
psychological objection
rephrasing question
sales objection
source objection
stalling objection
third-party answer
win-win negotiation

Sales Application Questions

1. Halfway through your sales presentation, your prospect stops you and says, "That sounds like a great deal and you certainly have a good product, but I'm not interested now; maybe later." What should you do?
2. Assume you are a salesperson for a cloud computing company. You have finished your presentation, and the purchasing agent for Petro-Canada says, "Well, that sounds really good and you do have the lowest price I have ever heard of from a cloud computing vendor. In fact, it's $200,000 less than the other bids. But we have decided to stay with our current supplier, mainly because $200,000 on a $1 million computer system is not that much money to us." Let's further assume that you also know that other than price, their current supplier has significant advantages in all areas over your product. What would you do?

3. When a customer is not receptive to your product, there is some resistance. In each of the following situations, the customer has an objection to a product:
   a. The customer assumes she must buy the whole set of books. However, partial purchases are permitted.
   b. The customer does not like the colour and it's the only colour your product comes in.
   c. The customer doesn't want to invest in a new set of books because she doesn't want to lose money on her old set. You have not told her yet about your trade-in deal.

   In which situations does the objection arise from a misunderstanding or lack of knowledge on the customer's part? In which situation(s) does the product fail to offer a benefit that the customer considers important?
4. Which response is best when you hear the customer reply, "I'd like to think it over"? Why?
   a. Give all the benefits of using the product now.
   b. If there is a penalty for delaying, mention it now.
   c. If there is a special price deal available, mention it now.
   d. None of the above is appropriate.
   e. Depending on the circumstances, the first three choices are appropriate.
5. Cliff Jamison sells business forms and he's regarded as a top-notch salesperson. He works hard, plans ahead, and exhibits self-confidence. One day, he is making his first presentation to a prospective new client, the Canadian Steel Company. "Ladies and gentlemen," says Jamison, "our forms are of the highest quality, yet they are priced below our competitors' forms. I know that you are a large user of business forms and that you use a wide variety. Whatever your need for business forms, I assure you that we can supply them. Our forms are noted for their durability. They can run through your machines at 60 per minute and they'll perform perfectly."

   "Perfectly, Mr. Jamison?" asks a Canadian Steel executive. "Didn't you have some trouble at Ogden's last year?"

   "Oh," replies Jamison, "that wasn't the fault of our forms. They had a stupid operator who didn't follow instructions. I assure you that if our instructions are followed precisely you will have no trouble.

   "Furthermore, we keep a large inventory of our forms so that you need never worry about delays. A phone call to our office is all that is necessary to ensure prompt delivery of the needed forms to your plant. I hope, therefore, that I can be favoured with your order."

   Did Jamison handle this situation correctly? Why?
6. One of your customers, Margaret Port, has referred you to a friend who needs your Hercules Shelving for a storage warehouse. Port recently purchased your heavy-duty, 18-gauge steel shelving and is pleased with it. She said, "This will be an easy sale for you. My friend really needs shelving and I told him about yours."

   Port's information is correct and your presentation to her friend goes smoothly. The customer has asked numerous questions and seems ready to buy. Just before you ask for the order, the customer says, "Looks like your product is exactly what I need. I'd like to think this over. Could you call me next week?" Which of the following would you do? Why?
   a. Follow the suggestion and call next week.
   b. Go ahead and ask for the order.
   c. Ask questions about the reason for the delay.

Sales Online Exercise

Finding People, Organizations, Maps, Areas, Phone Numbers, and Addresses

Opposition or resistance to information or to the salesperson's request is a sales objection. Objections often arise because the salesperson has not researched the individual or organization. Some types of selling require a tremendous amount of research to create a sales presentation. The better your research, the fewer the objections, and thus the more likely you are to make the sale. The following URLs can help you in your research.

Of course, also use your favourite search engines to find out more about people, organizations, markets, and geographical areas.

People Finders

www.canada411.ca

www.whitepages.com

www.superpages.com

www.linkedin.com

Organization Finders

www.strategis.ic.gc.ca

www.superpages.com

Geographic Market Areas

www.statcan.gc.ca

Email

www.el.com

Maps

www.mapquest.ca/directions

www.maps.google.com

Further Exploring the Sales World

1. A national sales company is at your school wanting to hire salespeople. What are some objections that such a company might have toward hiring you? How would you overcome them during a job interview?
2. Think of three different types of businesses (such as a grocery store, a hardware store, and a stereo shop), and think of one product from each business. If you were that store's buyer, think of the major objections you would have or questions you would ask a product salesperson if you were asked to buy a large quantity and promote it. Now, as that salesperson, how would you overcome those objections?

Student Application Learning Exercises (SALES)

Part 6

Sales objections are defined as opposition or resistance from the buyer. To complete this part:

1. List three objections a buyer might give you. Use objections that relate to your product. Do not use general objections, such as "I do not like it." The objection should be specific, such as "I do not like the colour."

   Objection 1:
   Objection 2:
   Objection 3:

2. Write the buyer–seller dialogue for each objection. State the buyer's objection and then your response to it. Follow the four-step process, and include the buyer's response to your clarifying probe or rephrase.
   Buyer's objection 1:
   Your acknowledgement:
   Your probe or rephrase:
   Buyer's response:
   Your FAB:
   Trial close:
   Role-play the buyer giving you the above objections and your response. If possible, use video or voice recording to play back the dialogue. Does what you say sound natural and conversational to you? If not, adjust it.

CASE 10–1

ACE BUILDING SUPPLIES

This is your fourth call on Ace Building Supplies to motivate them to sell your home building supplies to local builders. Joe Newland, the buyer, gives every indication that he likes your products.

During the call, Joe reaffirms his liking for your products and attempts to end the interview by saying: "We'll be ready to do business with you in three months—right after this slow season ends. Stop by then and we'll place an order with you."

QUESTIONS

1. Which one of the following steps would you take? Why?
   a. Call back in three months to get the order as suggested.
   b. Try to get a firm commitment or order now.
   c. Telephone Joe in a month (rather than make a personal visit) and try to get the order.
2. Why did you not choose the other two alternatives?

CASE 10–2

ELECTRIC GENERATOR CORPORATION (B)

George Wynn is a salesperson for EGC whose primary responsibility is to contact engineers in charge of constructing commercial buildings. One such engineer is Don Snyder, who is in charge of building a new School of Business Administration facility. Don's Red Deer-based engineering firm purchased three new EGC portable generators for this project. George learned that Don's company will build four more buildings on the campus, and he felt that Don might buy more machines.

Salesperson: Don, I understand you have three of our new-model electric generators.

Buyer: Yeah, you're not kidding.

Salesperson: I'm sure you'll need additional units on these new jobs.

Buyer: Yeah, we sure will.

Salesperson: I've gone over the building's proposed floor plans and put together the type of products you need.

Buyer: The buyers are down in Calgary; you need to see them!

Salesperson: I was just in there yesterday and they said it was up to you.

Buyer: Well, I'm busy today.

Salesperson: Can I see you tomorrow?

Buyer: No need; I don't want any more of your lousy generators!

Salesperson: What do you mean? That is our most modern design!

Buyer: Those so-called new fuses of yours are exploding after five minutes' use. The autotransformer starter won't start–Did you see the lights dim? That's another fuse blowing.

QUESTION

George Wynn feels pressured to sell the new EGC generators. Don Snyder's business represents an important sale both now and in the future. If you were George, what would you do?

a. Have EGC's best engineer contact Don to explain the generator's capabilities.

b. Come back after Don has cooled down.

c. Get Don to talk about problems and then solve them.

d. Do you have any other ideas?

Source: © Shironosov/Getty Images

CHAPTER 11

Closing—the Beginning of a New Relationship

Katherine Perrin
Niagara College, Niagara Region, Ontario
Source: Courtesy of Katherine Perrin.

A Sales Success Story

From an early age, Katherine Perrin knew that she wanted a career that involved educating others. However, she did not know that her career was going involve educating others on the importance of sales as a skill set and the opportunities that exist in B2B sales as a career. Katherine is a graduate of the Business Administration Marketing and Public Relations post-graduate programs at Niagara College and is currently finishing her marketing degree part-time at Ryerson University. During her time at Niagara College, she was heavily involved in OCMC, Enactus, and the Great Canadian Sales Competition. Today, Katherine is marketing manager for Sales Talent Agency and the Great Canadian Sales Competition (GCSC).

If you asked Katherine four years ago if she would have considered sales as a career, she would have definitely said "no." She didn't see the relevance of sales in any of the fields that she was interested in (marketing, advertising, public relations, etc.). If you asked her if she would ever need sales or if she would use sales daily, she would have said "no" again. But she was wrong. In reality, she didn't yet understand what sales consisted of and what a sales career would look like. Working as an on-campus ambassador for the GCSC really helped her understand what sales actually is, and ultimately led to her current management position with that organization.

A large part of her career with the GCSC has been spent prospecting and developing school partnerships. As you might expect, selling a sales competition to students, professors, program coordinators, and others is not an easy task. That said, over the past six years there has been a massive shift toward sales as a career. The GCSC has seen over 11,000 students enter to-date; 25-plus schools have embedded Round 1 of the competition into their curriculum; over 80 schools have had students participate; and hundreds of students have been hired for sales positions.

Although the current role that Katherine holds may not be a direct sales role, 70 percent of her time is spent selling to key stakeholders. A major takeaway from her transition into the marketing department is the importance of having a cohesive sales and marketing team. Without consistent communication and a strong bond between the two departments, unwanted sales challenges may develop.

Katherine wholeheartedly believes that the future is bright for sales in colleges and universities across Canada. Sales jobs are consistently one of the most advertised opportunities in Canada and should be viewed as an amazing career choice for students when they graduate.

MAIN TOPICS

Essentials of Closing

When Should I Pop the Question?

SELL Sequence

What Makes a Good Closer?

Difficulties with Closing

Specific Closing Techniques

Prepare a Multiple-Close Sequence

Close Based on the Situation

Cross-Selling

Research Reinforces These Sales Success Strategies

Keys to Improved Selling

The Business Proposition and the Close

Closing Out the Sales Interview

LEARNING OBJECTIVES

If everything has been done to develop and give a sales presentation properly, then closing the sale is the easiest step in the presentation. After studying this chapter, you should be able to:

LO1 Explain when to close.

LO2 Explain why you must prepare to close more than once.

LO3 Describe what to do if, when you ask for the order, your prospect asks for more information, raises an objection, or says no.

LO4 Discuss the 12 keys to a successful close.

LO5 Explain the difference between aggressiveness and assertiveness.

LO6 Present, illustrate, and use several techniques for closing the sale in your presentation.

LO7 Construct a multiple-close sequence.

LO8 Explain how cross-selling benefits a salesperson.

FACING A SALES CHALLENGE

Jovan made his presentation for in-office coffee service to the office manager. As he neared the end of it, the office manager asked, "What's your price?" Jovan quoted the standard price, and immediately the manager said, "Your competitor's price is $10 cheaper!"

As Sumit, who represented a medical laboratory equipment company, finished her presentation, the pathologist asked her about the cost. She stated the list price and heard, "Your price is too high. I can get the same type of equipment for a lot less."

Ralph, who sells a line of office copying machines, was only halfway through his presentation when the director of administration asked for the cost. When Ralph quoted the price on the top-of-the-line model the administrator closed off the interview with the familiar phrase, "Your price is too high."

Jovan, Sumit, and Ralph are facing a real challenge. Their buyers said, "Your price is too high," indirectly saying, "No, I'm not interested."

In each situation, what would you do now?

(Continued at end of chapter.)

Successful salespeople do not give a presentation and then ask for the order. Rather, they cultivate selling techniques that help develop a natural instinct, sensitivity, and timing for when and how to close with each buyer. This chapter wraps up our discussion of the main sales presentation elements. We begin by discussing when to close, providing examples of buying signals and discussing what makes a good closer. Next, we discuss the number of times you should attempt to close a sale, along with some problems associated with closing.

To be a good closer, you must be able to handle objections. Objections frequently arise as the salesperson nears the end of the presentation, as in the case of Jovan, and after the close, as experienced by Sumit. However, as Ralph found out, price objections can pop up at any time. This chapter and the previous chapter on objections will help you solve the "Sales Challenge" above.

Essentials of Closing

closing:
The process of helping people make a decision that will benefit them.

Closing is the process of helping people make a decision that will benefit them. You help people make the decision by asking them to buy. As successful salespeople know, there are no magic phrases or techniques to use in closing a sale. Closing is the end result of your presentation. If everything has been done properly to develop a sales presentation, closing the sale is the next step in a logical sequence.

Although it seems obvious, some salespeople forget that prospects know the salesperson is there to sell them something. So, as soon as they meet, the prospect's mind already may have progressed beyond the major portion of the salesperson's presentation. At times, the prospect may be ready to make the buying decision early in the interview. Remember, whatever the nature of a sale, there will always be a point when it's necessary to get a commitment from the buyer.

When Should I Pop the Question?

LO1

So when should you attempt to close a sale? Simply, when the prospect is ready! More specifically, when the prospect is in the conviction stage of the mental buying process. A buyer can enter the conviction stage at any time during the sales presentation. As shown in Exhibit 11.1, you might ask someone to buy as early as the approach stage or as late as another day. Much of the time, however, the close comes after the presentation. An ability to read a prospect's buying signals correctly helps a salesperson decide when and how to close a sale.

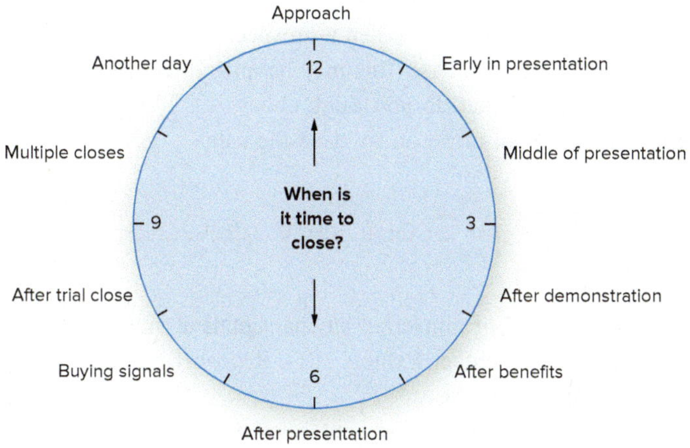

EXHIBIT 11.1
Close when the prospect is ready.

Reading Buying Signals

After prospects negotiate each stage of the mental buying process and are in the conviction stage, they often give you a signal. A **buying signal** refers to anything that prospects say or do to indicate their readiness to buy. Here are several ways a prospective buyer signals readiness to buy:

buying signal: Anything that prospects say or do that indicates they are ready to buy.

- **Asks questions** – "How much is it?" "What is the soonest I can receive it?" "What are your service and returned-goods policies?" At times, you may respond to a buying signal question with another question, as shown in Exhibit 11.2, to determine

EXHIBIT 11.2
Answering a prospect's buying signal question with a question.

BUYER SAYS	SALESPERSON REPLIES
• What's your price?	• In what quantity?
• What kind of terms do you offer?	• What kind of terms do you want?
• When can you make delivery?	• When do you want delivery?
• What size copier should I buy?	• What size do you need?
• Can I get this special price on orders placed now and next month?	• Would you like to split your shipment?
• Do you carry 8-, 12-, 36-, and 54-cm pipe?	• Are those the sizes you commonly use?
• How large an order must I place to receive your best price?	• What size order do you have in mind?
• Do you have Model 6400 in stock?	• Is that the one you like best?

your prospect's thoughts and needs. If your question is answered positively, the prospect is showing a high interest level and you are nearing the close.

- **Asks another person's opinion** - The executive calls someone on the telephone and says, "Come in here a minute; I have something to ask you." Or a person turns to their partner and says, "What do you think about it?"
- **Relaxes and becomes friendly** - Once the prospect decides to buy, the pressure of the buying situation is eliminated. A state of visible anxiety changes to relaxation because your new customer believes that you are a friend.
- **Pulls out a purchase order form** - If, as you talk, your prospect pulls out an order form, it is time to move toward the close.
- **Carefully examines merchandise** - When a prospect carefully scrutinizes your product or contemplates the purchase, this may be an indirect request for prompting. Attempt a trial close: "What do you think about . . . ?" If you obtain a positive response to this question, move on to close the sale.

The Trial Close—A Great Way to Obtain Buyer Feedback

A prospect may send verbal or nonverbal buying signals at any time before or during your sales presentation (remember Exhibit 11.1). Recognizing a buying signal should prompt you to attempt a **trial close**.

trial close: A technique that checks the attitude of your prospect toward the sales presentation.

As discussed in Chapter 9, during your sales presentation the trial close is an excellent test of your prospect's interest level in buying your proposition. It checks the pulse or attitude of your prospect toward the sales presentation. It helps to elicit the buyer's impressions. You perform a trial close by making a statement or posing a question that prompts the buyer to respond. The trial close should be used at these four important times:

1. After an important FAB
2. After addressing an objection
3. Immediately before attempting to close the sale
4. Whenever the salesperson needs buyer response during the presentation

The trial close allows you to determine (1) whether the prospect likes your product's FABs (the strong selling point); (2) whether you have successfully answered an objection; (3) whether any objections remain; and (4) whether the prospect is ready for you to close the sale. It is a powerful technique to induce two-way communication (feedback) and participation from the prospect.

If, for example, the prospect says little while you make your presentation, and if you get a no when you come to the close, you may find it difficult to change the prospect's mind. You have not learned the real reasons that the prospect is saying no. To avoid this, salespeople use the trial close to determine the prospect's attitude toward the product throughout the presentation.

Make Trial Closes Specific

The trial close asks for the prospect's reaction to what has just been presented by the salesperson. Most often what has just been presented is verbal–a FAB. Sometimes it may be nonverbal; for example, when the salesperson hands the buyer a testimonial letter and waits while it is read. In either case, a trial close is intended to shed some light on the buyer's "black box"–the internal decision process discussed in Chapter 3.

SELLING GLOBALLY

DOING BUSINESS IN KOREA

Doing business in Korea is still very different from doing business at home, even though the country has adapted well to Western business philosophies.

Relationships – Koreans appreciate an effort on your part to understand their way of life. Koreans will appreciate your effort to express simple phrases in Korean. For example, a simple *gam-sa-ham-di* (thank you) will go a long way in forming a friendship. Koreans also like to socialize. It is common for Canadian business people visiting Korea to engage in social activities with their Korean host. Joining them for an evening of drinking soju (Korean alcohol) and singing karaoke would be appreciated.

The business card – Receiving your business card is an excellent way for your Korean prospect to get to know your name, position, and status. The exchange of cards should be done almost formally, with a high degree of respect. A bilingual card would be ideal.

History – Be sensitive about Korea's historical relationship to Japan. Koreans often don't like things Japanese, so avoid comparisons between the two if the topic should arise. If you mention that you like the Japanese Toyota over the Korean Hyundai, you may as well pack your bags.

Business transactions – Relationships are important. You cannot cold call and it is best to have an introduction or referral. Koreans can be effective negotiators. Often, a Westerner may lose a negotiation due to style, rather than substance. Like the Chinese, Koreans are not big fans of formalized, written contracts. They would rather keep terms flexible, so it is important that agreements be understood fully by both parties.

An effective trial close, therefore, refers specifically to what occurs just before it is done. After an important FAB, the trial close will request the buyer's response to that specific benefit or advantage or feature. After a testimonial letter, the trial close will ask specifically for the prospect's reaction to the content of the letter. In other words, effective trial closes are specific, not general. "How do you like our colour selection?" is effective because it is specific to colours offered. "How does that sound?" is ineffective because it is too vague to provide the salesperson with valuable feedback.

Trial closes may be open or closed questions. Remember that the intention is to induce two-way communication. Skilled salespeople will use closed trial closes when they want brief responses from the prospect and open trial closes when they want the buyer to expand on his reaction. As they progress through their presentations, effective salespeople alternate between open and closed trial closes as needed to maintain momentum, check on their progress, and keep the buyer involved.

Skilled salespeople also use a variety of trial closes during their presentations to ensure they do not sound robotic. Overuse of phrases such as, "Can you see . . ." or "What do you think . . ." at the beginning of trial closes will sound repetitive and awkward to the buyer. Instead, by using a variety of different words and phrases, the salesperson will make the presentation more natural and conversational.

Trial Closes Are Not Needs Analysis or Closing

Trial closes are not needs-analysis questions. They are intended to obtain buyer feedback on the salesperson's offering, not to uncover buyer needs. For example, after presenting a FAB the salesperson should *not* ask, "Is this important to you?" If the buyer replies "No," then time has been wasted and the salesperson appears unprofessional. Equally troublesome is the probe, "Is this something that you are interested in?" The salesperson must know beforehand whether a FAB is of enough importance to present. As mentioned earlier, the salesperson learns this by conducting a needs analysis.

Trial closes are also not closes. They do not ask for the order. While an effective trial close such as "Which covering do you prefer, the vinyl or the leather?" may prompt the buyer to make a decision that could lead to a purchase, it does not request a commitment to buy, nor should it. A statement or question prompting the prospect to commit to buying is a close.

Remember the prospect's positive reactions. Use them later to help overcome objections and in closing the sale. Also, remember the negative comments. You may need to offset the negatives with the positives later in the presentation. Generally, however, you will not discuss the negative again.

If the prospect responds favourably to your trial close, then you are in agreement or you have satisfactorily answered an objection. Thus, the prospect may be ready to buy. However, if you receive a negative response, do not close. Either you have not answered some objection, or the prospect is not interested in the FAB you are discussing. This feedback allows you to better uncover what your prospect thinks about your product's potential for satisfying needs.

SELL Sequence

SELL sequence: A sequence of things to do and say to stress benefits important to the customer: show the feature, explain the advantage, lead in to the benefit, and let the customer talk by asking a question about the benefit.

One way to remember to incorporate a trial close into your presentation is the **SELL sequence**. Exhibit 11.3 shows how each letter of the word *SELL* stands for a sequence of things to do and say to stress benefits important to the customer. By remembering the word *SELL,* you remember to *show* the feature, *explain* the advantage, *lead* into the benefit, and then *let* the customer talk by asking a question about the benefit (trial close).

EXHIBIT 11.3
The SELL sequence: Use it throughout your presentation.

S	E	L	L
Show feature	Explain advantage	Lead into benefit	Let customer talk

Here are some examples of the SELL sequence in action:

Industrial salesperson to industrial purchasing agent: This equipment is made of stainless steel [feature], which means it won't rust [advantage]. The real benefit is that it reduces your replacement costs, thus saving you money [benefit]! Do you see how choosing stainless steel will save you money [trial close]?

Salesperson to consumer goods buyer: Our company will spend an extra $250,000 in the next two months advertising No Cling fabric softener [feature]. Plus, you can take advantage of this month's $1.20 per dozen price reduction [feature]. This discount means you will sell 15 to 20 percent more No Cling in the next two months [advantage], thus making higher profits and pulling more customers into your store [benefits]. How does our advertising and discount package sound to you [trial close]?

Once you use a trial close, carefully listen to what the customer says and watch for nonverbal signals to determine whether what you said has had an impact. If you have a positive response to your trial close, you are on the right track.

Remember, the trial close does not ask the customer to buy. It is a statement or question designed to determine the customer's opinion toward the salesperson's proposition (see Exhibit 11.4). It may prompt a signal that the prospect is ready to buy; however, its main purpose is to induce feedback from the buyer.

EXHIBIT 11.4

Examples of features, advantages, benefits, and trial closes that form a SELL sequence.

FEATURES (CHARACTERISTICS)	ADVANTAGES (PERFORMANCE CHARACTERISTICS)	BENEFITS (RESULT FROM ADVANTAGES)	TRIAL CLOSES (FEEDBACK QUESTIONS)
Nationally advertised consumer product	Will sell more product	Will make you more profit	What do you think of our advertising plan?
Air conditioner with a high energy-efficiency rating	Uses less electricity	Saves 10% on energy costs	How do you like the energy efficiency of our unit?
Product made of stainless steel	Will not rust	Reduces replacement cost	Do you like the fact that it is stainless steel?
Supermarket computer system with the IBM 3651 Store Controller	Can store more information and retrieve it rapidly by monitoring up to 24 checkout scanners and terminals and looking up prices on up to 22,000 items	Provides greater accuracy, register balancing, store ordering, and inventory management	Can you see how the increased power of the 3651 will improve your operations?
5% interest on money in bank when choosing NOW account	Earns interest that would not normally be received	Gives you one extra bag of groceries each month	What is your impression of this interest rate on your account?
Aerodynamically designed titanium golf club head	Increased club head speed, longer drives	Lower scores	How do you like the design?

What Makes a Good Closer?

In every sales force, some individuals are better than others at closing sales. Some persons rationalize this difference of abilities by saying, "It comes naturally to some people," or, "They've just got what it takes." What does it take to be a good closer?

Good closers have a strong desire to close each sale. They have a positive attitude about their product's ability to benefit the prospect. They know their customers and tailor their presentations to meet each person's specific needs.

Good closers prepare for each sales call. They take the time to carefully ascertain the needs of their prospects and customers by observing, by asking intelligent questions, and most of all, by earnestly listening. To be successful, salespeople should keep in mind their ABCs. *ABC* stands for *Always Be Closing*. Be alert for buying signals and close when the prospect is ready to buy (see Exhibit 11.5 on the next page).

Do not stop with the prospect's first no. If a customer says no, determine the nature of the objection and then return to the presentation. After discussing information relevant to overcoming the objection, use a trial close to determine whether you have overcome the objection, and then determine whether there are other objections. If resistance continues, remain positive and remember that every time you attempt to close, you are closer to the sale.

Ask for the Order and Be Quiet

No matter when or how you close, remember that after you ask for the order, it is important to be silent. Do not say a word. If you say something–anything–you increase the probability of losing the sale. You must put the prospect in a position of having to make a decision, speak first and respond to the close. If you say anything after your close, you take the pressure off the prospect to make that decision.

Imagine this situation: The salesperson has finished the presentation and says, "Would you want this delivery in two or four weeks?" The average salesperson cannot wait more than two seconds for the prospect's reply without saying something like,

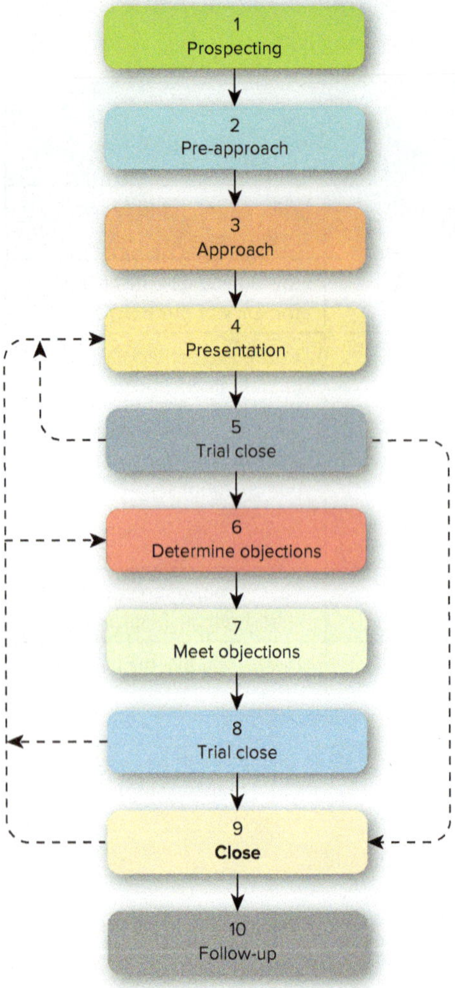

EXHIBIT 11.5

A positive response to the trial close indicates a move toward the close; a negative response signals that you should return to your presentation or determine the prospect's objections.

"I can deliver it anytime," or starting to talk again about the product. This destroys the closing moment. The prospect does not have to make the decision. There is time to think of reasons not to buy. By keeping quiet for a few seconds, the salesperson ensures that the prospect must make a decision.

All individuals experience the urge to say no, even when they are not sure of what you are selling or when they want what you propose. To help the prospect make the decision, you must maintain silence after the close. The professional salesperson can stay quiet all day, if necessary. Rarely will the silence last more than 30 seconds. During that time, do not say anything or make a distracting gesture; merely project positive nonverbal signs. Otherwise, you will lessen your chances of making the sale. This is the time to mentally prepare your responses to the prospect's reaction.

It sounds simple, yet it is not. Your stomach may churn. Your nerves make you want to move. You may display a serious look on your face instead of a positive one. You may look away from the buyer. Most of all, you may want to talk to relieve the uncomfortable feeling that grows as silence continues. Finally, the prospect will say something. Now, you can respond based on the reaction to your close.

Constantly practise asking your closing question, staying silent for 30 seconds, and then responding. This rehearsal will develop your skill and courage to close.

LO2 How Many Times Should You Close?

Courtesy and common sense imply a reasonable limit to the number of closes attempted by a salesperson at any one sitting. However, salespeople call on customers and prospects in order to sell their products.

To sell, you must be able to use multiple closes. Keep in mind that three closes is a minimum for successful salespeople. Three to five well-executed closes should not offend a prospect. Attempting several closes in one call challenges a salesperson to employ wit, charm, and personality in a creative manner. So, always take at least three strikes before you count yourself out of the sale. A good closer has a strong desire to close each sale. You should rarely accept the first no as the final answer. If you are professional, you should be able to close a minimum of three to five times.

Closing under Fire

To close more sales effectively, never take the first no from the prospect to mean an absolute refusal to buy. Instead, you must be able to close under fire. See Exhibit 11.6. In other words, you must be able to ask a prospect who may be in a bad mood or even hostile toward you to buy.

MAKING THE SALE

A MARK TWAIN STORY

Mark Twain attended a meeting where a missionary had been invited to speak. Twain was deeply impressed. Later he said, "The preacher's voice was beautiful. He told us about the sufferings of the natives and pleaded for help with such moving simplicity that I mentally doubled the fifty cents I had intended to put in the plate. He described the pitiful misery of those savages so vividly that the dollar I had in mind gradually rose to five. Then that preacher continued. I felt that all the cash I carried on me would be insufficient. I decided to write a large check. Then he went on," added Twain, "and on and on about the dreadful state of those natives. I abandoned the idea of the check. Again, he went on, and I was back to five dollars. As he continued, I went to four, two, and then one dollar. Still, he persisted to preach. When the plate finally came around, I took ten cents out of it."[1]

Take the experience of a consumer goods salesperson who suggested that a large drug wholesaler should buy a six-month supply of the company's entire line of merchandise. Outraged, the purchasing agent threw the order book across the room. The salesperson explained to the furious buyer that the company had doubled its promotional spending in the buyer's area and that it would be wise to stock up because of an upcoming increase in sales. The salesperson calmly picked up the order book, smiled, and handed it to the buyer saying, "Did you want to buy more?"

The buyer laughed and said, "What do you honestly believe is a reasonable amount to buy?" This was a buying signal that the prospect would buy, but in a lesser quantity. They settled on an increased order of a two-month supply over the amount of merchandise normally purchased. This example illustrates why it is important for the salesperson to react calmly to an occasional hostile situation.

EXHIBIT 11.6

Closing under fire. You can tell that this customer is unhappy with your product or with you. How do you save the sale and close?

Source: © Stockbyte/PunchStock RF

Difficulties with Closing LO3

Closing the sale is the easiest part of the presentation. It is a natural wrap-up to your sales presentation because it involves you solidifying details of the purchase agreement. Yet, salespeople sometimes have difficulty closing the sale for several reasons.

One reason salespeople may fail to close a sale and take an order is that they are not confident in their ability to close. Perhaps some earlier failure to make a sale has caused this mental block. They may give the presentation and stop short of asking for the order. The seller must overcome this fear of closing to become successful.

> *Closing requires preparation. When salespeople are well-prepared for the sales conversation, they increase the opportunity to close the sale.*

Second, salespeople often determine that the prospect does not need the quantity or type of merchandise, or that the prospect should not buy. So, they do not ask the prospect to buy. The salesperson should remember that *it is the prospect's decision and responsibility whether or not to buy.* Do not make the decision for the prospect.

Finally, the salesperson may not have worked hard enough in developing a customer profile and customer benefit plan–resulting in a poor presentation. Many times, a poorly prepared presentation falls apart. Be prepared and develop a well-planned, well-rehearsed presentation.

Keys to a Successful Close LO4

While there are many factors to consider in closing the sale, the following are essential if you want to improve your chances:

- Be sure your prospect understands what you say.
- Always present a complete story to ensure understanding.
- Tailor your close to each prospect. Eighty percent of your customers will respond to a standard close. It is the other 20 percent of customers you need to prepare for.

Prepare to give the expert customer all facts requested, to give the egotistical customer praise, to lead the indecisive customer, and to slow down for a slow thinker.

- Everything you do and say should consider the customer's point of view.
- Never stop at the first no.
- Learn to recognize buying signals.
- Before you close, attempt a trial close.
- After asking for the order, be silent.
- Set high goals for yourself, and develop a personal commitment to reach your goals.
- Develop and maintain a positive, confident, and enthusiastic attitude toward yourself, your products, your prospects, and your close.

Before we discuss specific techniques on how to ask for the order or close the sale, remember that you will increase your sales closings by using 12 simple keys to success, as shown in Exhibit 11.7.

As you see from these 12 keys, a successful close results from a series of actions that you have followed before asking for the order. Closing is not one giant step. If you don't make the sale, always remember to act professionally and be courteous and appreciative of the opportunity to present your product to the prospect. This keeps the door open for another time. Thus, Key 12 cannot be overlooked–always remember to leave the door open!

Often, salespeople believe that there is some mystical art to closing a sale. If they say the right words in the appropriate manner, the prospect will buy. They concentrate on developing tricky closing techniques and are often pushy with prospects in hopes of pressuring them into purchasing. Certainly, salespeople need to learn alternative closing techniques. However, what is most needed is a thorough understanding of the entire selling process and of the critical role that closing plays in that process.

A memorized presentation and a hurriedly presented product will not be as successful as the skilful use of the 12 keys to a successful close. A close look at the 12 keys illustrates that a lot of hard work, planning, and skilful execution of your plan occurs before you reach Key 11 and ask for the order. The point is that if salespeople understand how each of the 12 applies to them and their customers, and if they perform each successfully, they earn the right to close.

EXHIBIT 11.7

Twelve keys to a successful close.

1. Think *success!* Be enthusiastic.
2. *Plan* your sales call.
3. Confirm your prospect's *needs.*
4. Give a *great* presentation.
5. Use *trial closes* during and after your presentation.
6. Smoke out a prospect's *real* objections.
7. *Overcome* real objections.
8. Use a *trial close* after overcoming each objection.
9. Summarize *benefits as related to the buyer's needs.*
10. Use a *trial close* to confirm the benefits as related to the buyer's needs.
11. Ask for the *order* and then *be quiet.*
12. Leave the door *open.* Act as a professional.

MAKING THE SALE

CLOSING IS NOT ONE GIANT STEP

Too many salespeople regard the close as a separate and distinct part of the sales call: "I've discussed benefits and features, answered some objections, handled price, and now it's time to close."

Chronologically, of course, the close does come at the end. Closing is the natural outgrowth of the sales presentation. If the rest of the sales call has been a success, closing simply means working out terms and signing the order.

What about the salesperson who says, "I always have trouble closing. Everything's fine until it's time to close the sale." Chances are, there's no basis for the sale. "Everything's fine . . ." may merely be a way of saying, "I stated my case and the prospect listened. At least they never told me to pack up and go."

In fact, many times the close occurs automatically because it has become the easiest part of the sales presentation. Often, the prospect will close for the salesperson, saying: "That sounds great! I'd like to buy that" (see Exhibit 11.8). All the salesperson has to do is finalize the details and write up the order. Often, though, the prospect is undecided about the product after the presentation, so the skilful salesperson develops a multiple-close sequence.

Assertiveness or Aggressiveness?

LO5

Understanding the difference between assertiveness and aggressiveness can make or break a sale. Salespeople should strive for assertiveness. What is the difference between being assertive and being aggressive?

assertiveness: Expressing oneself in a direct and honest way; seeking a win–win outcome.

Assertiveness includes:

- Expressing our thoughts, feelings, and beliefs in a direct, honest, and appropriate way
- Respecting ourselves and others
- Working purposefully toward a win–win solution to problems
- Influencing, listening, and negotiating effectively so that others choose to cooperate willingly

EXHIBIT 11.8

Often the seller does not have to close. In this case, the product sold itself. After examining the business proposition, the prospect bought without the salesperson asking for an order.

Source: © Yuri Arcurs/Dreamstime.com/GetStock.com

aggressiveness: Expressing oneself in an inappropriate way; being forceful and demanding.

Aggressiveness includes:

- Expressing our thoughts, feelings, and beliefs in an inappropriate way
- Violating the rights of others
- Communicating an impression of disrespect, either actively or passively
- Putting our wants, needs, and rights above those of others
- Attempting to get our way by not allowing others a choice
- Striving for a win-lose solution (I'll be the winner; you'll be the loser)

Assertiveness Strategies

Use "I" Messages An "I" message is a good way to let people know what you are thinking. It is made up of three parts:

- **Behaviour** - "I think that by using our product, your company will experience . . ."
- **Effect** - "By delaying this decision, I think you might run the risk of . . ."
- **Feeling** - "I believe that adopting our solution will lead your company to much greater profits."

By using this kind of message, you are giving another person complete information, leaving no room for second-guessing or doubt. This is much more productive than simply expressing your frustration or resorting to a dubious closing technique.

Choose Assertive Words Carefully Use factual descriptions instead of judgments.

> "This product is the only one that can increase your profits." (Aggressive)
>
> "The product has reliably demonstrated that it can cut production costs by up to 20 percent in companies such as yours." (Assertive)

Avoid exaggerations.

> "We are the best in the world." (Aggressive)
>
> "We have been consistently rated in the top five sellers in our industry by the purchasing association." (Assertive)

Use "I," not "You"

> "Your company cannot grow without our product." (Aggressive)
>
> "I would like to show you how our product will help your company grow." (Assertive)

Test Your Assertiveness

These questions will help you to assess your assertiveness:

- When you differ with buyers you respect, are you able to speak up and share your own viewpoint?
- Are you able to refuse unreasonable requests made by buyers?
- Do you readily accept real criticisms and objections?
- Do you seek assistance when you need it?
- Do you have confidence in your own judgment and recommendations?
- If someone else has a better solution, do you accept it easily?
- Do you express your thoughts, feelings, and beliefs in a direct and honest way?
- Do you try to work for a solution that benefits all parties?

A "yes" response indicates an assertive approach.

SELLING TIPS

AN ASSERTIVENESS ACTION PLAN

Here are some communication techniques that can help you convey a positive, assertive attitude:

- Use suitable facial expressions, always maintaining good eye contact.
- Keep your voice firm but pleasant.
- Pay careful attention to your posture and gestures.
- Listen . . . and let people know you have heard what they said.
- Ask questions for clarification.
- Look for a win–win approach to problem solving.

Specific Closing Techniques

LO6

To successfully close more sales, you must determine your prospect's situation, understand the prospect's attitude toward your presentation, and be prepared to select instantly a closing technique from several techniques based on your prospect. By using a closing technique that fits the situation, you can save the sale and keep your customer satisfied.

Successful salespeople adapt a planned presentation to any prospect or situation that may arise. Some salespeople practice more than 10 closing techniques, each designed for a specific situation. In the next section, we will discuss a range of closing techniques.

In this section, we begin with a number of commonly used techniques. Then, we move to a number of techniques that may be applied in *specific types of situations.* Since different closing techniques work best for certain situations, salespeople prepare several options. By being prepared for each sales call, you are able to adapt to your customer and the specific situation. This level of preparation provides you with increased confidence and an increased opportunity to close the sales.

These closing techniques are used to ask a prospect for the order, whether the product sold is an industrial product or consumer product (see Exhibit 11.9 on the next page).

Commonly used techniques include:

- Summary-of-benefits close
- Alternative-choice close
- Probability close
- Negotiation close
- Technology close

Techniques used in specific situations include:

- Assumptive close
- Minor points close
- Compliment close
- Urgency close
- T-account or balance sheet close

Summary-of-Benefits Close

During the sales presentation, remember the main features, advantages, and benefits of interest for the prospect and use them during the close. Summarize these benefits in a positive manner so that the prospect agrees with what you say; then ask for the order. The summary close is possibly the most popular method to ask for the order.

EXHIBIT 11.9

Techniques for closing the sale: Which close should be used?

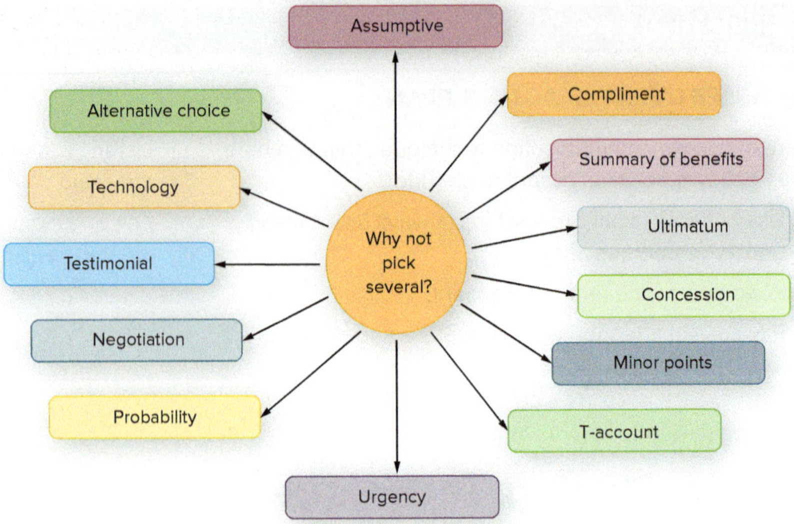

Emmett Reagan, sales trainer at the Xerox Training Center, says the major closing technique taught consists of these three basic steps of the summary close:

1. Determine the key product benefits that interest the prospect during the presentation.
2. Summarize these benefits.
3. Make a proposal.

summary-of-benefits close: A close wherein the salesperson summarizes the benefits of the product in a positive manner so that the prospect agrees with what the salesperson says.

Here is an example of using the **summary-of-benefits close** on a prospect. Assume that the prospect indicates during your sales presentation that she likes your profit margin, delivery schedule, and credit terms.

Salesperson: Ms. Stevenson, I'd like to recap our discussion. At the beginning of our discussion, you mentioned that any new product needed to meet your profit margin goals. Our new product delivers 48 percent. You also mentioned fast delivery. And I can commit to you that you will have the product in your distribution center within three weeks of the initial order. Finally, you mentioned you needed your vendors to provide favourable credit terms, and our firm offers a generous 2/30 net 90 payment policy. Am I missing anything? [Summary and trial close.]

Prospect: No. Those are the areas that I need for a new product.

Salesperson: With the number of customers in your store and our expected sales of the products due to normal turnover, along with our marketing plan, *I suggest you buy* [state the products and their quantities]. This will provide you with sufficient quantities to meet customer demand for the next two months, plus provide you with the profit you expect from your products. I can have the order to you early next week. [Now wait for her response.]

The summary close is likely the most popular type of close.

You can easily adapt the FAB statements and SELL Sequence for your summary close. The industrial equipment salesperson might say, "As we have discussed, our model's high-speed assembly system [feature] produces twice as many units in a similar amount of time as your current manufacturing system [advantage], saving you 15 to 30 percent in your manufacturing process [benefit] and helps you meet the pressures imposed upon you by your senior management to increase your plant's productivity [benefit of benefit]. What are your thoughts? [Trial close. If positive response, say:] "Would you like to move forward with this opportunity today?"

The sporting goods salesperson might say, "As we have said, this golf ball will give you an extra 10 to 20 yards on your drive [advantage], helping to reduce your score [benefit] because of its new solid core [feature]. How would it feel to take off a few golf strokes and improve your golf game? [Trial close. If positive response, say:] Will a dozen be enough?"

The air-conditioning salesperson could say, "This air conditioner has a high efficiency rating [feature] that will save you 10 percent on your energy costs resulting in a monthly savings of over $1,000 [benefit] because it uses less electricity [advantage]. What are your thoughts on this type of monthly savings? [Trial close. If positive response, say:] We can provide delivery within the week. Would you want the air-conditioning system delivered this week or do you prefer next week?"

One of the most popular methods of closing the sale, the summary-of-benefits technique, could be especially useful when you need a simple, straightforward close rather than a close aimed at a specific prospect's personality.

Alternative-Choice Close

In some selling situations, the salesperson possesses a strong relationship with the buyer. In these instances, the salesperson may be more straightforward because they understand the buyer, their needs, and their past buying history. Additionally, the conversation may be focused on a re-buy situation—when the buyer intends to buy the identical or similar product. In this type of situation, the alternative-choice close may serve as an option.

The **alternative-choice close** was popularized in the 1930s as the story spread of the Walgreen Drug Company's purchase of 800 dozen eggs at a special price. A sales trainer named Elmer Wheeler suggested to the Walgreen clerks that when a customer asked for a malted milk at a Walgreen fountain, the clerk should say, "Do you want one egg or two?" Customers had not even thought of eggs in their malteds. Now, they were faced with the choice of *how many eggs*—not whether or not they wanted an egg. Within one week, all 800 dozen of the eggs were sold at a profit. Here are two examples of the alternative close:

alternative-choice close: A type of close that does not give the prospect a choice of buying or not buying but instead asks which one or how many items they wish to buy.

- Which do you prefer—our current version of software or the version with the upgraded features?
- Would you prefer the Xerox 6200 or 6400 copier?

As you see, the alternative choice does not give prospects a choice of buying or not buying, but asks which one or how many items they want to buy. It says, "You are going to buy, so let's settle the details on what you will purchase." This approach assumes that a sale is imminent, such as the re-buy situation.

Take, for example, the salesperson who says: "Would you prefer the Xerox 6200 or 6400?" This question (1) assumes the customer has a desire to buy one of the copiers; (2) assumes the customer will buy; and (3) allows the customer a preference. If the customer prefers the Xerox 6400, you know the prospect is ready to buy, so you begin the close. A customer who says, "I'm not sure," is still in the desire stage, so you continue to discuss each product's benefits. However, you see that the customer likes both machines. Should the prospect appear indecisive, you can ask: "Can you share with me the areas you are unsure of?" This question probes to find out why your prospect is not ready to choose.

If used in an appropriate situation, the alternative-choice close is an effective closing technique. It provides a choice between items, never between something and nothing. By presenting a choice, you either receive a yes decision or uncover objections, which, if successfully met, allow you to come closer to making the sale.

Probability Close

probability close: A close that permits the prospect to focus on his or her real objections, which a salesperson attempts to reverse with a persuasive sales argument.

In some sales situations, the salesperson needs to assess the buyer's level of comfort or risk with certain solutions. In the **probability close,** you ask buyers to share their level of perceived risk on the entire solution or certain elements of the solution. This close may be used when the product or service is very technical or requires a sizable investment. The value of the probability close is that it allows the salesperson to understand the customer's ongoing concerns. We show an example of the probability close below. Please note that in the second element of the close, the buyer expresses some hesitation about distribution timelines. As you can see, this provides the salesperson with an opportunity to better meet the buyer's needs and move forward later.

What is the probability we will be doing business?

Salesperson: We have covered a great deal of information in this discussion. If I may, I'd like to propose that we take the three major elements of this proposal and ensure you are comfortable with them. Would this be acceptable to you?

Customer: That sounds great.

Salesperson: Fantastic. Now in terms of the promotional campaign, I'd like to understand your thoughts. On a scale of 1 to 10, how does the proposed campaign meet your business objectives in terms of driving the sales you need to meet your quarterly revenue numbers?

Customer: I really like the heavy investment of in-store promotions. This is exactly what I want my vendors to enact. I give it a 9.

Salesperson: Great. Now, let's transition to the implementation plan, primarily focused on the distribution timelines. We mentioned that your distribution centres can have the product within 11 business days of the first order date. Based on this timeline, what are your thoughts on a scale of 1 to 10 of this meeting your internal requirements?

Customer: About a 6, I'd ideally like it in the distribution centres within 9 business days.

Salesperson: Okay, this sounds like something we should discuss before we move forward.

Asking Questions Regarding Comfort and Level of Risk

Perhaps the purchase requires a sizable investment, you could ask buyers to rate their level of perceived risk in making the investment. For instance, a salesperson might ask, "I want to understand your thoughts at this time. On a scale of 1 to 100, what's your level of comfort in making this investment and moving forward today?"

Asking Questions Regarding the Probability of Conducting Business Together

When the prospect gives the famous "I want to think it over" objection, or some variation, try saying, "That would be fine. I understand your desire to think it over, but let me ask you this–when I call you back next week, what do you envision as the probability, in percentage terms, out of a total of 100 that you and I can work together to help you meet your needs with this solution?" Then pause, and don't say another word until the prospect speaks.

The prospect's response will be from three possible categories:

1. **More than 50 percent but less than 85 percent for buying** - If your prospects respond in this range, ask what the remaining percent is against buying, then pause and be silent. When you become skilled in this technique, you will see

prospects blink as they focus on their real objections. Many times, we hear that prospects want to think it over. It is not because they want to delay the decision; it is because they don't fully understand what bothers them. The probability close permits your prospects to focus on their real objections. Once you have a real objection, convert that objection with a persuasive sales argument.

2. **Above 85 percent but not 100 percent for buying** - If they're in this range, recognize that there is a minor probability against you. You might want to say, "As it is almost certain that we'll do business together, why wait until next week? What concerns do you have at this time? Or could we get a running start on this project together and move forward today?"
3. **Less than 50 percent for buying** - This is a signal that there is little, if any, chance that you will ever close this particular sale. The only appropriate tactic is returning to square one and starting the reselling process. It is amazing how many professional salespeople in a closing situation expect the prospect to say 80-20 as a probability in their favour, and instead they hear "80-20 against."

The probability close permits prospects to focus on their objections. It allows the true or hidden objections to surface. The more prospects fight you and the less candid they are about the probability of closing, the less likely they will buy anything.

Negotiation Close

Every sale is a negotiation. Most sales negotiations focus on two major themes: value and price. Customers often demand more value and lower prices. In their quest for more value at a lower cost, prospects often resort to unfair tactics and put heavy pressure on the salesperson. The purpose of a good sales **negotiation close** is not to haggle over who gets the larger slice of pie, but to find ways for everyone to have a fair deal. Both the buyer and seller should win. In order for this to occur, salespeople should understand the areas in which they can compromise. This requires a substantial knowledge of your firm's processes, policies, products, and implementation. Here are two examples of a salesperson using a negotiation close:

negotiation close: A close in which buyer and seller find ways for everyone to have a fair deal.

- If we could find a way in which we would eliminate the need for a backup machine and guarantee availability, would you be happy with this arrangement?
- Why don't we compromise? You know I am unable to offer you a discount, but I am more than happy to defer billing until the end of the month. Would you be willing to move forward with the agreement using these terms?

SELLING TIPS

YOUR PROSPECT'S NAME IS A POWERFUL CLOSING TOOL

Dale Carnegie, author of *How to Win Friends and Influence People,* taught his students, "If you remember my name, you pay me a subtle compliment; you indicate that I have made an impression on you." Your prospect's name is one of the most powerful closing tools because most of us are more interested in ourselves than anyone else.

Repeat your prospect's name several times—but don't overdo it—during your sales call. *Connect your prospect's name with the major benefit statements:*

- "This automatic dialing feature, Jim, will save you a lot of time."
- "Our warranty is designed to give you peace of mind, Susan."

Your prospect will not know that you are using a powerful psychological strategy referred to as *learned association* or *positive pairing.* If you have connected your prospect's name with three or four prominent product benefits, your customer will expect to hear something positive when you merely mention their name. When you approach the close, remember to use your prospect's name. Chances are that the sound of their name will again evoke positive feelings. By using this little-known secret of master sales closers, you will improve your chances of making the sale.

When you hit a tennis ball over the net, the kind of spin put on the ball determines the type of return shot received. In a negotiation, the attitude that you project determines the attitude you receive. Be positive! Be helpful! Be concerned! Show your interest in helping the prospect.

Technology Close

technology close: A close in which the buyer is shown past purchases, sales trends, purchase suggestions, and payment schedules by graphs and bar charts.

Picture this: You have just completed the discussion of your product, marketing plan, and business proposition. You summarize your product's main benefits to your customer. Now you bring out your laptop computer or tablet, placing it on the buyer's desk so they can see the screen, or you prepare to project the screen onto the wall. Using graphs and bar charts, you show the buyer past purchases and sales trends. Then you call up your recommended purchase suggestion. If appropriate, you can show payment schedules considering different quantity discounts. This **technology close** is very impressive to buyers.

The exact use of technology in closing a sale depends on the type of product and customer you're selling. Without a doubt, incorporating technology into your presentation will help you close more prospects and customers.

Assumptive Close

assumptive close: A type of close that assumes the prospect will buy.

Many times the salesperson has worked with a customer for a long time. In these instances, the salesperson has earned a high level of the customer's trust, and the salesperson can recommend and even place an order for the customer. Here, the assumptive close is especially effective. With the **assumptive close**, the salesperson assumes the prospect will buy. Statements can be made such as "I'd like to move forward with the recommendation and call your order in tonight" or "To meet the deadline we discussed, I'll have this shipped to you tomorrow." If the prospect does not say anything, assume the suggested order has been accepted.

In other instances, the customer may believe the salesperson is a valued partner. Due to this level of trust, the customer is often willing to move forward with the salesperson's recommendations. In this situation, the salesperson may state the following assumptive closes, "This is my recommendation for the product assortment and quantities that I suggest you need this month. I'd like to move forward with the order today," or "I'd like to send the following items to your distribution centres by the end of the week." Again, the assumptive close tends to be used within a more trust-based, long-term relationship.

Minor-Points Close

It is sometimes easier for a prospect to concede several minor points about a product than to make a sweeping decision on whether or not to buy. Big decisions are often difficult for some buyers. By having the prospect make decisions on a product's minor points, you can subtly lead into the decision to buy.

minor-points close: A close where the salesperson asks the prospect to make a low-risk decision on a minor element of a product.

The **minor-points close** is similar to the alternative-choice close. Both methods involve giving the buyer a choice between two options. The alternative-choice close asks the prospect to make a choice between *two* products, which represents a high-risk decision to some people that they may prefer not to make. However, the minor-points close asks the prospect to make a low-risk decision on a minor, usually low-cost element of a *single* product such as delivery dates, optimal features, colour, size, payment terms, or order quantity.

Single- or multiple-product element choices may be presented to the prospect. The automobile salesperson says, "Would you prefer the premium quality speakers or digitally integrated speakers within your new automobile?" The Xerox Business Products salesperson asks, "Are you interested in buying or leasing our equipment?" The home security system salesperson asks, "Would you like to install the 18- or the 24-camera system?"

This close is used widely when prospects have difficulty in making a decision or when they are not in the mood to buy. It is also effective as a second close. If, for example, the prospect says no to your first close because of difficulty in deciding whether or not to buy, you can close on minor points.

> *"Kind words are short and easy to speak, but their echoes are truly endless."*
>
> *MOTHER TERESA*

Compliment Close

compliment close: A close wherein the salesperson ends with a compliment to the prospect.

Effective salespeople adapt to their buyer. The **compliment close** is especially effective when you talk with a prospect who is a self-styled expert, who is quite dominant in the discussion, or who has a big ego. Would-be experts and egotistical prospects often desire recognition. By complimenting them, they listen and respond favourably to your presentation. The prospect with low self-esteem or one who finds it difficult to decide also responds favourably to a compliment. Here is an example of a consumer packaged goods salesperson closing a sale with a grocery retail buyer. Please note that the compliment should be sincere and targeted. Buyers can usually sense a false or insincere comment.

> **Salesperson:** Obviously, you have a wealth of experience within the grocery business. You have every linear foot of your store creating strong revenue gains and providing substantial profit levels. Ms. Stevenson, our products also will assist your store and your personal goals of increasing profitability. In fact, our profit will exceed your store's average profit-per-linear-foot by 25 points. And, the inventory turnover is 1.5 times greater than the average product in the competitive set. This added benefit of high turnover will further increase your cash flow–which you have said is important to you. [He pauses, and when there is no response, he continues.] Given the number of customers coming into your store, and our expected sales of these products due to normal turnover, along with our marketing plan, I'd like to recommend that you purchase 45 units per store. This will provide you with sufficient quantities to meet your customers' demands for the next two months, plus provide you with the expected profit from your products. [Now he waits for the response or again asks for the order using the alternative choice or assumptive close.]

All buyers appreciate your recognition of their better points. Conscientious merchants take pride in how they do business; customers entering the retail clothing store take pride in their appearance; people considering life insurance take pride in looking after their families. So compliment prospects relative to something that will benefit them as you attempt to close the sale. Remember, always make honest compliments. No matter how trusting you may think people are, nearly anyone can detect insincerity in a compliment. When a compliment is not in order, summarize the benefits of your product for a specific customer.

Urgency Close

For the right product, person, and situation, this is an appropriate close. Both retail and industrial salespeople can use this technique in situations in which deadlines, time constraints, inventory availability, or limited access to products and resources exist.

For instance, imagine you are representing a clothing manufacturer. You will need to communicate the time constraints associated with the availability of certain seasonal clothing lines. Prospects realize that factors such as seasonality, high sales demand, labour strikes, weather, transportation, inflation, and inventory shortages could make it difficult to buy in the future. In some instances, it is appropriate to communicate the deadline and convey a greater level of urgent action by using the urgency close.

How does the urgency close work? What happens if someone tells you that you cannot have something that you would like to have? You instantly want it! When you face an indecisive prospect that may not be able to access a product if they wait much longer or if you believe it is in a prospect's best interest to purchase a larger quantity due to limits on production or inventory, communicate that if they do not act now they may *not* be able to buy in the future. You can communicate this sense of urgency by using a **urgency close:**

urgency close: A close whereby a salesperson suggests that if a prospect does not act now, they may not be able to buy in the future, thus motivating the prospect to act immediately.

- This is the fastest selling style in our fall product line. Would you want them if I have them in stock?
- My customers have been buying all we can produce. If we don't act quickly, I'm not sure if we will have any inventory left to sell you.
- Well, I know you are thinking of ordering *X* amount, but would you please consider ordering (a larger amount) because we now have it in stock and I don't think we will be able to keep up with demand and fill your November order.
- Due to the increasing costs of commodities, the cost of this equipment will increase 10 percent next week. Would you consider writing the purchase order today so you can avoid the price increase that goes into effect next week?

By using the urgency close at the appropriate time, you may do your prospects a favour by encouraging them to buy now and thus avoid future uncertainties. However, it should be used honestly.

T-Account or Balance-Sheet Close

T-account close: A close that is based on the process that people use when they make a decision by weighing the pros against the cons.

The **T-account close** is based on the process that people use when they make a decision. Some sales trainers refer to it as the Benjamin Franklin close. In his *Poor Richard's Almanac,* Franklin said, "You know, I believe most of my life is going to be made up of making decisions about things. I want to make as many good ones as I possibly can." So, in deciding on a course of action, his technique was to take pencil and paper and draw a line down the centre of the paper. On one side he put all the pros, and on the other side he put all the cons. If there were more cons than pros, he would not do something. If the pros outweighed the cons, then he felt it was a good thing to do; it was the correct decision.

This is the process a customer uses in making a buying decision, weighing the cons against the pros. At times, it may be a good idea to use this technique on paper. Common column headings are pros and cons, debits and credits, or to act and not to act. For example, on a sheet of paper, the salesperson draws a large *T,* placing *to act* (asset) on the left side and *not to act* (liability) on the right side (debit and credit, in accounting terms). The salesperson reviews the presentation with the prospect, listing the positive features, advantages, and benefits the prospect likes on the left side and all negative points on the right. This shows that the product's benefits outweigh its liabilities, and it leads the prospect to conclude that now is the time to buy. If prospects make their own lists, the balance-sheet close is convincing. Here is an example:

Salesperson: Ms. Stevenson, here's a pad of paper and a pencil. Bear with me a minute and let's review what we have just talked about. Could you please draw a large *T* on the page and write "To Act" at the top on the left and "Not to Act" on the right? Now, you said you liked our fast delivery. Is that right?

TO ACT	NOT TO ACT
Fast delivery	Narrow assortment
Good profit	
Good credit	

Prospect: Yes.

Salesperson: OK, please write down "fast delivery" in the To Act column. Great! You were impressed with our profit margin and credit terms. Is that right?

Prospect: Yes.

Salesperson: OK, how about writing that down in the left-hand column? Now is there anything that could be improved?

Prospect: Yes, don't you remember? I feel you have a narrow assortment with only one style of broom and one style of mop. [Objection.]

Salesperson: Well, write that down in the right-hand column. Is that everything?

Prospect: Yes.

Salesperson: Ms. Stevenson, what in your opinion outweighs the other–the reason to act or not to act? [A trial close.]

Prospect: Well, the To Act column does. But it seems I need a better assortment of products. [Same objection again.]

Salesperson: We have found that assortment is not important to most people. A broom and mop are pretty much a broom and mop. They want a good quality product that looks good and that holds up continuously. Customers like our products' looks and quality. Aren't those good-looking products? [Trial close showing broom and mop.]

Prospect: They look OK to me. [Positive response–she didn't bring up assortment so assume you have overcome objection.]

Salesperson: Ms. Stevenson, I can offer you a quality product, fast delivery, excellent profit, and good credit terms. I'd like to suggest this: Buy one dozen mops and one dozen brooms for each of your 210 stores. However, let's consider this first: The XYZ chain found that our mops had excellent drawing power when advertised. Their sales of buckets and floor wax doubled. Each store sold an average of 12 mops. [He pauses, listens, and notices her reaction.] You can do the same thing.

Prospect: I'd have to contact the Johnson Wax salesperson, and I really don't have the time. [A positive buying signal.]

Salesperson: Ms. Stevenson, let me help. I'll call Johnson's and get them to contact you. Also, I'll go see your advertising manager to schedule the ads. OK? [Assumptive close.]

Prospect: OK, go ahead, but this stuff had better sell.

Salesperson: [Smiling.] Customers will flock to your stores [he's building a picture in her mind] looking for mops, polish, and buckets. Say, that reminds me, you will need a dozen buckets for each store. [Summary of benefits, keep talking.] I'll write up the order. [Assumptive.]

> *Life is like a field of newly fallen snow; where I choose to walk, every step will show. Tell the truth.*

Some salespeople recommend that the columns of the T-account be reversed so that the Not to Act column is on the left and the To Act column is on the right. This allows the salesperson to discuss the reasons not to buy first, followed by the reasons to buy, ending the presentation on the positive side. A contrary idea in the prospect's mind is like steam under pressure–explosive. So, when you remove the pressure by openly stating an objection, opposition vaporizes. An objection often becomes minor or disappears. Remember, however, if the customer says, "Well, I'm going to buy it," do not say, "Well, let's first look at the reasons not to buy." Instead, finalize the sale.

People may dislike you, be unhappy, and hard to get along with; be caring, joyous, and a pleasure to be with anyway.

Modified T-Account or Balance-Sheet or Checklist Close

Some salespeople modify the T-account close by only listing reasons to act in one column. They do not want to remind the prospect of any negative reasons not to buy as they attempt to close the sale. This is similar to a summary-of-benefits close. The only difference is that the product benefits are written on a piece of paper. For instance, think about a checklist written on a piece of paper. The checklist would contain the buyer's needs. As you review the buyer's needs, you would relay the way in which your solution meets each need.

This is a powerful sales tool because the prospects are mentally considering reasons to buy and not to buy anyway. Put the reasons out in the open so that you can participate in the decision-making process.

This close is especially useful as a secondary or backup close. For example, if the summary close did not make the sale, use this type of close. By doing so, you can ask the buyer to provide feedback on each element of your solution and how each element meets the needs.

Other Ways to Close

testimonial close: Presenting a prospect with statements from satisfied customers about your product.

There are a few other closing techniques that can be used such as the **testimonial close,** where you present the prospect with statements from satisfied customers about your product. For example, "Your neighbour, Mr. Smith, has been so pleased with our lawncare service, he mentioned that you can call him to ask any questions about our services as well." You can also show letters from previous customers using your product.

concession close: Offering a trade-off or incentive to result in an agreement to buy.

If your prospect is really sitting on the fence, it may be worthwhile to use a **concession close.** You can offer a concession in exchange for a deal or sometimes just offer a concession hoping that the prospect will see it as a sign of good faith and give you the deal anyway. For example, "I'll give you five free oil changes if you buy the car today." In this example we've made a trade-off. We've offered something IF they agree to buy.

ultimatum close: A closing technique that explains the potential negative consequences of not acting immediately.

Another final example, which needs to be used with caution, is the **ultimatum close,** which is similar to the urgency close. You explain the negative consequences of not acting now. This technique can be tricky and it sometimes can sound threatening to the buyers which can turn them off of you and your product. Some examples, "Don't forget Jim, that this sale ends tomorrow, after which I won't be able to offer this price." This type of close is not as common now as in previous years as there is now more emphasis on relationship building with customers.

LO7 Prepare a Multiple-Close Sequence

By keeping several different closes ready in any situation, you are in a better position to close more sales. Also, the use of a multiple-close sequence, combined with methods to overcome objections, enhances your chance of making a sale.

For example, you could begin with a summary close. If the buyer says no, you could rephrase the objection and then use an alternative close. If again the buyer says no and will not give a reason, you could use the four-step sequence method for overcoming objections. (See Chapter 10 for procedures on overcoming objections.)

Exhibit 11.10 gives an example of a multiple-close sequence developed by Jane Martin, who works for an electrical wholesaler. Notice that she uses both methods to overcome objections and closing techniques. First, she uses the summary-of-benefits close and then waits for a response. Martin does not rush. She realizes it is a big decision and is prepared to handle resistance and ask for the order several times. The buyer is sending out green signals, so Martin does not stop; she continues to respond to the buyer.

EXHIBIT 11.10
Multiple closes incorporating techniques for overcoming objections.

Salesperson: John, we have found that the Octron bulb will reduce your storage space requirements for your replacement stock. It offers a higher colour output for your designers, which reduces their eye fatigue and shadowing. Should I arrange for delivery this week or next week? [Close 1–Summary-of-benefits close.]
Buyer: Well, those are all good points, but I'm still not prepared to buy. It's too costly.
Salesperson: What you're saying is, you want to know what particular benefits my product has that make it worth its slightly higher price. Is that correct? [Rephrase.]
Buyer: Yes, I guess so.
Salesperson: Earlier, we saw that considering the extended life of the lamps and their energy savings, you can save $375 each year by replacing your present lamps with GE Watt-Misers. This shows, John, that you save money using our product. Right? [Trial close.]
Buyer: Yes, I guess you're right.
Salesperson: Great! Do you prefer installation this weekend or after regular business hours next week? [Close 2–Alternative close.]
Buyer: Neither; I need to think about it more.
Salesperson: I hear what you are saying. There must be some good reason that you're hesitating to go ahead now. Do you mind if I ask what it is? [Objection handling Steps 1 and 2.]
Buyer: I don't think I can afford new lighting all at one time.
Salesperson: In addition to that, is there another reason for not going ahead? [Objection handling Step 2.]
Buyer: No.
Salesperson: Group replacement is not a necessity; however, it does allow you to realize immediate energy savings on all of your fixtures. It saves you much of the labour costs of spot replacement because the lamps are installed with production-line efficiency. See what I mean? [Objection handling Steps 3 and 4.]
Buyer: Yes, I do.
Salesperson: Do you feel that installation would be better at night or on the weekend? [Close 3–Minor-points close.]
Buyer: I'd still like to think about it.
Salesperson: There must be another reason why you're hesitating to go ahead now. Do you mind if I ask what it is? [Objection handling Step 2.]
Buyer: Yes. My supervisor will not let me buy anything.
Salesperson: You agree you could save money for your company on this purchase–right?
Buyer: Yes.
Salesperson: Well, John, how about calling your supervisor now and telling her about how much money we can save in addition to reducing your storage space and the eye fatigue of your employees? Maybe both of us could visit your supervisor. [Close 4–Summary-of-benefits close.]

Source: © Arne9001/Dreamstime.com/ GetStock.com

Notice that the buyer finally gave the real reason for not buying when he said, "No. My supervisor will not let me buy anything." By professionally handling John's objections and politely continuing to close, Jane is in a position to talk with the real decision maker–John's boss.

Close Based on the Situation

Since different closing techniques work best for certain situations, salespeople often identify the common objections they encounter and develop specific closing approaches designed to overcome these objections. Exhibit 11.11 shows how different closing techniques are used to meet objections.

Assume, for example, that a buyer has a predetermined belief that a competitor's product is needed. The salesperson could use the T-account approach to show how a product's benefits are greater than a competitor's product. In developing the sales presentation, review your customer profile and develop your main closing technique and several alternatives. By being prepared for each sales call, you experience increased confidence and enthusiasm, which results in a more positive selling attitude. You can both help the customer and reach your goals.

EXHIBIT 11.11

Examples of closing techniques based on situations.

Situation / Closing approach	Alternative-choice	Compliment	Summary	Minor points	Assumptive	T-account	Urgency	Probability	Negotiation	Technology	Reason
Customer is indecisive	X		X	X		X	X	X	X		Forces a decision
Customer is expert or egotistical		X				X		X	X	X	Lets expert make the decision
Customer is hostile		X						X	X		Positive strokes
Customer is a friend					X			X	X		You can take care of the small things
Customer has predetermined beliefs						X		X	X	X	Benefits outweigh disbeliefs
Customer is greedy, wants a deal							X	X	X		Buy now
Customer is young, tech-savvy entrepreneur			X			X	X	X	X	X	Improved efficiency due to technology

LO8 Cross-Selling

I was at the hardware store the other day buying some taps for my kitchen sink. After selling me the taps, the clerk asked some questions. "Do you have enough propane at home to get the job done? How about lead-free solder? Have you considered some silicone caulking to prevent water from getting under your new taps?" These were all things I hadn't thought of and I ended up spending an extra $25 on materials, which perturbed me at first and I was a little upset with the sales clerk. It wasn't until I got home and finished the job that I realized I had in fact needed all these things and the clerk had done me a huge favour in suggesting them. An alert clerk simply doing some cross-selling probably saved me two or three trips back to the store and several hours of aggravation.

Cross-selling or **add-on selling** is an excellent way to increase the value of a sale, not only by selling more products but also by providing the customer with better service. Cross-selling involves suggesting extra or complementary products or services to a customer in addition to the main product they are purchasing. It is often useful, where applicable, to develop a script to take advantage of cross-selling opportunities. Developing a script for an add-on product or service can act as a bridge from the closed order to additional product or service selling.

cross-selling:
Occurs when a salesperson encourages a customer to purchase goods or services from other areas that may satisfy some of their needs; for example, selling a maintenance and supply agreement on a photocopier would serve as cross-selling.

add-on selling:
The process of generating additional revenues after you've closed a sale by selling additional complementary products or by increasing the value of the sale by simply selling more product.

Before attempting to use your cross-selling script, have the original order in hand. In other words, make sure you have achieved your primary objective first. Get the customer's commitment, get all the order details, and only then attempt the cross-sell. For example,

> Thank you, Ms. Kim, for the photocopier order. By the way, did you know that we offer first-time purchasers like yourself a 50 percent discount on copy paper ordered with the copier? It will not only save you money but also eliminate the need to find another supplier for paper–and our paper is specially formulated to take advantage of the many features of our machines. Would you like me to add a six-month supply of paper to the order?

The cross-sell should relate directly to the purchase, and the item should be relatively low cost in comparison to the original order (so that a major purchase decision is not necessary). A guideline is that the cross-sell should not increase the purchase amount by more than 25 percent. From a scripting point of view, the item is a related item and therefore needs little or no description. Leading off with "by the way" lends a casualness to the add-on that reduces the "hard sell" feeling that sometimes accompanies an add-on sale. The benefits are clearly expressed and, when it is done properly, most customers will perceive this as receiving extra value, not as being pushed into an order.

Prepare well before creating your cross-sell script. Examine the type of prospect to whom you will be selling. How knowledgeable are they? Will they see the add-on as an extra value, or as something requiring a little more thought? Will they require additional information to make the purchase decision?

Answers to these questions will dictate the type of add-on(s) that you may choose. For example, if your preparation had revealed that your prospect had been having a nightmare with the previous photocopier in terms of too much downtime, expensive repairs, paper jamming, and so on, your cross-sell script could include add-ons like an extended warranty agreement and your specially formulated paper. These add-ons appeal directly to the prospect's buying motives and will therefore be perceived as excellent value added.

Make cross-selling a habit. Be brief, to the point, and casual. It can have a tremendous impact on your sales figures and customer satisfaction levels. The following list provides some tips to help you cross-sell and up-sell:

1. **Close first and cross-sell later.** Do not attempt to up-sell or cross-sell until you have closed the first order. In our rush to up-sell we sometimes forget that the customer has an order to place. Selling additional items too early in the call might turn the customer off. You could lose the original sale.
2. **Follow the 25 percent rule.** The value of an add-on sale should not increase the overall order by more than 25 percent. Despite the fact that people are motivated to buy, too much up-selling may cause the customer to reconsider the entire purchase.
3. **Provide value.** On occasion, there will be an urge to use cross-selling and up-selling to move unwanted inventory. Never do this unless there is an inherent benefit to your customer. Don't saddle your prospect with unneeded merchandise just for your own benefit.

4. **Make sure it's related.** Limit your choice of add-on items to those that clearly relate to the original purchase. If a customer is buying machinery for her plant, don't try to sell her cleaning supplies for the washrooms just because you have some excess inventory of it.
5. **Plan ahead.** Cross-selling should be part of your sales plan. Appropriate up-sell products should be highlighted next to each major product in your sales notes.
6. **Be prepared.** Ensure that you are knowledgeable about the products or services that you are up-selling. Rehearse the skills necessary to get the customer to say yes. Be able to demonstrate how a particular add-on applies to and benefits the customer.
7. **Reap the rewards.** Your cross-selling efforts will be directly dependent on how motivated you are. Cross-selling and up-selling take additional time and effort. If you are not motivated, chances are the program will not succeed. Commit to the program and you are certain to increase your sales–and your compensation.

Research Reinforces These Sales Success Strategies

Although it is difficult to summarize all sales success strategies discussed throughout this book, one research report reinforces several key procedures that improve sales performance. This research sought to examine two key questions all salespeople frequently ask themselves: (1) What makes one sales call a success and another a failure? and (2) Do salespeople make common mistakes that prevent success?

To answer questions such as these, Xerox Learning Systems enlisted a team of observers to monitor and analyze more than 500 personal sales calls of 24 different sales organizations. The products and services sold ranged from computers to industrial refuse disposal.

Mike Radick, the Xerox senior development specialist overseeing the study, stated that the average successful sales call was 33 minutes long. During that call, the salesperson asked an average of 13.6 questions and described 6.4 product benefits and 7.7 product features. Meanwhile, the customer described an average of 2.2 different needs, raised 1.0 objections, made 2.8 statements of acceptance, and asked 7.7 questions.

The observers noted that the salesperson age, gender, or years of experience do not seem to matter. What matters is the ability to use certain skills and avoid common errors. These six common mistakes have prevented successful sales calls:

- **Tells instead of sells; doesn't ask enough questions** - The salesperson does most of the talking. Instead of asking questions to determine a customer's interest, the salesperson charges ahead and rattles off product benefits. This forces the customer into the passive role of listening to details that may not be of interest. As a result, the customer becomes increasingly irritated. For example, a person selling a computerized payroll system may tell a customer how much clerical time could be saved by using this service. However, if clerical time is not a concern, then the customer has no interest in learning how to reduce payroll processing time. On the other hand, the same customer may have a high need for more accurate recordkeeping and be extremely interested in the computerized reports generated by the system.
- **Overcontrols the call; asks too many closed-ended questions** - This sales dialogue resembles an interrogation, and the customer has limited opportunities to express needs. The overcontrolling salesperson steers the conversation to subjects the

salesperson wants to talk about without regarding the customer. When the customer does talk, the salesperson often fails to listen or respond, or doesn't acknowledge the importance of what the customer says. As a result, the customer is alienated and the sales call fails.

- **Doesn't respond to customer needs with benefits** - Instead, the salesperson lets the customer infer how the features will satisfy their needs. Consider the customer who needs a high-speed machine. The salesperson responds with information about heat tolerance but doesn't link that to how fast the equipment manufactures the customer's product. As a result, the customer becomes confused and loses interest, and the call fails. Research shows a direct relationship between the result of a call and the number of different benefits given in response to customer needs; the more need-related benefits cited, the greater the probability of success.
- **Doesn't recognize needs; gives benefits prematurely** - For example, a customer discussing telephone equipment mentions that some clients complain that the line is always busy. The salesperson demonstrates the benefits of their answering service, but the customer responds that busy lines are not important since people will call back. In this case, the customer is not concerned enough to want to solve the problem.
- **Doesn't recognize or handle negative attitudes effectively** - The salesperson fails to recognize customer statements of objection (opposition), indifference (no need), or skepticism (doubts). What isn't dealt with effectively remains on the customer's mind and, left with a negative attitude, the customer will not make a commitment. The research also shows that customer skepticism, indifference, and objection are three different attitudes. Each attitude affects the call differently; each one requires a different strategy for selling success.
- **Makes weak closing statements; doesn't recognize when or how to close** - In one extreme case, the customer tried to close the sale on a positive note, but the salesperson failed to recognize the cue and continued selling until the customer lost interest. The lesson is that successful salespeople are alert to closing opportunities throughout the call.

The most powerful way to close a sales call involves a summary of benefits that interest the customer. Success was achieved in three out of four calls that included this closing technique in Radick's study.

Keys to Improved Selling

How is the bridge from average to successful salesperson made? Xerox found it involves learning and using each of the following skills:

- Ask questions to gather information and uncover needs.
- Recognize when a customer has a real need and how the benefits of the product or service can satisfy it.
- Establish a balanced dialogue with customers.
- Recognize and handle negative customer attitudes promptly and directly.
- Use a benefit summary and an action plan requiring commitment when closing.[2]

Learn and use these five selling skills, use the other skills emphasized throughout the book, and develop your natural ability and a positive mental attitude to become a successful, professional salesperson.

The Business Proposition and the Close

For some salespeople, the discussion of the business proposition provides an excellent opportunity to close. The business proposition is the discussion of costs, markups, value analysis, or return-on-investment (ROI) profit forecast. It follows the discussion of a product's FABs and marketing plan. Remember, the marketing plan explains two things:

1. For wholesalers or retailers, how they should resell the product.
2. For end users, how they can use the product.

The product's FABs and marketing plan justify your suggested order. The business proposition is the third step within the presentation and very important to closing the sale. The three steps were discussed in Chapter 9.

Use a Visual Aid to Close

Using a visual aid works well in discussing the business proposition and when closing. Immediately after discussing the marketing plan for a heating system, the salesperson pulls out the profit forecaster shown in Exhibit 11.12. Notice that it is personalized with the account's name at the top.

The salesperson discusses each item on the profit forecaster. Then the salesperson says, "Based on your past sales, the profits you will earn, and our marketing plan, I suggest you buy 100 units for your three stores." The suggested order is written on the profit forecaster.

Now the salesperson remains silent. The buyer will respond with either "Yes," "No," or "That is too much to buy." While waiting, the salesperson should mentally go over what to say for each response that can be made by the buyer.

EXHIBIT 11.12

Example of a personalized visual. Using a visual is an excellent way to close. After discussing the financial information on the visual, close by suggesting what and how much should be ordered.

Source: Mila Supinskaya Glashchenko/Shutterstock

Closing Out the Sales Interview

A group of purchasing agents was asked about their biggest gripes about poor sales procedure. One item on their list was this: "They [salespeople] seem to take it personally if they don't get the business, as though you owe them something because they are constantly calling on you."[3]

Salespeople must learn that they simply cannot close every deal. Failure to close the deal should not jeopardize future relations with this and other potential prospects. Properly handling a no-sale situation can have a big impact on future sales. Attitude is everything here. Some salespeople react with anger, while some may attempt to make the prospect feel guilty or even stupid for making this decision. These reactions will seldom change the prospect's mind, but what they will do is make this prospect never want to do business with you in the future. In fact, this prospect may spread the word that you reacted this way so that others may want to stay clear of you (see Exhibit 11.13).

exit technique: A technique used by professional salespeople to keep the door open for future interactions with the prospect, in the event of not being granted the sale.

Using the **exit technique,** you might conclude by saying, "Mr. Smith, would you do one thing for your company? Would you please think about what we discussed? Please look over this material and the price sheet. I know (product name) is needed by your organization. Please call me if you have any questions. Would it be all right,

Mr. Smith, if I come by in a month or so to see what you think about (product name)?" Stand, smile, and compose yourself. While looking the buyer in the eyes and giving a firm handshake, say something like, "Thank you very much, Mr. Smith. I really enjoyed visiting with you. I look forward to seeing you next month!" Do not leave the room as if it is on fire. Leave slowly, professionally, with a smile on your face and a spring in your step. Be friendly with everyone you pass as you go to your vehicle. Call them by name if known.

EXHIBIT 11.13
Sometimes the salesperson will not make the sale, but it is important to leave the door open. If this software salesperson had not made a sale, he would have left the door open for a return sales call by being just as friendly when he left as he was when he arrived.

Source: © Stephen Coburn/Fotolia.com

After an unsuccessful close:

- Stay professional. Appreciate the prospect's reasons for not buying.
- Stay in touch. Let the prospect know that you're available for other needs.
- Stay cheerful. Don't become despondent or angry.
- Ask for referrals if you failed to close through no fault of your products.
- Leave your business card.
- Thank the prospect for their time.

After a successful close:

- Stay professional. Don't become flustered by your own success.
- Stay in touch. Let the customer know you're available for assistance.
- Stay cheerful. Be somebody who is a pleasure to deal with.
- Show appreciation for their time and business. People like to feel appreciated.
- Depending on the situation, it may be a good time to ask for referrals.

Regardless of the outcome of the sales interview, at the end of the day, salespeople should review their successes and failures and use this information to strengthen their ability to present effectively.

Get the Order—Then Move On!

Talking can stop the sale after the prospect has said yes. An exception would be asking the customer for names of other prospects. Once this is done, it is best to take the order and move on.

In continuing to talk, you may give information that changes the buyer's mind. So, ask for the order and remain silent until the buyer responds. If you succeed, finalize the sale and leave.

Summary of Major Selling Issues

Closing is the process of helping people to make decisions that will benefit them. You help people make those decisions by asking them to buy. The close of the sale is the next logical sequence after your presentation. At this time, you finalize details of the sale (earlier, your prospect was convinced to buy). Constantly look and listen for buying signals from your prospect to know when to close. It is time to close the sale any time the prospect is ready, whether at the beginning or the end of your presentation.

As you prepare to close the sale, be sure you have presented a complete story on your proposition and that your prospect completely understands your presentation. Tailor your close to each prospect's personality and see the situation from the

ETHICAL DILEMMA

STRETCH THE TRUTH TO CLOSE THE SALE?

You are seated across the table from a serious procrastinator. You have tried several closing techniques to no avail. She just can't seem to make up her mind. Throughout the presentation, you picked up on several cues suggesting that she wants the product and you know in your heart that her company could really use it.

Suddenly, you remember the "urgency close" technique. You hadn't really thought about it because you knew that you had plenty of merchandise in inventory and there were no price increases planned in the near future. You figure that if you presented this procrastinator with an urgent plea, it might push her over the edge and you could finally get her commitment.

Do you stretch the truth a lot to secure the order and tell her that there is some sort of time limit on the offer?

prospect's viewpoint. Remember that you may make your presentation and close too early, which causes a prospect to say no instead of "I don't understand your proposition, and I don't want to be taken advantage of." This is why you should never take the first no. It is another reason to use a trial close immediately before the close. But, no matter when or how you close, do so in a positive, confident, and enthusiastic manner to better serve your prospect and help you reach your goals. Learn and abide by the 12 keys to successful closing.

Plan and rehearse closing techniques for each prospect. Develop natural closing techniques or consider using closes such as the alternative-choice, assumptive, compliment, summary-of-benefits, minor-points, T-account, urgency, probability, negotiation, or technology close. Consider the situation and switch from your planned close if your prospect's situation is different from what you anticipated.

A good closer has a strong desire to close each sale. You should rarely accept the first no as the final answer. If you are professional, you should be able to close a minimum of three to five times. Make sure not to become upset or unnerved if a problem occurs when you are ready to close. Keep cool, determine any objections, overcome them, and try again to close—you can't make a sale until you ask for the order! Remember, whether the sales interview was successful or unsuccessful, how you close out the sales interview will have a big impact on your future sales ability.

MEETING A SALES CHALLENGE

Sumit had finished her presentation. Jovan and Ralph had not. At least Sumit was able to tell her whole story. Jovan and Ralph should have postponed discussing price. They may have lost all hope of making the sale.

In all three cases, the prospect said, "Your price is too high." Many buyers learn or are trained to say this to see whether the seller will decrease the price.

When the buyer said, "What's your price?" Jovan could have said, "It will depend on the type of service you need and the quantity purchased. Let's discuss that in just a minute." When the buyer said, "Your competitor's price is $10 cheaper!" Jovan could say, "I quoted you our base price. Your actual price will depend on the quantity purchased. We can meet and beat that price [the competitor's price]."

Sumit needs to find out more, such as what specific equipment and from whom. Equipment is different. So are service, terms, and delivery.

When Ralph's buyer says, "Your price is too high," Ralph needs to find out what the buyer is using for comparison. Ralph's buyer may not need the top-of-the-line model. So Ralph must get back to a discussion of the buyer's needs before determining the model and price.

PLAYING THE ROLE

Role A: A salesperson. Using a product that you have with you (cell phone, calculator, laptop, pen, pencil, etc.), develop a SELL sequence that would likely form part of a presentation of that product. Follow the SELL sequence by demonstrating any five of the following closing techniques:

- alternative-choice close
- assumptive close
- compliment close
- minor-points close
- negotiation close
- probability close
- summary of benefits close
- T-account close
- technology close
- testimonial close
- urgency close

Role B: A prospect.

Dramatize the SELL sequence and closing techniques to see how convincing you can be. Have your classmates analyze your close for its delivery, confidence, and conviction.

Key Terms for Selling

add-on selling	**concession close**	**T-account close**
aggressiveness	**cross-selling**	**technology close**
alternative-choice close	**exit technique**	**testimonial close**
assertiveness	**minor-points close**	**trial close**
assumptive close	**negotiation close**	**ultimatum close**
buying signal	**probability close**	**urgency close**
closing	**SELL sequence**	
compliment close	**summary-of-benefits close**	

Sales Application Questions

1. A salesperson must use a closing technique that is simple and straightforward and ask the prospect only to buy—not to buy *and* do something in addition to buying. In which of the following examples, if any, is the salesperson suggesting something to the buyer that is a close, rather than something the buyer must do in addition to buying?
   a. If you have no objection, I'll go out to the warehouse now to see about reserving space for this new item.
   b. To get this promotion off right, we should notify each of your store managers. I've already prepared a bulletin for them. Should I arrange to have a copy sent to each manager, or do you want to do it?
   c. To start this promotion, we should notify each of your store managers. I've already prepared a bulletin for them. On my way out, I can drop it off with the secretary.
   d. We should contact the warehouse manager about reserving a space for this new item. Do you want to do it now or after I've left?
2. Buying signals have numerous forms. When you receive a buying signal, stop the presentation and move in to close the sale. For each of the following seven situations, choose the appropriate response to your prospect's buying signal that leads most directly to a close.
   a. "Can I get it in blue?" Your best answer is
      (i) "Yes."
      (ii) "Do you want it in blue?"
      (iii) "It comes in three colours, including blue."

b. "What's your price?" Your best answer is
   (i) "In what quantity?"
   (ii) To quote a specific price.
   (iii) "For which grade?"

c. "What kind of terms do you offer?" Your best answer is
   (i) To provide specific terms.
   (ii) "Terms would have to be arranged."
   (iii) "What kind of terms do you want?"

d. "How big an order do I have to place to get your best price?" Your best answer is
   (i) A schedule of quantity prices.
   (ii) A specific-size order.
   (iii) "What size order do you want to place?"

e. "When will you have a new model?" Your best answer is
   (i) A specific date.
   (ii) "Do you want our newest model?"
   (iii) "This is our newest model."

f. "What is the smallest trial order I can place with you?" Your best answer is
   (i) A specific quantity.
   (ii) "How small an order do you want?"
   (iii) A variety of order sizes.

g. "When can you deliver?" Your best answer is
   (i) "That depends on the size of your order. What order size do you have in mind?"
   (ii) A specific delivery date.
   (iii) "When do you want delivery?"

3. Which of the following is the most frequently committed sin in closing? Why?
   a. Asking for the order too early.
   b. Not structuring the presentation toward a closing.
   c. Not asking for the order.
4. Is it a good closing technique to ask the customer at the right time, "Well, how about it? May I have the factory ship you a carload?" Explain your answer.
5. After completing a presentation that has included all of your product's FABs, should you immediately ask the customer, "How much of the product do you wish to order?" Explain your answer.
6. Each visual aid used during your presentation is designed to allow the customer to say yes to your main selling points. What should your visual aids include that allows you to gauge customer interest and help move to the close? What are several examples?
7. "Now, let's review what we've talked about. We've agreed that the Mohawk's secondary backing and special latex glue make the carpet more durable and contribute to better appearance. In addition, you felt that our direct-to-customer delivery system would save a lot of money and time. Shall I send our wall-sample display or would you be interested in stocking some 9 by 12s?"
   a. The salesperson's closing statement helps ensure customer acceptance by doing which of the following?
      (i) Summarizing benefits that the customer agreed were important.
      (ii) Giving an alternative.
      (iii) Assuming that agreement has been reached.
   b. The salesperson ends the closing statement by
      (i) Asking whether the customer has any other questions.
      (ii) Asking whether the product will meet the customer's requirements.
      (iii) Requesting a commitment from the customer.
8. "Assuming agreement has been reached" reflects the kind of attitude you should project when making a closing statement. When you make a close, nothing you say should

reflect doubt, hesitation, or uncertainty. Which of the following salesperson's remarks assume agreement?

a. "If you feel that Munson is really what you want . . ."
b. "Let me leave you two today and deliver the rest next week . . ."
c. "Well, if you purchase . . ."
d. "Well, it looks as if maybe . . ."
e. "We've agreed that . . ."
f. "When you purchase the X-7100 . . ."
g. "Why don't you try a couple, if you like . . ."

9. A good rule is, "Get the order and get out." Do you agree? Explain your answer.
10. The real estate salesperson is showing property to a couple who look at the house and say, "Gee, this is great. They've taken good care of this place and the rugs and drapes are perfect. Do you think they'd be willing to leave the rugs and drapes?" What should the salesperson do or say? Why?

Sales Online Exercise

Research Helps You Be a Better Closer!

Pick an event happening at your school and think of prospects to sell to or an organization you can approach to sponsor it. You might think of selling advertisements or tickets to events on campus, or getting contributions to a cause. Choose a prospect–someone or some organization that might buy what you are selling. Using the appropriate websites and your school's library, research the prospect.

Write a report to your boss on the sources you found useful in planning your sales presentation. Be sure to include how you would ask for the order, including what to buy and the quantity and how the prospect would benefit from the purchase.

Further Exploring the Sales World

1. Assume you are interviewing for a sales job and there are only five minutes remaining. You are interested in the job and know that if the company is interested, you will be invited to visit the company's local distribution centre and to work with one of their salespeople for a day. What are several closing techniques you could use to ask for the visit?
2. Visit several retail stores or manufacturing plants in your local area and ask their purchasing agents what they like and do not like about the closing when they are contacted by salespeople. See if they have already decided to buy or not to buy before the salesperson closes. Ask how a salesperson should ask for their business.
3. Develop a complete sales presentation that can be given in eight minutes. Include the buyer-seller dialogue. Make sure the appropriate components in Exhibit A are contained in the presentation. Use one of the three approaches shown in Exhibit A (on the next page) depending on your situation. For example, use the SPIN approach if this is the first time you have called this prospect. Use the SPIN or summary-of-benefits approach if this is a repeat sales call on a prospect or customer.

Your presentation must use several SELL sequences and should contain: a minimum of one evidence statement; two similes or analogies; and a demonstration of important benefits. The marketing plan also must incorporate one or more SELL sequences that tie the marketing plan back to the information uncovered in the approach and the first SELL sequence.

The business proposition is last and contains the appropriate discussion on price and value. Relate the business proposition to the information uncovered earlier in the presentation.

EXHIBIT A

Format of your sales presentation.

A. Approach

1. Situation question(s)
   Problem question(s)
   Implication question(s)
   Need–payoff question

2. Problem question(s)
   Implication question(s)
   Need–payoff question

3. Summary of benefits

B. Presentation

- SELL sequences
  - —Evidence statement
  - —Two similes, metaphors, or analogies
  - —Demonstration
  - —Visuals
- Marketing plan (incorporating SELL)
  - —Tie back to benefits
  - —Visuals
- Business proposition (incorporating SELL)
  - —Value analysis
  - —Return-on-investment
  - —Discounts
  - —Markups, margins
  - —Tie back to benefits
  - —Visuals
- Summarize benefits your buyer was interested in
- Discuss suggested order

C. Multiple-close sequence

- Close
- Objection
- Close
- Objection
- Close
- Etc.

Develop visuals for presenting your benefits, marketing plan, and business proposition. Anywhere within the presentation before the close, use a minimum of one objection, and answer one of the buyer's questions with a question.

Now, ask for the order using a summary-of-benefits close that includes a suggested order if appropriate for your product or service. Use a minimum of three closes. This requires you to develop *a multiple-close sequence* since the buyer has raised an objection or asked for more information after each close. Also, use different methods of handling objections. In the presentation, be sure to (1) have a professional appearance; (2) shake hands firmly and use direct eye contact before and after the presentation; (3) project positive nonverbal signs; and (4) use a natural level of enthusiasm and excitement in conversation.

Student Application Learning Exercises (SALES)

Part 7

Now it's time to ask for the order! Frequently, questions and objections arise when you ask someone to buy. Thus, you should anticipate questions and objections and be prepared to use several different closing and objection-handling techniques.

1. List the main benefits discussed in your presentation.
2. Select a closing technique, such as the summary-of-benefits close. Write out your close and label it with the name of the closing technique in parentheses. Use a trial close after completing the close to verify these are important benefits to the buyer.

Write out your trial close and label it using parentheses as shown in the Summary-of-Benefits Close section of this chapter.

3. Create a visual aid showing your suggested order. See Exhibit 11.12 for an example. This visual aid may be similar to or the same as the one you developed for discussing your price(s).
4. Now you are ready to construct your multiple-close sequence. First carefully study Exhibit 11.5. Now look at the example of a multiple-close sequence in Exhibit 11.10. The multiple-close sequence should be composed of the following:
   a. Your summary-of-benefits close
   b. Your trial close
   c. Your suggested order
   d. Use of the assumptive or alternative close
   e. Having the buyer ask a question or give an objection
   f. A response using another objection-handling technique
   g. A trial close to see whether you successfully handled the objection
   h. Asking for the order again using an unused closing technique; don't be pushy and use a calm, laid-back, friendly conversational style
   i. Repeating the close-objection-close-objection sequence if appropriate
5. Write up the above parts *a–i* in a script format. Role-play this dialogue until it sounds natural to you. This may require replacing the used techniques with new ones. Once the manuscript is finalized turn it in to your instructor.

CASE 11–1

THE GROOMING STORE

The Grooming Store, a large chain of personal-care retail stores, has mailed you an inquiry on personal-care items. They want to know about your electric shavers, moustache trimmers, and hair grooming kits. On arrival, you make a presentation to the purchasing agent, Christina Mercuri. You state that you have visited several of their stores. You discuss your revolving retail display, which contains an assortment of the three items Mercuri had mentioned in her inquiry, and relate the display's advantages and features to benefits for The Grooming Store.

During your presentation Mercuri has listened but has said little and has not given you any buying signals. However, it appears she is interested. She did not object to your price, nor did she raise any other objections.

You approach the end of the presentation and it is time to close. You have said everything you can think of.

QUESTIONS

1. What is the best way to ask Mercuri for the order?
   - *a.* "How do you like our products, Ms. Mercuri?"
   - *b.* "What assortment do you prefer, the A or B assortment?"
   - *c.* "Can we go ahead with the order?"
   - *d.* "If you'll just OK this order form, Ms. Mercuri, we'll have each of your stores receive a display within two weeks."
2. Discuss the remaining alternatives from Question 1, ranking them from good to bad, and state what would likely happen if a salesperson responded in that manner.

CASE 11–2

CENTRAL HARDWARE SUPPLY

Sam Gillespie, owner of Central Hardware Supply, was referred to you by a mutual friend. Gillespie was thinking of dropping two of his product suppliers of home-building supplies. "The sale should be guaranteed," your friend had stated.

Your friend's information was correct, and your presentation to Gillespie convinces you that he will benefit from buying from you. He comments as you conclude the presentation: "Looks like your product will solve our problem. I'd like to think this over, however. Could you call me tomorrow or the next day?"

QUESTIONS

1. The best way to handle this is to
   - *a.* Follow his suggestion.
   - *b.* Ignore his request and try a second close.
   - *c.* Probe further. You might ask: "The fact that you have to think this over suggests that I haven't convinced you. Is there something I've omitted or failed to satisfy you with?"
2. What would be your second and third choices? Why?

CASE 11–3

FURMANITE SERVICE COMPANY—A MULTIPLE-CLOSE SEQUENCE

Chris Henry sells industrial valves and flanges, tapes, and sealants. He is calling on Gary Maslow, a buyer from Shell Oil, to sell him on using Furmanite to seal all of his plant's valve and flange leaks. Chris has completed the discussion of the product's features, advantages, and benefits, the marketing plan, and the business proposition. Chris feels it is time to close. Chris says:

Salesperson: Let me summarize what we have talked about. You have said that you like the money you will save by doing the repairs. You also like our response time in saving the flanges so that they can be rebuilt when needed. Finally, you like our three-year warranty on service. Is that right?

Buyer: Yes, that is about it.

Salesperson: Gary, I suggest we get a crew in here and start repairing the leaks. What time do you want the crew here Monday?

Buyer: Not so fast–how reliable is the compound?

Salesperson: Gary, it's very reliable. I did the same service for Petro-Canada last year, and we have not been back for warranty work. Does that sound reliable to you?

Buyer: Yeah, I guess so.

Salesperson: I know you always make experienced, professional decisions, and I know that you think this is a sound and profitable service for your plant. Let me schedule a crew to be here next week or maybe in two weeks.

Buyer: Chris, I am still hesitant.

Salesperson: There must be a reason that you are hesitating to go ahead now. Do you mind if I ask what it is?

Buyer: I just don't know if it is a sound decision.

Salesperson: Is that the only thing bothering you?

Buyer: Yes, it is.

Salesperson: Just suppose you could convince yourself that it's a good decision. Would you then want to go ahead with the service?

Buyer: Yes, I would.

Salesperson: Gary, let me tell you what we have agreed on so far. You like our online repair because of the money you would save, you like our response time and the savings you would receive from the timely repair of the leaks, and you like our highly trained personnel and our warranty. Right?

Buyer: Yes, that's true.

Salesperson: When would you like to have the work done?

Buyer: Chris, the proposition looks good, but I don't have the funds this month. Maybe we can do it next month.

Salesperson: No problem at all, Gary; I appreciate your time, and I will return on the fifth of next month to set a time for a crew to start.

QUESTIONS

1. Label each of the selling techniques used by Chris.
2. What were the strengths and weaknesses of this multiple-close sequence?
3. Should Chris have closed again? Why?
4. Assume Chris felt he could make one more close. What could he do?

Source: © Caia Images/Glow Images

CHAPTER 12

Follow-up—Maintain and Strengthen the Relationship

Krystal Milo,
Vanier College,
Saint-Laurent, Quebec

Source: Courtesy of Krystal Milo

A Sales Success Story

Krystal Milo graduated from the three-year Business Administration: Marketing program at Vanier College in 2018. A big part of her learning process at Vanier came from participating in the BDC Case Competition, a Canada-wide case competition. In her second year at Vanier she volunteered at the competition and really started to take interest in the event. She worked hard in her Case class and further grew her skills. In her final year, Krystal, along with three other students, were selected to be part of the team representing Vanier at the competition. She was thrilled, and she and her team worked day-in and day-out training for the competition. Over the course of their training they completed nearly 50 cases and even trained during their holiday break.

In this type of stressful competition, preparation is everything—and Krystal and her team truly understood this. "The competition is so fast-paced! Essentially, we are put in a room, given a computer with no Internet, pens and paper, and a business case that we've never seen before. We're given 3 hours to read, analyze, and prepare a 20-minute PowerPoint presentation. At the end of the 3 hours, we are taken immediately to stand in front of a panel of industry experts to present our 20-minute case analysis, followed by a 5-minute question period." The BDC Case Competition is a two-day competition with 24 teams, and Krystal and her teammates placed first in a unanimous decision by the judges.

At the end of her last semester, Krystal and her classmates were expected to find a four-week marketing internship. Having participated in this case competition, she knew exactly what kind of internship she wanted to get. Krystal found an internship with two individual financial advisers, working as their web designer and social media manager. This internship allowed her vast creative liberty, which is something she was hoping for.

After completing the internship, one of the financial advisers she worked for, Averton Financial Services, hired her for a full-time position. Shortly after, she was promoted to her current position as marketing communications director. "The position is everything I could've hoped for in a job, especially because of my busy university-student schedule. All my jobs are on contract, which means I get paid per project and I can decide when and which projects I want to take on. What makes this job so great is all the liberty and leadership I am given the opportunity to use. I thrive in situations where I get to take control, and that's exactly what I get to do every day in my current position; I get to see jobs through, beginning to end, and am trusted to make important decisions as I see fit. Jobs range from web design to website management, social media management to creating entirely new innovative social media campaigns, and using and testing new platforms like Ulinc and LinkedIn Sales Navigator to find prospects fit to our target market and generate new leads."

Krystal has been working with Averton Financial Services for more than a year now and is very happy in her position. She is being challenged every day with new tasks and successfully tries new things outside of her comfort zone. "I couldn't have done it without the help of my college, the teachers, and especially my coaches for my case competition team. They believed in me and pushed me to be better and more strategic, and they allowed me to be a part of an event and competition that truly changed me and my outlook on marketing and my career path. The internship that I chose turned into a great job, but I wouldn't have chosen it prior to all the training and competition that I took part in. I discovered my love for selling and persuasive marketing while being a part of all this. Finding something that you both love and are good at is truly the recipe for success, and that is the most important piece of advice I could give to anyone."

MAIN TOPICS

Customer Satisfaction, Retention, and Engagement

Relationship Marketing and Customer Retention

The Product and Its Service Component

Excellent Customer Service and Satisfaction Require Technology

Understand the Importance of Post-Call Analysis

How Does Service Increase Your Sales?

Remember Why You Are Following Up

Turn Follow-up and Service into a Sale

Account Penetration Is a Secret to Success

8 Steps to Increasing Your Customer's Sales

Service Can Keep Your Customers

Cross-Sell Your Way to Increased Sales

If You Lose a Customer—Persevere

Handle Complaints Fairly

Build a Professional Reputation

Dos and Don'ts for Business Salespeople

LEARNING OBJECTIVES

Providing service to the customer is critical in today's competitive marketplace. After studying this chapter, you should be able to:

- **LO1** Understand the importance of customer satisfaction, retention, and engagement.
- **LO2** State why service and follow-up are important to increasing sales.
- **LO3** Discuss how follow-up and service result in account penetration and improved sales.
- **LO4** List the eight steps involved in increasing sales to your customer.
- **LO5** Explain how cross-selling as part of your follow-up campaign can contribute to higher sales volumes.
- **LO6** Explain the importance of properly handling customers' returned-goods requests and complaints in a professional manner.

FACING A SALES CHALLENGE

As a construction machinery salesperson, you know that equipment malfunctions and breakdowns are costly to customers. Your firm, however, has an excellent warranty that allows you to replace a broken piece of equipment with one of your demonstrators for a few days while the equipment is repaired. King Masonry has called you four times in the past three months because the mixer you sold them has broken down. Each time you have cheerfully handled the problem, and in less than two hours they have been back at work. Your company's mixer has traditionally been one of the most dependable on the market, so after the last breakdown, you let King Masonry keep the new replacement in hopes of solving any future problems.

The owner, Eldon King, has just called to tell you the newest mixer has broken down. He is angry and says he may go to another supplier if you cannot get him a replacement immediately.

How would you handle this situation?

(Continued at end of chapter.)

Customer retention, service, and follow-up are essential to the success of a salesperson in today's competitive markets. This chapter, the last in our discussion of the elements of the selling process, discusses the importance of follow-up and service, ways to keep customers, methods for increasing sales, and how to handle customer complaints. It ends by emphasizing the need to act professionally when servicing accounts.

Customer Satisfaction, Retention, and Engagement

LO1

Customer satisfaction refers to feelings toward the purchase. As illustrated in Exhibit 12.1, perceived purchase satisfaction is the customer's feelings about any differences between what is expected and actual experiences with the purchase. If satisfied, customers have an increased chance of buying in the future. If satisfied with repeat purchases, customers tend to continue to buy from the salesperson. Can you afford to lose a customer? Depending on the nature of the business, it can cost up to eight times more to acquire a new customer than it does to retain one. Remember that loyal customers are worth many times the price of a single purchase.

customer satisfaction: The feelings about any differences between what is expected and actual experiences with the purchase.

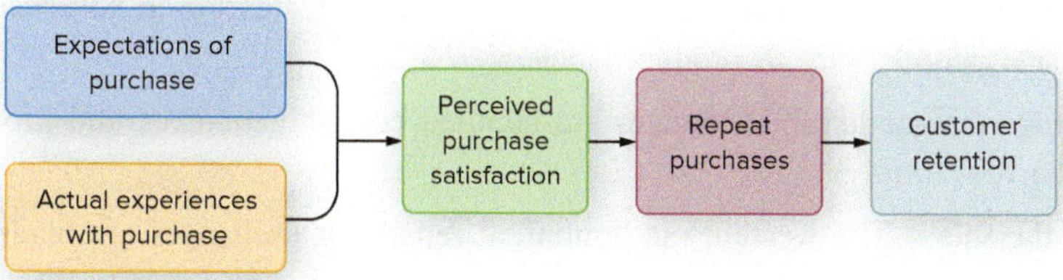

EXHIBIT 12.1

Customer retention: when the buyer is satisfied with purchases over time.

Satisfaction can result in a customer so loyal that it is very difficult for another seller to get their business. Thus, customer retention is critical to a salesperson's long-term success. Don't take retention for granted. There are too many opportunities and temptations today for customers to wander into a competitor's realm, which may cost you some business. Hence, not only is satisfaction and retention important, but so too is customer engagement. The more you keep your customer engaged with you and your products, the less likely it is they will wander.

Relationship Marketing and Customer Retention

Chapter 1 discussed these three levels of customer relationship marketing:

- **Transaction selling** - A customer is sold and not contacted again.
- **Relationship selling** - After the purchase, the seller finds out whether the customer is satisfied and has future needs.
- **Partnering** - The seller works continually to improve the customer's operations, sales, and profits.

Relationship marketing is a creation of customer loyalty and retention. Organizations use combinations of products, prices, distribution, promotions, and service to achieve this goal. Relationship marketing is based on the idea that important customers need continual attention.

An organization using relationship marketing is not simply seeking a sale or a transaction. It has targeted a major customer that it would like to sell to now and in the future. The company would like to demonstrate to the customer that it has the capabilities to serve the account's needs in a superior way, particularly if a *committed relationship* can be formed. Retaining customers is much less expensive and time consuming than finding new ones. Customer relationship marketing provides the key to retaining customers.

The Product and Its Service Component

product:
A bundle of tangible and intangible attributes, including packaging, colour, and brand, as well as the services and even the reputation of the seller.

When a customer buys a product, what is being purchased? A **product** (good or service) is a bundle of tangible and intangible attributes, including packaging, colour, and brand, and the services and even the reputation of the seller. People buy more than a set of physical attributes; they buy satisfaction, such as what the product does, its quality, and its image.

Note the phrase *and the services*. Buyers usually believe an organization ought to deliver a certain level of service with a product. Here are several expected services:

- **Product** - The product purchased has no defects.
- **Price** - The product gives fair value for the price.
- **Place** - The product is available when and where needed and promised.
- **Promotion** - The customer receives correct, honest information in advertisements, from salespeople, and on product labels.
- **Exchange transaction** - Exchanges are handled correctly, quickly, and professionally the first time.
- **After the sale** - The warranty is honoured; repairs or exchanges are made cheerfully; written information or a company representative is available to discuss how to put together, hook up, or use the product.

When buying something, you have certain expectations of what you are receiving for your money. So do organizations. Did the customer receive what was expected? The answer to this question determines the level of service quality perceived by the buyer.

Customer service (see Chapter 6) refers to the activities and programs provided by the seller to make the relationship satisfying for the customer. The activities and programs add value to the customer's relationship with the seller. Warranties, credit, speedy delivery, accurate invoices, financial statements, computer-to-computer ordering, parking, gift wrapping, and not being out of stock are services all designed to satisfy customers.

Expectations Determine Service Quality

The quality of service provided by an organization and its salespeople must be based on its customers' expectations. Customers expect a certain level of service from the seller. Their expectations frequently are based on information provided by the salesperson, past experience, word of mouth, and personal needs. When buyers perceive service received as what they expected, they are satisfied. Thus, service quality must match the customers' expectations.

Excellent Customer Service and Satisfaction Require Technology

Providing good service to customers in today's competitive marketplace is not enough—service must be excellent. Depending on the size of your customer base, it is often necessary to use technology to manage your relationship with your customers. As shown in Exhibit 12.2, customers often visit social media platforms such as Facebook and LinkedIn to post their grievances and expect the selling organizations to respond quickly.[1]

We have also discussed the usefulness of CRM (customer relationship management) software as it pertains to gathering data for use during the pre-approach stage of the selling process. The importance of this technology is shown by the intense competition among CRM software firms. This technology is useful in preparing for

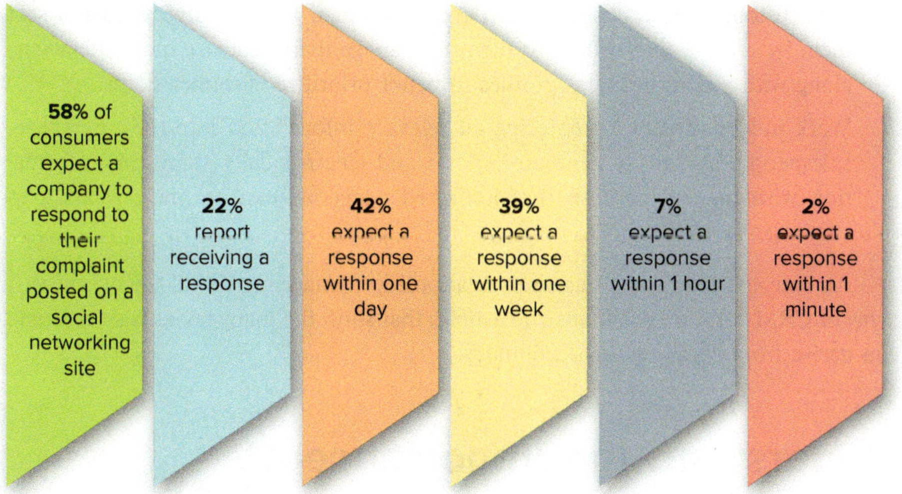

EXHIBIT 12.2

Technology may provide a means to enable the salespeople to communicate in a more responsive manner.

sales presentations, but is also often used in the areas of follow-up and relationship management.

With the proliferation of CRM software, salespeople are able to do the following:

1. Develop detailed databases with information about all of their customers and customers' purchases.
2. Organize mail-outs, phone calls, and follow-ups. Check out outreach.io to review software where salespeople can schedule, prioritize, and personalize emails and establish automated responses and follow-up. Vidyard.com is another new company that creates easy-to-send videos of business professionals to give a sales email a more personal message and capture the attention of customers.
3. Receive a notification when it is the best time to call customers after a sale.
4. Perform data mining, which involves looking for hidden patterns in a group of data; data mining can help salespeople find customers with similar interests, needs, and/or purchase patterns.
5. Through email, accept messages or direct messages when absent, then be alerted to the situation when logging into the system.

SELLING GLOBALLY

CUSTOMER SERVICE IN THE REAL WORLD

Hartness International is a supplier of case packers and other high-speed packaging equipment. The company has a commitment to be the "best supplier of packaging in the world."

In a large manufacturing company, equipment downtime can be as costly as $150 per minute. If a machine breaks down, how long will it take a technician to get there? Even if you get someone there in 24 hours, the loss in production can be as much as $200,000. To address this problem, Hartness has highly trained customer service personnel who can handle many common problems by telephone. For more difficult problems, Hartness uses videoconferencing. Each Hartness installation comes with a wireless camera and all the equipment needed to transmit images back to Hartness's offices in North Carolina. Technicians there direct in-plant maintenance and repair crews to fix problems. About 80 percent of problems can be fixed this way.

For the serious problems, the other 20 percent, Hartness has a local fleet of four aircraft that will fly technicians to plants without being held hostage to the regularly scheduled airlines.

Even when the customer is paying for the service, this method is a lot less expensive than downtime costs. If you're a sales representative for Hartness International, you can truly promise the highest level of service to your customers!

6. Sort customers; salespeople should know who their best customers are and sort them by criteria that will allow them to manage their database most effectively, along with generating sales profiles to better prioritize customer needs.
7. Work independently; by entering all relevant information into their database, salespeople can easily generate reports and electronically share this information with management so that informed decisions can be made relating to customer service.

An Internet search of "customer relationship management" will uncover a vast array of CRM software programs and articles that show the many benefits salespeople can derive from adopting this technology.

Understand the Importance of Post-Call Analysis

In a day where you rush from one sales call to another, it is important to discipline yourself to debrief properly after each key customer dialogue. Taking the time to think, plan, and strategize is an effective way to maximize sales. By employing a post-call analysis, you will come across as a true professional at the next face-to-face meeting.

Determine beforehand what it is important for you to accomplish during the sales call and develop your pre-call objectives as discussed in Chapter 7. Then, after each call, compare your call results to your call objectives. Develop a post-call analysis form to simplify this process (see below). List only questions that are relevant to your situation. Understand that this analysis will encourage you to look at your prospects and clients in ways you previously may not have considered. Determine what is most important to *you* and what you can use. Then, most importantly, act on the information.

Questions for Post-Call Analysis

1. Did you achieve your objective(s) for your meeting?
2. What did you learn about your client's decision-making process?
3. What did you learn about your client's timing of the decision?
4. Who are the key players in the decision-making process?
5. What did you learn about the decision roles within the process?
6. In what ways did you employ your questioning strategy?
7. What are the key solutions that you are considering for this client?
8. Summarize areas of uniqueness and/or competitive advantage.
9. What issues were brought up that could help or hinder you?
10. What is the potential for you and/or your products?
11. What do you need to follow up on?
12. What promises did you make that you need to keep?
13. Summarize your strategy to retain and/or grow this client.
14. Who else within your company should be involved with this client?
15. Who else might need to be involved from the client's organization or business?

Critique your own dialogue with your prospect. Make sure you did the following:

- Explain key FABs.
- Deal adequately with objections.

- Use trial closes in an effective manner.
- Attempt to gain commitment.

How Does Service Increase Your Sales?

LO2

Take a look at Exhibit 12.3. By now you are very familiar with it! You increase sales by obtaining new customers and selling more products to present customers. What is the best method for obtaining new customers? For many types of sales, customer referrals are best. Customers provide referrals when they are satisfied with the salesperson. So how important is it to your success and livelihood to take care of your customers? Even though it is last in the selling process, Step 10 is extremely important to a salesperson's success.

After Step 10 of the selling process, the salesperson moves back to Step 2, the pre-approach, when it's time to plan the next sales call on a customer. Meanwhile, the salesperson is also prospecting, as discussed in Chapter 6. Thus, the salesperson is involved in the ongoing process of finding new customers and taking care of present customers. With this review in mind, let's discuss service and follow-up techniques.

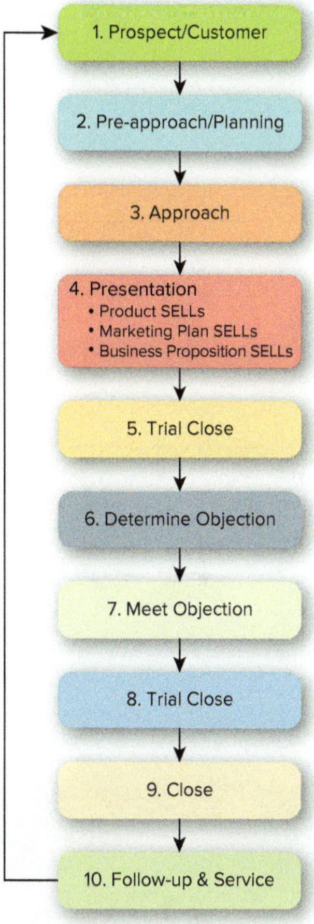

EXHIBIT 12.3

Sales come from current and new customers. Salespeople are constantly involved in follow-up and service and planning their next sales call on the customer; they also spend time prospecting.

Remember Why You Are Following Up

Having heard nothing for three months after buying a new car, a customer received a telephone call from the dealer reminding him that it was time for vehicle servicing. Although at first glance this could be viewed as a great service being performed by the dealer for the customer, is it? Is this a follow-up call or is it a prospecting call by the service department for more business? Perhaps it could be considered both.

A **follow-up** services the needs of customers after the sale in order to ensure customer satisfaction. As a salesperson, the last thing you want is recent customers experiencing difficulty with a product just purchased. The longer this situation continues, the worse their opinion becomes of the product, you, and your company. Two things can happen. First, customers will begin talking to anyone who will listen about the terrible experience they are having with your product. This is the beginning of a bad reputation for your business. Second, these customers may feel the need to complain, which leads to an angry call to you. Unfortunately, the timing of this call is likely more convenient for customers than for you. This may be a very important part of the day for you, as perhaps you are preparing for a major sales presentation to another customer. Having to address calls like this can be time consuming and frustrating.

> **follow-up:** One of the last steps in the selling process, involving servicing the needs of the customer after the sale in order to build a long-term relationship.

Fortunately, this whole negative situation can be avoided by salespeople who, with or without the aid of CRM software, develop a regular follow-up campaign. To do this, they must ask three important questions:

1. **Who?** Most of the time, the answer to this should be, "everybody who makes a purchase." However, in some instances, salespeople will have to establish some criteria as to which customers warrant a follow-up call and which do not. One must consider factors such as the nature of the product, the amount of the sale, the potential for future sales, etc. Most CRM systems today allow salespeople to sort their customer list by criteria that are useful to their type of business.
2. **When?** Although follow-up calls usually are appreciated, some may find them bothersome. "I just bought this product last week. What do you want now?" To prevent problems from developing, salespeople should make their first follow-up call a few days after their customer has taken delivery

and had a chance to use the product. Any further delay might provide time to formulate negative attitudes. Of course, some products may require a call sooner and some later, depending on the nature of the product. A local pizza franchise made it a habit of calling customers about one hour after their pizza had been delivered to ensure customer satisfaction—a call that was often appreciated. A car, or piece of machinery, on the other hand, would require a longer waiting period so that the customer has a chance to experience the product.

3. **How?** How salespeople follow up is often determined again by the type of customer and the nature of the product. Some of the options include a telephone call, personal visit, letter or personal note, fax, text, or email. It is best to personalize the follow-up as much as possible. A telephone call is probably the most time efficient and practical in most situations. Designate time each day or every few days to make these calls. This is an excellent use of any downtime that salespeople experience during the day. You can also use software to help you plan your day and remind you to call or email. A personal visit may be appropriate where the sale or product was very large, such as a piece of major machinery, or for a regular customer. Often, it is a nice touch to send a personalized, handwritten note to a customer. Using email can be useful, but its impersonal nature makes it less effective.

The Call

What do you say? Remember that one of the main purposes of making this call is to maintain your relationship with the customer. Show that you care. It's your job to care. Typically, a follow-up call should be short so you're not considered bothersome.

Turn Follow-up and Service Into a Sale

High-performing salespeople can convert follow-up and service situations into sales (see Exhibits 12.4 and 12.5).

EXHIBIT 12.4

A sample follow-up call.

PURPOSE	EXAMPLE
Introduction: Some prospects may need reminding who you are and where you're from.	"Hello Mrs. Marks, this is Gillian Mullet from Star Enterprises. Last week we delivered the photocopier that you ordered three weeks ago."
Identify your purpose for calling.	"The reason I'm calling is to make sure that everything went well with the delivery and that everyone is enjoying the many features of the copier."
Check their satisfaction level.	"Do you or any of your employees have any questions about its operation? Is it doing the job you wanted it to do?"
Show appreciation. People like to feel appreciated.	"Well, I'd like to thank you once again for your business. I'm sure you and your employees will be very happy with your decision to purchase the LV200."
Inform the buyer that you're available for help. Be positive.	"Just so you know, if you have any questions about the copier, you can reach me at [contact information]."
Leave the door open for future opportunities with this buyer or others.	"I'm glad that everything is working out fine. If you or anyone you know needs any of my products, feel free to call at any time. I'll check back with you in a few months to see how things are going."

A large jewellery retailer gives some examples:

> I send customers a thank-you card immediately after the sale, and after two weeks, I call again to thank them and see if they are pleased with their purchase. If the purchase is a gift, I wait before contacting the customer, or I contact the spouse. This has been a key to my success in building a relationship and in farming or prospecting. Very often I get a lead.
>
> Here is how it works. In two weeks they have shown it around to someone who has made a comment. I start with, "Is everything OK?" Then I say, "Well, I know Judy [or Jack] is really proud of it, and I'm sure she's [he's] shown it to someone—parents, family, friends. I was curious whether there is anyone I could help who is interested in something. I'd like to talk to them or have you call and see if they'd like me to call them." If I've done a good job, the customer feels good about letting me call this individual and will help me. If I wait too long to call, they say, "Well, someone was asking about it, but I've forgotten who it was."
>
> My biggest sale to a single customer was $120,000. It took about two weeks. A man initially called asking for 12 diamonds to give two stones to each of his children. In handling this, I found some other pieces I felt were good for him—a ruby ring, a 4.62-carat sapphire ring, a gold and diamond bracelet, and two other rings. He bought everything. Thus, much of my success comes from follow-ups, suggestion selling [when someone comes in for something and they buy other things], or service situations. Once you realize you can turn routine situations into sales, retail selling becomes exciting and challenging.[2]

EXHIBIT 12.5

Follow-up calls can be productive. Here, a sales rep follows up her sale with an email outlining additional uses for the product before heading off to meet another customer.

Source: © Darren Baker/Fotolia.com

Follow-up and service help satisfy the needs of customers. Another way to help customers involves account penetration.

Account Penetration is a Secret to Success

LO3

Follow-up and service create goodwill between a salesperson and the customer, which increases sales. By contacting the customer after the sale to see that the maximum benefit is derived from the purchase, a salesperson lays the foundation for a positive business relationship. Emmett Reagan of Xerox says:

> Remember that there is still much work to be done after making the sale. Deliveries must be scheduled, installation must be planned, and once the system is operational, we must monitor to ensure that our product is doing what is represented. This activity gives us virtually unlimited access to the account, which moves us automatically back to the first phase of the cycle. We now have the opportunity to seek out new needs, develop them, and find new problems that require solutions. Only this time, it's a lot easier because, by now, we have the most competitive edge of all, a satisfied customer.[3]

The ability to work and contact people throughout the account, discussing your products, is referred to as **account penetration**. Successful penetration of an account allows you to properly service that account by uncovering its needs and problems.

account penetration: The ability to work and contact people throughout the account, discussing your products.

SELLING TIPS

FOLLOW UP BY TELEPHONE—SOME SIMPLE STEPS

1. **Have an objective.** Don't call just because you feel you should. Have a purpose for the call and review it before you pick up the phone.
2. **Prepare.** Make sure you have listed what you want to incorporate into this call. Don't just start talking, or you may end up having wasted your and your customer's time.
3. **Be ready.** It's good to set aside a certain part of the day or week to make follow-up calls and it shouldn't be a task that you're dreading. Most customers appreciate the attention—you should find this one of your more enjoyable sales tasks.
4. **Be conversational.** Stick to your purpose but listen carefully. Don't try to monopolize the conversation—you may become annoying.
5. **Remember that you've already made the sale.** At this point, you should be working on developing your relationship. The call should sound like two friends are speaking candidly to each other, not like one is trying to push the other into something.
6. **Watch your timing.** Call at a time when your customer is not likely to be extremely busy. You've already taken some of their time and you don't want to come across as an annoyance.
7. **Think about what's next.** Decide on the next step you'll be taking with this customer. You're here to help them, not sell them, so make this known. Ask if there's anything else you can do to provide value to them and if not, ask if you can call them at some future time.
8. **Seek referrals.** If this call goes smoothly and you sense an opportunity, it may be a good time to ask for a referral. Perhaps you should ask in a more passive way so it doesn't appear that this was really the purpose of the call in the first place. "If you hear of anyone who could use . . . please pass my name along."

Achieving successful account penetration is dependent on knowledge of that account's key personnel and their situation. If you do not have a feel for an account's situation, you reduce your chances of maximizing sales in that account.

Tailor the presentation to meet buyers' objectives and provide benefits to them. By knowing your buyers, their firms, and other key personnel, you uncover their needs or problems and develop a presentation that fulfills the needs or solves the problems. Account penetration is determined by the following:

- Your total and major-brand sales growth in an account
- Distribution of the number of products in a product line, including sizes used or merchandised by an account
- Level of cooperation obtained, such as reduced resale prices, shelf space, advertising and display activity, discussion with their salespeople, and freedom to visit with various people in the account
- Your reputation as the authority on your type of merchandise for the buyer

As a general rule, the greater your account penetration, the greater your chances of maximizing sales within the account. Earning the privilege to move around the account freely, either physically or by phone, allows you to uncover prospect needs and to discuss your products with people throughout the firm. As people begin to know you and believe that you are there to help, they allow you to take action that ultimately increases sales, such as expanding shelf space or talking with the users of your industrial equipment in the account's manufacturing facilities. A good sign that you have successfully penetrated an account is when a competitor dismally says, "Forget that account; it's already sewn up." You have created true customer loyalty.

SELLING TIPS

CAN SOMEONE PLEASE HELP ME?

Customer: May I speak to Alain, please? I want to reorder.

Supplier: Alain isn't with us anymore. May someone else help you?

Customer: What happened to Alain? He has all my specs; I didn't keep a record.

Supplier: Let me give you Roger; he's taken over Alain's accounts.

Customer: Roger, you don't know me, but maybe Alain filled you in. I want to reorder.

Salesperson: You want to reorder what?

Customer: I want to repeat the last order, but increase your number 067 to 48.

Salesperson: What else was in the order?

Customer: Alain had a record of it. It's got to be in his file.

Salesperson: Alain isn't here anymore, and I don't have his records.

Customer: Who does?

Salesperson: I don't know. I'm new here, so you'll have to fill me in on your requirements. Are you a new customer?

Customer: Does four years make me new?

Salesperson: Well, sir, you are new to me. How long ago did you place your order?

Customer: Last month.

Salesperson: What day last month?

Customer: I don't remember; Alain always kept track of it. Maybe I could speak to the sales manager?

Salesperson: You mean Mort?

Customer: No, I think his name is Enzo.

Salesperson: Enzo left us about the same time as Alain. I can ask Mort to call you, but I'm sure he doesn't have your file either.

Customer: Roger, have you ever heard that your best prospect is your present customer?

Salesperson: Is that true?

Customer: I don't think so.

Multiply this conversation by the millions of times it happens each year, and you have the biggest deterrent to sales in North America.

8 Steps to Increasing Your Customer's Sales

LO4

To maximize your sales to a customer, develop a customer benefit program. This means helping the account to use in its business or sell to its customers a level of merchandise equal to its maximum sales potential. There are two methods:

1. Have current customers buy *more* of a product than they currently use.
2. Have current customers buy the same products to use for different purposes. For example, a Johnson & Johnson retail sales representative may encourage accounts to stock the firm's baby shampoo in both the infant care and adult toiletries sections of their establishments.

Source: Jackbluee/Dreamstime.com/GetStock.com

It is often not difficult to sell repeat orders; however, to maximize sales in an account with a retailer, for example, you must persuade the customer to consistently promote your product through advertisements, displays, and reduced prices. To increase sales with a customer, the following steps can be taken. Each step cannot be used in all situations, but using some can increase sales.

Step 1

Develop an account penetration program. Develop a master plan for each account consisting of specific actions to take toward developing friends within the account and increasing sales.

Step 2

Examine your distribution. Review the merchandise currently used or carried in inventory. If the account is not using or carrying some of your merchandise, concentrate on improving your distribution. For example, if you have four sizes of a product and the account carries only one or two of them, develop a plan to persuade the customer to carry all four sizes. A general goal may be having each account carry all sizes of your products.

Step 3

Keep merchandise in the warehouse and on the shelf. Never allow the account to run out of stock. Stockouts result in lost sales for your firm and account. Routine calls on customers help to avoid stockouts. If the account is critically low on merchandise, telephone in an emergency order. Quick service can maintain, or even increase, your credibility as a sales professional.

Step 4

Fight for shelf space and shelf positioning. If you are selling consumer goods, constantly seek the best shelf space and aisle position. On each sales call, stock the shelf, keep your merchandise clean, and develop merchandising ideas. For example, during a routine visit to a client's store, a consumer-goods salesperson found that one of his products with a list price of $2 was being sold for $1.79. This enterprising salesperson taped a small sign to the shelf showing both prices and later discovered that sales of the product increased. This device is now used routinely for all of this salesperson's products.

Step 5

Assist the product's users. If you sell business products, help users learn to operate them properly. Make users aware of product accessories that might aid them in performing a function in a safer, better, or more profitable manner. This type of account servicing can increase both account penetration and sales.

Step 6

Assist the reseller's salespeople. To ensure enthusiastic promotion of your firm's products, work closely with your account's sales force. Experience indicates that manufacturers' salespeople who cultivate the friendship of the reseller's salespeople and provide them with product knowledge and selling tips are more successful than salespeople who call only on buyers. For example, a successful pharmaceutical salesperson suggested to all retail salespeople involved in a certain account that as they hand a customer a prescription for an antibiotic they say, "When taking these antibiotics, you also should double up on taking your vitamins." Well, most customers are not taking vitamins, so when they say, "I don't have any vitamins," the salesperson hands them a bottle of vitamins, saying, "I take these myself and highly recommend them to you." Of course, this manufacturer's salesperson previously gave the retail salespeople sample bottles of vitamins. This sales tip accounted for an increase of more than 300 percent in vitamin sales for this reseller.

Step 7

On each sales call, demonstrate your willingness to help the account through your actions. Your actions–not just words–are what build respect or distaste for you. Pull off your coat and dust, mark, stack, and build displays of your merchandise, and return damaged merchandise for credit. Let the buyer know that you are there to help increase retail sales.

Step 8

Obtain customer support. By working hard to help your customers reach their goals through doing the activities just discussed, you will find that they help and support you. You help them; they help you. This type of relationship benefits you and the customer.

Again, there is no guarantee that doing everything suggested in this text will always result in a sale. Nevertheless, conscientious use of sound selling principles *will* increase your likelihood of overall success.

Vincent Norris of Scientific Equipment Corporation sent us a copy of his secret to sales success. Although follow-up is at the bottom of his list of secrets shown in Exhibit 12.6, it is extremely important, as you can see.

• Think positively	. . . and follow up
• Plan carefully	. . . and follow up
• Present thoroughly	. . . and follow up
• And follow up	. . . and follow up
. . . and follow up	. . . and follow up
. . . and follow up	. . . and follow up
. . . and follow up	. . . and follow up

EXHIBIT 12.6

A super sales success secret.

SOCIAL MEDIA INSIGHTS FOR SALESPEOPLE

SOCIAL MEDIA AND CUSTOMER ENGAGEMENT

Using social media is an excellent way to stay in touch with your customers once you've sold them something and established the beginning of a relationship. While traditional, personal follow-up is still an excellent way to stay in touch, there are many social media tools available that can serve to keep your customers engaged. Here are a few examples:

1. Work with your customers. Provide more information than what may be readily available. Using one of the social media platforms, perhaps you could offer weekly tips on how to get the most out of your products—perhaps leading to more profitability for your customers. They're likely to stay engaged with this type of information.
2. Provide educational material. Use your expertise to present information on current products as well as potential new products. Even industry and market information could be shared with customers to "keep them in the loop." It would likely become regular reading for them and of course, provide you with almost constant exposure.
3. Interact. Make it a practice to answer frequently asked questions. Perhaps you could even set time aside each week to answer one-off questions for clients. This practice is sure to be appreciated.

These are just a few examples of how salespeople can keep their customers engaged after a sale using social media. Customers would appreciate this and there would be fewer reasons for them to feel abandoned and seek help elsewhere.

Service Can Keep Your Customers

You work days, weeks, and sometimes months to convert prospects into customers. What can you do to ensure that they buy from you in the future? After landing a major account, consider these six factors:

1. **Concentrate on improving your account penetration.** As discussed earlier, account penetration is critical in uncovering prospect needs or problems and consistently recommending effective solutions through purchasing your products. This allows you to demonstrate that you have a customer's best interests at heart and are there to help.

2. **Contact new accounts frequently on a regular schedule**. In determining the frequency of calls, consider the following:
   - Present sales or potential future sales to the account
   - Number of orders expected in a year
   - Number of product lines sold to the account
   - Complexity, servicing, and redesign requirements of the products purchased by the account

   Since the amount of time spent servicing an account may vary from minutes to days, be flexible in developing a call frequency for each customer. Typically, invest sales time in direct proportion to the actual or potential sales represented by each account. The most productive number of calls is reached at the point where additional calls do not increase sales to the customer. This relationship of sales volume to sales calls is referred to as the *response function* of the customer to the salesperson's calls.
3. **Handle customers' complaints promptly**. This is an excellent opportunity to prove to customers that they and their businesses are important and that you sincerely care about them. The speed with which you handle even the most trivial complaint shows the value that you place on that customer.
4. **Always do what you say you will do**. Nothing destroys a relationship with a customer faster than not following through on promises. Promises made and subsequently broken are not tolerated by professional buyers. They have placed their faith (and sometimes their reputation) in you by purchasing your products, so you must be faithful to them to ensure future support.
5. **Provide service as you would to royalty**. By providing your client with money-saving products and problem-solving ideas, you can become almost indispensable. You are an adviser to listen to rather than an adversary to haggle with. Provide all possible assistance.
6. **Show your appreciation**. A buyer once said to a salesperson, "I'm responsible for putting the meat and potatoes on your table." Customers contribute to your success, and in return, you must show appreciation. Thank them for their business and do them favours. Here are several suggestions:
   - Although you may be hundreds of kilometres away, make contact immediately whenever you've thought of or seen something that may solve one of your customers' problems.
   - Email links to information that may interest your customers even if the material has no bearing on what you're selling. They could be items from trade journals, magazines, newspapers, or newsletters.
   - Write congratulatory notes to customers who have been elected to office, promoted to higher positions, given awards, and so on.
   - Send newspaper clippings about your customers' families, such as marriages, births, and activities.
   - Send holiday or special-occasion cards. If you limit yourself to just one card for the entire year, send a Canada Day card. This makes a big impression on customers.
   - Send annual birthday cards. To start this process, subtly discover when your prospects were born.
   - Prepare and email a brief newsletter, perhaps quarterly, that keeps customers informed of important matters.

These are just a few of the many practical ways you can remember customers. The important point is to personalize whatever you send. It doesn't take much thought, energy, or time to send a card, newspaper clipping, website link, or copy of an article. The secret to impressing customers is to personalize the material with a couple of sentences in your own handwriting. Be sure it's legible!

Cross-Sell Your Way to Increased Sales

LO5

Encouraging existing customers to spend more can have a dramatic effect on your sales volumes. However, to successfully cross-sell you have to get your timing right. As we know, it is far more costly to get a new customer than it is to keep an existing one. Therefore, it should become a natural part of every salesperson's follow-up campaign to cross-sell—that is, encourage more business from the customers you already have. This statement is probably true of most businesses, no matter what field they're in. It's a question of knowing what to sell and when to sell it. Cross-selling is synonymous with up-selling and full-line selling. The underlying purpose of these is to look for opportunities to add value to the sale, both for you and for your customer.

Cross-selling should become a natural process—if you are selling photocopiers, selling a maintenance plan would be a natural extension for those requiring frequent maintenance. If you sell machinery, you might try to sell lubricants and an extended warranty. Often all it takes to gain that extra sale is to tell the customer about the product or service.

Some people worry that they will irritate customers by cross-selling. Actually, the reverse is usually true—you are demonstrating an interest in them and showing that you are aware of their requirements, and this is usually appreciated. Cross-selling involves six fundamentals:

1. Know your products.
2. Know your customers and their business.
3. Ask questions and listen for clues.

Send a text message—make use of any downtime.

Source: © Diego.cervo/Dreamstime.com/GetStock.com

4. Assess customers' needs and suggest only appropriate products.
5. Treat the sale as a suggestion so that clients will feel comfortable about volunteering the information and will find it easy to accept the offer.
6. Don't make it difficult for the customer to say no. Most customers do not want to be hounded, which will only hurt the relationship.

To get the most from cross-selling, identify the customers who are most appropriate. Using your CRM software, you might identify people who have bought certain products that lend themselves to cross-selling. Your database should flag you on the follow-up to make appropriate cross-selling suggestions.

To make a particular cross-sell more tempting, relate it directly to the customer's needs. For example, if you're selling productivity software to a client, you might also offer them training sessions, or day planners and organizers.

Timing is essential. While you can cross-sell at any time, there are particularly suitable moments:

- Many companies have stringent budgeting procedures, so if you push your extra sales at the wrong time you may be up against company policy. To avoid this, try to find out when your client's budgeting takes place. If you time your proposal right, they will have money in hand and maybe even spare budget for extras.
- Move when the need is present. For example, when the end of the calendar year is approaching, selling new day planners, organizers, and calendar refills not only will be profitable for you but also will satisfy a legitimate need for your customer.

Another Benefit of Questions

You can increase the chances of making a cross-sale by asking questions. Asking if people want anything else can only gain you business. You won't lose whatever product or service the customer has already purchased, so there is only an upside. Perhaps near the end of a follow-up call you could simply ask, "Is there anything else you might need at this point?" and perhaps even make a suggestion or two. Cross-selling is one of the easiest and least intrusive marketing techniques. If it's well thought out and executed, it can greatly benefit your bottom line.

If You Lose a Customer—Persevere

All salespeople suffer losses, either of a sale or of an entire account to a competitor. Four things can win back a customer:

1. **Visit and investigate**. Contact the buyer and your friends within the account to determine why the customer did not buy from you. Find out the real reason.
2. **Be professional**. If you have completely lost the customer to a competitor, let the customer know you have appreciated past business, that you still value the customer's friendship, and that you are still friendly. Remember to assure this lost account that you are ready to earn future business.
3. **Don't be unfriendly**. Never criticize the competing product that your customer has purchased. If it was a bad decision, let the customer discover it. Making sales means never saying, "I told you so!"
4. **Keep calling**. Treat a former customer like a prospect. Continue to make calls normally; present your product's benefits without directly comparing them to the competition.

Like a professional athlete, a professional salesperson takes defeat gracefully, moves on to the next contest, and performs so well that victories overshadow losses. One method of compensating for the loss of an account is to increase sales to existing accounts.

MAKING THE SALE

FOLLOW-UP: AN OFTEN IGNORED STEP

National Sports Distributors supplied sporting equipment to private schools across Canada through the National Association of Private School Athletics (NAPSA). It operated on five-year-long supply contracts. Kim Sangster, the marketing professional for National, was responsible for handling this contract. Kim thought that this contract had been managed effectively, having had no major complaints over the past several years. Kim made a point of calling on each province's association whenever travelling through the area (approximately once each year). When the contract came up for renewal, NAPSA insisted on two-year contracts from then on and, despite Kim's best efforts, the new contract was lost to a competitor that in fact had higher prices than National. Kim was perplexed and very upset by the decision.

What may have happened? Can you suggest what Kim's next steps should be?

Handle Complaints Fairly

LO6

Customers may be dissatisfied with products for any number of reasons:

- The product delivered is a different size, colour, or model than the one ordered.
- The quantity delivered is less than the quantity ordered—the balance is back-ordered (to be delivered when available).
- The product does not arrive by the specified date.
- Discounts (trade or promotional payment) agreed on are not rendered by the manufacturer.
- The product does not have a feature or perform a function that the customer believed it would.
- The product is not of the specified grade or quality (does not meet agreed-on specifications).

Whenever you determine that the customer's complaint is honest, make a settlement that is fair to the customer. "The customer is always right" is a wise adage to follow. Customers actually may be wrong, but if they honestly believe they are right, no amount of haggling or arguing will convince them otherwise. A valued account can be lost this way.

Occasionally, a dishonest customer may require you and your company not to honour a request. One of the authors relates the following experience.

> Retailer A once purchased some of my firm's merchandise from Retailer B, who had a fire sale and eventually went out of business. Retailer A insisted he purchased it from me and that I return close to $1,000 of damaged goods to my company for full credit. He actually had paid ten cents on the dollar for it at the fire sale. I told Retailer A that I would have to obtain permission from the company to return such a large amount of damaged goods.
>
> That afternoon, a competitive salesperson told me that Retailer A had asked him to do the same thing. I informed my sales manager of the situation. He investigated the matter and found out about Retailer B, who had sold most of

> his merchandise to Retailer A—who happened to be my customer. I went back and confronted Retailer A with this and said it was company policy only to return merchandise that was purchased directly from me. This was a rare situation, yet you must occasionally make similar judgments considering company policy and customer satisfaction.

Remember, unhappy customers are much more likely to tell others about their bad experience than satisfied customers are to tell about their good experience. Therefore customers should always get the benefit of the doubt. Complaints can actually be a positive thing and, in a sense, should be welcomed. If the same complaint arises repeatedly, perhaps it's time to change something so that the complaint is dealt with before it is raised again. Always have a plan for problem solving. For example:

- Obtain as much relevant information from your customer as possible. Listen very carefully.
- Remain calm and stay professional at all times. Remember, it's not likely they are complaining about you. The complaint is probably about your company or product—so don't personalize the situation.
- Express sincere regret for the problem. Thank them for bringing the situation to your attention.
- Display a service attitude (a true desire to help).
- Review your sales records to make sure the customer purchased the merchandise.
- Handle the complaint quickly and cheerfully if the customer is right. Provide an appropriate solution.
- Follow up to make sure the customer is satisfied.

Take care of your customers—especially large accounts. They are difficult to replace and are critical to success. When you take care of accounts, they take care of you as they know you'll look after them in tough situations.

ETHICAL DILEMMA

I APPRECIATE YOUR BUSINESS

People buy from you for many reasons, but primarily because of your excellent products and the service you and your company provide to customers. You follow the Golden Rule: "Do unto others as you would have them do unto you." You feel that customers put the food on your table. They are responsible for the good income you earn. You appreciate that and always try to show your gratitude for their trust and business.

You have occasionally been taking one of your customers, whom you like personally, out to lunch. Recently, this customer's purchases have increased from $50,000 to $650,000 a year. You want to show your appreciation by buying your customer two season tickets for the local Canadian Football League team. The buyer and his spouse are avid football fans. However, if your other clients and co-workers found out, they might view the gift as unprofessional.

What would be the most ethical action to take?

1. Get a season ticket for yourself and for your client. That way, you can always justify it as a "business meeting" if people ask.
2. Buy your client and his spouse the season tickets. You are just trying to show your appreciation for his business.
3. Do not buy the season tickets. It is unprofessional to mix work and social ties. Instead, write your client a nice thank-you letter stating that you appreciate his continued business.

Do you have any other suggestions?

Build a Professional Reputation

This text stresses the concept of sales professionalism. Sales professionalism directly implies that you are a professional person—due the respect and ready for the responsibilities that accompany the title. In speaking before a large class of marketing students, one sales manager for a large university textbook publishing company continually emphasized the concept of sales professionalism. This man stated that a professional sales position is not just an 8-to-5 job. It is a professional and responsible position promising both unlimited opportunity and numerous duties. This veteran emphasized that a sales job is an especially good vocational opportunity because people are looking for "someone we can believe in; someone who will do what she says—a sales professional."

To be viewed as a professional and respected by your customers and competitors, consider these ten important points:

1. Be truthful and follow through on what you tell the customer. Do not turn off your conscience when you start work each day.
2. Maintain an intimate knowledge of your firm, its products, and your industry. Participate in your company's sales training, and take continuing education courses.
3. Speak well of others, including your company and competitors.
4. Keep customer information confidential; maintain a professional relationship with each account.
5. Never take advantage of a customer by using unfair, high-pressure techniques.
6. Be active in community affairs and help to improve your community. For example, live in your territory, be active in public schools, and join worthwhile organizations such as the Chamber of Commerce, environmental organizations, and so forth.
7. Think of yourself as a professional and always act like one. Have a professional attitude toward yourself and your customers.
8. Remember your online presence counts too. You are visible to all via social media. Do not compromise your reputation with unflattering comments, pictures, or other content.
9. Provide service "above and beyond the call of duty." Remember that it is easier to maintain a relationship than to begin one. What was worth attaining is worth preserving. When you do not pay attention to customers, they find someone who will. The professional salesperson never forgets a customer after the sale.
10. Don't take your best customers for granted. Often, salespeople will unwittingly mistreat their best customers because "they're already customers." They don't offer price breaks and may not even provide their best service. If you continue to do this, you may lose these "best" customers to your competition.

Source: © Yuri Arcurs/Dreamstime.com/GetStock.com

Dos and Don'ts for Business Salespeople

What do purchasing agents expect of business salespeople? A survey of purchasing agents showed that they expect results. The following list shows the most important traits that purchasing agents found in their top business salespeople:

- Willingness to advocate for the buyer within the supplier's firm
- Thoroughness and follow-through after the sale
- Knowledge of the firm's product line

- Market knowledge and willingness to keep the buyer up to date
- Imagination in applying products to the buyer's needs
- Knowledge of the buyer's product line
- Preparation for sales calls
- Regularity of sales calls
- Diplomacy in dealing with operating departments
- Technical education–knowledge of specifications and applications

The survey also asked purchasing agents what they did not like salespeople to do in sales calls. The results, as shown in Exhibit 12.7, are "The Seven Deadly Sins of Business Selling."[3] Purchasing agents want salespeople to act professionally, to be well trained, to be prepared for each sales call, and to keep the sales call related to *how the salesperson can help the buyer.*

Professional selling starts in the manufacturer's firm. A professional attitude from the manufacturer reinforces professionalism among the sales force. One such company is B.J. Hughes, a division of the Hughes Tool Company. B.J. Hughes manufactures and sells oil-field equipment and services to companies in the oil and gas industry. Exhibit 12.8 presents Hughes's checklists of *dos* and *don'ts* for its salespeople. By providing these checklists, the company encourages them to act professionally.

EXHIBIT 12.7

The seven deadly sins of business selling.

THE SEVEN DEADLY SINS OF BUSINESS SELLING
1. **Lack of product knowledge** - Salespeople must know their product line as well as the buyer's line or nothing productive can occur.
2. **Time wasting** - Unannounced sales visits are a nuisance. When salespeople start droning about golf or grandchildren, more time is wasted.
3. **Poor planning** - A routine sales call must be preceded by some homework–see whether the call is necessary.
4. **Pushiness** - This includes an overwhelming attitude, backdoor selling, and prying to find out a competitor's prices.
5. **Lack of dependability** - There is a failure to stand behind the product, keep communications clear, and honour promises.
6. **Unprofessional conduct** - Knocking competitors, drinking excessively at a business lunch, sloppy dress, and poor taste aren't professional.
7. **Unlimited optimism** - Honesty is preferred to being a good news bearer who promises anything to get an order. Never promise more than you can deliver.
A FEW COMMENTS FROM PURCHASING AGENTS
• "They take it personally if they don't get the business; it's as though you owe them something because they constantly call on you."
• "I don't like it when they blast through the front door like know-it-alls and put on an unsolicited dog-and-pony show that will guarantee cost saving off in limbo somewhere."
• "Many salespeople will give you any delivery you want, book an order, and then let you face the results of their 'short quote.'"
• "They try to sell *you,* rather than the product."
• "After the order is won, the honeymoon is over."
• "Beware the humble pest who is too nice to insult, won't take a hint, won't listen to blunt advice, and is selling a product you neither use nor want to use, yet won't go away."

SALESPERSON'S CHECKLIST OF DOS	SALESPERSON'S CHECKLIST OF DON'TS
Know the current products/services and their applications in your area. Look for the new techniques/services your customers want.	Never bluff; if you don't know, find out.
Maintain an up-to-date personal call list.	Never compromise your, or anyone else's, morals or principles.
Listen attentively to the customers.	Don't be presumptuous—never with friends.
Seek out specific problems and the improvements your customers want.	Never criticize a competitor—especially to a customer.
Keep calls under five minutes unless invited to stay.	Do not take criticisms or turndowns personally—they're seldom meant that way.
Leave a calling card if the customer is not in.	Do not worry or agonize over what you cannot control or influence. Be concerned about what you *can* affect.
Identify the individual who makes or influences decisions and concentrate on that person.	Do not offend others with profanity.
Entertain selectively; your time and your expense account are investments.	Do not allow idle conversation to dominate your sales call. Concentrate on your purpose.
Make written notes as reminders.	Don't try to match the customer drink-for-drink when entertaining. Drink only if you want to and in moderation.
Plan work by the week, not by the clock. Plan use of available time. Plan sales presentations. Have a purpose.	Don't use high-pressure tactics.
Ask for business on every sales call.	Never talk your company down—especially to customers. Be proud of it and yourself.
Follow through with appropriate action.	

EXHIBIT 12.8

B.J. Hughes's checklist of dos and don'ts help it to be a customer-oriented company

Words of Sales Wisdom

Salespeople are often guided by their eagerness to sell. Some salespeople view selling as a competitive sport—they have to win. After all, salespeople are only human. They want to be successful. They have bills to pay and people to support. Many feel under pressure to sell, and others are driven by greed. "Yes, I am here to help," said a salesperson, but "I am here mainly to sell."

This book, however, offers sales wisdom you can use to learn how to help others through the purchase of their products and services rather than how to sell in pursuit of their own self-interest. Caring for people is the beginning of sales wisdom. The purpose of this book has been to teach you how to become an effective salesperson and experience long-term career success by doing what is right and just and fair. This book strives to help new salespeople gain knowledge and discretion and to help seasoned salespeople add to their learning.

proverb:
A short, wise, easy-to-learn saying that calls a person to think and act.

Sales Proverbs

A **proverb** is a short, wise, easy-to-learn saying that calls a person to think and act. The following are a few proverbs of sales wisdom:

- Customer choice among suppliers has never been greater.
- You lose *X* percent of sales or customers per year.
- People do not care how much you know until they know how much you care.
- You do business with the one you trust and you trust the one you know.
- 80 percent of your profits comes from about 20 percent of your customers.
- Obtaining new customers and selling more products to present customers are the ways to increase sales.
- Like a ripple in water, satisfied customers will tell others about their positive experiences.
- It is always easier to sell a satisfied customer than an unsatisfied one or a prospect.
- The cost of acquiring a new customer is higher than keeping a present customer.

What does this mean to the salesperson? Take excellent care of your current customers!

knowledge:
Knowing something gained through experience and/or training.

wisdom:
The ability to make good use of knowledge.

Knowledge versus Wisdom

Knowledge is good, but there is a vast difference between **knowledge** (having these facts) and **wisdom** (applying these facts to taking care of customers). You may amass knowledge, but without wisdom your knowledge is useless. You must learn how to live out what you know. In this age of information, knowledge is plentiful but wisdom is scarce. Wisdom means far more than simply knowing a lot. It is a basic attitude that affects every aspect of life. The foundation of knowledge and wisdom is to honour and respect everyone.

Wisdom Is Learned

In sales, you gain wisdom through a constant process of growing. First, you must trust and honour people. Second, you must realize that your purpose is to help people. Third, you must make a lifelong series of right choices and avoid moral pitfalls. Fourth, you must learn from your errors and recover. People do not develop all aspects of sales wisdom at once. A sales career involves both science and art that take time to learn.

Exhibit 12.9 helps illustrate the importance of follow-up and service. The business relationship begins after you sell to someone. This is referred to in Exhibit 12.9 as commitment.

If the salesperson is to have the privilege of selling again, the customer must answer positively to questions like these:

1. Can I trust this person?
2. Did the product and salesperson do what was presented?
3. Does the salesperson truly care about me?

If the customer answers yes to these questions, certainly they will allow the salesperson to make future presentations. Will the customer always buy? No. But if the customer feels the salesperson is trustworthy and cares, they often will give the salesperson the benefit of the doubt and buy rather than taking a chance on another salesperson.

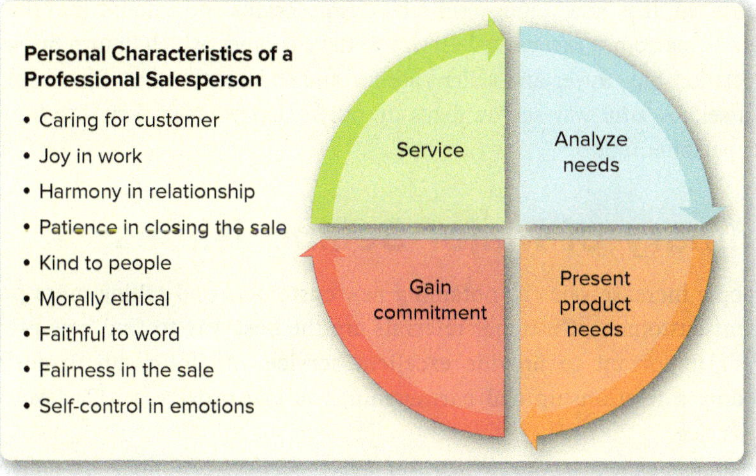

EXHIBIT 12.9

If customers are truly important, their needs come first. Sellers should care about customers as much as themselves.

True Caring Builds Relationships and Sales

What is the purpose of the sales call? Is it solely to make a sale? Or is the sales call meant to help someone? There is a big difference! The potential buyer can often see this difference.

Exhibit 12.9 shows that the salesperson first analyzes the prospect's, customer's, or organization's needs. Although this can take time, it is critical. It is somewhat like a medical doctor getting someone to have X-rays and blood analysis before determining the exact problem and prescribing a course of action. Once the prospect feels the salesperson understands their needs, they have more confidence in what the salesperson recommends.

After the sale, customers look to see if you are the same as before the sale. People like to buy and be remembered, not sold and forgotten. A relationship should be stronger, not weaker, after the sale. This is why Chapter 1 pointed out that today's salespeople need personal characteristics allowing them to do the following:

- Care for the customer, take joy in your work, and find harmony in the relationship.
- Have patience in closing the sale, be kind to all people, and have moral ethics.
- Be faithful to your word, fair in the sale, and self-controlled in emotions.

Do these success characteristics describe you? Do you have all, or part, of them? Can you develop the missing ones? The desire to serve others is a quality we all admire. However, only when you enjoy serving others does your service take on a radiant goodness that gives a contagious glow. This glow shows you care!

Caring Is Seen

Caring about the customer is more than simply warm feelings; it is an attitude that reveals itself in action. How can sellers care about a customer as much as themselves? By helping when it is not convenient, by giving the best price, by devoting energy to their welfare, and by making sure the customer is satisfied. These are just a few ways the seller shows caring for the customer.

Caring Is Hard to Do

This kind of caring is hard to do. That is why people notice when the seller does it. This is how customers know the salesperson places their welfare first and know the seller can be trusted. It is how a long-term relationship begins and extends into the future. Through caring comes exceptional service to the customer, which in turn brings peace to the relationship. Buyer and seller care for and trust each other. Live from day to day in a self-forgetful way so you focus on others, not yourself. Let "live for others" be your personal motto.

Summary of Major Selling Issues

Salespeople increase sales by obtaining new customers and selling more products to present customers. Customer referrals are the best way to find new prospects. Thus, it's important to provide excellent service and follow-up to customers. By building a relationship and partnership, you can provide a high level of customer service.

Customers expect service. When you deliver service, customers are satisfied and continue to buy; this results in retention and loyalty. Follow-up and service create goodwill between salesperson and customer that allows the salesperson to penetrate or work throughout the customer's organization. Account penetration helps the salesperson to better service the account and uncover its needs and problems. A service relationship with an account leads to increases in total and major-brand sales, better distribution on all product sizes, and customer cooperation in promoting your products.

To serve customers best, improve account penetration. Contact each customer frequently and regularly; promptly handle all complaints. Always do what you say you will do, and remember to serve customers as if they were royalty. Finally, remember to sincerely thank all customers for their business, no matter how large or small, to show your appreciation.

Should customers begin to buy from a competitor or reduce their level of cooperation, continue to call on them in your normal professional manner. In a friendly way, determine why they did not buy from you, and develop new customer benefit plans to recapture their business.

Always strive to help your customers increase their sales of your product or to get the best use from products that you have sold to them. To persuade a customer to purchase more of your products or use your products in a different manner, develop a sales program to help maximize sales to that customer. This involves developing an account penetration program; increasing the number and sizes of products purchased by the customer; maintaining proper inventory levels in the customer's warehouse and on the shelf; achieving good shelf space and shelf positioning; communicating clearly with people who directly sell or use a product; willingly assisting wholesale and retail customers' salespeople in any way possible; willingly helping customers; and developing a positive, friendly business relationship with each customer. By doing these eight things, your ability to help and properly service each customer increases.

Today's professional salesperson is oriented to service. Follow-up and service after the sale maximize your territory's sales and help attain personal goals.

MEETING A SALES CHALLENGE

What a tough situation! You have to keep servicing the equipment if you want to keep King Masonry as a customer. If the customer is misusing the mixer and causing it to break down, you must train the operators of the mixer and explain to Eldon King what is happening. Before saying anything to King, get his permission to talk with the mixer operators. Find out why the machine is breaking down.

PLAYING THE ROLE

The situation: As a newly hired salesperson in a local camera shop, you have just completed your first two major sales of a new top-quality digital camera. The total sale for each amounted to $2,400. Over the next few days, you recalled studying the importance of the follow-up call in your college sales course. You're thinking that you should call the customers about a week after purchase. You've now got to figure out what to say during these calls.

Role A: You, the camera salesperson. Prepare your follow-up calls. You don't know what your customer is thinking.

Role B: The happy customer. You've had the camera for a week and are reasonably satisfied with it.

Role C: The unhappy customer. You've had the camera for a week and still don't have a clue how it works and are becoming increasingly agitated about the whole purchase to the point that you're considering returning it for a refund.

Dramatize these sales calls in class. Have your classmates analyze the dialogue and make recommendations for improvement.

Key Terms for Selling

account penetration	**knowledge**	**proverb**
customer satisfaction	**product**	**wisdom**
follow-up		

Sales Application Questions

1. What is account penetration? What benefits can a salesperson derive from it?
2. List and briefly explain the factors salespeople must consider to ensure that customers buy from them in the future.
3. What must a salesperson do after losing a customer?
4. A good way for a salesperson to create goodwill is by helping customers increase their sales. What are the steps for the salesperson who attempts to increase customer sales?
5. This chapter discussed several reasons that a salesperson must project a professional image. Why is being a sales professional so important?
6. Return to Exhibit 12.7, "The Seven Deadly Sins of Business Selling." Think of an experience you had with a salesperson who displayed a poor sales image. How did the salesperson's attitude affect your purchase decision?
7. You have just learned that one of your customers, Tom's Discount Store, has received a shipment of faulty goods from your warehouse. The total cost of the merchandise is $2,500. Your company has a returned-goods policy that allows you to return only $500 worth of your product at one time unless a reciprocal order is placed. What would you do?
   a. Call Tom's and tell them you will be out to inspect the shipment in a couple of days.
   b. Ask Tom's to patch up what they can and sell it at a reduced cost in an upcoming clearance sale.
   c. Send the merchandise back to your warehouse and credit Tom's account for the price of the damaged goods.
   d. Go to Tom's as soon as possible that day, check the shipment to see whether there are any undamaged goods that can be put on the shelf, take a replacement order from Tom's manager, and phone in the order immediately.
   e. Call your regional sales manager and ask what to do.

8. Review the section on cross-selling. Imagine yourself as a sales representative in the following scenarios:
   a. You have just sold a water bottling machine to a water bottling company.
   b. You have just sold 25 hot tubs to a chain of fitness centres.
   c. You have just sold 40 high-volume photocopiers to a multi-location insurance company.

   For each scenario, try to determine how you could use cross-selling to increase the value of your sale to each customer. Develop a follow-up call with a sample script showing how you would approach each customer. What would you sell? When would you call? To whom would you speak? Is there anything else you should consider to maximize service and increase your sales to these customers?

Sales Online Exercise

What Is the Best Method to Determine Feedback?

Providing service after the sale to customers is important, no matter what type of company, product, or service you represent.

Some organizations, such as J.D. Power in the automobile industry, specialize in analyzing a company's customers' satisfaction (see www.jdpower.com).

For this assignment, determine how one or more companies determine the satisfaction of their customers with their product(s) and service. Find a company that requires that people answer an online satisfaction questionnaire.

Other suggested sites are:

www.customer-care-research.com/
www.customercare.com

Write a brief report to your boss on your findings. State what you feel would be the best way for a company of your choice to determine its customers' satisfaction.

Further Exploring the Sales World

1. Contact the person in charge of the health and beauty aids department of a local supermarket or drugstore. In an interview with this person, ask questions to determine what service activities salespeople perform in the department. For example, do they build product displays, put merchandise on the shelves, straighten products on the shelves, and keep a record of how much product is in the store? Also, determine how the department head believes that salespeople can provide the best service.
2. Contact the person in charge of marketing in a local bank. Report on the role that service plays in attracting and retaining bank customers.

Selling Experiential Exercise

How Do You Feel About Follow-up?

Often, salespeople are reluctant to follow-up on customers because they are worried about uncovering problems and dealing with what could become potentially difficult customers. Answer each of the following questions with a "Yes" or "No" response.

	Yes	No
1. I would follow up on customers that I perceived to be potentially difficult with a positive attitude and belief that I could turn the situation into a positive one.		
2. In dealing with customers, I would seek to determine their true needs before offering a service solution.		
3. I would do additional research on behavioural styles and recognize their importance in delivering quality service.		
4. When emotions ran high during a service transaction, I would use strategies such as those discussed in this text.		
5. I would consciously monitor my language and seek feedback from my peers on it to ensure that I use positive phrases when communicating.		
6. When dealing with a difficult customer during a follow-up call, I would maintain my professionalism and actively listen in order to better serve their needs.		
7. When working with co-workers, I would afford the same courtesies and professionalism that is required for external customers.		
8. To ensure that I fully understand and react appropriately to problems in the workplace, I would use a step-by-step problem solving model.		

Source: *Customer Service* by Robert W. Lucas, 3rd Edition, McGraw Hill Irwin, Page 203.

If you answered "Yes" to most of the questions, congratulations! You have the mindset that will allow you to confidently follow up on each sale and deal with any problems in a confident and service-oriented manner.

If you answered "No," you would be wise to seek out further resources to enhance your understanding of the importance of customer service to sales success.

CASE 12–1

CANADA ADHESIVES CORPORATION

Marilyn Fowler recently became a sales representative for the Canada Adhesives Corporation (CAC) and covers Nova Scotia and New Brunswick. After completing a three-week training program, Marilyn was excited about the responsibility of reversing a downward sales trend in her territory, which had been without a salesperson for several months.

The previous salesperson was fired because of poor sales performance and had not left behind any information regarding accounts. After contacting her first 20 or so customers, Marilyn came to some major conclusions: None of these customers had seen a CAC salesperson for six to nine months; they had CAC merchandise that was not selling; and they had damaged merchandise to return.

These customers were hostile toward Marilyn because the previous salesperson had used high-pressure tactics to force them to buy, and as one person said, "Your predecessor killed your sales in my business. You said you would provide service and call on me regularly, but I don't care about service. In fact, it's okay with me if I never see anyone from your company again. Your competition's products are much better than yours, and their salespeople have been calling in this area for years trying to get my business." Marilyn was left wondering whether she was working for the right company.

QUESTIONS

1. If you were Marilyn, what would you do to improve the sales in your territory?
2. How long would your effort take to improve sales and how would you sell it to your sales manager?

CASE 12–2

SPORT SHOE CORPORATION

You are a salesperson for the Sport Shoe Corporation. On your desk is a letter marked "Urgent," from the athletic director of Simon Fraser University, and it pertains to the poor quality of football shoes that you sold to him. The director cites several examples of split soles and poor overall quality as his main complaints. In closing, he mentions that since the season is nearing, he will be forced to contact the ACME Sport Shoe Company if the situation cannot be rectified.

QUESTIONS

What actions would be appropriate for you? Why?

a. Place a call to the athletic director assuring him of your commitment to service. Promise to be at Simon Fraser at his convenience to rectify the problem.

b. Go by the warehouse and take the athletic director a new shipment of shoes and apologize for the delay and poor quality of the merchandise.

c. Write a letter to the athletic director assuring him that SSC sells only high-quality shoes and that this type of problem rarely occurs. Assure him you'll come to his office as soon as possible but if he feels ACME would be a better choice than Sport Shoe, he should contact them.

d. Don't worry about the letter because the athletic director seems to have the attitude that he can put pressure on you by threatening to switch companies. Also, the loss in sales of 20 to 40 pairs of football shoes is a drop in the bucket compared to the valuable sales time you would waste on a small account like Simon Fraser.

PART FOUR

Keys to a Successful Selling Career

Professional salespeople are managers of themselves, their time, and their customers. They work in a variety of industries and in a variety of sales jobs such as retail selling, not-for-profit, B2B selling, and many more. However, most of the fundamentals of selling remain the same no matter what is being sold. Selling skills need to be adapted to all kinds of situations.

In this last part of the text, discussion covers how to manage yourself in terms of time and territory management. Also, different types of selling jobs are examined a little more closely.

This part includes

© Undrey | Dreamstime.com

CHAPTER 13

Time, Territory, and Self-Management

Gregory Rocha
Concordia University, Montreal, Quebec.

Source: Courtesy of Gregory Rocha.

A Sales Success Story

Like many students, Gregory Rocha struggled with deciding what career he wanted to pursue, and in what industry. He knew it would be something in business, but he didn't think he would end up in a sales position, especially in the pharmaceutical industry. Gregory holds a Bachelor of Commerce degree from Concordia University, and is currently finishing his MBA part-time online with the Australian Institute of Business. During his time at Concordia, Gregory was involved in case competitions where he learned the power of storytelling in sales pitches in order to convey messages to an audience. He was also involved in the co-operative education program, which led him to internships at Novartis Pharmaceuticals where he discovered this industry.

During his time at university, Gregory had no idea that he would find himself in a career in sales and use that as a means to make a difference in the world.

Selling medications to health care practitioners is not your typical sales journey, and once he understood this, everything became clear. For Gregory, his work is a sales journey about helping health care practitioners find the right pharmaceutical solutions for their patients, and helping patients live their lives to the maximum considering their diagnoses. Moving from university to reality, there was confusion about what a sales position actually would entail for Gregory. Holding the position of a pharmaceutical sales rep helped Gregory close that gap, and after understanding the skillset and importance of sales in a B2B landscape, and how it is the backbone of most companies, it led him to the marketing position he holds today as brand manager.

In the sales role, Gregory learned that sales is actually interlinked in almost every aspect of the job, both in front and not in front of customers, as well as in his personal life. Gregory learned that in order to have a successful sales call, he needed to understand the journey the customer was on, where they were located in that journey, and what obstacles were in the way to bring them to the end result. To do this, he needed empathy and strategic thinking, and he also needed to manage the gatekeepers along the way. Another surprising realization for Gregory was that he also needed to sell his business plans inside his company to defend what he was planning to do. The end result of getting the sale was very fulfilling, as Gregory knew that patients could now live either a longer life or a better quality life because they were taking the best possible medication available.

Moving from sales to marketing, one of the biggest and immediate takeaways for Gregory was how sales taught him the importance of selling by understanding the customer journey. In the role of brand manager, Gregory has to sell his ideas internally to the sales force, management, and colleagues by understanding where they are located in the journey, and how best to move them to that end result. If this cannot be done Gregory will not succeed in his role, as he needs others to implement the strategy; but, first, people must be sold on the strategy.

Gregory strongly believes that a career in sales, whether long term or short term, requires a particular skillset that all students who are intending to go into any type business should obtain. Sales is also a very fulfilling career, as it provides a way to make a difference and directly bring happiness, peace, or satisfaction to people. All industries consistently have openings and opportunities for sales positions, and once a person has this skillset, it will help them achieve bigger and better things in the future.

MAIN TOPICS

Customers Form Sales Territories

Elements of Territory Management

The Management of Time

Technology can Enhance Time Efficiency

Self-Management

What's Happening in Sales

LEARNING OBJECTIVES

A salesperson's ability to manage time and territory is important to success. After studying this chapter, you should be able to:

LO1 Discuss the importance of the sales territory.

LO2 Explain the major elements involved in managing the sales territory.

LO3 Discuss the importance of self-management and time management to salespeople.

LO4 Discuss some recent trends in the sales profession.

FACING A SALES CHALLENGE

"How can I manage my time to take better care of my customers?" thinks Alice Jenson. "It seems that each day that I work, I get farther and farther behind."

Alice recently took over the sales territory of Rudy Kavanagh, who retired and moved across the country after 35 years of calling on customers. He kept all records in his head. Alice had to contact the 200 customers in the sales territory with no information other than their past sales. After several weeks, Alice had seen 95 percent of the customers once and 25 percent a second time. Two weeks ago, complaints started coming in that Alice had not followed up on her last calls or had not been back to see them.

Alice started telephoning people. That helped some, but customers wanted to see her. She almost stopped prospecting for new customers because she felt it was easier to keep a customer than get a new one. However, as sales started to decline, Alice realized customers were beginning to buy from her competitors. Alice is in trouble—and it is getting worse.

What should Alice do to keep customers, have time to prospect, and increase sales?

(Continued at end of chapter.)

Planning your workday and managing your time and customers are key to your success. According to a national survey of thousands of salespeople, managing time and territory is the most important factor in selling. Because of things such as the rapidly increasing cost of direct selling, decreasing time for face-to-face customer contact, continued emphasis on profitable sales, and the fact that time is always limited, it is no wonder that many companies are concentrating on improving how salespeople manage time and territory.[1]

Suppose you were given a bank account that receives a fresh deposit of $86,400 every day. You are free to spend the money any way you want, but the unspent balance is not carried forward to the next day. Regardless of what you have spent by the end of the day, the balance is reset daily at $86,400. What would you do with such a bank account?

Now consider the fact that each dollar represents the number of seconds in one day: $24 \times 60 \times 60 = 86{,}400$ seconds. Once they are "spent" they disappear, and the balance is reset at 12:00:01 A.M. every day. How do you spend your time?

LO1

Customers Form Sales Territories

sales territory: A group of customers or a geographical area assigned to a salesperson.

A **sales territory** comprises a group of customers or a geographical area assigned to a salesperson. Exhibit 13.1 lists seven important reasons for establishing sales territories.

1. To obtain thorough coverage of the market	
2. To establish each salesperson's responsibilities	
3. To evaluate performance	
4. To improve customer relations	
5. To reduce sales expense	
6. To allow better matching of salespeople to customers' needs	
7. To benefit both salespeople and the company	

EXHIBIT 13.1

Reasons companies develop and use sales territories.

To Obtain Thorough Coverage of the Market

With proper coverage of territories, a company will reach the sales potential of its markets. The salesperson analyzes the territory, identifies customers, and meets customers' needs. Division into territories also allows management to easily realign territories as customers and sales increase or decrease.

To Establish Each Salesperson's Responsibilities

Salespeople act as business managers for their territories, and are responsible for maintaining and generating sales volume. Salespeople's tasks are defined clearly. They know where customers are located and how often to call on them. They also know what performance goals are expected. This can raise the salesperson's performance and morale.

To Evaluate Performance

Performance is monitored for each territory. Actual performance data are collected, analyzed, and compared to expected performance goals. Individual territory performance is compared to district performance, district performance is compared to regional performance, and regional performance is compared to the performance of the entire sales force. With computerized reporting systems, the salesperson and a manager can monitor individual territory and customer sales to determine the success of selling efforts.

To Improve Customer Relations

Customer goodwill and increased sales are expected when customers receive regular calls. From the customer's viewpoint, the salesperson *is,* for example, Procter & Gamble. The customer looks to the salesperson, not to Procter & Gamble's corporate office, when making purchases. Over the years, some salespeople build such goodwill with customers that prospects will delay placing orders because they know the salesperson will be at their business on a certain day or at a specific time of the month. Some salespeople even earn the right to order merchandise for certain customers.

To Reduce Sales Expenses

Sales territories are designed to avoid duplicating efforts so that two salespeople do not travel in the same area. This lowers selling costs and increases company profits. Such benefits as fewer travel kilometres, fewer overnight trips, and regular contact with productive customers by the same salesperson can improve the firm's sales-cost ratio.

To Allow Better Matching of Salespeople to Customers' Needs

Salespeople are hired and trained to meet the requirements of the customers in a territory. Often, the more similar the customer and the salesperson are, the more likely the sales effort is to succeed.

To Benefit Both Salespeople and the Company

Proper territory design aids in reaching the firm's sales objectives. Thus, the company can maximize its sales effort, while the sales force can work in territories that allow them to satisfy personal needs, such as a good salary.

Why Sales Territories May Not Be Developed

There are disadvantages to developing sales territories for some companies, such as in the real estate or insurance industries. First, salespeople may be more motivated if not restricted by a particular territory; they can develop customers anywhere. In the chemical industry, for example, salespeople may sell to any potential customer. However, after the sale is made, other company salespeople are not allowed to contact that client. Second, the company may be too small to be concerned with segmenting the market into sales areas. Third, management may not want to take the time, or may not have the know-how, for territory development. Fourth, personal friendships may be the basis for attracting customers. For example, life insurance salespeople may first sell policies to their families and friends. Nevertheless, most companies establish sales territories such as the one assigned to Alice Jenson in Facing a Sales Challenge at the beginning of this chapter.

SELLING TIPS

WHAT MAKES A GREAT SALES ENVIRONMENT?

Many argue that the best sales environment is one where you can make enormous amounts of money. This is not always the case. While income is certainly a motivating factor, there are other things that contribute to happiness in the sales environment:

1. Working in a collegial atmosphere with teamwork being part of the relationship
2. Knowing what is expected
3. Having the training and materials needed to make the sale properly
4. Feeling empowered in your relationship with your customers rather than simply being an intermediary between them and your company
5. Receiving recognition for a job well done; this doesn't have to be monetary in nature but people do like to be recognized
6. Being treated well, and not being made to feel like a number or business unit; people like to be treated like people
7. Receiving support for personal and professional growth; an environment that supports life-long learning or community involvement is highly motivational
8. Receiving respect for your knowledge and opinions; having a meaningful say in company operations is very rewarding
9. Feeling secure; knowing that your company's success is related to your personal success allows for a feeling of job security
10. Interacting socially at work; a combination of professional conduct and personal friendship is highly rewarding

Sales managers can learn from these ideas. Building a positive sales environment is a tough task, but incorporating some of these insights will help.

LO2 Elements of Territory Management

For the salesperson, territory management is a continuous process of planning, executing, and evaluating the sales and service provided to customers. By completing each of the seven key elements involved in territory management, as shown in Exhibit 13.2, the salesperson ensures customers will be provided excellent service. Additionally, prospects will be found in the territory that may eventually become customers.

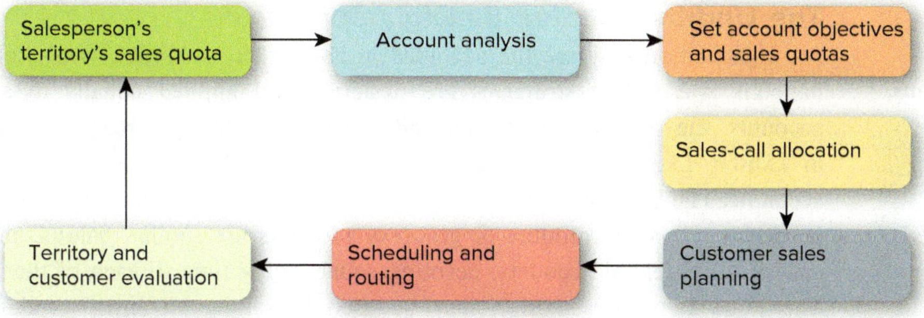

EXHIBIT 13.2
Elements of territory management for the salesperson.

Building relationships with customers requires spending time with them. As discussed in Chapter 11, a good business friendship is like a personal friendship. Time is required to get to know each customer and his or her needs. But there is only so much time in the day, week, month, and year. This requires you to make the hard decision on how to spend your business time. You determine that you require a strategic plan to determine how to manage your territory. The first step is to set goals or quotas.

Salesperson's Sales Quota

A salesperson is responsible for generating sales in a territory based on its sales potential. The salesperson's manager typically establishes the total sales **quota** that each salesperson is expected to reach.

quota: An expected level of performance often established by sales managers for their sales force.

Once this quota is set, it is the salesperson's responsibility to develop territorial sales plans for reaching the quota. Although there is no best planning sequence to follow, Exhibit 13.2 presents seven factors to consider in properly managing the territory for reaching its sales quota.

A salesperson's **goal setting** should be:

goal setting: Establishing what one wants to accomplish and what activities need to be performed in order to reach desired career or performance goals.

Specific - You must know exactly what your goal is. (e.g."Increase sales by 10 percent.")

Measurable - You must be able to quantify your goals. (e.g. "Develop five new customers per month.")

Achievable - Setting an unrealistic goal simply sets you up for failure and doesn't accomplish anything.

Relevant - Is the goal consistent with the purpose or mission of the salesperson? If you've set an irrelevant goal, there's really no purpose or motivation to reaching it.

Time Bounded - Setting proper goals, with a time constraint on them, provides a personal challenge and more motivation. (e.g., "Increase sales by 10 percent by August 31, 2021 and achieve top-level status.")

Account Analysis

Once a sales goal is set, the salesperson must analyze each prospect and customer to maximize the chances of reaching that goal. First, a salesperson should identify all prospects and present customers. Second, a salesperson should estimate present customers' and prospects' sales potential. This makes it possible to allocate time between customers, to decide what products to emphasize for a specific customer, and to better plan the sales presentation.

Two general approaches to **account analysis**–identifying accounts and their varying levels of sales potential–are the undifferentiated selling approach and the account segmentation approach.

account analysis: The process of analyzing each prospect and customer to maximize the chances of reaching a sales goal.

EXHIBIT 13.3
Undifferentiated selling approach.

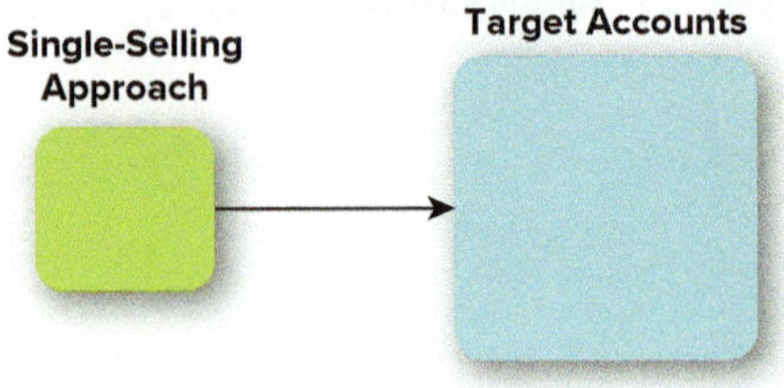

The Undifferentiated Selling Approach

An organization may see the accounts in its market as similar. When this happens and selling strategies are designed and applied equally to all accounts, the salesperson uses an **undifferentiated selling** approach. Notice in Exhibit 13.3 that the salesperson aims a single selling strategy at all accounts. The basic assumption underlying this approach is that the account needs for a specific product or group of products are similar. Salespeople call on all potential accounts, devoting equal selling time to each of them. The same sales presentation may be used in selling an entire product line. The salesperson feels they can satisfy most customers with a single selling strategy. For example, many door-to-door salespeople use the same selling strategies with each person they contact (a stimulus-response sales presentation).

undifferentiated selling: The process of applying and designing selling strategies equally to all accounts.

Salespeople whose accounts have homogeneous needs and characteristics may find this approach useful. The undifferentiated selling approach was popular in the past, and some firms still use it. However, many salespeople feel that their accounts have different needs and represent different sales and profit potentials. This makes an account segmentation approach desirable.

The Account Segmentation Approach

account segmentation: The process of applying different selling strategies to different territories.

Salespeople using the **account segmentation** approach recognize that their territories contain accounts with heterogeneous needs and differing characteristics that require different selling strategies. Consequently, they develop sales objectives based on overall sales and sales of each product for each customer and prospect. Past sales to the account, new accounts, competition, economic conditions, price and promotion offerings, new products, and personal selling are among the key elements in the analysis of accounts and territories.

Salespeople classify customers to identify profitable ones. This classification determines where the salesperson's time is invested. One method of segmenting accounts is by:

1. Key account -
   a. Buys over $200,000 from us annually.
   b. Loss of this customer would substantially affect the territory's sales and profits.
2. Unprofitable account -
   a. Buys less than $1,000 from us annually.
   b. Little potential to increase purchases to more than $1,000.
3. Regular account -
   a. All other customers.

The salesperson would not call on the unprofitable accounts. The **key accounts** and regular accounts become target customers.

key accounts: Your largest customers, the loss of which would greatly affect a territory's sales and profits.

Once the accounts are classified broadly, categories or types of accounts are defined in terms such as extra large (key), large, medium, and small, which we refer to as the **ELMS system**. For example, management may divide the 3,000 total accounts in the firm's marketing plan into these four basic sales categories, as shown in Exhibit 13.4. There are few extra large or large accounts, but they often account for 80 percent of a company's profitable sales even though they represent only 20 percent of total accounts. This is known as the **eighty/twenty principle**. The number of key accounts in an individual territory varies, as does responsibility for them. Even though the key account is in another salesperson's territory, a key account salesperson may call on the extra-large customer. Typically, this approach is taken because of the account's importance or because of an inexperienced local salesperson.

ELMS system: The process of dividing broad account classifications into varying sized accounts.

80/20 principle: 80 percent of sales often come from 20 percent of a company's customers.

CUSTOMER SIZE	YEARLY SALES (ACTUAL OR POTENTIAL)	NUMBER OF ACCOUNTS	PERCENTAGE
Extra large	Over $200,000	100	3.3
Large	$75,000-200,000	500	16.6
Medium	$25,000-75,000	1,000	33.3
Small	$1,000-25,000	1,400	46.6

EXHIBIT 13.4

Account segmentation based on yearly sales.

Accounts can be segmented whether or not the firms are actual customers or prospects. As shown in Exhibit 13.5, actual customers are further segmented based on sales to date and sales potential. Prospects also are segmented into the ELMS classification, and each account's potential sales are estimated.

	CUSTOMERS		
ACCOUNT CLASSIFICATION	SALES TO DATE	POTENTIAL SALES	PROSPECT POTENTIAL SALES
Extra large			
Large			
Medium			
Small			

EXHIBIT 13.5

Basic segmentation of accounts.

Multiple Selling Strategies

Exhibit 13.6 illustrates how multiple selling strategies are used on various accounts. Salespeople know the importance of large accounts; in fact, meeting sales objectives often depends on how well products are sold to these customers. As a result, companies often develop their sales force organizational structure to service these accounts–incorporating elements such as a key-account salesperson.

Selling strategies vary depending on the account. The bulk of sales force resources (such as personnel, time, samples, and entertainment expenses) should be invested in the key accounts, and the needs of these large accounts should receive top priority.

Company positioning relative to competition must receive careful consideration. Competitors also will direct a major selling effort toward these accounts. Thus, salespeople should strive to create the image that they, their company, and their products are uniquely better than the competition. One way to accomplish this is to spend more time on each sales call and to make more total sales calls during the year, thus providing a problem-solving approach to servicing accounts.

Selling larger accounts is different from selling medium and small accounts. However, these smaller accounts may generate 20 percent, and sometimes more, of a company's sales and must not be ignored.

EXHIBIT 13.6

Account segmentation approach.

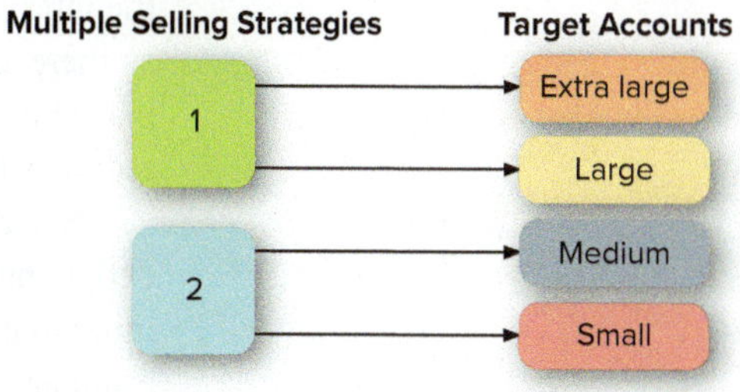

Develop Account Objectives and Sales Quotas

The third element of territory management is developing objectives and sales quotas for individual products and for current and potential accounts. Objectives might include increasing product distribution to prospects in the territory or increasing the product assortment current customers purchase.

Develop an effective plan to allocating efforts across goals, activities, and time periods.

Sales Call Allocation

sales call allocation: A plan to allocate sales calls within territories based on number of accounts in the territory, number of sales calls made on customers, time required for each sales call, frequency of customer sales calls, travel time around the territory, nonselling time, and return on time invested.

The fourth element of territory management is **sales call allocation**, that is how salespeople develop a plan to allocate sales calls within territories. Increasing the number of sales calls each day and the number of new accounts obtained for the year are other examples of objectives salespeople develop to help meet sales quotas. In recalling his early days as a salesperson, Shelby H. Carter, Jr., former Xerox senior vice president of sales of U.S. field operations, said, "I placed a sign on my car's visor that read, 'Calls are the guts of this business.' We lived in Baltimore," he recalls, "and I drove 40 miles every day to get to Annapolis. You've got to make extra calls," he told his salespeople, "because one more call a day is five a week, 20 a month, and 240 calls a year. If you close 10 percent of the people you contact, you have an extra 24 sales a year."

A sales territory is a cost- and revenue-generating profit centre. Because of this, priorities must be established on account calls to maximize territory profits. These seven basic factors need to be considered in call allocation:

1. Number of accounts in the territory
2. Number of sales calls made on customers
3. Time required for each sales call
4. Frequency of customer sales calls
5. Travel time around the territory
6. Nonselling time
7. Return on time invested.

Sales call efforts are in direct proportion to the actual or potential sales that the account represents.

Analysis of accounts in the territory has resulted in determining the total number of territory accounts and their classification in terms of actual or potential sales. Now, the number of yearly sales calls required, the time required for each call, and the intervals between calls can be determined. Usually, the frequency of calls increases as there are increases in (1) sales and/or potential future sales, (2) number of orders placed in a year, (3) number of product lines sold, and (4) complexity, servicing, and redesign requirements of products.

Since the time spent servicing an account varies from minutes to days, salespeople must be flexible in developing call frequencies. However, they can establish a minimum number of calls they want to make on the various classes of accounts. For example, the salesperson determines that the frequency of calls for each class of account in the territory, as shown in Exhibit 13.7, should be one contact a month for all but the small accounts.

Typically, the salesperson's sales call efforts are in direct proportion to the actual or potential sales that the account represents. The most productive number of calls is reached at the point at which additional calls do not increase sales. This relationship of sales volume to sales calls is the **sales response function** of the customer to the salesperson's calls.

sales response function: The relationship between sales volume and sales calls.

CUSTOMER SIZE	CALLS PER MONTH	CALLS PER YEAR	NUMBER OF ACCOUNTS	NUMBER OF CALLS PER YEAR
Extra large	1	12	2	24
Large	1	12	28	336
Medium	1	12	56	672
Small	1*	4	78	312
Total			164	1,344

*Every 3 months.

EXHIBIT 13.7

Call allocation by salesperson.

Customer Sales Planning

The fifth major element of territorial management is developing a sales-call objective, a customer profile, and a customer benefit program, including selling strategies for individual customers. (See Chapter 7 for further discussion of customer sales planning.) You have a quota to meet, have made your account analysis, have set account objectives, and have established the time you will devote to each customer; now, develop a sales plan for each customer.

Scheduling and Routing

The sixth element of territory management is scheduling sales calls and planning movement around the sales territory. **Scheduling** refers to establishing a fixed time (day and hour) for visiting a customer's business. **Routing** is the travel pattern used in working a territory. Some sales organizations prefer to determine the formal path or route that their salespeople travel when covering their territory. In such cases, management must develop plans that are feasible, flexible, and profitable to the company and the individual salesperson, and satisfactory to the customer.

scheduling: The establishment of a fixed time for visiting a customer's business.

routing: The travel pattern used in working a sales territory.

In theory, strict formal route designs enable the company to (1) improve territory coverage; (2) minimize wasted time; and (3) establish communication between management and the sales force in terms of the location and activities of individual salespeople. In developing route patterns, management needs to know the salesperson's exact day and time of sales calls for each account; approximate waiting time; sales time; miscellaneous time for contacting people such as the promotional manager, checking inventory, or handling returned merchandise; and travel time between accounts. This task is difficult unless territories are small and precisely defined. Most firms allow considerable latitude in routing.

> *"You've got to be careful if you don't know where you're going cause you might not get there!"*
>
> *YOGI BERRA*

Typically, after finishing a workweek, the salesperson fills out a routing report and sends it to the manager. The report states where the salesperson will work (see Exhibit 13.8 on the next page). In the example, on Friday, December 16, the salesperson is based in Toronto and plans to call on accounts in Toronto for two days during the week of December 26. Then, they plan to work in Ottawa for a day, spend the night, drive to Montreal early the next morning and make calls, and be home Thursday night. The last day of the week, the salesperson plans to work in Toronto. The weekly route report is sent to their immediate supervisor. In this manner, management knows where the salesperson is and, if necessary, can contact them.

EXHIBIT 13.8

A weekly route report.

TODAY'S DATE DECEMBER 16		FOR WEEK BEGINNING DECEMBER 26
DATE	CITY	LOCATION
December 26 (Monday)	Ottawa	Home
December 27 (Tuesday)	Ottawa	Home
December 28 (Wednesday)	Kingston	Holiday Inn/South
December 29 (Thursday)	Brighton	Home
December 30 (Friday)	Ottawa	Home

Some firms may ask the salesperson to specify the accounts to be called on and at what times. For example, on Monday, December 26, the salesperson may write, "Toronto, 9 A.M., LEVER BROS., Markham, 2 P.M., Pillsbury." Thus, management knows where a salesperson will be and what accounts will be visited during a report period. If no overnight travel is necessary to cover a territory, the company may not require any route reports because the salesperson can be contacted at home in the evening.

Territory and Customer Evaluation

Territorial evaluation is the establishment of performance standards for the individual territory in the form of qualitative and quantitative quotas or goals. Actual performance is compared to these goals for evaluation purposes. This allows the salesperson to see how well territory plans were executed in meeting performance quotas. If quotas were not met, new plans must be developed.

Many companies routinely furnish managers and individual salespeople with reports on how many times during the year salespeople have called on each account and the date of the last sales call. Management can monitor the frequency and time intervals between calls for each salesperson.

As an example, a national pharmaceutical company supplies its sales force with a net sales by customer and call report shown in Exhibit 13.9. The report lists each

EXHIBIT 13.9

Net sales by customer and call frequency: May 1, 2020.

	PIERCE (GP, TORONTO)	PETERSON (PEDIATRICS, LONDON)	DEMARCO (GP, WINDSOR)	AMATO (GP, WINDSOR)	HEATON (GP, GUELPH)
Calls:					
Month	2	1	1	0	2
Year-to-date	8	4	4	4	9
Last call	4/20	4/18	4/18	3/10	4/19
Net sales in dollars:					
Current month	60	0	21	0	500
Year-to-date:					
This year	350	200	75	1,000	2,000
Last year	300	275	125	750	1,750
Entire last year	2,000	1,000	300	1,000	5,000

customer's name, address, and medical specialty. The desired number of monthly calls on a given customer and the actual number of calls to date are noted. Net sales are broken down into last year's sales, the current month's sales, and year-to-date sales. Finally, the date the salesperson last called on each customer is reported.

Using the report, you can see that Pierce is a Toronto physician in a general practice. He should be called on twice a month, and he has been seen eight times over the past four months. He purchased $60 worth of merchandise this month, and his purchases so far are $50 more than last year. He was last called on April 20 of the current year. Using this type of information, which might include 200 to 300 customers for each salesperson, management and salespeople can continually review sales-call patterns and customer sales to update call frequency and scheduling.

ETHICAL DILEMMA

A BREAKDOWN IN PRODUCTIVITY

You are a hard worker, often putting in 60 hours a week. On your first sales job and with the company only five months, you realize the importance of getting off to a good start. You have sold an average of 30 percent over your sales quota for the past three months. One reason is your hard work. Another reason is that the salesperson that preceded you in this territory either neglected accounts or just renewed old orders, never striving to upgrade current accounts. Most customers complained that they hadn't seen a salesperson from your company for months before you began to call on them.

Last month one of the older salespeople jokingly suggested that you slow down—you are making everyone look bad. You have noticed a breakdown in productivity among your fellow salespeople, who seem to be goofing off to extremes. Although it doesn't affect you directly, it will ultimately have an adverse impact on the department's productivity. Your boss likes good news and frequently asks you for ideas on how to increase sales in other territories. Because you are new and have not yet established yourself as a loyal employee, you have kept quiet in the past, hoping to win the trust of your co-workers. Tomorrow you have a meeting with your boss about your territory's productivity and you are sure he is expecting input about the other territories.

What would be the most ethical action to take?

1. Tell your boss nothing. State that your territory must be particularly active right now and that you think the other territories must just be slow right now. It does not affect you, so why should you get involved?
2. Tell your boss that your numbers have been so high because you have been working very hard and putting in long hours. Let him know that you have noticed that the other salespeople have been slacking and, in fact, have told you to "slow down." After all, it isn't right that they are abusing their positions and hurting the company's profits.
3. Suggest to your boss that he have some type of new sales incentive plan. This way, maybe the other salespeople will stop "goofing off" and you don't have to say anything.

03

The Management of Time

"Time is money" is a popular saying that applies to our discussion because of the costs and revenue the individual salesperson generates. A good salesperson is a skilled time manager who knows how to manage time wisely to maximize territorial profits. Thus, the effective salesperson consistently uses time well. How does the effective salesperson manage time?

Many salespeople develop daily, weekly, and monthly call plans or general guidelines of customers and geographical areas to be covered as part of their **time management** process. The salesperson may use them to make appointments with customers in advance, to arrange hotel accommodations, and so forth. Weekly plans are more specific, and they include the specific days that customers will be called on. Daily planning starts the night before, as the salesperson selects the next day's

time management: The process of using a given period of time for maximum effectiveness.

prospects, determines the time to contact the customer, organizes facts and data, and prepares sales presentation materials.

"In our initial training we teach people how to be organized, set a list of priorities and plan their activities, and we encourage them to think outside of the box. They need to think about tomorrow, next week, down the road and to set objectives and anticipate needs before they occur," explains Jeff DeRoux, information and technology manager for the Preston, Washington-based SanMar Corporation. DeRoux believes that good organization, long- and short-range planning, and setting priorities are absolutely necessary in eliminating time wasting.[2]

Exhibit 13.10 lists six time management skills that can help sales professionals in achieving productivity and efficiency.

"It's been said," says Tupperware's Terry Fingerhut, "21 days make a habit–good or bad. In three weeks, the results of the work I did or didn't do today will show up. If I spent my time well, three weeks from today I'll have positive results. If I wasted my time, three weeks from today I'll have negative results. The conclusion–each day, every day–is produce *now* at your best. In three weeks and every week thereafter you'll have a string of truly positive results."

Qualify the prospect. Salespeople must be sure their prospects are qualified to make the purchase decision, and they must determine whether sales to these accounts are large enough to allow for an adequate return on time invested. If not, they do not call on these prospects. It is often thought of as the biggest time waster for salespeople to spend their time with unqualified prospects. Time is money and the salespeople must be diligent in their research to determine who is qualified to buy.

Use waiting time. Have you seen salespeople waiting to see buyers? Have you ever noticed their actions? They work while waiting: studying material about their products, completing call reports, or organizing material for the sales presentation. Also, they quickly determine whether buyers they wait for will be free within a reasonable time. If not, they contact other customers.

Have a productive lunchtime. Salespeople often take prospects to lunch. However, the results of one study show that the business lunch does not lead directly to a sale, but to the buyer and seller knowing each other better, which builds confidence and trust. In turn, this may lead to sales in the long run. During a business lunch,

EXHIBIT 13.10

Six time management skills that can help sales professionals in achieving success.[3]

Source: ©Rawpixel Ltd/Alamy Stock Photo

1. Be selective in prioritizing time
2. Spend time on high-priority tasks
3. Have a better sense of the time needed to complete tasks
4. Avoid overcommitting to nonessential tasks at the expense of core work tasks
5. Develop an effective plan to allocating efforts across goals, activities, and time periods
6. Have a systematic account for the outcomes you aim to achieve before allocating time to achieve these outcomes

salespeople must keep an eye on the clock and not monopolize too much of the buyer's time. They should not have a lunchtime cocktail. In fact, in some companies, a luncheon cocktail or any use of alcohol or other drugs is against company policy. A salesperson's lunch is time to review activities and further plan the afternoon. It is a time to relax and start psyching up for a productive selling afternoon.

Complete records and reports. Records and reports are a written history of sales and of the salesperson's activities. Effective salespeople do paperwork during nonselling times; evenings are best. Many companies note these records and reports in performance evaluations of salespeople, and the salesperson should keep them current. The company, however, should hold paperwork to a minimum.

Return on Time Invested

Time is a scarce resource. To be successful, the salesperson uses time effectively to improve performance. In terms of time, costs also must be accounted for. That is, what is the cost both in time and money of an average sales call?

Break-even analysis determines how much sales volume a salesperson must generate to meet costs. The difference between cost of goods sold and sales is the gross profit on sales revenue. Gross profit should be large enough to cover selling expenses. **Break-even analysis** is a quantitative technique for determining the level of sales at which total revenues equal total costs. Break-even point is computed in dollars with this formula:

break-even analysis: A quantitative technique for determining the level of sales at which total revenues equal total costs.

$$\text{Break-even point (in dollars)} = \frac{\text{Salesperson's fixed costs}}{\text{Gross profit percentage}}$$

To illustrate the formula, let's use the values shown here for sales and costs, with gross profit being the difference between a salesperson's sales revenue and costs of goods sold in the territory, expressed as a ratio of gross profit to gross sales in percentage form:

Sales	$600,000
Cost of goods sold	
Gross profit	$180,000
Gross profit (percentage)	(180,000 ÷ 600,000) or 30%

Assume the salesperson's direct costs are as follows:

Salary	$60,000
Transportation	12,000
Expenses	15,000
Direct costs	$87,000

Substitute in the formula:

$$\text{BEP} = \frac{\$87{,}000}{.30} = \$290{,}000$$

If the salesperson sells $290,000 worth of merchandise, it exactly covers the territory's direct costs. A sales volume of $290,000 means that the salesperson produces a gross margin of 30 percent, or $87,000. Sales over $290,000 contribute to profit.

Assume that the salesperson works 46 out of 52 weeks (considering time off for vacations, holidays, and illness) for 230 days each year; also assume a five-day week and an eight-hour day in which six calls are made. There are 1,840 working hours per year and 1,380 sales calls (230 × 6 calls) made each year in the territory. To determine a salesperson's cost per hour, divide direct costs ($87,000) by yearly hours worked (1,840 hours). The cost per hour equals $47.28. The break-even volume per hour is as follows:

$$\text{Break-even volume per hour} = \frac{\text{Cost per hour}}{\text{Gross profit percentage}} = \frac{\$15.76}{.30} = \$157.60$$

Thus, the salesperson must sell an average of $157.60 an hour in goods or services to break even. Carrying this logic further, the salesperson must sell an average of $1,260.80 each day, or $210.13 each sales call to break even.

Technology Use Can Enhance Time Efficiency

Today's organizations understand the importance of technology to enhance the salesperson's time efficiency. With field sales costs still rising and no end in sight, more companies are investing in sales technology to supplement personal selling efforts. **Sales technology** is described as the transformation of manual sales activities to electronic processes through the use of various combinations of hardware and software applications.[4]

sales technology: The transformation of manual sales activities to electronic processes through the use of various combinations of hardware and software applications.

Sales technology tools help salespeople with routine as well as strategic tasks, allowing them to focus on actual selling time. Examples of such automation tools include programs such as sales route planners and calendaring tools such as Salesforce, Outreach, and Calendly. Applications such as calendaring and routing tables can transform salespeople's typical sales routines and thus reduce downtime.

Sales technology helps salespeople by managing information about a larger number of customers. Salespeople equipped with such valuable information are able to easily relate to customers and can be more responsive to critical issues, thereby shortening the duration of each sales call. Salespeople using the CRM system may also be able to save time by speeding the process of sales call planning. For example, CRM use may help a salesperson configure product offerings that are better customized to customer needs. CRM systems also allow information-sharing across a sales organization. Information-sharing is important because it provides the knowledge about the customer throughout the organization, and therefore can reduce the potential for mistakes.

While each firm and its salespeople have to decide which sales technology is applicable to their sales process, most salespeople benefit from adopting the following practices:

- Ask yourself, "Can this interaction be conducted virtually?" Available web conferencing and online meeting software (e.g., GoToMeeting) make it simple and cost-effective to serve distant customers.
- Consider the resources invested in each customer. You may wish to mostly assign smaller accounts that contribute less than 5 percent of business to inside-sales salespeople.
- Create a valuable information resource. Consider prospecting, marketing data gathering, and call scheduling with a CRM technology system.

Using Technology for Territory Management Activities

For today's salespeople, companies such as Mapline and Badgersales offer route planners and schedulers. Salespeople can quickly and easily visualize their sales territory by integrating important information, such as customer lists, maps, and their calendar, into one mobile app. With the help of such technology tools, it is easier for salespeople to adjust to schedule changes. For example, in the event of an appointment cancellation, a salesperson could use the technology to find potential appointments or leads in the same geographic areas. Salespeople also receive reminders when they are not meeting the timelines set on their daily schedule.

The next software technology used in territory management is called territory analysis. Territory analysis software helps a salesperson understand each customer within the territory, the cost to serve the customer, and the revenue each customer generates. In addition, the software allows the salesperson to understand the performance of the entire territory. Territory analysis software allows salespeople to easily upload their customers' list and analyze data based on purchase volume, purchase types, and, purchase frequency. With this software, salespeople can continually see their sales performance, and it enables them to make adjustments based on the data.

Using Technology for Non-Selling Activities

Sales technology tools can also provide an opportunity for salespeople to reduce their administrative tasks. A critical objective of the salesperson is to develop and maintain business relationships and revenue flows. Yet, in order to do so, the salesperson must manage a great deal of information about their customers, their distributors, and other key processes. Sales technology software provides a more automated, organized means to handle these activities and thereby reduce the administrative burden on the salesperson.

Using the Telephone for Territory Coverage

The telephone can be a great time-waster or time-saver, depending on how it is used. The increasing cost of a personal sales call and the increasing amount of time spent travelling to make personal calls are reasons for the efficient territory manager to look to the telephone as a territory coverage tool. More and more companies are developing telephone sales and marketing campaigns to supplement personal selling efforts. These campaigns use trained telephone communicators and well-developed telephone marketing techniques. Usually, they require a company-wide effort.

Although each salesperson has to decide on the types of calls and accounts that lend themselves to telephone applications, most people benefit from adopting the following practices as minimal territory coverage:

- Satisfy part of the service needs of accounts by telephone.
- Assign smaller accounts that contribute less than 5 percent of business to mostly telephone selling.
- Do prospecting, market data gathering, and call scheduling by telephone.
- Carefully schedule personal calls to distant accounts. If possible, replace some personal visits with telephone calls.
- With new technologies, the possibilities are endless in terms of improving territory coverage. With programs such as Skype or the iPhone's Face Time, it is much easier to communicate with distant customers both verbally and visually using a smart phone, tablet, or computer.

Source: Ldprod/Shutterstock.com

The telephone and computer are important selling tools for salespeople. Many sales jobs require extensive travel; however, even in airports, travelling salespeople can keep in contact with their offices, access computer files containing customer information, and record customer information.

Self-Management

self management:
The development of a personal time management plan, setting priorities based on supervisors' expectations, keep a watchful eye on industry trends, and have a vision for the future.

Apart from time and territory management practices, successful salespeople should also manage themselves. In a demanding and rewarding profession such as professional selling, it is critical for salespeople to pay attention to **self-management** and develop a personal time management plan, set priorities based on their supervisors' expectations, keep a watchful eye on the industry trends, and have a vision for the future. In the following sections, we detail a number of areas that will be increasingly important for the emerging salesperson.

Personal Time Management

A salesperson views time, customers, and relationships as critical resources. When salespeople manage their time effectively, they create opportunities to better serve their customers, meet their post-sales service commitments, and accomplish their objectives. Salespeople often use time management software, such as an online calendar application, to plan their time, ensure they carry out their commitments to others, and meet their responsibilities.

In many organizations, salespeople use calendar and time management systems such as Microsoft Outlook and Google Calendar. While these time management systems are continually improving their capabilities, the software allows salespeople to do the following:

- Send invitations and appointments to customers.
- Reserve and schedule blocks of time to work on key projects.
- Reserve conference rooms within their company.

- Review the availability of their (internal) colleagues to meet on certain times and dates (i.e., search their schedules).
- Provide reminders of key deadlines.
- Receive meeting invitations from customers.
- Review their daily, weekly, and monthly meeting schedule.
- Access their list of internal and external contacts and their associated information.
- Develop and prioritize a task list or to-do list of their projects.

Regardless of your intended profession, we suggest that you begin using an online time management system. Time management is a critical skill to develop. Further, employers will be interested in knowing that you already possess the skill set.

What Might Your Sales Manager Tell You?

In our discussions with sales managers, we've found a number of consistent themes regarding new salespeople. In this section, we outline some of the reoccurring topics discussed with sales students and entry-level salespeople.

- **Take initiative.** Don't be afraid to act, make a recommendation, and get involved. Management wants you to become an active member in the organization.
- **Accept feedback and coaching.** The great sales organizations and sales managers want to help you develop your skill set and become more effective. In order to build your skill set, they will set up training as well as coaching opportunities. They believe in investing in you and hope you will accept the feedback in order to improve.
- **Do your due diligence.** In order to be a knowledge broker, you need to prepare, prepare, prepare. Don't take a customer relationship for granted. Your customer wants you to be a valued partner. The onus is on you to consistently create value for the customer.
- **Manage your time–well.** One of the fantastic elements of a sales career is the flexibility related to scheduling and time. You will need to develop your skills in managing your time and effort in order to meet the results expected from you.
- **Ask if you need help.** It's likely that most salespeople have confronted the same situations that you are dealing with. Be proactive and ask your colleagues and managers when you have a challenge or are unsure of the next step(s). You belong to a team.
- **Be honest and ethical.** Relationships are built on trust. Trust is extremely difficult to develop and easy to destroy. Be honest and ethical regardless of the situation–whether you are with the customer or you are alone. You have a long career to consider.
- **Meet deadlines.** We will all have milestones that we need to achieve. Set reasonable deadlines and be proactive when challenges occur. Forgiveness often comes easier when it's requested two weeks before a deadline rather than two hours before a deadline.
- **Understand the business–you are a key part of it.** You will need to be an ongoing learner. Business changes on an ongoing basis. Continually challenge yourself. Learn about your customer and your firm and understand key business processes–especially how your firm earns its money.
- **Understand your attitude.** Develop an earnest, appreciative attitude. Learn what bothers you and develop coping skills to manage frustration during challenging times.

- **Be careful with your use of technology.** Technology is advancing ahead of processes, protocols, and etiquette. Always consider the impact of your personal use of technology on the customer. Does your use of technology adhere to honest and ethical practices? Does your use of technology create trust or does it erode trust in the relationships with your customers and your colleagues?
- **You won't hit a home run every time.** It's impossible to close every sale. Instead, enjoy the successes and learn from the failures. However, keep an ongoing learning attitude. You will always be developing your sales skills.
- **Leverage the technology and tools.** Your company will provide a number of tools and technology to help make you more productive and effective. Don't be wary of learning and integrating sales technology into your skill set.
- **Leverage your internal resources.** You will have a group of colleagues that are invested in helping you and the business become successful. Use their collective intelligence, skill sets, and capabilities to help you build and maintain strong customer relationships.
- **Be a professional.** Again, you have a long career to consider. Consider the impact of your actions, words, and deeds upon yourself, your customers, your colleagues, and your career. For example:
  - Are you on time for your meetings?
  - Do you follow the guidelines or processes required by your customer and your employer?
  - Do you submit quality work?
  - Do you meet expected milestones and deadlines?
  - Do you follow-up and ensure you meet your commitments?

Executive Presence

executive presence: A certain aura that the salesperson is perceived as possessing, including qualities like professionalism, ability, and authority.

The term *executive presence* has entered a number of our discussions with senior sales professionals. **Executive presence** refers to a certain aura that the salesperson is perceived as possessing. These qualities include professionalism, ability, and authority.

For instance, some salespeople meet with C-level executives (i.e., chief financial officers, chief operating officers, chief executives officers, chief marketing officers, and chief information officers). In these types of conversations, the salesperson needs to possess a certain level of executive presence. These salespeople must develop a level of professionalism and business presence; they must demonstrate that they are credible and bring value to the business relationship.

Some research suggests that executive presence is (a) the perception held by others about you; (b) the perception results from your initial interaction with a group as well as your ongoing interactions, and (c) the perception (held by others) that you have a certain level of gravitas and influence.[5]

As an emerging salesperson, you need to remember that executive presence is about how others perceive you. For instance, do your customers perceive you as being credible? Do your colleagues perceive you to be genuine? And do your supervisors perceive you as possessing the needed skills, attitudes, and attributes to accept increasing levels of responsibility?

Perhaps, the true question lies in asking yourself, "Am I developing the skills and qualities of a high performing professional?" As we discuss in the previous section, your managers want you to be prepared, be a lifelong learner, be honest and ethical, accept feedback, and follow-up on your commitments. All of these qualities will serve you well in your interactions with customers, colleagues, and supervisors.

You have a long career to consider. Now is the time to set your goals for your professionalism, your goals for lifelong learning and development, and your understanding of business and the marketplace.

Emotional Intelligence

Emotional intelligence is another prevalent topic within the sales industry. **Emotional intelligence** (often called EI) is the combination of four abilities: (1) your ability to perceive other's emotions, (2) your ability to identify your emotions, (3) your ability to understand what's causing your emotion, and (4) your ability to manage your emotions.[6] EI serves as a skill the salesperson can use in interactions with customers, colleagues, and supervisors.

emotional intelligence (EI): A combination of four abilities: (1) your ability to perceive other's emotions (2) your ability to identify your emotions (3) your ability to understand what's causing your emotion and (4) your ability to manage your emotions. EI serves as a skill the salesperson can utilize to interact with customers, colleagues and supervisors.

As you probably have guessed, a salesperson who can identify their customer's emotions and then suitably adapt their sales conversation has an opportunity to be more effective. Similarly, a salesperson may find a customer interaction overwhelming or frustrating. Rather than venting, the high EI salesperson can identify their emotion and its driver. By managing their emotions, the salesperson can better maintain their composure and continue the sales conversation.

Like any skill, enhancing your EI capacity requires practice, awareness, and coaching. However, it's becoming a skill that is increasingly valued within sales organizations. EI serves as a skill that can increase your effectiveness with your customer base.

Networking

Sales is an interaction-based profession, and **sales networking** is the continuous method of making and using contacts. As a salesperson, you be will immersed in a series of relationships–with your customers, with your colleagues, with your vendors, with your business partners, and with your family and friends.[7] Simply put, you will be working constantly with others–in face-to-face interactions, in virtual interactions through video-conferencing, and via teleconferences and individual phone calls.

sales networking: The continuous prospecting method of making and utilizing contacts.

As such, it's important to be able to build relationships, maintain a wide array of relationships, and be willing to assist those individuals within your network. These relationships will be invaluable to you throughout the course of your career. The people who make up your relationship network will allow you to do the following:

- Learn from them.
- Leverage their expertise to help you with your projects and customers.
- Ask for their assistance, guidance, and counsel.
- Experience greater levels of satisfaction with your job.[8]

But remember: networking is your personal array of relationships–from individuals you have just met to those you consider to be close friends and confidantes–and relationships are based on trust and communication. Effective salespeople remember that relationships are a mutual commitment. They ask themselves how they can help those in their network, how they can share their expertise, and how they can create value for others. Always keep in mind that building and maintaining relationships requires the **mutual investment** of effort, time, and resources.

mutual investment: A requirement for building and maintaining relationships requiring effort, time and resources.

What's Happening in Sales

LO4

Sales continues to evolve. In this section, we briefly highlight a few thoughts to consider as you are developing your vision for the future and start building your sales skill set.

artificial intelligence system (AI): The software to better understand customers behaviours and help salespeople understand how they can better help their customers.

predictive analytics: The software technology that can predict the plausible future opportunities to assist the customers and provide salespeople with the needed tools to do so.

Artificial intelligence and predictive analytics are evolving. Software provides an opportunity to learn more about your customers. Another evolving technology tool lies in artificial intelligence and predictive analytics. Firms are integrating the **artificial intelligence system** to better understand their customers and help their salesforce understand how they might help them. For instance, banks are integrating predictive analytics and artificial intelligence systems, such as Salesforce's Einstein software.[9] The goal is to better integrate and understand all of the ways that the firm and its customer base interact. With this learning, the **predictive analytics** software can predict the next plausible opportunity to assist the customers and provide their frontline salespeople with the needed tools to do so. For the upcoming salesperson, the software offers another tool to become more customer-focused and create value.

Inside sales provides an interesting growth opportunity. A number of firms continue to build their inside sales centres.[10] Rather than invest solely in a widely dispersed field sales force, firms are investing in more centralized inside sales centres. Inside sales people sell remotely using a wide array of social media, web technology, video conferencing, and other technology tools. For salespeople, inside sales provides a unique learning opportunity to enhance their professional selling skill set by developing expertise in leveraging technology throughout the sales process.

Will marketing and sales departments integrate a little more? An opportunity exists to create more collaboration between the departments. Marketing and sales serve vital roles in a company's ability to drive sales. Now, the question lies in how to further leverage their collective value. While sales provide the capability to create relationships and drive revenue, marketing possesses the ability to differentiate a product and communicate its value. As firms increasingly develop strategies to attract new customers and cement relationships, an ideal time exists to create a collaborative relationship between marketing and sales. For the upcoming salesperson, this opportunity should open a number of opportunities in content strategy, digital prospecting, and customer-focused activities.

Buyers continue to evolve. Buyers are leveraging technology to learn about options and services and to move forward with their decision-making processes. Technology has also impacted the buying process. Buyers and buying committees (i.e., buying centres) are leveraging technology to evaluate product options, seek expert opinions, and inform themselves–all from their desk, laptop, or even coffee shop. This has allowed the buying process to move forward, often without the involvement of the seller. For the upcoming salesperson, it's important to understand how to use technology to monitor and interpret new and existing customers' digital actions. Further, as the use of buying committees continues, the upcoming salesperson needs to be able to work with a broad array of buyers with distinct roles and responsibilities. Relationship adaptability will continue to be a critical skill set.

Customer-focused, value-creating, adaptable salespeople are key. Regardless of the changes in business, we believe it's a fantastic time for the upcoming salesperson. Undoubtedly, the upcoming salespeople will be asked to enhance their knowledge base on an ongoing basis, to learn how to muster internal and external resources, and to develop increasingly customized solutions for their customers. But despite the continued transformation in technology, buying processes, and business structure, we suggest that sales remains a fantastic career. For the earnest upcoming salesperson, the development of professional selling skills will remain a great investment across your career. The ability to communicate, to listen, to problem-solve, to share expertise, and to adapt to various buyers will continue to drive value in any relationship. We applaud your investment of time and effort in learning about professional selling and we sincerely hope you continue a lifelong development of your sales skill set.

Summary of Major Selling Issues

Proper time and territory management is critical for the salesperson to maximize territorial sales and profits. A sales territory comprises a group of customers or a geographical area assigned to a salesperson. It is a segment of the company's total market. A salesperson within a territory must analyze the various segments, estimate sales potential, and develop a marketing mix based on the needs and desires of the marketplace.

Companies develop and use sales territories for numerous reasons. Assigning territories allows the company to obtain thorough coverage of the market, to fully reach sales potential, and to establish salespeople's responsibilities. Territories mean that performance can be monitored and customer relations improved through regular calls from the salesperson. This helps to reduce sales expenses by avoiding duplicated effort in travelling and customer contacts. Finally, territories allow better matching of salespeople to customer needs, and benefit salespeople and the company.

Nevertheless, there are disadvantages to developing sales territories. Some salespeople may not be motivated if they feel restricted by a particular territory. Also, a company may be too small to segment its market, or management may not want to take time to develop territories.

Time and territory management is continual for a salesperson; it involves seven key elements:

1. Establish the territory sales quota.
2. Perform account analysis, which involves identifying present and potential customers and estimating their sales potential. In analyzing these accounts, salespeople may use the undifferentiated selling approach if they view accounts as similar or, if accounts have different characteristics, they use the account segmentation approach.
3. Develop objectives and sales quotas for individual accounts.
4. Allocate time in the territory, managing time, planning schedules, and using spare time effectively.
5. Develop the sales-call objective, profile, benefit program, and selling strategies for individual customers. Salespeople have to learn everything they can about customers and maintain records on each one. Once this is done, they can create the proper selling strategies to meet customers' needs.
6. Schedule the sales calls at specific times and places, and route the salesperson's movement and travel pattern around the territory.
7. Evaluate the territory and customer sales results periodically to see if the system is working and whether aspects need adjustment. Use established objectives and quotas to determine how effectively the salesperson performs. Compare actual performance to these standards for evaluation purposes.

The increasing cost of a personal sales call and the increasing amount of time spent travelling to make personal sales calls are reasons why efficient salespeople look to technology as a sales tool. Sales technology tools help salespeople with routine as well as strategic tasks, allowing them to focus on actual selling time.

ETHICAL DILEMMA

TECHNOLOGY HELPS WIN THE DAY

You have been working for an established mid-sized food processor for the past three months. As a young rookie in the company, you have been assigned to one of the more complex sales territories with extensive travelling. Most of the other sales reps are older, and many have been with the company more than 20 years. The previous salesperson assigned to this territory averaged only about six sales calls per day because of the long travel times. Because of your youth, you have been able to average seven calls per day and hence, have been enjoying a slightly higher income than your predecessor.

One weekend you decided to use Googlemaps to map out your sales routes. You found that it cut down on travel time as it helped plan the quickest routes to your destinations regardless of location. It proved so effective that, before long, you could make up to 10 calls per day without any problems. Now you find yourself in a quandary. Should you continue to make your seven calls per day and finish early so you can relax with your friends in the afternoon? Or should you make your 10 calls, which will probably cause your manager to put more pressure on your colleagues to increase their own performance? After all, you have the toughest territory and you are "burning it up."

What should you do?

MEETING A SALES CHALLENGE

How Alice Jenson manages her time will determine her productivity. Alice should tell her boss about the situation. Then she should analyze her accounts to classify them according to past sales and sales potential. Now she can allocate her time by concentrating on her extra-large and large accounts, contacting each as often as necessary. The medium-sized customers might be seen every one to two months, and the small ones might be seen less frequently or be contacted by telephone. If needed, Alice's boss could be asked to contact some customers. Alice's situation illustrates why companies require salespeople to do so much record keeping. After each sales call, Alice needs to update the customer profile, as shown in Chapter 7, to have current information on all customers.

PLAYING THE ROLE

The situation: You are the sales manager for Acme printing company. You oversee six salespeople, each of whom is responsible for an established territory. Your sales force is considered a good one—highly motivated and professional. However, one of your reps, Howard, has been a cause for concern recently. You've noticed that he has been arriving late for work more frequently and two of his customers have called in recently to discuss the fact that he smelled of alcohol during sales calls. You decide to ask around and you find out that Howard's marriage is in trouble and he's been drinking fairly heavily.

His sales have slipped recently so you decide to call Howard in for an appointment on Friday afternoon. One of your options is to fire him—after all, he's costing you business.

What other options do you have?

Role A: The sales manager.

Role B: Howard.

Having prepared for the appointment, role-play the actual meeting. Once Howard shows up, demonstrate what you would do and how you would handle the situation. Be prepared to defend your actions to the class.

Key Terms for Selling

80/20 principle
account analysis
account segmentation
artificial intelligence system(AI)
break even analysis
ELMS system
emotional intelligence (EI)
executive presence
goal setting
key accounts
mutual investment
predictive analytics
quota
routing
sales call allocation
sales networking
sales technology
sales response function
sales territory
scheduling
self management
time management
undifferentiated selling

Sales Application Questions

1. How could you use technology to better manage your customers and your territory? Explain how you could use technologies such as a CRM system and other sales technology tools to save time and to manage a sales territory.
2. What is a sales territory? Why do firms establish sales territories? Why might sales territories not be developed?
3. Briefly discuss each of the elements of time and territory management and indicate how these seven elements relate to one another.
4. What is the difference between the undifferentiated selling approach and the account segmentation approach for analyzing accounts? When might each approach be used?
5. Assume a sales manager determines that in a given territory each salesperson sells approximately $500,000 yearly. Also, assume that the firm's cost of goods sold are estimated to be 65 percent of sales and that a salesperson's direct costs are $35,000 a year. Each salesperson works 48 weeks a year, eight hours a day, and averages five sales calls per day. Using this information, how much merchandise must each salesperson sell to break even?
    a. For the year?
    b. Each day?
    c. Each sales call?
6. What is a key account?
7. What are the factors to consider when a salesperson allocates time?
8. What is the purpose of customer sales planning?
9. Define *scheduling* and *routing.*

Sales Online Exercise

Time Is Money, So Make Every Minute Count!

Time wasted trying to find a prospect's address and location can cost a salesperson valuable resources. For this assignment, find three potential customers for your organization within a 75-kilometre radius of the city where you currently live. Choose another two potential customers who live in each of two provinces or territories next to the province or territory you live in.

Using Google maps or another travel mapping app, create a travel schedule that would allow you to contact these five potential customers in a two-day period.

Research the standard industrial classifications for each organization and individual.

Write a memo to your boss showing the addresses of each potential customer, plus the route you will use on the day you will be at that customer's business.

Further Exploring the Sales World

1. Visit a large retailer in your community and ask a buyer or store manager what salespeople do when they make a sales call. Determine the number of times the retailer wants salespeople to visit each month. Are calls from some salespeople preferable to others? If so, why?
2. Contact a salesperson and sales manager and report on each one's philosophy toward managing time and territory. Ask each person to calculate how much it costs to contact one prospect and, on the average, what amount must be sold each day to break even.

Selling Experiential Exercise

Make a chart similar to the one below and record the time you spend on various activities for one week. Each day, place codes on your chart to indicate the time spent on each activity. Some codes are suggested here; add any codes you need. At the end of the week, write your total hours in that column. If any activity takes up a great deal of time–such as "Personal"–subdivide it by assigning additional activities such as sports, phone, or socializing. Now that you have a good idea of how you spend your time, decide whether you want to make some changes.

Time Management

Name ________________ Week beginning ____

(Date)________________

	MON	TUE	WED	THUR	FRI	SAT	SUN	ACTIVITY	CODE	TOTAL HOURS
6:30–7:00 a.m.								Class	CL	______
7:00–7:30								Sleep	SL	______
7:30–8:00								Study	SU	______
8:00–8:30								Work	W	______
8:30–9:00								Personal	P	______
9:00–9:30								______	______	______
9:30–10:00										
10:00–10:30										
10:30–11:00										
11:00–11:30										
11:30–12:00										
12:00–12:30 p.m.										
12:30–1:00										
1:00–1:30										
1:30–2:00										
2:00–2:30										
2:30–3:00										
3:00–3:30										

	MON	TUE	WED	THUR	FRI	SAT	SUN	ACTIVITY	CODE	TOTAL HOURS
3:30–4:00										
4:00–4:30										
4:30–5:00										
5:00–5:30										
5:30–6:00										
6:00–6:30										
6:30–7:00										
7:00–7:30										
7:30–8:00										
After 8:00*										

*Note: If you need to, make another sheet.

CASE 13–1

YOUR SELLING DAY: A TIME AND TERRITORY GAME*

Your sales manager is working with you tomorrow only, and you want to call on customers with the greatest sales potential (see Exhibit A) because you are on a straight commission. The area of your territory that you want to cover contains 16 customers (see Exhibit B). To determine travel time, allow 15 minutes for each side of a square. Each sales call takes 30 minutes. You can leave your house at 8:00 a.m. or later. If you take time for lunch, it must be in 15-minute time blocks (15, 30, 45, or 60 minutes). Your last customer must be contacted by 4:30 p.m. to allow you enough sales time. Your customers do not see salespeople after 5:00 p.m. You travel home after 5:00 p.m.

EXHIBIT A

Customers' sales potential.

CUSTOMER	SALES POTENTIAL	CUSTOMER	SALES POTENTIAL
A	$4,000	I	$ 1,000
B	3,000	J	1,000
C	6,000	K	10,000
D	2,000	L	12,000
E	2,000	M	8,000
F	8,000	N	9,000
G	4,000	O	8,000
H	6,000	P	10,000

*Case copyright © 1997 by Charles M. Futrell.

EXHIBIT B

A partial map of your sales territory.

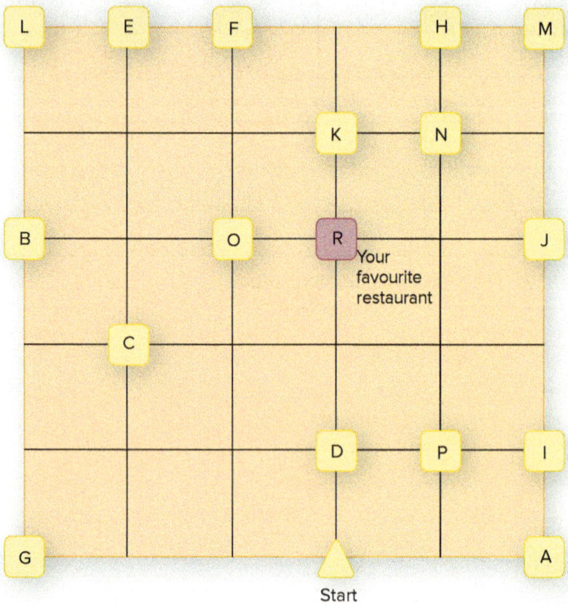

QUESTIONS

1. Develop the route that gives the highest sales potential for the day your boss works with you.
2. For the next day, develop the route allowing you to contact the remaining customers in this part of the territory.

CASE 13–2

NAOMI BEAUPRÉ'S DISTRICT—DEVELOPMENT OF AN ACCOUNT SEGMENTATION PLAN

Naomi Beaupré sat listening to her boss talk about the new time and territory management program being implemented by her company. Her boss was saying, "Since we want to eventually establish priorities for our accounts in order to make time-investment decisions, we must classify the accounts into categories. A simple *A, B, C, D, E* designation of categories is the most commonly used approach, with *A* accounts the most valuable.

"The basis for setting the values or limits for each category is the distribution of sales or concentration patterns in most industries. In general, business in our company is distributed approximately as shown in Exhibit A. Generally, the top 10 percent of the accounts will generate 65 percent of sales, and the top 30 percent will generate 85 percent of the sales in any given territory. Salespeople may use this rule-of-thumb breakdown of accounts in determining the classification system for their accounts. Once the potential for all their accounts has been calculated, their territory should break down like this:

- *A* accounts = top 10 percent of the accounts
- *B* accounts = next 20 percent of the accounts
- *C* accounts = next 50 percent of the accounts
- *D* accounts = next 10 percent of the accounts
- *E* accounts = last 10 percent of the accounts

EXHIBIT A

Distribution of sales.

CUSTOMER CLASSIFICATION	PERCENTAGE OF CUSTOMERS	PERCENTAGE OF TOTAL SALES VOLUME
A	10	65
B	20	20
C	30	10
D	10	3
E	10	2
	100	100

"Naomi, I want you to have each of your salespeople take a close look at his or her sales-call cycles. As I have explained, a call cycle is a round of calls in which all *A* accounts are called on at least once and some, but not all, *B, C, D,* and *E* accounts are called on. When a salesperson has visited all of his or her *A* accounts, the cycle is completed. Then, a new cycle begins and the series of calls repeats. Since not all *B, C, D,* and *E* accounts are called on in every cycle, the specific accounts to be seen in these classifications differ from cycle to cycle. A call cycle, therefore, is established around the call frequency patterns of *A* accounts."

Suppose that a group of accounts is classified in this way:

ACCOUNTS	EXPECTED VALUE
A	$100,001 and over
B	$50,001-100,000
C	$30,001-50,000
D	$20,001-30,000
E	Under $20,000

The call frequency patterns, therefore, based on potential and return on time invested, may be as follows:

ACCOUNTS	WEEKS BETWEEN CALLS	NUMBER OF ACCOUNTS
A	2	10
B	4	20
C	6	45
D	8	12
E	10	10

Thus, a call cycle in this territory will cover two weeks. This means that in every two-week cycle the salesperson will call on these accounts:

- All of the *A*s
- Half of the *B*s
- One-third of the *C*s
- One-quarter of the *D*s
- One-fifth of the *E*s

QUESTIONS

1. Develop a table showing a salesperson's call cycle using the call-frequency patterns.
2. Discuss why this should be done.

Source: © Hill Street Studios/Gary Kious/Blend Images/Getty Images RF

CHAPTER 14

Retail, Business, Services, and Nonprofit Selling

Sara Matheson
St.Clair College
Zekelman School
of Business and IT,
Windsor, Ontario

Source: Courtesy of Sara Matheson

A Sales Success Story

Sara Matheson is a graduate of the three-year Business Administration: Marketing program at the Zekelman School of Business and IT at St. Clair College. She has always been passionate about sales and customer service, and she loves working with people. She began her career in sales in 2009 as a part-time membership marketing associate at Costco Wholesale. She was responsible for the sale and upsell of Costco memberships and credit cards. This position gave Sara the opportunity to sell both inside the warehouse and outside at various local employers.

When Sara graduated in 2011, she was ready to take the next step in her career. In September of that year, Sara accepted a role as a sales account manager at Cypher Systems Group, where she became a Registered Insurance Broker. In this role, she worked in an inbound contact-centre environment, selling auto and home insurance to people from coast to coast in Canada. This position helped further strengthen Sara's sales skills by teaching her firsthand the importance of establishing rapport—and overcoming the challenges of doing so solely over the phone.

As Sara explains, "One of the first sales skills that I developed in this role was the ability to smile through the phone. Insurance is not a tangible item, nor something that many people enjoy purchasing, but as a sales person, I was able to overcome this by quickly establishing a rapport with the customer and making sure they were fully educated on the insurance process the entire way. I found the most success when I made the call not just about insurance, but took the time to know the customer. Asking how their day is going, complimenting them on their vehicle, talking about sports to learn what their favourite team is, or wishing them a happy birthday—these things go a very long way. I made sure to always make note in their files of the personal items that I learned about them. That way, on our next phone call, I could speak to these items again. I could almost hear their smiles through the phone!"

Sara continued in this role until 2015, when she was promoted into a supervisory role as a cross-divisional outbound sales team leader. In this role she was responsible for leading a team of outbound sales representatives who drove leads into two insurance brokerages at Cypher Systems Group. Sara was able to apply theory of constraint thinking to overcome team challenges and developed tools to help make the team's job quicker and easier. These tools helped provide more leads to brokers, which ultimately converted into paying customers. Due to this growth, her team was expanded from two to five insurance brokerages at Cypher Systems Group.

As Sara continued on her professional development, in 2016 she accepted a role as service team leader where she was responsible for leading a team of service account managers. She was able to uniquely apply her sales experience in this role, which proved to help the team with cross selling to existing policyholders. Sara also became involved in the planning, research, and implementation of new organizational initiatives for process improvement. "My professional growth with Cypher Systems Group was a direct result of having a genuine interest in doing not just a good job, but a GREAT job!" says Sara.

In 2017, Sara made the decision to expand her wings and explore a career outside of Cypher Systems Group. She accepted a role as manager of business development at a local human resources firm where she was responsible for establishing and maintaining business relationships. This role became pivotal in rounding out Sara's sales skills as she was cold calling and walking into establishments in an effort to land a meeting and, ultimately, sign a business deal. This gave Sara the opportunity to learn about many different industries. "At 10 a.m. I could be at a local automotive manufacturer learning about seat assembly, at 11 a.m. I'm at a restaurant learning about chef duties, and by 1 p.m. I could be at a local tomato greenhouse," says Sara. "I'm like a sponge when it comes to learning. I had not personally worked in many of the industries that I was hiring for. When establishing trust with these business owners, it became my job to learn their industry and the various roles. This was a fantastic experience that I am forever grateful for!"

In 2018, Sara decided to follow her passion and returned to Cypher Systems Group where she became a commercial sales team leader. In this supervisory role, she led a team of commercial insurance brokers. "This role was a perfect fit for me, as I was able to coach my team on the importance of learning the industries that we were insuring."

In August 2018, Cypher Systems Group was acquired by HUB International and was rebranded as HUB Customer Central. Sara continued in her role until March 2019, when she was promoted to sales resource administrator, reporting to the senior vice president."This role is like a dream come true for me as a professional. I am responsible for opportunity development and implementation of support functions, while maintaining current relationships across HUB and partnered group clients across Canada. I am entrusted to represent our company across Canada and act as the ombudsperson to resolve any concerns."

Throughout her professional sales career, Sara has been commended on her positivity. Sara identifies one skill that she firmly believes is critical to her success: "Smiling. I know it sounds simple, but coming to work every day with a big smile (and leaving life's challenges outside of work) not only makes my day better, but it makes my team and customers want to work with me! Secondly, being a person of your word is crucial. We are not just given trust; this is something that we must earn. If I make a commitment to get something done, I always ensure it is done to its entirety and finished with a sincere smile."

MAIN TOPICS

What Is Retailing?

Career Opportunities

The Retail Salesperson's Role

Technology Builds Relationships

The Basic Retail Selling Process

What's Different about the Business Market?

Selling Business Products Is Different

Steps that Business Purchasing Agents Use in Making Buying Decisions

Whom Should I Talk To?

Purchasing Agents Are Rational Buyers

Why Do Producers Buy?

Selling Services Is Challenging

Nonprofit Selling—It's about Time!

Selling Is Selling

LEARNING OBJECTIVES

Retail selling can be challenging and rewarding depending on the particular retailer. Salespeople sell many types of goods and services in business, nonprofit, and consumer markets. After studying this chapter, you should be able to:

LO1 Discuss the importance of personal selling in retailing.

LO2 Describe the retail selling process.

LO3 Discuss the differences between business and consumer products, as well as their markets.

LO4 Explain what an RFP is and outline how to respond to one.

LO5 Explain the steps business purchasing agents use in buying decisions.

LO6 Explain the differences between services and nonprofit selling.

LO7 Discuss the term crowdfunding as it relates to nonprofit selling.

FACING A SALES CHALLENGE

Susan Chung was very surprised to learn that at least two people she worked with made more than $4,000 a month selling electronics and computers in a retail store located in a mall. She felt lucky to earn $400 a month. Going to school allowed her to work only 50 hours a month, but the holidays were approaching and her manager said she could work 40 to 50 hours a week after finals.

Being paid the minimum wage and a commission, as well as participating in an occasional sales contest, had not resulted in big bucks for Susan. But if her co-workers were making 10 times her salary, she had room for improvement. In analyzing her procedures, Susan realized that she waited for someone to enter the store and approached quickly, asking, "May I help you?" Ten percent of the customers knew what they wanted, so Susan showed it to them, asked questions, and let the prospects make up their own minds. About 15 percent of the people she waited on bought. Most people, however, said no when Susan asked, "May I help you?" Not wanting to seem pushy, she did not disturb shoppers as they looked around the store but waited for them to ask for her help.

Can you suggest to Susan how she might increase her sales and earn more money?

(Continued at end of chapter.)

This chapter examines selling careers in four organizational settings: retail, business, services, and nonprofit. Since you are probably most familiar with retail selling, let's begin there.

What Is Retailing?

Many of us have worked retail, earning the minimum wage and not being challenged by the job. However, thousands of retail sales jobs are challenging and financially rewarding. Hard work, product knowledge, selling skills, and a good sales commission plan can make it possible to earn $50,000 to more than $1,000,000 a year in retail sales. This chapter introduces you to the selling skills used by retail salespeople making big bucks.

Retailing refers to any individual or organization selling its goods or services directly to final consumers for their personal, nonbusiness use. The distinguishing characteristic of a retail sale is that a retail transaction involves the final consumer—the retail customer. A retail sale may occur over the telephone, through the mail, on a street corner, on the Internet, in a private residence, or in a traditional retail store.

retailing: Any individual or organization selling goods or services directly to final consumers for their personal, nonbusiness use.

Goods and services sold to final consumers for their personal, nonbusiness use vary from items such as T-shirts and jogging shoes to stocks and bonds, legal services, cosmetics, cars, real estate, and wedding cakes. A person selling cosmetics to a department store shopper is engaged in retailing, as is a real estate agent selling a $400,000 house. This section focuses on retail transactions that occur in a retail store.

Career Opportunities

Retail stores in Canada account for more than $605 billion in sales each year.[1] The many salespeople associated with retailing are employed by firms as diverse as huge discount stores, upscale chain department stores, and mom-and-pop operations. Sales career opportunities in the business, services, and nonprofit areas are excellent. Approximately 2.1 million people are employed in retail trade in Canada as clerks, sales representatives, and sales or store managers.[2] Jobs may increase faster as nonprofit organizations discover the benefits of having a sales force.

Financial Rewards Are Excellent

As in other forms of professional selling, the financial rewards and promotional opportunities for the retail salesperson are excellent. Earnings as a retail salesperson vary depending on the type of product sold, the compensation plan (straight salary, salary plus commission, or straight commission), and the organization. Salary ranges can vary from minimum wage (between roughly $11 to $15 per hour, depending on the province/territory) to more than $1,000,000 a year. When you are in a store, ask salespeople whether they are on an hourly salary or commission plan. Those on commissions could be making big bucks if they are (1) order getters, (2) prospectors, and (3) able to obtain referrals.

Nonfinancial Rewards Are Many

Financial compensation is only one part of the reward received as a retail salesperson. Nonfinancial rewards offered by a retail career are numerous. They include excellent training programs, rapid assumption of responsibility, recognition, opportunity for personal growth and development, travel, and satisfaction from work.

The Retail Salesperson's Role

The role requirements of retail salespeople vary greatly. Some jobs require the salesperson to act only as an order taker. Other jobs require highly skilled people who can successfully identify and arouse customers' needs and persuade them to purchase and satisfy those needs. Generally, a retail salesperson is involved, to some extent, in providing service, working stock or managing inventory, personal selling, and completing transactions. The following sections elaborate on each of these four retail sales functions.

Service

To build clientele–and thus earn top money–retail salespeople need to (1) develop repeat sales from present customers, (2) get new customers through referrals from customers, and (3) sell prospects entering or calling the store. Salespeople do these things by being able to close prospects and provide great service to customers.

Working and Knowing Stock

Maintaining a variety of neatly displayed items for sale to consumers and reordering or replacing stock items when depleted is a tedious, time-consuming, and important function of many retail salespeople. The appearance of a store, or a department within a large store, reflects on the retail salesperson and helps the consumer to develop a good first impression, thereby boosting the retailer's chance of making sales. Working stock also aids a retail salesperson in gaining knowledge of the company's products and their location within the store.

LO1 Personal Selling

Of the four functions of the retail salesperson, personal selling is most important. In most cases, the retail salesperson should consider using the same major parts of the sales presentation used by the business salesperson, beginning with the approach. Before continuing, please read Making the Sale for an example of creative retail selling.

MAKING THE SALE

CREATIVE SUGGESTION SELLING

A salesperson approached a young customer in a large department store and asked whether she could help her by writing up the sale of a $50 necktie, so she could wait on another customer. She quickly introduced the customer to another salesperson at the counter and walked over to the other customer.

As he began writing up the sale, he looked up and said, "This is a beautiful tie you have selected. What is he going to wear with it?" The woman reached into her purse and pulled out a swatch of fabric. He looked at it a moment and said, "There's an ancient madder pattern that comes in two colour combinations that would go very well with this suit." He pulled out the two ties as he was talking with her. She readily agreed and took both of them—at $50 each.

He asked, "Doesn't he need some new shirts to go with his new suit?" The customer replied, "I'm glad you asked; he does need some, but I haven't been able to find any white ones with French cuffs. Do you have any size 15/33?" He showed her two qualities, pointing out the difference in the cloths. She selected three shirts at $60 each. "Does he ever wear coloured shirts?" he inquired. "Yes; if you have this same shirt in blue, I'll take two."

The sale progressed from there to include gold-filled cuff links, a travel robe to match the ancient madder ties, pyjamas, and slippers. The total sale was $1,000, versus the $50 the original salesperson was willing to settle for. Even more importantly, this salesperson made a new customer for the department and himself. That is creative suggestion selling at its very best.

Not once in the course of the sale did he oversell. He related to the customer's desires and wants and knew the content of the stock well enough to fulfill her requirements. Above all, he had the heart of a salesperson who not only thoroughly enjoys the excitement of meeting the expressed request of the customer, but also has the imagination to conceive of other things the buyer might find of interest. This type of selling technique can be taught; unfortunately, it doesn't happen very often.[3]

Accurately Completing Transactions

When a customer is ready to make a purchase, the salesperson must complete the transaction before the sale can be completed. A retail transaction should be handled quickly, smoothly, and accurately to avoid frustrating the customer and possibly losing the sale. This is a good checklist to follow when transacting a sale:

- Collect customer information clearly and accurately.
- Accept payment.
- If change is required, count it accurately, and do not place the money received from the customer in the cash drawer until you have made change and the customer has accepted it.
- When accepting a credit card, debit card, gift card, or cheque make sure all necessary forms are signed by the customer.

Many retailing institutions encourage the use of charge accounts by qualified customers. If that is the case, encourage new customers to participate in your store's charge program by asking them to fill out a credit application. Later that day, you could drop these customers a short thank-you card requesting their regular patronage. This type of retail service builds long-lasting relationships between salespeople and customers.

Technology Builds Relationships

Retailers use technology to strengthen customer loyalties and build relationships. Here's an example. A chain of 30 fashion stores in five provinces created its Call Customer Program in which salespeople maintain ongoing relationships with their regular customers. All sales associates maintain personal *call books* that include detailed customer information such as size, colour, and style preferences; previous purchases; names of family members; employment; and important dates to remember.

(Contact-management software—see Chapter 5—is great for recording customer information.) The associate acts as a purchasing agent for customers, contacting them about special events or when appropriate merchandise arrives, or reminding them of important personal dates (e.g., the birthday of a spouse). Associates often act as personal shoppers, selecting items throughout the store for customers.

Some retailers have salespeople view merchandise at their central warehouse showroom via satellite, make selections for specific customers, and then contact customers.

SELLING TIPS

THE RETAIL APPROACH—A DEVELOPING ART

Historically, retail selling has been known as transactional selling—once the deal is done, that's it, move on to the next customer. Today, many successful retail salespeople are recognizing the value in practising relationship selling at the retail level. For example, you probably own a cell phone and/or a tablet, and/or a laptop computer. Did you or do you buy all your electronics from the same store or even the same salesperson? With technology changing so quickly, how many home electronics products do you think you'll purchase in your lifetime?

Practising relationship selling can result in a very comfortable living. Retail relationship selling begins with the first time you approach your customer. What makes for an effective approach? The first minute or so is critical for relationship building.

1. **The greeting** – Greet customers within 30 seconds of their entering the store or your area. Let them get comfortable in the store and then greet them. Don't be overbearing like you're trying to make a quick sale. Customers do not like this and may leave quickly. Introduce yourself to personalize the relationship.
2. **Your manner** – Be friendly, sincere, and professional. Forget the fake smiles and phoney greetings; prospects see right through them. This is your chance to make a good first impression so don't blow it! Appearance is important too. Would you want to do business with you, now and into the future?
3. **Rapport** – Try to get your prospect to relax. He or she is probably used to being defensive in retail buying situations. You want prospects to feel comfortable dealing with you, so don't rush them.
4. **Questioning** – Too many retail salespeople are more apt to sell what they want to sell rather than what a prospect wants to buy. Good questioning and listening skills are critical here. Both show empathy and will ensure greater satisfaction.
5. **Body language** – This says a lot about you. Fidgeting, slouching, and constantly looking around indicates your impatience and disinterest—hardly things you want to demonstrate if you plan to develop a relationship.
6. **Facial expression** – Use eye contact and a friendly smile to show your sincerity and make the prospect comfortable.

Keep in mind that the retail approach is your opportunity to plant the seeds for a long-term relationship with this customer. This is how good incomes are earned in retail selling.

LO2 The Basic Retail Selling Process

Why do you shop at a particular retail store? Why do you buy from a particular salesperson? Your reasons will differ depending on the type of product you shop for, such as gasoline, a bank account, a wedding ring, or an automobile.

- **The salesperson** - Is this the right salesperson for me to trust and from whom to buy? Does this salesperson have integrity, judgment, and knowledge concerning my situation?
- **Company** - Is this the store for me?
- **Product** - Will this product fulfill my needs?
- **Price** - Should I shop around for price? Will this store lower the price shortly? What about terms and returns?
- **Time to buy** - Should I buy now?

- **Service** - Will the company and salesperson help me if I need further help?
- **Trust** - Can I trust this salesperson, store, and product?

You probably have other reasons to add to the list. However, successful retail salespeople consider these patronage motives when using a selling process similar to these 10 steps:

1. Prospecting
2. The approach -
    a. Attitude
    b. Appearance
    c. Manner
3. Presentation -
    a. Agreement of need
        i. Bring sales presentations into focus on product needed
    b. Selling the store
        i. Your reputation
        ii. Company reputation
    c. Fill the need
        i. Stress benefits of features and advantages of products and store using SELL sequence.
4. Use a trial close
5. Respond to objection
6. Use your trial close to determine whether you've handled objection
7. Close the primary sale
8. Suggestion selling -
    a. Suggest other items to buy
9. Wrap it up -
    a. Remove fears, uncertainties, doubts
    b. Complete the transaction
10. Follow-up and service after the sale

Carefully orchestrated and executed, these 10 steps can bring you success and satisfied customers.

SOCIAL MEDIA INSIGHTS FOR SALES PEOPLE

SOCIAL MEDIA IN THE RETAIL REALM

While social media networking is certainly used by many large and successful retailers, what about individual salespeople? Do they use it independently to increase their sales? Those making minimal wages who simply act as order takers probably do not. However, those working on a commission basis often use it to boost their sales as well as their income levels.

Imagine a sales rep that may work on commission in a large electronics store. The company itself probably has its own corporate social media presence to build company sales. However, a wise salesperson could, if not against company policy, also make use of their own personal social networks to boost their commissions also. How?

- Ensure that all personal contacts are aware of what they sell and where they sell it.
- Engage customers with tips and advice on product usage.
- Post announcements on upcoming sales and promotions.
- Share other relevant news and information—in other words, create a following.

These are just a few ways a retail salesperson can use social media. Depending on the nature of the product, it is highly likely that retail salespeople can employ the same social media strategies that many of their B2B counterparts use.

SELLING GLOBALLY

THE FORMER SOVIET UNION, EASTERN EUROPE, AND THE THIRD WORLD

Despite essential differences between the former Soviet Union, its former satellites in Eastern Europe, and developing countries, all share similar business problems: low productivity, poor-quality products, and, in many cases, a physically run-down manufacturing location with a poor—or nonexistent—infrastructure.

North American retailers wanting to open stores in these countries should expect (1) a bureaucratic tone to the negotiating process, (2) different negotiation methods, and (3) differing expectations on the part of the negotiator. Remember that your partners from these countries may have real security concerns. Their jobs—even their careers—may still depend on the success of the individual negotiation.

Since red tape can be an obstacle, expect to waste a lot of time when dealing with the bureaucracy. Even if there are progressive, liberal laws and regulations, many of these bureaucrats continue to use discretion in approving key parts of foreign investment activities. A significant delay, however, shouldn't necessarily jeopardize the whole transaction.

Settlements are usually written in a highly detailed way; this applies to everything from feasibility studies to multimillion-dollar equipment and construction contracts. Don't expect the negotiation process to move quickly or smoothly. Negotiations are likely to continue right up to (and often through) the drafting of the final contract. Accept the possibility of a slow pace with a lot of attention given to what may seem like insignificant details.

LO3

What's Different about the Business Market?

business market: The market where all profit and nonprofit organizations buy goods and services for a specific purpose.

The **business market**, sometimes called the *industrial, producer,* or *organizational market,* consists of all business users. Business users are profit and nonprofit organizations that buy goods and services for one of three purposes:

- **To make other goods and services** - Campbell's buys fresh vegetables to make soup, and Air Canada buys airplanes to transport people.
- **To sell to consumer or other industrial users** - Safeway buys canned tuna to sell to consumers, and Boeing sells its airplanes to organizations such as Air Canada.
- **To conduct the organization's operation** - The British Columbia Institute of Technology buys office supplies and electronic office equipment for the registrar's office, and a dentist buys supplies to use in the office.

business marketing: The marketing of goods and services to business users.

In the business market, salespeople can deal with both consumer products and business products. **Business marketing** is the marketing of goods and services to business users, as contrasted to ultimate consumers.

Because the business market is largely unknown, average consumers are apt to underrate its significance. Actually, this market is huge in total sales volume and the number of firms involved in it. About 50 percent of all manufactured products are sold to the business market. In addition, about 80 percent of all farm products and virtually all minerals, forests, and sea products are business goods. These are sold to firms for further processing.

The basic types of goods and services purchased by buyers in the producer market are shown in Exhibit 14.1. In addition to raw materials and components, producers purchase facilities (such as buildings), capital equipment, and a wide array of periodic services such as repairs, legal services, and advertising.

• Entering goods
Raw materials: • Farm products (wheat, cotton, livestock, fruits, vegetables) • Natural products (fish, lumber, crude petroleum, iron ore)
Manufactured materials and parts: • Component materials (steel, cement, wire, textiles) • Component parts (small motors, tires, castings)
• Foundation goods
Installations: • Buildings and land rights (factories, offices) • Fixed equipment (generators, drill presses, computers, elevators)
Accessory equipment: • Portable or light factory equipment and tools (hand tools, lift trucks) • Office equipment (calculators, desks)
• Facilitating goods
Supplies: • Operating supplies (lubricants, coal, paper, pencils) • Maintenance and repair items (paint, nails, brooms)
Business services: • Maintenance and repair services (window cleaning, calculator repair) • Business advisory services (legal, management consulting, advertising)

EXHIBIT 14.1
Classification of goods and services in the business market.

Selling Business Products Is Different

Selling products to businesses is often different from selling directly to customers. Let's examine the demand, types of purchases, and product characteristics of the business product.

Demand for Business Products

Three important factors distinguish the demand for business products from the demand for consumer goods. When selling in the business market, consider the influences on the demand for your products and services in order to properly plan a sales presentation.

Derived Demand

The demand for many business goods and services is linked to consumer demand for other products–it is a **derived demand**. For example, General Motors purchases tires for its cars. The number of tires it purchases is determined by the customer demand for new General Motors cars. While we as consumers also buy tires, we buy them as replacements for worn tires on our own cars. This is an example of the same product being defined in a different way. General Motors' demand is based on the eventual consumer demand for its products (derived demand).

derived demand: Demand linked to consumer demand for other products.

Inelastic Demand

The demand for many business products is **inelastic demand**. An increase or decrease in the price of a product usually does not generate a proportionate increase or decrease in sales for the product. The Chevrolet produced by General Motors has many parts. The cost of each part represents a fraction of the total cost. If there is

inelastic demand: Demand that does not change in direct proportion to a change in price.

an increase or decrease in the price of a single part, such as the interior cloth, the demand for the car is not significantly influenced. Even if the cost of the cloth doubled (assuming it did not represent a large proportion of production costs), and was passed along to the consumer, the car's sales price would increase by a small amount, having little effect on consumer demand.

Joint Demand

joint demand: Demand that occurs when two or more products are used together to produce a single product.

The demand for many business products is also affected by **joint demand**. Joint demand occurs when two or more products are used together to produce a single product. For example, General Motors manufactures automobiles and needs numerous component parts–tires, batteries, steel, glass, and so on. These products are demanded jointly.

The salesperson selling products that are demanded jointly must understand the effect of joint demand on the market. When a customer purchases a product, there is an opportunity to sell companion products. An example is the grocery retailer who purchases computerized cash registers. They require the purchase of associated items such as a small computer, cash registers, product scanners, and other supplies to operate the equipment in the grocery store.

Major Types of Business Purchases

new-task purchase: A type of purchase made when a product is bought in conjunction with a job or task newly performed by the purchaser.

straight-rebuy purchase: A routine purchase of products bought regularly.

modified-rebuy purchase: A type of purchase made when regular purchasing patterns are slightly changed to suit customers' present needs.

Business purchases are usually one of three general types–new-task purchases, straight-rebuy purchases, or modified-rebuy purchases.

The **new-task purchase** is made when a product is bought in conjunction with a job or task newly performed by the purchaser. A long period is frequently needed for the salesperson to make this type of sale since the buyer is often cautious, especially when confronted with an expensive product or large quantities. This is the most challenging selling situation, since buyers want to consider all alternative suppliers and may need substantial information from each supplier. The salesperson may have to submit a prototype of the product, tender a price bid, and make several presentations over an extended period before the final purchase decision. New-task purchases include buying capital equipment, construction materials for a new job site, and even an entire plant facility.

The **straight-rebuy purchase** is a routine purchase of products bought regularly. This sale is normally casual order taking. Often, buyers negotiate a blanket purchase order (BPO) agreement, which establishes the price and terms of the sale for a set period. Buyers require little time and information to make a purchase decision. This type of purchase might include continually used raw materials, office supplies, or MRO (maintenance, repair, and operations items such as spare parts for machinery).

The **modified-rebuy purchase** is somewhat like the straight-rebuy purchase procedure. The buyer seeks a similar product but wants or needs to negotiate different items. The buyer may want a lower price, faster delivery, or better quality. For example, a firm that buys oil field drilling bits from a supplier each month (straight-rebuy situation) decides it needs a better-quality drilling bit. The firm goes to the same supplier and others to see whether a better-quality bit is available and at what price (modified-rebuy situation). The drilling company still wants drill bits, but looks for a slightly different product to suit its present needs.

LO4

Requests for Proposals (RFPs)

request for proposal (RFP): Purchasing process often used for large purchases when large organizations invite bids on a project.

If your company becomes involved in a **request for proposal (RFP)** process, certain issues require careful attention. To maximize your chances of being selected from among other candidates and to avoid getting into a situation that could prove extremely time consuming and costly, consider the following points.

An RFP is a document issued by a company or government agency asking suppliers to send in bids for a contract to supply products or services over a designated period. Included in the RFP may be proposed products or services; proposed budgets; and specific costs, fees, time schedules, and so on.

An RFP can range from being an informal process (a few suppliers are interviewed and a selection is made from among them) to a highly formal process (where a larger number of suppliers are requested to make formal presentations to a board). Occasionally, an RFP is a multi-step process, involving several presentations. In this case, a large initial group of suppliers will be narrowed down in stages until a few select suppliers are asked to give final presentations.

More involved selection processes require a greater time commitment from each participant. It is common for total presentation preparation to cost a significant percentage of what a supplier would expect to make during the first year of a contract. For this reason, instructions in RFPs should be followed to make the process as productive and cost-effective as possible.

When you receive an RFP, what is your response supposed to look like? The list below shows steps to take in response to an RFP, although the content will change for each RFP.

1. **Background** - Briefly go over the general requirements. For example, Canadian Petroleum Company would like a local area network installed to connect all of the computers in one office to share disk space and printers and perform automatic backups.
2. **Scope** - Address in detail each item in the RFP and how you intend to manage it. Use diagrams to illustrate your configuration. This will be the longest section of your proposal and will probably have several subsections.
3. **Schedule** - When do you anticipate starting the project? How long will each task take? Make a table of your expected schedule for completing the project.
4. **Staff** - This may be an optional section. Some firms like to see who will be working on the project, along with their credentials and qualifications. This is more important for government projects. Resumés may be necessary here.
5. **Cost** - Break down the cost by equipment and labour time to come up with your expected budget. Include payment terms, discounts for early payment, and other cost or payment information.
6. **Supporting information** - Add any supporting information here (for example, if you're trying to convince a potential client to use a specific type of networking technology, support your reasoning here with third-party quotations, research, and testimonials). You can also add references to similar projects you have completed for other firms, as well as those results. Include any supporting documentation from clients, clippings from newspapers, and so on.

Product Characteristics

Business products, like business markets, have certain characteristics that a salesperson must consider when selling to buyers of these goods. These product characteristics differ from consumer product characteristics. Business products are (1) technical, (2) in need of specifications and bids, (3) complex in pricing, and (4) standardized.

Technical Products

Compared to consumer goods, business sales are more technical. The business salesperson must have more product knowledge training than a salesperson of consumer goods. Discussing complex production information with knowledgeable customers, which demands considerable expertise, is essential to success. These sales reps are generally referred to as technical sales representatives.

These products are standardized.

Source: © Krzysztof Zmij/iStockphoto

A new office building is unique

Source: © Prebranac/Dreamstime.com/GetStock.com

EXHIBIT 14.2

The characteristics of some products make selling them a challenge. How do these products differ?

Specifications and Bids

Many business goods are bought based on specifications. These specifications may be determined by the customer, or they may be commonly accepted industry standards. They may be tremendously complex, such as the design of a specialized hydraulic pump, or as simple as requiring a particular colour.

Bids based on stated specifications usually are submitted by several selling firms to the purchasing firm. Each seller bids on a homogeneous, similar product. Depending on the buyer's wishes, bids may range from a similar oral quote given over the phone to a formalized written quotation or a sealed bid held in the buyer's office and opened on a specific closing date along with all other bids. If the purchasing agent does not want to accept any of the bids, suppliers may be asked to submit second bids. Purchasing firms typically use this system to identify the product's true market price.

If all other factors are equal, the company submitting the lowest bid wins the contract. However, other factors frequently affect the buying decision. The product's performance and quality level, for example, may be important considerations in the buying decision. H.J. Heinz of Canada Ltd. may pay a supplier several cents more per bushel for a higher grade of tomatoes so that it can charge a premium price for its products at the retail level.

Complex Pricing

Because of a product's technical nature, its inelastic demand characteristic, the buyer's expertise, and the fact that competitive bidding often is involved in the purchase process, pricing is complex. Final price to the customer can be based on estimates of long-term agreements, present and future labour and material costs, availability of materials, expected salvage value of present equipment, product service agreements, cost-effectiveness of production facilities, and return on investment.

In considering the many factors affecting the price of a business product, a sales manager may give the company's sales force a range of prices to use in negotiations. Avoid trying to use low price alone to make a sale. After all, your selling skills determine success in the long run.

Standardization

Many business products tend to be homogeneous. When compared to competing products, they show high similarity (see Exhibit 14.2). When a new product or product feature is introduced to the market, its initial advantage quickly may be lost. It is easy for competitors to improve a product slightly and market it as their own. Most of the time, the salesperson sells products that are similar to a competitor's products.

LO5 Steps that Business Purchasing Agents Use in Making Buying Decisions

Business goods have market and product characteristics that differ from consumer goods. Therefore, the buying decision is somewhat different. The eight steps involved in purchasing business products are:

1. Recognition of the problem or need
2. Determination of the characteristics of the needed product

3. Determination of product specifications,
4. Search for and qualification of potential sources
5. Acquisition and analysis of the proposal
6. Selection of supplier(s)
7. Establishment of an order routine
8. Evaluation of product performance

Exhibit 14.3 shows the steps in the business buying process, along with the three business buying situations. For the straight rebuy, Steps 2 through 7 can be eliminated. In this situation, a need is recognized, such as a low inventory of a product, and the order is automatically processed. The salesperson supplying a product on a straight rebuy basis contacts the customer periodically to check inventory and to make sure that the order is processed quickly. This procedure strengthens a customer's loyalty to and reliance on a seller, indirectly warding off competition. Salespeople must continually watch for the possibility that present customers may reassess their needs and find some problem with a product, and thus seek another supplier. By routinely contacting the customer, the salesperson becomes aware of changes in the buyer's attitude.

In the new-task and modified-buying situations, several competing suppliers' salespeople may present the prospect with information. The salesperson helps determine the buyer's needs and shows the buyer how the product fulfills the need. The salesperson needs to work closely with everyone who has an influence on the buying decision. When no firm has an initial edge on an industrial order, the salesperson who spends the *right* amount of time with the *right* people often walks away with the order. This person probably spent some time learning *whom* to talk to. Knowing the right people in an organization is vital to a salesperson's existence. With experience, most good salespeople learn whom they need to contact. But how does the beginning salesperson find these influential people? The next section provides some answers.

EXHIBIT 14.3

Business buying process and situations.

	TYPE OF BUYING SITUATION		
STEPS IN BUSINESS BUYING PROCESS	NEW TASK	MODIFIED REBUY	STRAIGHT REBUY
1. Recognition of a problem or need	yes	yes	yes
2. Determination of characteristics of the needed product	yes	yes	no
3. Determination of product specifications	yes	yes	no
4. Search for and qualification of potential sources	yes	yes	no
5. Acquisition and analysis of the proposal	yes	yes	no
6. Selection of supplier(s)	yes	yes	no
7. Establishment of an order routine	yes	yes	no
8. Evaluation of product performance	yes	yes	yes

Whom Should I Talk To?

Many salespeople contact only the buyer or purchasing agent, who often just places the order. The purchasing agent may not actually decide what to buy. It is important to talk to anyone who might influence the purchase decision.

In determining whom to see and how much time to spend with each person, the salesperson should learn who influences the purchase decision and the *strength of each person's influence.* People who may influence the purchase of a product include:

initiator:
The person proposing to buy or replace a product.

deciders:
Those persons actually involved in making the decision to buy.

influencers:
People who influence the decision to buy a product.

buyer:
The purchasing agent.

gatekeeper:
A person who influences where information from salespeople goes and with whom salespeople will be allowed to talk.

users:
People who must work with or use the product.

- **Initiator** - The person proposing to buy or replace the product
- **Deciders** - The people involved in making the actual decision, such as the plant engineer, purchasing agent, and someone from top management
- **Influencers** - Plant engineer, plant workers, and research and development personnel who develop specifications needed for the product
- **Buyer** - The purchasing agent
- **Gatekeepers** - People who influence where information from salespeople goes and with whom salespeople talk (see Chapter 7); receptionists, administrative assistants, and purchasing agents are gatekeepers
- **Users** - Those people who must work with or use the product; for example, plant workers or administrative assistants

It is crucial that the salesperson get by the gatekeepers to talk to the initiators, users, influencers, buyers, and deciders. For example, users of a company's copy machine (initiators) may become dissatisfied with its quality of copies. An administrative assistant (influencer) mentions that Xerox makes an excellent copier that the firm can afford. After a conference with several major users of the current duplicating machine, the office manager (decider) confers with the representatives of several competing copy machine firms and decides to lease the Xerox machine. A purchase order is forwarded to the corporate home office, where a purchasing agent (buyer) approves the machines. Which person should the Xerox salesperson have visited in selling the machine? In this example, each person who participates in the purchase decision should have been contacted–the administrative assistant, major users, and office manager–and the salesperson should have explained the product's benefits to each person.

Purchasing Agents Are Rational Buyers

When selling to the producer market, the salesperson deals with well-trained, knowledgeable, and rational buyers. Purchasing agents in large corporations are often specialists, and are experts in dealing with salespeople. See Exhibit 14.4.

Purchasing agents carefully examine information presented to them, and they expect quality sales presentations from salespeople they see. Buying decisions are made based on practical business reasons, unlike the emotional decisions often made by consumers. As a result, the time required to make a purchase decision is usually longer than in the consumer setting. This is because industrial buyers carefully compare their firm's needs with the features, advantages, and benefits of competing products–a process that takes time.

EXHIBIT 14.4
This purchasing agent is an expert on products used in manufacturing. The salesperson must know the product and how it can best be used by the customer.
Source: © AP/Ted S. Warren/ The Canadian Press

Why Do Producers Buy?

Buyers in the producer market seek to buy for many reasons. Some common reasons usually evolve from an aspect of the product's cost and quality. Specific primary buying needs or motives include the following:

- Increasing profits
- Increasing sales
- Producing a quality product
- Helpfulness of the salesperson
- Improving the operation's efficiency (resulting in cost reductions)
- Service
- Payment terms
- Trade-in allowances
- Delivery service
- Lowest price

To be a successful salesperson, determine each buyer's important buying needs. Then develop a sales presentation emphasizing your product's features, advantages, and benefits, and how your products can fulfill the buyer's needs. One of the best and most often used methods of presenting your product's benefits to the buyer is value analysis or showing your prospect how your product provides them with the best value.

Selling Services Is Challenging

LO6

Most people think of selling physical products, such as candy, cars, or copiers. Yet recently we've seen the phenomenal growth of careers in selling services. With its schools, post offices, and social agencies, government is in the service business. With its charities and churches, the nonprofit sector is in the service business. A good part of the business sector, with its airlines, banks, insurance companies, and law firms, is in the service business. In fact, almost 79 percent of the labour force is now in the service sector.[4]

A service is an action or activity done for others for a fee; rock bands and barbers perform services. As you will see, the production of services may or may not be linked to a physical product.

Exhibit 14.5 shows a mix of goods and services on a continuum ranging from relatively pure goods to relatively pure services. There are few pure goods or services, since each usually requires the other. In taking a college course, for example, you may buy a textbook. Similarly, buying salt, soup, and toothpaste requires supporting services, such as totalling up what you owe and bagging the good(s) at the checkout.

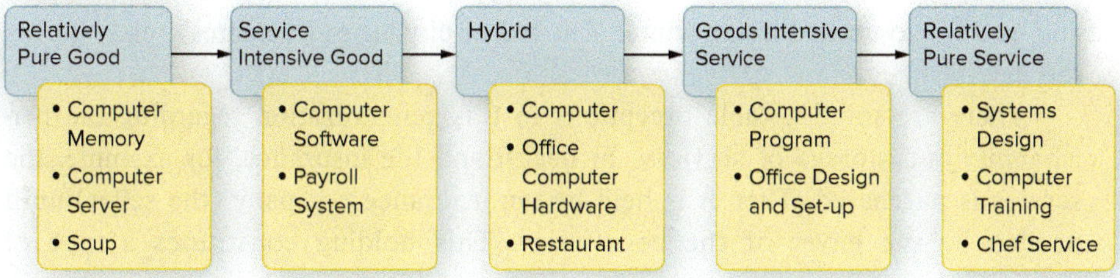

EXHIBIT 14.5
A goods–service continuum.

Characteristics of Services

The special nature of services creates special selling challenges and opportunities, which are substantially different from those used to sell goods.

Intangibility

Because services are essentially intangible, customers cannot sample–taste, feel, see, hear, or smell–services *before* they buy them. Salespeople must concentrate on the benefits to be derived from the service, rather than emphasizing the service itself. An insurance salesperson thus may stress service *benefits* such as guaranteed payment of a child's post-secondary expenses or a retirement income of so many dollars per month. Telecom salespeople discuss how business users can cut selling costs by using their company's long-distance calling system.

Inseparability

Services often cannot be separated from the person of the seller. Moreover, some services must be created and dispensed simultaneously. For example, dentists create and dispense almost all their services at the same time.

From a sales standpoint, inseparability frequently means that direct sale is the only possible channel of distribution, and a seller's services cannot be sold in very many markets. This characteristic also limits the scale of operation in a firm. One person can repair only so many vehicles in a day or treat only so many patients.

As an exception to the inseparability feature, the service may be sold by a person representing the creator-seller. A travel agent, insurance broker, or rental agent, for instance, may represent and help promote the service that will be sold by the institution producing it.

Heterogeneity

A service industry, or even an individual seller of services, cannot standardize output. Each unit of the service is somewhat different from other units of the same service. For example, an airline does not give the same quality of service on each trip. All repair jobs a mechanic does on automobiles are not of equal quality. An added complication is the difficulty of judging the quality of a service. (Of course, we can say the same for some goods.) It is particularly difficult to forecast quality in advance of buying a service. For example, a person pays to see a ball game without knowing whether it will be an exciting one, well worth the price of admission, or a dull performance.

Perishability and Fluctuating Demand

Services are highly perishable, and they cannot be stored. Haircuts not provided, empty seats in a stadium, and idle mechanics in a garage all represent business lost forever. Furthermore, the market for services fluctuates considerably by season, by day of the week, and by hour of the day. Many ski lifts lie idle all summer, and golf courses go unused in the winter. The use of city buses fluctuates greatly during the day.

There are some notable exceptions to this generalization regarding the perishability and storage of services. In health and life insurance, for example, the service is purchased. Then it is held by the insurance company (the seller) until needed by the buyer or the beneficiary. This holding constitutes a type of storage.

The combination of perishability and fluctuating demand creates product-planning, pricing, and promotion challenges for service company executives. Some organizations have developed new uses for idle plant capacity during off-seasons. Thus, during the summer, several ski resorts operate their ski lifts for hikers and sightseers who want access to higher elevations. Advertising and creative pricing also stimulate demand during slack periods. Hotels offer lower prices and family packages for weekends. Telephone companies offer lower rates during nights and weekends. In some university towns, apartment rates are reduced in the summer.

Selling Services Is the Most Challenging

Selling services is the most challenging sales job you could have because of the characteristics of services. The salesperson, for example, cannot show and physically demonstrate services. Intangibles–including insurance, financial investments, car repairs, and health services–are often difficult for many prospects to understand.

Nonprofit Selling—It's about Time!

A **nonprofit organization** does not have profit as a goal; therefore, it neither intends nor tries to make a profit. Most of the nonprofit organizations sell services rather than tangible products. Here are examples:

nonprofit organization: In this type of organization, profit is not a goal; most sell services rather than tangible products.

- **Cultural** - Museums, zoos, symphony orchestras, opera and theatre groups (e.g., 4th Wall Chamber Music)
- **Religious** - Churches, synagogues, temples, mosques
- **Charitable and philanthropic** - Welfare groups (e.g., Salvation Army), research foundations (e.g., Canadian Cancer Society, Easter Seals), fundraising groups (e.g., United Way)
- **Social cause** - Organizations dealing with family planning, civil rights, stopping smoking, preventing heart disease, environmental concerns, or support for or opposition to abortion or nuclear energy
- **Social** - Fraternal organizations, civic groups, clubs
- **Political** - Political parties, individual politicians

Business versus Nonprofit Selling

In terms of buyer behaviour, a major difference between business and nonprofit customers involves the groups that the particular organization must deal with. As we know, it is important for salespeople to understand their business buyer and how their customer's business runs. Business executives have traditionally defined their basic markets as comprising their present and potential customers. They have thus directed their selling efforts primarily toward this one group. In contrast, most nonprofits are involved with *two* major markets in their marketing effort. One of these groups consists of the **nonprofit contributors** (of money, labour, services, or materials) to the organization. Here the nonprofit organization's task is that of attracting resources and volunteers.

nonprofit contributors: The providers of a nonprofit organization's resources.

The other major target market is the organization's **nonprofit clients**–the recipients of the organization's money or services. This recipient market is much like that of the customers of a business company. However, nonprofit organizations–such as churches, Girl Guides groups, or symphony orchestras–are unlikely to refer to their client-recipients as customers. Instead, these organizations use such terms as *parishioners, members,* or *audience*.

nonprofit clients: The recipients of nonprofit organizations' money and services.

This distinction between business and nonprofit selling is significant for this reason: A nonprofit organization must develop two separate sales programs–one looking back at its contributors and the other looking forward at its clients.

Importance of Nonprofit Selling

The attention that is finally being devoted to nonprofit selling is long overdue. Thousands of these organizations handle billions of dollars and affect millions of people. Often the operation of these organizations is inefficient; a large part of the money collected by a nonprofit organization typically goes to cover its administrative expenses rather than to serve the intended customers. This creates a dual social and economic loss–donors' gifts are wasted and clients are not served efficiently.

The importance of selling is clear when nonprofit organizations fail to do an effective sales job. The result may be additional social and economic costs and wastes. If the death rate from smoking rises because the Canadian Cancer Society and other organizations cannot persuade people of the harm of smoking, we all lose. When good museums or good symphony orchestras must cease operating because of lack of contributions or lack of attendance, again there are social and economic losses.

By developing an effective sales program, a nonprofit organization can increase its chances of (1) satisfactorily serving both its contributor and its client markets and (2) improving the overall efficiency of its operations.

Generally speaking, people in most nonprofit organizations do not realize that they are running a business and should employ business management techniques.

LO7

Crowdfunding—Leading the Future of Nonprofit Sales

crowdfunding: Generating sales by delivering your sales message to the masses via the internet. Examples include gofundme.com and kickstarter.com used for new businesses as well as nonprofit companies.

Crowdfunding (and crowdsourcing) are relatively new forms of finding ways to increase donations to a nonprofit cause or to help deliver your message to the masses. Websites like gofundme.com and kickstarter.com both have had much success with mass message delivery and selling their ideas or causes to the general public. Many new technology companies began with funding from these types of crowdsourcing websites. The future looks bright for many of these sites to continue to build and establish businesses and relationships online.

GoFundMe was extremely powerful and influential after the 2018 Humboldt Broncos bus crash in Saskatchewan, where 16 young lives were lost. The entire world felt Canada's loss and rallied to raise funds for the families of the deceased and the survivors of the crash, which included 13 players, coaches, and support staff. By raising $15.2 million from 142,000 donors across 80 countries, the fundraiser became the single largest fundraiser in GoFundMe history.[5] Messages encouraging people to show support for those lost or injured in the Humboldt tragedy by placing hockey sticks by their front doors were also delivered through online mass messaging.[6]

After the tragic bus crash involving the Humboldt Broncos hockey team, Canadians showed their solidarity for the victims and their families by leaving hockey sticks next to their front doors.

Source: THE CANADIAN PRESS/ Jonathan Hayward

How Selling Is Used

Personal selling is frequently used in fundraising efforts. Sometimes a door-to-door campaign is used. During the holiday season, Salvation Army volunteers collect donations in the downtown area or malls of many cities. Potential large donors often are approached by salespeople.

Many nonprofit organizations also use personal selling to reach their public clients. These personal representatives may not be called salespeople, but that is what they are. Personal selling is used to recruit new members for organizations such as the YMCA and Girl Guides. Business executives approach other members of the business community for donations to the United Way.

Using salespeople to reach either contributors or clients poses some management problems for a nonprofit organization. In effect, the organization has to manage a sales force–including recruiting, training, compensating, supervising, and evaluating performance. Unfortunately, not many nonprofit organizations think in these terms, nor are they as yet qualified to do this management job.

SELLING TIPS

NONPROFIT SELLING

Many salespeople working for nonprofit groups don't consider themselves salespeople, yet they are. They are the people responsible for raising funds, increasing memberships, and making the nonprofit "profitable." Many of the techniques used in selling other products are also used in this line of selling as well. Here are some tips for those of you who will be employed in the nonprofit sector. Do they look familiar?

1. **Qualify** – Just as you would in a normal business setting, you need to find out if the prospective donor or contributor has the money and motivation to give to your cause. If they don't, move on to others who do.
2. **Research** – Before approaching your prospect, be sure that you understand them and/or their organization. Check their history of giving or donating and the importance they place on it.
3. **Present** – Planning your presentation is important. Be sure you present to their identified motives. Match their needs to the organization you represent.
4. **Close** – Don't forget to ask for what you're looking for, whether it's money, time, space, or some other type of donation.
5. **Follow up** – They've given, so make sure you thank them and continue to thank them. Public acknowledgement adds value to your "customer" and good follow-up will increase the likelihood of future "sales."

Selling Is Selling

No matter whether you are persuading someone to give you money for a copier, an insurance policy, or a charity–you are selling. Personal selling refers to the personal communication of information to persuade a prospective customer to buy something–a good, service, idea, or something else–that satisfies the individual's needs. Whenever you are doing this, you are selling.

ETHICAL DILEMMA

THE SCOOP

You work in a large electronics chain store. You and your colleagues work on a commission basis. On a particular busy Saturday morning, you observe one of your colleagues, Anne, spend about an hour with a newlywed couple who are interested in buying cell phones. Anne spends time going over the different rate plans and the features and benefits of several different styles of phones. The couple seem hesitant as it is the first time they have bought something with this many choices. After an hour, they tell Anne that they will consider all the information and if they decide to buy, they will return on Tuesday with their decision.

The following Monday, business is kind of slow and you recognize the newlyweds as they enter the store. You know this is Anne's day off. You see that they look around for Anne and, not being able to find her, they approach you and ask if you can help. You answer a few questions for them and they decide that they'd like to buy their two phones. You end up spending about 20 minutes with them.

Two thoughts go through your mind:

1. Should I write up the order and keep the commission (scoop her sale)? Anne will probably never find out!
2. If I can start a relationship with this couple, they may buy many things from me over the next few years. Anne will probably never find out!

What will you do here? Justify your reasoning.

Summary of Major Selling Issues

The retailer is extremely important to the Canadian economy, accounting for billions of dollars in sales each year. As a career, retailing offers excellent financial and personal rewards to people who are willing to work hard, have the ability to manage people, and understand the principles of selling.

The retail salesperson's job activities vary from store to store, yet they usually include making transactions, contacting customers, handling complaints, working stock, and personal selling. The fundamentals of selling discussed in earlier chapters and mentioned in this chapter are used by the retail salesperson just as they are used by the business salesperson.

Business products include the raw materials, supplies, equipment, and services used in production, as well as finished goods and services intended for the producer, reseller, and government markets. The producer market contains individuals and organizations that purchase products and services for the production of other goods or services. Characteristics of the producer market include derived demand, inelastic demand, and joint demand. Products are technical in nature and frequently require specifications and bids, complex pricing, and standardization.

The business buying decision may be a complex and lengthy process. It usually involves eight basic steps, depending on whether it is a new-task, a modified-rebuy, or a straight-rebuy situation. It is important for the salesperson to locate individuals who influence the buying decision and to determine the strength of each one's influence in order to allocate the right amount of time and effort needed to solve a customer's problems. Buyers are concerned about costs and product quality, which can result in increased profits and more efficient operations. A value analysis can be used to show the buyer that the salesperson's product is cost-efficient.

A service is an action or activity done for others for a fee. Services can be characterized as intangible, inseparable, heterogeneous, or perishable, and their demand fluctuates compared to physical goods. Nonprofit organizations do sell others on contributing resources, such as money, labour, and materials. They also sell clients on using their services.

MEETING A SALES CHALLENGE

Many retail salespeople earn excellent incomes. It usually depends on what they sell, their store, compensation plan, product knowledge, and selling skills. Assuming Susan Chung knows her products, she needs to develop a selling process to allow her to increase her sales.

Susan needs to prospect, using customers and people who come into the store but do not buy. She can keep a prospect file, take the names of people who are interested in something, and telephone or mail something to them to see whether they are interested in a new product or one that has gone on sale.

Susan should be creative when someone enters the store. She should introduce herself and she should call prospects by name, learn to remember names, and use those names if they return. She should ask questions to determine someone's needs, and not be afraid to handle objections positively. Susan needs to use suggestion selling.

If they buy, she should mail a thank-you letter, email, or call to thank them. Maybe she can uncover another prospect and have people ask for her when they need something. Susan must provide service after the sale.

It takes months, even years, to build a clientele. Yet using the 10-step retail selling process will help Susan enjoy her work more and feel she is becoming a sales professional. She should certainly try to use selling skills to work with people buying for the holidays and during the store's January sales.

PLAYING THE ROLE

The situation: Read the Ethical Dilemma: The Scoop in this chapter. Assume that you have decided to scoop Anne's sale in this situation. Now it is two weeks later and one evening while you're both working, the newlyweds return with their phones. They see Anne, so approach her with some questions that they have about a couple of the phones' features. A little bewildered, Anne obliges them and spends another half hour explaining how to use the phones.

The next day, Anne discovers that it was you who processed the original order so she approaches you to give her the commission on that sale.

Role A: You (the "scooper"). Prepare a defence of your actions.

Role B: Anne. Prepare an argument for your request for the commission.

Dramatize this scene to see if you can come to a reasonable resolution. Have your classmates observe and determine if the solution is reasonable or not.

Key Terms for Selling

business market	**inelastic demand**	**nonprofit contributors**
business marketing	**influencers**	**nonprofit organization**
buyer	**initiator**	**request for proposal (RFP)**
crowdfunding	**joint demand**	**retailing**
deciders	**modified-rebuy purchase**	**straight-rebuy purchase**
derived demand	**new-task purchase**	**users**
gatekeeper	**nonprofit clients**	

Sales Application Questions

1. Discuss the differences between selling for a retailer and selling for an industrial firm.
2. Suggestion selling is frequently used in retail selling. Explain suggestion selling and give an example of it. Can suggestion selling be used in business-to-business selling as well? Explain.
3. Lynn Madden received four sweaters as holiday gifts. One was too small and she is now on her way to Feldman's Department Store to return it. As usual, the store is full of people with complaints about broken merchandise and wanting to return gifts that they can't use. Lynn spots a clerk in the clothing department and asks where to go for a refund. Annoyed, the busy clerk tells her to go to the window at the back of the store for a refund.
   a. Do you think the clerk did the proper thing?
   b. Analyze the situation and discuss what you believe the clerk could have done differently.
   c. Explain how Lynn Madden, the clerk, and the store may have been hurt in the situation.
4. Ravi Singh has been looking for a new sport coat for weeks. He has finally found one he really likes at Herb's Haberdashery.

   Buyer: I really like this coat.

   Salesperson: It's one of the best we carry. I think you've made an excellent choice.

   Buyer: I've been looking for quite a while, but I'm not sure this is what I really need.

Salesperson: I don't think you can go wrong with this coat, Mr. Singh. You mentioned that you liked its quality, and it really does show off your good taste.

Buyer: I am tired of shopping, and it is a good buy . . . OK, I'll take it.

Salesperson: That's wonderful; I'm sure you'll be extremely happy with your decision. Will that be cash or charge?

a. What did the salesperson do correctly in this situation?

b. What opportunities were overlooked?

5. What three types of demand can affect business products? Illustrate each type with an example.
6. Assume you have been offered sales jobs with three different organizations. One sells computers, one sells insurance, and one sells medical equipment to doctors. Describe the differences in the jobs.
7. Assume that the president of your college has put you in charge of selling your college's teaching facilities to a very large organization that is interested in a facility for 22 weekends per year. This would mean a large financial windfall for your college.
   a. Who, from your college, would you want included on your sales team?
   b. Explain what each team member could contribute.
8. Assume you are a representative for Canadian Blood Services. You have been asked by your superior to make a presentation to a local business encouraging people to donate blood. Suggest three FABs you could use in your presentation.
9. Recent events have inspired you to help advocate for a cause. You have been asked to create a crowdfunding campaign to raise funds for this cause. How would you begin?

Sales Online Exercise

Comparing Places to Live for Your Salespeople

As a newly appointed national sales manager, you anticipate that you will often hire salespeople for different locations within Canada. To better help you provide information to new hires and transferees, it pays to have an understanding of the various areas of Canada. Use www.canada-city.ca to research different cities in Canada. Develop a sales plan that accentuates the positive aspects of these cities to potential new hires or when transferring sales representatives.

For specific information on workforce issues, incomes, and so on, go to www.statcan.ca, www.monster.ca, or www.indeed.ca and search for the employment outlook for different types of sales jobs in different regions of Canada.

Further Exploring the Sales World

1. Visit three different types of retailers in your community, pose as a customer, and report on the selling techniques used by each salesperson you encounter. Comment on what each person could do to improve the sales presentation.
2. Visit a large retailer in your community that trains its employees in using selling techniques. Report on the company's reasons for sales training, how it trains, and what is included in its sales training program.
3. Select a good, a service, and a product sold by nonprofit organizations and compare their features, advantages, and benefits. How would you demonstrate a main benefit of each?
4. Check out www.gofundme.com fundraisers in your area in Canada. Are there any causes that you would support? Why or why not? Were you surprised by the number of causes in your area? Do you think people find it a convenience or a nuisance to donate in this way?

Selling Experiential Exercise

What Are Your People Skills?

How well do you understand people, observe their behaviour, and address their personal and professional growth? This self-test can help you see your skills. On a separate sheet of paper, write your score for each question.[7]

		STRONGLY AGREE			STRONGLY DISAGREE
1.	I think that people often are unaware of their true motivation.	4	3	2	1
2.	Psychological factors often play more of a role in job performance than in the job's required skills.	4	3	2	1
3.	I make a conscious effort to understand the basic needs of others.	4	3	2	1
4.	I am able to empathize with other people, even when I don't share their viewpoints.	4	3	2	1
5.	I consciously try to organize my thinking around others.	4	3	2	1
6.	People often reveal themselves by small details of behaviour.	4	3	2	1
7.	I am usually aware of people's strengths and weaknesses.	4	3	2	1
8.	Most people aren't easy to read.	4	3	2	1
9.	I notice when someone gets a new haircut, eyeglasses, or clothes.	4	3	2	1
10.	After a meeting, I can usually accurately report how others responded to the discussion.	4	3	2	1
11.	People may present themselves in a certain way that doesn't show who they really are.	4	3	2	1
12.	I try not to read my own attitudes into other people's behaviour.	4	3	2	1
13.	I often think about the implications of my past impressions of people on the job.	4	3	2	1
14.	When dealing with others, I try to consider how different they may be from me.	4	3	2	1
15.	I don't judge someone until I have enough information to form a sound judgment.	4	3	2	1
16.	I often think about ways to foster other people's personal and professional growth.	4	3	2	1
17.	I see people for their potential—not how they can be of use to me, but how they can fulfill their life goals.	4	3	2	1
18.	You can't change someone else.	4	3	2	1
19.	When making decisions about people, I deliberately consider a wide range of factors.	4	3	2	1
20.	I consciously try to help people use their strengths and address their weaknesses.	4	3	2	1
	Total Score ______________				

Results - If you scored:

- 75 to 80 - You're probably strong in solving people problems.
- 61 to 74 - You have potential strengths in this area.
- 40 to 60 - You have potential weaknesses in this area.
- 20 to 39 - You have weaknesses to work on in solving people problems.

Now relate what you've learned to your work experiences by setting goals and intermediate targets. Then adjust!

CASE 14–1

PLIMPTON'S TIRE SERVICE

Lauren Yakobosky put on the brakes to stop her car. It was a rainy day and the car seemed to slide a bit too far. When she got home she checked her tires. Sure enough, they were worn almost bare. "Have I had these tires this long?" Lauren thought to herself. The answer to that question didn't matter. It was obviously time to buy new tires.

Lauren drove her 1966 Mustang to a nearby tire store she had heard advertised many times. She entered the store ready to buy a set of inexpensive, nylon, four-ply tires. She didn't feel she needed more expensive radial tires, because she drove the Mustang only in town, almost exclusively to and from work. While she didn't need a top-of-the-line tire, she did want whitewalls. She thought whitewalls made her car look better. The conversation went like this:

Lauren: Hello, I'm looking for some new tires.

Salesperson: What type of car?

Lauren: A '66 Mustang . . . I think the diameter is 14 inches. Oh, I'm looking for an inexpensive tire.

Salesperson: [*Walking over to a display*] These are our cheapest tires.

Lauren: That's a little more than I wanted to spend. [*She pauses, waiting for a reply; getting none, she continues:*] Well, I guess I'll have to shop around.

QUESTIONS

1. Would this salesperson have sold you? Why or why not?
2. What did the salesperson do wrong in this case?
3. If you were the salesperson, what would you have done?

CASE 14–2

COMPETITION SHOES, INC.

The ad read, "Competition Shoes–We know what it takes to keep you running." Marc Mulletini looked at his running shoes and knew they only had a couple of kilometres left in them.

Marc had only recently taken up running, but he was now addicted and generally ran 25 to 30 kilometres a week. He realized that his running shoes were not high quality, and now that he was a serious runner, he wanted the proper equipment–and that meant better shoes. He decided to see if Competition Shoes had what he needed. That night, he went to the store:

Salesperson: Hello, what can I help you with this evening?

Buyer: I am looking for a new pair of running shoes.

Salesperson: Do you have a particular shoe you would like to try on?

Buyer: To be honest with you, I've been running for only three months, and I don't know very much about running shoes.

Salesperson: How much do you run a week?

Buyer: I'm up to about 30 kilometres.

Salesperson: That's a lot of running for a beginner. Do you plan to compete in the future?

Buyer: Well, I started running for the exercise, like so many people do, but I really enjoy running, and I would like to prove to myself that I can finish a marathon.

Salesperson: So you would like to compete.

Buyer: Come to think of it, I guess I would.

Salesperson: Where do you do most of your running—on a track, grass, or pavement?

Buyer: There is a high-school track a few blocks from my house, but I have to run on the street to get there and back.

Salesperson: Mr. Mulletini, I have two shoes that I believe will work very well for you [*showing Marc two shoes from the display*]. This Nike shoe is very sturdy and generally holds up well for people who put in as many kilometres as you do each week. This Big Paw Olympian [*showing Marc the other shoe*] is just as sturdy and has this wide, vibration-reducing heel. This heel will save your feet and legs a lot of stress. It's especially made for running on hard surfaces.

Buyer: I'll try on the Olympian model. I'll probably need a size 10. [*The salesperson gets the shoes, and Marc tries them on.*]

Salesperson: How do they feel?

Buyer: Great! [*realizing the difference between these shoes and his old pair*] I'll take them.

Salesperson: That's wonderful! I know they will suit your needs. Now come over here, I want to show you our new, thick, runners' socks. With your running schedule, I think you will need three pairs of new socks.

QUESTIONS

1. What did the salesperson do correctly in this situation? Do you think any errors were made?
2. If you were looking for a new pair of running shoes, would you have bought from this salesperson? Why?
3. How did the salesperson show professionalism in this situation? How did this salesperson differ from the one in Case 14–1?

APPENDIX A

Sales Arithmetic and Pricing

Salespeople want to exchange something for something–usually their products for the customer's money. Organizations and consumers (and even you) want to know, "How much is this going to cost?" Salespeople have to be prepared to discuss all aspects of costs and prices. Consequently, salespeople need some knowledge of the basics of sales arithmetic and pricing.

This appendix discusses sales arithmetic and pricing concepts that are useful in sales to (1) resellers, such as wholesalers and retailers, and (2) end users, such as businesses and non-profit organizations.

Types of Prices

Although a firm may engage in many pricing practices, all companies have a list price, net price, and prices based on transportation terms. Five of the most common types of prices include:

- **List price** - a standard price charged to all customers
- **Net price** - the price after allowance for all discounts
- **Zone price** - the price based on geographical location or zone of customers
- **FOB shipping point** - the shipping process in which the buyer pays transportation charges for goods, the title for which passes to the customer when the goods are loaded onto the shipping vehicle
- **FOB destination** - the shipping process in which the seller pays all shipping costs

These prices are established by the company, and allow the salesperson to quote prices according to company guidelines.

In Canada, the *Competition Act* prohibits price discrimination and other trade practices that reduce competition. For example, selling the same quantity of similar products at different prices to two different buyers is illegal.

A company can justify different prices if it can prove to the courts that its price differentials do not substantially reduce competition. Often, companies justify price differentials by showing the courts one of two things:

1. One customer buys more of a product than another. For the customer purchasing larger quantities, a firm can manufacture and market the products at a lower cost. These lower costs are passed on to the customer in reduced prices.
2. A company must lower prices to meet competition.

Thus, if justified, companies can offer customers different prices. They typically do this through discounts.

list price:
A standard price charged to all customers.

net price:
The price after allowance for all discounts.

zone price:
The price based on geographical location or zone of customers.

FOB shipping point:
The shipping process in which the buyer pays transportation charges for goods, the title for which passes to the customer when the goods are loaded onto the shipping vehicle.

FOB destination:
The shipping process in which the seller pays all shipping costs.

Discounts Lower the Price

Discounts are a reduction in price from the list price. In developing a program to sell a product line over a specified period, marketing managers consider discounts along with the company's advertising and personal selling efforts. The main types of discounts allowed to buyers are quantity, cash, trade, and consumer discounts.

discounts:
A reduction in price from the list price.

Quantity Discounts: Buy More, Pay Less

Quantity discounts result from the manufacturer's saving on production costs because it can produce large quantities of the product. As shown in Exhibit A-1, these savings are passed on to customers who buy in large quantities using discounts. Quantity discounts are either non-cumulative or cumulative.

One-time reductions in prices are **non-cumulative quantity discounts**, which are commonly used in the sale of both consumer and industrial goods. A salesperson might offer $0.10 per kilogram off potato salad on any truckload-sized order, or one free case of facial tissue with the purchase of 10 cases of facial tissue.

non-cumulative quantity discount:
A one-time price reduction.

The salesperson is expected to use these discounts as inducements for the retailer to buy in large quantities. The sales goal is to have the prospect display and locally advertise the product at a price lower than normal. Ideally, the retailer's selling price should reflect the price reduction allowed because of the quantity discount.

Cumulative quantity discounts are discounts received for buying a certain amount of a product over a stated period, such as one year. Again, these discounts reflect savings in manufacturing and marketing costs.

cumulative quantity discounts:
Discounts received for buying a certain amount of a product over a stated period.

To receive a 10 percent discount, a buyer may have to purchase 12,000 units of the product. Under the cumulative discount, the buyer would not be required to

EXHIBIT A–1
Various promotional allowances are available to resellers.

GREAT NEW DEAL ON DECONGESTANTS! FOUR DOUBLE-STRENGTH SIZES TO STRENGTHEN YOUR PROFITS!					
PROMOTIONAL ALLOWANCES					PROMOTIONAL SUPPORT
FREE-GOODS ALLOWANCE*	PLUS ADVERTISING ALLOWANCE†		PLUS MERCHANDISING ALLOWANCE		
	OPTION A	OPTION B‡	REDUCED PRICE FEATURE	DISPLAY	
350 mL liquid $8\frac{1}{3}$% off invoice	Up to $1.25 per dozen	$1.00 per dozen	$0.75 per dozen reduced-price feature	$0.75 per dozen floor or end cap display	Direct to consumer national TV promotion . . . 1.705 GRPs
150 mL liquid $8\frac{1}{3}$% off invoice	Up to $0.75 per dozen	$0.50 per dozen	$0.50 per dozen reduced-price feature	$0.50 per dozen floor or end cap display	88% reach 1.7 billion impressions
60 tablets $8\frac{1}{3}$% off invoice	Up to $1.25 per dozen	$1.00 per dozen	$0.75 per dozen reduced-price feature	$0.75 per dozen floor or end cap display	Year-round physician detailing and sampling
24 tablets $8\frac{1}{3}$% off invoice	Up to $0.75 per dozen	$0.50 per dozen	$0.50 per dozen reduced-price feature	$0.50 per dozen floor or end cap display	Major trade and medical journal advertising support

Also available—up to 2 percent billback allowance for four-colour roto advertising or consumer coupon programs.
Unlimited purchases allowed for claiming billback allowances.
Retail buy-in period: July 16 through August 31, 2020.
Advertising performance period: July 16 through November 9, 2020.
Claim deadline: 45 days following appearance of ad.
Contact your representative for complete details.
*Through participating wholesaler.
†All ads should feature both liquid and tablets.
‡Provided advertising coverage is in at least 75 percent of the applicant's trading area.

purchase the 12,000 units at the same time but would purchase instead 1,000 units each month, for example. As long as the agreed-on amount is purchased within the specified time, the 10 percent discount on each purchase applies. A cumulative discount allows the buyer to purchase the products as needed rather than in a single order.

Cash Discounts Entice the Customer to Pay

cash discounts on time: Discounts earned by buyers who pay bills within a stated period.

Cash discounts on time are earned by buyers who pay bills within a stated period. For example, if the customer purchases $10,000 worth of goods on June 1 and the cash discount is 2/10, net 30, the customer pays $9,800 instead of $10,000 if they pay within 10 days. Thus, 2/10, net 30, translates into a 2 percent discount if the bill is completely paid within 10 days of the sale. If the payment is not made within 10 days, the full $10,000 is due in 30 days.

Trade Discounts Attract Channel Members' Attention

trade discounts: Discounts on the list retail price offered to channel members.

The manufacturer may reduce prices to channel members (intermediaries) to compensate them for the services they perform. These are **trade discounts**. The trade discount is usually stated as a percentage off the list retail price. A wholesaler may be offered a 50 percent discount and the retailer offered a 40 percent discount off list price. The wholesaler's price to its retail customers is 10 percent above its cost or 40 percent off the list price. The wholesaler earns a 10 percent gross margin on sales to retail customers. Channel members are still eligible to earn the quantity and cash discounts.

Consumer Discounts Increase Sales

consumer discount: A one-time price reduction passed on from the manufacturer to channel members or directly to the customer.

Consumer discounts are one-time price reductions passed from the manufacturer to channel members or directly to the consumer. Cents-off product labels are price reductions passed directly to the consumer. A package marked 15 cents off each product or $1.80 off a dozen uses a consumer discount. See Exhibit A-2.

The manufacturer expects channel members to reduce the price from their normal price. A mass merchandiser might normally sell a product with a list price of $2.50 for $1.98. The manufacturer might then want salespeople to persuade the retailer to price the product 15 cents lower than the $1.98, or at a price of $1.83.

EXHIBIT A–2
Types and examples of discounts.

TYPES OF DISCOUNTS	DISCOUNT EXAMPLES
Quantity discount: Non-cumulative (one-time)	• Buy 11 dozen, get 1 dozen free • 20 percent off on all purchases • $5 off invoice for each floor-stand purchase
Cumulative (yearly purchases)	• 5 percent discount with purchase of 8,000 units • 8 percent discount with purchase of 10,000 units • 10 percent discount with purchase of 12,000 units
Cash discounts	• 2/10 end-of-month • 2/10, net 30
Trade discounts	• 40 percent off to retailers • 50 percent off to wholesalers
Consumer discounts	• 15 cents off regular price marked on product's package • 10-cents-off coupon

Cents-off coupons that the consumer brings to the retail store are another example of a temporary price discount. In both the cents-off label and coupon examples, the manufacturer ensures that the price reduction is passed on to the consumer. This occurs because channel members may not have promoted the product or reduced the price, keeping the quantity or off-invoice savings for themselves. An offer of a cents-off product label and coupons is used by the salesperson to sell larger quantities to customers. For a summary of discounts and examples of each, see Exhibit A-2.

Resellers: Markup, Margin, and Profit

The dollar amount between a product's cost and its selling price is sometimes referred to as markup and sometimes as margin. These two terms are frequently used interchangeably; however, this is incorrect and could be a costly mistake for a salesperson to make.

Markup is the dollar amount added to the product cost to determine its selling price. **Margin** is the dollar amount subtracted from the selling price that yields the product cost. The dollar amount of markup or margin will be the same for any given product.

margin:
The dollar amount subtracted from the selling price that yields the product cost.

Markup and margin are often expressed as a percentage, however, and this is where confusion can get a salesperson into trouble. It is important to remember that markup is a percentage of the product cost and margin is a percentage of the selling price. The percentage amount of markup or margin will never be the same for a given product!

While markup and margin have different meanings, they both represent gross profit. **Gross profit** is the money available to cover the costs of marketing the product, operating the business, and profit. **Net profit** is the money remaining after the costs of marketing and operating the business are paid.

gross profit:
The money available to cover the costs of marketing the product, operating the business, and profit.

net profit:
Money remaining after the costs of marketing and operating the business are paid.

Exhibit A-3 presents an example of markup and margin for each channel-of-distribution member. Each channel member has a different percentage markup and margin. The product that costs the manufacturer $3 to produce eventually costs the consumer $12. The manufacturer's selling price represents the wholesaler's cost. Price markups enable the wholesaler to pay business operating costs, cover the product's cost, and make a profit. The wholesaler's selling price of $6 becomes the retailer's cost. In turn, the retailer marks up the product to cover its cost and the associated costs of doing business (such as for stocking the product and for allocating fixed costs per square metre), and to maintain a desired profit level.

As mentioned earlier, markup percentage is based on product cost, whereas margin percentage is based on product selling price. It is important to know the methods of determining markup and margin percentages. Using a manufacturer's cost of $3,

EXHIBIT A-3

Example of markup on selling price in channel of distribution.

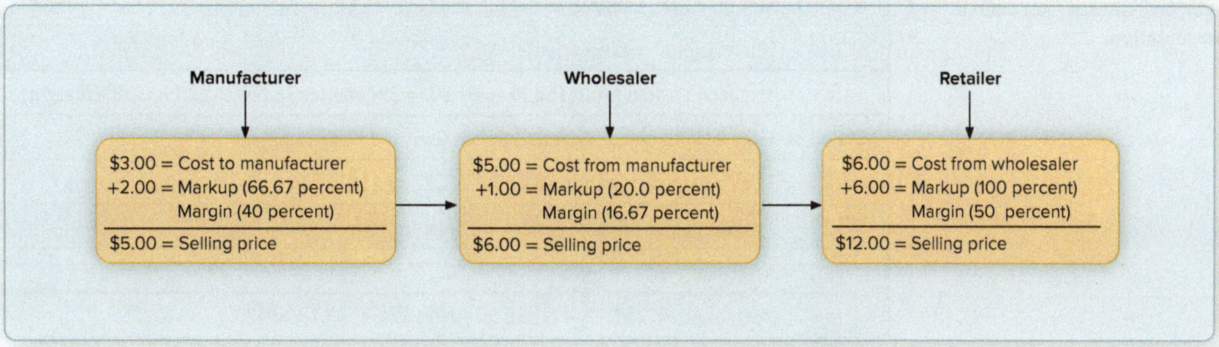

a markup of $2, and a selling price of $5 shown in Exhibit A-3, the methods of determining percentage markup can have different results:

$$\text{Percentage margin on selling price} = \frac{\text{Amount added to cost}}{\text{Selling price}} = \frac{\$2.00}{\$5.00} = 40 \text{ percent}$$

$$\text{Percentage markup on cost} = \frac{\text{Amount added to cost}}{\text{Cost}} = \frac{\$2.00}{\$3.00} = 66.67 \text{ percent}$$

Channel members want to buy goods at low prices and establish selling prices at a competitive level that allows for a reasonable profit. Such objectives result in retailers having different markups and margins on different goods. For example, a retailer may have markups of 10 percent on groceries, 30 percent on cameras, and 50 percent on houseware items. Based on the type of store (discount–high volume; specialty–low volume; department–high service), markups and margins may vary greatly depending on the volume of sales and degree of service rendered.

In preparing the sales presentation for an individual customer, the salesperson should consider all the discounts available to suggest a promotional plan for the retailer. For example, the advertisement shown in Exhibit A-1 illustrates several of the discounts a retailer can receive with the purchase of four decongestants. The salesperson can use these discounts in the sales presentation by suggesting that the retailer advertise the products at a reduced price and place the promotional displays by each of the store's cash registers.

Markup and Unit Price

Sellers, especially consumer-goods salespeople, like to talk in terms of the cost and profits earned from an individual unit. However, wholesalers and retailers do not buy one product at a time. Depending on the customer's size, manufacturers may sell resellers several dozen or thousands of dozens at a time. The cost and profits of an individual unit may not be useful for wholesalers, but they become extremely important to retailers since their customers buy the product one at a time.

Here is how it works. Assume you are selling a consumer product to a large chain of grocery stores. As shown in Exhibit A-4, your normal price for each unit is $1.80 and the retailer sells it for $2.19, 10¢ less than the manufacturer's $2.29 suggested selling price. This gives a normal profit of 39¢ or an 18 percent margin [($2.19 – $1.80 = 39¢)

EXHIBIT A–4

Example of using unit cost. Consumer-goods salespeople often break down costs and talk of unit costs and profits. Here is the arithmetic one salesperson used in their presentation.

$ 1.80 = Regular price of each unit
-$0.53 = Special promotional allowance
$ 1.27 = Deal cost
$ 2.29 = Manufacturer's suggested selling price
$ 2.19 = Normal retail selling price
18% = Retailers' normal profit ($2.19 – $1.80 = 39¢ margin) (39¢ ÷ $2.19 = 18% margin)
$ 1.39 = 3-day special price suggested for retailer to advertise product
8.6% = 3-day sale profit margin ($1.39 – $1.27 = 12¢) (12¢ ÷ $1.39 = 8.6% margin)
$ 1.89 = 2-week special price suggested for in-store promotion.
33% = After-sale profit margin ($1.89 – $1.27 = 62¢) (62¢ ÷ $1.89 = 33% margin)
18% = Normal profit ($2.19 – $1.80 = 39¢) (39¢ ÷ $2.19 = 18%)

then divide by \$2.19 (39¢ ÷ \$2.19 = 18 percent)]. Subtracting the 53¢ promotional allowance gives the retailer a deal cost of \$1.27.

The normal profit, or margin, is 18 percent. If the product is sold at \$1.89 for an additional two weeks, the margin reflecting the 53¢ promotional allowance equals 33 percent. If the retailer buys the product and does not reduce the price, the manufacturer is throwing away 53¢ a unit or \$6.36 a dozen.

What are the salesperson's objectives? To have the retailer: (1) buy a larger quantity than normal; (2) reduce the price for a three-day \$1.39 advertised promotion; and (3) run a two-week, in-store promotion at \$1.89. The retailer's sale price of \$1.39 would provide an 8.6 percent profit and the \$1.89 produces a 33 percent profit margin. The manufacturer, the retailer, and the retailer's customers all win in this deal.

The information in Exhibit A-4 (except for the arithmetic in parentheses) was on a sheet of paper with the buyer's company name at the top. The seller showed how the buyer could purchase a large quantity and make 8.6 percent profit by selling each item for \$1.39 instead of the normal \$2.19. The retailer's customers save 80¢ (\$2.19 − \$1.39 = 80¢). After the three-day sale, the retailer increases the price to \$1.89 for two weeks and makes 33 percent instead of the 18 percent margin.

Markup and Return on Investment

Consumer-goods salespeople can also use return on investment (ROI) in their presentations. **Return on investment (ROI)** refers to a sum of money expected from an investment over and above the original investment. ROI is often expressed as a percentage; however, a dollar return on investment can also be used by salespeople. The information shown in Exhibit A-5 illustrates the actual ROI used by a salesperson. Continuing the previous example, the salesperson wants the customer to have a three-day advertised special and a two-week in-store price reduction, and to buy a large quantity for normal stock. The purchasing agent buys for a chain of 100 grocery stores.

return on investment (ROI): The additional sum of money expected from an investment over and above the original investment.

Normally, the chain sells on average 1,500 dozen in six weeks. The salesperson believes that the promotion and price reduction will increase sales to 3,000

EXHIBIT A-5

Profit forecaster for granola bars shown to buyer.

	THREE-DAY SPECIAL	ONE-MONTH SPECIAL	NORMAL
Total stores	100	100	100
Deal dates	June 1 through June 30		
Regular cost per dozen	\$21.60	\$21.60	\$21.60
Less allowance (\$0.53)	-6.36	-6.36	
Deal cost per dozen	\$15.24	\$15.24	\$21.60
Feature price	\$1.39	\$1.89	\$2.19
Cases purchased	500[a]	1,000	1,500
Total investment	\$7,620[b]	\$15,240	\$32,400
Total gross sales	\$8,340[c]	\$22,680	\$39,420
Total gross profit	\$720[d]	\$7,440	\$7,020
Return on investment (ROI)	9.5%[e]	48.8%	21.7%

[a] 5 cases per store
[b] 500 × \$15.24 = \$7,620
[c] 500 × 12 = 6,000; 6,000 × \$1.39 = \$8,340
[d] \$8,340 − \$7,620 = \$720
[e] \$720 ÷ \$7,620 = 9.5%

dozen. As seen in Exhibit A-5, the salesperson asks the retailer to invest $55,260 ($7,620 + $15,240 + $32,400). Sales are projected to be $70,440 ($8,340 + $22,680 + $39,420), with profits of $15,180 ($720 + $7,440 + $7,020). The retailer's return on investment is 27.5 percent, as shown here:

$$
\begin{aligned}
\$70{,}440 &= \text{total gross sales} \\
-\ \underline{\$55{,}260} &= \text{total investment} \\
\$15{,}180 &= \text{total gross profit} \\
27.5\% &= \text{ROI } (\$15{,}180 \div \$55{,}260)
\end{aligned}
$$

Discounts, payment plans, markups, margins, unit prices, and return on investment are important for salespeople to understand thoroughly. Customers are extremely interested in receiving this information during the salesperson's presentation.

Organizations: Value and ROI

value analysis: An investigation that determines the best product for the money.

Business salespeople often include a value analysis in the sales presentation. A **value analysis** determines the best product for the money. It recognizes that a high-priced product may sometimes be a better value than a lower-priced product. Many firms routinely review a value analysis before deciding to purchase a product.

The value analysis evaluates how well the product meets the buying company's specific needs. It addresses questions such as:

- How do your product's features, advantages, and benefits compare to the product currently used?
- Can your product do the same job as your buyer's present product at a lower price?
- Does the buyer's current equipment perform better than required? (Is the equipment too good for present needs?)
- On the other hand, will a higher-priced, better-performing product be more economical in the long run?

As you can see from the examples in this appendix, frequently you must analyze the buyer's present operation carefully before suggesting how your product might improve efficiency, enhance the quality or quantity of the product produced, or save money.

In discussing how to present a value analysis to a buyer, Patrick Kamlowsky, who sells drilling bits for oil and gas wells, said:

> *It's not as simple as it may appear to make a recommendation and have the oil company adhere to it. You must be thorough in the presentation and present the facts in an objective manner. After all, their money is at stake. The presentation must be logical and based on facts that are known; it must be made with as little speculation as possible.*
>
> *What is difficult is presenting a recommendation to one who has spent 30 or more years in the oil field and has drilled all over the world. I am confronted with the challenge of explaining to this man that the methods he has employed for years may not be the best application where he is currently drilling. The presentation of the recommendation must therefore be thorough and to the point. When talking to him, I do not imply that his method is outdated or wrong, but that I believe I can help him improve his method. To be successful, I must establish two things very quickly–his respect and my credibility. Showing him my proposal and supporting evidence, and permitting him the time to evaluate it, are vital. I don't wish to come on too strong, just show him that I genuinely want to help.*

A salesperson can develop numerous types of value analyses for a prospective buyer. Three types frequently used are (1) product cost versus true value, (2) unit cost, and (3) return on investment.

Compare Product Costs to True Value

All buyers want to know about costs. The value analysis developed for a customer should present cost in a simple, straightforward manner. A product's costs are always relative to something else; thus, cost must be judged in value and results. The base cost of your product should never be the determining factor of the sale. Buying a product solely on cost could cause a customer to lose money.

Never discuss costs until you have compared them to the value of a product. In this manner, the customer intelligently compares the true worth of the proposed investment in your product to its true monetary cost. In effect, a good purchase involves more than initial cost; it represents an investment and you must demonstrate that what you sell is a good investment.

Exhibit A-6 provides an example of how a salesperson might compare the cost of a copier (Product X) with a competitive copier (Product C). It illustrates how you can demonstrate to a buyer that your product is a better value than one would think from looking only at purchase price. Another value analysis technique is to further break down a product's price to its unit cost.

Unit Costs Break Down Price

One method of presenting a product's true value to a buyer is to break the product's total costs into several smaller units or the **unit cost**. Assume you sell a computer system that costs $1,000 per month and processes 50,000 transactions each month. The cost per transaction is only 2¢.

Return on Investment Is Respected

Return on investment refers to a sum of money expected from an investment over and above the original investment. Buyers are interested in knowing the percentage return on their initial investment. Since the purchase of many business products is an investment in that it produces measurable results, salespeople can talk about the percentage return that can be earned by purchasing their products.

Again, assume you sell computer equipment requiring a $10,000 per month investment. Benefits to the buyer are measured in hours of work saved by employees, plus the resulting salary saving. First, have the buyer agree on an hourly rate, which

EXHIBIT A–6

Cost versus value of a small copier.

	PRODUCT C	PRODUCT X
Initial cost	$2,695	$3,000
Type of paper	Treated paper	Plain paper
Copy speed	12 copies per minute	15 copies per minute
Warm-up time	Instant	Instant
Cost of each copy	3¢ a copy	1¢ a copy
Monthly cost (assuming 10 000 copies)	$300	$100

Conclusion: The difference in the purchase price of the two copiers is $305 ($3,000 - $2,695). Product X saves $200 on monthly copy costs. The savings on monthly copy costs pay for the higher-priced Product X in 1.5 months. In 15 months, savings on the monthly copy equal the purchase price of Product X. Therefore, Product X is less expensive in the long run.

includes fringe benefit cost; let's say salaries average $5 an hour for employees. The hours saved are then multiplied by this hourly rate to obtain the return on investment. If hours saved amounted to 2,800 per month, it is a savings of $14,000 per month (2,800 hours × $5 hourly rate). You could develop a table to show the potential return on investment:

Value of hours saved	$14,000 per month
Cost of equipment	−$10,000 per month
Profit	$ 4,000 per month
Return on investment ($14,000 ÷ $10,000)	140 percent

Subtracting the $10,000 cost per month from the return of $14,000 per month provides a $4,000 a month profit or a 140 percent return on investment. This is taken one step further by considering return on investment after taxes–calculated like this:

$$\frac{\$14{,}000(1 - \text{Tax rate})}{\$10{,}000}$$

This return on investment presents the buyer with a logical reason to buy. Remember to let the customer make the cost estimates. The buyer must agree with the figures used for this to be effective in demonstrating the real value of buying your product.

Key Terms for Selling

cash discounts on time
consumer discount
cumulative quantity discounts
discounts
FOB destination
FOB shipping point
gross profit
list price
margin
net price
net profit
non-cumulative quantity discount
return on investment (ROI)
trade discounts
unit cost
value analysis
zone price

Sales Application Questions

1. Many companies offer customers various discounts from their normal or list price to entice them to buy. Discuss the main types of discounts offered.
2. Should the salesperson mention a discount at the beginning, middle, or end of a sales presentation? Why?
3. It cost a company $6 to manufacture a product that it sold for $10 to a wholesaler who sold it to a retailer for $12. A customer of the retailer bought it for $24. What was the markup on selling price for each member of this product's channel of distribution?
4. Determine the markup of a product that costs your customer $1 with the following potential suggested resell prices: $1.25, $1.50, $2. How much profit would the wholesaler or retailer make selling your product at each of the three suggested resell prices?
5. Assume you sell hardware supplies to grocery, drug, and hardware retailers. Tomorrow, you plan to call on the Real Hardware chain–your largest customer. To reach your sales quota for this year, you must get a large order. You know the purchaser will buy something; however, you want him to purchase an extra amount. Furthermore, you know the company is 120 days overdue on paying for what you shipped months ago, and your company's credit manager will not ship more merchandise until the company pays the bill. How would you handle the sales call? Include in your answer where you would discuss the overdue-bill problem in your sales presentation.

Also include what you would do if the buyer said, "I haven't paid for my last order yet! How can I buy from you today?"

6. List and define five commonly quoted types of prices.
7. The following examples are several types of discounts. In each situation (a) explain what type of discount is used, (b) determine by what percentage the *cost* of the product has been reduced, as well as savings per unit, and (c) answer other questions asked for each situation.
   a. Bustwell Inc., a regional business computer firm, is attempting to sell a new computer-operated gasoline pump meter to a convenience store chain, Gas 'N' Go. The device will help reduce gasoline theft, give an accurate record of each sale, and aid in determining when Gas 'N' Go should order more gasoline. Gus Gas, of the convenience chain, seems interested in your initial proposal but believes the price may be too high. The cost of each computer is $1,000, but you could sell Gas 50 computers for $45,000. The Gas 'N' Go chain owns 43 stores and is building eight more that will open in about one month.
   b. The Storage Bin Warehouse in your territory has reported a number of break-ins in the past three months. As a salesperson for No-Doubt Security Products, you believe your extensive line of alarm systems and locks could benefit the warehouse greatly. You make an appointment with the manager at the Storage Bin for early next week. During your preparation for the sales call, you discover that the warehouse currently uses poor-quality locks and has no security system. You plan to offer the manager a security package consisting of 150 Sure-Bolt deadbolt locks (for the company's 150 private storage rooms) at a price of $10 each, and a new alarm system costing $5,000. The terms of the sale are 2/10, net 30. How would the total cost change if the terms of the alarm system alone were changed to 5/10, net 30 (and the locks remained 2/10, net 30)? What is the cost of the security package if the Storage Bin takes 25 days to pay for the purchase?
   c. You are a salesperson for Madcap Arcade Games, selling video games and pinball machines. A local business wants to open an arcade and would like to buy a new game about every two weeks. A new game costs $3,000. You can offer a 5 percent discount (an end-of-year rebate) if at least 25 games are purchased from you during the next year. What will the discount be in dollars?
   d. The XYZ company is having its year-end sales push. As a salesperson for XYZ, a manufacturer of consumer goods such as toothpaste, shampoo, and razor blades, you have been instructed to give a "buy 11, get 1 free" discount to half of your accounts. The remainder of your accounts, because of their small volume, are offered 10 percent off all purchases. Compare the two situations. Which is the better deal?
8. As a salesperson for the Electric Generator Corporation, you have decided to attempt to sell your EG 600 generator to the Universal Construction Corporation. The EG 600 costs about $70,000. You estimate that operating and maintenance costs will average $3,000 a year and that the machine will operate satisfactorily for 10 years. You can offer a $65,000 price to Universal if it purchases 10 to 20 machines. Should Universal purchase more than 21 machines, its cost would be $58000 per generator. The generators currently used originally cost $65,000, have a life of seven years, and cost $5,000 each year to operate. As far as you know, Universal's present supplier cannot offer them a quantity discount.
   a. Develop a value analysis table comparing the two generators.
   b. In your presentation, what are the selling points you would stress?
9. Value analysis is an effective sales tool. Define value analysis and describe its use in a selling situation.

CASE A–1

CLAIRE COSMETICS

June Sathi was hired recently by a national cosmetics manufacturer. She just graduated from college. Having no previous work experience, she always feels nervous about making sales presentations. Her large customers make her especially nervous. However, for the first month she was in her territory, June only took orders, which relieved much of the pressure, and the salesperson whom June replaced had done an excellent job; customers seemed to accept June because of this.

In today's mail, June received information on products the company wants the sales force to emphasize next month. She has been instructed to review the material and come to next week's sales meeting prepared to discuss the information. Of the four products to concentrate on, one product will receive special emphasis. Claire Super Hold hair spray will have the following sales promotion aids and price allowances:

- Floor stand containing twelve 230 mL and thirty-six 350 mL sizes
- Counter display containing six 230 mL and six 350 mL sizes
- $1 floor stand and counter display off-invoice allowance
- 10 percent co-op advertising allowance requiring proof of advertising
- 10 percent off-invoice discount for each dozen of each size purchased

The 230 mL size has a suggested retail price of $1.39 and has a normal invoice cost of 83¢ or $9.96 a dozen. The more popular 350 mL size retails for $1.99 and costs $1.19 each or $14.28 a dozen. June knows that she, like each salesperson, will be called on at the meeting to give her ideas on how to sell this product in front of the 10 salespeople in her district. Her boss will be there and, it is rumoured, the national sales manager will be in the area and may attend. This is making June really nervous.

QUESTIONS

1. What can June do to prepare herself for the meeting to reduce her nervousness?
2. If you were attending the meeting, what ideas would you present?

CASE A–2

McBATH WOMEN'S APPAREL

Getting a new, improved product into a chain of stores that has never carried her line of women's apparel is a new experience for Lynn Morris. Lynn was promoted to key account sales representative for McBath Women's Apparel this month.

She has worked for McBath since graduating from college three years ago. As a novice salesperson in a large metropolitan market, she inherited a sales territory in which all the major department stores carried the popular McBath line. By displaying a service attitude, Lynn kept all her original accounts and managed to help several outlets increase sales of McBath products, but she was never given the opportunity to sell to new accounts.

Now, she has accepted the key account sales position in another region of the country (a key account is one that generates a large volume of sales for the company). Also, she has the responsibility of selling to a large chain of department stores (Federale) that has never carried McBath products. Maurice Leverett, vice president of marketing at McBath, is counting heavily on adding the Federale chain because the company's president is intent on continuing McBath's rapid sales growth.

Lynn firmly believes that her products are the best on the market. She is concerned, however, about the sales interview she has scheduled with the chief purchasing agent at Federale, Mary Bruce. Despite McBath's high-quality image and its reputation for having a dependable, hard-working sales force, Mary Bruce has turned down other McBath salespeople several times over the past six years, saying, "We already stock four manufacturers' lingerie. We are quite happy with the lines we now carry and with the service their salespeople provide us. Besides, we only have so much floor space to devote to lingerie and we don't want to confuse our customers with another line."

Lynn has decided to make her company's new display system her major selling point for several reasons:

- Several high-ranking McBath executives (including Leverett) are strong backers of the new display and want it in all retail outlets.
- The stores currently using the display for test-marketing purposes have shown an increase in sales for McBath products of 50 percent.
- Federale will not have to set aside much space for the new system, and it can be installed, stocked, and ready for use in less than one hour.
- The display will increase shopping convenience by allowing shoppers easy access to the well-known, trusted line of McBath products with the aid of clear, soft-shell plastic packaging and easy-to-understand sizing.
- A new advertising campaign will start in a few weeks and will emphasize the revolutionary display. Other promotions, such as coupons and special introductory sales, will also be tried.

QUESTIONS

1. Lynn believes a good presentation will be critical for her to sell Bruce the new display. How should she structure her presentation? What are the key selling points to discuss?
2. Assume you are Maurice Leverett. Give an example of each of the four major types of discounts discussed in this chapter that your salespeople could use to help put the new display into retail stores. Which type of discount will be most effective, and which least effective? Explain your reasoning.
3. How can Lynn use quantity (cumulative and noncumulative), cash, trade, and consumer discounts to her advantage?

CASE A–3

ELECTRIC GENERATOR CORPORATION

The Electric Generator Corporation was founded in the early 1970s to develop and market electrical products for industrial and commercial markets. Recently, the company has developed a new electric generator, the EGI, with a revolutionary design. While its initial cost is $2000 higher than any competing generator, reduced maintenance costs will offset the higher purchase price in 18 months. The Electric Generator sales force has been instructed to concentrate all effort on selling this new generator as the company believes it has a sales potential of $500 million.

Ontario salesperson Sandy Hart has as her main customer the E.H. Zachary Construction Company of Toronto, which is the largest non-union construction firm in the world. Because of the importance of potential Zachary purchases of the EGI (estimated at $1 million), Sandy's boss asks her to spend two days developing a plan for contacting and selling to Zachary. Monday morning, she is expected at the regional sales office to present this plan to her boss, the regional sales manager, and the divisional sales manager. The latter two people will critique the presentation, and then the four of them will finalize a sales plan that Sandy will present to Zachary's buying committee.

QUESTIONS

1. If you were Sandy, what would be your suggested sales plan?
2. How would a value analysis enter into your presentation?

CASE A–4

FRANK'S DRILLING SERVICE

Frank's Drilling Service specializes in drilling oil and gas wells. Salesperson Dushan Bednarsky is preparing to contact the drilling engineer at Oilteck, an independent oil company. Dushan has learned that Oilteck plans to drill approximately 12 new wells in the next six months.

Dushan estimates that each oil well will require a drilling depth of approximately 3,000 metres. The drilling service the company uses charges $2.70 per metre, plus $1,200 per hour for personnel to operate the equipment. They take about 16 days to drill each well.

Frank's charges $1,200 per hour for personnel and their costs are $3 per metre. Dushan believes his drilling crews save customers time and money because they can drill a 3,000 metre well in 12 days.

QUESTIONS

1. Using the above information, develop a value analysis that Dushan could use to sell to his customer.
2. What are several features, advantages, and benefits Dushan should discuss with Oilteck's drilling engineer?

APPENDIX B

Personal Selling Experiential Exercises

Sell Yourself on a Job Interview

You will play the roles of a sales job applicant and a recruiter.[1] You may interview any organization, but the hope is you will choose to interview an organization with which you would like to interview for a job sometime in the future. For your role as an applicant, develop a one- to two-page professional-looking resumé. Before you are to be interviewed, turn in a copy of the resumé to your instructor to give to your interviewer to go over before the meeting. Also give the instructor a one- to two-page description of the company at which you are applying for a beginning sales job. Assume this is your first interview with the company and you have never met the recruiter. It will last approximately five to eight minutes.

Recruiter

Create a business card to give to the applicant sometime during the interview.

Resumé

Bring an original copy of the resumé with you to the interview. During the interview, be prepared to point out one or more selling points in the resumé that relate to the interviewer's question(s) or to major point(s) you will discuss about yourself during the interview.

Personal Business Card

Here are few format ideas for your business card (see Exhibit B-1). Place your name in bold near the top. Underneath your name, have your address, telephone number, and email address in a regular typeface. Now include the name of your school in bold, followed by your degree, such as BBA in Marketing, and graduation date. On the back of the card, you may wish to include a bulleted list of items such as your GPA, courses relating to the job, and main job(s) experience. In effect, you are creating a mini-resumé.

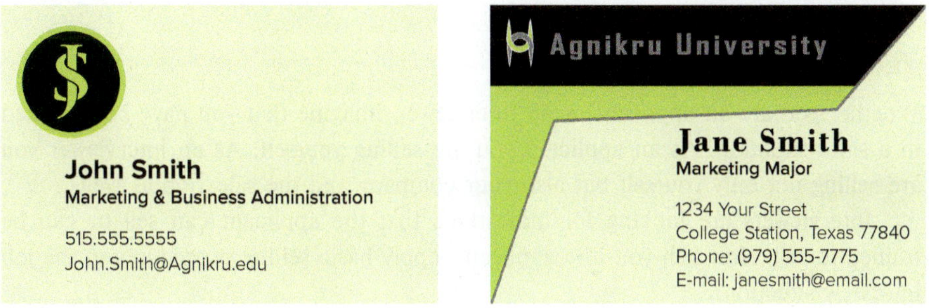

EXHIBIT B–1

Portfolio

You may want to consider creating a bound portfolio of school projects you have completed during your work career and coursework, or a one-page summary of key projects and the skills you learned from the projects. At the appropriate time during the interview, go over one or more of the projects that best relates to this job. If you have no projects, use a fake portfolio. Make up facts related to the project(s) for discussion with the recruiter.

The resumé and portfolio serve as visuals that aid in creating the image of you as a creative, highly motivated person who has thoroughly prepared for this interview and is very interested in obtaining a job with the organization. You will leave both the resumé and the portfolio with the interviewer. They will be returned to you after the interview. You are encouraged to develop other creative elements for your presentation.

I Want the Job

Before the interview is over, consider letting the recruiter know "you are very interested in the job." The interviewer may not feel this is true if you do not show knowledge about the organization and the job. However, if you can demonstrate in-depth knowledge about the company, the job, products, and customers, such a statement will be taken positively by the recruiter. Some organizations will not hire someone unless that person states: "I want this job." If true, you also would declare this in a later interview.

Grade Beginning and Ending

Your grade for this exercise begins when you shake hands for the greeting and ends when you shake hands to end the interview. You should act in a professional manner the entire time.

Follow-Up

After the interview, create a professional thank-you letter or email. In order to know the interviewer's address, ask for a business card sometime during the interview. Within one day after the interview, mail or email the thank-you letter to your instructor. For the letter's inside address and salutation, use the recruiter's name as shown on the business card.

Two weeks after the interview send a follow-up email to your recruiter. Use the recruiter's name in the email (To: Mr. Smith). The email actually goes to your instructor. Assume you have not heard anything back from the recruiter after the interview, and you want to know if the recruiter has received your follow-up letter and has any other questions to ask you. Also, assume that you are interested in being further considered for the sales job and that the recruiter said they would let you know if you are still being considered for the job within two weeks after the interview.

You Are Selling

Whether you are an applicant or an interviewer, imagine that you have been placed in a sales situation. As an applicant you are selling yourself. As an interviewer you are selling not only yourself but also your company and the sales job as well.

Interviewers are looking for indications that the applicant can sell or can be trained to sell. How can you–the applicant–apply basic selling procedures to the job interview situation?

You can look, dress, and groom like, and have the attitude of, a successful person. Showing the interviewer you have prepared for the interview indicates how you might prepare to make a sales call on a customer. Using the resumé and portfolio during the interview helps distinguish you from others interviewing for the job. Finally, you should "close" the sale by asking for the order (job).

Sales Call Objective

An applicant typically goes through several interviews before being offered a job. Consider this your first interview. What is your sales call objective for the first interview? It is to be asked back for a second interview! The end of the interview is an excellent time for you to illustrate your sales skills.

Futrell's Closing Sequence

One way to demonstrate your sales skills is by using "Futrell's Two-Question Interview Closing Sequence." At the end of most first interviews the recruiter will ask something like, "Do you have any questions?" You should respond as follows:

- "Yes, I have two questions. What is the next step in the interview process?"

  Wait for the reply. Then ask,

- "Based on my background, my resumé, and what we have talked about today, how could I improve my skills to increase the chance of being asked back for a second interview?"

Should the interviewer not ask if you have a question, you should say something such as "I have two questions" or "May I ask two questions before I go?"

Resumé, Follow-Up Letter, Email

There are many formats of resumés to choose from that will best highlight your qualifications and experience. No matter which of these you decide to use, there are some things that should be included in any format. The following is a checklist of these necessary items.

Resumé Checklist

- **Personal data** - Include your name, permanent and local addresses, phone number, and email address.
- **Education** - Begin with the most recent school attended. List the name and location of college or university (city and province are sufficient), degree received, your major and minor, and dates of attendance or month and year graduating, and your grade point average. May include relevant course work (six to eight important classes). Include honours achieved, such as dean's list, class rank, awards, and scholarships. Include special training, licensure, or certifications.
- **Experience** - Begin with the most recent. List full-time, part-time, internship, and co-op jobs. Do not include part-time work unless it's particularly relevant. Include dates of employment, company or organization name, city and province of location, and your job title. Describe your duties using phrases, beginning with action verbs, in present or past tense, depending on the time of the experience.
- **Activities** - List your professional affiliations, clubs/organizations, campus activities, and dates of involvement. Include any offices you held or committees you

chaired. You may want to briefly describe the activity and what you did using action verbs.

- **Skills** - Include any technical skills, such as computer software applications, hardware, and/or languages. List any language fluencies.
- **Personal categories** - These sections can be used to demonstrate valuable attributes, for example, military experience, publications and presentations, relevant projects completed, and major accomplishments.
- **Miscellaneous** - Optional information includes willingness to relocate, willingness to travel, dates of availability, and/or special interests.
- **References** - A statement "References available upon request" is common. However, if space is limited, this statement is not necessary. Rule of thumb: For the interview, have references available on a separate sheet.

Other Tips

- Use brief descriptive phrases instead of complete sentences. Avoid using personal pronouns–*I, me, my, their.*
- Have someone critique your resumé to check for spelling and/or grammatical errors.

Appearance Checklist

- Always buy good-quality paper for resumés.
- Select a subdued-coloured paper, such as white, pale beige, or light grey. Resumés are traditionally white. Print the resumé in *black ink* only.
- Limit your resumé to one page unless a second page is essential for relevant details and extensive work experience.

Action Verbs

Use action verbs when describing your experiences and accomplishments on your resumé, in your letters, and during your interview. Skills you will bring to an employer will consist of three basic types: people, things, and ideas. The following are common verbs used to describe these skills.

- **People** - administered, conducted, motivated, promoted, directed, coordinated, supervised, advised, explained, affected, managed, taught, activated, programmed, organized, conducted, stimulated, accomplished, adapted, adjusted, advertised, analyzed, assisted, catalogued, collaborated, calculated, consulted
- **Things** - built, constructed, compiled, specified, designed, changed, improved, prepared, calculated, completed, invented, created, programmed, revised, expedited, drafted, edited, enlarged, established, evaluated, examined, expanded, facilitated, familiarized, formulated, generated, governed, guided
- **Ideas** - established, wrote, proposed, coordinated, illustrated, modified, analyzed, adapted, investigated, explained, defined, devised, innovated, implemented, created, educated, synthesized, initiated, integrated, interviewed, maintained, manipulated, marketed, monitored, negotiated, obtained, persuaded, presented, presided

Resumé Formats

There are many different types of resumés. The most common type of resumé used is the chronological, which focuses on work history and experiences. A second type, which will become more widely used as technology expands, is the scannable. The scannable resumé is printed ready to be read by a computer. Here are suggestions for both of these types.

Chronological Résumés

The chronological resumé is the most common format and the one that is most familiar to employers (see Exhibit B-2). It focuses on work history and experience and is organized by type of experience. Examples of categories of experience are education, technical experience, work experience, and activities.

EXHIBIT B–2

Example undergraduate resumé.

Jane Smith

OBJECTIVE

Sales in the fashion industry.

EDUCATION

Bachelor of Business Administration Degree in Marketing — May 20xx

Brock University, St. Catharines, Ontario — GPA: 3.0 overall; 3.2 major

WORK EXPERIENCE

Department of Marketing, Brock University

Student Worker — January 20xx-May 20xx

- Worked for two professors within the department
- Duties included grading papers, making copies, inputting data, and editing

Recreational Centre, Brock University

Personal Trainer — January 20xx-December 20xx

- Scheduled appointments with (# of) clients per shift
- Met with (# of) individual clients on a weekly basis
- Planned a workout schedule for each client to help client reach fitness goals

Payless Shoes, St. Catharines, Ontario

Buying Office Intern — May 20xx-September 20xx

- Analyzed sales trends and markdowns and used data for merchandising
- Correlated with (# of) vendors the sending of samples and shipping orders
- Created and presented (# of) advertisements for newspapers and magazines
- Keyed and processed orders and distributions; approximately 3 per shift

LEADERSHIP ACTIVITIES

President, Canadian Marketing Association	20xx-present
Vice-President, Retailing Society	20xx-20xx
Intramural Sports	20xx-20xx
Member, Business Students Society	20xx-20xx

HONOURS

Alpha Mu Alpha, National Marketing Honour Society

Marketing Department Distinguished Student, — Fall 20xx

TECHNICAL EXPERIENCE

Microsoft Word, PowerPoint, Excel, Access

234 Your Street, St. Catharines, ON L2S 3A1
905-555-5555
janesmith@email.com

This type of resumé has advantages and disadvantages. It can provide prospective employers with a clear and concise assessment of your experience. It also highlights most students' major asset: their education. On the downside, if you do not have a steady or relevant work history, this will be emphasized in the chronological resumé.

To write this type of resumé, first list your education, work experience, and activities. Then go beyond just listing the experiences and write what you gained in each experience that proves you have qualities that the employer desires.

Scannable Resumé

As technology advances, an increasing number of employers are requesting scannable resumés (see Exhibit B-3). In many cases, your resumé will no longer be initially reviewed by an employer, but rather by a computer. **Remember: Computers read resumés differently than people do!** To make sure that no important information about you is lost in the scanning process and to increase your chances of

EXHIBIT B–3

Example scannable resumé.

Jane Smith
1234 Your Street
St. Catharines, ON L2S 3A1
Phone: 905-555-5555
Email: janesmith@email.com

EDUCATION

Bachelor of Business Administration Degree in Marketing May 20xx
Brock University, St. Catharines, Ontario
GPA: 3.0 overall; 3.2 major

COMPUTER SOFTWARE SKILLS

Microsoft Word, PowerPoint, Excel, Access

WORK EXPERIENCE

Department of Marketing, Brock University

Student Worker, January 20xx–May 20xx
Worked for different professors within the department. Duties included grading papers, making copies, inputting data, and editing.

Recreational Centre, Brock University

Personal Trainer, January 20xx–December 20xx
Scheduled appointments with clients. Met with individual clients weekly to help them achieve their fitness goals.

Payless Shoes, St. Catharines, Ontario

Buying Office Intern, May 20xx–September 20xx
Analyzed sales trends and markdowns. Correlated with vendors the sending of samples and shipping orders. Created and presented advertisements for newspapers and magazines.
Keyed and processed orders and distributions.

ACTIVITIES & AFFILIATIONS

Canadian Marketing Society
Retailing Society
Intramural Sports
Business Students Society

OTHER INFORMATION

Financed most of my university expenses, past 2 years 100%
Strong interest in languages and travel; willing to relocate

being electronically selected, the following are suggested guidelines for writing a scannable resumé:

- Use plain white paper, 8½″ × 11″.
- Do not fold the page; use large envelopes.
- Do not use borders, graphics, or landscape printing.
- Select an unembellished typeface (such as Arial, Courier, Helvetica, ITC Bookman, ITC Avante Garde Gothic, New Century Schoolbook, Optima, Palatino, Times, Univers).
- Avoid *italics* and underlining.
- Use **bold** sparingly.
- Put your name and address on each page.
- Clearly state functional and geographic preferences.
- Include degrees, majors, and GPAs.
- List computer software and hardware skills.
- Include job titles, employers, dates, and accomplishments, as usual, and additional sections for activities, honours, and the like.

Written Communication Is an Excellent Sales Tool

It may be necessary to write many letters during your job search. Some companies may prefer that you correspond by email, and proper email formats will also be discussed. Your best bet is to follow the lead of the recruiter in regard to communication.

Always address letters to a specific person and include that person's job title. They should be only one page in length. There are several different styles of letter writing, but the favourite is the block style because it is the easiest. In block style, all lines begin at the left margin. Professional-looking business letters are very organized and contain standard parts (see Exhibit B-4 on the next page).

Return Address

In this section, beginning on line 11, type your street address and city, province, and postal code. Do not type your name as part of the address. On line 13, the next line after your address, type the date. Do not use abbreviations, except for the official provincial abbreviation.

Inside Address

This part of the letter is where you type the address of the person receiving your letter. Include the person's name and position in the organization. Be careful with the spelling of the recipient's name and always include a courtesy title such as *Mr., Ms.,* or *Mrs.*

Salutation

Place the salutation two lines below the inside address. Type "Dear" followed by the person's courtesy title and last name. When using block letter style, do not add a colon after the person's name, unless you are on a first-name basis with that person.

Body

This portion of the letter should be single-spaced with double line spacing between paragraphs.

EXHIBIT B–4

Example follow-up letter format.

Line 11

Student Address 2
Student Address 3
Date

1 Line

Contact Name
Contact Title
Company Name
Company Address 1
Company Address 2
Company Address 3

1 Line

Dear Mr./Ms. Contact Last Name

1 Line

First paragraph: Express appreciation for the interview. Indicate the position for which you applied. Include favourable remarks about the products/services, position responsibilities, and facilities and employees, where applicable.

1 Line

Second paragraph: Reemphasize your strongest qualifications. Draw attention to the match between your qualifications and the job requirements. Use the opportunity to provide or offer supplemental information.

1 Line

Third paragraph: Reiterate your interest in the position. Repeat a phone number (or add a different number where you can be reached during certain hours if appropriate). State your plan to follow-up. Indicate that you will call during a certain time period to check the status of your candidacy.

1 Line

Concluding paragraph: Restate your appreciation for the interviewer's time and consideration.

1 Line

Sincerely

3 Lines

Student Name

Complimentary Close

The complimentary close should come two lines after the last line of the letter. For a formal letter, use a closing such as "Sincerely" or "Cordially."

Signature

Type your name three to four lines below the complimentary closing. Sign the letter in the space above your typed name.

Enclosure Notation

If you are including something with your letter, such as your resumé, make a note of this two lines below your typed name. This serves as a reminder to the recipient to look for your attachment. You may type out the word "Enclosure" or "Attachment," or you can abbreviate it by typing "Enc." or "Att." To indicate the number of attachments, add a colon after the notation (for example, Enclosure: 1 Resumé).

Thank-You Letters Are Important

Every time you meet with a recruiter, follow-up with a thank-you letter (see Exhibit B-5). If you are interviewed by more than one person, then write or thank each person individually in a letter sent to the main contact person. A thank-you letter can be the final factor in the decision-making process. For example, if you and another recruit have practically the same skills and qualifications, and you sent a thank-you letter and the other recruit did not, chances are you will get the job. Your letter should reflect your desire to work for the organization and once again highlight the skills and attributes that make you the best candidate for the job.

EXHIBIT B–5

Example thank-you letter.

1234 Your Street
St. Catharines, ON L2S 3A1
April 3, 20xx

Mr. John Doe
Manager of Human Resources
Industry Fashions

555 Main Street
Toronto, ON M2S 3A1

Dear Mr. Doe,

Thank you for the interview for the position of sales representative. Industry Fashions is a dynamic company with outstanding products. I would love to work as a sales rep for such a wonderful organization.

The interview strengthened my enthusiasm for the position and interest in working for Industry Fashions. Industry Fashions seeks only the most qualified recruits, and I believe that my education and experience are a good match for your company.

Hearing back from you would be very exciting. The phone number is 905-555-5555. Please call at your convenience.

Thank you again for your time and consideration.

Sincerely,

Jane Smith

Email Messages

In today's "e-world," some of the corresponding you do with future employees may be done by email (see Exhibits B-6 and B-7 on the next page). Because email is constantly developing as a communications medium, its formatting and usage are always changing. The following suggestions are just a basic guide to help you construct your email messages when you are unaware of the format the particular organization you are corresponding with uses.

"To" Line

In this portion of the email, include the receiver's email address. You may personalize this line by typing the name of the receiver first, followed by the receiver's email address in angle brackets: John Smith <johnsmith@email.com>.

EXHIBIT B–6
Example email follow-up.

From: Student Name <student@email.com>
Sent: March 1, 20xx
To: Recipient Name <recipient@email.com>
Cc:
Subject: Concise but interesting subject

Dear Mr./Ms. Contact Last Name

First paragraph: Express appreciation for the interview. Indicate the position for which you applied. Include favourable remarks about the products/services, position responsibilities, and facilities and employees, where applicable.

Second paragraph: Re-emphasize your strongest qualifications. Draw attention to the match between your qualifications and the job requirements. Use the opportunity to provide or offer supplemental information.

Third paragraph: Reiterate your interest in the position. Repeat a phone number (or add a different number where you can be reached during certain hours if appropriate). State your plan to follow-up. Indicate that you will call during a certain time period to check the status of your candidacy.

Concluding paragraph: Restate your appreciation for the interviewer's time and consideration. Make sure your message is not longer than two screens in length.

Sincerely,
Student Name

"From" Line

This section contains your email address and is automatically inserted by most systems.

Cc

Cc is an acronym for *carbon copy* or *courtesy copy*. The single *c* for any kind of copy is becoming the most commonly used copy notation. Type the email addresses of the

EXHIBIT B–7
Example email thank-you letter.

From: Jane Smith <janesmith@email.com>
Sent: March 1, 20xx
To: John Doe <johndoe@industryfashions.com>
Cc:
Subject: Thank you for the interview.

Dear Mr. Doe

Thank you for the interview for the position of sales representative. Industry Fashions is a dynamic company with outstanding products. I would love to work as a sales rep for such a wonderful organization.

The interview strengthened my enthusiasm for the position and interest in working for Industry Fashions. Industry Fashions seeks only the most qualified recruits, and I believe that my education and experience are a good match for IF.

Hearing back from you would be very exciting. The phone number is 905-555-5555. Please call at your convenience.

Thank you again for your time and consideration.

Sincerely,
Jane Smith

people who need to receive a copy of the message in this line. There is also a *Bcc* function, which stands for *blind carbon copy*. This allows you to send a copy of your email message to someone without the receiver's knowledge.

Subject

In this line, briefly state the subject of your message. Include enough information so that the receiver will understand why you are writing and will be interested in reading what you have sent.

Salutation

You may include a brief greeting at the beginning of your message. Some writers use a salutation much like that of a letter, such as "Dear Mr. Smith." You may choose to include the receiver's name in the first line instead of using a salutation, for example, "Thanks, Mr. Smith, for meeting with me last week." There is a division in the way to treat an email message: Some treat them more like letters (with a salutation), whereas others write them as if they were memos (with no salutation).

Message

Cover only one topic in your message. Try to keep your message very concise and no more than two screens in length. To help you with this, many systems have features such as cut, copy, paste, and word-wrap. Do not get too carried away with formatting because the receiver's system may not support different fonts or colours.

Closing

Close your message as you would a letter, with a closing followed by your name and email address. If you do not include your email address and your system does not transmit your address to the recipient, they will not be able to reply to you.

HOW TO CREATE A PORTFOLIO

A portfolio is a binder or book that shows off your work and abilities. It goes beyond a cover letter and a resumé. A portfolio is a job-hunting tool that you develop that gives employers a picture of who you are: your experience, your education, your accomplishments, and your skills. Not only does it show the employer who you are, but it displays what you have the potential to become. It is designed to do one thing: **support you as you market yourself!**

Top Six Reasons to Have a Portfolio

1. Distinguish yourself from the competition.
2. Turn the interview into an offer.
3. Increase the salary offer by impressing the interviewer.
4. Offer tangible proof of your abilities.
5. Potentially help you get promoted.
6. Help you find the position that is right for you!

Where to Begin

Start developing your portfolio by first doing a self-assessment. Evaluate what you have to offer and what the best ways are to market your assets. Decide which of your skills and experiences will relate to the needs of the interviewer, or what you would most like the interviewer to see. If you don't have much work experience–most students don't–you'll need to mine your schoolwork, volunteer work, and hobbies for evidence of the relevant skills you know you have. For example, if you did event promotions for a campus organization, include a copy of a flyer or poster you designed.

The following is a list of items you may want to include:

- **Table of contents** - For easy reference
- **Career summary and goals** - A description of what you stand for (such as work ethic, organizational interests, and management philosophy) and where you see yourself in two to five years
- **Traditional resumé** - A summary of your education, achievements, and work experience, using a chronological or functional format
- **Scannable resumé** - A text-only version of your resumé
- **Skills, abilities, and marketable qualities** - A detailed examination of your skills and experience; include the name of the skill area, the performance or behaviour, knowledge, or personal traits that contribute to your success in that skill area, and the background and specific experiences that demonstrate your application of the skill
- **Samples of your work** - A sampling of your best work, including reports, papers, studies, brochures, projects, and presentations; include print versions and USB memory sticks, videos, and other multimedia formats if appropriate
- **Testimonials and letters of recommendation** - A collection of any kudos you have received from customers, clients, colleagues, past employers, professors, and so on; some experts suggest including copies of favourable employer evaluations and reviews
- **Awards and honours** - A collection of certificates of awards, honours, and scholarships
- **Conferences and workshops** - A list of conferences, seminars, and workshops you've participated in and/or attended
- **Transcripts, degrees, licenses, and certifications** - A description of relevant courses, degrees, licences, and certifications
- **Test results** - Professional or graduate school testing results
- **Newspaper clippings** - Articles and/or photos that address your achievements
- **Military records, awards, and badges** - A description of your military service, if applicable
- **References** - A list of three to five people (including full names, titles, addresses, and phone/email) who are willing to speak about your strengths, abilities, and experience; at least one reference should be a former manager

Organize Your Portfolio

1. Keep your portfolio in a professional three-ring binder.
2. Come up with an organizational system of categories to put your items together, such as: Work Experience, Education, Awards and Certificates, Special Skills, Personal Accomplishments, Background. Use tabs or dividers to separate the categories.

3. Your portfolio should be no more than 25 pages. The shorter it is the better, because an employer will really absorb only 6 to 10 samples.
4. Every page should have a title, a concise caption, and artefact. Captions should explain the process you went through and the resulting benefits, such as: "This is a flyer I designed for the promotion of the Canadian Marketing Association Membership drive. We gained over 50 new members that year." Use the same type of action verbs you would use in a resumé.
5. Photocopy full-page samples to a smaller size, if needed.
6. Make the layout and design consistent, and don't get overly decorative–keep it clean and use lots of white space.
7. You may also consider including a USB memory stick with samples of your work. An online portfolio is another option.
8. Once you have put together your portfolio, create a title page, a table of contents, and an introduction. The introduction provides an opportunity to tie together your portfolio contents and summarize your qualifications.

Finishing Touches

- Have a faculty member or someone at the career centre review and critique your portfolio.
- Develop a condensed version of your portfolio that contains your most important accomplishments to leave with your interviewer. It could be in an inexpensive report cover or folder. This provides something physical to remind the interviewer that you were there. It also provides an occasion for an additional contact in a week or so to arrange for its pickup. Make sure you do not include original materials of which you only have one copy!
- Mention that you have a portfolio in the reference section of your resumé as well as in your cover letter.

How Do I Use My Portfolio during the Interview Process?

- Bring the condensed version of your portfolio with you to the interview and be prepared to present all the information within it to the interviewer. You may not always want to leave a condensed version of your portfolio. Level of interest in the position and cost should help you decide.
- Announce at the beginning of the interview that you have a portfolio and would like to present it at some point during the interview.
- You can use your portfolio to support your responses. For example, the interviewer might say, "I see that you have worked on your school newspaper. What were your favourite writing assignments?" You might reply, "My favourite assignments include this article (turn portfolio toward the interviewer and show the interviewer the article in the portfolio), which required a lot of research, and this creative writing piece (show article), which I wrote for a special edition."
- If you are unable to present it during the interview, begin the time allotted for questions by mentioning that you would like to present your portfolio.

Glossary

A

80/20 principle 80 percent of sales often come from 20 percent of a company's customers.

acceptance signals Signs that your buyer is favourably inclined toward you and your presentation.

account analysis The process of analyzing each prospect and customer to maximize the chances of reaching a sales goal.

account penetration The ability to work and contact people throughout the account, discussing your products.

account segmentation The process of applying different selling strategies to different territories.

action The last of the prospect's mental steps—when the prospect buys your product.

add-on selling The process of generating additional revenues after you've closed a sale by selling additional complementary products or by increasing the value of the sale by simply selling more product.

advantage The performance characteristic of a product that describes how it can be used or how it will help the buyer.

aggressiveness Expressing oneself in an inappropriate way; being forceful and demanding.

alternative-choice close A type of close that does not give the prospect a choice of buying or not buying but instead asks which one or how many items they wish to buy.

Amiables A buyer personality type focused more on relationships and less on facts; amiables have a strong need to feel recognized and valued and they tend to be trusting, friendly, and optimistic negotiators.

analogy A comparison between two different situations that have something in common.

Analyticals A buyer personality type focused on the details; analyticals tend to process information slowly and to be methodical, unemotional, organized and systematic.

approach Opening of the presentation from first talk with the prospect to discussion of the product or service.

artificial intelligence system (AI) The software to better understand customers behaviours and help salespeople understand how they can better help their customers.

assertiveness Expressing oneself in a direct and honest way; seeking a win–win outcome.

assumptive close A type of close that assumes the prospect will buy.

attention The first mental step in the buying process. From the moment the salesperson begins to talk, they should try to quickly capture and maintain the prospect's attention.

autosuggestion A kind of suggestion that attempts to have prospects imagine themselves using the product.

B

B2B selling Business-to-business selling, occurs when salespeople (representing a business) sell to other businesses.

B2C selling Business-to-consumer selling, occurs when salespeople (representing a business) sell to consumers (i.e., the end user).

benefit A favourable result the buyer receives from the product because of a particular advantage that has the ability to satisfy a buyer's need.

benefit selling A method of selling whereby a salesperson relates a product's benefits to the customer's needs using the product's features and advantages as support.

black box The unobservable, internal process taking place within the mind of prospects as they reach a decision whether or not to buy.

blog A frequently updated personal journal using the Internet; intended for people to read.

body language Nonverbal communication that includes facial expression, appearance, handshake, and body movement.

boomerang method The process of turning an objection into a reason to buy.

breach of warranty A situation in which a product does not perform as promised by the company's representatives.

break-even analysis A quantitative technique for determining the level of sales at which total revenues equal total costs.

bribe The process of giving something to somebody to get them to do something.

bundling Offering several products as one combined product.

business market The market where all profit and nonprofit organizations buy goods and services for a specific purpose.

business marketing The marketing of goods and services to business users.

buyer The purchasing agent.

buying centre A group composed of all the people performing different roles in the buying process (e.g., user, buyer, decider, influencer, gatekeeper) based on their expertise and responsibilities within their firm.

buying signal Anything that prospects say or do that indicates they are ready to buy.

C

calendar management Scheduling appointments, telephone calls, or "to-do" lists.

call reluctance A feeling of not wanting to contact a prospect or customer.

career path The upward sequence of job movements during a sales career.

cash discounts on time Discounts earned by buyers who pay bills within a stated period.

caution signals Signs that a buyer is neutral or skeptical toward what the salesperson says.

CCC GOMES A stakeholder acronym: customers, creditors, community, government, owners, managers, employees, and suppliers.

cell yell Yelling into a cell phone thinking that yelling is necessary to be heard.

centre of influence method A method whereby the salesperson finds and cultivates people in a community or territory who are willing to cooperate in helping to find prospects.

closed-ended questions Questions that can usually be answered with yes or no or by a very short response. Also known as *direct questions*.

closing The process of helping people make a decision that will benefit them.

cloud A technology approach that enables a more mobile, portable opportunity for salespeople by allowing access to software anywhere, as long as the individual is connected to the Internet.

code of ethics A formal statement of the company's values concerning ethics and social issues.

cognitive dissonance Tension on the part of a buyer regarding whether the right decision was made in purchasing a product.

cold canvass prospecting method A method whereby the salesperson contacts as many leads as possible with no prior knowledge of the business or individual called upon.

collect information The process by which buyers visit retail stores, contact potential suppliers, or talk with salespeople about a product's price, size, advantage, and warranty before making a decision regarding buying.

communication The act of transmitting verbal and nonverbal information and understanding between seller and buyer.

compensation method The method of offsetting negative product aspects with better benefit aspects.

compliment close A close wherein the salesperson ends with a compliment to the prospect.

complimentary approach An approach that opens with a compliment that is sincere and therefore effective.

computer-based presentations Dramatic and interactive presentations created at relatively low cost with the help of sales force automation using a computer.

concession close Offering a trade-off or incentive to result in an agreement to buy.

condition of the sale A situation wherein an objection becomes a condition of the sale, such that if the condition is met the prospect will buy.

conference call A teleconference or meeting conducted from multiple locations using the telephone.

consultative selling The process of professionally providing information to help customers make intelligent actions to achieve short- and long-term objectives.

consumer buying The purchasing activities of individuals and households for their personal use or consumption or to meet the collective needs of the household unit, such as a family or individual.

consumer discount A one-time price reduction passed on from the manufacturer to channel members or directly to the customer.

consumer sales promotion A promotion that includes free samples, coupons, contests, and demonstrations to consumers.

conventional moral development level The second level of an individual's moral development. At this level, an individual conforms to the expectations of others, such as family, employer, boss, and society, and upholds moral and legal laws.

conviction The fourth mental step in the buying process. In the conviction step of the prospect's mental buying process, the salesperson should strive to develop a strong belief that the product is best suited to the prospect's specific needs. It is established when no doubts remain about purchasing the product.

cooling-off period A period during which the buyer may cancel the contract, return any merchandise, and obtain a full refund.

countersuggestion A suggestion that evokes an opposite response from the prospect.

CPSA Canadian Professional Sales Association.

creative imagery A relaxation and concentration technique that aids in stress management in which a salesperson envisions successful coping in various sales situations.

creative problem solvers Individuals who have the ability to develop and combine nontraditional alternatives to meet the specific needs of the customer.

credibility A salesperson's believability, established through empathy, willingness to listen to specific needs, and continual enthusiasm toward his or her work and the customer's business.

cross-selling Occurs when a salesperson encourages a customer to purchase goods or services from other areas that may satisfy some of their needs; for example, selling a maintenance and supply agreement on a photocopier would serve as cross-selling.

crowdfunding Generating sales by delivering your sales message to the masses via the internet. Examples include gofundme.com and kickstarter.com used for new businesses as well as nonprofit companies.

cumulative quantity discounts Discounts received for buying a certain amount of a product over a stated period.

curiosity approach An approach whereby the salesperson asks a question or does something to make the prospect curious about the product or service.

customer benefit approach An approach whereby the salesperson asks a question that implies that the product will benefit the prospect.

customer benefit plan A plan that contains the nucleus of information used in the sales presentation.

customer profile An outline that gives relevant information regarding the firm, the buyer, and individuals who influence the buying decision.

customer relationship management (CRM) A technology system that helps companies manage information about existing and potential customers.

customer satisfaction The feelings about any differences between what is expected and actual experiences with the purchase.

customer service The activities and programs provided by the seller to make the relationship a satisfying one for the customer.

D

deciders Those persons actually involved in making the decision to buy.

decoding process Receipt and translation of information by the receiver.

demonstration The process of showing a product to a prospect and letting them use it, if possible.

derived demand Demand linked to consumer demand for other products.

desire The third mental step in the buying process. It is created when prospects express a wish or wanting for a product.

direct denial The method of overcoming objections through the use of facts, logic, and tact.

direct question A question that usually can be answered with yes or no or by a very short response; also known as a *closed-ended question*.

direct suggestion An approach that suggests prospects buy rather than tells them to buy.

direct-mail prospecting The process of mailing advertisements to a large number of people over an extended geographical area.

disagreement signals Signs that the prospect does not agree with the presentation or does not think the product is beneficial.

discounts A reduction in price from the list price.

discretionary responsibility Behaviours that are purely voluntary and guided by the desire to make social contributions not mandated by economics, law, or ethics.

dodge Doesn't deny, answer, or ignore the objection, but temporarily dodges it.

dramatization The theatrical presentation of products.

Drivers A buyer personality type focused on results and the bottom line; Drivers have a strong concern for positive outcomes and are quick to decide, even with minimal detail; winning is important for Drivers, who tend to be impatient, self-confident, and assertive.

E

economic need The buyer's need to purchase the most satisfying product for the money.

electronic mail (email) Messages sent electronically through a computer system that delivers them immediately to any number of recipients.

ELMS system The process of dividing broad account classifications into varying sized accounts.

emotional intelligence (EI) A combination of four abilities: (1) your ability to perceive other's emotions (2) your ability to identify your emotions (3) your ability to understand what's causing your emotion and (4) your ability to manage your emotions. EI serves as a skill the salesperson can utilize to interact with customers, colleagues and supervisors.

empathy The ability to identify and understand another person's feelings, ideas, and circumstances.

employee rights Rights desired by employees regarding their job security and the treatment administered by their employer while on the job.

encoding process Conversion of ideas and concepts into information.

endless chain referral method A method of prospecting whereby a salesperson asks each buyer for a list of friends or colleagues who might also be interested in buying the product.

enthusiasm A state of mind wherein a person is filled with excitement toward something.

ethics The code of moral principles and values that governs the behaviours of a person or a group with respect to what is right or wrong.

ethics committee A group of executives appointed to oversee company ethics and provide rulings on questionable ethical issues.

ethics ombudsman An official given the responsibility of corporate conscience who hears and investigates ethical complaints and informs top management of potential ethical issues.

evidence statements Statements that substantiate claims made by the salesperson; also called *proof statements.*

exclusive dealing Prohibiting a channel member from carrying competitive products.

executive presence A certain aura that the salesperson is perceived as possessing, including qualities like professionalism, ability, and authority.

exhibitions and demonstrations A situation in which a firm operates a booth at a trade show or other special-interest gathering staffed by salespeople.

exit technique A technique used by professional salespeople to keep the door open for future interactions with the prospect, in the event of not being granted the sale.

Expressives A buyer personality type focused on perceptions, status and approval; Expressives tend to be impulsive, colourful, egocentric, and spontaneous, and often buy for the sake of prestige or status.

Expressives A buyer personality type focused on perceptions, status, and gaining approval; Expressives tend to be impulsive, colourful, and egocentric, with spontaneous perconalities, and they often buy for the sake of status or prestige.

extensive decision making Decision making characteristic of buyers who are unfamiliar with a specific product and who must therefore become highly involved in the decision-making process.

F

FAB selling technique A technique stressing features, advantages, and benefits of a product.

Facebook A social networking site that facilitates building relationships, communicating with clients, and prospecting for new customers.

feature Any tangible or intangible characteristic of a product.

feedback Verbal or nonverbal reaction to communication as transmitted to the sender.

"Ferris wheel" concept An analogy that compares prospecting to the management of a ferris wheel; as riders (customers) exit the ferris wheel, the attendant (salesperson) must replace them in order to keep the ride profitable.

financial rewards Rewards given or compensation given by a company.

five-question sequence The five-step process of overcoming objections in which facts, logic, and tact are used.

FOB destination The shipping process in which the seller pays all shipping costs.

FOB shipping point The shipping process in which the buyer pays transportation charges for goods, the title for which passes to the customer when the goods are loaded onto the shipping vehicle.

follow-up One of the last steps in the selling process, involving servicing the needs of the customer after the sale in order to build a long-term relationship.

formula presentation A presentation by which the salesperson follows a general outline that allows more flexibility and tries to determine prospect needs.

G

gatekeeper A person who influences where information from salespeople goes and with whom salespeople will be allowed to talk.

geographic information system (GIS) Allows salespeople to view and manipulate customer or prospect information on an electronic map.

goal setting Establishing what one wants to accomplish and what activities need to be performed in order to reach desired career or performance goals.

gross profit The money available to cover the costs of marketing the product, operating the business, and profit.

H

hearing The ability to detect sounds.

hidden objection An objection that disguises the actual objection either with silence or triviality.

I

incentive A reward that serves to motivate someone.

indirect denial An apparent agreement with the prospect used by the salesperson to deny the fundamental issue of the objection.

indirect suggestion A statement by the salesperson recommending that the prospect undertake some action while making it seem that the idea to do so is the prospect's.

inelastic demand Demand that does not change in direct proportion to a change in price.

influencers People who influence the decision to buy a product.

information evaluation A process that determines what will be purchased as the buyer matches this information with needs, attitudes, and beliefs in making a decision.

initiator The person proposing to buy or replace a product.

Instagram A video and photo sharing site popular with business and consumers alike due to its simplicity.

intelligent questions Questions relating to a prospect's business that show the salesperson's concern for the prospect's needs.

interest The second mental step in the buying process. It is important for the salesperson to capture the prospect's interest in their product. If this link is completed, prospects usually express a desire for the product.

intimate space A spatial zone up to 0.5 metres, about an arm's length from a person's body, that is reserved for close friends and loved ones.

introductory approach The most common but least powerful approach; it does little to capture the prospect's attention.

J

joint demand Demand that occurs when two or more products are used together to produce a single product.

K

key accounts Your largest customers, the loss of which would greatly affect a territory's sales and profits.

knowledge Knowing something gained through experience and/or training.

L

lead A person or organization that might be a prospect.

libel A written act of defamation such as in a newsletter, blog, or published announcement.

limited decision making Decision making characteristic of a buyer who invests a moderate level of energy in making the decision to buy because, although the buyer is not familiar with each brand's features, advantages, and benefits, they know about the general quality of the good.

LinkedIn A social networking site that facilitates professional networking.

list price A standard price charged to all customers.

listening Ability to derive meaning from sounds that are heard.

logical reasoning Persuasive techniques that appeal to the prospect's common sense by applying logic through reason.

M

MAD An acronym for the three questions that determine whether a prospect is a qualified one; a qualified prospect needs the money, authority, and desire to buy.

margin The dollar amount subtracted from the selling price that yields the product cost.

markup The dollar amount added to the product cost to determine its selling price.

medium The form of communication used in the sales presentation and discussion, most frequently words, visual materials, and body language.

memorized presentation A type of presentation in which the salesperson does 80 to 90 percent of the talking, focusing on the product and its benefits rather than attempting to determine the prospect's needs.

message Information conveyed in the sales presentation.

minor-points close A close where the salesperson asks the prospect to make a low-risk decision on a minor element of a product.

misrepresentation Statements made by salespeople that exaggerate the capabilities of their products or services and false statements made to close a sale.

modified-rebuy purchase A type of purchase made when regular purchasing patterns are slightly changed to suit customers' present needs.

money objection A price-oriented objection.

morals People's adherence to right or wrong behaviour and right or wrong thinking.

mutual investment A requirement for building and maintaining relationships requiring effort, time and resources.

N

need arousal A situation in which a salesperson triggers a psychological, social, or economic need in the buyer.

need-satisfaction presentation A flexible, interactive type of sales presentation in which a prospect's needs are thoroughly discussed.

needs The basic requirements of human life—food and water, shelter, clothing, security, interaction with others, and self-fulfillment.

negotiation The act of reaching an agreement mutually satisfactory to both buyer and seller.

negotiation close A close in which buyer and seller find ways for everyone to have a fair deal.

net price The price after allowance for all discounts.

net profit Money remaining after the costs of marketing and operating the business are paid.

netiquette Proper rules and manners for communicating over the Internet.

new-task purchase A type of purchase made when a product is bought in conjunction with a job or task newly performed by the purchaser.

no-need objection An objection in which the prospect declares they do not need the product and implies the end of the selling effort but that may actually be either a hidden or a stalling objection.

noise Factors that distort communication between buyer and seller, including barriers to communication.

non-cumulative quantity discount A one-time price reduction.

nonfinancial rewards Rewards that are generated by the individual, not given by the company; also called psychological income or intrinsic rewards.

nonprofit clients The recipients of nonprofit organizations' money and services.

nonprofit contributors The providers of a nonprofit organization's resources.

nonprofit organization In this type of organization, profit is not a goal; most sell services rather than tangible products.

nonverbal communication Unspoken communication such as physical space, appearance, handshake, and body movement.

O

objection A statement by your buyer indicating resistance to your proposal.

observation method The process of finding prospects by a salesperson constantly watching what is happening in the sales area.

open-ended question A question that opens up two-way communication by beginning the question with who, what, where, when, how, or why.

opinion approach An approach whereby a salesperson shows that the buyer's opinion is valued.

order getter An individual who gets new and repeat business using a creative sales strategy and a well-executed sales presentation.

order taker An individual who asks what the customer wants or waits for the customer to order.

organizational buying All of the activities of organizational members as they define a buying situation and identify, evaluate, and choose among alternative brands and suppliers.

organizational buying process The problem-solving procedure the firm uses to meet its goals and objectives as it relates to making purchases.

organizational buying situation The firm's perception of a business problem (also called a need).

orphaned customers Customers who are abandoned as a result of a salesperson's leaving the company.

P

parallel referral sale A method of selling that makes the sale and gains referrals.

partnering The third level of selling where the seller works continually to improve the customer's operations, sales, and profits.

pass up The option of a salesperson not to pursue a presentation or sale or not to respond to an objection.

personal productivity Improvement of an individual's performance through more efficient data storage and retrieval, better time management, and enhanced presentations.

personal selling The personal communication of information to persuade a prospective customer to buy something that satisfies that individual's needs.

personal space An area 0.5 to 1.5 metres from a person; it is the closest zone a stranger or business acquaintance is normally allowed to enter.

persuasion The ability to change a person's belief, position, or course of action.

PIPEDA Personal Information Protection and Electronic Documents Act (PIPEDA) is the federal privacy law for private-sector organizations. It sets out the ground rules for how businesses must handle personal information in the course of commercial activity.

plan A method of achieving an end.

postpone the objection The option of a salesperson to respond to an objection later during the sale presentation.

practical objection An overt objection based on real or concrete causes.

pre-approach Planning the sales call on a customer or prospect.

preconventional moral development level The first level of an individual's moral development. At this level, an individual acts in their own best interest and thus follows rules to avoid punishment or receive rewards. This individual would break moral and legal laws.

predictive analytics The software technology that can predict the plausible future opportunities to assist the customers and provide salespeople with the needed tools to do so.

premium An article of merchandise offered as an incentive to the user to take some action.

premium approach An approach in which the salesperson offers a prospect something as an inducement to buy.
prestige suggestions A technique in which the salesperson has the prospect visualize using products that are used by people whom the prospect trusts.
Prezi A cloud-based presentation software package that allows salespeople to design engaging presentations.
price The value or worth of a product.
price discrimination The act of selling the same quantity of the same product to different buyers at different prices.
principled moral development level The third level of an individual's moral development. At this level, an individual lives by an internal set of morals, values, and ethics, regardless of punishments or majority opinion.
probability close A close that permits the prospect to focus on his or her real objections, which a salesperson attempts to reverse with a persuasive sales argument.
probes Questions that help salespeople obtain information from the prospect, develop two-way communication, and increase prospect participation.
probing The act of gathering information and uncovering customer needs using one or more questions.
problem–solution presentation A flexible, customized approach involving an in-depth study of a prospect's needs, requiring a well-planned presentation.
product A bundle of tangible and intangible attributes, including packaging, colour, and brand, as well as the services and even the reputation of the seller.
product approach An approach in which the salesperson places the product on the counter or hands it to the customer, saying nothing.
product objection An objection relating directly to the product.
proof statements Statements that substantiate claims made by the salesperson; also called *evidence statements.*
prospect A qualified person or organization that has the potential to buy a salesperson's product or service.
prospecting The process of identifying potential customers.
prospect's mental steps The five steps or phases that salespeople believe constitute a purchase decision.
proverb A short, wise, easy-to-learn saying that calls a person to think and act.
psychological objection A hidden objection based on the prospect's attitudes.
public space Distances greater than 3.5 metres from a person.
purchase The fifth and last step in the mental buying process. Once the prospect is convinced, the salesperson should plan the most appropriate method of asking the prospect to buy or act.
purchase decision A buyer's decision to purchase something
purchase satisfaction Gratification based upon a product that supplies expected, or greater than expected, benefits.

Q

qualified prospect A prospect who has the financial resources to pay, the authority to make the buying decision, and a desire for the product.
quota An expected level of performance often established by sales managers for their sales force.

R

receiver The person a communication is intended for.
reciprocity An agreement whereby a person or organization buys a product if the person or organization selling the product also buys a product from the first party.
redirect question A question that guides the prospect back to selling points that both parties agree on.
referral A person or organization recommended to you by someone who feels that this person could benefit from you or your product.
referral approach An approach that uses a third person's name as a reference to approach the buyer.
referral cycle The process that provides guidelines for a salesperson to ask for referrals in four commonly faced situations experienced by salespeople.
relationship marketing The combination of products, prices, distributions, promotions, and service that organizations use to create customer loyalty.
relationship selling Salespeople build a long-term relationship with clients by acting as consultants, partners, and problem solvers.
rephrasing question A question whereby the salesperson rephrases what the prospect has said in order to clarify meaning and determine the prospect's needs.
request for proposal (RFP) Purchasing process often used for large purchases when large organizations invite bids on a project.
retailing Any individual or organization selling goods or services directly to final consumers for their personal, nonbusiness use.
return on investment (ROI) The additional sum of money expected from an investment over and above the original investment.
routine decision making The process of being in the habit of buying a particular product, so attitudes and beliefs toward the product are already formed and are usually positive.
routing The travel pattern used in working a sales territory.

S

sales call allocation A plan to allocate sales calls within territories based on number of accounts in the territory, number of sales calls made on customers, time required for each sales call, frequency of customer sales calls, travel time around the territory, nonselling time, and return on time invested.
sales call purpose Sales call purpose is to make a contribution to the welfare of a person or organization.
sales networking The continuous prospecting method of making and utilizing contacts.
sales objection The prospect's opposition or resistance to the sales person's information or request.
sales presentation The actual presentation of the sales pitch to the prospect.
sales presentation mix The elements the salesperson assembles to sell to prospects.
sales process A sequence of actions by the salesperson that leads toward the prospect taking a desired action and ends with a follow-up to ensure purchase satisfaction.
sales response function The relationship between sales volume and sales calls.
sales technology The transformation of manual sales activities to electronic processes through the use of various combinations of hardware and software applications.
sales territory A group of customers or a geographical area assigned to a salesperson.
sales training The effort put forth by an employer to provide the opportunity for the salesperson to acquire job-related culture, skills, knowledge, and attitudes that result in improved performance in the selling environment.
scheduling The establishment of a fixed time for visiting a customer's business.
self management The development of a personal time management plan, setting priorities based on supervisors' expectations, keep a watchful eye on industry trends, and have a vision for the future.
SELL sequence A sequence of things to do and say to stress benefits important to the customer: show the feature, explain the advantage, lead in to the benefit, and let the customer talk by asking a question about the benefit.
shelf facings The number of individual products placed beside each other on the shelf.
shelf positioning The physical placement of the product within the retailer's store.

shock approach An approach that uses a question designed to make the prospect think seriously about a subject related to the salesperson's product.

simile A direct comparison statement using the words like or as.

Skype A software application that uses the internet for voice calling, video calling, group calling, video conferencing, text messaging, and more.

slander An act of defamation that is verbal or spoken.

SMART A technique to set the sales call objectives by making sure the objectives are specific, measurable, achievable, realistic, and timed.

smartphone A cell phone that also has computer functions including Internet access, calendar management, GPS, email, customer account information, and other advanced functionality.

Snapchat A popular social media platform that allows users to text and send photos easily; photos and videos are deleted by default; while this app is popular with younger generations, it is not as suitable for a professional audience.

social listening The monitoring, interpreting and seeking understanding of buyer-based action and communication.

social media Technology that allows social interaction and communication over the World Wide Web (for example, Facebook, LinkedIn, and Twitter).

social networking Meeting and communicating with different people, often done using the Internet.

social responsibility A business's obligation to maximize its positive impact and minimize its negative impact on society.

social sales technology Any social interaction-enhancing technology that can be deployed by sales professionals to generate content and develop networks.

social space A zone that is 1.5 to 3.5 metres from a person and is the area normally used for sales presentations.

source The origin of a communication.

source objection A loyalty-related objection by which the prospect states a preference for another company or salesperson, and may specify a dislike for the salesperson's company or the salesperson.

space invasion A situation in which one person enters another person's personal or intimate space.

space threats Situations in which a person threatens to invade another's spatial territory.

SPIN An acronym describing a sequential questioning approach used by salespeople; situation, problem, implication, needs payoff.

stakeholder Any group within or outside the organization that has a stake in the organization's performance.

stalling objection An objection that delays the presentation or the sale.

stimulus–response model A model of behaviour that describes the process of applying a stimulus (sales presentation) that results in a response (purchase decision).

straight-rebuy purchase A routine purchase of products bought regularly.

strategic Programs, goals, and problems of great importance to customers.

strategic customer relationship A formal relationship with the customer, the purpose of which is joint pursuit of mutual goals.

success Setting a goal and accomplishing it.

suggestive proposition A proposition that implies that the prospect should act now.

summary-of-benefits close A close wherein the salesperson summarizes the benefits of the product in a positive manner so that the prospect agrees with what the salesperson says.

surfing the Internet Exploring the different websites found within the web of links on the Internet.

T

T-account close A close that is based on the process that people use when they make a decision by weighing the pros against the cons.

tablet A general-purpose computer contained in a single panel that uses a touch screen as the input device.

technology close A close in which the buyer is shown past purchases, sales trends, purchase suggestions, and payment schedules by graphs and bar charts.

telemarketing A marketing communication system using telecommunication technology and trained personnel to conduct planned, measurable marketing activities directed at targeted groups of consumers.

telephone prospecting The process of reaching potential customers over the phone.

teleprospecting The process of reaching potential customers over the phone. The process tends to use a greater range of traditional selling elements, including needs discovery and solution provision.

territorial space The area around oneself that a person will not allow another person to enter without consent.

territory manager A person who plans, organizes, and executes activities that increase sales and profits in a given territory.

testimonial Using a third-party statement as proof to substantiate a claim.

testimonial close Presenting a prospect with statements from satisfied customers about your product.

text messaging Short message service (SMS) communications sent between cell phones.

textiquette Etiquette for text messaging.

third-party answer The technique of responding to an objection with testimony from authoritative sources.

three realms The three aspects involved in selling; salespeople must have the ability to sell the company, the company's products, and themselves.

tied selling Selling in which a buyer is required to buy additional products not wanted when purchasing particular items.

time management The process of using a given period of time for maximum effectiveness.

trade discounts Discounts on the list retail price offered to channel members.

trade sales promotion A promotion that encourages resellers to purchase and aggressively sell a manufacturer's products by offering incentives such as sales contests, displays, special purchase prices, and free merchandise.

transactional selling The first level of selling where customers are sold a product or service and not contacted again.

trial close A technique that checks the attitude of your prospect toward the sales presentation.

Twitter A social media microblogging service that lets users send "tweets" up to a maximum of 280 characters.

U

ultimatum close A closing technique that explains the potential negative consequences of not acting immediately.

undifferentiated selling The process of applying and designing selling strategies equally to all accounts.

unique selling proposition (USP) A statement about why a prospect should buy from you—it offers a reason why your product or company is both different and better than your competition's.

urgency close A close whereby a salesperson suggests that if a prospect does not act now, they may not be able to buy in the future, thus motivating the prospect to act immediately.

users People who must work with or use the product.

V

value analysis An investigation that determines the best product for the money.

virtual office A venue (home, vehicle, hotel room, or even local coffee shop) where salespeople are able to conduct business with the help of technology.

visuals Also called visual aids, these are illustrative material that aids a prospect in increasing memory retention of a presentation.

W

wants Not required to sustain life. Discretionary items on the "would like to have" level–gourmet meals and fine wine, a spacious home in a prestigious neighbourhood, designer fashions, and so on. We are not born with wants–we learn them. Our knowledge, experiences, culture, and personality all influence what we want.

whistle-blowing Employee disclosure of illegal, immoral, or illegitimate practices on the employer's part.

win-win negotiation A negotiation result where both parties have gained and neither party perceives that they gave up too much.

wisdom The ability to make good use of knowledge.

worldview People's different beliefs about the world around them.

written communication A thank-you letter or email mailed immediately after an initial call.

Y

YouTube A worldwide video-sharing community that salespeople can use to enhance their sales.

Z

zone price The price based on geographical location or zone of customers.

Notes

Chapter 1

1. See www.salary.com
2. Government of Canada, Key Small Business Statistics - January 2019, at https://www.ic.gc.ca/eic/site/061.nsf/eng/h_03090.html#point1-1 (accessed May 2019); Canadian Federation of Independent Business (CFIB) homepage, at https://www.cfib-fcei.ca/en (accessed May 2019).

Chapter 2

1. "'We are all doing it': Employees at Canada's 5 big banks speak out about pressure to dupe customers," Go Public, March 15, 2017, CBC News online. https://www.cbc.ca/news/business/banks-upselling-go-public-1.4023575
2. https://www.cbc.ca/news/business/big-banks-osc-excess-fees-1.4180732
3. "'I'm Not Aware Of That': Starbucks Employees Receive Racial Bias Training," May 29, 2018. NPR online. https://www.npr.org/2018/05/29/615263473/thousands-of-starbucks-stores-close-for-racial-bias-training.
4. "Amazon to pay $1-M penalty over pricing practices in Canada." *The Toronto Star.* January 12, 2017. https://www.thespec.com/news-story/7062562-amazon-to-pay-1m-penalty-over-pricing-practices-in-canada/
5. "Amazon is investigating claims that employees deleted reviews and sold sales data to sellers," *The Verge* online. September 16, 2018. https://www.theverge.com/2018/9/16/17867358/amazon-investigation-employee-seller-bribery-internal-data-deleting-negative-reviews
6. For an in-depth discussion of worldview, see Charles Colson and Nancy Pearcey, *How Now Shall We Live?* (Nashville, TN: LifeWay Press, 1999).
7. Based on L. Kohlberg, "Moral Stages and Moralization: The Cognitive-Development Approach," *Moral Development and Behavior: Theory, Research, and Social Issues,* ed. T. Lickona (New York: Holt, Rinehart and Winston, 1976). Also see Jerry R. Goolsby and Shelby D. Hunt, "Cognitive Moral Development and Marketing," *Journal of Marketing,* January 1992, pp. 55–68.
8. Also see Thomas R. Wotruba, "A Comprehensive Framework for the Analysis of Ethical Behavior, with a Focus on Sales Organizations," *Journal of Personal Selling & Sales Management*, Spring 1990, pp. 29–42; and Michael A. Mayo and Lawrence J. Marks, "An Empirical Investigation of a General Theory of Marketing Ethics," *Journal of the Academy of Marketing Science*, Spring 1990, pp. 163–72.
9. Theresa Tedesco, "Canadians see misconduct in the workplace, but few are reported: study," *Financial Post* online. July 4 2013. https://business.financialpost.com/news/fp-street/canadians-see-misconduct-in-workplace-but-few-are-reported-study; Schroders, "Global Investor Study: The global rise of sustainable living," https://www.schroders.com/en/us/insights/global-investor-study/2017-findings/sustainability/, retrieved October 2018.
10. *Canadian Charter of Rights,* http://canada.justice.gc.ca/Loireg/charte/const_en.html
11. Canadian Human Rights Commission web site. What Is Harassment? https://www.chrc-ccdp.gc.ca/eng/content/what-harassment-1. Accessed October 2, 2018.
12. Canadian Human Rights Commission web site. What Is Harassment? https://www.chrc-ccdp.gc.ca/eng/content/what-harassment-1. Accessed October 2, 2018.
13. Also see Leslie M. Fine and Janice R. Franke, "Legal Aspects of Salesperson Commission Payments: Implications for the Implementation of Commission Sales Programs," *Journal of Personal Selling & Sales Management,* Winter 1995, pp. 53–58.
14. John Jobs, "Watch Those Buyers," *Sales & Marketing Management,* October 1997, pp. 34–38.
15. "Twenty-five per cent of seafood sold in Metro Vancouver is mislabelled," UBC News. June 19, 2018. https://news.ubc.ca/2018/06/19/twenty-five-per-cent-of-seafood-sold-in-metro-vancouver-is-mislabelled/
16. https://www.ontario.ca/laws/statute/90s01
17. Les Andrews, "Watch What You Say," *Distribution*, April 1997, p. 23.
18. Charles H. Schwepker, Jr., O. C. Ferrell, and Thomas N. Ingram, "The Influence of Ethical Climate and Ethical Conflict on Role Stress in the Sales Force," *Journal of the Academy of Marketing Science*, Spring 1997, pp. 99–108.
19. Based on Bart Victor and John B. Cullen, "The Organizational Bases of Ethical Work Climates," *Administrative Science Quarterly,* 33 (1988), pp. 101–125. © Johnson at Cornell University.
20. CBC News. "TTC launches employee whistleblower line," July 22, 2013. https://www.cbc.ca/news/canada/toronto/ttc-launches-employee-whistleblower-line-1.1338612.

Chapter 3

1. David Mothersbaugh and Delbert Hawkins, *Consumer Behaviour: Building Marketing Strategy,* 13th ed. (New York: McGraw-Hill, 2016).
2. F.E. Webster, Jr. and Y. Wind, "A General Model for Understanding Organizational Buying Behavior," *Journal of Marketing*, 1972, pp. 12–19.
3. Elina Jaakkola, "Purchase Decision-Making within Professional Consumer Services: Organizational or Consumer Buying Behaviour?" *Marketing Theory*, March 2007, pp. 93–108.
4. R. Agnihotri, M. Krush, and R.K. Singh, "Understanding the Mechanism Linking Interpersonal Traits to Pro-Social Behaviors among Salespeople: Lessons from India," *Journal of Business & Industrial Marketing* 27, no. 3 (February 2012), pp. 211-27.
5. F. E. Webster, Jr. and Y. Wind, "A General Model for Understanding Organizational Buying Behavior," *Journal of Marketing,* 1972, pp. 12–19.
6. Adapted from J.R. Schermerhorn, J.G. Hunt, and R.M. Osborn, "Managing Organizational Behavior" (New York: Wiley, 1991), p. 123.

Chapter 4

1. Gerhard Gschwandtner, *Nonverbal Selling Power* (Englewood Cliff, NJ: Prentice Hall, 1995), p.3.
2. Kranz, Michal. " Trump's Handshakes with World Leaders Are Legendary —Here's a Roundup of the Most Awkward Ones," Business Insider website. November 16, 2017. https://www.businessinsider.com/trump-awkward-handshakes-photos-2017-11
3. G. R. Miller and M. A. Hewgill, "The Effect of Variations in Nonfluency on Audience Ratings of Source Credibility," *Quarterly Journal of Speech* 50 (1964). pp. 36–44.
4. Mark Fidelman, "Study: 78% of Salespeople Using Social Media Outsell their Peers." *Forbes* website. May 19, 2013. https://www.forbes.com/sites/markfidelman/2013/05/19/study-78-of-salespeople-using-social-media-outsell-their-peers/#7214ae12a39e
5. Mark Fidelman, "Study: 78% of Salespeople Using Social Media Outsell their Peers." *Forbes* website. May 19, 2013. https://www.forbes.com/sites/markfidelman/2013/05/19/study-78-of-salespeople-using-social-media-outsell-their-peers/#7214ae12a39e
6. Barb Darrow, "LinkedIn Claims Half a Billion Users." Fortune.com. April 24, 2017. http://fortune.com/2017/04/24/linkedin-users/
7. Facebook Newsroom website. Company Info. accessed September, 2018. https://newsroom.fb.com/company-info/
8. Number of estimated Skype users registered worldwide from 2009 to 2024 (in billions). Statista website. https://www.statista.com/statistics/820384/estimated-number-skype-users-worldwide/, retrieved February 2019.
9. Instagram website. Info Center, Our Story. Accessed January 2019. https://instagram-press.com/our-story/
10. Snapchat website. What Is Snapchat? accessed February 2019. https://whatis.snapchat.com/

11. Adapted by permission of the publisher, from the "Listening Self-Inventory" from *Supervisory Management*, January 1996, American Management Association, New York, NY. All rights reserved. www.amanet.org.

Chapter 5

1. Based on Charles Futrell's conversation with Jack Smith of the Colgate Company about his first month's selling.
2. Also see Sanjay K. Dhar and Stephen J. Hoch, "Price Discrimination Using In-Store Merchandising," *Journal of Marketing*, January 1996, pp. 17–30.
3. Portions of this section where adapted from George W. Colombo, *Sales Force Automation* (New York: McGraw-Hill, 1994).
4. Mary E. Shoemaker, "A Framework for Examining IT-Enabled Market Relationships," *Journal of Personal Selling and Sales Management* 21, no. 2 (January 2001), pp. 177–85.
5. Lauren Hahn, "Tuning Up Sales Skills," *Sales and Marketing Management*, March 2006, p.17.

Chapter 6

1. Also see Malcolm Fleschner, "High-Level Selling," *Selling Power*, February 2, 2010. Online at https://www.sellingpower.com/2010/02/01/4423/high-level-selling.
2. Donald L. Brady, "Determining the Value of an Industrial Prospect: A Prospect Preference Index Model," *Journal of Personal Selling & Sales Management*, August 1987, pp. 27–32; and Roger Pell, "It's a Fact... Qualified Referrals Bring More Sales in Your Company," *Personal Selling Power*, March 1990, p. 30.
3. "Trade Shows: Creating Sales Leads," *Marketing Communications*, November 1993, pp. 36–40.
4. http://www.bizjournals.com/boston/bog/mass-high-tech/2012/05/teleprospecting-versus-telemarketing.html
5. Also see Herbert E. Brown and Roger W. Brucker, "Telphone Qualifications of Sales Leads" *Industrial Marketing Management*, August 1987, pp. 185–90.
6. Ken Krogue, "What Is Inside Sales? The Definition of Inside Sales," February 26, 2013. https://www.forbes.com/sites/kenkrogue/2013/02/26/what-is-inside-sales-the-definition-of-inside-sales#5d061cc566d8
7. Portions of this section are adapted from Scott Krammick, *Expecting Referrals: The Resurrection of a Lost Art* (Fredericksburg, VA: Associate Publishing, 1994).
8. R. Agnihotri, P. Kothandaraman, R. Kashyap, and R. Singh, "Bringing 'Social' into Sales: The Impact of Salespeople's Social Media Use on Service Behaviors and Value Creation," *Journal of Personal Selling & Sales Management* 32, no. 3, (June 2012), pp. 333–48.

Chapter 7

1. Adapted from Robert H. Schuller, *Success Is Never Ending, Failure Is Never Final* (New York: Bantam, 1988), p. 227.
2. Marilyn Price-Mitchell, "Goal-Setting Is Linked to Higher Achievement," *Psychology Today*. Posted March 4, 2018. Available online at https://www.psychologytoday.com/us/blog/the-moment-youth/201803/goal-setting-is-linked-higher-achievement.
3. Robert W. Palmatier, Rajiv P. Dant, Dhruv Grewal, and Kenneth R. Evans, "Factors Influencing the Effectiveness of Relationship Marketing: A Meta-Analysis," *Journal of Marketing* 70, no. 4 (October 2006), pp. 136–53.
4. https://www.yesware.com/blog/four-ways-salespeople-can-beat-call-reluctance/
5. Adapted from Joseph P. Smith, *Dress for Business* (Menlo Park, Calif.: Crisp Publications, 1997), p. 23.
6. Adapted from John A. Firestone, *Sales Fundamentals* (Menlo Park, Calif.: Crisp Publications, 1993), p. 12.

Chapter 8

1. Adapted from G.M. Grikscheit, H.C. Cash, and W.J.E. Crissy, *Handbook of Selling: Psychological, Managerial, and Marketing Bases* (New York: Wiley, 1981).
2. Example provided by Professor Richard D. Nordstrom, California State University–Fresno.
3. Adapted from Grikscheit, Cash, and Crissy, *Handbook of Selling: Psychological, Managerial, and Marketing Bases.*
4. Adapted from Charles F. Stanley, *In Touch* (Atlanta: GA: In Touch), March 2006, p. 44.
5. Adapted from Grikscheit, Cash, and Crissy, *Handbook of Selling: Psychological, Managerial, and Marketing Bases.*
6. Example provided by Professor Richard D. Nordstrom, California State University–Fresno.
7. David Fitzpatrick, IBM Executive in Residence, Howard University, Washington, DC, and Charles M. Futrell, 2004.
8. For a complete discussion, see Neil Rackham, *SPIN Selling* (New York: McGraw-Hill, May 1988).
9. Also see Tony Alessandra, Phil Wexler, and Rich Barrera, *Nonmanipulative Selling* (Englewood Cliffs, NJ: Prentice Hall, 1997).

Chapter 9

1. Patricia M. Doney and Joseph P. Cannon, "An Examination of the Nature of Trust in Buyer-Seller Relationships," *Journal of Marketing*, April 1997, pp. 35–51.
2. Jacklyn Boice, "Story Selling Happily Ever After," *Selling Power*, June 2001, p. 21.

Chapter 10

1. Adapted from Tom Hopkins, *How to Master the Art of Selling* (New York: Warner Books, 1994), p. 191.

Chapter 11

1. Adapted from John L. Johnston, *Works of Mark Twain* (New York: Harper & Row, 1989), p. 133.
2. Mike Radick, "Training Salespeople to Get Success on Their Side," *Sales & Marketing Management*, August 15, 1993. Also see Neil Rackham, *SPIN Selling* (New York: McGraw-Hill, 1988).

Chapter 12

1. Right Now Technologies (2010), Customer Experience Report: North America, 2010, Harris Interactive.
2. Charles M. Futrell, *ABC's of Relationship Selling* (Burr Ridge, Ill.: Richard D. Irwin, Inc., 1997), p. 373.
3. Charles M. Futrell, *ABC's of Relationship Selling* (Burr Ridge, Ill.: Richard D. Irwin, Inc., 1997), p. 373.

Chapter 13

1. Charles M. Futrell, "Survey of America's Top Sales Forces," private research project, 1998.
2. William F. Kendy, "Time Management," *Selling Power*, July/August 2000, pp. 34–36.
3. A.A., Rapp, D.G. Bachrach, & T.L. Rapp. "The Influence of Time Management Skill on the Curvilinear Relationship between Organizational Citizenship Behavior and Task Performance," *Journal of Applied Psychology* 98, no. 4 (July 2013), p. 668.
4. Mark L. Rivers, and Jack Dart. "The Acquisition and Use of Sales Force Automation by Mid-Sized Manufacturers," *Journal of Personal Selling and Sales Management* 19, no. 2 (Spring 1999), p. 59.
5. G. Dagley and C. Gaskin, "Understanding Executive Presence: Perspectives of Business Professionals," *Consulting Psychology Journal: Practice & Research* [serial online]. 66, no. 3 (September 2014), pp. 197–211.
6. John D. Mayer, and Peter Salovey, "What Is Emotional Intelligence?" In *Emotional Development and Emotional Intelligence: Educational Implications,* edited by Peter Salovey and David Sluyter (New York: BasicBooks, 1997), pp. 3–34.
7. Gerrard Macintosh, and Michael T. Krush, "Networking Behavior and Sales Performance: Examining Potential Gender Differences," *Journal of Marketing Theory and Practice* 25 (December 2017), pp. 160–170.
8. Gerrard Macintosh, and Michael T. Krush, "Examining the Link between Salesperson Networking Behaviors, Job Satisfaction, and Organizational Commitment: Does Gender Matter? *Journal of Business Research* 67, no. 12 (December 2014), pp. 2628–2635.

9. Penny Crosman, "U.S. Bank Bets AI Can Finally Deliver 360-Degree View," *American Banker* 182, no. 139 (December 2017), p. 1.
10. Jeff Green, "The New Willy Loman Survives by Staying Home," *Bloomberg Businessweek,* no. 4312 (January 14, 2013), pp. 16–17.

Chapter 14

1. Statistics Canada, "The Daily—Retail trade, December 2018," at https://www150.statcan.gc.ca/n1/daily-quotidien/190222/dq190222a-eng.htm?indid=3660-1&indgeo=0.
2. Statistics Canada, "Labour force characteristics by industry," at https://www150.statcan.gc.ca/t1/tbl1/en/tv.action?pid=1410002301.
3. Adapted from Stanley Marcus, "Fire a Buyer and Hire a Seller," *International Trends in Retailing,* Fall 1986, pp. 49–55.
4. Statistics Canada "Labour Force Characteristics," at https://www150.statcan.gc.ca/t1/tbl1/en/tv.action?pid=1410002301.
5. Daily Hive Staff, "These were Canada's top GoFundMe fundraisers of 2018." December 7, 2018, Daily Hive online, at https://dailyhive.com/montreal/canada-top-gofundme-fundraisers-2018.
6. The Canadian Press. "Here are the top five GoFundMe campaigns," April 11, 2018. National Post online, at https://nationalpost.com/pmn/sports-pmn/hockey-sports-pmn/here-are-the-top-five-gofundme-campaigns.
7. Adapted from Wayne Rodgers, *People Management* (Menlo Park, Calif.: Crisp Publications, 1994), p. 25.

CHAPTER SOURCES

Chapter 2

- *Making the Sale: Do I Really Have to Buy That?* Source: Financial Consumer Agency of Canada. http://www.fcac-acfc.gc.ca/Eng/forConsumers/topics/yourRights/Pages/TiedSell-Ventesli.aspx
- *Selling Tips: EthicsCentre.ca–Canadian Centre for Ethics and Corporate Policy.* Source: Adapted from the EthicsCentre CA.

Chapter 4

- *Social Media Insights for Salespeople: Communicating with Customers through Social Media.* Source: Hainla, Liis. "21 Social Media Marketing Statistics You Need to Know in 2019." July 5, 2018–updated February 7, 2019. www.dreamgrow.com/21-social-media-marketing-statistics/.

Chapter 14

- *Selling Globally: The Former Soviet Union, Eastern Europe, and the Third World.* Source: Adapted from Wayne Rodgers, *People Management* (Menlo Park, Calif.: Crisp Publications, 1994), p. 25.

Index

U

V

W

X

Y

Z